Active Credit Portfolio Management in Practice

JEFFREY R. BOHN

ROGER M. STEIN

WILEY

John Wiley & Sons, Inc.

Published by John Wiley & Sons, Inc., Hoboken, New Jersey.
Published simultaneously in Canada.

For general information on our other products and services or for technical support, please
contact our Customer Care Department within the United States at (800) 762-2974, outside
the United States at (317) 572-3993 or fax (317) 572-4002.

Wiley also publishes its books in a variety of electronic formats. Some content that appears in
print may not be available in electronic books. For more information about Wiley products,
visit our web site at www.wiley.com.

Library of Congress Cataloging-in-Publication Data:

Bohn, Jeffrey R., 1967–
    Active credit portfolio management in practice / Jeffrey R. Bohn, Roger M. Stein.
        p. cm. – (Wiley finance series)
    Includes bibliographical references and index.
    ISBN 978-0-470-08018-4 (cloth/website)
    1. Credit–Management.   2. Portfolio management.   3. Risk management.
I. Stein, Roger M., 1966–   II. Title.
    HG3751.B64 2009
    332.7–dc22

                                                                    2008042838

Printed in the United States of America

10 9 8 7 6 5 4 3 2 1

For
Brenda, Brittany, and Ian
—JRB

For
Michal, Ariel, and Tamir
—RMS

Contents

CHAPTER 7
PD Model Validation   361

CHAPTER 8
Portfolio Models   455

Foreword

Jeff Bohn and Roger Stein are ideally positioned to provide us with this artful treatment of credit risk modeling. The book is a masterful collection of accessible and practical guidance placed on strong conceptual foundations. As leading entrepreneurs and practitioners in the quantification of credit risk, and at the same time among the top scholars writing widely on the topic, Jeff and Roger have been riding a wave of exceptional changes in credit markets. The design of many new financial products, the explosive growth of trading in credit derivatives, a major change in bank capital requirements for credit risk, and a surge of new theoretical and empirical research have combined to make this the place to be among all areas of financial markets for the decade up to 2007. And then came the serious credit crisis in which we find ourselves. Roger and Jeff have been through it all.

The credit crisis of 2007–2008 has set us back on our heels. Issuance of structured credit products, not just in the subprime area, is down dramatically, just as issuance of collateralized mortgage obligations fell over a cliff after the 1994 blowout of David Askins' Granite Fund. Numerous regulators, commercial banks, rating agencies, bond insurers, and buy-side investors are under exceptional scrutiny for their risk management and other failures. It is time to take stock of what we as modelers could have done better. In this excellent book, Jeff and Roger provide state-of-the-art guidance on how to measure credit risk, borrower by borrower and also at the portfolio level.

In my opinion, products were designed, rated, priced, and risk-managed with too much confidence in our ability to reasonably capture default correlation using the current generation of models and methods of data analysis. Had we better models for default correlation, some of the overhanging risks would have been better understood and avoided. Alternatively, with at least a better appreciation of the weaknesses of the models that we have been using, the tide of issuance of relatively complex products might have been stemmed somewhat. Would someone in any case have suffered the ultimate losses on subprime mortgage assets? Those losses were larger than they would have been without such a ready market for structured products, offering credit spreads that might have been appropriate for the risks as measured, but not for the actual risks. Laying off those risks through a food chain of structured products reduced the incentives of the direct lenders and servicers of the underlying loans to screen and monitor the borrowers and to limit credit appropriately.

The failure of our current generation of models to better measure default correlation is not restricted to products backed by subprime credit. For example, the market for collateralized debt obligations (CDOs) backed by corporate debt is also ripe for a crisis of confidence. It would take only a somewhat surprising string of corporate downgrades or defaults for investors, already spooked by the subprime crisis, to reprice bespoke corporate-debt CDOs in a manner that would make the distortions in this market during the events surrounding the GM downgrade of May 2005 seem like a mere hiccup.

Indeed, by mid-2008 the issuance of bank-loan collateralized loan obligations (CLOs) has fallen off significantly in parallel with the virtual disappearance of issuance of subprime-backed CDOs.

In concept, structured credit products like CDOs are well suited to transferring credit risk away from banks and other credit intermediaries, and placing it in the hands of buy-and-hold investors who are less crucial to the provision of liquidity to financial markets. Those investors can indeed be offered properly designed and rated products that are suited to their risk appetites and financial sophistication. Long-run institutional investors such as insurance companies, pension plans, and endowments can be rewarded with extra spreads for holding assets that are relatively illiquid, for they don't need as much liquidity and should not pay for what they don't need. For now, however, the well has been tainted.

Going forward, we need to pay more attention to the development and use of models with stronger conceptual foundations, fed by better and more relevant data. This excellent book by my long-valued colleagues, Jeff Bohn and Roger Stein, is a good place to start.

DARRELL DUFFIE
Lausanne
June 2008

Preface

Sen ri no michi mo ippo kara. *(Even the thousand mile road starts from a single step.)*

—Japanese Proverb

In theory there is no difference between theory and practice. In practice there is.

—Yogi Berra

Several years ago, a commercial banker asked one of us why he needed to calculate expected loss for his loan portfolio since he didn't "expect" to lose anything. Shortly after this conversation, this banker's bank experienced an unprecedented default in its portfolio, and this default impacted the profitability of the bank. The bank quickly moved to introduce more quantitative analytics to manage its risk and the banker who hadn't expected any loss took early retirement.

Up until the past 10 years or so, calculating any portfolio level analytic, such as portfolio expected loss, was considered by many to be irrelevant to the executives driving the businesses at large financial institutions. Credit analysis consisted of qualitative characterization of a borrower's health coupled with a few financial ratios they saw as necessary to keep regulators happy. The world has changed.

Today credit analysis encompasses both qualitative and quantitative analysis. Most executives at large financial institutions expect to see analytics such as portfolio expected loss. They also request estimates of unexpected loss (also known as portfolio volatility) and the likelihood of extreme losses (tail risk) that may impair the institution's ability to run its business. The most recent credit crisis notwithstanding, it is a rare financial executive who does not now require a quantitative characterization of the overall risk faced by that institution. Financial institutions without the infrastructure to measure, monitor, and manage their credit exposure run the risk of sudden demise or possible takeover.

New strategies and instruments facilitate active diversification of a credit portfolio to better weather the current crisis and prepare for the next one.

Financial institutions are in the midst of an unprecedented shift in the way they are managed and evaluated. In this book, we present a collection of ideas, models, and techniques for understanding and interpreting these changes.

With the rapid growth in quantitative credit risk management, we found in writing this book that many of our colleagues in academia and banking have also been busy writing. In fact, a number of excellent texts have been written in the past several years that provide a rich theoretical context for a diversity of credit models. Our goal in writing this book is perhaps far more modest but specific. We have tried to produce a practical text that presents a number of compelling ideas and descriptions in a way that makes clear how these techniques can be applied *in practice*. We have framed most of the discussions in the context of real business applications requiring the implementation of tools to support credit trading, active credit portfolio management (ACPM), and management of economic capital. When useful, we have included key derivations in the context of our model descriptions; however, more detailed understanding of the mathematics behind many of these models will require referencing one of the books or papers that we include in the References list.

Thus, our goal has been to write a book that provides substantial insight into our experiences in implementing credit-risk models and methodologies from the trenches, without necessarily providing a full complement of rigorous mathematical results in each case. By the same token, however, this is not intended to be a recipe book on financial engineering or a statistics manual. We have tried to limit our presentation of detailed algorithms to those that are not widely covered in other sources. So, for example, we do not discuss how to implement algorithms such as loess, the bootstrap, or Newton-Raphson, but do provide details on how to calibrate PD models to ratings from a number of different perspectives, or how to estimate asset volatility effectively for a structural model.

As in many endeavors, we will almost certainly disappoint some readers, but hope (in expectation) to generally satisfy most. There is a joke about three statisticians who go hunting. They spot a bird overhead in the distance. The first statistician steps up, fires, and shoots 50 feet in front of the bird. The second steps up, fires, and shoots 50 feet behind the bird. The third steps up, looks through his binoculars and declares, "We got him."

We hope to do better than this!

To illustrate the practical challenges of using these models, we provide specific advice on various details of implementation, which we include in boxes throughout the text. We have also included a composite case study based on our experience working with financial firms building and managing credit, capital, and portfolio management systems. This case study and the practical examples throughout the book reflect the synthesis of our collective experience from interacting with hundreds of banks and financial institutions over the past 20 years.

This approach mirrors the evolution of credit models, tools, and systems in recent years. The models and analytics have become more standardized and more widely understood. Many of the good books we mention are available to take readers deep into the derivations of these models (see Duffie and Singleton 2003; Lando 2004; and Schonbucher 2003 for more detailed and comprehensive descriptions of the literature and derivation of credit models). The conceptual foundation of why these tools should be used has become more widely accepted. This was not always the case; however, the wave of research in credit modeling over the past decade and a half, led by these authors and their academic colleagues, has resulted in a body of theoretical work that is far better developed than it has ever been.

In industry, we now find that the bigger practical challenge is implementing systems that actually *make use* of these new analytics and tools in a way that realizes their conceptual promise. As many practitioners have discovered as they begin to implement credit analytic systems and procedures within financial firms, the size of the gap between theory and practice can be large. Our goal is to help fill this gap.

The broad concepts underlying ACPM and its associated economic capital management approaches are easy to enumerate and easy to explain. We consider five important ideas to be our catalysts for the value-enhancing characteristics of the models and frameworks we describe in this book:

1. Default probabilities are dynamic and, for many asset classes, can be accurately estimated.
2. Credit exposure correlations and loss given default can be estimated (though with considerably less precision than default probabilities), leading to a quantification of a credit portfolio's risk.
3. Active management of credit portfolios can lead to higher return per unit of this quantified portfolio risk.
4. Economic capital is a scarce resource for a financial institution attempting to build a profitable business and is determined by a target credit quality.
5. Managing a portfolio of credit-risky instruments and managing a portfolio of business franchises require different business models, managers, and cultures to be successful. Transfer pricing of risk is an efficient tool for separating incentives associated with the credit portfolio and the portfolio of businesses.

In this book, we discuss the approaches to measuring quantities such as default probabilities and correlations that we have found most useful, and we attempt to provide insight as to how they can be used to facilitate active portfolio management and economic capital allocation. Along the way we will explore related themes such as quantitative risk management, valuation, and credit trading. The dynamic nature of default probabilities (from peak to trough of the credit cycle, typical default probabilities may change by a factor of five or six), coupled with the empirical fact that cross-sectionally they can range over a large spectrum (the range is typically one basis point to thousands of basis points) creates an opportunity in which implementation of powerful default probability models will lead to substantial savings as a financial institution minimizes its bad lending decisions.

Many financial institutions choose to implement single-obligor risk management systems only. Somehow, in practice, focusing on the stories behind each name tends to trump a less personal portfolio perspective. While we believe that any effort to implement best-practice systems is a positive step (even if that system focuses just on quantifying single-obligor risk), we will repeatedly emphasize our view that a portfolio view of credit is ultimately the best and most prudent way to manage a financial institution exposed to credit risk. Said another way, it is hard to make money (and avoid large losses) consistently by only focusing on single-name credit decisions without reference back to a portfolio.

The emphasis on the portfolio perspective of credit arises from the nature of the credit return distribution. Any quantitative analysis of credit begins with the skewed, non-normal return distributions typical of both individual credit exposures and portfolios of those exposures. (While correlations of credit exposures tend to be lower than the correlations of other types of securities such as equity, when coupled with the asymmetric payoff of credit exposures, they can create substantial skewness in the loss distributions of these assets.) Herein lies the source of diversification benefits from large portfolios. A holder of a credit portfolio continues to benefit in terms of diversification as more small and minimally correlated exposures are added to the portfolio. With symmetric distributions such as those exhibited by equities, the incremental benefit of diversification is quite small once the portfolio is in the hundreds of names (some researchers argue incremental diversification benefit stops in the tens). In contrast, the probability of correlated extreme losses is small in credit portfolios, but not negligible and certainly not economically insignificant. Unlike an equity portfolio with a (fairly) symmetrical return distribution, a so-called fully diversified credit portfolio may still have substantial volatility due to this nondiversifiable component of its correlation structure.

Ironically, credit markets originate credit in a decidedly undiversified way. As a consequence, holding the (local) market-weighted portfolio of outstanding credit produces dangerously concentrated portfolios. These circumstances contrast with the equity market where the market-weighted portfolio is well diversified. The implication is that while active management does not seem to produce much benefit for equity portfolios, it does produce substantial benefit for credit portfolios. This observation sets the stage for the importance of implementing systems, models, and tools to support active credit portfolio management.

However, although our knowledge and technical abilities regarding credit-risk quantification have expanded dramatically, there remain substantial hurdles. Paramount among these is the practical difficulty in estimating and validating correlation models, which are essential to effective portfolio management. In the case of single-obligor default risk modeling, we now often have enough data to draw conclusions about the performance of a model. (This was not always the case. As recently as a decade ago, default probability models were sold in terms of their conceptual coherence or anecdotal behavior. As more data became available, these conceptual discussions were backed up by the development of rigorous validation frameworks and techniques, which moved the discussions from model coherence to empirical performance.) In contrast, even today, we are still in the conceptual stage of understanding many correlation models. Partly due to the nature of correlations and partly due to a lack of data, often we cannot make strong statements about correlation models on the basis of rigorous validation. Nonetheless, correlations are an integral part of good portfolio models and we must often make do with the best tools that are available, augmented with judgment and experience.

Another practical difficulty in implementing active credit portfolio management has more to do with the psychology of lenders than the limitations of our mathematics. Financial institutions thrive on the creation of customer relationships, and executives love a good story. Shifting to a portfolio perspective often replaces some of the anecdotal discussions of industry structure, a company's product, and the personality of a CEO with reams of data presented in an abstract way. Executives at leading financial institutions understand the importance of portfolio-based decision making, but they and their staff still lean toward single-obligor analyses. While industry experience and common sense are crucial to using credit models wisely, they cannot generally, in and of themselves, form the basis of credit policies for complicated portfolios of correlated assets.

In our judgment, it is useful for organizations to segment the portfolio management function into a central group, while at the same time providing relationship managers with incentives to cross-sell services into their client base. In this way, the anecdote- and relationship-based approaches can still have relevance alongside those of the individuals with more of a quantitative bent who will migrate to the portfolio management function. The economic capital allocated to support the relationship business, which generates fee income from selling financial products and services, can then be differentiated from the economic capital allocated to support the central management of the credit risk in the portfolio.

The portfolio perspective does not release a bank's management from the responsibility to stay vigilant as to the possibility of fraud and poor monitoring, which some have asserted were common in the run-up to the subprime difficulties witnessed in recent years. Rather, the portfolio perspective—informed by quantitative characterization of the return and risk profiles of a bank's portfolio—should be part of senior management's toolkit. Models serve the specific purpose of distilling information and reducing the level of complexity in understanding the return and risk of a portfolio exposure. Unfortunately, model output can sometimes become a crutch for managers unwilling to drill into the details of a transaction or portfolio strategy. This book is one attempt at demystifying key credit models so that more participants in the financial markets can better understand the underlying drivers of the risks to which they are exposed.

In a number of places in this book, we make a point of relating abstract financial theory to quantifiable financial costs and benefits that can be used for the purpose of better aligning incentives with share-value maximizing behavior. The result should be a more valuable financial institution.

WHY ACTIVE CREDIT PORTFOLIO MANAGEMENT?

Several trends in the financial markets reflect the growing recognition of the benefit of active credit portfolio management (ACPM). There are a number of reasons for this. First, analyses of past banking crises highlight one major common source of bank failures: too much portfolio concentration. If a bank develops a strong business in a particular area, and if it does its job well, over time it will generate concentrated exposure to this area as the bank and clients seek each other out in these areas of specialization. In a global market, the correlations may be less apparent, but no less dangerous. Actively managing a portfolio mitigates this concentration risk to the extent possible.

Second, the development of credit derivatives such as credit default swaps (CDSs) and synthetic collateralized debt obligations (CDOs) has presented a new set of tools for managing diversification. Recent difficulties in the structured finance market have dented some of the enthusiasm for CDO and collateralized loan obligation (CLO) structures. The broader credit crisis of 2007 and 2008 has cast doubt on the usefulness of CDSs. Nonetheless, when used for hedging, rather than as investment vehicles in and of themselves (particularly when the investment is highly levered), users of synthetic structures and credit derivatives can improve diversification relatively cheaply compared to transacting in the underlying assets individually. However, along with these powerful instruments comes responsibility. Participants in this market for credit derivatives must continue to work on building a robust and viable market with natural buyers and sellers trading in all market conditions and at reasonable leverage levels. Much of the analysis that benefits portfolio analysis can also be applied to these synthetic versions of credit portfolios. On the other hand, when these instruments are used to "take a position" on the market directly, rather than to hedge an existing position, they can actually increase concentration and can work against prudent portfolio management practice.

Third, financial institutions that manage their credit portfolios appear historically to weather economic downturns more effectively. One of the more recent economic downturns in the United States, following the dot-com bust at the start of the new millennium, highlighted the resilience of U.S. commercial banks with diversified portfolios. This recession was marked by a lack of bank failures, due in no small part to how credit exposure was managed. More recent banking difficulties have been partly a consequence of disappearing liquidity in the financial markets; however, many of the larger failures were also a consequence of large portfolios with concentrated exposure to the U.S. real estate market. One of the authors has heard from some credit portfolio managers that they were never given the opportunity to manage credit exposure that entered their institution's portfolio in the form of tranches in structures with mortgages as collateral. These same managers have successfully minimized losses in portfolios of large corporate loans that have historically been the source of concentration risk in bank portfolios. Hopefully, more financial institutions will begin to manage all of their credit exposures from a portfolio perspective (not just large corporate exposure).

Despite the advances in managing credit portfolios, the recent difficulties triggered by the subprime crisis in the United States suggests that many institutions still have work to do in terms of managing their exposure to liquidity risk that arises when too many market participants end up on the same side of every trade. In the end, however, even the best risk management systems are still only a component of a business strategy. Management still must take firm control of the institution and rely actively on both risk control systems and sound business judgment to provide guidance.

Ultimately, the emphasis on ACPM derives from a premise that underlies our thinking with respect to banking: Bank managers should be making decisions to maximize the value of the bank's equity shares. This emphasis by bank managers will result in substantially different portfolios than those at banks whose managers focus on maximizing the amount of assets held in the bank's portfolio.

That is, a large bank portfolio does not necessarily translate into higher bank market capitalization. The fact that defaults are rare and the somewhat abstract nature of how capital underlies the ability of a bank to make a loan make it difficult for some bank managers to understand why concentration risk in a portfolio is such a bad thing. Since bank failures are very uncommon, a manager may see healthy income from a large, concentrated portfolio for years before a cluster of defaults throws the bank into difficulty. The bank's share price should, however, reflect this risk. Without proper incentives, a bank manager may conclude that he should capture as much income as possible now and worry later if the bank portfolio deteriorates. Our perspective, reflected throughout this book, is that share price, not portfolio size or portfolio income, should be integrated into a bank's performance management and compensation framework as a natural mechanism by which credit risk can be managed. Since the share price reflects the market's assessment of the firm's equity value, including the risk of insolvency, focusing on share price will align incentives of the bank's senior management and its line staff with the objectives of the shareholders.

Finance theory suggests that ACPM and the models used to separate the credit portfolio from a bank's (or other financial institution's) other businesses will lead the bank toward a higher share price. It is our view that operating in an environment where managers make decisions that lead to a higher market capitalization will, on balance, be best for the bank, its employees, and the country or countries in which it is located. It will also lead institutions away from a short-sighted search for profit at the expense of longer-term risk, given the objectives of management and the appetite of the shareholder base. Active credit portfolio management makes these trade-offs explicit and transparent.

OBJECTIVE OF THIS BOOK

As any new field of analysis develops, pockets of inefficiency and mischaracterization persist. Quantitative analysis is both revered and reviled. Some practitioners extol the virtues of returning to qualitative analysis of credit. Others dismiss existing models as oversimplifications of the world and insist that credit risk management demands more complex solutions—or much simpler ones. We tend to view the correct balance as sitting somewhere in the middle. A large swath of credit analysts still focus on fundamental analysis only. The number of vendors of credit analytics has increased, each pitching its own version of a credit risk management platform. Despite the increase in analytic firepower, the field is new enough to make standardization of approaches and techniques difficult in practice. The trends in the market married with the availability of analytics and tools make understanding the concepts underlying these models an essential part of financial education today.

Our objective in writing this book is to provide a coherent and comprehensive (to the extent possible) framework for understanding and implementing effective credit risk management and credit portfolio management systems, evaluating credit trades, and constructing credit portfolios. It is worth repeating that this book is not intended to be an exhaustive survey of the broad literature on credit models or of all frameworks that have been developed or used. The References section at the end of the book provides sources to satisfy the reader's curiosity about other models and frameworks.

In our discussions, we tend to focus a bit more on a structural approach to analyzing credit risk, supplemented by other methods we think are useful in particular applications where the structural framework falls short. As it turns out, there are many applications where we will recommend the reduced-form modeling approach or a data-driven econometric one. A well-trained analyst will be comfortable with a variety of models and frameworks. While our preferred framework is grounded in economic explanations of default, our discussions of other frameworks are generally motivated by the challenge of making use of existing data. While we often find structural models most appealing from an intuitive perspective, in a number of settings such models cannot be practically implemented and thus pragmatism, rather then dogma, guides us. When helpful in highlighting our recommended approach, we discuss some other popular implementations of the models for certain applications.

In order to increase the reader's understanding of the models ultimately in use, we have tried to provide an (extremely) abbreviated history of how the models have evolved over time. We hope that this contextualization of how models have changed will improve the reader's grasp of the underlying concepts. We have not necessarily been comprehensive in these descriptions (again we refer the reader to the texts cited in the References to expand on our exposition); but we have highlighted the key developments that lead us to where we are today in terms of how models are used in practice.

MODELS IN PRACTICE

In all of these discussions, we warn the reader that we have developed strong views over the years and that we tend not to hide our opinions. We have acquired almost 20 years' experience in the credit arena and have developed deep-seated views about what a financial institution should and should not do to build value in a credit-related business. We plan to share this perspective. By way of disclosure, we note that in practice, an effective, *practical* framework will be rough around the edges with the odd inconsistency here and there (usually to deal with available data or the lack thereof). Sometimes two seemingly incompatible models can have value in specific contexts, resulting in retention of both models despite the fact that they may not be consistent with each other from a theoretical perspective. In fact, we recommend that financial institutions look to multiple models and incorporate stress testing and reality checks frequently when building credit risk systems as a method for mitigating model risk.

Importantly, though, all models are not created equal and some models are better avoided. How can we make a determination as to the quality and usefulness of a particular model? Over time, we have developed the view that five criteria for evaluating a model or framework in the context of actual implementation of a credit risk and portfolio management system are useful:

1. Possibility of objective evaluation.
2. Interpretability of model output.
3. Relevance of model output to real and important business decisions.
4. Contribution to financial institution's value.
5. Reasonable cost relative to benefit of using the model.

Notice that criterion 1 immediately leads us down the applied modeling path. Many elegant mathematical credit models cannot currently (and in some cases may never) be tested, for lack of the right data. Other models reflect esoteric issues irrelevant to the real world of lending and trading.

Implicit in these five criteria is the view that objective evaluation will be facilitated by quantitative analyses and that those analyses will validate the performance of the model. Many times, however, we encounter quants who stop at criterion 1: quantitative validation. Their institutions will suffer for this narrow focus. The list is vitally important and speaks to the manner in which a model or framework changes and orients an organization.

In the end, a model will only be as good as the way in which it is used. The nature of the model—its fit along the dimensions previously outlined—can materially impact the probability of it being used well. One consequence of our perspective is that sometimes less elegant models from a theoretical (usually mathematical) perspective will be judged superior to models that reflect a theoretical infrastructure appealing to academicians. A good model will become integrated into the way a financial institution is managed on a day-to-day basis.

These five criteria lead us to the following conclusions:

1. Whenever possible, use models based on observable data and, if possible, choose market data.

2. Models should be transparent—no black boxes. Models should provide some sort of explanation for their output in addition to the output itself.
3. Economic, causal models tend to be more useful.
4. Simple models are, all else equal, better; however, the world is complicated and models should not be too simple.
5. Managers should align carefully the way in which the models are used with organizational incentives.

The last conclusion will make choosing models, frameworks, and systems very much an exercise in adaptation. Both models and organizations will need to be adapted to each other. We will provide our own insights based on the experience of observing this adaptation and evolution at financial institutions around the world. While our work has tended to be weighted toward interaction with large, global financial institutions, in our experience, financial institutions of all sizes will benefit from moving toward a quantitative orientation in credit and portfolio management coupled with incentives that target maximization of share value.

BASEL II AND OTHER REGULATIONS

While regulations and regulatory authorities are a necessary part of the financial system, we will only refer to regulations in passing. Many other books explain the intricacies of bank regulation in general and Basel II in particular (e.g., Ong and KPMG 2004). Please look to those publications for details on strategies for regulatory compliance. This book is not intended as a source for in-depth explanation of bank regulations. In fact, we view bank regulation similarly to financial accounting—something that has to be done, both for the sake of the bank and the broader financial system, but not something that should be the main driver of an institution's business decisions. Regulatory capital should be measured so that if a bank discovers it is facing constraints in this dimension, it can take measures to secure regulatory capital relief. Decisions as to which businesses to develop and which transactions to do should be driven from economic capital models (subject to regulatory compliance).

Unfortunately, the good intentions and insights of the Basel committee are sometimes buried beneath the need for local regulators to turn these principles into guidelines that are practically implementable in their local markets. These interpretations, and the limitations of the local environments in which they are executed, sometimes create distortions in the markets as financial institutions scramble to respond to (and sometimes try to arbitrage) the rules.

Regulatory capital should not be mistaken for market-based economic capital. While it is important to distinguish between economic and regulatory capital, we will only touch briefly on Basel II in the context of some of our discussions. We find that in practice the value of Basel II, which is high, stems mostly from the discipline that it creates within organizations as well as the allocation of budgets to risk management groups that are typically underfunded and understaffed. Regardless of our perspective, Basel II is a development that most financial institutions with a global presence will implement in some form and to which they will thus pay close attention. We support the efforts of knowledgeable bankers to engage in working with the Bank for International Settlements (BIS) and their own local regulators to continue to develop useful and practical rules for determining regulatory capital. That said, from a business perspective, most of an institution's effort and budgets for capital management systems will typically end up being focused on economic capital and its return.

OUR APPROACH TO EXPLAINING IDEAS

The exposition in this book will tend toward practical examples with minimal presentation of lengthy mathematical proofs. Of course, mathematical derivations can sometimes highlight conceptual points, and the field of credit risk management is at its core mathematical. Some readers may judge that we have been too liberal in our use of mathematical formulations while others will thirst for more technical detail. Wherever possible, we have tried to provide references to other work that can satisfy a more mathematical reader's desire to achieve a better understanding of any particular model's foundations. While both of us have taught in academic environments for many years, our focus in presentation here is more on how a particular theoretical construct or model can help solve a real business problem rather than on the elegance of various theories from an intellectual or aesthetics standpoint. As a consequence of this rather pragmatic perspective, we have tried to highlight the applications of various models in the context of our real-world experience.

After providing an overview in Chapter 1 of credit analysis, credit portfolio management, and associated concepts, we move to the models and frameworks used in this area. Before we tackle the specifics of the models, the second chapter discusses a number of organizational issues associated with ACPM in practice to set the stage for the other discussions. Each subsequent chapter then addresses a different aspect of the tools and frameworks that can change the processes and systems used by financial institutions today. The first several of these cover the range of PD and valuation models used in these credit portfolio management systems: structural, econometric, and reduced-form. Since differentiating the usefulness of models becomes key to effective system implementation, we have set aside an entire chapter on model validation. Though applied work on estimating loss given default (LGD) is still in its early stages of development, we have also included a short chapter that discusses this problem and some approaches to modeling LGD.

The penultimate chapter of the book focuses on the portfolio modeling question with an emphasis on correlation, estimation of loss distributions, and touches on how structured credit works. The final chapter presents a case study of a bank implementing these tools to build an ACPM and economic capital allocation function. This case study is a composite drawn from a number of actual implementations completed at a number of financial institutions with which we have worked. The composite nature of the case study allows us to highlight the range of issues when implementing these systems that often go beyond just choosing models.

HOW TO USE THIS BOOK

As we mentioned a number of times in this Preface, several more detailed and more comprehensive texts than ours have been written on credit already (see our References for a list). While we did not sit down to write another such book, we did hope to write this text to serve as a valuable field guide for practitioners, an industry-focused text for business schools, and an excellent complement to several of the other more theoretical texts. Moreover, we provide detailed discussions of the practical issues on which we have not seen other authors previously opine.

The first two chapters are essential background reading for the rest of the book. After these chapters, the reader may choose to read the rest of the book in any order, though our recommendation is for readers to get comfortable with single-obligor credit modeling before moving on to the discussions of credit portfolio modeling. Regardless, each chapter is designed to stand on its own. In fact, readers who read the book cover to cover will find some of the discussions and concepts repeated in several chapters. This is not an accident. Our experience in teaching this material is that some repetition of material— for example, of material on correlation or risk-neutral concepts—improves the reader's ability to retain understanding. For readers who pick and choose what they wish to learn, the complete discussion in each relevant context minimizes the need to flip back and forth through the book (although we expect that this jumping around in the text cannot be completely avoided).

Supplemental materials are provided to complement the text. In particular, we offer review questions and problems at the back of each chapter.

Other materials, such as computer source code, can be found on the web site www.creditrisklib.com. As it turns out, we have not been able to find a single computational tool that seems to suffice for building models for all the applications covered in this field. Even between the two of us, we find the need to use a number of platforms. That is why you may find code written with several different languages and tools. Instead of bemoaning the lack of standardization, we accept our fate, celebrate the diversity of coding platforms, and try to use each to its best effect. Since we are continually updating and adding to these materials, we recommend you refer back to our web site often. We retain the copyright to this code; however, it can be used without charge as long as you prominently provide attribution whenever you use all or a portion of these materials. We also encourage you to add to our growing store of credit risk tools on the web site. Please send contributions you wish to share with the public to modelingcode@creditrisklib.com. Finally, if you have comments or corrections on the text, please let us know at bookcorrections@creditrisklib.com.

Acknowledgments

Who would have guessed 30 years ago that the interaction of John A. ("Mac") McQuown, Oldrich Vasicek, Fischer Black, Myron Scholes, and Robert Merton would have created such a lasting impact on the world of credit? We are grateful to all of them for building the foundation for modern, quantitative credit risk and portfolio management. The addition of Stephen Kealhofer to this list of quantitative finance visionaries rounds out a powerful group of thinkers who have given us much of the tools and vocabulary to write this book. We express our thanks and acknowledge our intellectual debt to this group. We also thank John Rutherfurd and Mac McQuown for facilitating the creation of the company, Moody's KMV, that enabled the two of us to work together.

Over the years, many people at Moody's and KMV have contributed to the stockpile of credit knowledge reflected in this book. We thank all the members and former members of these companies who worked with us on developing better implementations of quantitative credit tools. In particular we thank Deepak Agrawal, Jalal Akhavein, Navneet Arora, Richard Cantor, Lea V. Carty, Ren-Raw Chen, Peter Crosbie, Ashish Das, Douglas Dwyer, Ken Emery, Greg Gupton, David Hamilton, Shota Ishii, Felipe Jordão, Sean Keenan, Andrew Kimball, Ahmet Kocagil, Kyle Kung, Matt Kurbat, Som-Lok Leung, Amnon Levy, Douglas Lucas, Christopher Mann, Albert Metz, Hans Mikkelsen, Bill Morokoff, Norah Qian, Jody Rasch, Alex Reyngold, Joachim Skor, Jorge Sobehart, Ben Zhang, and Jing Zhang. In addition, we thank the many clients of Moody's and MKMV that worked in intellectual partnership with us over the years as many of these ideas became instantiated in tools and processes facilitating quantitative risk management and active credit portfolio management. We also thank the following current and former colleagues at Shinsei Bank: Roger Browning, Mark Cutis, Rahul Gupta, Nick James, and Thierry Porte.

During the course of this project we received valuable feedback from a number of colleagues. In particular, several of them read large portions of this text and provided extensive comments on the content: Ed Altman, Marcia Banks, Richard Cantor, Ashish Das, Darrell Duffie, Douglas Dwyer, Gus Harris, David Keisman, Andrew Kimball, David Lando, Terry Marsh, and Jing Zhang. We are grateful for your time and patience in crafting your feedback which greatly improved the book.

Over the past eight years we both have benefited greatly from the feedback of members of Moody's Academic Advisory and Research Committee (MAARC), both during presentations at our semiannual meetings and through individual correspondence on particular topics. We would like to thank past and present members of the committee for their continued support and feedback: Pierre Collin-Dufresne, Darrell Duffie, Steve Figlewski, Gary Gorton, David Heath, John Hull, David Lando, Andrew Lo, William Perraudin, Mitchell Petersen, Raghu Rajan, Stephen Schaefer, Ken Singleton, Jeremy Stein, and Alan White. MAARC has been a constant source of feedback and new ideas.

Jeffrey R. Bohn also thanks the students in U.C. Berkeley's master's in financial engineering program who took his credit risk modeling course for providing feedback on the manner in which much of this material is described. Roger M. Stein thanks the students in the NYU Stern School of Business who took the courses he taught on modeling and attended his lectures over the past decade and who, through questions (and occasional blank stares), helped shape the presentation of this content.

Portions of the material here appeared in earlier published articles in a number of journals. We are grateful to the editors of the *Journal of Banking and Finance*, the *Journal of Investment Management*, and the *Journal of Risk Model Validation* for granting permission, where necessary, to use this material.

We also thank our editors, Bill Falloon, Emilie Herman, and Michael Lisk of Wiley who gave us excellent guidance on developing the material and shaping it into book form.

We created the "word cloud" images at the beginning of each chapter at www.wordle.net

While we have tried to make this book as useful as possible, there is no single recipe for most of the problems we discuss. Rather than attempt to offer a one-size-fits-all blueprint, we have tried to provide sufficient detail and practical advice to motivate readers to think about and implement some of the tools in this book and to begin to take informed action. However, as with any technical field, there is always a gap between reading about something and doing it. Setting up an active credit portfolio management function requires hundreds of small and large decisions, and these require more specialized and customized expertise than can fit into any general text.

This field still has a ways to go. We look forward to maintaining and extending associations with the members of the global credit community to overcome the long list of issues still to be resolved in this dynamic field of quantitative credit risk modeling.

Importantly, we express a number of strong views in this text. *These views are wholly our own, and do not represent the views of our current or former employers (Moody's Investors Service, Moody's Risk Management Services, Moody's KMV, and Shinsei Bank) or any of their affiliates. Accordingly, all of the foregoing companies and their affiliates expressly disclaim all responsibility for the content and information contained herein.*

CHAPTER 1

The Framework: Definitions and Concepts

Commercial credit is the creation of modern times and belongs in its highest perfection only to the most enlightened and best governed nations. Credit is the vital air of the system of modern commerce. It has done more, a thousand times more, to enrich nations than all of the mines of the world.
—Daniel Webster, 1934 (excerpt from speech in the U.S. Senate)

Theories of the known, which are described by different physical ideas, may be equivalent in all their predictions and are hence scientifically indistinguishable. However, they are not psychologically identical when trying to move from that base into the unknown. For different views suggest different kinds of modifications which might be made and hence are not equivalent in the hypotheses one generates from them in one's attempt to understand what is not yet understood.
—Richard Feynman, 1965

Objectives

After reading this chapter, you should understand the following:

- Definition of credit.
- Evolution of credit markets.
- The importance of a portfolio perspective of credit.
- Conceptual building blocks of credit portfolio models.
- Conceptually how credit models are used in practice.
- The impact of bank regulation on portfolio management.
- Why we advocate active credit portfolio management (ACPM).

1

WHAT IS CREDIT?

Credit is one of the oldest innovations in commercial practice. Historically, credit has been defined in terms of the borrowing and lending of money. Credit transactions differ from other investments in the nature of the contract they represent. Contracts where fixed payments are determined up front over a finite time horizon differentiate a credit instrument from an equity instrument. Unlike credit instruments, equity instruments tend to have no specific time horizon in their structure and reflect a claim to a share of an entity's future profits, no matter how large these profits become. While some equity instruments pay dividends, these payments are not guaranteed, and most equity is defined by not having any predetermined fixed payments.

In contrast, traditional credit instruments facilitate transactions in which one party borrows from another with specified repayment terms over a specific horizon. These instruments include fixed-coupon bonds and floating-rate loans (the coupon payments are determined by adding a spread to an underlying benchmark rate such as the U.S. Treasury rate or LIBOR[1]). Corporations are well-known issuers of these types of debt instruments; however, they are not the only borrowers. The past several decades have seen an explosion of consumer credit (particularly in the United States) in the form of home mortgages, credit card balances, and consumer loans. Other borrowers (also called *obligors*) include governments (usually termed *sovereigns*) and supranational organizations such as the World Bank. The credit risk of these instruments depends on the ability of the sovereign, corporation, or consumer to generate sufficient future cash flow (through operations or asset sales) to meet the interest and principal payments of the outstanding debt.

As financial engineering technology has advanced, the definition of credit has expanded to cover a wider variety of exposures through various derivative contracts whose risk and payoffs are dependent on the credit risk of some other instrument or entity. The key characteristic of these instruments is that, here again, the risk tends to lie in a predetermined payment stream over the life of the security or contract. Credit default swaps (CDS) exemplify this trend which aims to isolate the credit risk of a particular firm, the *reference obligor*, by linking a derivative's value to the solvency of the reference obligor, only. These contracts require the *protection buyer* to pay a regular fee (or spread) to the *protection seller*. In the event the reference

---

[1] The London Interbank Offer Rate (LIBOR) is the rate at which large banks are willing to lend to each other. The interest rate swap market provides an indication of how LIBOR is expected to change over time.

obligor defaults (per the specification of the CDS contract), the protection seller is required to make the protection buyer whole per the terms of the contract. Conceptually, the contract represents an insurance policy between the buyer (the insured) and the seller (the insurance provider). Extending the metaphor, the regular fee represents an insurance premium and the payout in the event of default represents an insurance claim under the policy. While a myriad of contract types now trade in the market, fundamentally they all represent a view on the credit risk of the underlying reference obligor.

While a CDS refers to a single name, derivative contracts on indexes of many named obligors can also be purchased as contracts on a specific basket of assets. These instruments expand the ability of credit portfolio managers to manage a large number of exposures without always resorting to hedging on a name-by-name basis or selling assets outright.

A related set of securities requiring financial engineering are broadly defined as *structured credit*. Popular forms of structured credit (also known as *securitization*) include collateralized debt obligations (CDOs) and asset-backed securities (ABS). In recent times, the credit crisis has made discussion of CDOs and ABSs more common in the media. Many commentators have called for drastic measures to curtail the use of structured credit. While abuse of these instruments can increase risk in institutions and markets, structured financial products can also be used responsibly to reduce risk in the financial system. Some regional banks, for example, have successfully hedged the concentration risk in their portfolios that results from most of their loans being originated in a single geography. They do this by selling some of their portfolio risk via structured credit. Other investors have purchased this risk and integrated it into their own portfolios as diversifying investments, creating lower volatility portfolios with improved return per unit of risk profiles. All market participants benefit from this kind of trading. Of course, these instruments can be abused when combined with excessive leverage or when market participants attempt to speculate using structures they do not fully understand.

But even the *simplest* of financial instruments such as equity can be inappropriate for particular investors in certain situations. The same is true of structured credit. We try to be careful to distinguish the *purpose* from the *characteristics* of particular instruments.

Conceptually, the basic structure of these instruments is straightforward: A number of securities or derivative contracts called *collateral* are placed in a structure called a *special purpose vehicle* (SPV) or *special purpose company* (SPC), creating a corporate vehicle to direct the cash flows from the collateral. In its simplest form, the purpose of the SPV is to borrow cash, typically through debt issuance, and to use this cash to purchase the collateral: some type of credit-sensitive obligation. The collateral may be provided by a financial institution, such as a bank that issues mortgages, or purchased in the secondary market, such as the case of corporate bonds.

Why could not a financial institution just issue the bonds directly rather than through an SPV? The purpose of an SPV is typically to create *bankruptcy remoteness* for the issuance of the debt. This means that the ownership of collateral is legally transferred from, say, the bank that made the loans, to the SPV. The objective is to ensure that if the bank goes into default, the collateral will not be considered part of the assets of the bank. Said another way, the SPV structure ensures that the collateral will be used only for the benefit of the holders of the structured securities issued by the SPV, regardless of where it was originated.

The SPV uses the cash flow from the collateral to pay back the debt as the collateral generates payment income through, for example, amortization and interest payments. The cash flow from the collateral is paid out to holders of each class of the liability structure (called a *tranche*) of the SPV per a set of rules called a *cash flow waterfall*. The tranching of debt creates a priority of payments (or of loss positions) such that more junior tranches (i.e., those lower in the capital structure) absorb losses first, followed by the next most senior, and so on. The motivation behind these structures is the desire to change the return/risk profile of the collateral into a set of securities or tranches with different return/risk profiles, with lower tranches exposed to more risk and higher tranches enjoying greater protection from collateral losses. In many structures there are also rules that specify that all cash be directed to more senior tranches if the performance of the collateral begins to deteriorate, providing still further protection for the higher tranches. It should be obvious that the analysis of many types of structured instruments is therefore quite similar to the analysis of a portfolio of assets in any financial institution but with the added complication of waterfalls and other structural provisions.

The names of these structures, such as CDO or ABS, reflect this collateralized nature of these instruments. Each specific structure name refers to the nature of the collateral:

- CLO: Collateralized loan obligation.
- CBO: Collateralized bond obligation.
- CDO-squared: CDO of tranches issued by other CDOs.
- RMBS: Residential mortgage–backed security.
- CMBS: Commercial mortgage–backed security.

Even without the added complexity of a securitization, credit instruments can be fairly complicated on a stand-alone basis. For example, many corporate bonds incorporate an attached call option designed to give the issuer the opportunity to pay back the debt earlier, should market conditions favor doing so. The call option identifies a price at which the issuer (i.e., obligor or borrower) can purchase back the debt. In an environment of falling interest rates or improving credit quality for the borrower, this option opens the door for the borrower to take advantage of better terms as they become available. For example, a fixed-rate bond will rise in price as interest rates fall. At some point, the issuer of a callable bond will find it advantageous to purchase back the debt so they can reissue at the lower rate. The call option provides this opportunity. As another example, many bank loans are structured with triggers and other features that change the payoff of the loan conditional on various metrics related to the borrower's performance. Such loan covenants may increase the loan's coupon rate if the financial performance of the firm, based on a predefined metric such as a leverage ratio (e.g., total debt/total equity or total debt/total assets), deteriorates.

Sometimes a credit exposure does not even reflect actual cash being loaned right away. Instead of a straight term loan, a bank may extend a commitment to lend with a variety of conditions as to the terms of borrowing. We typically refer to loans where cash is actually disbursed as *funded* and commitments to lend as *unfunded*. Note, however, that a contractual commitment to lend exposes the bank to risk even if funds have not actually been transferred to the obligor.[2] As this brief discussion highlights, credit exposures like these can be decomposed into a risk-free debt instrument and a collection of other (e.g., default, prepayment, interest rate, etc.) options. In fact, most credit instruments represent a portfolio of options.

Credit exposure also arises in the context of more traditional derivative transactions such as equity options and interest rate swaps. When such a derivative is *in-the-money*,[3] the market risk (i.e., risk arising from changes in quantities driving the value of the derivative) must be separated out from the credit risk. This implicit credit risk may become significant when systemic events impact the entire market. The recent financial crisis has highlighted how the solvency of large counterparties to derivatives transactions can have widespread impact on the financial system overall. The most recent global credit crisis is not, however, the only example in modern times of increased

---

[2] A common oversight of some banks is to ignore their unfunded commitments since the commitments are made to potential borrowers at times when these borrowers are financially healthy. The problem that can arise is that these obligors tend to borrow at times when they face difficulties.

[3] The counterparty who is *out-of-the-money* owes payments to the counterparty who is *in-the-money*, such as would be the case, for example, for the holder of the fixed-rate leg of a floating-fixed-rate interest swap when fixed rates were above floating rates.

counterparty-default risk. The latter part of 1998 also saw a substantial increase in the likelihood of counterparty default. After Russia defaulted on its domestic currency debt and LTCM (a large hedge fund) came to the brink of insolvency, many investment banks appeared to face unprecedented difficulty. In this situation, the risk of a counterparty not paying became significant. Counterparty credit risk always exists, and even if a derivative counterparty does not default, the value of an in-the-money derivative may be adversely affected by the difficulties faced by the counterparty. A firm or counterparty does not have to default in order to result in a loss of value for a particular credit-risky instrument. Counterparty credit risk has become a much more important topic as the volume of derivatives has mushroomed and market participants have become more cognizant of this risk.

The salient feature of all these different types of credit exposure is the shape of the distribution of losses. Credit exposures are typically characterized by skewed, fat-tailed return distributions. That is, the lender or originator of an exposure has a high probability of receiving its principal back plus a small profit over the life of the exposure and a low probability of losing a significant portion of the exposure. An example of a credit loss distribution can be seen in Figure 1.1.

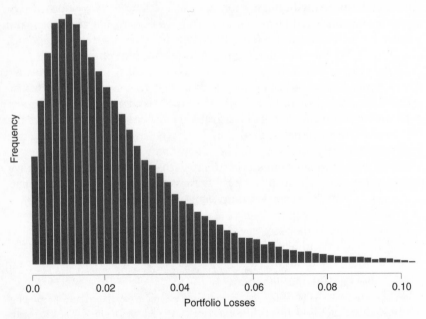

FIGURE 1.1   Simulated Loss Distribution

Said another way, many borrowers have a high chance of repayment but if they do fail, they tend to fail severely. The correlation among these types of exposures tends to be quite low compared with, say, the correlation of equity exposures. However, ironically, the diversification of these exposures tends to take a larger number of names than is the case with equity or other instruments with less skewed payoffs. This low correlation coupled with the chance of losing a substantial amount on any one exposure makes these securities particularly well suited for management in the context of a large, *well-diversified* portfolio. If a bank's portfolio contains only small bits of each exposure, the occasional extreme loss for any one exposure will tend not to affect the portfolio's overall performance. Thus, diversification buys stability in the portfolio's loss profile. Importantly, unlike the case of other instruments, even a well-diversified portfolio will typically exhibit significant skewness *that cannot be diversified away*. We return to this conclusion a number of times throughout this book.

EVOLUTION OF CREDIT MARKETS

While the idea of debt extends back into ancient societies, the more modern notion of credit really began in preindustrial Europe in the context of commercial payments. Credit was typically extended by way of deferred payment for goods sold or advance payment for future delivery of goods purchased (see Kohn 2001 for more details on the history of banks and credit). Over time these debts began to be treated as fungible and would be assigned to other merchants, and eventually systems of settlement evolved. Deposit banking developed in response to the need for assignment of third-party debt among strangers. Since the bank became the counterparty for multiple transactions, it could net a large number of payments without resorting to final cash settlement.

This set of circumstances enabled preindustrial banks to offer a solution to the endemic problem of liquidity risk faced by merchants, namely a short-term lack of cash preventing completion of a particular transaction. Since depositors in the bank found it convenient to leave their money with the banker so that settlement of transactions could be done without having to lug around actual coins, the bank now had a store of deposits to use as the basis of an overdraft loan. The bankers discovered that they could extend credit beyond the quantity of actual coins or gold on deposit since most depositors did not demand all of their deposits most of the time. Here we find the beginnings of leverage in financial institutions. Since the banker knew his clients well, the bank could use its knowledge of the capacity of a potential borrower (who is also likely a depositor) to repay a loan and allow this individual to periodically overdraw his account. Eventually, these short-duration, relatively small overdraft loans were supplemented and then overtaken by longer, larger commercial loans. (Again refer to Kohn 2001 for more details on the evolution of banks and credit markets.)

From these humble beginnings, credit evolved along a myriad of dimensions. Credit could be extended not only in the form of loans, but also in the form of bonds traded in a global capital market. Computers replaced written ledgers and money become *tokenized*—represented as digitized bits stored in a hard drive. However, the characteristics of credit remain the same. Yet along with this technological progress developed a capacity for higher volume lending. As a result, a number of difficulties appeared as the institutions and markets developed for the origination and management of credit and this evolution progressed.

The first difficulty the financial world encountered was that of *bank runs*. Since the process of lending depends on depositors not demanding their money in cash all at once, the reputation of the bank, and depositor's confidence in its solvency, is critical. If a large enough number of depositors perceive a bank to be unsound and demand their cash all at once (creating a run on the bank), that bank may fail even if the perception is false. The creation of a lender of last resort such as a central bank and the provision of deposit insurance from the government are institutional responses to this bank failure risk due to runs on banks.

The second difficulty developed from the challenge in managing potentially large losses on the bank's loan book. In these cases, the trouble arises when a sizable portion of a bank's portfolio of loans simultaneously cannot be repaid as promised. In this case the bank, in a sense, becomes the victim of its own success. Typically, a bank develops expertise in originating loans within a particular geography and sector. For example, large Japanese banks in the 1980s became very good at lending money to large Japanese trading companies. While economic times were good, this concentration of loans in one geography and one sector did not seem to pose a problem. However, such concentrations obviously create significant correlation in the payoffs of the loans in the portfolio. When Japan's economic bubble burst and the 1990s uncovered the disastrous impact of holding a concentrated portfolio, large Japanese banks watched the loans in their portfolios deteriorate together. This problem is by no means unique to Japan. It is hard to find any country with a functioning banking system that has not seen this kind of bank crisis at some point in its financial history. Origination expertise in a particular area leads to concentrations that create problems when that sector or geography becomes troubled.

The third difficulty concerns the inefficiencies in the market for corporate credit. The corporate bond market developed in parallel to the expansion in the origination of bank loans. In preindustrial Europe, some merchants traded bills of exchange with each other. Over time, a dealer market emerged for corporate debt. The problem with this market was a lack of standardization and in turn a lack of transparency in pricing. These inefficiencies resulted in a lack of liquidity, making it difficult to trade in and out of positions and to thus manage a portfolio of corporate debt.

These challenges notwithstanding, debt markets continued to mature, albeit at a leisurely pace. However, the 1990s ushered in a new era for corporate credit markets in which several trends converged to create an environment where credit could be priced and managed in a relatively efficient manner. The first trend involved the successful implementation of objective, quantitative analytic tools to facilitate rigorous evaluation of credit exposures. This environment arose from the marriage of modern finance and powerful computer technology. However, the ability to analyze the risk of a credit portfolio was only the first step; a portfolio manager also needed to have the ability to act on this analysis and trade at a reasonable cost. This second step, which has only become fully implemented in the past decade due to the availability of cheap telecommunications, has created a trend that facilitates inexpensive trading in credit-risky instruments. While corporate bonds have always been traded, a market in secondary trading of corporate loans has also developed.

The third step in this evolution was the ability to complete the cycle of analysis and trading and to thus diversify *portfolio* holdings. Modern financial theory emphasizes the power of portfolio diversification. A variety of financial institutions ranging from banks to pension funds now manage their portfolios using measures of diversification. This third trend has set the stage for a dramatic increase in the number of market participants trading credit for reasons other than just exiting a distressed position (although corporate distress will always motivate a significant number of trades).

In recent years, some of the most sophisticated banks have used portfolio analysis technology to devise transfer pricing mechanisms allowing them to separate the management of the bank's credit portfolio from the creation of valuable service businesses. (We discuss this organizational change in more detail later in this chapter.) Clearly, today the motivation for trading credit goes beyond avoiding a default and ranges from perceived market inefficiencies to portfolio rebalancing designed to improve the return/risk profile of an institution's entire credit portfolio.

Another important trend has been the change in the regulatory environment as financial regulators come to grips with the importance of measuring and managing credit risk. The first global bank accord, known as Basel I, defined a simple notion of how much capital a bank should hold, given the credit risk of its loan book. Currently, a more complex accord known as Basel II is being debated. While regulators have now acknowledged the feasibility and importance of estimating quantitative measures of credit such as probability of default (PD) and loss given default (LGD), the most advanced banks have already been running systems that not only evaluate PDs and LGDs, but also incorporate the correlations among exposures in their portfolios. Some regulators have made efforts to incorporate a portfolio view into bank regulations, but the progress has been slow. The benefit of this new regulatory focus on credit is that it motivates many financial institutions to invest in the systems that enable them to do better credit portfolio management. Regulators have also improved market transparency. In the United States, regulatory pressure resulted in the creation of the Trade Reporting and Compliance Engine (TRACE) data initiative requiring bond dealers to post their transaction prices for corporate bonds.

A fifth trend is the sudden appearance of a deep and liquid market in corporate credit derivatives. At the time of this writing, the CDS market exceeds USD$60 trillion in notional value. The availability of credit indexes such as the iTraxx and CDX makes it much easier to hedge portfolio exposure. Synthetic CDOs have become common transactions in the world of credit management. These instruments create a mechanism for more efficient management and transfer of risk exposure. A portfolio manager can now isolate the credit risk components of price from other types of risks impacting the value of a bond or a loan (e.g., market risk and liquidity risk). In this way, portfolio decisions are no longer held hostage by the inability to trade a particular risk by itself. Furthermore, research can now begin to sort out the relationships among credit risk and some of these other kinds of risks. The draining of liquidity in the structured credit market in 2007 and 2008, particularly for collateralized loan obligations, has set the market back somewhat as the ability to hedge with structured credit has diminished. More recently, questions have arisen regarding potential misuse of leverage in constructing portfolios of CDS contracts, and more investment and transparency is needed in the infrastructure of settling CDS trades. These challenges have made all market participants more focused on how to better develop this important tool for managing credit risk.

Though still evolving, the markets for corporate credit risk, whether they involve bank loans, bonds, or credit derivatives, are becoming more liquid and more transparent. This does not imply that they are anywhere near fully mature. The development of these markets has not been smooth, as exemplified by the recent credit crisis resulting in the dramatic reduction in issuance volume in many sectors of the market for CDOs in late 2007 and the overall difficulties across most credit markets in 2008. That said, the CDS market remains the primary place to trade corporate credit risk and it appears to be here to stay despite recent drops in volume. This market is generally much more liquid than other markets involving credit. While these markets still have much room for improvement (particularly outside of the United States), we have the benefit today of tools and the understanding to manage a portfolio of corporate credit exposures actively in a way that substantially decreases the risk of extreme losses. Tools and methods are also being developed for analyzing portfolios of ABS and retail exposures, though the quantitative literature on these types of exposures lags in many cases that of the corporate literature.

The challenge lies in choosing the right models and systems to support this active corporate portfolio management effort. Even more important is modifying the way that risk is managed within a financial organization in a manner that motivates employees to make decisions that result in efficient allocation of the bank's economic capital. In our judgment, proper organizational incentives informed by useful portfolio insight will lead to less risky, more valuable banks.

DEFINING RISK

Throughout our discussions in this book, we define risk as the possible change in value of a security or asset over a particular time horizon. Change in value is not the only way to define risk. Some practitioners have focused on risk as defined only in terms of the probability of default (i.e., firms with low PDs (high ratings) are safe and those with high PDs are risky). The trouble with this definition is that a portfolio can store up "time bombs," in effect, that are not readily appreciated until it is too late when many firms in the same industry or geography default at the same time. Since the probability of default of one loan is the same regardless of the concentrations in a portfolio, the potential for large losses on a portfolio can change dramatically with portfolio correlation. Furthermore, the tracking of credit migration or changes in value prior to maturity becomes essential to capturing the true risk of a portfolio through time. Otherwise, the portfolio manager may be surprised by a cluster of sudden defaults. In this context, an approach that considers both the underlying risk and the change in the values of securities within a portfolio is a superior focus for risk assessment than just the risk of defaults within a portfolio.

Other authors have argued that risk should be defined only in terms of a decline in value. However, our experience suggests that a focus on only downside variance (sometimes called semivariance) ignores important information about the future. For example, Internet firms in the late 1990s experienced a few years of skyrocketing growth in value. Their later fall was even faster than their rise. Focusing just on downside variance in those cases would have led to a severe underestimation of overall risk.

In the case of *credit risk*, this change in value derives from the changing probability that the obligor will fulfill its obligation to pay interest and ultimately repay principal. This is fundamentally different along a number of dimensions than *market risk*, which encompasses changes in a security's value as driven by variables such as interest rates, equity prices, commodity prices, and foreign exchange. Financial practitioners have settled on models and systems in the field of market risk much more quickly than in the field of credit risk. The availability of data and liquid markets in instruments such as interest-rate swaps and other derivatives has made it easier to introduce quantitative hedging and portfolio management techniques in the field of market risk for equity and other instruments, while the absence of data and the more complicated statistical relationships made it more difficult historically to do the same for credit risk. That said, recent advances in both fields have produced a convergence of models and systems. Increasingly, we are encountering demands to integrate credit and market risk.

We touch briefly in this book on the state of this integration. Our primary interest lies in understanding how interest rates and credit spreads are related. The portfolio factor model structure we introduce in Chapter 8 can be modified to handle both credit-risky securities and market-risky securities. The challenge lies in defining the function that transforms *factor realizations* (i.e., economy- or sector-wide shifts in the drivers of default) into a security value. The increasingly heterogeneous (in terms of asset classes) nature of most financial institutions' portfolios makes it even more important to build models with the flexibility to handle a variety of instruments. As part of our exploration of reduced-form models (Chapter 6), we also discuss the similarities between market-risk models and some of the reduced-form models used for credit risk.

As previously noted, in credit risk modeling, we attribute much of the change in value of credit-risky securities to changes in the likelihood that the obligor will pay its coupons and repay principal. Some models, such as structural models, rely on specific economic reasoning to describe why an obligor defaults—namely that the market value of the borrower's assets falls to a point at which it no longer covers the total amount of its obligations. Other more statistically focused models such as reduced-form models do not rely on a specific causal economic relationship, but rather focus on default as an unpredictable event that can be captured in a coherent mathematical model that is consistent with financial theory. Even so, reduced-form models tend to focus on processes that drive credit quality. They can also be extended to include processes that drive the state of market liquidity.

What can substantially muddy this modeling challenge is the possibility of a liquidity-based default or liquidity-based change in security value. In a circumstance in which market liquidity has dried up, a firm with sufficient market value may still default because it cannot roll over its short-term debt as it comes due. The claims represented in the issued loans and bonds of a particular obligor may still relate to that obligor's valuable assets, but the absence of liquidity in the market prevents a portfolio manager or credit trader from finding new financing or selling positions in its portfolio to cover existing claims. These liquidity-driven difficulties may result from different processes than the ones driving changes in credit quality (although the credit problems and liquidity difficulties are often related). From a model perspective, we attempt to separate (when possible) the effect of credit factors from the effect of liquidity factors on estimates of relevant metrics that characterize risk and value.

A WORD ABOUT REGULATION

Given the importance of banks to most national economies, governments have an interest in ensuring the prudent management of these institutions. Such efforts to reduce systemic financial risk often focus on instituting regulations. At the international level, the Bank of International Settlements (BIS) has taken on the task of coordinating proposals for bank regulations internationally. These proposals may or may not be implemented in each domicile; however, the ideas spark discussion throughout the regulatory community. As mentioned earlier in this chapter, in the late 1980s, BIS published a global banking accord designed to eliminate the advantage Japanese banks seemed to hold in gaining access to cheap funding. Basel I, as the accord is now called, outlined for banks the appropriate levels of capital they should hold for given classes of risk. It did this in broad terms with the goal of creating a common language of regulatory capital risk rather than of outlining detailed risk management strategies.

However, in hindsight, while it was an important step forward, the blunt nature of Basel I created opportunities for regulatory arbitrage in which a bank could take advantage of situations in which the rules unintentionally led institutions *away* from economically profitable transactions.

In recent years, the BIS has struggled to finalize the next generation of regulation, Basel II. Basel II is intended to create more sensible guidelines within which banks can develop systems for credit risk assessment and economic capital allocation. The promise of Basel II lies in aligning the regulatory guidelines with the way in which decisions are actually made at financial institutions. Unfortunately, the tendency of government entities to create broad-ranging proposals that attempt to satisfy many different interest groups has resulted in regulations that some market participants feel fall short along certain dimensions. One positive result of the Basel II efforts is the impact it has had on the way in which senior bank managers think about and now focus on the notion of quantitative credit risk modeling and capital allocation. As a consequence, risk management efforts within banks now receive better funding to build and implement systems that not only facilitate regulatory compliance, but that can also be used to implement economic capital systems, which in turn result in more efficient and, importantly, less risky banks.

To our knowledge, most regulators still do not publicly promote the idea of active portfolio management.[4] Their efforts focus more on establishing rules that reduce systemic risk in the financial markets. However, the regulatory perspective with respect to quantitative risk management has become far more sophisticated than it was at the time Basel I was introduced. In fact, some of the leading researchers on credit risk now reside within central banks and other regulatory bodies. As a result we expect that over time, newly formed organizations such as the International Association of Credit Portfolio Managers (IACPM) will assist banks in the process of coordinating with regulators to improve the dialogue around implementing new systems and new organizational structures.

WHAT ARE CREDIT MODELS GOOD FOR?

One of the authors recalls an experience a number of years ago teaching a group of old and wizened loan originators at a bank implementing quantitative tools for credit risk management. In the middle of the training session, one frustrated participant complained that we "rocket scientists" were

---

[4] In fact, Basel II has relatively less to say about portfolio correlation in general, compared to PD and LGD estimation.

destroying relationship banking. He went on to proclaim that a computer model could never match his capability for assessing a company's credit quality. While his track record was never verified to our knowledge, we are aware of several studies[5] at banks that show that *on balance*, subjective credit risk assessment alone is decidedly inferior to quantitative-based approaches (in a later chapter we explore in more detail how to evaluate models). Further, the credit officer's first statement in this anecdote about the destruction of relationship banking seemed to imply a simplified view of how models should be used.

While some computer scientists still assert "true" artificial intelligence is possible in the near term, typical businesspeople do not expect that a model or computer will fully replace a human being in the credit assessment process in the foreseeable future or that this would even be a good thing. In fact, relationship banking is alive and well and relies primarily on the strength of human intuition. Rather than destroying relationships, quantitative models change the way a bank can be organized and, more importantly, change the way credit analysts and relationship managers can do their jobs. Well-implemented systems improve the development of relationship banking and increase the efficiency and accuracy of credit analysts. Good models can provide a means to reduce some of the more tedious aspects of credit analysis and focus the analyst on the obligors, data, and processes that need attention as the bank manages its risk.

With quantitative models at the foundation of a bank's credit assessment process, qualitative assessment can be overlaid when appropriate. It is crucial that when such systems are developed and implemented, they facilitate ongoing rigorous assessment of how well models are performing and what the models' limitations are, regardless of whether they are quantitative, qualitative, or a mixture.

Qualitative assessment becomes more important when evaluating borrowers where market observable information is lacking. Even in these circumstances where data is scarce, a quantitative model can assist in directing the conversation to meaningful characterizations of what drives a borrower's risk. In many ways, these models become a *lingua franca* for risk discussions throughout the bank and transaction discussions outside the bank. We find that the most successful institutions benchmark (on a regular basis) internal models to ensure that the language of risk maintains the same meaning from transaction to transaction. Models are best used in environments in which

---

[5] Such studies are often internal and thus are not often published externally; one standard older reference on a nonfinance topic is Dawes (1979).

the organization maintains a balance of healthy skepticism—reviewing the models underlying this language of risk and reconsidering model assumptions regularly—and healthy enthusiasm for the efficiency and insights that quantitative approaches to credit risk management can bring to their credit processes and internal communication about risk. If implemented correctly, this language of risk can be used to transform a financial institution's business, moving it from origination of single exposures to *active credit portfolio management.*

ACTIVE CREDIT PORTFOLIO MANAGEMENT (ACPM)

Throughout this chapter we refer back to the importance of managing a portfolio and improving its diversification. In the equity market, symmetric return distributions coupled with the diversified nature of what is available in the market often means that active management does not pay high dividends. In fact, most active equity managers *under*perform their risk-adjusted benchmark.

Credit is different. Credit markets do not originate well-diversified portfolios, and the asymmetric nature of credit return distributions makes avoiding a deteriorating credit material to overall portfolio return. Moreover, the lack of good benchmarks makes it difficult to offer index funds that do not suffer from substantial idiosyncratic risk. These characteristics of credit markets create an opportunity to earn outsize returns given a particular level of risk on a portfolio of credits that is actively managed. This starts with models and systems that discriminate good from bad obligors. Further returns can be earned by refining the correlation estimates—a difficult but achievable proposition to some degree for certain segments of the credit markets.

Another important reason that active management is beneficial in the world of credit has to do with the heterogeneous nature of liquidity across credit-risky instruments. While robust liquidity models are still being researched, good credit models can move a manager a step closer to identifying profitable trades and reduce the uncertainty with respect to the question of liquidity. In many circumstances, these models provide an interpretive framework to discern the different factors driving value and focus analysis. Developing these strategies in the context of portfolio trades helps reduce the idiosyncratic impact of inexplicable behaviors of particular securities. A portfolio perspective complemented with quantitative systems sets the stage for generating high Sharpe (return per unit of volatility) and Vasicek (return per unit of tail-risk contribution or return per unit of capital) ratios for a credit portfolio that is actively managed.

LIQUIDITY

Defining liquidity can be difficult. In general, we think of liquidity as a measure of the depth of a market and the ease with which a trade can be made. For some, liquidity is the label researchers place on the things that economists or financial modelers cannot explain (i.e., the residual in their analyses). With the development of a variety of markets pricing risk associated with the same names (e.g., equity, bonds, loans, CDSs), we have begun to catch glimpses of pricing differences that are a function of differences in liquidity. We do not yet have the full framework to sort out these differences. In the meantime, we are left with cruder methods, such as matrices of liquidity premia that reflect geography, industry, and size of the obligor.

While we currently do not have fully developed models of liquidity, we do understand the following:

1. Many theoretical credit models underestimate credit spreads, in part because they do not account for a liquidity premium.
2. Large transactions or trades tend to be heavily impacted by lack of market liquidity.
3. While available approaches are still evolving, some measure of liquidity (even if *ad hoc*) should be incorporated into mark-to-market and transfer pricing frameworks.
4. With the availability of CLOs and bespoke synthetic CDOs, we can develop an estimate of the cost of hedging through these vehicles that can assist us in finding an indirect estimate of the illiquidity premium. The difficulty lies in disentangling the credit risk premium from the illiquidity premium.

The topic of liquidity will continue to be a focus of research as more financial institutions build up their portfolio management capabilities. The dramatic changes in liquidity seen throughout the credit markets since late 2007 should provide important new data on liquidity premia.

While still in its infancy, the development of ACPM groups within financial institutions and the increasingly common discussions of the importance of tracking a portfolio's mark-to-market value suggest that some banks will start to look more like trading houses than classical commercial lending institutions. This shift will continue to blur the difference among different types of financial firms. Hedge funds, large corporations, insurance companies, asset managers, and investment banks are joined by commercial banks as financial institutions discover the value in separating the *management of their credit portfolios* from the *development of franchise businesses.* In some cases (e.g., hedge funds), the only business of a firm may be managing a portfolio, while in other cases (e.g., large financial conglomerates) the ACPM business is just one of many. Though still developing slowly, this convergence bodes well for the global capital market's ability to originate, distribute, and manage credit risk without creating dangerous concentrations in any one location.

An implication of this shift in managing a bank's portfolio separately from developing its franchise businesses (which includes the business of loan origination) is that a bank moves from an originate-and-hold strategy to an originate-to-distribute (also called "originate-and-distribute") strategy. This means that loans may be sold or hedged right after origination and not necessarily held to maturity. Said differently, the bank now manages its portfolio or credit risk based on portfolio concerns rather than assuming it will hold each originated loan to maturity.

Some critics have pointed to the originate-and-distribute model of commercial banks as a key cause of credit market difficulties such as the recent subprime crisis. In a world where the portfolio managers (whether they are CDO collateral managers or ACPM portfolio managers) do not rigorously evaluate the securities for which they have responsibility or where outright fraud is perpetrated by borrowers, an originate-and-distribute model can result in agency problems in which market participants do not pay sufficient attention to (or have transparency into) what kinds of borrowers are creating credit exposure. The problem that can arise when this happens on a large scale is that dramatic market corrections that occur in a systemic manner across the economy can have undesirable external impact in other parts of the financial markets. The only environment in which the originate-and-distribute model can function is one in which there is ample transparency with respect to instruments and assets and in which the incentives and structure of the lending process makes fraud difficult and its penalties severe.

While this is a tall order, unfortunately, the alternative of returning to the originate-and-hold model leaves the economy open to a greater risk of widespread systemic problems as commercial banks end up holding concentrated portfolios that cannot withstand cyclical economic downturns. The numerous bank crises seen throughout history illustrate this risk. Each system has its strengths and weaknesses. Our view, however, is that the originate-and-distribute model has much more to offer to counterbalance the possibilities of widespread market difficulties. Recent events will more than likely increase market transparency and set the stage for much more robust institutional response to liquidity crises. In our view, while the originate-and-distribute model must still evolve to provide more closely aligned incentives for market participants, turning back to the former model of originate-and-hold will not do much to improve the resilience of financial markets.

The tools we describe in this book and the framework we suggest for their application within banks and other financial institutions provide a means to achieving ACPM by coordinating a set of models and systems with organizational change to improve dramatically the growth opportunities at a bank. The mechanism lies in aligning incentives at the nonportfolio business and relationship manager levels with the overall objective of a bank's management to build new and growing channels of cash flow. In the process of making these system and organizational changes, the bank will manage its credit portfolio such that the likelihood of extreme loss can be significantly reduced (though some systematic risk will always remain).

The ACPM function becomes critical to making the most of the models and systems available. The necessity of holding concentrated portfolios to leverage internal bank local expertise disappears. Discussions about business strategy and new transactions become much more meaningful as a quantitative framework provides context for framing and testing assertions. By coupling this with a performance evaluation system tied into this framework, the bank's management can credibly justify higher valuation in the equity market and lower spreads in the debt market. This objective of higher share valuation becomes the ultimate motivation for moving the bank to an active portfolio management mind-set and investing in the models and internal processes to make this happen.

FRAMEWORK AT 30,000 FEET

At a conceptual level, the models discussed in this book provide insight into the return and risk trade-off among exposures in a credit portfolio. The stand-alone risk of a particular exposure tends to be the easiest to understand and act upon. Most analysts look to their wins in terms of which names they labeled correctly as high or low risk. The industry tends to remember the analyst who identified a deteriorating credit well before this deterioration was reflected in that obligor's loan, bond, or CDS price. A financial professional who identified problems at WorldCom or Ford before they became newspaper headlines will emphasize this in describing his abilities as a credit analyst.

The problem with these isolated examples is the lack of focus on the overall performance of the portfolio. If an analyst is consistently negative about all obligors, he will successfully identify the handful of big names that default. But that analyst has not necessarily helped that financial institution: Anyone can recommend avoiding all prospective borrowers. While it would be unusual for an analyst to deem all prospects poor risks, many qualitative assessments can tend toward the negative. Some analysts will use this negative bias to highlight the borrowers that do default. A similar difficulty will arise from an always optimistic analyst. Stand-alone risk assessment should clearly distinguish the strong from the weak borrowers. The ability to make this distinction should be regularly benchmarked and tested regardless of whether the assessment is done by a model, an analyst, or both.

What we and others have discovered over the past 20 years is that by itself, qualitative, stand-alone risk assessment typically does not (on average) lead to better-performing portfolios. Analysts who can regularly separate winners from losers in high volume are few and far between. More importantly, from a bank's perspective, the risk of any particular exposure is less interesting than is the performance of the portfolio as a whole. Thus, single exposures should be evaluated in the context of a portfolio, which requires characterization of credit exposure correlations. Stand-alone risk is only one piece of the portfolio puzzle. Moreover, we need measures that place each exposure on the same scale. The framework we emphasize in this book enables an analyst to calculate a portfolio value distribution. This distribution reflects the likelihood of different value outcomes over a specified time horizon.

The probability of a loss exceeding the point on the distribution associated with a target threshold can be interpreted as the probability that the portfolio will become insolvent—in other words, that the capital will be exhausted in the remote event of an extreme loss beyond the threshold. (In the next section we describe how this threshold may be set.) Each exposure's contribution to aspects of the portfolio loss distribution reflects a consistent, portfolio-referent measure of risk. We will refer to these portfolio-based risk measures as *risk contribution*.

Later we will be more specific about how we calculate risk contribution. At this stage, risk contribution can be interpreted as the post-diversification contribution of an exposure to a portfolio's overall risk—that is, the exposure's contribution to overall portfolio risk after accounting for how much the exposure adds to or subtracts from the portfolio's overall diversification. Risk contribution reflects the marginal risk of an exposure. An important point is that this marginal risk or risk contribution measure will be specific to a unique portfolio. What looks like a good addition at the margin in a Japanese bank portfolio may be a terrible loan to make for a U.S. bank portfolio.

Given the importance of understanding the concept of risk contribution, consider two examples where a portfolio risk contribution measure will motivate different conclusions than a stand-alone risk measure.

Japanese banks in the 1990s tended to hold portfolios heavily concentrated in large, Japanese companies. Some of these companies such as Toyota were quite safe on a stand-alone basis. However, the risk contribution of a safe, large company such as Toyota to a Japanese bank portfolio at this time would likely have been larger than the risk contribution of a moderately risky mid-size European company. The stand-alone measure for Toyota may imply it is a good addition to the portfolio, while the portfolio-referent risk measure may suggest that a riskier, non-Japanese company is a better choice. The portfolio perspective accounts not just for an exposure's stand-alone risk, but also the correlation and concentration of that exposure in the context of a given portfolio. Typically the correlation across geographies is lower than the correlation across industries within any particular geography.

Consider a similar example in the United States: U.S. banks in the 1970s tended to hold portfolios of high-quality, large U.S. corporate borrowers. Some of these banks even characterized themselves as diversifying across industries, but did not validate their assertion of effective portfolio diversification in any objectively quantitative way. We now know that the risk contribution of one more large corporate borrower in the context of these U.S. bank portfolios was typically higher than the risk contribution of a small to mid-size company even if the smaller company was from an industry already heavily represented in the portfolio. (Typically the correlation across company size groups within the same industry is lower than the correlation across industries for a given company size group.) A portfolio perspective requires uncovering the underlying factors that drive correlation across the portfolio. (Sometimes this risk is labeled *systemic* or *systematic*.)

With this conceptual understanding of why the risk side of the equation should focus on the portfolio, we now introduce the notion of *return*.

At its core, the motivation behind putting money at risk is to earn some kind of return. We can measure both the cash payments and the change in value of a credit-risky security when calculating return. In the context of the framework we develop in this book, the value of a security or asset is a function of the size and likelihood of cash payments we expect to receive as a consequence of holding that security or asset. In order to place all securities in a portfolio on the same measurement scale, we specify a time horizon. The change in value of a particular security over that time horizon requires us to know the value at the starting time of analysis (often referred to as the *as-of date*) and the time horizon date in the future over which the risk analysis is performed. These valuation exercises require a model to convert the characteristics of a particular security and its concomitant risk into a currency value.[6] Many default probability models are variants of valuation models.

Returning to our discussion: While the total return for a particular exposure is a useful first measure, we need to make two adjustments before we can draw any strong conclusions about a particular exposure. First, we must adjust the return for the time value of money. Conceptually, this means subtracting a measure of the risk-free return—that is, return earned from investing in a risk-free security. (In practice, we lean toward subtracting a measure of the cost of funds for the bank as that is the cost of securing the funds to put at risk.) Second, we must adjust for the amount we expect to lose. (Because there is credit risk associated with credit-risky securities and because there is an upper bound on the payoffs, the risk of a loss is always positive. This expected loss is the cost of running a credit business.) The result is a measure of return over a particular time horizon of analysis that is the premium earned for taking credit risk. The credit risk premium is what we expect to earn above and beyond the cost of funds and the exposure's expected loss.

Now we have the conceptual pieces for building a high-performance (lower risk/higher return) credit portfolio. We will always be faced with some constraints limiting the type of credit exposures that can be placed in the portfolio (e.g., limits on position sizes, availability of borrowers in some sectors, etc.). Subject to these constraints, we can compare the credit risk premium to the risk contribution for each existing exposure as well as each possible new exposure to determine which exposures to hold and which to sell out of the portfolio or buy protection on.

A final criterion for identifying a useful return or risk measure is that the measure can be coherently aggregated to characterize the health of the overall portfolio as well as subportfolios. For example, stand-alone risk cannot be coherently aggregated—in other words, a portfolio's stand-alone risk is not a simple weighted average of each of its exposure's stand-alone risks. Risk contribution, however, can be aggregated based on each exposure's weight in the portfolio. Expected return can also be aggregated based on the portfolio exposures' weights. In general, return measures are easier to aggregate than risk measures since return measures typically represent mean quantities, while risk measures typically represent higher moments of distributions (e.g, the ninety-ninth percentile). In this book, we focus on

---

[6] In credit we often convert the currency value into a spread, which is another way to represent the same value subject to several conditions. We discuss the notion of spread in detail several times throughout this book.

measures that meet this criterion. We introduce several different approaches for modeling each component of this framework. We also describe how to interpret and implement these measures in ways that will materially improve the performance of a financial institution actively managing its credit portfolio.

BUILDING BLOCKS OF PORTFOLIO RISK

Understanding the portfolio framework requires definitions of the key components used for credit portfolio analysis:

- Probability of default (PD): The probability that an obligor will not meet a stated obligation. In the case of a loan, the obligor is the borrower and the obligation is to pay a regular coupon and repay the principal at maturity. A PD will have a time horizon attached to it.
- Loss given default (LGD): The amount lost when an obligor fails to meet a stated obligation. Many times the focus is on recovery, or 1-LGD.
- Time horizon of analysis (H): Meaningful credit portfolio analysis requires the specification of a time horizon over which the analytics are calculated. Later we will be more specific with respect to the criteria for specifying H. Most analyses begin with the assumption that H is one year. Note that we often denote time with the letter T. In this book, we distinguish time to maturity as T from time horizon of analysis, which is H.
- Default correlation: The co-movement into default of two obligors.
- Value correlation: The co-movement in the value of the credit-risky securities within a portfolio.

With these definitions, we can sketch out the framework for evaluating a credit portfolio. Initially, we will determine expected loss, which is a primary cost of building a credit portfolio.

- Expected loss (EL): PD times LGD. This quantity is typically calculated over the time horizon, H. In this definition, we assume that the exposure at default (EAD) is par. This definition can be modified for other instrument types.
- Economic capital: The amount of (value) cushion available to absorb extreme losses—that is, absorb losses after using other sources of reserves such as provisions based on EL and earnings from exposures. The economic capital amount is calculated based on a target probability associated with an estimated portfolio loss distribution (estimated

for the time horizon, H). That is, the economic capital corresponds to the present value (of amounts at time H) of the loss level at which the probability of exceeding that loss level equals the target probability.

As we have alluded, it may be tempting to interpret EL as a measure of risk; however, it is better thought of as a measure of the cost of building credit portfolios. Then when we discuss capital as a cushion for unexpected losses, we have a clean separation of costs and capital.[7] The occasional surprise loss (or losses) becomes the focus of portfolio risk assessment. The following are two preferred measures of portfolio risk:

1. Unexpected loss (UL): A measure of the volatility or standard deviation for a portfolio loss distribution.
2. Tail risk (TR): A measure of the likelihood of extreme losses in the portfolio (this is similar to the concept of value-at-risk or VaR; we will also introduce the concept of conditional VaR or CVaR, which is sometimes referred to as *expected shortfall*). Tail risk corresponds to the area of the portfolio loss distribution from which we typically calculate economic capital.

Figure 1.2 shows a graphical depiction of a portfolio value distribution with an indication of the UL and TR. Note that this figure displays the value distribution. We often analyze a portfolio loss distribution, which is a linear transformation of the value distribution. Simply explained, to convert a value distribution to a loss distribution, we identify a loss point (i.e., the point at which we start counting losses), and subtract that point from each point in the value distribution. A typical candidate loss point is the risk-free value of the portfolio at the horizon date. We discuss these calculations in more detail in Chapter 8.

---

[7] It is important to highlight that in this discussion and throughout this book we focus on *economic capital*, which is reflected in the market capitalization of a financial institution. Economic capital typically differs from *book capital*, which is an accounting concept. Book capital is not really the value cushion available to absorb extreme losses; book capital reflects the accumulation of accounting entries that have a backward-looking bias. Whether the financial institution possesses the resources to absorb loss depends entirely on the current ability of the financial institution to make use of its equity's market value. Another type of capital results from regulations. This is known as *regulatory capital*. Calculation of regulatory capital results from an attempt on the part of regulators to determine a minimum cushion that will coincide with economic capital.

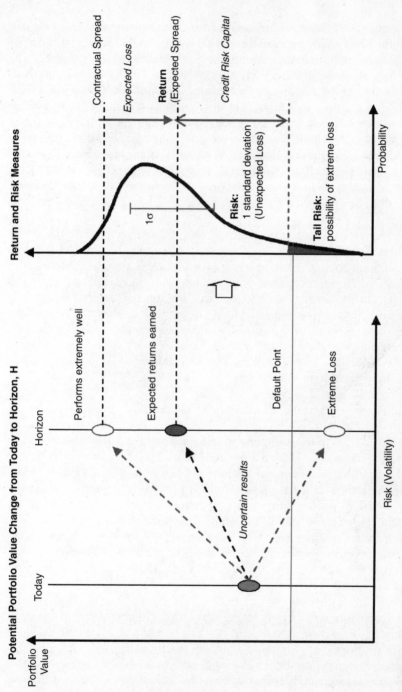

FIGURE 1.2 Portfolio Value Distribution with Unexpected Loss and Tail Risk

Both of these measures are essential for characterizing the risk of a credit portfolio, but they are necessarily summary statistics. In fact, the entire portfolio loss distribution contains important information about the risk of the portfolio; however, a financial institution with a credit portfolio needs to develop one or two analytics that can be communicated throughout the firm. Since tracking the entire loss distribution over time can be difficult in a conceptual sense (practically speaking, we can certainly calculate the portfolio loss distribution at different points in time; the difficulty arises in understanding the implications of changes in the distribution), focusing on measures such as UL and TR provides a current assessment of the portfolio risk as well as some historical context (e.g., the UL is higher or lower than before, which provides some sense of how the portfolio risk has changed).

Since we have only discussed UL and TR abstractly thus far, let us consider how the measures are interpreted in practice. Unexpected loss tells us something about the variation we expect to see in the size of most losses experienced by the portfolio. Since a large portion of a bank's earnings derive from the financial portfolio, this variation will directly impact the bank's earnings volatility. In this way, UL provides guidance as to how the composition of an existing portfolio will impact a bank's earnings' volatility. However, a portfolio that experiences little volatility, but every once in a while is hit with a loss so large so as to put the entire bank at risk, is not a portfolio a bank should be interested in holding. We turn to TR for a characterization of this extreme loss risk.

In recent years, the interpretation of TR has arisen from the ideas underpinning *value-at-risk* modeling, which is often called VaR. To better understand VaR in a credit context, we need to take a short digression to review the motivation behind a financial firm's target capital structure.

The owners of a financial institution's equity make use of debt to improve the return on their equity. Banks, for example, typically have a depositor base to provide fairly low-cost debt. But even if depositors are not the primary source of a bank's funding, the degree of leverage will typically affect a bank's credit quality, which in turn will determine how much a bank will pay (in terms of ongoing interest expense) for its debt. While this book tends to emphasize concepts in the context of banking institutions, the principles are equally relevant to any institution building a capital structure to support a credit portfolio. In theory, different levels of leverage in the bank's capital structure will directly impact the cost of funding for that bank. At some level of leverage, the cost of funding becomes so high that the bank cannot profitably employ those funds. Furthermore, at some level of high leverage, the credit quality of the bank will be so low so as to reduce or eliminate many profitable areas of business such as entering into derivative transactions, serving as custodian for assets, or generally providing services that require a strong balance sheet and a strong reputation.

Thus we have two countervailing motivations for deciding on the degree of leverage in a bank's capital structure. On the one hand, equity holders want to use as much leverage as possible to improve their return. On the other hand, these same equity holders realize that their ability to run a profitable business depends on maintaining a suitable level of credit quality, which constrains the desired degree of leverage. More fundamentally, the event of bankruptcy by the bank would cause the equity holders to lose all of their investment.[8] For these reasons, we can assume that at some point a bank can have too much leverage.

Though we do not have a coherent theory of optimal bank capital structure, we assume that a bank will desire to maintain a strong investment-grade level of credit quality to profitably construct a portfolio and build service businesses. While not rigorously verified empirically, our experience suggests that in many bank managers' views, this level does not need to be the highest (Aaa in the parlance of rating agencies) for all banks. That is, the cost of obtaining and maintaining a Aaa rating may exceed its benefit in some cases. Casual observation of market spreads for debt issued by different financial institutions suggests that a strong A borrower often pays about the same spread as a Aa or Aaa borrower in many settings. In a similar vein, Aaa, Aa, and strong A borrowers appear to have the same kind of access to banking-related service businesses. The extra capital needed to achieve a Aaa rating may materially impact the bank's overall return on equity while not necessarily changing its funding cost structure or range of business opportunities.[9] Figure 1.3 provides more intuition with respect to the relationship of economic capital and rating on the bank's debt.

A related issue that has taken center stage in the recent credit crisis of 2007 and 2008 is the benefit of having diversified sources of funding. In the months and years before summer 2007, a financial institution could often fund itself entirely in the wholesale finance market, borrowing directly from other financial institutions or investors. Many of the institutions offering this type of funding have either stopped doing so or been acquired. Surviving

---

[8] Some debate continues as to whether holding bank equity in a portfolio of investments changes the incentives so that the risk of bankruptcy of any one bank is overshadowed by the possibility of better returns across a number of bank equity investments.

[9] Note that certain businesses require that counterparties be rated Aa or Aaa. For example, some investors require Aaa-rated securities for their investment portfolios. Banks interested in providing guarantees on instruments that target such investors may require a Aaa rating to be able to do so.

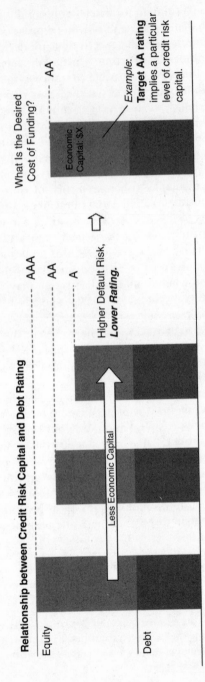

FIGURE 1.3 Relationship between Credit Risk and Capital and Debt Trading

financial institutions maintained a diversified mix of funding sources anchored with deposit-based funding. While we are not aware of any systematic research at this time, we suspect that in some cases, a higher rating such as Aa or even Aaa will make a difference going forward in a bank's ability to access funds at reasonable (i.e., profitable) cost. The key point is a bank's management should think carefully about its overall objectives and contingencies when considering what its target probability of default should be.

Why have we taken this digression in our discussion of VaR and TR to discuss bank capital structure? If we accept the assumption that a bank targets a capital structure that results in a strong (but not necessarily the strongest possible) investment-grade credit quality, we can interpret bank equity as the cushion available to absorb portfolio losses. In other words, equity value can be considered a reflection of the bank's available economic capital. The size of this equity or economic capital cushion makes the credit quality of the debt dependent on the likelihood that the portfolio will suffer a loss so large as to exhaust all the available equity value. This likelihood is a direct function of the bank portfolio's composition—that is, which securities or assets are held and in what quantities. If we convert this likelihood into a specific target probability, we can use our portfolio loss distribution to help determine which loss threshold corresponds to a specific target probability of exhausting all available economic capital. The same is true of other financial institutions.

Assuming that a particular probability of exhausting all capital is the same as the probability of a financial institution defaulting on its outstanding debt, we can convert a given target probability into a simplified "rating" for easier interpretation. For example, using a market-based measure of default probability, a one-year target probability of 0.15 percent is roughly associated with an A rating.[10] If a bank's management concludes that an A rating is sufficient to run a profitable business given its portfolio composition, then it will adjust its leverage (i.e., issue more or pay down debt) such that the probability of exhausting its equity is 0.15 percent (or 0.02 percent or another level, depending on the bank's view of which PD maps into which risk category). In this way, the portfolio loss distribution leads to a VaR interpretation of the risk for the debt issued by the bank. Please refer to Figure 1.4 for a graphical characterization of this relationship. Note that

---

[10] We base this statement on our research using MKMV's Expected Default Frequency (EDF) measure of the probability of default. The typical one-year EDF for the past 10 to 15 years for an A-rated borrower has been about 0.15 percent. However, this depends on the measure chosen. For example, the historical average issuer weighted historical one-year default rate for a Moody's A-rated instrument was about 0.02 percent between 1986 and 2006.

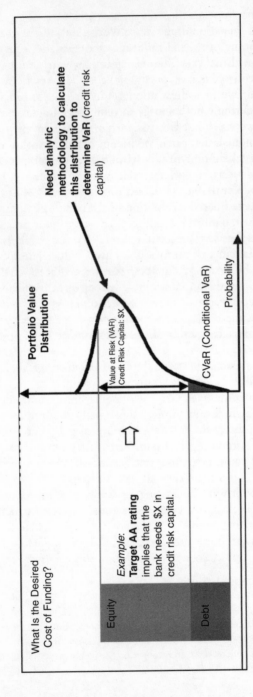

FIGURE 1.4 Relationship of Simple Bank Capital Structure to the Value at Risk (VaR) Characterized by a Target Probability for Portfolio Value That Indicates Bank Insolvency (Equity Value of Zero)

the target probability matches the area under the curve that is shaded in at the extreme edge of the value distribution. Portfolio value realizations that are below the beginning of the debt in this simple example will correspond to the equity losing all its value. As we have stated, the time horizon of analysis is typically one year.

Tail risk is what we measure to determine how a particular exposure contributes to this extreme portfolio loss event at a particular target probability. Thus far, we have not been too rigorous about defining TR. In Chapter 8 we distinguish TR calculated from conventional VaR (i.e., the contribution to the likelihood of a portfolio loss exceeding a particular threshold, which is associated with a specific target probability) from *conditional VaR* or CVaR (sometimes called *expected shortfall*—the contribution to the amount expected to be lost conditional on the portfolio loss being beyond the threshold). Tail risk calculated based on VaR does not distinguish between losses that may be considerably beyond the target-probability threshold. Tail risk calculated based on CVaR, by contrast, tells us whether the loss will likely be just a bit beyond the threshold or whether it will substantially exceed the threshold. We explore the details of this difference in Chapter 8. In recent years, various researchers have raised concerns regarding the coherency and usefulness of VaR-based measures. As a result, a number of practitioners are now inclined to focus on CVaR.

Once a target probability is chosen, the amount of capital required can be calculated by examining the quantile of the loss distribution corresponding to this probability. (Note that this approach assumes that the target quantity is a PD. In some environments, targets are described in terms of expected loss, in which case a more complicated calculation is required.) Given the preceding discussion, we find it convenient to consider bank equity value as the measure of capital that the bank needs to ensure a particular target probability of capital exhaustion given the composition of the bank's portfolio.[11]

Once we have determined an aggregate capital amount for a given portfolio, we can next look to allocate that capital to each exposure in the portfolio. For example:

- If we are focused on UL or volatility as our measure of risk, we may choose to base capital allocation on a given exposure's contribution to

---

[11] Note that as we move out into the far tail, caution is warranted since the drivers of extreme losses may be different than in our general model assumptions. Stress-testing should be considered along with correlation models for extreme losses.

UL, which is sometimes called *risk contribution* (RC). This approach will favor exposures that do not vary in value much over time, such as loans to large, high-quality corporate borrowers.

- Alternatively, we may choose to allocate capital based on a given exposure's contribution to portfolio TR, which is sometimes called *tail-risk contribution* (TRC). This approach will favor exposures that do not have correlation with the portfolio or do not represent a large concentration.

Ultimately, the choice of objective function is a management decision, so it is important that the management of a financial institution all share a comfortable understanding of the underlying meaning of each of these measures.

USING PDs IN PRACTICE

In the previous section, we provided a first introduction to the language of credit portfolio risk. Now consider an example of how this language can be used in practice. When a financial firm shifts to a quantitative orientation of risk assessment, PDs become the foundation for evaluating and monitoring obligors. Probabilities of default move considerably through the credit cycle: From trough to peak of the cycle, the typical market-based PD of a public firm in a sector or geography may change by as much as a factor of five or six. Probabilities of default also vary considerably across different classes of obligors.[12]

This change over time and change across obligors at any given point in time make it important to estimate PDs accurately. The first step in doing so is to rank current and prospective obligors in terms of their PDs. In most banks, PDs are converted into internal ratings. This bucketing of PDs creates more stability in the estimates and facilitates better communication with nonquantitative employees at the bank. (For those interested in bucketing PDs, we discuss a number of approaches to doing so in Chapter 4.) However, it also discards a good deal of information on the credit quality of the borrower.[13]

---

[12] For example, MKMV's EDF values (one commonly used measure of PDs) range from 1 basis point (0.01 percent) to 3,500 basis points (35 percent).

[13] One of the authors was once speaking with a banker who complained that PDs moved much more frequently than ratings. The author responded, "You don't have to look at them every day." By bucketing PDs, banks effectively do this.

EVOLVING APPRECIATION FOR CREDIT MEASURES IN BANKS

As a bank develops more experience with PDs, the tendency is toward converting them into financial values such as bond prices or CDS spreads. This value orientation is the primary focus of credit hedge funds and other teams that trade credit.* Note that the first step of simply ranking by PD provides a rough way of determining which credit exposures are more likely to get into trouble. Converting a PD into a value offers an extra dimension that facilitates comparison to existing market prices since it describes in financial terms the *cost* of the risk. Eventually, the most sophisticated users of these analytics will incorporate both the physical PDs and their corresponding valuations into a portfolio model by introducing exposure weights and correlations.

*For valuation applications, the physical PD must be converted into a *risk-neutral* PD and an LGD needs to be estimated. We discuss valuation, risk-neutral measures, and so on in more detail in a later section.

Probabilities of default are an integral, if not the most important, part of a portfolio model. Using PDs, an analyst can not only make a relative statement about obligor risk (e.g., this small manufacturing company is a better risk than that medium-size business services firm), but he can also quantify the differences (e.g., this small manufacturing company is one-third as likely to default as that medium-size business services firm). Layering in the portfolio view facilitates analysis in the context of diversification (e.g., while the medium-size business services firm is much riskier than the small manufacturing company on a stand-alone basis, in the context of this European bank portfolio both firms contribute about the same level of risk).

The final piece of the puzzle concerns return: How much will a bank earn from each credit exposure? Valuation helps sort out this question. We can use PDs in the context of a valuation model to determine how much an exposure is worth today and how much we expect it to be worth at a particular date in the future. This expected gain or loss can be added to the expected cash flow stream to determine the overall expected return from holding a particular credit security. We can also incorporate these models into simulation engines so that we determine values conditional on the realization of various factors that reflect a particular state of the economy. Probabilities of default are the threads that run throughout the fabric of all these risk models.

In evaluating the quality of various PD models, we typically make a distinction between a model's power and its calibration. The power of a PD model tells us how well it distinguishes good from bad borrowers. In Chapter 7, we describe evaluation tools known as *power curves* that statistically characterize a model's power. A powerful PD model is not necessarily well calibrated. A well-calibrated model produces probability estimates that agree well with the observed default rates for obligors. If the model is used only for ranking the risk of obligors, poor calibration will not make a large difference as long as the model properly distinguishes the obligors. However, if the objective is to allocate economic capital or to value a security or exposure, both power and calibration matter. A poorly calibrated model will produce values that will not correspond to market prices. Moreover, portfolio analyses may be skewed if the valuations do not conform at all to existing market prices.

VALUE, PRICE, AND SPREAD

In the course of our model discussions, we will return often to the theme of valuation. The objective of most credit analyses in a portfolio context is to determine how the value of individual exposures and the overall portfolio will change over time. An important concept in this context is the transformation of actual or physical or actuarial PDs, which measure the actual probability of default events into risk-neutral or risk-adjusted PDs, which measure the probability of default implied by market prices after accounting for uncertainty. When assessing risk, we estimate the actual, *physical* PDs. When we estimate a credit instrument's value, we also use PDs; however, we first convert these actual PDs into *risk-neutral* PDs. While the physical PD represents the estimate of the expected rate of default for a particular entity, this conversion to risk-neutral PDs for the purpose of valuation reflects the inherent risk aversion of investors. This adjustment reflects the fact that risk-averse investors require an extra premium beyond payment for expected loss to compensate them for the risk associated with purchasing a security that may lose value in excess of everyone's expectations. In other words, investors require additional compensation for accepting a gamble versus a sure thing with the same expected payout. The change of measure from physical to risk-neutral PDs can be accomplished in a variety of ways, but the key objective is to adjust the probability for the (extra) risk that needs to be implied in order to adjust for risk aversion. We will be careful to distinguish actual from risk-neutral PDs.[14]

As we stated before, the value of a credit instrument derives from the likelihood of receiving cash payments over time in the future. This value may be reflected in a market price, in quotes provided by market participants, or it may be the output of a model. Unlike accounting measures, valuation-based measures can fluctuate substantially. For example, if in general the market is demanding a higher premium for credit risk due to pessimism about the economy, *all* of the loans in a bank's portfolio may be affected.

In several of our discussions, we will talk about *value, price,* and *spread.* These terms have multiple definitions and tend to be used in ambiguous and sometimes confusing ways in the finance literature. In this section, we define these terms as we will use them in this book.

When we discuss *value,* we refer to a measure that reflects the model framework's assessment of the present value of the future risk-adjusted cash flows expected to be generated by the asset or security under analysis. *Price,* by contrast, is the amount at which an asset or security is bought or sold in a market. The asset or security's value does not necessarily equal the price at which one could buy or sell the asset or security at any given point in time. Instead, value provides an indication, per a model, of the price at which the asset or security *should* be bought or sold, but which may not reflect the actual current market price due to various market conditions. A useful model will generate values to which prices converge over some reasonable time horizon (usually less than a year). In some cases, the asset is not traded (e.g., the market value of an entire firm[15] or the bank loans of a small firm) and in some cases the security's price is driven by factors outside a model (e.g., market liquidity effects). These are two examples of many in which value may differ from price. Of course, the model generating a particular value may be wrong and never converge to any observable price. (We recommend rejecting models to which relevant prices never converge.)

While most people tend to think in terms of a price or value in currency terms (which for credit is typically quoted on a scale of 100—thus, a price that is 98 percent of par value would be quoted as "98"), we typically

---

[14] If you are not familiar with this concept, please refer to one of the financial texts referenced in this book. Hull (2005) and Neftci (2000) are good choices.

[15] In many instances throughout this book, we refer to "securities" and "assets" in a portfolio, which we use to mean a financial instrument. We also refer at times to the "asset value" of a firm, which reflects the value of the firm's entire enterprise. An asset in a portfolio is in most cases different than the assets of a firm (unless the portfolio is composed of owning many firms in their entirety). Readers should be aware of this distinction when they encounter the term *asset.*

convert price or value into a spread relative to a risk-free benchmark. The word *spread* is perhaps the most overloaded (and sometimes abused) word in finance. For example, the difference between a bid and an offer on a security is called a spread; however, we do not focus for the most part on this type of spread and when we do, we refer to this type of spread as the *bid-offer spread*. In contrast, most of the time when we refer simply to a *spread*, we generally mean the extra premium with respect to a reference benchmark (e.g., a risk-free rate) that represents a suitable conversion from the benchmark to the security's value or price.

To calculate a spread, we must first specify a risk-free benchmark. While most of the finance literature adopts the U.S. Treasury curve or possibly another reserve-currency sovereign such as the UK gilt curve, we maintain that credit models are best fit to spreads relative to a corporate-risk-free rate. This corporate-risk-free rate is the rate at which a risk-free corporate borrower could borrow. (While this type of borrower does not exist in practice, we can consider near risk-free borrowers as a benchmark.[16]) The swap curve is a good first approximation to this curve.

Once we have determined the appropriate risk-free benchmark, r_f, we can convert a price or value into a spread. We do this conversion in the context of a particular model for the price or value of debt, D. We can sometimes solve for spread analytically (e.g., in the case of zero-coupon bonds); but for most debt securities—particularly ones with coupon, C—we must find the spread, s, such that the functional relationship holds: $D = f(r_f, s, T, C, \text{etc.})$

In the case of callable or putable bonds, we incorporate the optionality into the calculation to estimate what is termed an *option-adjusted spread* (OAS). The OAS calculation generally requires some kind of *lattice* or *tree* construction depicting the possible paths and path probabilities for the debt value. If the debt security does not have optionality attached to it, fitting the spread in the context of a lattice construction results in what is termed a *Z-spread*.

In the context of the models in this book, we are careful to distinguish the following spreads:

- *Total spread (TS)*. We usually call the spread to the U.S. Treasury (or some similar reserve-currency sovereign curve) the total spread. This spread includes compensation for a variety of risks extending beyond just credit risk. In a portfolio modeling context, we define TS relative

---

[16] At MKMV we coined the term *0-EDF rate* to describe this benchmark. The 0-EDF curve seems to be 10 to 20 basis points less than the swap curve (see Bohn 2000b). We can think of this curve as 0-PD or rates for a corporate borrower that has a PD of 0.

to a 0-EDF curve (see footnote 16) or swap curve.[17] If we define TS in this way, the difference between the benchmark and the U.S. Treasury curve can be considered compensation for less liquidity in the corporate debt market.

- *Expected spread (ES)*. As we discuss in Chapter 8, we subtract expected loss (EL) from TS to arrive at ES. This spread reflects the premium for holding credit exposures. This spread may comprise both a credit component and a liquidity component specific to the firm under evaluation.
- *Credit spread*. Part of the challenge in credit modeling is isolating that part of the spread compensating credit risk only. Strictly speaking, we define the credit spread as that portion of the total spread related just to credit risk. It is composed of the EL and the premium earned for holding credit risk.
- *Liquidity spread*. Unfortunately, we do not have good models of liquidity, so this spread tends to be the residual of the ES that cannot be explained by the credit model. Conceptually, there is likely to be some premium earned for exposure to liquidity risk. In practice, we may inadvertently characterize portions of the TS or ES as liquidity spread when in fact our model is misspecified.
- *Zero-coupon spread*. When discussing term structures of spreads, we normally characterize the zero-coupon spread as that which would be earned on a zero-coupon debt security at different maturity dates.
- *Par spread*. An alternative way to characterize the term structure of spreads is in terms of the spread earned on a floating-rate bond such that the price of the bond is equal to par—that is, equal to 100. We call this characterization the par spread.

We will be explicit about which type of spread is calculated when discussing model calculations. In most modeling discussions, we will refer to the spread associated with a debt security. Spreads tend to put all securities on a similar measuring scale for comparison. While not a perfect measure even in a credit-modeling context (it is sometimes better to think about a term structure of spreads), most practitioners focus on spreads and they tend to be a good way to refer to the output of credit valuation models. We sometimes distinguish spreads that come from models (i.e., *value-based* spreads) and spreads that come from market prices (i.e., *price-based* spreads). In a portfolio context, we tend to focus on ES to determine the relevant marginal

---

[17] The reference to a *swap* here refers to swapping a fixed-rate obligation for a floating-rate obligation (or vice versa). Swap curves define the rates at which an approximately AA obligor can borrow. While some credit risk is reflected in these rates, they are generally good proxies for the corporate risk-free or 0-PD rates.

return we expect to earn relative to the risk contributed to the portfolio. Expected spread is a common component of metrics used to evaluate a credit portfolio's performance.

DEFINING DEFAULT

Central to the various discussions in this book is the concept of an event of default. A simple definition of default is the nonpayment of interest or principal on a credit obligation. We have found, however, that sometimes default can be usefully defined in different ways. Another possible definition of default is bankruptcy. For example, a firm may behave differently in a bankruptcy resulting in full liquidation of its assets than if it just defaulted on one or two outstanding debt issues. This may, in fact, be mandated by law. The difference in behavior may materially impact the recovery obtained in the event of default. Thus, in such a context it may be useful to examine the difference between probability of bankruptcy and probability of default.

Situations can also arise in which a firm appears to have defaulted in an economic sense, but not in practical terms. Consider a bank that becomes insolvent, but whose country's government continues to inject funds to keep the institution running. (Recall Japan in the 1990s.) This bank is economically in default while still making good on its obligations. Firms may also restructure their debt in such a way as to adversely affect the value of their debt without actually defaulting. This restructuring may be interpreted as a technical default despite the fact that interest and principal continue to be paid.

Further complicating definitional issues is that conventions may differ from country to country regarding when a firm is considered to be in default. For some countries, the convention may be to interpret any missed payment as an immediate default while other countries may wait until the payment is 90 or 120 days late.

It is important to understand clearly the definition of default when interpreting model output and evaluating model performance. Definitions may differ depending on the circumstances. As long as the definition is consistent with the procedures taken to estimate and use the model in question, the definition of default may vary without difficulty.

PORTFOLIO PERFORMANCE METRICS

We have touched on a measure of the extra premium or expected spread (ES) earned to hold a risky security in a portfolio. We have also characterized contribution to portfolio volatility, or risk contribution (RC), and contribution to portfolio tail risk (TRC). The RC and TRC can be used to allocate economic capital, usually defined as a capitalization rate (CR), to a particular exposure. Finally, we characterized the portfolio's stand-alone risk or unexpected loss (UL) and a particular portfolio's target probability–based economic capital (C). The question remains: How do we use these measures in practice? While we delve into these measures in more detail toward the end of this book, we introduce them briefly here to motivate the material that follows.

Performance cannot be managed if it is not measured and benchmarked. In the equity portfolio management business, performance is measured in terms of return per unit of volatility, known as the Sharpe ratio (named after the Nobel laureate, William Sharpe). In the case of equity portfolios, the Sharpe ratio is compared to an index that matches a portfolio manager's style of equity investing and the manager is evaluated based on whether he over- or underperformed relative to the index. While many retail investors still tend to look only at historical return, sophisticated investors evaluate equity portfolios on the basis of their return per unit of volatility relative to an appropriate benchmark.

In the world of credit, notions of return per unit of risk and benchmarks are still quite new. Nonetheless, the Sharpe ratio measure has started gaining popularity for credit portfolios. To port the Sharpe ratio to the credit context, analysts make a few modifications. Return is measured in terms of ES: not just the risk-free rate but also expected loss is subtracted from total return. The denominator for the portfolio is UL.[18] (At the exposure level, UL is replaced by RC.)

Once the Sharpe ratio is calculated, though, a more fundamental difficulty arises in that there is a lack of an appropriate benchmark. While many credit indexes do exist, they tend to suffer from the endemic problem that the market does not originate well-diversified portfolios. Unlike in the equity world, where indexes can be constructed that more or less diversify away idiosyncratic risk, in the credit world, a borrower such as Ford may account for several percentage points of the market portfolio in exposure value terms. Thus the benchmark is overshadowed by the idiosyncratic risk of its largest constituents. Traded CDS indexes are rapidly developing into benchmarks which may not suffer from the diversification problems of current bond indexes. That said, the issues' changing liquidity and their relative

---

[18] Note that the calculation of the Sharpe ratio for a credit portfolio maintains the conceptual underpinning of the traditional Sharpe ratio: return divided by risk. However, in our context, we replace the traditional measures of excess return and the standard deviation of returns with measures appropriate to credit risk.

newness make them not always the most reliable choice at present, though they will likely eventually develop into benchmarks in the future.

Where does this leave us?

First, we can begin with the portfolio's current Sharpe ratio as a reasonable target for motivating each transaction within the bank. In this way, each new transaction should earn at least as much return per unit of volatility risk as the current portfolio.

An alternative benchmark is the Sharpe ratio for the "best" possible[19] portfolio that the firm can construct given its constraints. All financial institutions have constraints governing what and how much they can own. This benchmark pushes the institution toward building the best possible portfolio available to it. Each transaction's Sharpe ratio (calculated in this case as ES/RC) is compared to this best-case portfolio's Sharpe ratio (calculated as ES/UL). This approach to decision making works for motivating value-adding transactions.

For single transactions and subportfolios, the performance can be measured against the larger portfolio or the best-case portfolio. But how can we benchmark the larger portfolios? The lack of good market credit indexes requires construction of something like a well-diversified market portfolio. Though we will provide some ideas and guidance based on what is best practice today, this field of benchmarking still leaves much to be desired.

An alternative measure of performance to the Sharpe ratio is something we call the Vasicek ratio (named after its developer, Oldrich Vasicek, a pioneer in the field of modern quantitative finance). A Vasicek ratio is analogous to a Sharpe ratio in the sense that it is a measure of return per unit of risk. But in this case, we replace the volatility-based denominator with a capital number reflecting a calculation of the portfolio tail risk. In the early 1990s, a similar measure was developed at Banker's Trust, called *risk-adjusted*

---

[19] We have purposely refrained from using the word *optimal* as it is still difficult to construct an optimal credit portfolio. We discuss this further in Chapter 8. At this point, we should clarify the difference between *ex ante* and *ex post* measures of performance. In this discussion, we have tended to focus on *ex ante* measures, which are reflected in expected performance over a given time horizon. We recommend using *ex ante* measures to drive efficient decision making. *Ex post* measures describe what actually happened over a given time horizon. Here we must focus on realized return and realized volatility. Several practical difficulties arise when calculating realized quantities that we discuss in more detail later in the book. The point to remember here is that while portfolio construction can only be done based on *ex ante* measures, employee compensation should be paid on realized (*ex post*) performance relative to a benchmark. This motivates the firm to ensure that the credit decision-making tools it uses are as accurate and realistic as possible.

return on capital (RAROC). The credit modeling firm KMV introduced a variant of this measure in the mid-1990s called *return on risk-adjusted capital* (RORAC). (The authors have even come across *risk-adjusted return on risk-adjusted capital* (RARORAC).) The "rocks" and "racks" measures tend to include the risk-free return component of asset value growth, and many of these metrics mix in a variety of expenses and capital calculations that can sometimes distort decision making. In the end, most of these adjustments tend to diminish the usefulness of the measure.

The Vasicek ratio is much more straightforward. It is defined as ES/C, so the estimation effort stays focused on properly calculating the capital, or C. We will have much to say about components of this calculation throughout this book. The conceptual point to take away from this discussion is that the Vasicek ratio provides some sense of the return earned on capital that has been put at risk to support a particular transaction or portfolio. A credit portfolio manager still faces the difficulty of choosing the proper benchmark and, similar to results using the Sharpe ratio, the best choices for a benchmark would appear to be the entire portfolio's Vasicek ratio or the best-case portfolio's Vasicek ratio.

A further benefit of the Vasicek ratio is the ease with which this concept of return on economic capital can be extended to nonportfolio businesses within the firm. In Chapter 2 we will discuss how a transfer pricing mechanism within the firm can centralize the management of credit risk in an active credit portfolio management (ACPM) function. This differentiation enables the firm to measure separately capital allocated to the portfolio and capital allocated to each of the nonportfolio businesses. The operating cash flow earned by these nonportfolio businesses becomes a measure of return. One can then calculate a business-based Vasicek ratio, assuming the capital allocation can be properly estimated. In this way, a common notion of return to capital informs performance evaluation and strategy discussions throughout the firm.

A related metric to the Vasicek ratio and one that can also serve as a common measure for evaluating portfolio and nonportfolio businesses is *shareholder value added* (SVA), or economic profit. Shareholder value added is calculated by first calculating a net income number adjusted downward for expected loss (similar in concept to the calculation of ES). Next, the cost of capital allocated against a portfolio or business (defined as allocated capital times the cost of that capital) is also subtracted from the net income. The residual is the economic profit or SVA of that activity.

While the Vasicek ratio provides some sense of the percentage return earned on capital allocated, SVA provides a sense of the absolute level of contribution to shareholder value. A business may have a high Vasicek ratio but be so small as to not materially increase shareholder value. In contrast, a lower Vasicek ratio business may have a high SVA given its size. In our view, though, the Vasicek ratio provides a sense of the ongoing opportunity associated with a particular business, as a high growth rate will eventually result in a high SVA (all else equal). Both the Vasicek ratio and SVA are useful tools for benchmarking performance.

DATA AND DATA SYSTEMS

Many of the modeling choices we recommend follow from our attempts to accommodate real-world data limitations. One of the primary factors behind the gap between many models introduced in the financial literature and those used in practice is the difficulty researchers have in finding sufficient data to estimate some academic models. Over time the models driving risk analytics have become more widely accepted and in some cases, somewhat commoditized. However, the manner in which the models are implemented in systems and the manner in which the organization changes to make use of the models continue to be debated. We will illustrate in several different contexts how we think data should influence this debate.

In our judgment, it makes sense to have a bias toward market observable information. While private information about management plans or new products and other qualitative analysis can be useful supplements, we have been firmly convinced over years of work with dozens of clients using a wide variety of analytic approaches that quantitative, observable data (as long as the historical period is sufficiently long) provides the best starting point and foundation for modeling in almost every case. This does not mean that qualitative analysis has no value. Rather, we find that it is hard to achieve consistent and repeatable performance across a large portfolio using subjective measures alone. Given this bias, we tend to choose and recommend models that rely on market data.

In circumstances where market data is not available, such as when modeling private small and medium enterprises (SMEs), our experience suggests large pools of data from several different sources constitute the best data foundation from which to start. Some banks erroneously believe that their own portfolio is large enough so that they have sufficient internal data to build robust credit models. In the process of collecting data for corporate (as well as retail) credit modeling, we have found that multiple banks' data provided substantial improvement in out-of-sample performance of default probability models. We discuss an example of this in Chapter 7. In the absence of market data, we have found that the best approach relies on collecting a diverse and large sample of data that usually requires collaboration among several institutions and/or government entities.

Significant investment in data collection, data cleaning, and data systems will be a common implication of our recommendations. No matter how robust a model appears or how confident an analyst is of a particular approach, bad data will quickly render the model and system useless. Since credit events happen so infrequently, the modeling exercises in this context tend to be focused on outliers. Any system whose calibration is heavily impacted by outliers becomes highly sensitive to data quality. We will demonstrate in several contexts the importance of this point and how to practically address it.

With this introduction as background, we now turn to the question of how an ACPM function is implemented in practice. This chapter and Chapter 2 provide the overall context for the model and system discussions that follow in subsequent chapters.

REVIEW QUESTIONS

1. What distinguishes credit risk from market risk?
2. What distinguishes credit risk from liquidity risk?
3. What is an asset-value driven default?
4. What is a liquidity-driven default?
5. Explain why the nature of credit instrument return distributions make them difficult to hold in isolation (i.e., not in portfolios).
6. What is the purpose of holding capital?
7. How does economic capital differ from book capital and regulatory capital?
8. Why are credit portfolios more amenable to active management than are equity portfolios?
9. Generally speaking, over which dimension should a credit portfolio be diversified and why?
10. Explain the difference between unexpected loss (UL) and tail risk (TR).
11. Describe the motivation behind the creation of a CDO.

CHAPTER 2

ACPM in Practice

The professional traders make their money, not by escaping losses, but by making their profits outbalance their losses.

—John Moody

Statistical thinking will one day be as necessary for efficient citizenship as the ability to read and write.

—H. G. Wells, 1952

Objectives

After reading this chapter, you should understand the following:

- What active credit portfolio management (ACPM) is.
- Why ACPM is important.
- How a bank can be organized to implement ACPM.
- What metrics should be used to facilitate ACPM.
- How ACPM groups should be evaluated.

In 1478, the London branch of the Medici Bank was finally liquidated as the branch's portfolio had deteriorated beyond repair. The problems had started earlier, in the 1460s, with the War of the Roses. During that time, the banking family had lent money both to King Edward IV and to many of the rebels he fought. As the war progressed, Edward continued to demand loans in exchange for allowing the Medici to continue to receive wool export licenses, which were highly valued. Edward ultimately defeated the rebels, but then fell into even greater debt to the Medici. Eventually, he effectively defaulted. To make matters worse for the Medici, the rebel borrowers, whose loans the Medici had also underwritten, were slaughtered after the War and their property seized. Thus, the Medici could collect from neither Edward nor the rebels. The Medici Bank suffered the consequences of deploying its surplus cash in a correlated and concentrated portfolio. (See De Roover 1948 for a fascinating account of the Medici Bank's demise.)

This historical anecdote highlights the pitfalls of banking without a portfolio perspective. The Medici rightly focused on their relationship with King Edward IV to secure export licenses. They granted loans in order to enjoy a benefit from having this relationship. Unfortunately for them, the size of their credit exposure grew too large and thus it created concentration risk in their portfolio. This portfolio concentration risk was exacerbated by lending to Edward's enemies. These other loans increased the correlation in the bank's portfolio. Now the bank's portfolio was exposed to the risk of a war that ultimately destroyed the solvency of both the king and his enemies at the same time. (If only the Italians had had a hedging strategy that they could have used to lay off their English royalty risk.)

One might argue that the Medici could have foreseen the folly of lending to both sides of a conflict and that this banking debacle amounted to nothing more than poor business judgment. However, unforeseen events can dramatically impact portfolios in a similar manner. On September 1, 1923, a 7.9-magnitude earthquake rocked the southern Kanto area of Japan, killing more than 100,000 people in Tokyo and Yokohama. This earthquake destroyed assets equal to nearly 40 percent of national income for 1923. By April 1927 the Wakatsuki government faced a severe financial crisis resulting directly and indirectly from this earthquake. Unable to garner support for an aggressive bank assistance plan, the Wakatsuki cabinet resigned on April 18, 1927. Several banks subsequently closed their doors. The most surprising bank to close in these difficult times was Fifteen Bank, which was also known as the "Aristocratic bank" because its owners were almost exclusively aristocrats. The bank had recently absorbed three new banks and appeared solid from the outside. What the public did not know was that 30 percent of this bank's loan portfolio consisted of exposures in various forms to the businesses of a single family, the Matsukata. Furthermore, the remainder of Fifteen Bank's portfolio also consisted of big loans to large, established Japanese businesses, most of whom were also directly impacted by the single event. This concentration, while seemingly unimportant in times of economic strength, sank the bank in a time of natural disaster and government instability. (See Tamaki 1995 for more details on the history of modern Japanese banking.)

Until the 1990s, banks never seemed able to escape the inevitability of these types of portfolio meltdowns through a repeating cycle of relationship lending. A bank would work hard to build relationships with lucrative clients. These relationships led to loans. These loans tended to strengthen relationships and led to other bank business with the existing clients. At the same time, having developed a franchise in a specific sector or geography, a bank tended to increase its loans into the geography and sector in which it had developed this successful lending business. At some point, bank customers in this chosen geography and sector inevitably cycled into economic difficulty, at which point the bank experienced solvency-threatening losses and would be liquidated, acquired, or bailed out. This story has repeated in different countries at different times and almost always results in crisis. We saw variants of this story in the United States in the 1970s and 1980s and Japan in the 1990s.

A consequence (we assert) of these cyclical bank crises is relatively low equity valuations for banks in the public stock markets (in terms of price to book or EBITDA[1] multiples). We propose that the market fears the disruption of future cash flows arising from this tendency to concentrate portfolio risk as a bank exploits its relationships to generate not just interest income, but also fee or service income. The noninterest income is the potentially more valuable cash flow stream, but the portfolio concentration risk seems to overwhelm this driver of value.

Despite the apparent inevitability of bank crises and failures, advances in the 1990s in analytics, technology, and organizational structure produced a class of banks in the United States and Europe that separated the management of bank portfolio risk from the management of bank revenue streams earned from a bank's various franchises for products and services. By the 2000s, the rapid growth of the credit derivative market and the increasing liquidity in all credit markets created an environment where a properly outfitted bank could build and hedge many of its successful franchise businesses without necessarily succumbing to the portfolio concentration risk that has plagued modern banking. While recent events in 2007 and 2008 have highlighted difficulties with maintaining liquidity in the various markets for credit, the overall trend for financial institutions is toward developing the systems and organizations to manage their respective credit portfolios.

An important organizational feature of many banks that have weathered recent economic difficulties is the ACPM function. ACPM becomes the mechanism for centrally managing a bank's portfolio risk. The availability of new credit instruments, when responsibly used, has turned a theoretical possibility into a practical requirement.

Financial institutions that implement ACPM strategies accrue benefits that extend beyond simple credit risk reporting. First, ACPM enables a financial institution to better weather financial crises that occur on a regular basis as the economy cycles from boom to bust. Second, with more stability

---

[1] Earnings before interest, taxes, depreciation, and amortization.

ACPM

The basic concept of active credit portfolio management is simple: all credit risk can to some degree be priced based on the cost of hedging the risk. To the extent that a business unit wants to enter business that it feels is attractive, or to lend to a client it feels will generate large future revenues through other activities, the business unit should pay for the hedging cost of each transaction as one of the expenses associated with its business. Whenever the value of the expected benefit does not exceed the cost the firm must bear for hedging the credit risk associated with doing a transaction, the business unit should not do the deal.

If ACPM techniques and the markets that support them had been developed in the time of the Medici, the Italian bankers making loans to the English (and their enemies) would have had increasingly higher hedging expenses for each loan made (since it increased the concentration in the portfolio and thus required more aggressive hedging) and at some point would have found the cost of hedging to exceed the benefit of the wool export licenses, which in turn would suggest the need for more diversification.

in portfolio performance, a financial institution can focus on building its franchise businesses, which constitute the engine of value creation for these types of firms. Third, the ability for credit originators to distribute risk throughout the market in small, digestible chunks, when done responsibly, reduces overall systemic risk as large financial institutions' stability becomes less tied to the fortunes of a particular country, industry, or market segment.

The management of credit risk is typically the primary concern of most large financial institutions today. Market risk, liquidity risk, and operating risk are also important concerns for these institutions. The recent lack of liquidity in some segments of the structured finance markets highlights the importance of developing a centralized view on all exposures. While we may not have the tools to model liquidity risk as rigorously as market and credit risk, the active monitoring and management of an institution's portfolio—regardless of which division originated the exposures—can go a long way in mitigating both liquidity and operating risk. Moreover, transparency regarding the characteristics of an exposure, which is not always available even today, regardless of whether it is a loan or a structured credit tranche is an essential requirement for managing that exposure's risk. Finally, centralized management of an institution's credit portfolio lays the foundation to better understand the liquidity risk and the interconnected market risk that may also exist in that portfolio.

This chapter is intended to delve a little deeper into the salient issues associated with ACPM from a practical organizational perspective and to provide context for making particular organizational, system, and model choices. Importantly, while we have strong views on how financial institutions can benefit by managing credit risk and, by extension, managing their organizational policies and structures with respect to credit risk, we are not proposing to prescribe more generally how these institutions should be managed. Day-to-day management of each institution requires a more specific understanding of particular circumstances and business environments. Rather, our experience gives us a concrete perspective on the things a firm can do to better align its risk management practice and its overall business practices. These general principles can then be tailored to the specific circumstances an institution faces. To this end, we make some observations about how this alignment may be done more effectively when approached from an organization-wide perspective. Against this backdrop, our objective in this chapter is to outline how ACPM is changing the way the risk management and pricing functions at large financial institutions can be managed and regulated.

INTERNATIONAL ASSOCIATION OF CREDIT PORTFOLIO MANAGERS

While we present a number of useful ideas regarding ACPM in this chapter, there are still many issues in this context that need more elaboration. Moreover, the field of ACPM continues to evolve. We encourage those in this field to speak with others building ACPM teams and join organizations like the International Association of Credit Portfolio Managers (IACPM). IACPM is a great source of information since it holds regular conferences, conducts surveys, and periodically publishes material on a range of topics germane to this function. Interested readers can browse www.IACPM.org for more information. For a comprehensive overview of the sound practices advocated by IACPM, we refer the reader to its publication entitled "Sound Practices in Credit Portfolio Management" (2005). This publication identifies general practices when implementing ACPM. IACPM provides an important source of the current thinking regarding credit portfolio management.

The rest of this chapter describes the characteristics of ACPM as it is (and should be) implemented in actual financial institutions. Before we dive in, we first start by discussing the drivers of bank value. This background is important as it explains why an institution should be motivated to manage its credit portfolio centrally. It also has implications for how a financial institution's senior management can best leverage the activities of its ACPM function to provide evidence to the market that will likely lead to a higher share valuation.

BANK VALUATION

Many of the recommendations in this book rest on the premise that a bank or financial institution should manage itself to maximize, long term, the value of its equity. In particular, banks (and other financial institutions with credit exposure)[2] should manage their credit risk (and trade this off against profit opportunities) in a manner that maximizes this long-term value. This share-value maximization perspective leads us to explore the manner in which the market, in turn, values a bank. Even a nonpublic financial institution can benefit from operating to maximize shareholder value. Basic financial theory suggests that, all else equal, the growth and stability of cash flow generated by a bank should result in a higher equity valuation (see Copeland, Koller, and Murrin 2000 for details). The difficulty lies in disentangling the many drivers of value.

Some researchers and most if not all regulators may be less concerned with the market capitalizations of banks and more with the risk of individual banks, and possibly how that risk aggregates within a particular financial system. (See Carey and Stultz 2005 and Gorton and Winton 2002 for surveys of the issues concerning bank risk.) Fortunately, the two are directly related and this implies an alignment of incentives: Banks cannot

---

[2] This section specifically discusses banks. Much of the work and thinking in this area has been developed in the context of banking. That said, and as we indicate throughout this book, many if not all of the ideas and principles discussed here and in other chapters have applicability to any financial institution that originates, trades, or manages credit portfolios. The bulk of information and experience with respect to ACPM specifically has been with banks and a handful of insurance companies who manage their credit portfolios in a similar way. In sections such as this one where the ideas and practice have developed specifically in the context of banking, we will tend to leave out reference to other types of financial institutions. We believe that in general most of these ideas can be easily extended to any financial institution struggling with management of its credit exposure.

sustainably increase market capitalization without adequate risk manage-ment. The ideas presented in this book primarily focus on the *credit risk of a bank* only to the extent that a bank's riskiness impacts its share price. Given the importance of banks to the world economy and most regional economies, we might expect to find extensive research in this area. While some research has been published (see, for example, Kane and Unal 1990; Dewenter and Hess 1998; and Megginson, Poulsen, and Sinkey 1995), it is far from extensive when compared with other areas of finance. In fact, most researchers who delve into topics ranging from general equity valua-tion to capital structure often explicitly *exclude* banks and other financial institutions due to their unique characteristics.

Why do banks prove to be so difficult to analyze from a valuation perspective? The answers to this question are important to disentangling the myriad influences driving bank valuation. Before we can look for answers to this question we need to elaborate a bit more on the nature of banking as a business.

Banks reflect a mix of heterogeneous businesses. On the one hand, they are well known for taking in deposits with short maturities and using these funds to undertake a variety of lending activities to governments, corporations, and individuals at longer maturities. These deposit and lending activities are typically composed of the following:

- A retail deposit business providing a way for individuals to earn a return on their savings and an inexpensive source of funding for the bank.
- A loan origination business providing a way for borrowers to obtain financing.
- A portfolio business providing a way for a bank to earn a premium for taking risk in lending.

However, banks have also leveraged (pun intended) their relationships with both depositors and borrowers to build other kinds of service busi-nesses. For example:

- Cash management services.
- Foreign exchange services.
- Merger and acquisition advisory services.
- Investment banking services (underwriting, structuring, etc.).
- Financial product distribution channels.
- Wealth management advisory services.

As illustrated in the case of the Medicis' efforts to secure wool export licenses, the relationship developed on the basis of lending can lead to other profitable business transactions. The important distinction we make, however, is between deriving noninterest income from a customer relationship on the one hand, and managing a portfolio of financial assets (that are accumulated as a by-product of providing the services and selling products to the customer) on the other.[3] (We do note, however, that the types of businesses a bank can develop will often be restricted by the regulatory entities supervising the bank. For example, the United States prohibited commercial banks from developing investment banking capability for most of the twentieth century. Repeal of the 1933 Glass-Steagall Act in 1999 eliminated this prohibition. A similar regulation, Article 65, in Japan, did the same thing. Other examples can be found around the world.)

In summary, a bank builds value in its shares by managing its portfolio to reduce the risk of extreme portfolio losses and providing incentives for its business managers to build profitable businesses based on noninterest income. In order to do this, a bank must be able to separate the function of generating revenue by *originating* loans and other products from that of *managing the risk* resulting from carrying the loans on the bank's balance sheet. An ACPM function becomes a key component of this organizational framework.

ORGANIZING FINANCIAL INSTITUTIONS: DIVIDING INTO TWO BUSINESS LINES

As we outlined in the last section, a typical financial institution can be analytically evaluated as two distinct business lines. One business line manages the portfolio of the firm's *financial assets*, while the other manages a portfolio of the firm's *franchises*. Examples of valuable franchises at large financial institutions include retail banking services, loan origination services, cash management services, merger and acquisition advisory services, and so forth—the list is long and varied. These franchises constitute the means by which a financial institution increases its value. (It turns out that even the know-how associated with managing a financial asset portfolio can be turned into a franchise.) For some franchises, such as those focused on building fee income from large borrowers, a financial institution may have to take on large, lumpy exposure to one or a few counterparties. However, in order to make this work, the lending franchise needs to be able to offset

---

[3] As we discuss later in this chapter, our own research suggests that the risk and value of financial firms is far more accurately modeled when default models explicitly accommodate this two-franchise view of the firm.

the concentration risk from these exposures. In this case, managing the diversification of the loan portfolio is an essential component of making the overall interaction with the borrower profitable.

The key insight here is that the two business lines should be functionally separated but related via some kind of *transfer-pricing* mechanism (which we describe more fully later on) that provides the appropriate incentives to manage the bank's risk exposure and to which we will return later. For many financial institutions, the creation of credit exposure is one of the by-products of the manner in which a particular franchise business is built. For example, a loan origination service will naturally create a credit exposure in the form of a loan. Historically, a bank originating a loan was stuck with the concentrations arising from the activities of particular origination teams. With the models, tools, and technology available today, however, the two aspects of this origination—the management of the risk associated with originating a loan and the franchise business of origination services—can be managed separately such that the franchise business can grow without the creation of a poorly diversified credit portfolio.

Why bother to separate these two business lines analytically? The answer lies in the inherent differences in philosophy, objective, and skill sets associated with managing the two lines. Once these differences are understood, the management infrastructure for the two lines can be tailored to their particular characteristics.

The Portfolio Business Line

If we first focus on the portfolio business line, we can readily determine that a portfolio should be diversified and then managed in such a way so as to improve the return per unit of risk. (We define *return* and *risk* more specifically in a moment.) The natural consequence of this orientation, which follows directly from modern finance theory (and folk sayings about eggs and baskets), is a reduction in the concentration of particular exposures. Since the credit markets tend to originate poorly diversified portfolios (note the large amount of debt in the market from borrowers such as Ford, GM, NTT, and TEPCO), the likelihood for a large financial institution to hold a dangerously undiversified portfolio is high.

An active approach to rebalancing a credit portfolio will naturally arise from viewing the portfolio as a separate business line. The performance of the portfolio can then be objectively compared to benchmarks designed to reflect the currently available investment opportunities. In this way, the tendency toward subjective evaluation of credit exposures is replaced with more objective approaches to maximize the return per unit of portfolio risk. With proper implementation of both information and financial technology,

ACPM can be implemented at low cost (i.e., on the order of tens of basis points of the total portfolio exposure). Some institutions may even consider outsourcing this portfolio management function to more efficient teams at institutions with strong track records, and transparent mechanisms for oversight. One implication here is that large, complex financial institutions should be encouraged to adopt quantitative models, the associated technology infrastructure, and the corporate culture to implement a strong portfolio management function and to use these within a broad "risk culture" that accommodates both the strengths and the limitations of these models.

One of the practical questions that arise in the context of ACPM in a financial organization concerns the placement of the ACPM unit. Some institutions already have a portfolio risk function that sometimes appears to be the best place for the ACPM function to be located. We actually recommend against this choice. The difficulty in placing ACPM within the risk management group is that that group is not a profit center. As a consequence, the business units will tend to reclaim the interest income that derives from ACPM—especially in times of difficulty—rendering the ACPM function no more than an *ad hoc* hedging effort at best and a weak gatekeeper at worst. Another practical problem with this placement involves the background and training of the staff. Risk management staff do not typically have a trading orientation, which is often necessary to manage a successful portfolio.

The next logical place to build the ACPM function is the institutional banking division (often called *C&I* for "corporate and institutional banking"). While still not ideal placement, at least this division is a profit center and tends to attract the type of staff needed to manage the portfolio. A bank that chooses this placement, however, must take care in how it establishes this function.

One dangerous path that we recommend strongly against is to create a *separate* portfolio management function *within* each sub-business unit. We have seen a number of banks take this approach during the initial phase of adopting a portfolio perspective. In such instances, the temptation was to indulge some of the stronger business units by allowing them to set up a portfolio management function within their sub-business unit. For example, a strong energy lending team may decide to manage its energy exposures in a portfolio with a dedicated portfolio manager. (In one extreme case, we actually saw a bank recast many of its loan origination specialists as "portfolio managers.") The problem is, though, that sub-business unit heads will often have incentives to run the group's hedging strategies without concern for the impact on the bank's *overall* portfolio. The result is haphazard portfolio management that neither mitigates the bank's concentration risk nor improves the return per unit of risk earned on the bank's portfolio.

If a bank chooses to build its ACPM function within its institutional banking division, it also makes sense to centralize the function across all sub-business units. In essence, ACPM can be thought of as another sub-business unit whose franchise is to manage all exposures that the other business units generate.

In such a configuration, all loans originated in the institutional division are first "priced" to determine how much risk they contribute to the overall portfolio and how much this risk costs to hedge. The loans can then be transfer-priced into the ACPM portfolio so that in cases where the initial loan pricing fails to cover the contribution to the bank's overall portfolio risk, the difference can be booked as an expense to the sub-business unit doing the origination or trade. (We discuss the mechanics of transfer pricing in a later section.) The relationship managers in that sub-business unit can then be compensated on their ability to sell a mix of products at costs (hedging and other) that result in reasonable profits. In many institutions, large corporate loans or revolvers are almost always priced too low from a risk contribution perspective. The generation of cash flow from noninterest income is the key to building profitable customer relationships.

Other possible locations for ACPM team placement include the finance group and treasury. While placement of the ACPM function within the finance, treasury, or the C&I division can work, the ideal organizational structure designates ACPM as a *separate business unit altogether*. In this organizational form, all bank credit exposures—not just those to large corporate bodies—can be transfer-priced into a central portfolio. In this way, the management of all credit risk happens centrally and each business unit throughout the bank can transparently assess profitability after accounting for the potential credit cost of extending loans and funding commitments.

In a few respects, some investment banks have approached this kind of organizational structure when taking on credit risk exposure in the course of building fee-based business franchises. Of course, some investment banks have also failed. A sound organizational structure with proper incentives while necessary is not a sufficient condition for a profitable enterprise—an institution still needs strong managers who can see beyond models and systems to run a successful business.

In practice, however, this level of centralization—the ACPM unit as a separate business unit—may be difficult to achieve in the near term. Many institutions today are too new to the notion of ACPM, and for them, the best approach still remains starting within the institutional banking division. As time goes on, we may eventually see some of these more forward-thinking organizational structures.

The Franchise Business Line

If we define one general business line as portfolio management as we did in the previous section, we can differentiate it from the other: a *service type* of business line that characterizes each of the several customer-service-oriented franchises within a typical bank. This other type of business line presents a completely different set of challenges. This category of business line leverages relationships developed in the context of taking deposits and making loans.

In order to maximize the value of this type of business line, a financial institution must first identify its core competencies and comparative advantages and then determine how to leverage these into franchises that continue to grow over time. Whereas the portfolio management function benefits from the availability of technology and benchmarks, a franchise business requires more entrepreneurial managers who have a vision rooted in a passion for meeting some particular customer demand. Franchise businesses will likely be more costly to staff and manage. They will require other functions such as sales and marketing. They may also require more traditional brick-and-mortar assets (although the Internet has opened up new opportunities for virtualization in some cases).

Because of its profile, a portfolio of franchise businesses will typically exhibit volatility in value that is an order of magnitude greater than the volatility in the portfolio of the bank's financial assets.[4] The compensation for this increased volatility is the prospect of a growing business for which, if the expectations are good, investors should be willing to pay a multiple of current earnings.

An important characteristic of the distribution of future values for franchise businesses is the symmetry of these values with respect to both upside and downside value realizations. In other words, the distribution of these values behaves in some ways like a typical equity investment, where an initial cash outlay is about equally likely to double as it is to be reduced by half. A portfolio of credit exposures, by contrast, has a high probability of earning a small amount and a low probability of losing a large amount—in other words, low upside and large downside. Hence, the focus on management of

---

[4] At MKMV, in an analysis of over 100 large financial institution portfolios, the majority of which were from commercial banks, with a few from investment banks, asset managers, and insurance companies, we found the typical asset volatility estimate to be in the range of 2 to 7 percent. In contrast, publicly traded service businesses exhibited typical volatility in the value of their franchise businesses in the range of 30 to 50 percent.

the credit portfolio is management of downside risk. In contrast, in the case of a portfolio of franchise businesses, the upside and downside should be approximately balanced, reducing the overall risk to the financial institution and to the economy as a whole.

The bulk of a financial institution's operating risk should lie in its franchise businesses and its overall management of the organization. Organizational management requires skills and techniques that are difficult to measure and quantify in the same way that we can measure and quantify market and credit risk. In recent years, operational risk modeling has been introduced as a means for managing some of the risk associated with operating the firm's overall portfolio of businesses. (As an aside, regulation tends to focus less on the nature of these businesses, as they typically do not contribute much to systemic risk in the economy.) We are still in the early years of understanding how best to use key performance indicators (KPIs) to manage operational risk. That is all the more reason for a financial institution to make sure it has the types of managers running its franchise businesses who are comfortable with building businesses in a world of incomplete information. Note that the portfolio business and the corporate functions of financial institutions (e.g., finance, accounting, treasury, human resources, etc.) are subject to operational risk that goes beyond the operational risk inherent in each franchise business. The nature of operational risk faced by the franchise businesses may differ from the operational risk faced by an institution's corporate functions.

In summary, our view is that financial institutions will be best served by leveraging global credit markets to improve the return per unit of risk on their portfolio of financial assets, and by facilitating the creation of franchise businesses that leverage the institution's core competencies. The link in this structure is the implementation of transfer pricing of the risk between the portfolio business line that hedges and manages credit risk capital and the franchise business lines that put the bank's credit capital at risk in the course of building their businesses. Current financial technology facilitates the estimation of reasonable transfer prices for a wide range of securities that may or may not be entirely liquid. We discuss the models used for these applications in later chapters.

EMPHASIS ON CREDIT RISK

Why our emphasis on credit risk? Fundamentally, banks consider how to actively manage all risk to which they are exposed: market, credit, and liquidity. As it turns out, for most financial institutions, the bulk of the exposure in their financial portfolios reflects credit risk. For example, large financial institutions are typically not good repositories for interest-rate risk since the vast, liquid markets in interest-rate derivatives make it possible for most interest-rate risk to be hedged away. A prudent financial institution will hedge this risk so that interest rate movements (over which management has no control) do not drive the institution's profitability. Given these market circumstances, the primary financial risk faced by large financial institutions is credit risk.

In the case of a commercial bank, the institution's portfolio is primarily composed of credit exposures.[5] Investment banks have not historically had the same level of credit exposure as commercial banks; however, recent shifts toward providing credit facilities to some clients together with the credit exposure to counterparties in their derivatives book has increased their credit exposure, as has the increase in credit-derivative trading. The recent credit crisis of 2007 and 2008 has resulted in the major U.S. investment banks disappearing, being acquired by commercial banks, or turning into bank holding companies. In any case, the trend has been to increase the degree to which credit risk becomes a key risk faced by all banks. Other nonbank financial institutions (NBFI) have increased their credit exposure as the size of consumer finance portfolios have ballooned (particularly in the United States) and the availability of credit derivatives and structured products in the form of credit default swaps (CDS), asset-backed securities (ABS), and collateralized debt obligations (CDO) have proliferated. Insurance companies have long parked corporate bonds on their balance sheets, and recent interest in ACPM has lured them into expanding their credit exposure as well. The appearance of credit-strategy hedge funds and the increased participation of pension funds in the credit markets have also expanded the number of players in the credit space as well as increased the potential for heightened credit market volatility. While beyond the scope of this book, even large corporations find themselves increasingly exposed to credit risk in the form of accounts and trade receivables as well as direct investment in credit derivatives and credit portfolios. The population of potential market participants motivated to trade credit risk is now large and varied. These circumstances have set the stage for the continued development of a robust market for credit risk on a global scale.

---

[5] Note that we differentiate between the market risk associated with an equity investment or an interest-rate-sensitive instrument and that of the change in market value of a credit-risky instrument due to changes in either the credit environment or the credit quality of the borrower, which we consider to be a form of credit risk.

MARKET TRENDS SUPPORTING ACPM

Three recent market developments herald the rapid expansion of methods for managing credit risk:

1. The increased transparency of the U.S. corporate bond market following the implementation of the Trade Reporting and Compliance Engine (TRACE)[6] initiative in July 2002.
2. The rapid growth in the number of traded credit default swaps (CDS). (Outstanding CDS notional amount has gone from virtually nothing in 2000 to over $60 trillion in 2008, although the total outstanding has pulled back some in the wake of the 2007 and 2008 credit crisis.)
3. The recent availability of corporate credit indexes and synthetic collateralized debt obligations (CDO) written on these indexes or on portfolios of names relevant to most large financial institutions.

In the past, credit markets have been hampered by lack of transparency in pricing, making it difficult to mark a portfolio to market let alone hedge or trade a particular exposure. With the advent of TRACE and the increased number of data vendors collecting, filtering, and disseminating data, financial institutions have a much better opportunity to make sensible, cost-effective decisions with regard to changing their portfolio composition. With the combination of better data, more powerful credit analytics, and a growing number of traded credit instruments, a financial institution can now cost-effectively mark to market, hedge, and trade large segments of its portfolio. While the credit crisis of 2007 and 2008 has highlighted the difficulties that can present themselves in marking portfolios to market in times of crisis (particularly when the portfolios contain structured credit), the longer-term prospects for managing regularly marked portfolios are much better than before the development of the CDS market and the different initiatives focused on improving transparency in pricing. While there is still a ways to go, this most recent crisis has created more momentum for improving transparency throughout the various markets for credit, particularly with respect

---

[6] In September 1998, the U. S. Securities and Exchange Commission (SEC) requested the National Association of Securities Dealers (NASD) to provide more transparency into the transactions in the corporate debt market. The NASD agreed to start an initiative called TRACE to disclose corporate bond transaction prices from July 1, 2002. Today the transaction prices of most corporate bonds traded in the United States are available via TRACE and can be obtained from the web site of the Financial Industry Regulatory Authority (FINRA), www.finra.org. FINRA was created in July 2007 with the consolidation of the NASD and the member regulation, enforcement, and arbitration functions of the New York Stock Exchange.

to how instruments are structured and priced. The challenge going forward is in determining how best to organize a financial institution such that its senior management has incentives both to improve portfolio performance on a risk-adjusted basis and to build solid franchise businesses.

As financial institutions have developed better methods for allocating capital on an economic basis, the relevance of some older financial regulation has declined, which in part has led to the push toward the new Basel II framework. Our discussion of ACPM thus far has focused on the importance of encouraging large financial institutions to acquire and implement not just single-obligor credit risk models but also economically focused portfolio models. In our judgment, the health of these institutions will be driven by sensible management of their portfolio risk on an economic basis with a focus on building robust franchise businesses.

Quantitative risk and portfolio models, combined with appropriate oversight and reality checks, provide the means to building a robust ACPM function, and effective management of credit portfolios requires these quantitative tools. The balance of this chapter discusses the interplay of the analytics and organization in implementing a successful ACPM function.

FINANCIAL INSTRUMENTS USED FOR HEDGING AND MANAGING RISK IN A CREDIT PORTFOLIO

Among the most challenging classes of credit portfolios to actively manage are bank portfolios. A bank portfolio contains mostly loans, often to private borrowers. Thus, the ACPM group within a bank will be faced with challenges that arise from the risk inherent in a loan portfolio. These challenges follow from characteristics of loans that make them difficult to manage in a portfolio:

- There is a lack of standardized terms and conditions. Loans tend to be customized to particular borrowers. With increased syndication of loans, more standardized contracts have become common; however, compared to traded bonds, loans still have widely differing fee structures, collateral arrangements, and covenants.
- Loans are hard to trade. The lack of standardization is a primary reason behind the lack of liquidity in the secondary loan market. While more loans have started trading in recent years, in practice, an ACPM group will have more difficulty buying and selling individual loans than it would buying or selling comparable bonds or CDS.

- Data on loans is often difficult to collect. Many loans are originated to small and medium enterprises (SMEs). Since these obligors are not often tracked in market data vendors' databases, a bank is left to manage with its own data collection infrastructure to build models to characterize risk on an ongoing basis. Since each bank relies on its own models, two banks may disagree on the creditworthiness of a loan or even on the scales on which this credit quality is measured. As a result, it is sometimes difficult to complete trades regarding many of the names in the loan portfolio. With the advent of widely used vendor models now achieving ubiquity in some sectors, this challenge has begun to abate.
- Borrowers not familiar with modern portfolio theory may resist the bank's desire to sell or hedge their loans. In recent years, an increased level of understanding in the financial services industry has mitigated this perception problem; however, in some markets and regions it can still hamper the management of a bank's portfolio.
- Many hedging instruments such as synthetic CDOs and CDSs have become the target of criticism. Difficulties in some sectors of the structured credit market have created (for some) a perception problem for all structured credit and credit derivatives. While we recommend that the instruments used for ACPM generally be straightforward and transparent, less informed bank managers may have concerns about trading in any structured credit or derivative instruments.

Despite these challenges, current market conditions and perceptions are much more conducive to ACPM than they were a little over a decade ago when many of these ideas were first suggested. The models and systems that we describe in this book become an important starting point for all financial institutions seeking to understand the return/risk profile of their portfolio. Even if a bank's management believes it cannot manage its portfolio in accordance with market-based metrics, simply understanding the portfolio in this context will make strategy discussions more meaningful.

Even before a bank starts actively managing its credit portfolio, it can use portfolio-level analysis to direct the organization toward value-creating businesses and away from value-destroying businesses. A key step forward in doing so is the creation of an ACPM function within the institution with which to begin implementing the discipline of transfer pricing. As an introduction to the concepts of ACPM, the bank may begin to measure the transfer price of various exposures to the bank. This in turn can lead to more disciplined lending. In some cases, relationship managers will stop rolling over credit lines and renewing loans for customers whose transfer price vastly exceeds the spreads and fees earned from the relationship. From there, the ACPM group can start exploring opportunistic trades in names where liquidity is available that improve the bank's risk profile and diversification efficiently.

Individuals new to the concepts of ACPM sometimes assume that a perfectly efficient and liquid market will eliminate the need for this kind of management. In fact, the correlation impact inherent in credit portfolios implies that a particular portfolio will always benefit from diversifying trades where risk is reasonably priced. In practice, credit markets are far from efficient, so a good portfolio manager will capture not just the diversification benefit, but also extra spread from exploiting market inefficiencies.

Once the ACPM team is fully operational with the necessary models and support systems, its trading can range from outright sales of loans to replicating trades in other instruments. For example, buying protection in the CDS market on a company related to a large exposure in the portfolio may be a way to hedge the large exposure in cases where there may be business sensitivities about directly hedging that company's risk. As another example, the portfolio manager may be able to identify sectors and geographies that will add to the portfolio's diversification, provided the bank can credibly analyze the instruments in question. Experience suggests that this can be overdone; diversifying trades should not be made in new areas just because casual analysis suggests that the portfolio does not have those types of exposures. A new position outside the bank's area of expertise should not be added to the portfolio unless the trade makes sense from a business perspective and can be evaluated comfortably.

More importantly, the ACPM team, over time, will develop expertise in basket swaps, nth to default swaps,[7] and synthetic CLOs, which can be efficient financial tools for managing chunks of portfolio risk. The hedges may be managed separately in a rebalanced book to improve the efficiency of those hedges. The best performance will come from a team that responsibly trades loans, bonds, CDSs, and portfolio derivatives—in other words, its transactions are based on sound analysis grounded in best-practice models and systems.

---

[7] These types of swaps involve the protection seller taking on exposure to a portfolio of names instead of just one name. A basket swap contains a "basket" or group of obligors that are the reference entities for the protection seller who will absorb losses from defaults of any obligor in the group. An nth to default swap is similar except the protection seller only covers losses if the second, third, or nth obligor (depending on how n is defined) in the group defaults.

MARK-TO-MARKET AND TRANSFER PRICING

An important implication of moving to a quantitative assessment of portfolio return and risk concerns the adjustment of the financial institution's perspective to a mark-to-market (MTM) approach to portfolio management. Except for their market risk books, many financial institutions continue to manage large portions of their portfolios on an historical book value basis. A transition to an MTM orientation forces the portfolio manager to evaluate the portfolio each day on a forward-looking basis. As the credit quality waxes and wanes for different borrowers, the portfolio implications will change, regardless of the circumstances under which the exposures were first originated. This change in value may occur due to exogenous factors such as a change in the competitive structure in the marketplace or change in the general level of interest rates, for example. Of course, it may also change due to the borrower changing the way it manages its business. This highlights the need to track these changes on a real-time basis. In this way, prudent hedging and trading can take place before difficult circumstances turn into crises.

While MTM sounds attractive in theory, in practice it can be exceedingly difficult to implement. Changes in market value can sometimes be hard to accept, as, for example, in the case of a borrower whose valuation has dropped but who continues to pay its coupons on time without difficulty. If a financial institution has transfer-priced the exposure into a central portfolio (so that those individuals personally involved in providing other services to the borrower are not directly involved in the management of the risk exposure), it is much easier for everyone to accept the MTM perspective. Such transfer pricing also ensures that those originating loans and services are aware of the costs, from a risk perspective, of a particular business opportunity to the bank overall. Relationship managers may still choose to grant a loan at a loss, but that cost will now be explicit and they can use it in determining whether the prospect of future business is sufficient to offset current cost.

Conceptually, transfer pricing places a cost on the use of capital inherent in the extension of credit to an obligor. More specifically, a transfer price recognizes the actual cost to a bank's portfolio resulting from adding a particular exposure. The spread on the loan will offset this cost and in some cases (rarely for corporate loans) exceed the transfer cost. The idea we introduce in this chapter is that originating a loan that stays on the bank's balance sheet consumes some of the bank's capital. If that loan is placed in a centralized portfolio and managed accordingly, economics and common sense imply that its spread should be sized so that the return per unit of risk (appropriately measured) for that loan is at least as good as or better than the typical return per unit of risk earned by all the exposures in the portfolio (otherwise the portfolio's risk/return profile will decline). By instituting a transfer price, the ACPM function will not be disadvantaged as it takes on loans from the origination teams. The relationship managers originating the loan will be properly motivated to either charge a profitable spread or find other noninterest income (or both) so that each customer relationship adds to, instead of subtracts from, overall bank share value.

In theory, the appropriate method for calculating a transfer price would contemplate a measure of spread per unit of contribution to overall portfolio risk. As we discussed in Chapter 1, this contribution may be defined as a loan's contribution to portfolio volatility, known as risk contribution (RC), or as contribution to the probability of extreme loss, known as tail risk contribution (TRC). Without delving into the technical details of these metrics (which we do later in Chapter 8), a transfer price calculation might begin with the expected spread (ES) level needed to generate a Sharpe ratio (ES/RC) or a Vasicek ratio (ES/TRC) that at least equals the overall portfolio Sharpe ratio or Vasicek ratio, respectively. (We discuss in Chapter 8 the advantages and disadvantages of the two ratios, but for now assume that one or the other is chosen.) The transfer price would then equal this required ES level plus the expected loss (EL) for that exposure.

While such simple calculations are appealing from a theoretical perspective, in practice, this approach turns out not to work very well. The practical difficulties arise for at least two behavioral reasons. First, transfer pricing is usually opposed by the relationship managers since it constitutes a radical change in how they typically build their loan business. The focus shifts from size of loans made to the economic or risk-adjusted profitability of loans. Most successful implementations of transfer pricing result from strong support at the CEO level, which means many bank employees affected only grudgingly accept it. Given this background, transfer pricing based on something like a Sharpe or Vasicek ratio comes across as esoteric and hard to understand. Further, different stakeholders in the bank will have to accept the output of underlying models that can sometimes be difficult to validate. For example, both RC and TRC require a calculation of correlation, which requires acceptance of models that are still relatively new. These concerns can be overcome in certain circumstances, but generally implementations will become bogged down in seemingly endless model and data discussions.

The second behavioral reason concerns the tendency of this kind of transfer-pricing algorithm to unintentionally produce incentives for building suboptimal businesses. Since correlation becomes an important factor in this calculation, and different geographies and asset classes from the existing portfolio tend to have lower correlations (all else equal), the transfer price for these less familiar loans will be relatively smaller. This may motivate relationship managers to seek out unusual loans in areas where they and the bank may not have the expertise for evaluation and monitoring. Conversely, the relationship managers may reduce loans to obligors in markets where the bank does have expertise and this expertise is leading to other fee-based businesses.

This approach may, in fact, be what the management of the financial institution wants; but it is important to understand how to measure the *full customer profitability* before a bank can effectively implement an RC- or TRC-based transfer-pricing approach. Since most banks are not close to having the full customer profitability available on a risk-adjusted basis, transfer pricing with RC or TRC may result in undesirable outcomes. Since transfer pricing itself is still an important first step to building a more valuable bank, where do we turn?

Market-based pricing (such as that reflected in the CDS market) for any purpose has the strong advantage of objectivity. Everyone can observe and evaluate the price. If the bank's portfolio exactly matches the diversification characteristics of the overall CDS market, then the CDS spread (in an efficient market) will equal the required ES (based on RC or TRC—depending on whether the market is pricing to volatility or extreme loss) plus EL. In practice, each institution's portfolio will differ from the market's portfolio, but the CDS spread also has another important interpretation: It is a good proxy for the cost of hedging—in many cases, it may reflect the actual cost of hedging. In any case, the CDS spread becomes an effective way to transfer-price originated loans into the portfolio. While the bank may still need to rely on modeled CDS spreads for obligors without traded CDSs in the market, this kind of credit-curve fitting to CDS spreads tends to be easier to explain and defend than pricing based on RC or TRC.

As banks and the market become more sophisticated, we may eventually arrive at transfer prices more in line with the portfolio metrics. In the meantime, the CDS market provides one excellent source for incorporating proper incentives in a bank originating a credit portfolio. Whichever metric is used to determine a transfer price, the goal is the replacement of subjective analysis of cross-subsidization (across an institution's business groups) with objective analysis so that the institution moves in a direction that increases its value.

Many times, we have heard stories of banks willing to lend at unprofitable spreads to secure other more profitable business such as cash management contracts. After rigorous analysis, we often found that some of these supposedly valuable customer relationships were never actually profitable. A transfer-pricing mechanism highlights this kind of inefficiency by eliminating the subjectivity in this analysis and disciplining the organization to

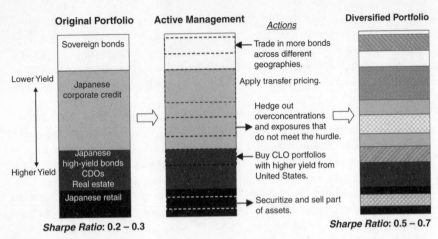

FIGURE 2.1   Process of Improving the Performance of a Japanese Bank Portfolio

filter out unprofitable customer relationships. The result should be a higher share price. Figure 2.1 provides a high-level view of possible changes to a Japanese bank portfolio.

This figure reflects the type of portfolio one might find at a medium to large Japanese bank. As can be seen in the first bar, most of the risk in the original portfolio arises from exposure in Japan. The concentration risk associated with the Japanese exposure in general and the corporate credit specifically should be the focus of a well-functioning ACPM strategy. The actions the ACPM group can take are listed in the second bar. Diversification and the return/risk profile of the portfolio is improved by hedging out specific chunks of concentrated risk with CDS, buying portfolio exposures in geographies and sectors that have low correlations with the existing portfolio, and selling part of the overall concentrated, Japanese portfolio risk with instruments such as synthetic CLOs. Transfer pricing assists in aligning incentives throughout the loan origination process to reflect the actual cost to the portfolio of particular exposures. These efforts should improve the portfolio Sharpe ratio by a factor of 2 to 3.

Consider another real-life example of how this works. A large bank in Germany that shifted its organizational structure to accommodate a centralized portfolio management function in the late 1990s began by working with its corporate relationship managers to understand how each client added value. The bank implemented a transfer pricing mechanism using CDS spreads such that a particular loan exposure's transfer price constituted the cost of hedging that exposure in the CDS market. If a loan were originated at LIBOR plus 100 basis points, but it cost 120 basis points to hedge the loan in the CDS market, then the (negative) 20 basis point difference is the net charge back to the relationship manager. In essence, the transfer price of the loan is based on the market price of hedging the loan. For this trade to make sense, this manager would need to find other products and services (e.g., cash management, foreign exchange trading, merger and acquisition advisory, etc.), presumably from the same client, that would cover the 20 basis point cost *plus* earn a profit. If the relationship manager ultimately earns more than the 20 basis point net cost, then the relationship will add value to the bank's traded equity.

In contrast, if the relationship manager were to continue to manage the risk exposures by focusing on cash flow (i.e., if the relationship manager were responsible for the continued coupon flow from the loan as well as the associated risk of default), it would likely be difficult for the manager to accept a change in value (i.e, agree that it mattered) of an exposure as long as that borrower continued to pay its bills. This is a bit paradoxical since the manager would probably readily agree that the credit quality of *publicly traded* debt can change quite substantially even though the borrowers continue to pay. Yet for some reason, we have found that this logic is harder for relationship managers to accept with respect to their own clients. They will, of course, welcome an MTM approach in cases where the value of a position has increased. But the incentives become skewed when a manager accepts only the upside change in value and rejects the downside changes. In any case, clearly aligning incentives and educating bank staff on the importance of transfer pricing and the related concept of MTM will go a long way in reducing internal resistance.

A common objection to MTM in a bank portfolio context focuses on the lack of liquidity in many types of loans. While less true today than 10 years ago, a large proportion of loans still may not be liquidly traded. Even today, sudden changes in liquidity for particular asset classes (such as the loss of liquidity in late 2007 in the market for CDO tranches and the broader liquidity problems in the entire range of credit markets in 2008) can make it difficult to provide regular, credible marks. The solution lies in developing an MTM *waterfall* where the internal MTM system moves through a waterfall of choices of valuation approaches from most liquid to least liquid or modeled, seeking to apply the most liquid and most relevant choice to each exposure. The waterfall ensures that the MTM system does not suffer from applying the same approach to each exposure. In times of crisis, some leeway will be necessary to account for the lack of information on how to price a security. That said, the MTM discipline will create a culture focused on market-based changes of value that will ultimately increase the overall value of the financial institution. In addition to improving portfolio monitoring by providing a regular snapshot of the portfolio's changing value, MTM discipline will make it easier for relationship managers and business heads to understand and accept transfer pricing of originated credit into an ACPM portfolio.

Moving to an MTM approach is important for instilling the right level of discipline in portfolio management. In this way, reasonable comparisons to performance benchmarks can be implemented. While it may first appear to create more earnings volatility due to the changes in portfolio value being realized as they occur rather than hidden in a book-value world (that only realizes loss when a borrower cannot pay), the truth is that the underlying volatility in portfolio value (and therefore in the value of the overall financial institution) is always present though it has not always been measured. Astute analysts have understood this fact and awarded lower multiples to financial institutions whose portfolio values have exhibited excessive volatility, even if only implicit. An MTM environment creates a higher level of transparency, which should be positively received by financial analysts and regulators.

METRICS FOR MANAGING A CREDIT PORTFOLIO

A number of measures of exposure and portfolio risk have been suggested in industry and academia, and every summary measure of risk has benefits and drawbacks. Our own experience suggests that measures of risk contribution and tail risk contribution at the exposure level and unexpected loss and economic capital at the portfolio level are versatile and informative. These measures are components of the core performance metrics we recommend for a credit portfolio (we list them again for reference):

- Portfolio Sharpe ratio = portfolio expected spread / portfolio unexpected loss
- Exposure Sharpe ratio = exposure expected spread / exposure risk contribution
- Portfolio Vasicek ratio = portfolio expected spread / portfolio capital
- Exposure Vasicek ratio = exposure expected spread / exposure tail risk contribution

An additional useful ratio is something we call a *capital efficiency ratio* (CER). This ratio is calculated by taking the percentage of capital a particular exposure uses divided by the weight of that exposure in the portfolio. The CER characterizes how much more capital the exposure uses relative to its weight in the portfolio. More efficient exposures will have a CER less than one (they use proportionally less capital than their exposure weight percentage in the portfolio).

Managing a credit portfolio requires tracking individual exposures via these metrics and looking for problems and opportunities among different groups of exposures. Useful groupings for such activities include groupings by sector, geography, and risk rating classes. At the overall portfolio level, the portfolio manager monitors both the Sharpe ratio and the Vasicek ratio. In practice, many institutions, particularly banks, do not fully track return data (e.g., MTM value of exposures, spreads, fees, and coupons) as well as they could. Often it is difficult for them to report exposure income data on a transaction by transaction basis. Sometimes, changes in spreads for step-up facilities are not well recorded. And MTM systems can suffer from lack of frequently updated data. These difficulties will sometimes make the ES calculations less reliable than the TRC calculations so that TRC should be tracked separately, together with Sharpe, Vasicek, and CEF ratios.

A simple example will highlight how these measures are used. Assume a large Japanese bank's portfolio consists predominantly of loans to Japanese companies (similar to the one in Figure 2.1). Next assume that this bank is presented with the opportunity to lend money to two new companies, one European and the other Japanese, that are similar in every way (i.e., same size, same industry, same default probabilities, etc.) except in their country of operation. The exposure stand-alone unexpected loss estimates for these two companies will be almost identical. In contrast, the exposure portfolio-referent risk contribution numbers may be substantially different.

Our research at MKMV, which has been corroborated by other financial researchers, demonstrated that correlations tend to be lower across countries than across industries. Thus in this scenario, the European company will look much better in the sense that its risk contribution with respect to the Japanese bank portfolio will be substantially lower than the risk contribution of the Japanese prospective borrower. In our own experience working with bank portfolios, we found that corporate borrower risk contributions for typical large financial institution portfolios can be as low as 5 percent of the borrower's stand-alone unexpected loss. That is, in the context of a particular portfolio, the portfolio has the ability to diversify away much of the risk of an instrument having low correlation with other exposures in the portfolio. In some cases, the portfolio can diversify away 95 percent of the instrument's stand-alone risk. The typical range for this diversification benefit for large financial institution portfolios is 30 to 95 percent of stand-alone unexpected loss.

The strength of the risk contribution measure is its intuitive interpretation and its mathematical tractability. Given the nature of correlation, individual instrument unexpected loss estimates do not add up to the portfolio unexpected loss. Correlation (or lack thereof) drives the benefits of creating portfolios. In the case of credit exposures, correlations are typically low, making them amenable to placement in large portfolios. Said differently, given low correlations in credit exposures (but asymmetric payoffs associated with them), a financial institution may continue to see diversification benefit even when holding a portfolio of tens of thousands exposures.

The weakness of the risk contribution measure is its lack of information with respect to the possibility of extreme loss. Tail risk contribution addresses this extreme loss potential.

Tail risk contribution may generate results that seem at first glance to be counterintuitive. Seemingly lower risk exposures are sometimes identified as risky while seemingly higher risk ones are not. For example, exposure to large, low-risk borrowers such as NTT or IBM may result in a relatively low risk-contribution estimate, but the size of the exposure may also result in a relatively high TRC estimate. What is driving this result? In states of the economy where circumstances are extremely difficult, holding large chunks of what had been low-risk borrowers exposes the financial institution to the threat of insolvency more than a small position in a higher-risk borrower. Furthermore, the large, low-risk borrower may be more highly correlated with the rest of the portfolio.

If we look back at the history of banking crises, we see a common tendency among banks to have originated portfolios of large, correlated corporate exposures. In difficult economic times, these *seemingly* well-diversified portfolios (in terms of industry concentration, which has historically been the dimension along which banks diversify) did not weather well the losses that arose due to the correlated nature of corporate distress. The need to withstand not just typical volatility but also rare distressed states of the economy (in which many obligors default at the same time) is what drives the use of TRC and economic capital calculations. Properly used, these measures can provide a good sense of the risk of extreme loss for a financial institution.

This is why we find that the Vasicek ratio (VR), which places TRC, rather than UL in the denominator, useful in providing a characterization of the return per unit of contribution to extreme loss risk. Well-placed hedges can substantially reign in the overall portfolio tail risk and reduce the TRC of highly concentrated exposures.

The capital efficiency ratio (CER) provides some sense of which names in the capital usage vastly exceed the exposure's weight. Like the VR, the CER helps to identify names that should be hedged. The CER provides more of a sense of the size of the concentrated risk positions. A portfolio may contain an exposure with a moderate VR but a high CER, just because the name takes up quite a bit more capital in a relative sense than what might be expected given the weight of the exposure.

The preceding are specific examples of return/risk metrics that are useful for managing a portfolio. Simply put, the portfolio manager should have incentives to buy or hold exposures with high Sharpe and Vasicek ratios and sell exposures with low ratios, as highlighted in Figure 2.2.

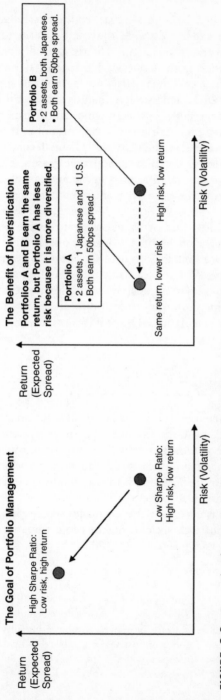

The Goal of Portfolio Management

High Sharpe Ratio:
Low risk, high return

Low Sharpe Ratio:
High risk, low return

Return
(Expected
Spread)

Risk (Volatility)

The Benefit of Diversification

Portfolios A and B earn the same return, but Portfolio A has less risk because it is more diversified.

Portfolio A
• 2 assets, 1 Japanese and 1 U.S.
• Both earn 50bps spread.

Portfolio B
• 2 assets, both Japanese.
• Both earn 50bps spread.

Same return, lower risk   High risk, low return

Return
(Expected
Spread)

Risk (Volatility)

FIGURE 2.2 Example of Improving a Portfolio's Sharpe Ratio and Diversification

This figure highlights the goal of a portfolio manager when using a Sharpe ratio. In the left-hand graph, the goal is to migrate the portfolio to the low-risk, high-return quadrant. The right-hand graph illustrates the benefit of diversification in this context. The lower-risk portfolio A reflects the lower correlation, so that the portfolio earns the same spread as portfolio B but has lower risk. One can do similar analysis in the context of the Vasicek ratio, where the risk measure is the economic capital instead of volatility.

This strategy over time will improve the overall portfolio ratios. Note that the capital and tail risk calculations will be dependent on the target probability of insolvency chosen for analysis. For example, a financial institution's management may be interested in the amount of capital necessary to absorb losses that occur 99.95 percent of the time (roughly this results in a AA rating). The tail risk contribution calculation in this case will reflect the contribution of loss of an exposure to extreme loss events that occur only 0.05 percent of the time. One may also find it useful to look at the contribution to extreme loss events that occur 1 percent of the time or 10 percent of the time. With the tools and measures we have been discussing it is possible for managers to understand more clearly the impact of correlation and concentration in both normal and severe economic circumstances. We will return to the calculation of these measures in Chapter 8 on portfolio modeling.

DATA AND MODELS

The ability to implement useful systems rests on data and model availability. While data and models are still not available for every exposure type found in large financial institution portfolios around the world, the past decade has seen a number of advances that facilitate the analysis of the vast bulk of corporate credit exposure. Our bias is toward models that rely on observable data, especially observable market data.[8]

We have found it useful, in circumstances where data is not available for a specific domain (e.g., some forms of project finance), to use analyst

---

[8] We have found that the very best analysts are often aware of details about the strategy of a borrower or developments in an industry that can be difficult for the general investing community to assimilate into prices. However, such cases are rare and it is usually difficult to generalize this specific knowledge beyond a portfolio of closely followed firms. Even these analysts, moreover, can have difficulty incorporating the impacts of developments in other industries or geographies in their assessments of credit quality. Of course, the average analyst is, by definition, not among the very best.

input within a structured setting, such as an expert system or scorecard. In these circumstances, it is often most productive to make available quantitative models to augment the qualitative analysis and provide different perspectives. Organizations that are most effective at this type of analysis also develop systems to evaluate the performance of these analysts and their subjective judgments over time.

In all cases, regardless of whether the analysis is done qualitatively or quantitatively, senior management will likely require that analysts communicate the conceptual underpinnings of their credit analysis without hiding behind reams of statistical data or vague gut feelings. A good economic explanation (what economists call a *story*) should always accompany model output.

The key inputs to these portfolio models are term structures of default probabilities (PDs). Today, a financial institution can build or buy one or several PD models for both public and private corporations operating in most geographies, including most emerging markets. In many cases, particularly the case of public firm models, the value of these models today is less in the financial theory that underlies them (since the generic analytics have become more widely known) and more in the implementation and data processing. As a result, much of the action for a financial institution involves gaining a high level of confidence that the inputs its models are using reflect extensive data filtering and are refreshed on a regular basis. The economies of scale associated with maintaining global coverage for default probabilities typically make it substantially more cost-effective for most financial institutions to buy corporate models from vendors with long track records rather than build their own systems, at least for broadly covered markets. Since exposure to corporate borrowers constitutes one of the major sources of risk in a typical financial institution's portfolio, the mature state of models and the availability of robust data analytics make it possible for most financial institutions to begin doing meaningful portfolio analysis at a reasonable cost.

While the analytics for loss given default and correlation estimation are not as mature as those available for default probability estimation, these inputs are often available for private and public exposures in major economies around the world. Some other exposure types for which analytics are now becoming available include retail and commercial real estate. Analytics have also been recently developed for understanding structured products such as collateralized debt obligations and asset-backed securities, though these models continue to develop and be refined. Here again, the costs of maintaining large databases of underlying portfolios for each transaction and, in the case of cash transactions, the cost of coding and testing the unique waterfall for each transaction suggest economies of scale and scope. As a result, as in the case of corporate credit risk, it may be more cost-effective for institutions with exposures to structured products to outsource this function by purchasing software and data from established vendors. (Note that this does not imply the models should be followed blindly—only that the data collection and software development may be uneconomical for institutions to implement on a one-off basis.) The next few years will likely see substantial advancement in modeling these types of exposures plus others (e.g., sovereigns, project finance, hedge funds). We are at a point today where coverage is available for enough of a typical large financial institution's portfolio to facilitate meaningful portfolio analysis on an institution-wide basis. Both senior managers of these institutions and regulators should encourage these organizations to build a quantitatively sound foundation for managing their portfolios.

Importantly, as we wield these various models, it is tempting to think that we have captured all of the components of risk. However, the most important piece of education that a quantitative analyst (or *quant*) can impart, both to businesspeople and to other members of a quant team, is that models are not guarantees. They are abstractions of reality that can help users understand complicated phenomena. The real world is always more complex than that which can be modeled on a whiteboard or a computer. The statistician George Box is reported to have said, "Essentially, all models are wrong, some are useful."[9] When a weather researcher simulates a hurricane on his computer, he does not expect to get wet. In the same way, when we simulate a loss distribution, we do not expect that the real loss distribution will look exactly like the one we simulate. We also do not expect that our model has encompassed all of the many, many factors that can affect portfolio losses.

This does not mean we should throw up our hands and give up. Rather, it suggests that in addition to understanding what the models we use do, we should also understand what they cannot do—their limitations. With our increasing ability to model more and more precise quantities and more and more complex relationships comes a tendency to forget that all models are wrong. Furthermore, even robust models can be undermined by poor and incomplete data, so data quality should be a key objective. Our experience is that models are most useful when modelers and users are able to find a reasonable balance between healthy skepticism and enthusiastic open-mindedness.

---

[9] This is quite a statement considering that the source, George Box (1919–), has made (and continues to make) numerous seminal contributions to statistical theory in areas ranging from quality control to time-series analysis to Bayesian methods. Some of his better-known contributions include Box-Jenkins time series methods and Box-Cox transformations.

EVALUATING AN ACPM UNIT

When a bank implements ACPM, performance management can change throughout the organization to reflect the new incentives introduced by the ACPM activities. We have discussed how transfer pricing to a central portfolio better aligns incentives for relationship managers so that they focus on how to sell products and services to generate cash flow streams that on balance add to shareholder value. This makes sense. However, the effectiveness of the ACPM unit itself must also be evaluated, and this process can be challenging for a number of reasons:

- Losses are infrequent and thus the primary output of the unit, loss minimization, is difficult to observe. Given the nature of credit portfolios, a well-managed portfolio will only experience losses every once in a while. Even a poorly managed portfolio built in a relatively quiescent time period (from a credit cycle perspective) may experience significant losses only every several years. Thus, the benefit of hedging costs incurred in years in which few losses occurred in the target geographies and sectors represented in the ACPM portfolio is sometimes hard to evaluate.
- It is not obvious how much to actually hedge. Since a well-implemented transfer-pricing program transfers exposure risk from relationship managers to the ACPM group, the loan business may have difficulty understanding why it has to pay the full hedge cost of a particular exposure. A well-managed credit portfolio will most likely not contain hedges for all of the risk in the portfolio as the portfolio manager searches out opportunities to improve the return per unit of risk for the portfolio; fully hedging the book eliminates the portfolio's risk, rendering the existence of a portfolio management group somewhat meaningless, although at a very high cost. A fully hedged book should return about the risk-free rate, in theory.
- Effective evaluation of credit portfolio performance requires marking to market. Shifting to the ACPM paradigm essentially requires a shift from a book-value, originate-and-hold perspective on capital to a market-value, buy-and-sell perspective. This change in perspective should be accompanied by a shift to tracking the value of the portfolio—in other words, marking the portfolio to market on a regular basis. Moving to an MTM perspective can be both technologically and culturally challenging since it can be difficult for many bank staff and managers not familiar with portfolio management and trading. All members of the loan business will benefit from education regarding the benefits of tracking value over time rather than suffering from surprises in loan books that can drive a bank into insolvency.

In designing specific approaches for evaluating ACPM units, which is inevitably an institution-specific task, it is important to distinguish *ex ante* or *prospective* measures from *ex post* or *retrospective* measures. Thus far in the introduction and this chapter, we have discussed several important measures: expected spread (ES), unexpected loss (UL), capital (C), Sharpe ratio (for the portfolio it is ES/UL), and Vasicek ratio (ES/C). These measures are typically calculated over a horizon into the future and thus are *ex ante* measures. However, performance measures should also track realized or *ex post* performance. Mathematically, ES is replaced with realized spread and UL is replaced with the realized portfolio volatility. To be effective, the realized numbers should be calculated with a regularly marked value of the portfolio. The MTM perspective will provide a better sense of how well the portfolio is being managed. Extreme portfolio losses can also be recorded and evaluated.

Once the data, models, and systems are up and running, an ACPM group's performance can be evaluated in terms of both the *ex ante* and the *ex post* measures. Tracking the portfolio Sharpe and Vasicek ratios—preferably relative to benchmarks—is a good place to start to measure how well the team is performing. Next come the *ex post* measures, such as a realized Sharpe ratio (realized spread adjusted for expected loss, which should be considered an expense, divided by realized volatility) and realized Vasicek ratio (realized spread divided by the capital allocated at the beginning of a year). Ultimately, the performance should be linked into some kind of shareholder value added (SVA) measure that is calculated as follows:

$$SVA = \text{net income} - (\text{allocated capital} \times \text{cost of capital})$$

The challenge lies in reaching consensus on how each component is calculated and what constitute reasonable benchmarks and deviations from those benchmarks.

One valid concern a bank's senior management should raise is how to develop performance evaluation models without relying too much on the ACPM team itself. Given how new these analytics are and the shortage of trained credit quants, often the ACPM team contains the individuals who can develop the models for evaluating the ACPM team performance. It is always better for the risk management group or the finance group to take responsibility for evaluation. In some institutions, the CFO also becomes the chief performance officer and in such a setting staffs a division that can develop suitable analytics for evaluating not just the ACPM team, but also the rest of the business divisions in the firm. Another possibility is to create a separate analytics or research team that serves many different divisions in

CALCULATING SVA

In an MTM framework, the portfolio realized return can serve as the beginning point for determining the net income contributed by the ACPM team. By subtracting off the relevant expenses allocated to the team over the return period, we can derive a reasonable first approximation to net income. For the second term in the SVA equation, a good simulation tool can be used to estimate the portfolio value distribution, and from this distribution the allocated capital can be calculated. The cost of capital can be proxied by the bank's cost of equity.

To compare these quantities, they must be measured over the same time period. What time period should be used? If systems are up to the challenge, quarterly evaluation of these measures seems to strike a good balance between timeliness and smoothing of noise. In practice, annual or semiannual evaluations may be the best an institution can achieve in the near term. In the end, these measures may be tied to the compensation of the team, so it is important to consider carefully how each component of these metrics is calculated and tracked.

A powerful advantage of SVA is that it can be calculated for all business units in an institution (not just the ACPM unit). That way, a common metric can be deployed to compare performance in terms of contribution to shareholder value across the entire institution. For businesses that make extensive use of the overall financial institution's balance sheet and implicitly absorb a relatively large amount of capital, SVA helps to objectively sort out which activities are actually adding value. The ACPM unit's performance can be effectively evaluated in this context.

the institution (finance, risk, businesses, etc.). In this way, the calculations will likely be more consistent and objective.

MANAGING A RESEARCH TEAM

As credit portfolio management has become more quantitative in its orientation, the availability of a strong research team comprised of quantitative analysts has become more important for large financial institutions. For some institutions, these teams are outsourced to consultancies or analytics vendors. However, most large financial institutions prefer to build their own research team and then augment its capability with consultants and analytics vendors. In many cases, such as the estimation of default probabilities, it is cheaper to purchase data and analytics from vendors that can spread their development costs across multiple financial institutions. Even so, a quant or group of quants will need to be employed at the financial institution to combine in a meaningful way the data and analytical output. In particular, most ACPM functions will require access to a research team.

Both of us have managed research teams ranging in size from a few individuals to 50 or 60. Interestingly, while potential job candidates and academics have often asked what the philosophy is that leads to the functioning of an effective commercial research team, we are seldom asked these questions in industry. Our own sense is that business professionals feel that managing a group of quants is similar to managing any other group of knowledge workers, and thus they extrapolate from their own experiences.

In our work, we have been fortunate to have had the opportunity to manage both quant and non-quant groups of highly skilled, highly motivated individuals. However, we have found that managing a research group is different in kind than managing other types of smart people. We are not experts in organizational theory or psychology so we do not have the type of pithy organizational metaphor that is popular among management consultants. However, we do feel we can offer some insight into aspects of managing a research group that seem important to us. Ironically, we do start by defining the problem of research in terms of a common consulting framework: the TCQ triangle.

The Triangle

The thing that is perhaps hardest for nonresearchers to understand about research is that it is exceedingly difficult to plan. This is because, by definition, the motivation to do the research is to better understand some phenomenon that is less well understood. As such, the process of research is a self-correcting one in which new insights lead to reassessments of both the feasibility of the original goal and the best way to get there.

For example, trying to estimate the shape of the tail of a distribution can involve a fair amount of experimentation with different estimators, dynamic estimation schemes, and other factors. In the course of doing these experiments, it may become clear that the originally conceived approach will not work. Or it could become clear that the new approach will require much more testing and calibration than originally thought. This dynamic nature can make conversations between researchers and businesspeople challenging. Often, a researcher will have only a rough estimate of the time a project may take. Paradoxically, it is typically the things that businesspeople think are easy that take the most time—and *vice versa*.

A feature of these interactions that can prove to be particularly troubling is that it can be exceedingly difficult for business consumers of the research to evaluate its quality because they often do not understand the technical details involved in the research they need. Like most activities, funding research involves trade-offs. The dimensions over which the business has control are:

- *Time* to deliver.
- *Cost* to deliver.
- *Quality* of deliverable.

This is sometimes called the TCQ triangle, shown in Figure 2.3.

Here is the catch: Though the triangle has three vertices, you can only choose *two*. In other words, if a firm wants to do a project quickly and cheaply, the quality will likely be poor. If it wants the project done quickly and to a high standard, the cost will likely be quite high, and so on. Of course, some projects cannot be done arbitrarily quickly at any cost (e.g., growing a crop) due to physical constraints.

Since organizations are used to measuring cost and time, the natural inclination of businesspeople is to economize over these two dimensions at the expense of the much less well understood quality dimension. In principle, there would be nothing wrong with this approach if the decision makers understood well the trade-offs they were making. Indeed, in some settings, a rough, quick-and-dirty analysis is exactly what is required for a particular application. Unfortunately, many businesspeople make this trade-off not because they understand it to be appropriate, but because they do not always understand the implications (costs) of choosing this path.

FIGURE 2.3 The TCQ Triangle

We have often observed businesspeople, their eyes glazed over, making comments such as, "Well it may not be academically correct, but it will be close enough." What they often fail to grasp, however, is that in many cases, the impact of lowering quality is not an abstract aesthetic one. Rather it can be the difference between well informed decision making and quite flawed inferences based on incorrect results. For example, corporate default probability estimation has a high payoff to accuracy. Understanding whether the probabilities are accurate can sometimes be difficult for a person who is not a technical manager. However, a poor corporate default probability model will have sizable negative consequences for an ACPM effort.

Imagine a quality scale of 1 to 10, where 10 is the best-quality research. While businesspeople often think researchers are striving for, say, a 10 on this scale, when a 7 will do, researchers are often indicating that a particular approach will not even result in a 3! History has shown repeatedly that in cases where science was subordinated to expediency, the results, while not always immediate, can be catastrophic. The space shuttle Challenger and Columbia disasters are stark examples of this. (For an excellent discussion of this phenomenon in the Challenger context, see Starbuck and Milliken 1988. For a more general discussion of engineering failures, see Petroski 1992.) This sentiment was captured succinctly by Richard Feynman in the last line of his appendix to the Presidential Commission's report on the Challenger disaster: "... nature will not be fooled." (Feynman 1986). Much of the job of the quant in a business organization is to educate businesspeople regarding the implications of different approaches to solving specific quantitative problems.

Three Simple Rules

Given these constraints, how can one best optimize the performance and structure of a commercial research team? We have developed three basic rules for managing a research group given the reality of the TCQ triangle:

1. Make sure the environment is a good one.[10]
2. Make sure people have everything they need to do good work.
3. Research managers must do research (but also stay out of the way).

It is important to note that in our discussion of the ACPM side and relationship management side of a financial institution, we have focused on financial incentives—return per unit of risk and transfer pricing being two

---

[10] Classic business joke: Q: How do you make a million dollars and pay no taxes? A: Step 1: Make a million dollars...

key innovations for driving performance-based compensation. The research team should also have some of their compensation driven by these factors. However, the nature of many researchers is such that the overall circumstances in which they work can also be highly valuable to them. In our experience, portfolio managers, relationship managers, and traders tend to be more motivated by the financial incentives and will be less affected by the issues embodied in implementing the three rules above. Researchers, in contrast, will be heavily impacted by whether they work in a group that follows these rules. We have seen firsthand how quickly research groups disintegrate as the circumstances revert to a more standard business management approach.

An important point to emphasize here is that the collective institutional memory embodied in a research group has substantial value and cannot be inexpensively re-created. Unlike many other types of work in a financial institution that rely on documented processes and basic skills such as salesmanship, research productivity relies heavily on experience, specifically in the context of the projects relevant to a particular institution. A small team of four or five researchers who have worked together for years may generate more and better output than a 20- or 30-person team of newly hired researchers. As long as the objectives are clear, continuity in the team will pay huge dividends over time.[11]

Rule 1: Environment   One of the authors was recently speaking on a "How I Became a Quant" panel at a well-known research center at a major university. The event was organized to give prospective quants some insight into how various industry researchers came to work in their fields and what it was like to practice professional research on a daily basis. Interestingly, while the interest of many of the attendees centered around how to maximize the financial return on their education, many of the panelists ranked the financial rewards as lower, relative to the intellectual challenges of the work. This contrast between those who actually practice research successfully and those who view it from the outside is not uncommon.

Organizations can also fall prey to thinking that substantially reduces the productivity of a research group. By viewing the research function as a typical support function, they engage in the following limiting approaches:

- Accepting relatively high rates of turnover (e.g., 10 to 20 percent per year).

---

[11] One risk an institution runs as it creates research groups is that the researchers veer off into research topics not directly related to the issues relevant to the ACPM effort. Objectives should always be focused on business problems relevant to the financial institution.

- Motivating members of the research group primarily with compensation alone.
- Planning based on formulaic assessments of task requirements.
- Organizing around rigid managerial structures

This type of thinking results in environments not conducive to productive research teams. Most successful research teams are characterized by a strong sense of collegiality and collaboration. In order for a research environment to be favorable for innovation and dynamic productivity, the environment must be one that encourages researchers to collaborate, exchange ideas, experiment, and fail. It should be led in a way that ensures that everyone gets credit for their contributions and has responsibility and control over their research agendas. The culture should be one of erring on the side of giving colleagues too much credit for work or ideas: authors should be arguing about whose name should go first on a publication, with each insisting that the *other's* go first. In such a setting, the main role of the research head is to provide vision and direction by setting out priorities and projects for the team and to oversee and help out on specific research projects.

In this context, the single most important factor in determining the success of a research team is the composition of its staff. This is so for the obvious reason that more talented individuals tend to produce higher-quality output and do so more efficiently. However, this is true for several other reasons as well.

As it turns out, researchers value, perhaps more highly than some other types of knowledge workers, having good colleagues around them who can vet their work, challenge their ideas, and spur them on to better and more interesting problems. To understand why this makes sense in a research setting, it is useful to consider how applied research is done. Contrary to the Hollywood depiction of researchers slaving away alone in their secluded labs, research is a much more collaborative process. Furthermore, applied work tends to involve far more engineering than might be the case in an academic setting. Rather than the image of a sole figure hunched over a desk, a more useful image is that of a team of individuals, each at their desks, but coming together frequently to vet ideas, ask questions, and seek advice from each other.[12]

In order for this type of organization to work, the group needs a critical mass. As any Boy Scout knows, it is almost impossible to start a fire

---

[12] A Hollywood film that actually depicts this dynamic fairly well is *Fat Man and Little Boy* (1989), which recounts the story of Robert Oppenheimer's team of scientists involved in the Manhattan Project.

with a single log, or even two. It is similarly difficult to generate the collaborative energy necessary to maintain a dynamic, world-class research team with only one or two researchers. Without a deep and diverse enough bench, individuals end up working on isolated projects, and opportunities to collaborate become minimal. Furthermore, interesting research points that come up during the process, some of which may be important from a business perspective, may not get the full attention they require due to resource constraints. A larger research group also allows for projects that may not be directly related to the tasks at hand. Research teams need to be staffed with some slack resources so that when the need arises, from a tactical perspective, they can be quickly deployed to pressing projects. However, during normal times, some portion of the research group should be working on innovative research that aims to extend the knowledge of the firm about areas of interest or develop new tools for specific needs. While we would not encourage excessive digressions into areas not directly related to a research agenda grounded in the bank's corporate strategy, a small amount of novel research may pay huge dividends.

An important point in this context is that a good research manager can guide noncore efforts that may still be indirectly related to a bigger research picture. In fact, it is hard to imagine a successful research team that is not given leeway to spend some percentage of its time on new ideas or more basic research. Without this, the potential for new innovations is reduced dramatically. We have found that new product and service ideas emerge from research groups at least as often as they do from marketing and sales units. In the best environments, the researchers collaborate closely with product development staff. In such environments, even a single successful blue-sky project can pay enormous organizational and financial dividends.

In our experience, the point at which a group of researchers moves from being a bunch of smart people to a research team is somewhere around the point where it grows to seven or eight researchers (plus data professionals, programmers, etc.). This is the point at which economies of scope begin to prevail and it makes sense to include specialists in the team (e.g., an expert on volatility or an expert on optimization). Naturally, these are just rules of thumb, and the ability to enjoy these benefits will depend critically on the volume and type of work that is required of the group. We have seen organizations where teams of 4 or 5 quants are able to do excellent work while teams of 20 or 25 are so overwhelmed with demands from the organization as to be inefficient at even simple projects.

In our judgment, for such a team to be effective, it must not only reach a critical mass, but it must also have continuity. This implies minimal turnover. It is difficult to overstate the cost of losing a team member who has deep experience with both the domain and the work styles of the other team members. Inevitably, the work of modeling and analytic system development involves hundreds of small decisions and modeling conventions. As team members work together they get to know not only their colleagues, but the ways in which they approach problems and communicate results. While it is possible to hire quants with excellent skills, there is no quick way to infuse this meta knowledge to new team members. For this reason, teams of quants typically end up working together over and over again, even if they change organizations, because it is just so much easier to get things done and to produce good-quality work together.

Rule 2: Resources   The second essential component of an effective research team is ample access to resources of various sorts. Here we define *resources* quite broadly, from physical infrastructure such as computers and software, to data resources such as pricing services or historical data sets, to access to senior people in the organization (including the head of research) when needed. Without raw materials, even the best research team will be unproductive. Clearly these types of resources are in high demand within most organizations. Thus, the challenge for the manager becomes determining the best mechanisms by which to convince the broader organization that these resources should be made available to the research team.

To do this, a research head must become integrated into the business units and act as an ambassador—both for the group and for the research it produces—to the rest of the organization. This involves substantial investments in both communication and education. On the one hand, senior members of the firm must be educated in the value of a particular research stream and be able to understand in a tangible fashion what will be delivered and how it will add value. On the other hand, members of the research team must be educated in the realities of the business application of the research and how best to deliver easy-to-interpret results to the rest of the business.

Researchers need to spend time on a regular basis to update businesspeople on the progress of certain key projects and to repeat (sometimes several times) the underlying analytic issues and the quantitative principles that underlie them. We have found it most useful to create working groups that meet regularly and are composed of members of the business unit and members of the research team. These groups can hash out the details of implementation and explore with each other the alternative potential solutions to various issues that may arise.

Ironically, though this section is related to resources, it is really about product development and internal (and external) marketing of the research team. Expectation management is central to this since, as we mentioned earlier, it can be quite difficult for line managers to evaluate the content and quality of research. Things that seem intuitively easy can turn out to be quite hard to implement. Simply stated, a research team leader can follow a simple strategy: Communicate early. Communicate clearly. Communicate often.

If these things are done well, the firm will naturally come to rely on and trust the judgment of the research team, and adequate resources will tend to flow to the group. When they do not, the business will eventually realize the limitations of the low-resource approach that it is undertaking. However, the business may also discover that it is hard to modify this quickly. The challenge lies in overcoming the fact that research groups are typically not profit centers, and in communicating to senior management how the group adds tangible value to the firm.

Rule 3: Research Managers Must Do Research (But Also Stay Out of the Way) Unlike many other fields in which, as a talented manager rises in an organization, his direct work on the line diminishes with the broadening of managerial responsibilities, some of the most successful quant team leaders continue to conduct research. This is true even for the most senior heads of research at some of the largest financial institutions in the world.[13] At first, this seems counterintuitive: If a bank division manager were still involved with line work such as examining loan applications it would probably seem odd. Yet often managers of quant teams spend a portion of their time doing precisely this analogous type of line activity.

To some degree there may be a bit of a walk-the-walk phenomenon at play. More fundamentally, however, since the primary output of the group is ideas, the manager must be able to understand the domain in sufficient detail to be able to contribute to the collaboration. More importantly, it is vital that the manager be able to estimate accurately how difficult a task is and how long it might take. Finally, the head of research will typically be the one who needs to make calls on how best to balance pragmatic needs of the business with the aesthetic sensibilities of researchers who wish to do rigorous work. Without having the credibility of actually doing the research, it is difficult to maintain trust and morale while asking colleagues to compromise on the purity of their research.

As important as participating in research is, it is even more important that the manager know when to stay out of the way. If the team is a good one,

---

[13] While this is true in many cases, it is certainly not true in every case and varies by financial institution.

then once the problem has been set up for a researcher, the head of research should give the researcher the latitude to solve the problem. Typically, once a project in one of our teams is started, we get involved only in one of three ways: (1) as collaborators in cases where we have a specific skill set that would benefit the project; (2) as reviewers at various points in the project to provide peer review on the quant work; or (3) as navigators and mediators if the project has veered off course. Research team members are free to ask for help from any team members, including the manager, but do not feel that someone is looking over their shoulder or prescribing how to do the research.

While the preceding discussion may seem somewhat pedantic (it did to us as we wrote it), we have found that these simple rules, if adhered to, tend to produce teams that function effectively, experience low turnover, and produce high-quality work.

CONCLUSION

Where do we go from here? Financial institutions should be encouraged to increase their disclosure with respect to their portfolio risk and their strategy for building franchise businesses. Over time this increased transparency should lead to higher market valuations for those institutions taking the steps to ensure they are managing their portfolio risk in an objective and rigorous way. Further, this rigorous portfolio management will improve financial institutions' ability to build valuable franchise businesses. These businesses will be engines of growth for such institutions. This orientation demands transfer-pricing mechanisms, customer profitability analysis, entrepreneurial managers for building franchise businesses, and a dedicated effort to implement active credit portfolio management.

To support this effort, a financial institution will benefit from having a well-managed research group. This group can be an important resource for an ACPM team. It is important to remember that models and systems are tools. Senior management will gain from these tools, but the tools cannot replace business intuition, common sense, and strong organizational skills. As the markets, tools, and systems evolve, the nature of ACPM will also change. Even so, the basic objectives of quantifying the portfolio return/risk profile and managing to improve the overall portfolio performance will not change. Implementing ACPM in this context provides a means to unlock the value-creation power of the firm's capital. Otherwise, the financial institution may risk one of three undesirable outcomes: low market valuation, takeover, or insolvency. Market-based portfolio solutions lead to better managed, more efficient, and more valuable financial institutions.

REVIEW QUESTIONS

1. Name at least two reasons why a bank should pursue ACPM.
2. Explain why an ACPM function should be centralized.
3. What is the mechanism for efficiently centralizing the management of a firm's credit portfolio?
4. What is it about loans that make them more difficult to trade than bonds?
5. Why do we consider a return on capital performance metric (e.g., Vasicek ratio) in addition to a return per unit of volatility performance metric (e.g., Sharpe ratio) when evaluating a portfolio?

EXERCISES

Assume a U.S. bank credit portfolio manager approaches you about improving his portfolio's diversification. He wants to add a corporate bond issued by a large, German obligor. However, he has heard from other U.S. traders that some U.S. institutions have had trouble with understanding the nuances of German corporate law when enforcing the terms of a bond indenture.

1. Specify a trade using instruments that are not German corporate bonds that will generate the same type of payoff profile as a German corporate bond.
2. Highlight two potential sources of differences in the payoff of the replicating strategy and the corporate bond.

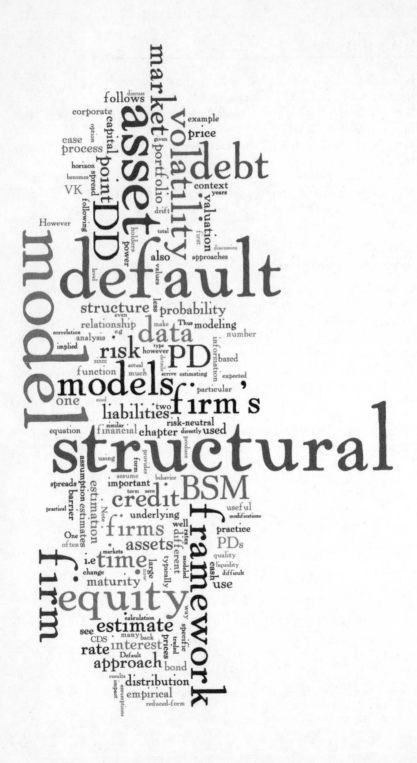

CHAPTER 3

Structural Models

*One of the secrets of analysis consists ... in the art of skillful
employment of available signs.*

—Leibniz

*Two investors with quite different utility functions and different
expectations for the company's future but who agree on the
volatility of the firm's value will for a given interest rate and
current firm value agree on the value of [a] particular security
[which is a function of the firm value and time].*

—Robert Merton, 1974

Objectives

After reading this chapter,[1] you should understand the following
concepts:

- Definition of structural models of default.
- The basics for building a structural model of default.
- Strengths and weaknesses of structural models.
- How to estimate structural models of default.
- Thoughts on handling liquidity in the structural framework.
- Definition of a hybrid structural model.

One of the obstacles to building a strong, centralized portfolio management function (or devising profitable portfolio trading strategies) involves

---

[1] Portions of the material in this chapter were drawn from P. Crosbie and J. R. Bohn,
2003. Modeling Default Risk, *Modeling Methodology*, San Francisco: Moody's
KMV. All materials contributed by Moody's Corporation and/or its affiliates are
copyrighted works used with permission. All rights reserved.

finding a way to evaluate all of the different types of exposures in a credit portfolio using a common measurement scale. At the broadest level, two types of approach have been adopted in practice: those focusing on top-down analysis of portfolios and those focusing on bottom-up analysis of individual exposures, aggregated to the portfolio level.

The first approach exploits results from the actuarial sciences to construct a top-down view of the portfolio. In this framework the aggregate behavior of the portfolio is statistically calibrated to produce desired behavior without detailed reference to the individual characteristics of the individual assets. In some cases, where detailed information is not available at the asset level, this may be the only option a modeler has. However, in our view, this type of approach ignores useful information that a bank, fund, or analyst may have on individual exposures. This is especially true of the optionality that an instrument may have (e.g., prepayment risk) which may not be fully expressed in historical data. While useful in some settings, for corporate exposures of the type we consider in this book, it is typically the case that a bank or other financial institution will have loan- and bond-specific information. Furthermore, top-down approaches fall short in terms of providing a window into an obligor's credit quality and that obligor's contribution to the portfolio's overall risk which is central to ACPM. The practical implementation of active portfolio management demands analysis at the obligor and transaction level in order to provide *actionable* information, rather than simply providing a description of the overall risk of a portfolio. For this reason, we do not focus on the top-down portfolio approaches in any detail in this text. Interested readers are encouraged to read Saunders (1999), which compares several portfolio modeling approaches including a top-down method.

A second solution that makes use of the exposure-level information we have been discussing depends on the aggregation of results applied to individual exposures in a bottom-up approach. This type of approach starts by modeling the risk and value of each individual exposure in a portfolio and then folds all the individual exposures into a framework enabling portfolio-level analyses. Bottom-up models require more data and more granular specification of each exposure in the portfolio. Despite the greater data requirements, this type of model can, over time, create more efficiency in the overall credit risk analysis process. An important reason for this is that such a model provides a framework for meaningfully integrating both objective empirical data and judgment from analysts. This objective input increases the efficiency of the analyst. This input also facilitates the systematic evaluation of an analyst's judgment, which can improve a manager's ability to discern an analyst's capability and to weight appropriately the analyst's input. In simplest terms, a bottom-up or individual firm model transforms observable data on exposures into usable metrics for credit risk assessment and active credit portfolio management. In this book, we cover several broad categories of exposure-level models including structural, reduced-form, and econometric. We begin with structural models in this chapter.

STRUCTURAL MODELS IN CONTEXT

In the early 1970s, Fischer Black, Myron Scholes, and Robert Merton laid the foundation of structural models in their seminal papers discussing the option-like relationship of a company's equity to its underlying asset value (see Black and Scholes 1973 and Merton 1974). In the early 1990s, Stephen Kealhofer, John Andrew ("Mac") McQuown, and Oldrich Vasicek extended this model framework and provided a practical implementation of it. They made this tool available as a commercial, structural model-based default probability called the Expected Default Frequency™ (EDF™). Their company, KMV, led the way in formulating practical implementations of a structural model. They were not the first nor the last to construct practical structural credit models. However, the KMV[2] EDF is probably the best-known practical implementation of the structural model framework.

Structural models provide estimates of an obligor's probability of default (PD). Furthermore, when combined with models or assumptions about a risk-free term structure, a market risk premium, loss given default (LGD), and, in the case of unfunded commitments, exposure at default (EAD),[3] structural models also provide a natural framework for estimating a credit-risky security's value. (The other fundamental building block in credit modeling is correlation, which we discuss in later chapters in the context of portfolio analysis and model validation. As we will see in Chapter 8, structural models can also aid in correlation modeling.)

We focus primarily here on models of corporate default with some discussion of how certain techniques can be extended to other types of

---

[2] KMV was purchased by Moody's in 2002; today the company that sells credit analytics is known as Moody's KMV or MKMV.

[3] Note that exposure at default (EAD) is either a mechanical issue, as in the case of the amortization schedule of a loan or the sinking fund of a bond, or an issue that is a broad function of interest rate movements, as in the case of an interest rate swap contract or floating-rate bond. However, in the cases of revolvers, lines of credit, or commitments to lend, we have less developed models compared to the other three components of credit risk modeling and tend to rely on statistical characterizations of borrower behavior.

exposures (e.g., sovereign credits, retail exposures, commercial real estate, etc.) or various definitions of default. As we discussed in Chapter 1, default definitions can impact the way a model is estimated and the way its output is interpreted. Since default events and their consequences are often determined by both legal and financial factors, different market conventions have evolved for defining default in different markets. The definition used by a modeler can dramatically affect the utility of a model, depending on how well the definition matches the application.[4]

To orient the reader, note that throughout the text we characterize default modeling approaches as falling somewhere on a spectrum that ranges from idealized causal models to purely data-driven models. Causal models are rooted in economic explanations of default based on firm value and capital structure, while data-driven techniques tend to take observable data (prices, financial statements) as generated by a hidden mechanism and use these to infer quantities relating to the default likelihood of a firm. Since our bias is toward using market-observable (or obtainable) data, we define our spectrum in terms of how the data are used.[5]

Causal models, the focus of this chapter, are generally described as *structural* models. The structure of the model defines how various quantities that describe the firm or instrument (and which are captured in the data) relate to each other in an economically meaningful way. In contrast, data-driven models rely more on the statistical regularity of data relationships themselves, which may or may not be rooted in economic theory. An important subset of data-driven models are described as *reduced-form* models, in which default time is parameterized with a default intensity. Darrell Duffie and Ken Singleton first introduced the structural and reduced-form labels in the *Review of Financial Studies* in 1999 (Duffie and Singleton 1999) for a class of models they and other authors introduced in the 1990s (see Chapter 6). Since the introduction of the reduced-form approach, the definitions of the term have become somewhat confused. Initially, the distinction between reduced-form and structural models was made based on whether default was endogenously or exogenously determined. Today, many authors use

---

[4] Sometimes it is possible to adjust a model's output to reflect the different probabilities of default associated with one definition versus another. We discuss this in Chapter 4. However, if the definition of default itself incorporates other factors, adjustment of the *output* may not be the most efficient way to deal with this issue.

[5] Other default approaches can be developed for asset classes without rich data based on a fundamental, qualitative assessment of a firm. We do not consider these models in detail in this book. See Kurma, Stein, and Assersohn (2006) for an example.

reduced-form to characterize any intensity-based model, which is not strictly accurate. In subsequent chapters, we discuss econometric, intensity-based, and rating-based models, which all can be categorized as reduced-form.

In our view, the terms *structural* and *reduced-form* are typically defined in the credit risk modeling context as follows (see the box for a short discussion on the history of the definitions for structural and reduced-form). Structural models link specific variables for a firm within a causal structure to the firm's specific probability of default. Reduced-form models, by contrast, begin with the assumption that the time of default is unpredictable so the best one can do is specify the intensity process governing the possibility that a firm within a particular class will default. While some models blur this distinction—particularly hybrid approaches, which we cover toward the end of this chapter—we use this popular convention of distinguishing causal models known as structural from intensity models known as reduced-form.

The promise of the structural modeling approach lies in its ability to produce output that is intuitive for users to interpret and diagnose. Effective credit modeling focuses largely on understanding outliers and how these impact the broad behavior of a portfolio. Structural models provide a framework for sorting out the source of outlier behavior and a means for understanding at an economically sensible level the drivers of risk for both individual exposures and the portfolio. Data-related problems are rife in the processes associated with managing a credit portfolio. Use of a framework not grounded in economics (i.e., beyond a set of statistical relationships) makes it more likely that data errors may lead portfolio managers astray. ACPM groups benefit greatly from the analytical firepower housed in a causal framework.[6]

Structural models offer elegant descriptions of firm behavior and default and have shown themselves, given appropriate practical modifications, to perform well for default prediction and valuation (when good market prices are available to compare). In times of market turmoil, structural-model-based values will likely differ substantially from observed market prices; however, these models can continue to provide some guidance as to where prices may return once the turmoil abates. That said, a structural model may not be appropriate for certain pricing applications in difficult and illiquid markets as the model values will tend to diverge too much from observed

---

[6] Of course it is not always possible, or even desirable, to implement a structural model for a specific asset class or portfolio. Interpretability is only one of a number of constraints that must be managed.

CHANGING DEFINITIONS OF STRUCTURAL AND REDUCED-FORM

In the world of 1970s finance, the adjective *structural* was sometimes used to describe economic models that exhibited an empirical track record of parameter stability. Sometimes structural referred to models that made use of structural equations: systems of equations that were related to each other through economic theory and which were used to model portions of the economy (e.g., supply and demand). *Reduced-form* models would strip away portions of the economic theory to arrive at simpler models that solved for the endogenous variables in the structural model, thus eliminating them from the equations. These parameters were then estimated econometrically. Thus, reduced-form models were distinguished by relative parameter instability and relative lack of obvious theoretical underpinnings. (Over time, though, this definition was superseded by one that focused on whether or not the model mapped back to a measure of utility, with reduced form models lacking this property. In this usage, the term reduced-form model indicated some other kind of model that did not ultimately track back to utility.)

Thus, before the explosion in credit risk modeling of the last decade, structural models in the finance literature were generally those that solved for endogenous variable relationships. Reduced-form models reflected exogenously specified variable relationships. In the 1990s, the credit risk modeling literature began referring to causal economic models as structural. Reduced-form became associated with intensity-process models, which tended to exhibit relatively less focus on the drivers (causes) of default and viewed default as a randomly arriving surprise. Collectively, the finance community seems to have moved away from the origins of these definitions in economic modeling, and this can cause some confusion when reading some of the older literature. Today, advocates of one or the other of these approaches sometimes endow these terms with quasi-religious dogmatic interpretations. Structural modelers claim superiority to reduced-form advocates and vice versa.

Regardless of how we define the models in this and the following chapters, both categories of models have their place in credit risk modeling and ACPM. We are hopeful that practitioners and academics alike will continue to expand the functional perspective of how specific models can be matched to particular objectives.

prices. As is often the case, model choice depends on the objective of the manager or trader using the model. All equal, though, the ability to diagnose the drivers of the model in an intuitive, economic context is a key advantage of structural models.

Current structural models of default generally draw on options pricing theory to describe the relationship between the debt holders of a firm and its owners, conditional on the capital structure of the firm. Though many structural models share a similar framework, researchers in academia and industry have introduced many variants to accommodate different views relating to the nature of default-triggering events and capital structure relationships. These models also address differences that researchers have observed between model predictions and actual observable outcomes, particularly with respect to market prices. As we cover the various structural models in this chapter, we also discuss their practical implications as well as some of the additional research and engineering that is typically required practically to produce reasonable predictions.

In this chapter we discuss a number of well-known structural models for estimating default probabilities and debt valuation. These models also integrate well into a portfolio framework and, properly implemented, are less prone to difficulties that can arise from sparse data, sizable outliers, and unintuitive output. This capacity to integrate across a large portfolio makes structural models particularly well suited for determining overall portfolio risk as well as for understanding the contribution of individual exposures to this overall risk.

This chapter builds the foundation for quantitative credit risk analysis and credit portfolio management. Developing robust models for characterizing single obligor risk is essential for creating strong risk management systems and effectively implementing active credit portfolio management, and structural models provide one powerful means to doing this. The key to successful model implementation is balancing theoretical and practical issues.

A BASIC STRUCTURAL MODEL

For the purposes of this book we define a structural model in a credit risk modeling context as a model that reflects an economic explanation of default. Specifically, this model framework assumes a causal relationship, among a set of variables, that results in an economic default for a borrower. The most well-developed models in this category focus on corporate entities or firms (we focus on models of corporate default in this book), but the principle of building a model reflecting an economically motivated, causal explanation of default can be applied to any type of borrower.[7]

An important characteristic of this framework is the perspective that the market provides useful information to identify firms likely to default. In order for these models to be useful, we *do not* need to assume that the market is attempting to predict default directly in its pricing. Rather we need only stipulate that the market is attempting to fairly value a firm, most typically through its equity.

We will begin with the simple model that a firm will default in an economic sense if its market value is such that it can no longer cover its obligations (liabilities). In such a case, liquidating the firm would result in negative equity, which would typically create a situation in which the firm's owner would prefer to walk away from the liabilities of the firm rather than repay them, as the value of equity cannot practically fall below zero.

Before we wade into the models, consider the recent default of Bally Total Fitness Holdings[8] in the context of a structural framework. In April 2007, the company missed interest payments on its outstanding subordinated notes. This financial difficulty arose from the increased competition in the fitness industry and specific business issues associated with the company. This difficulty faced by the company impacted its expected cash flows, which resulted in a reduced value of the entire Bally enterprise. MKMV used a structural model to transform this asset value information, based on the firm's equity prices, into a probability of default that is called an Expected Default Frequency or EDF. These circumstances caused the firm's EDF value to rise dramatically prior to it actually defaulting. The rapid decline in the market value of the firm combined with an increase in the volatility of this value resulted in a clear signal of credit deterioration, as indicated by the rising default probability. A risk manager or portfolio manager tracking a metric such as EDF may have had time to consider measures to mitigate the risk associated with the sudden and prolonged deterioration of the firm.

While not the case with Bally Total Fitness, many firms that default will also increase their liabilities as their market value declines. (While less common today than in the past, we have observed that often firms with deteriorating asset value find ways to *increase* their liabilities. In many cases, the firm has access to an accommodating banker who will believe the reasoning

---

[7] Note that such models can also be used to explain other borrower behaviors such as loan prepayment. In the case of mortgage analytics, such structural models of prepayment have, in fact, found popularity both in academia and in industry (Kalotay, Yang, and Fabozzi 2004).

[8] Information for this default example was provided by MKMV.

of the firm's management: that the firm will be back on its feet soon and that, furthermore, the market valuations are undeservedly harsh. Alternatively, bankers and other creditors may legitimately feel that a capital infusion with an uncertain future prospect is preferable to a certain default in the present.[9])

Fundamentally, however, when a firm is experiencing distress, we often observe that the firm's asset value moves closer to its liabilities (i.e., default point), indicating a marked increase in its default risk—that is, the value of equity is dropping rapidly. A structural model framework facilitates estimation of these components and provides a coherent approach for transforming this market information into usable estimates of the probability of the firm actually crossing into default.

Structural Model Input

As a first step in understanding the details of specific structural models and their implementation, it is useful to review the analytic input and output we expect from such models. First, we describe the model input (note that some of these variables cannot be directly observed and must thus be estimated or implied from market data).

- *Market value of assets.* This is the total estimated economic value of a firm's assets (equity plus liabilities). This is different from the value of the *equity* of the firm, which typically reflects one claim on the firm's assets among other claims in the firm's capital structure and thus does not directly reflect the degree of leverage the firm employs. In the special example of a firm 100 percent financed by publicly traded equity, the value of the equity will equal the value of the firm's assets.
- *Asset volatility.* This is the variability of the market value of a firm's assets. It is a measure of the stability of the asset levels. Firms with high asset volatility are more likely to experience wide swings (up or down) in the value of their assets. Here again, due to capital structure differences among firms, two firms with the same equity volatility but substantially different capital structures would generally have different asset volatility. Asset volatility is typically related to the industries and countries in which the firm operates as well as to the firm's size.
- *Default point.* This quantity represents an estimate of the asset value at which a firm's shareholders will theoretically decide to cede control

---

[9] This correlation of market value of assets and total liabilities will become important when we discuss modifications to the Black-Scholes-Merton framework.

of the firm to the firm's creditors. The default point reflects a stylized view of the firm's liabilities coming due at some horizon of interest. While a firm may have various tranches of liabilities, each with its own maturity, the liabilities that are of most relevance from a default prediction perspective are those that come due on or before the date for which we wish to make the default probability estimate. For example, in calculating a one-year probability of default, we might be relatively less concerned about a zero coupon bond maturing in 10 years, since it is unlikely to force a firm into default in the coming year because the firm will make no payments on it before year 10. In some structural models, the default point is generalized to a notion of a *default barrier* that reflects a point at which a process related to firm value (but not necessarily firm value itself) falls to a level where default becomes the rational choice of action.

In summary, *market value of assets*, *asset volatility*, and *default point* are the three key inputs to a structural model of default. In practice it can be difficult to observe these directly, so we often have to rely on either assumptions or the use of a similar or related model to turn an observable quantity, such as equity price, into the inputs we need, such as market value of assets and asset volatility.

Structural Model Output

Having reviewed the basic inputs, we now turn to the analytic output of structural models:

- *Distance to default (DD)*. This is the distance of the *expected market value of assets* for the borrower from the borrower's *default point at the time horizon of analysis*, scaled by the volatility of the borrower's market asset value. In its simplest form, DD is the number of standard deviations the borrower's market asset value is away from hitting its default point at the time horizon of analysis. If this number is large, it suggests that the firm would have to deteriorate significantly to experience distress. If it is small, it suggests that even a mild shock could be sufficient to push the firm into default. The concept of a DD underlies structural models and can, by itself, be used as an indicator of a borrower's credit quality.
- *Physical probability of default (PD)*. This measure provides an indication of the actual frequency of default for a particular borrower. Sometimes we refer to physical probabilities of default as *actual* or *real-world* probabilities of default. Conceptually (and literally in several structural

models), PD is a transformation of the borrower's DD. The DD is the quantity most often calibrated to observed default probabilities. The physical PD is used in risk assessment, some valuation applications, and the estimation of loss distributions used in portfolio and capital analyses.

- *Risk-neutral probability of default (PD^Q)*. This measure is an estimate of the risk-neutral assessment of the probability of default. In our notation, we distinguish a risk-neutral PD with a Q superscript, indicating a change of measure—that is, probabilities drawn from a different distribution.[10] If we estimate a physical PD from equity prices, we need to adjust it with an estimate of the *market price of risk*, which indicates how much investors are demanding as compensation for taking on risk. In this sense, the risk-neutral PD accounts for *overall* risk aversion of investors as it relates to the *specific* firm being examined. We use risk-neutral probabilities in the context of valuation as this allows us to discount probability-adjusted cash flows at the default risk-free rate, r or r_f, which substantially simplifies the calculations. Note that this adjustment from PD to PD^Q occurs only in the context of valuation. Risk-neutral PDs can also be estimated directly from traded credit instruments such as bonds or credit default swaps (CDSs). Backing out physical PDs from CDS-implied risk-neutral PDs, which is what is sometimes done in reduced-form models (Chapter 6), also requires an estimate of the market price of risk but proceeds in the opposite direction.

- *Cumulative probability of default (cpd for physical and cpd^Q for risk-neutral)*. Typically, a PD is reported in its annualized form; however, in practice we may need to convert the PD into its cumulative form and a subscript t (e.g., cpd_t) will be added to make clear the specific date to which a PD is applied. For a constant term structure of PDs, the relationship of annualized and cumulative PDs is:

$$cpd_t = 1 - (1 - pd)^t$$

- *Loss given default (LGD)*. When a borrower defaults, the loss incurred by the lender constitutes the LGD for that exposure. A tricky aspect of LGD estimation and interpretation is whether to focus on the price of the defaulted security shortly after the event of default or the ultimate loss incurred after efforts have been made to recover as much as possible. Traders of credit instruments tend to focus more on the price of

---

[10] For an introduction to changing probability measures and risk-neutral probabilities, please refer to Hull (2005) or Neftci (2000).

defaulted securities, while bankers tend to focus on ultimate recovery. However, determining how best to represent the discounted value of the ultimate recovery is nontrivial. A structural model may be used to determine LGD based on the conditional values of the underlying assets in states where the asset value has fallen below the default barrier. Said another way, LGD can be determined based on the expected value of the asset value distribution below the default point. In practice, however, LGD is usually estimated separately (see Chapter 5) and used as an input for valuation applications.

- *Value.* We distinguish value (which is a function of the obligation's expected risk-adjusted cash flows) from price (which is observed in a market).
- *Price.* The amount a buyer is willing to pay to buy a security and the amount at which a seller is willing to sell a security. The important point about price is that it may or may not reflect what a model or analyst thinks the true or intrinsic value is. The price is what the market says it is.
- *Spread.* By assuming a reference risk-free rate, we can convert value or price into a spread with respect to that risk-free rate. We will distinguish a *credit spread* from a spread that may include compensation for liquidity and other noncredit risks. (Refer back to Chapter 1 for the details of moving between value and spread.)

A structural model makes use of market information and the characterization of a firm's capital structure to produce estimates of the outputs just described. These outputs can be used in a variety of applications ranging from basic risk assessment to credit portfolio management and security valuation. We now introduce the most basic structural model and then move to extensions that have made these types of models more useful in practice.

BLACK-SCHOLES-MERTON

In the early 1970s, Fischer Black, Myron Scholes, and Robert Merton introduced the original insight that a firm's capital structure represents a series of options on the firm's assets. Equity, for example, can be viewed as a call option on the firm's assets with a strike price equal to its debt (Black and Scholes 1973, Merton 1974). In their model, which we call the BSM model, default occurs if the market value of assets falls to a point below the face value of debt at the maturity date of the debt. In other words, shareholders choose to default on debt when the value of the firm is less than the amount of the firm's contractual obligations. This insight continues to anchor structural credit models.[11]

A second important aspect of the BSM model (important also in corporate finance modeling) is the independence of a firm's asset value from the firm's capital structure (also known as the Modigliani-Miller theorem; see Modigliani and Miller 1958 for details). In brief, because the market value of the firm's assets is a function of the expected cash flow forecasted from those assets, the capital structure only serves to carve up the way in which this value is assigned back to debt holders and equity holders. Thus the asset value itself is determined exogenously in the BSM framework and should not affect the valuation of the assets of the firm. The degree of leverage merely determines how this total value is shared among the claimants to the firm's cash flow—namely equity holders and debt holders. (We remind the reader that these abstractions from the real-life behavior of firms serve as a starting point that is often modified depending on data and analyst insight.)

An interesting implication inherent in this framework is that the relationship between debt and equity can be recast as one in which both the liabilities and equity of the firm can be viewed as options on the firm. We have already described equity as a call option on the underlying firm's assets. What about the debt? Debt, D, can be decomposed into two components:

1. An otherwise risk-free security with the same face value, D^*, and the same maturity, T, as the risky debt we are analyzing.
2. A put option on the firm's assets struck at the debt value.

The lender or purchaser of the firm's debt implicitly writes (sells) this option to the firm's shareholders, who can "put" the firm's assets back to the debt holder in the event the value of those assets fall below the face value of the debt. This option is similar to a credit default swap in which the buyer of protection will receive the face value of the debt in the event of default. In the case of a lender or debt holder, this protection is implicitly written (sold) to the firm's owners as might be done explicitly with a CDS contract.

We can characterize the value of debt in terms of these two components as follows:

$$D = e^{-r_f T} D^* - CDS$$

---

[11] Folklore has it that Black and Scholes did not initially include the firm failure application of their model in the original manuscript, but that they later did so when a journal referee commented that the original options pricing framework was not substantial enough on its own and would benefit from additional applications.

The value of the debt of the firm is equal to the present value of a risk-free bond with the same face value less the price of a CDS on the firm with a notional amount equivalent to the face value of the debt.

Since asset value A is distributed across debt D and equity E, we can write the following equality:

$$A = D + E$$

or

$$D = A - E$$

Then, substituting for D and rearranging, we arrive at the following:

$$A = e^{-r_f T} D^* - CDS + E$$

or

$$E + e^{-r_f T} D^* = CDS + A$$

Readers familiar with options pricing theory will recognize this relationship as the familiar *put-call parity*, which implies that selling a put and buying a call (or vice versa) should net zero profit.

The BSM framework provides a natural interpretation of the relationship between debt and equity in the context of this well-known option-based, functional relationship. A popular trading strategy called *capital structure arbitrage* leverages this relationship to determine when debt and equity are mispriced with respect to each other. Since both debt and equity ultimately derive their value from the same underlying firm asset value, when they diverge, capital-structure arbitrageurs make bets on the likelihood that eventually the two sets of claims will converge to their appropriate values relative to each other. Some evidence in the late 1990s suggested capital structure arbitrage was, in fact, a profitable trade. More recent data, however, suggests that most of these relative mispricings have disappeared. Too many traders and investors now recognize the inter-relationship between different components of the capital structure (as BSM describes) and look across both the debt and equity markets with the knowledge of how these should relate to each other. Even occasional divergence across the debt and equity markets will still create these kinds of capital structure arbitrage trading opportunities.

A More Detailed Examination

While the Black-Scholes-Merton model in its original, highly stylized form turns out to have limitations when used in practice for predicting default, its conceptual underpinnings are integral parts of the many and varied versions of structural models that have evolved since its introduction. As such, it is essential to understand the basic building blocks of the model in order to move on to applying the more practical variants.

We now turn to some of the more relevant details of the original model. The quantity of greatest interest, which we wish to estimate based only on financial statement data and market prices, is the *distance to default* (DD) which, as we describe in more detail in a moment, can be computed as

$$DD = \frac{\ln\left(\frac{A}{X}\right) + \left(\mu_A - \frac{1}{2}\sigma_A^2\right) T}{\sigma_A\sqrt{T}}$$

Note that we define the face value of the debt, which becomes the *Default Point* in this DD calculation as X. We choose X instead of D^*, which we used earlier, to avoid confusion and we will continue to use X as we make the definition of the default barrier more general. (For reference, some authors use F to represent this same quantity, given that it reflects the face value of the outstanding debt; in the BSM framework we explicitly assume the default barrier is the face value of the firm's one class of debt. Also, the use of X reinforces the options theoretic foundations of the approach, as the strike price of an option is often designated by either an X or a K in much of the options pricing literature.) At this point in our discussion, take as given that we have made reasonable assumptions to arrive at this definition of DD; we will return to this later.

We now examine each component of this definition in turn. (In some cases in this and other sections, we present analytic results without proofs, which we defer to appendixes. See Appendix 3A for a more detailed derivation of DD within the BSM model.)

We begin with a characterization of the market value of the firm's assets, A. In this model, A is assumed to follow geometric Brownian motion:

$$dA = \mu_A A dt + \sigma_A A dz$$

Next we determine the contractual amount of the firm's debt obligation, X. In the BSM model, debt is assumed to be zero-coupon. (This is convenient mathematically as, since zero coupon bonds only make payment at maturity, it implies that the only time at which a firm defaults is at the maturity of the debt, eliminating the need for a *first passage* treatment of the default process. Subsequent models relax this assumption.)

The debt's time to maturity, T, is the time at which A is compared to X to determine whether the firm is in theoretical default. Note that this model assumes that equity is a European option—that is, it can be exercised only at T—which is generally consistent with the assumption of a zero-coupon bond, though not required. That means that a borrower may see its asset value fall below its debt level one or more times before the debt maturity date without defaulting as long as the asset value returns to a level at or above X by time T. Obviously, this assumption is not consistent with the way in which firms evolve in the real world. (Later we will relax this assumption as well when we discuss other models that reflect modifications to the BSM framework.) The governing differential equation developed in this framework is (see Appendix 3A, Black and Scholes 1973, or Merton 1974 for details):

$$\frac{1}{2}\frac{\partial^2 E}{\partial A^2}\sigma_A^2 A^2 + \frac{\partial E}{\partial A}rA + \frac{\partial E}{dt} - rE = 0$$

One other functional relationship is needed to produce a measure of the volatility of the firm's market value. The volatility of the market value of the firm's assets, σ_A, is related to the volatility of the firm's equity through the firm's leverage (A/E) and the delta $\partial E/\partial A$ (i.e., sensitivity) of the firm's equity with respect to its assets. This provides a convenient, though sometimes misinterpreted, relationship between a firm's equity volatility and its asset volatility:[12]

$$\sigma_E = \frac{\partial E}{\partial A}\frac{A}{E}\sigma_A$$

Recall the Modigliani-Miller theorem: Since a firm's asset volatility is primarily driven by the nature of its business and its overall operations, we do not expect it to move around too much over short periods of time (with some exceptions, such as in sectors like telecommunications and during certain time periods like the dot-com boom in 1999 and 2000). Equity volatility, however, is affected directly by shifts in capital structure: Moving from zero to 50 percent leverage, all else equal, will approximately double

---

[12] Note that a firm can have stationary asset volatility and still have nonstationary equity volatility as the firm changes its leverage over time.

equity volatility. The quality of any structural model depends primarily on the quality of the σ_A estimate.[13]

The expected growth rate of a firm's assets is a component of the BSM model as well, in the sense that it provides a baseline of the distance between the future value of the firm and the default point. In practice, this growth rate or drift, μ_A, turns out to be fairly difficult to estimate. This task is similar to the (difficult) task of estimating expected return in the equity market. If an analyst does this accurately, he will be well rewarded by trading on this information. In practice, our experience is that it is quite difficult to differentiate forecasted empirical growth rates from firm to firm.

Fortunately, μ_A turns out to be the least important variable to the quality of the BSM output for the horizons of typical interest in credit modeling.

Misspecifying this variable will have only minor impact on PD estimation and valuation for shorter time horizons of up to two or three years. As the time horizon moves beyond about three years, though, the asset drift term will start to have more influence on the final output. However, the bulk of analyses that credit analysts and credit portfolio managers require will be concerned with time horizons shorter than three years. As is the case in classic option pricing, asset volatility is much more important to default prediction than is asset drift.

The BSM framework illustrates the general approach to structural modeling using equity price data. It follows two distinct steps for estimation:

1. Using equity price data, the system of equations relating asset value, equity value, asset volatility, and equity volatility can be used to estimate an implied asset value and an implied asset volatility.
2. These two estimates of A and σ_A can then be used together with the default point, X, and the time horizon of analysis, T, to calculate a DD we presented earlier:

$$DD = \frac{\ln\left(\frac{A}{X}\right) + \left(\mu_A - \frac{1}{2}\sigma_A^2\right) T}{\sigma_A\sqrt{T}}$$

(Again, Appendix 3A provides the detail on the actual derivation of the DD quantity in the BSM framework.) Note that this framework can

---

[13] In practice, modelers who work in detail with the dynamics of structural models spend the majority of their data production efforts to ensure a quality estimate of asset volatility.

also define a functional relationship between equity *value* and debt *value*, which we explain shortly. It turns out that the standard techniques for solving two equations in two unknowns do not produce stable estimates of the unobservable quantities we need. Later in this chapter we describe techniques associated with implementing the estimation procedure for DD in a way that produces usable output given real-world data limitations.

Distance to default becomes the key focus in default prediction using structural modeling approaches. Not all structural model frameworks result in such elegant, interpretable formulae; however, most of them reflect this basic causal relationship between asset value and the default barrier. A smaller DD (assets closer to liabilities, given volatility) implies a higher probability of default while a larger DD implies a lower probability of default.

Under the BSM framework, DD is taken to be Gaussian distributed (i.e., it follows the normal distribution). Thus, a PD is calculated as follows:

$$PD = \Pr(A \leq X) = \Phi(-DD)$$

This convenient distributional assumption is clearly unrealistic. This becomes clear when we observe that empirically the majority of publicly traded firms have DDs greater than 4. That is, the majority of firms would be assigned a PD of (approximately) zero, since the probability of observing a downward move of four standard deviations is about 0.00003 under the normal distribution. Figure 3.1 shows the difference between a normal distribution for transforming to a default probability and a more fat-tailed (in this case t with 1 df) distribution. Since it is both intuitively and empirically difficult to assert that most firms have a PD of zero, practically applying this approach requires us to seek an alternative distributional assumption to translate DD to PD.

Later in this chapter, we describe an example of an empirical approach pioneered at MKMV that makes use of default data to map DDs into a PD. For example, under MKMV's empirical distribution and using the VK model described later in this chapter, a DD of 4 converts into an EDF of almost 1 percent. Only a small fraction of the sample of publicly traded firms have EDF values at the limit of 0.01 percent, which will correspond to a DD larger than 14 and can range up to 16. However, before we get too far ahead of ourselves, we return to the BSM model and note that in the BSM model, the DD is transformed into a PD simply using the normal distribution.

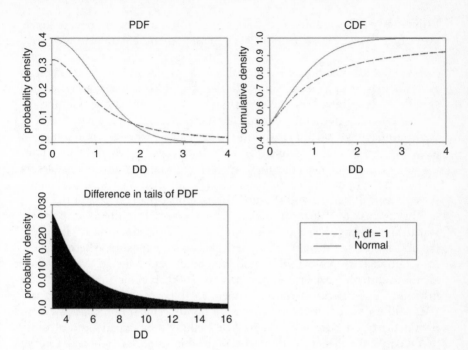

FIGURE 3.1 The Difference between Normal Distribution and a More Fat-Tailed Distribution

VALUATION

Earlier in this chapter we discussed the difference between price and value. A *price* reflects an actual or prospective transaction. *Value* focuses on a modeled price—that is, the price to which the modeler expects the market will converge (if it is not already there), which represents the longer-term economics of the asset. Our structural model discussion thus far has bounced between PDs and valuation. It is useful to discuss the subtleties of valuation before we move on to modifications and extensions of the BSM framework.

Throughout this book, we both implicitly and explicitly recommend the adoption of a mark-to-market (MTM) approach to managing credit where possible. This approach requires valuation models. We return to this valuation question often in different contexts as we illustrate application of different models in credit risk assessment and credit portfolio management.

Estimation of PDs is a first necessary step, but not a sufficient one, to arrive at usable values. PD estimation is also easier than valuation in a relative sense.

As we have mentioned earlier, structural models can be formulated to generate PDs or to generate values. In the case of PD estimation, we can be specific in describing how the quantity calculated reflects the assumptions we have made, given that default has been defined in a particular way (e.g., nonpayment of principal and interest). If we change an assumption (e.g., assume default is defined by legal bankruptcy), we are clear about the implications for the estimate of the PD. We can then test the results by observing the frequency of the specific corporate distress behavior. In some sense, a model focused on PD estimation is a pure play on default risk.

In the case of valuation, however, things are not quite as straightforward. We typically see a price that reflects an amalgamation of all of the factors that drive the value of a particular credit exposure. These include, for example, risk premia and liquidity. The difficulty lies in disentangling all these different drivers. As recently as 2000, reliable prices for credit instruments were scarce. Data providers such as Bloomberg, Reuters, and IDC sold evaluated prices for corporate bonds. This meant that raw data obtained from dealers was reviewed or evaluated by experts and possibly modified. While this evaluation process produced more reliable data in the aggregate as it was less likely that egregious outliers leaked into the database, it was not always clear which data points reflected a real market price and which ones represented an analyst's best guess as to what the price would be if a trade had happened.[14] Thus, a modeler was never quite sure whether he was testing or fitting a model to the market's price or to another analyst's model.

With the advent of the TRACE initiative in the United States, which required disclosure of actual traded bond prices, and the explosive growth of the CDS market for which data can be obtained through firms such as MarkIt Partners and Moody's Credit Quotes (formerly BQuotes), we now benefit from having multiple market views on the same obligor. More data from different markets provides a partial solution to the valuation challenge. For many large debt issuers in most developed countries, we can find a traded

---

[14] In a number of markets, evaluated prices are still the best form of information, and the data provided by reputable valuation firms is central to some aspects of these markets. In some cases, it is not clear that certain markets will evolve sufficiently to permit market-based pricing. For example, the municipal bond markets are characterized by a very large number of very small bond issues. These tend not to be widely held and thus trade fairly infrequently.

equity price, a traded corporate bond price, a CDS spread, and possibly even a quote on a loan traded in the secondary market.

While some may quibble about the quality and availability of data for particular names, with the advent of more liquid trading in credit, the overall situation has significantly improved. The recent credit crisis of 2007 and 2008 has thrust us back in time somewhat in terms of finding liquidly traded prices on credit. That said, a return to normalcy will (we hope) return us to market conditions that produce an improved quality, quantity, and transparency of data. How exactly can we make use of all this data?

To see how, we start with a simple characterization of value for a zero-coupon corporate bond. For expositional purposes, we will stay within the BSM framework for this discussion: If the firm does not default before maturity, T, than it will pay back the face value of the bond, which we will assume to be 1. If the firm does default, the holder of the bond will receive $1 - LGD$, the residual of the value, after loss given default. Table 3.1 outlines the possible payouts and their associated probabilities.

In the earlier section describing the BSM model, we focused on using the model to derive an estimate of the PD itself. Now Table 3.1 gives us a conceptual way to link the PD to a valuation equation. In Appendix 3A, we derive the following BSM equations relating equity and asset values:

$$E = A_0\Phi(d_1) - Xe^{-rT}\Phi(d_2)$$

$$d_1 = \frac{\ln A_0 + \left(r + \frac{1}{2}\sigma_A^2\right)T - \ln X}{\sigma_A\sqrt{T}}$$

$$d_2 = \frac{\ln A_0 + \left(r - \frac{1}{2}\sigma_A^2\right)T - \ln X}{\sigma_A\sqrt{T}} = d_1 - \sigma_A\sqrt{T}$$

If the zero-coupon bond we are valuing were the *only* debt in the firm's capital structure, we could use these equations to value this debt. We would

TABLE 3.1 Simple Payout Matrix for a Zero-Coupon Corporate Bond

	No Default at Maturity	Default at Maturity
Payout	Face Value = 1	Recovery = 1 – LGD
Probability	Probability of Survival = 1 – PD	Probability of Default = PD

first solve for A_0 based on observed equity prices. Note again that we cannot simply invert this system of equations given the nature of the functions. As we show later, conditional on observing equity prices, we can solve for the market value of the firm's assets. With a value for A_0 and the market observable E, we solve for the value of the debt, D, as follows:

$$D = A_0 - E$$

This equation holds because of the Modigliani-Miller assumption that a firm's asset value is independent of its capital structure.

Some readers might be uncomfortable since this model abstracts substantially from the real world we observe. This sentiment is not unreasonable. We are introducing it here as a means to begin building a conceptual understanding of the interrelationships. Let us emphasize, however, that this simple formulation fails not because of the *general framework*, but rather because of the *simplifying assumptions* of the model. In particular, most firms' capital structures cannot be reduced to a single class of zero-coupon debt and a single class of non-dividend-paying equity. As importantly, there are a number of other factors ranging from interest rate volatility to market liquidity that affect debt value.

Converting from Physical to Risk-Neutral PDs

Though we can write down the equation that allows us to solve for the value of the firm's debt in the simple setting in which we separate a zero-coupon bond into two possible payoffs, we still need to do a bit more work before we can actually use it to estimate debt and equity values. Foremost is the need to convert the *physical* PDs produced by the inversion of the DD into *risk-neutral* PDs suitable for valuation. In the BSM framework if we assume the underlying firm asset returns are correlated with a global market for corporate assets, we can convert physical PDs into risk-neutral PDs (PD^Q) by including two additional quantities: a risk premium in the form of the market price of risk, λ, and R, the correlation of the firm's asset value to the systematic risk of the market, as follows:

$$cpd_T^Q = \Phi\left(\Phi^{-1}\left(cpd_T\right) + R\lambda\sqrt{T}\right)$$

Note that we convert annualized PDs into cumulative PDs so that we can produce estimates of value for any time to maturity—not just one year. The details of the derivation can be found in Appendix 3B.

The intuition is straightforward: Applying the normal inverse function to the physical PD produces a negative DD (refer back to our discussion of moving between DDs and PDs). We then adjust this negative DD by adding the product of the firm's systematic risk (i.e., an indication of how much of the firm's asset value is driven by factors driving the economy) and the market price of risk (i.e., an indication of the level of compensation demanded by investors per unit of risk). We then scale this to the time horizon of interest ($\sqrt{T}$), in this case the time to maturity for the zero-coupon bond. This product is always positive so that the inner term is now larger (smaller in absolute value). Thus, when we take the normal function of the modified argument, the result is a risk-neutral PD that is always larger than the physical PD.

It is useful to reflect on the functional form of the (standard) normal inverse, $\Phi^{-1}(\cdot)$, and its impact on the risk-neutral conversion. We do not require here that the physical PD be generated by a model that assumes the DD is normally distributed. (Of course, a model such as BSM, which does imply a normally distributed DD, will be most consistent with this risk-neutral probability specification.) That said, the process of taking the normal inverse, modifying the argument, and taking the normal distribution function requires only that the shape of the actual DD distribution, not the shape of the resulting PD distribution, be approximately normal in the same region. Rigorous mathematicians will not like the looseness in this argument; however, the empirical power of the approach suggests that this works quite well in practice, which is a criterion we weight highly (see Bohn 2000b for details). The value of this transformation approach lies both in its empirical usefulness and in the economic interpretation of each component of the calculation.

Taken as a whole, the overall coherence of the framework that generates this functional relationship turns out to be a good place *to start* in valuation analysis. In later sections and in Chapter 6, we will see that most methods for moving between physical and risk-neutral probabilities have limitations: They can be either unintuitive (i.e., the translation is buried in complicated mathematics with no readily available economic interpretation) or rather arbitrary (i.e., based on convenient mathematical assumptions, such as that of the normal distribution, with little economic foundation to motivate the convenient assumptions). Having said all of this and despite this "roughness around the edges," these models turn out to be useful in appropriate settings. One challenge in bringing finance theory into practice is that we must manage the trade-off between model interpretability and model precision. The BSM model is elegant, if abstract, and thus enjoys better transparency than many other more evolved models: It is easier to interpret the

BSM input and output than is the case for many more realistic models. However, other less intuitive models will often do a better job fitting the actual data. The objective of the analysis will determine where on the spectrum of transparency and accuracy a particular model's application requires it to be.

Bringing It All Together

Returning to the valuation of the zero-coupon bond, we have almost all the components necessary to develop an approach to valuation. First, we use LGD (which we will denote as L) to split the bond into a default-risk-free component and a risky component with a probability of default PD. Thus far, we have not been precise enough about the PD necessary for valuation. If the time to maturity is one year, then the annualized and cumulative PDs are typically the same. However, this circumstance will be the exception rather than the rule. In order to accommodate any length of maturity, we will characterize the PD as a cumulative quantity, cpd_T^Q. (Refer back to the earlier section that describes annualized and cumulative PDs.) See Table 3.2.

With the risk-neutral probability of default converted into a risk-neutral probability of survival $(1 - cpd_T^Q)$, we can now speak in terms of the discounted value of the total value of what the bondholder receives, which is the default-risk-free portion $(1 - L)$ plus, to the extent it survives, the risky portion, L. To arrive at a value, we discount both portions by the default-risk-free rate, r. (We use the default-risk-free rate since we have already converted the physical PD to risk-neutral values.) For simplicity, we assume the zero-coupon bond pays 1 at maturity, T. Combining the value of the two components produces the following valuation equation to value a zero-coupon debt issue, D:

$$D = e^{-rT}(1 - cpd_T^Q L)$$

TABLE 3.2   Valuing Each Component of a Simple Zero-Coupon Corporate Bond

	Default-Risk-Free Component	Risky Component
Payout	$(1 - L)$	L
Probability (risk-neutral)	1	$1 - cpd_T^Q$
Value	$e^{-rT}(1 - L)$	$e^{-rT}L\left(1 - cpd_T^Q\right)$

This equation has an elegant economic interpretation: The value of the debt is comprised of an otherwise default-risk-free bond less the debt's risk-neutral expected loss. Alternatively, we can assume the risk-neutral expected loss reflects the value of a CDS that pays out the LGD, *L*, in default.

While this equation is helpful in illustrating the conceptual underpinnings of this simple valuation approach, it is not typically used in practice due to its very simplicity. However, this functional form *can* be used to estimate an implied market price of risk, λ. To do so we can use the following four steps:

1. Calculate a physical PD from equity prices using a structural model.
2. Model or assume a reasonable LGD (often a value between 40 and 60 percent).
3. Observe (a) option adjusted spreads (OAS) on traded bonds or (b) CDS spreads, along with prices for risk-free securities.
4. Solve for λ using steps 1 to 3 and the equation relating risk-neutral and physical PDs: $cpd_T^Q = \Phi(\Phi^{-1}(cpd_T) + R\lambda\sqrt{T})$

The noise in typical bond and CDS can be substantial, so this data requires cleaning, which entails some work. Consequently, estimating the market price of risk with this equation generally requires a relatively large number of observations and robust data estimation techniques.

The flexibility of this simple valuation framework lies in the ease with which different estimates of PD, LGD, and λ (market price of risk) can be mixed within a single framework. For example, the equity market can be used to estimate a relatively clean PD (i.e., one not contaminated by LGD assumptions, which would be the case in the bond or CDS markets since these instruments' values rely on the multiplication of PD and LGD; more assumptions or an extended model is required to break apart PD and LGD for these instruments). This PD can then be used in conjunction with CDS data to estimate either implied LGD values or implied λ. Alternatively, the CDS market can be used to estimate a PD based on suitable assumptions for LGD and λ.

The point here is not to emphasize one particular data source over another, but rather to highlight the many approaches an analyst can take. In practice, the CDS and equity markets tend to produce more reliable data than the corporate bond and secondary loan markets. The bigger challenge for many institutions lies not in the traded assets in their portfolios, but in addressing sizable subportfolios of loans issued to firms that do not have traded equity or traded CDSs. These unlisted firms require other approaches

DEALING WITH NOISE IN CREDIT MARKET DATA: ROBUST ESTIMATION

Economic and financial data are notorious for their noise. Measurement error, inefficient markets, and statistical and accounting manipulation are a few of the reasons the data can be unreliable. Thus, estimation work in this field requires substantial cleaning and filtering. The tendency of many researchers and analysts is either to ignore the data unreliability and report results as if the problem did not exist, or to avoid any heavy data analysis while emphasizing stylized facts and stories.

An alternative approach is to use some simple robust data estimation techniques and to expend more effort diagnosing the input and output. What are some of these techniques?

Cohort creation

1. Gather data into cohorts along combinations of dimensions that produce reasonably homogeneous groups. Some of the more useful and common dimensions are:
   - Geography.
   - Sector or industry.
   - Size (total sales works well for nonfinancial firms, and total book assets is reasonable for financial firms).
   - Credit quality (e.g., credit rating). This dimension can be difficult if your ultimate goal is an estimate of credit quality!
   - Asset volatility.
2. Once the data are grouped into cohorts, calculate measures of central tendency, μ, of each cohort for the variable of interest x, at each point in the time series, if appropriate. In the case of credit, we recommend a median or similar robust measure for μ to reduce the effect of issues such as outliers and skewness.
3. Replace the value of x with μ for all observations in the cohort.

Winsorization

Another technique is to *Winsorize* the data. To do this:

1. Sort the data by the quantity of interest, x, (e.g, spread or PD).
2. Calculate an upper bound (e.g., 95th percentile or 99th percentile of x).

3. Replace all values greater than the upper bound with the upper bound.
4. Calculate a lower bound (e.g., 1st percentile or 5th percentile of x).
5. Replace all values lower than the lower bound with the lower bound.

The idea of Winsorization is to retain the data points associated with extreme observations while eliminating the potentially large statistical impact on the results of observations if we suspect they are the result of unreliable data. Obviously, this technique should be used with caution and only when the analyst has reason to suspect that the extreme observations do not reflect reality and are erroneous.

A third technique, sometimes called *shrinkage estimation*, relies again on cohorts and population-level statistics to control for potential outliers. Shrinkage is a technique used in a variety of contexts in econometrics. The basic idea is to replace an individual observation with a blend of the original value and the population average to create a modeled version of the quantity. Thus, an individual observation may be improved by blending the raw empirical data and the modeled quantity to arrive at something more reliable. The basic operation works as follows:

1. Estimate some either long-run (e.g., 15- or 20-year) or cross-sectional (e.g., industry or geography) population value, μ, for the quantity of interest x.
2. Determine the appropriate shrinkage factor, α, to use to blend the population value with the original value.
3. Calculate the modeled value as $x^* = (1 - \alpha)x + \alpha\mu$

Of course, most of the challenge is in determining appropriate values of α and μ, which can become intricate and involve a fair amount of empirical work. We will see this technique in more detail when we discuss volatility estimation in the context of the Vasicek-Kealhofer model later in this chapter. Chapter 4 also discusses strategies for cleaning data and for automating portions of the process.

covered in Chapter 4 and later on in this chapter (e.g., the Wilcox model or comparables approaches).

Extending BSM Valuation Beyond Zero-Coupon Bonds

To bring BSM a little closer to a realistic representation for valuation, we can make a generalization. Thus far, we have focused on a single class of liabilities: zero-coupon bonds. In practice, we require tools that can address a variety of credit instruments. Zero-coupon bonds are a rare and exceptional class of credit instruments for corporations. Fortunately, the simple BSM valuation framework retains its elegance and parsimony in its more generalized form.

We will *extend* the previous structure of dividing the valuation task into two components: default-risk-free and default-risky. However, instead of a single class of zero-coupon bond, we will specify a series of *cash flows*, C_t, that occur at each payment date, t. We will continue to assume that the instrument matures at time T. The difference now is that the credit instrument (e.g., a firm's debt) will now pay out cash at *various* times between its origination date and maturity date rather than only at time T. See Table 3.3.

Consider a coupon paying bond. The cash flow stream is comprised of the coupon payments from now until maturity plus the final principal payment. The cumulative default probability must be calculated out to the time of each payment. A key simplifying assumption in this framework is that the holder of the instrument (i.e., the creditor) will receive the $(1 - L)$ fraction of all the cash payments regardless of the timing of default. Those familiar with fixed-income instruments may observe that the timing of default on a coupon-paying bond will make a significant difference in the valuation of the bond. This is true. If a firm defaults at a date far away

TABLE 3.3 Valuing Each Component of a Generic Credit-Risky Bond

	Default-Risk-Free Component	Risky Component
Payout	$\sum_{t=1}^{T} C_t(1 - L)$	$\sum_{t=1}^{T} C_t L$
Probability (risk-neutral)	1	$1 - cpd_T^Q$
Value	$(1 - L)\sum_{t=1}^{T} e^{-r_t t} C_t$	$L \sum_{t=1}^{T} e^{-rt} C_t \left(1 - cpd_t^Q\right)^*$

*If L is itself time varying, this term can be moved inside the summation and subscripted by t.

from maturity, the bond holder will stop receiving coupons altogether and will focus on retrieving some portion of the principal, while a firm defaulting close to the bond's maturity date will have already paid most of its coupons.

One can solve a version of this model assuming a richer characterization of the interaction of default timing and coupon payment (we have left this derivation to the reader as a problem accompanying this chapter); however, it turns out that the added complexity often does not buy much in practice. Loss given default is difficult to estimate precisely and tends to have high variance even when the estimates are reasonably sophisticated. Further, valuation reflects a mathematical expectation so that even if we assume recovery of some portion of *all* of the coupons, we can lower our LGD estimate with respect to principal such that the overall recovery expectation is closer to what we observe from defaulted companies. The convenience of being able to divide a debt instrument into its default-risk-free and its risky portions typically outweighs the slight costs of not reflecting the timing of default in valuation applications.

This more general, non-zero-coupon form provides one possible technique for valuing other credit-risky instruments. Real estate loans, project finance, and sovereign loans can also be handled in this framework assuming that one can generate a credible estimate of the PD and LGD. While the underlying BSM model is a little trickier to implement in evaluating these noncorporate securities, it is not impossible. The key is to stay with the same structure of asset value, asset volatility, and default point. At the very least, this structure can serve as a starting point for having consistent and rigorous discussions regarding the drivers of credit risk underlying the value of these types of securities.

MODIFYING BSM

The simplifying assumptions of BSM that appear to have, in the fullness of time, rendered the model less relevant in practice have also provided jumping-off points that have motivated a number of researchers to modify the framework's theoretical structure to move it closer to a model that could provide a better approximation of the real world, though typically at the expense of some measure of interpretability.

Why was this necessary?

On the empirical side, the lack of data in the early years following the model's introduction prevented extensive analysis. Despite the data difficulties, Jones, Mason, and Rosenfeld (1984) tested a version of the BSM model using corporate bond data. The authors found that the model substantially underestimated the observed spreads to U.S. Treasuries for these bonds. This work initially discouraged later researchers from taking the framework too seriously for practical applications.

A number of researchers introduced extensions to the model over the next decade, and researchers began to reexamine the usefulness of structural models again as these models succeeded in producing predictions that came closer to observed data, but often still not close enough to be practically useful. The view that structural models could not be used for practical applications began to change substantially in the 1990s with the introduction of the modified framework introduced by KMV, which incorporated modifications suggested by Oldrich Vasicek and Stephen Kealhofer and was accompanied with commercial quality software and data feeds. More recent research has breathed some life back into the practical application of the structural framework, with appropriate modifications (see Kealhofer 2003a, 2003b and Ericsson and Reneby 2004.)

However, even today, a steady stream of empirical research continues to cast doubt on the practical viability of structural models more generally (Anderson and Sundaresan 2000; Eom, Helwege, and Huang 2004; Huang and Huang 2003). This has led to a search for more complete models. One promising point of departure is that of the hybrid approach, where characteristics of both structural and reduced-form models are combined (Duffie and Lando 2001) or where structural and econometric approaches are combined (Sobehart et al. 2000; Stein 2004; Duffie et al. 2007). Despite the limitations of the simpler structural models, however, numerous financial institutions around the world have successfully implemented and tested credit risk management systems based on the structural framework. For example, to our knowledge, the structural model framework has been, by far, the basis of the most commonly used commercial approach to estimating PDs for public firms. We will return to these points later.

Before doing so, we first consider several of the more important extensions to the BSM framework, each of which addresses and relaxes different BSM model assumptions. We begin with the assumption that default can only occur at the maturity date of the debt.

FIRST PASSAGE TIME: BLACK-COX

The assumption that default can only occur at maturity constitutes a major limitation of the classic BSM framework. In 1976, Black and Cox (BC) modified the BSM framework to allow for default before time T. Their original idea (Black and Cox 1976) focused on the possibility of a borrower violating its safety covenants; however, this framework can be extended to any situation where a default barrier is hit before the maturity date. We call models of this type *first-passage-time* models since they cast the default problem as one of estimating the probability and timing of the first time that a firm's assets pass through the default point, even if this occurs before time T. Under BSM, in contrast, the market value of a firm's assets can fall through the default barrier at any time before T, but subsequently increase back above the default barrier before T, and under the model this would not constitute a default. This case is not realistic as a firm will typically default at whatever time its market asset value falls through its default barrier.

A simple extension of BSM is to assume no asset value drift and that the default barrier absorbs the asset value (i.e., the firm cannot recover if its asset value falls through the default barrier). In this case, the PD calculation changes as follows (note that the simple absorbing PD is defined as pd_a):

$$pd_a = 1 - [P(\ln A_T > \ln X, \inf \ln A_t > \ln X)], \text{ where } t < T$$

$$pd_a = 1 - [P(\ln A_T > \ln X) - P(\ln A_T < \ln X)] = 1 - (1 - pd - pd) = 2pd$$

Unfortunately, we need a more realistic model in practice. Black and Cox move us in this direction of realism. Black-Cox adds two new components to the BSM framework, moving it closer to reflecting the real world:

1. A default boundary condition exists before the time to maturity.
2. Asset value can be reduced either by dividends paid continuously to equity holders or interest paid continuously to debt holders.

Introducing the First-Passage Condition and Continuous Dividends

Recall that under BSM, the governing differential equation for the firm's equity value is

$$\frac{1}{2}\frac{\partial^2 E}{\partial A^2}\sigma_A^2 A^2 + \frac{\partial E}{\partial A}rA + \frac{\partial E}{dt} - rE = 0$$

Now consider adding a barrier, $K = Xe^{-\gamma(T-t)}$, that constitutes the market value of the firm's assets below which the firm will be liquidated. The fact that the barrier changes with time due to discounting following the preceding specification produces mathematical tractability in the solution to the problem. Under the BSM model, the barrier was the face value of the debt, F (recall that we defined the barrier $X = F$ under BSM). Thus, under BSM we had the following boundary condition for valuing the firm's equity:

$$E = \max(A_T - F, 0)$$

Thus, the firm can only default at the maturity date, T. The first modification of BSM under BC adds to this condition. With BC we retain the BSM condition and add a second condition: If $A_t \leq Xe^{-\gamma(T-t)}$ then $E_t = 0$.

The second modification that the BC model introduces, a continuously paid dividend, impacts the specification of the differential equation. With a continuously paid dividend, a, the differential equation becomes

$$\frac{1}{2}\frac{\partial^2 E}{\partial A^2}\sigma_A^2 A^2 + \frac{\partial E}{\partial A}(r - a)A + \frac{\partial E}{dt} - rE + aA = 0$$

These two modifications produce substantially more complexity in the solution. As we discuss at the end of this section, under BC the equity value is the same as that of a down-and-out call option.

Let us now consider the debt in this setup under Black-Cox. If we want to use the BC formulas directly to solve for debt value, then we will need to specify the equations for the debt. Solving directly for the value of the debt, D, we use a similar differential equation to the one used for equity with different boundary conditions reflecting the same assumptions:

$$\frac{1}{2}\frac{\partial^2 D}{\partial A^2}\sigma_A^2 A^2 + \frac{\partial D}{\partial A}(r - a)A + \frac{\partial D}{dt} - rD = 0$$

Similar to BSM, we have the boundary condition at the time to maturity, which implies that the debt holder receives either the face value of the debt, F, or the value of the firm at T: $D_T = \min(A, F)$. The second boundary condition indicates that if the firm value hits the barrier at any time up until maturity, the firm is liquidated and the debt holders receive the barrier value: If $A_t \leq Xe^{-\gamma(T-t)}$, then $D_t = Xe^{-\gamma(T-t)}$. Adding these two modifications—absorbing default barrier and a continuous dividend payment—generates several mathematical challenges for solving the differential equations. Before we tackle direct valuation of debt or equity, let us first consider the simpler (relatively speaking) calculation of a PD.

We can estimate the PD directly by determining the probability that $A_t \leq K = Xe^{-\gamma(T-t)}$ where t is any time from the current date of valuation up until the maturity date, T. Let us consider the formula for this calculation of *cpd* assuming the BC setup:

$$
\Pr(A_t \leq K) = cpd_t = 1 - \left[\Phi \left(\frac{\ln \frac{A}{K} + \left(\mu_A - a - \frac{1}{2}\sigma_A^2 \right) t}{\sigma_A \sqrt{t}} \right) \right.
$$

$$
\left. - \left(\frac{A}{K} \right)^{\left(\frac{-2\left(\mu_A - a - \frac{1}{2}\sigma_A^2 - \gamma \right)}{\sigma_A^2} \right)} \Phi \left(\frac{\ln \frac{K}{A} + \left(\mu_A - a - \frac{1}{2}\sigma_A^2 \right) t}{\sigma_A \sqrt{t}} \right) \right]
$$

Since the mathematical derivation and more in-depth discussions of the variants of this equation are not central to the discussion here, we refer interested readers to the model details described in Black and Cox (1976) and Lando (2004). (Note that relative to the originally published paper we have adjusted the presentation of the formula for readability.)

As we saw before in the BSM framework, we may want to solve for debt directly in addition to generating a PD estimate. Solving the BC partial differential equation (PDE) for debt is complicated by the presence of the finite maturity date, T. In practice, a much more usable version of the formula can be solved by assuming the debt is perpetual. In fact, the perpetual version of the BC model lends itself to the inclusion of a continuously paid coupon on the debt. Of course, one could always solve the PDE numerically and handle everything: finite time-to-maturity, absorbing barrier, dividend payments, and debt coupon payments. The problem is for a numerical solution technique the analyst will often require substantial (sometimes unavailable) computing resources to generate values for each asset in a typical institutional portfolio even without sensitivity analysis, which is much harder to do. Moreover, an analyst will face difficulties in diagnosing model output. As an alternative, we discuss one analytical solution that does not face these implementation difficulties.

Given the model setup described (i.e., absorbing barrier and continuous dividend payment), we follow BC's assumption that the firm issues only zero-coupon debt. The idea here is to moderate the mathematical complexity with the argument that the omitted interest payments will not be as strong of a constraint as an absorbing barrier that may reflect a "safety covenant." While a solution was originally published in Black and Cox (1976), Lando (2004) provides a more concise version of the debt valuation formula that also differs somewhat from the formula originally published by Black and Cox:

$$
D = X \frac{e^{b\mu}}{e^{b\tilde{\mu}}} \left[\Phi \left(\frac{b - \tilde{\mu}T}{\sqrt{T}} \right) + e^{2\tilde{\mu}b} \Phi \left(\frac{b + \tilde{\mu}T}{\sqrt{T}} \right) \right]
$$

where

$$b = \frac{\ln \frac{X}{A} - \gamma T}{\sigma_A}; \quad \mu = \frac{r - a - \frac{1}{2}\sigma_A^2 - \gamma}{\sigma_A}; \quad \tilde{\mu} = \sqrt{\mu^2 + 2\alpha}$$

While BC highlight this setup without interest payments, they later discuss solving a version that assumes that the firm's debt is perpetual and pays a continuous coupon, c (note that in this case we specify c as the currency amount of payments, not as a rate applied to the asset value). This eliminates the $\frac{\partial D}{\partial t}$ term. The PDE now becomes the following ordinary differential equation (ODE):

$$\frac{1}{2}\frac{\partial^2 D}{\partial A^2}\sigma_A^2 A^2 + \frac{\partial D}{\partial A}\left[(r - a)A - (c + d)\right] - rD + c = 0$$

In this context, the question of boundary conditions becomes even more interesting. If we assume the equity holders can sell assets to pay coupons and dividends until the asset value is 0, then the boundary conditions are as follows:

1. $D(0) = 0$: Only when the asset value is 0 does everything stop since the equity holders will continue to sell assets to fund the coupon payments.
2. $\frac{\partial D}{\partial A}(A) \rightarrow 0$ as $A \rightarrow \infty$: As asset value goes to infinity, the debt value approaches its otherwise risk-free value.

BC show the solution to this ODE to be the following:

$$D = \frac{c}{r}\left[1 - \frac{\Gamma\left(k - \frac{2(r - a)}{\sigma_A^2} + 2\right)\left(\frac{2(c + d)}{\sigma_A^2 A}\right)^k}{\Gamma\left(2k - \frac{2(r - a)}{\sigma_A^2} + 2\right)} \right.$$

$$\left. \times M\left(k, 2k - \frac{2(r - a)}{\sigma_A^2} + 2, -\frac{2(c + d)}{\sigma_A^2 A}\right)\right]$$

where k is the positive root of $\sigma_A^2 k^2 + \left[\sigma_A^2 - 2(r - a)\right]k - 2r = 0$
          $\Gamma(\cdot)$ is the gamma function
          $M(\cdot, \cdot, \cdot)$ is the confluent, hypergeometric function

In practice, the first boundary condition is not realistic. In line with the initial (non-perpetual) version of the BC model, a more realistic boundary condition assumes a barrier, X, at which the equity holders stop paying coupons and cede control of the assets to the debt holders. In this case, the boundary conditions become the following:

1. $D(X) = \min\left(X, \frac{c}{r}\right)$: Asset sales are not allowed to pay the coupons after the firm's asset value hits the barrier so that the barrier indicates the point at which the equity holders stop paying coupons.
2. $D(A) \to \frac{c}{r}$ as $A \to \infty$: Similar to the second condition above, the value of debt approaches its otherwise risk-free value as the asset value goes to infinity.

If we define this second version as D^*, BC show that debt value can be calculated as follows:

$$D^*(A) = \frac{c}{r} + \lambda \left(D(A) - \frac{c}{r} \right)$$

where

$$\lambda = \left(\frac{X - \frac{c}{r}}{D(X) - \frac{c}{r}} \right)$$

From the equations, one can readily see that the debt with the safety covenant that creates the non-zero barrier is more valuable than the debt for a firm where the equity holders can take the asset value down to 0 to pay coupons.

Returning to the value of the equity in this framework, we can rely on the solution to a down-and-out call option (see Hull 2005 or Wilmott 2001 for details on this kind of option) to determine a relationship between equity value and asset value. In this way, a more realistic model can still be used to "back out" asset value and asset volatility that appears in the BSM formula for a DD. By calculating DD in this way, we can potentially improve the PD we estimate assuming we have a suitable data sample to calibrate an empirical distribution. We will explore this idea in more detail when we discuss the Vasicek-Kealhofer approach later. Importantly, the structural framework properly modified for empirical realities can still be an effective tool for estimating PDs and debt values.

BC provide a useful framework for understanding characteristics of real-world debt while still retaining the convenience and speed of analytical solutions. In our experience, the perpetual version of these equations reflects the best trade-off of avoiding mathematical complexity and maintaining real-world applicability. Adding the absorbing barrier and firm payouts (e.g., dividends and interest) to the basic BSM model moves us in a direction that creates greater flexibility for capturing the range of risk reflected in the various obligors found in a typical credit portfolio.

Model Implications

The implication of the BC model is that a PD under the more realistic assumptions will be higher than under BSM. This makes sense, since BSM is a special case of BC and, under BC, default can happen under all the conditions of BSM as well as in additional cases. However, the nature of the recovery assumptions may sometimes result in counterintuitive changes in spreads relative to BSM. That is, the BC model results in lower spreads (higher debt prices) than BSM (all else equal). If we straightforwardly assume the creditor receives all the asset value at the time the firm hits the default barrier without bankruptcy costs, then the creditor will be better off than under the BSM framework.

This difference arises from the European-option nature of the BSM model. That is, the equity holders retain some option value related to the assets since default cannot occur until the maturity date of the debt. If we assume bankruptcy costs and add more structure to the recovery characterization, it is possible to see higher spreads with the BC model than with a comparable BSM characterization. Note that these modifications typically make use of an exogenous specification of recovery. More sophisticated LGD models may be implemented by keeping recovery endogenous to the model; however, counterintuitive results should be carefully analyzed.

The BC modifications of an absorbing barrier prior to maturity of the firm's debt and of paying a dividend are two important extensions to the BSM framework. As we discuss later, these assumptions are important components for capturing realistic credit spread dynamics as well as distinguishing the credit quality of firms that pay out significant dividends from those that do not.

PRACTICAL IMPLEMENTATION: VASICEK-KEALHOFER

In addition to BC, Ingersoll (1977) highlighted the benefit of using absorbing barriers in the context of this structural model approach. Ingersoll also introduced modifications to extend this framework to handle convertible and callable securities. These modifications extended the BSM framework in a way that better captures the characteristics of real-world securities. However, it is not until the work of Vasicek in 1984 that we arrive at a model that was usable in practice. Building on Vasicek's 1984 paper, Stephen Kealhofer and KMV developed a powerful and realistic approach for harnessing the information in the equity market to shed light on corporate credit quality. They built this framework by introducing a number of practical extensions and empirical estimation techniques to the BC and Ingersoll frameworks. This section details the features of the Vasicek-Kealhofer (VK) extension of the BSM model (see Vasicek 1984 and Kealhofer 2003a, 2003b for more information on this approach). Note that the characterization of the model that follows is based on published material distributed by MKMV. In practice, MKMV makes other modifications to the implementation of this model to produce Expected Default Frequency (EDF) values. These modifications to the VK model are made to improve its performance but are not publicly disclosed.

Similar to BC, the VK model begins with an absorbing barrier characterization of the relationship of firm asset value to the firm's default point. VK further modifies the framework by assuming multiple classes of liabilities in the capital structure rather than one class of plain vanilla debt and one class of non-dividend-paying, common equity that are common to previous models. The VK model assumes that the firm pays dividends. Convertible debt or convertible preferred stock (i.e., securities that can dilute the equity holders) are assumed to convert as the asset value of the firm becomes large. The dilution factor assumes the whole convertible issue converts into common equity.

With these modifications, we arrive at a messy equation for equity and asset value, which is not fully disclosed publicly. However, in this discussion, we are focused less on the actual equation and more on the techniques that VK and MKMV developed to arrive at usable and meaningful output. Regardless of which equation we use to relate equity and asset values, we can follow the same process outlined before to use equity values as a means to back out asset value and asset volatility.

At this point, we turn to some of the more practical issues that arise when estimating these models. The VK implementation incorporates important components to make the PD estimates and the debt value estimates more applicable to the real-world demands of credit risk assessment, credit trading, and ACPM. Much of the value in structural models lies in the facilitation of objective analyses and conversations about obligors and specific exposures. If the framework departs too much from the way firms behave in practice, it becomes difficult to have meaningful debates on the merits of particular transactions.

The following are specific aspects of the VK implementation that address practical concerns.

- *Capital structure.* The BSM framework assumes two simple classes of claims: debt and equity. In the BSM framework, these claims are assumed not to pay dividends or interest. Actual corporations issue a variety of claims in their capital structure. The tenor of liabilities will have different impacts on the likelihood of firm distress. The extent to which a firm pays coupons or dividends on the liabilities and equity in its capital structure will also impact the likelihood of firm distress. To develop a more realistic framework, the VK model assumes five classes of liabilities: short-term liabilities, long-term liabilities, convertible securities, preferred stock, and common stock.

- *Cash payouts.* The BSM framework assumes no cash payouts on the capital structure claims. The VK framework assumes different payouts for debt, preferred stock, and common stock. (Note that the amounts are *not* entered as rates on the underlying asset value.)
- *Default point.* The BSM framework assumes a firm will default on its debt when the value of this firm's assets falls to the level of the firm's face value of debt. As we highlighted earlier, firms have multiple classes of debt and the tenor will affect the likelihood of default. Internal empirical research shed light on default and more realistic corporate capital structures. KMV had the benefit of a large corporate default database in which researchers found that firms did not default when their asset value fell to the value of their total liabilities. Somehow firms are able to stay afloat even though they start to have difficulty meeting long-term obligations. That said, firms tend to default before their asset value falls to the book value of their *short-term* liabilities. In distress, many of a firm's long-term liabilities become short-term liabilities as covenants are broken and debt is restructured. While there are a variety of methods for empirically specifying the default point, empirical analysis suggests that the best approach (using model power as the criterion) was to use separate algorithms for nonfinancial firms and financial firms. In general, a floor is placed on the default point at a given percentage of total adjusted liabilities (see box for a discussion of adjusting liabilities).

    For nonfinancial firms, the default point in the VK model is approximated as short-term liabilities plus one-half of long-term liabilities. For financial firms, the actual tenor of liabilities is difficult to discern. As a consequence, the approach used in the VK model is to specify the default point as a percentage of total adjusted liabilities. In practice, this percentage differs by subsector (e.g., commercial banks, investment banks, nonbank financial institutions, etc.).

- *Default time.* The BSM framework rests on a European option framework so that default can only occur at the maturity date. This assumption allows a firm's asset value to fall through its default point and then recover to a level above the default point before the debt's maturity date. This assumption does not coincide with real corporate default behavior. In practice, a firm will tend to default at the point at which its asset value hits its default point, regardless of whether that time is before the

ADJUSTED LIABILITIES AND DEFAULT POINTS

When specifying Default Points, a modeler must eventually face the question of which liabilities to use in the calculation. While it may seem that *all* balance-sheet liabilities should enter the calculation, real-world capital structures contain liabilities that will not force the firm into distress. Two examples are deferred taxes and minority interest. In both cases, states of the world in which the firm is in distress will coincide with these liabilities going away. When evaluating actual samples of defaulted firms, research suggests that the power of a structural model is improved by subtracting out deferred taxes and minority interest before calculating a Default Point.

Even after doing this, though, in practice, focusing only on stated liabilities recorded on a firm's balance sheet will typically not produce the most powerful structural model possible. One situation where balance-sheet liabilities can be insufficient involves firms with significant off-balance-sheet liabilities. For example, some airlines sell their airplanes to a leasing company and then lease them back from that company. These operating leases can constitute a sizable liability. While small amounts (i.e., less than 20 percent of total liabilities) of off-balance-sheet liabilities do not appear to materially impact a structural model calculation, large levels of off-balance-sheet liabilities can make a difference and should be included in the DD calculation. The primary difficulty with this adjustment results from limited data availability—many firms obfuscate their level of off-balance-sheet liabilities and most data vendors do not maintain this type of data in accessible form.* As a result, it is useful to adjust vendor data after reading the footnotes and other commentary on a firm's financial reports.

A final potential adjustment to this calculation would be to incorporate analysts' (external to the firm or within the firm itself) forecasts of future liabilities. Unfortunately, this measure also suffers from limited data availability; however, its impact can be substantial. This adjustment uses analyst forecasts or even firm forecasts on liabilities in order to specify a default point based on what the liabilities are *expected to be* in the future. Since a PD is estimated over a specified time horizon and the DD is determined based on the expected asset value relative to the default point at the time horizon of interest, *pro forma* or forecasted liabilities (assuming the forecast is based on sound analysis) will typically produce superior power in a structural model.

*One exception with which we are familiar is *Moody's Financial Metrics* which provides analyst-adjusted financial statement data for rated firms.

maturity of the firm's debt. Like BC, VK assume that default can occur at any time, which means the model now includes an absorbing barrier. While this assumption substantially increases the complexity of the mathematical formulae used for relating equity and asset values, the improvement in the model performance justifies this increased complexity.

- *Equity maturity date.* In the BSM framework, equity has an implicit maturity equal to the debt's maturity. In order to regain some ground in reducing the framework's mathematical complexity, the VK model assumes that equity is perpetual (which is a more realistic assumption as well).

- *Convertible securities.* Earlier we discussed the more accurate characterization of a firm's capital structure, which includes convertible securities. In this context, the VK model adds another boundary condition that reflects the possibility of full conversion of these convertible securities as a firm's asset value becomes very large. This possible dilution of outstanding common equity is an important addition to the model structure for firms that have issued substantial convertible debt and/or convertible preferred stock.

- *DD distribution.* One implication of the BSM framework is that distance to default is normally distributed. Empirical research, however, found that nearly 60 percent of its sample of over 25,000 firms have DDs that are 4 or greater. Recall that under the normal distribution, a DD of 4 is nearly equal to zero. Thus, 60 percent of the world's traded firms would have an effective PD of zero. This is not a realistic outcome from an empirical perspective, which suggests a need for a more robust approach to converting DDs into PDs. We discuss this next.

One successful approach involves returning to actual default data to convert DDs into usable PDs. To do this, we need only assume that DD at least discriminates good companies from bad so that the ranking is accurate. (We explore this question of discriminatory power in more detail in Chapter 7.) If the DDs have no discriminatory power from the outset, transforming them into PDs will not produce any more useful information. As it turns out, DDs discriminate well.

An innovation in the VK model is the use of a default database to estimate a DD distribution empirically (see the box on empirical DD estimation for more detail on estimating an empirical distribution). Ideally, we would like a better model that generates a distribution closer to what we observe empirically. To date, we have not found such a model that can capture (1) the steepness of the distribution as DD approaches zero and (2) the long tail as DD extends beyond 4, so empirical calibration fills the gap. In the final analysis, the empirically calibrated DD distribution produces usable PDs that have found their way into a variety of applications ranging from straightforward risk assessment to valuation and portfolio management. Pure theoreticians sometimes take issue with the fudging of this final result; however, our experience in practice has verified the value of this shortcut to estimating a usable PD.

This type of empirical calibration is a familiar one in the statistics literature. As we discuss in Chapter 4 on econometric models, a rich theoretical literature has evolved around such approaches (sometimes referred to as *generalized additive models* or *kernel density estimators*). One way to think about this calibration is that the VK model is a single-factor econometric model, where the single factor is the VK DD (Stein 2004).

ESTIMATING AN EMPIRICAL DD TO PD DISTRIBUTION

The initial challenge for estimating an empirical DD distribution is in finding data on default. In recent years, rating agencies such as Moody's have made default samples commercially available on rated companies. Other firms such as KMV (now MKMV) spent considerable effort privately collecting large samples of default data on both rated and unrated firms (only about 25 percent of public firms are rated). In any case, the data has to be collected from somewhere and these types of samples continue to be expensive to collect and are quite rare. That said, many banks have their own internally collected samples of default. While a few large, multinational banks may have enough breadth in their client base to collect a sample without particular biases, most banks will produce heavily biased distribution estimates if they rely only on their internally collected data. Pooling databases can partially address this challenge. (See Chapter 4 for techniques for estimating default probability by pooling and for calibrating models when the sample data and the target universe have different default rates.)

At a bare minimum, a sample (ideally unbiased) of 400 defaults in a range of credit qualities is needed to develop a reasonable estimate of the empirical DD distribution. A sample of at least 1,000 defaults is recommended, and even higher numbers are recommended for more heterogeneous populations.

(Continued)

ESTIMATING AN EMPIRICAL DD TO PD
DISTRIBUTION (*Continued*)

The method of converting DDs to PDs is straightforward. First, determine the time horizon of estimation. Ideally, the sample should cover at least one full credit cycle. Preferably, the sample should cover two or more full credit cycles. It is important to match the time horizon of estimation with sufficient data to develop a robust estimate of the empirical DD distribution. For example, 10 years of data may be sufficient to estimate one-year PDs; however, one may want to collect data from a longer historical period to estimate five-year PDs. Once a time horizon is determined, the chosen structural model can be used to calculate DDs for all firms in the sample at the start of each period. Next, the number of defaults over the target time horizon is recorded for each DD cohort. Our recommendation is that this be done with no larger than one-half standard deviation intervals from 0 to 16, resulting in 32 cohorts.

One choice that impacts the statistical properties of the estimation is whether to generate overlapping estimates. Consider the example of one-year PD estimation. Overlapping estimates would result from starting on the first day of the sample, generating an estimate for each DD cohort over the subsequent year, and then calculating the next estimate from one month later (or one week or one day; however, data limitations generally make monthly the shortest reasonable frequency). The second estimate includes some information from the first estimate, and so on throughout the sample. The alternative is to generate the first-year estimate and then start one year later for the next sample. Our recommendation is to use the overlapping estimation process to generate more estimates with the realization that the resulting confidence intervals will be impacted by this choice since the estimates will be correlated from period to period due to the overlapping structure.*

Once we have walked through the sample and generated a number of estimates for default frequency for each DD cohort, we next fit a function to arrive at the empirical distribution. Our preferred

---

*One way to think about this is that rather than having N samples (e.g., for 20 years of data and a five year horizon, $N = 15$), we only have $N * b$, where $b < 1$ is a function of the positive correlation. In the theoretical limit, if the correlations were 100 percent, we would only effectively have one independent sample rather than the N that we might count.

method is to take the median default frequency for each default cohort as a starting point. We then use a function such as the Weibull, a third- or fourth-order polynomial, or a nonparametric estimator, to fit the distribution function relating DD to default frequency.

Fitting the edges of the distribution often requires additional care. Typically one has to make adjustments in order to fit at the far end (i.e., DD greater than 10) and arrive at sensible estimates. On the near end (i.e., DD less than 1), the data also becomes quite noisy. Our experience is that it becomes difficult to fit a DD around 0.5, so our recommendation has been to cap the PD at a number around 20 to 40 percent. The specific problem in the low DD range is that one does not observe much differentiation among firms with DD close to 0, 0.5, or to 1.

The approach outlined here is not the only method to deal with noisy data and small samples. For example, more effort is likely warranted to evaluate the confidence intervals at different DD ranges to develop a better sense of how to fit the distribution function. As we noted earlier, the primary difficulty arises from having to jointly fit a steep curve at low DD levels and a flat, long curve at high DD levels. On suitably large samples, this approach does produce PD estimates that are useful in practical risk assessment and risky debt valuation applications. Indeed, the distributional estimate may be improved by using credit spreads (from liquid markets such as those for CDSs) to better parameterize the fit.

In summary, the challenges in estimating an empirical DD distribution are threefold:

1. *Collecting a large enough sample to ensure high confidence in the estimates.* Chapter 7 on validation explores some properties of estimation in this context. In our experience, a well-calibrated model requires at least 1,000 defaults, with a minimum of 400.
2. *Developing a reasonable approach for interpolating and extrapolating the distribution.* The difficulty with DD distributions is the steep nature of the curve at low DD levels near 1 and the flat long tail beyond 4.
3. *Managing outliers.* As we note repeatedly, credit modeling is mostly about dealing with outliers. In DD distribution estimation, decisions as to how to deal with outliers can sometimes materially impact the final output.

The VK model constitutes one of the more popular extensions of the BSM and BC modeling frameworks. The model has provided a number of interesting insights about drivers in the credit market along with useful approaches for financial engineering techniques for estimating various interesting quantities in the context of structural models. We have already touched in this section on some of the challenges in estimating an empirical DD distribution. Next we explore the implications of this framework, more ideas on estimation, and a discussion on effective use of this model in the context of ACPM.

Why Isn't DD Normally Distributed?

We have highlighted a number of times an important implication of assuming that asset value follows geometric Brownian motion: The resulting DD is normally distributed. Empirical evidence strongly suggests that this is not a valid implication. In our discussion of the VK implementation, one solution to this disconnect between theory and empirics is to estimate the DD distribution directly. This approach produces both a statistically powerful and a practically useful model, particularly when we relax the assumption of DD normality. For the purposes of diagnosing model performance and setting the stage for other model extensions, we will explore two economically plausible reasons why the distribution of DD is likely not normal.

The first possibility arises from the interaction of a firm's asset value with its Default Point. The model frameworks we have described so far have assumed that the default point is deterministic, if not static. In reality, default points are dynamic in some interesting ways. When a firm's asset value is in distressed territory, the firm often seems to find ways to secure more loans, thereby increasing its Default Point. This negative correlation between asset value and default point makes it more likely that a firm with a reasonably large (i.e., low-risk) DD at the beginning of the year may still find itself in default by the end of that year. Unfortunately, the correlation between Default Point and DD does not appear to be stable.

Interestingly, the negative correlation appears to swing into positive territory for firms whose asset values are growing from the mid to large range. Many growing firms also appear to seek to increase their liabilities (and thus their Default Point) to finance further growth and capitalize on the firm's growing opportunities. At the upper end of the scale, though, firms with substantial asset value (i.e., Microsoft) do not exhibit the same degree of correlation between asset value and default point since at this mature stage, borrowing money is typically not the most important aspect of their planning. Thus, the correlation between asset value and default point moves

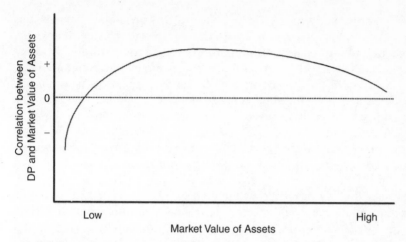

FIGURE 3.2 Stylized Relationship between Asset Value and Default Point

back toward zero as a firm's asset value becomes very large. Figure 3.2 represents this relationship graphically.

We could imagine a *two*-factor, structural model of default (one factor being asset value and the other being Default Point) that incorporates dynamic leverage into the picture. We can also imagine adding more structure to firm leverage in these models by making it mean-reverting. In fact, models of this type have been developed in the literature. The trouble is that capturing this interesting correlation structure requires a level of model complexity that may exceed its benefit for most applications. Regardless of the modeling difficulties in a two-factor structural model, these dynamics constitute one likely explanation for the non-normality demonstrated in the empirical DD distribution. The fact that a firm may substantially increase its Default Point as its asset value falls can create a situation where a firm with a high DD could still fall into default within a short time horizon, which is a case not likely if we only assume its asset value follows a standard diffusion process.

A second possible explanation deals directly with the characterization of the asset value process itself. In the structural models covered thus far, we have assumed asset value follows geometric Brownian motion. Thus, the diffusion process does not allow for sudden and dramatic moves in asset value. The real world is not quite so well behaved. Sudden declines in asset value such as seen in recent years at WorldCom, Enron, or Lehman Brothers suggest the possibility of jumps in asset value. This jumpiness in asset value could explain a non-normal DD distribution. Later in this chapter, we explore a model that assumes a firm's asset value follows the combination of a standard diffusion process and a jump diffusion process.

Some mathematical purists criticize the VK model's grafting of an empirical distribution at the last step of the model estimation as an *ad-hoc* and indefensible modeling approach. We are more sanguine. The VK-based DD quantity by itself has proven to be a powerful tool for discriminating between good and bad obligors (see Kealhofer 2003a for details of this empirical work). Converting this DD into a well-calibrated PD is an important but separate step from that of evaluating the measure's discriminatory power. In Chapter 7, we distinguish a model's power from its calibration. In this case, the DD can demonstrate model power independently from its calibration. While we would prefer to have a distribution generated directly from the model framework, the evidence does not support this approach. The empirically calibrated distribution, however, does seem to work (see Bohn 2000b and Kealhofer 2003b for details) in the context of debt valuation and portfolio risk estimation.

Estimating Asset Value and Asset Volatility

Irrespective of the model used to relate equity value and firm asset value, PD estimation using the models described in this chapter relies on the ability of a modeler to convert observable equity and balance sheet data into estimates of unobservable asset value and asset volatility. In this section, we discuss two possible techniques for implementing this estimation. Note that while this step enables us to estimate a firm's asset value at time 0, we will ultimately look to calculate a DD and PD for specific time horizons in the future. Thus, small differences in the accuracy of the estimation can become magnified by the time we extend the estimation to some future horizon. In practice, model users often require an estimate of the term structure of PDs that may extend out beyond a few years. The quality of estimates from these kinds of equity-based PD models rapidly deteriorates beyond five to seven years, given the static nature of the default point, so longer-term PDs are usually the result of extrapolation routines applied to the reliable data in the first one to seven years of a PD term structure.

For reference, we reproduce the general mathematical relationships among equity values and volatility and asset values and volatility that we have introduced in this chapter:

$$E = f(A, X, \sigma_A, \ldots)$$

$$\sigma_E = \frac{A}{E} \frac{\partial E}{\partial A} \sigma_A$$

Each of the structural models we describe in this chapter can be characterized in this way. The trouble the modeler faces is that this seemingly innocuous system of equations typically turns out not to be invertible. This suggests some sort of iterative numerical solution. In the next few pages, we discuss two possible approaches to estimating firm asset value and firm asset volatility from this system of equations.

In our discussion of Default Points, we observed that the power of the model may be improved by using forecasted or *pro forma* estimates of a firm's liabilities. The motivation in this case is to use forward-looking estimates to improve the predictive power of the model. Market data such as equity prices are even better examples of forward-looking estimates of a firm's prospects and thus a better indicator of the underlying firm asset value. To the extent possible, it is useful to look for forward-looking estimates of the variables that enter a structural model, providing we are confident in the quality of the estimates.

To arrive at a forward-looking estimate of the equity volatility, we can use the *implied volatility* calculated from at-the-money equity options. This procedure works as follows:

1. Develop criteria for assessing the appropriate level of liquidity in the option market for the firm, below which options are too thinly traded to get reasonable volatility estimates.
2. Using at-the-money options on the firm's equity, calculate implied volatility from a standard model such as Black-Scholes for firms that meet the criteria in step 1.
3. Plug in the implied volatility for equity volatility in the system of equations relating equity and asset value. In particular, estimate the implied asset value and asset volatility based on the observed equity value and the other observed inputs such as liabilities used to calculate the default point, but use the *implied* equity volatility rather than the historical volatility. (Solving for the asset value and volatility here requires an iterative technique such as Newton-Raphson.)

This appears to improve predictive power for firms that qualify. In one informal study, we found that this approach worked quite well for firms that have liquidly traded options available on their equity.

Unfortunately, the number of firms in this category is small and mostly in the United States. Any financial institution requiring estimates of PDs for a large number of publicly traded firms will find most of its portfolio missing if it can only produce PDs for firms with liquidly traded equity options. What can we do, then, for the majority of firms in order to better estimate asset value and asset volatility? We now turn to a second approach that requires only that we have a time series of equity data.

This second approach (developed by Vasicek and Kealhofer) also relies on an iterative solution technique; however, a number of extra steps are added. Much of the effort in this second approach focuses on improving the out-of-sample predictive power of the overall model. In a sense, the extra steps compensate for the fact that the estimate derived from historical equity return data would otherwise be backward-looking. In fact, comparisons of this second approach and the implied volatility approach showed no statistical difference in predictive power for firms with estimates of implied volatility.

We return to the system of equations relating equity value and asset value. Note that any of the models discussed thus far are candidates; in our own research, we have focused on estimating volatility under the VK model. Unlike in the previous case, we do not make an explicit direct estimate of equity volatility. This seems odd at first glance. Why do we not just calculate historical volatility based on the equity time series that we collect? The short answer is that raw, historical equity volatility turns out not to be as good a predictor of future volatility as the one we describe here.

In fact, much has been written on the topic of generalized autoregressive conditional heteroskedasticity (GARCH) modeling in the context of equity volatility estimation (see Engle 2001 for an introduction to the field and references to papers for an overview of the topic). These conditional volatility models assume specific time-series structure in the way that equity volatility moves around. However, while these techniques extend both our practical and theoretical understanding of the behavior of equity volatility, the trouble from a credit modeling perspective is that equity volatility can move around quite a bit because the firm is changing its leverage. In addition, the changes in other implicit factors underlying market perceptions of firm value can also shift dynamically. It is convenient to find a mechanism to capture this behavior in an estimation process. A secondary drawback of the GARCH class of models for this application is that the target time horizons for credit model estimation tend to be greater than a year at which some of the more notable GARCH-like behavior is less pronounced. Vasicek and Kealhofer developed a method[15] in the early 1990s that addresses many of these concerns.

---

[15] In 2002, Vassalou and Xing distributed a working paper that outlines a similar iterative estimation approach. Because neither Vasicek and Kealhofer nor KMV published this method, some researchers erroneously attribute the development of this approach to Vassalou and Xing. The method has been circulated in written form to KMV clients since the mid-1990s.

Now let us return to the discussion of the Vasicek-Kealhofer estimation procedure. First let us look at the setup. What do we observe? A time series of equity values. Consider the relationship between change in asset value and change in equity value: Each time the firm's asset value changes, the equity value changes as a function of the delta, or $\frac{\partial E}{\partial A}$. That is, equity value changes in proportion to the functional relationship that links equity and asset values. Mathematically, we can characterize this relationship as follows:

$$r_E E = r_A A \frac{\partial E}{\partial A}$$

where r_E and r_A are equity returns and asset returns, respectively.

Rearranging terms, we find that equity returns are a function of asset returns, leverage, and the firm's equity delta with respect to its underlying asset value. We can then calculate a volatility (i.e., standard deviation) of those returns reflecting the following mathematical relationship:

$$\sigma_E = \frac{A}{E} \frac{\partial E}{\partial A} \sigma_A$$

With a time series of equity values, we can construct a time series of equity returns. We then run the equity value equation backwards to determine an implied asset value. The two equations—equity value as a function of asset value, and equity volatility as a function of asset volatility—become the foundation for iteratively solving for a firm's asset value and asset volatility.

In brief, the Vasicek-Kealhofer estimation procedure works as follows:

1. Collect 156 weeks (i.e., three years) of equity returns for the firm.[16]
2. Calculate the realized annualized volatility for the 156 weeks as the initial guess for the asset volatility. Depending on data availability and quality, monthly data may be a better choice than weekly data. In this case, we recommend using five years of data for a total of 60 observations.
3. Using an initial guess for asset volatility in the context of the system of equations (note that technically any reasonable guess will work[17]), calculate 156 weeks of asset values and convert these into asset returns.

---

[16] We prefer to use the continuous return version, which is calculated as follows: $r_E = \ln \frac{E_t}{E_{t-1}}$.

[17] For example, scaling the equity volatility by the leverage of the firm is also a reasonable place to start.

Then calculate the volatility of those returns. The calculated volatility is then compared to the initial guess. If the two diverge, a subsequent change is made to the initial guess and the process is repeated until the two differ by a small amount (as in most numerical methods, the tolerance is a function of the level of precision required).

4. Users can optionally enhance the approach using techniques that improve the robustness of the estimates. For example, outliers within the time series can be eliminated or tempered in the process of fitting asset value and asset volatility.

5. An important part of the implementation of the VK model is based on the empirical finding that the VK model's predictive power can be further increased by blending the raw, empirical volatility with a *modeled volatility*, a technique called *shrinkage*, as described in the box on data. We delve into the details of modeled volatility in the next subsection. In this calculation process, the final volatility used in the DD calculation is a weighted average of the raw volatility and the modeled volatility. The weights can vary depending on the domain. For U.S. companies, for example, the weights tended to be about 70 percent raw and 30 percent modeled. For Japanese companies, the weights were 50 percent each. Each geography tends to have a different weighting based on empirical research on relative model power.

Importantly, we have found that the quality of the estimate is heavily influenced by the extent to which data are filtered and cleaned. For example, large corporate transactions such as spin-offs, acquisitions, and substantial share repurchases require adjustments or the output will be corrupted. Trimming outliers in the process of finding the asset volatility produces another significant boost to the quality of the output. In practice, over 90 percent of the data processing functions typically focus on producing quality asset volatility estimates. Much of this quality goes back to data analysis and data processing—not to the individual model specification. Said differently, a simpler model may still produce meaningful output if careful attention is paid to data quality. The more complex specification suggested by VK and the more involved estimation process just outlined then builds on this data foundation.

Modeled Volatility

Structural model power depends heavily on the quality of the asset volatility estimate. In practice, the combination of trimming outliers (discussed in the previous section) and of developing a modeled volatility estimate results in an asset volatility estimate that produces a version of the VK model that performs as well as the version that uses option implied volatility. The challenge in constructing modeled volatility lies in choosing dimensions that facilitate the categorization of data into cohorts that are reasonably homogeneous. Research completed at KMV in the context of implementing the VK model resulted in the choices of geography, industry, and size as the dimensions, which produce good empirical results for the VK model. Once these dimensions are defined, the modeling proceeds by first constructing industry and geographic cohorts and then using nonlinear least squares to relate the firm size to the volatility quantity.

Consider each of the cohort dimensions.

As we will find in correlation modeling, geography is a useful first dimension. Some art is required to trade off quantity of data and granularity of geographic categorization. For example, we often do not have enough data in the different Asian economies (outside of Japan) to produce cohorts of sufficient size. Thus, we may create a cohort called Asia Ex-Japan. In principle, we want to create cohorts for each individual country and as equity markets continue to develop around the world, we move closer to this ideal. While not surprising, we found in unpublished research that the distribution of traded firms' asset volatilities within Japan differs substantially from that of the United States and Europe. This type of empirical fact suggests the great importance of categorization by country. The following is a list of recommendations for geographic cohorts:

- North America
- Japan
- Asia ex-Japan
- Australia and New Zealand
- Europe
- Middle East and Africa
- Central and South America

The next dimension we consider is industry. While not as powerful as geography in producing homogeneous cohorts (it is surprising at first to some bankers who naturally think of diversification in terms of sectors), industry provides a second layer to distinguish firms from each other. Again, there is some art involved in trading off quantity of data and granularity. Often, we end up combining multiple industries into a sector to achieve this balance. The most important division occurs with the broad sectoral divisions of financial, nonfinancial, and utilities. Next, we break down financial and nonfinancial into industries. Commercial banks are quite different from nonbank financial institutions (NBFIs). Manufacturing companies are quite different from service businesses, and so on. Unfortunately, the more granular industry categorizations do not always provide the desired homogeneity with respect to volatility estimates. The following is a list of cohorts that generally categorizes the data into relatively homogeneous subgroups:

- Financial: banks, insurance companies, NBFIs, securities companies.
- Nonfinancial: manufacturing; service businesses; technology, media, and telecommunications (TMT); wholesale/retail; transportation; chemicals; pharmaceuticals; agriculture.
- Utilities.

Once we have constructed cohorts, the next step is to estimate a function relating firm size to asset volatility within each cohort. For nonfinancial firms, we typically choose total revenue as a descriptor of firm size. This data item is less likely to be manipulated in the financial reporting process. Financial reporting for financial firms produces a different set of challenges. For financial firms, total revenue is not as useful since it is less well defined and thus can be easily manipulated. For these firms, we typically choose total book assets to develop some sense of the size of their portfolio. Often we normalize these quantities or place them on a log scale. We then fit a functional relationship between size and asset volatility using a flexible technique such as nonlinear least squares or loess. Note that in principle, one could also do this estimation in the cross-section by using dummy variables for geography and industry. Our experience is that as size becomes smaller, asset volatility rises at an increasing rate (all else equal).

Once we have estimated the functional relationships, we can use them to estimate a *modeled volatility* for a firm based on its geography, industry, and size. This modeled quantity is blended with the raw empirical asset volatility to arrive at the final asset volatility used in the DD calculation. Essentially, the other firms in the cohort assist us in refining our estimate of asset volatility, improving its forward-looking predictive power in the context of our DD model. The weight of the modeled volatility in the blended calculation requires empirical research on the incremental benefit of adding modeled volatility to the different cohorts. One way to do this is to build a predictive model that takes as independent variables firm-specific and modeled volatility and seeks to estimate, say, the volatility one year in the future.

A side benefit of this modeled volatility estimation effort is the ability to assign asset volatilities to firms without traded equity (e.g., small and medium enterprises that are privately owned or newly listed firms). One approach is to develop estimates of asset value based on some kind of multiples-based formula using financial statement data such as earnings before interest, taxes, depreciation, and amortization (EBITDA) or a similar operating cash flow number. (Note that other approaches are conceivable to estimate asset value; however, our view is that the cash-flow-based multiples approach currently appears to be the most promising.) One can then create a DD (and thus a PD) for privately held companies.

While the asset volatility estimate tends to be relatively robust for unlisted firms, it turns out that the asset value estimate's quality can vary widely.[18] Other approaches, such as the econometric method described in Chapter 4, perform more consistently in terms of predictive power across a wide range of unlisted firms (Stein et al. 2004). One can envision creating a more powerful comparables-based model for calculating DDs on unlisted firms by developing a more complex model for estimating asset value. That said, we have not yet seen a model in this framework that can outperform its econometric counterpart.

Drift and Default Point

A minor complication that arises when estimating a DD after having successfully estimated a firm's implied asset value and implied asset volatility involves the specification of the firm's asset value drift—that is, the expected growth rate of the underlying firm's asset value. We require this expected growth rate since we are searching for a PD with respect to the future level of asset value relative to the firm's default point. When we estimate a PD, we typically have a particular time horizon in mind. The most popular time horizon for ACPM applications is one year since this horizon corresponds approximately to the time many market participants believe it would take for a financial institution (or holder of a credit portfolio) to rebalance its capital structure in the event of an extreme loss event. For valuation purposes, we typically estimate PDs from six months out to 5, 7, or 10 years. In either case, we need an estimate of a firm's asset value drift in order to calculate the DD at the target time horizon.

Similar to phenomena that the finance community has uncovered in equity return research, credit researchers have shown that our ability to distinguish *ex ante* differing growth rates is limited. In fact, were a researcher able to successfully estimate this parameter, he might productively pursue trading strategies instead of worrying about modeling credit risk. Fortunately, though, PD estimation does not appear to be overly sensitive to

---

[18] This is the underlying framework for KMV's legacy Private Firm Model and it is used for implying asset volatility for private firms, based on the firm PD, in MKMV's RiskCalc 3.1 models.

misspecification of the drift term. As is the case in option pricing in general, the most important parameter in estimating credit risk in a structural framework turns out to be the underlying reference entity's volatility, which in the case of PD estimation is the underlying firm's asset volatility. In general, most sensible model approaches to specifying drift—such as making the drift a function of the firm's beta or reflecting empirical observation by industry—will work reasonably well. However, regardless of the approach, modelers need to include "frictions" such as cash payouts (e.g., dividends) in the calculation of the expected asset value at the target time horizon. Despite its relatively small impact at short horizons, imprecision with respect to drift specification becomes problematic the further out into the future the target time horizon becomes.

This difficulty arises from the interplay of a positive drift rate and a static Default Point. The further into the future we project without changing the Default Point, the farther away the expected asset value moves from the firm's Default Point. Depending on the numbers, the DD can become so large as to render the resulting PD indefensibly low. This behavior implies that for any credit quality cohort, eventually the term structure of credit spreads will become hump-shaped. That is, at some time horizon, the annualized PD will start moving downward as the tenor increases due to the presence of a positive drift and static default point. Recall that the BSM framework predicts downward sloping and hump-shaped credit-spread term structures for lower credit qualities. For these lower-credit-quality obligors, the hump will occur in the two- to four-year tenors. For all obligors, regardless of credit quality, the effect resulting from positive drift and static default point will generally kick in around the 10- to 15-year tenors.

A promising solution lies in developing a richer characterization of Default Point dynamics, which we discussed in the context of why DD is not normally distributed. A rough approximation may be to build a step function into the Default Point specification in which the Default Point increases at higher tenors. Some firms (mostly in the United States) report projected liabilities going out several periods into the future. Some analysts also provide their estimates of projected liabilities. All of this information can be useful in specifying Default Points for calculation of longer-dated PDs. One could even assume a functional form such as the exponential or consider some kind of mean-reverting process for Default Point evolution. While imperfect along a number of dimensions, we continue to anticipate the arrival of research that reveals a better solution integrating Default Point dynamics with changes in asset value. Until that time, however, a power user of these models will be careful to understand their limitations and to specify approximations when necessary to improve the applicability of a structural model at longer tenors.

Convergence

Before we move on to other examples of modifications to the BSM framework, it is useful to discuss the question of convergence of modeled prices and market prices in the context of the VK implementation. Much of the debate over whether a model is useful in practice revolves around whether and to what extent actual prices (observed in the market) *converge* to modeled prices over time (i.e, when the model price and the market price differ meaningfully, whether the market eventually comes around to the model's price or the other way around). In our previous discussion of value and price, we highlighted the fact that prices are set in a market while value is a theoretical quantity resulting from the use of a model. Nothing guarantees the two will always agree. If a modeled price or value persistently diverges from an actual price, the model is not very useful unless this divergence consistently provides a meaningful signal.

In our own work on pricing under the VK model, we typically used two criteria for evaluating whether to pursue a particular modification to the model or estimation process:

1. Does the change improve model predictive power?
2. Do the modeled PDs that result from the change improve the agreement of a reasonable valuation model with market prices observed in the debt or CDS markets?

The first criterion involves the ability of the model to differentiate between defaulting and nondefaulting firms. The second of the criteria centers on convergence. While one can imagine many approaches for defining specific targets in the context of convergence, in our own research we developed a rule of thumb in which we have identified instances of divergences between model and market prices lasting one to two years as a trigger for highlighting areas of potential improvement in the model or estimation process. Sometimes, after investigation, the answer turns out to be explained by instances of fraud, which is not something with which this framework is equipped to deal. Often, however, changing a specification such as how the Default Point is calculated materially improved the quality of the estimate and thus the rate of convergence between market and model prices. In any case, our view is that managing to these kinds of criteria substantially improves the prioritization of what to investigate. A specific example is useful for illustrating how this process can work.

A common criticism of the PDs generated by the VK model in the late 1990s focused on the model's consistently high PD estimate relative to bond spreads (and later CDS spreads) for many financial firms. In fact, this bias became so pronounced that some market participants erroneously concluded the model had become ineffective for these firms, even though in reality the power of the model (i.e., the ability to distinguish good from bad borrowers) was equally high for financials and nonfinancials. The problem was, however, that the level of spreads implied by the financial-firm probabilities did not make sense. After a number of years of persistent divergence, we drilled into the data to determine the source of the problem. Initially, we suspected the Default Point specification to be the source of the error; but we found that alternative specifications of this quantity did not materially improve the fit to observed credit spreads and had the negative side effect of reducing the model's power. Ultimately, we traced the problem to how the asset volatility was being estimated. The following description provides details of this finding.

Because the total enterprise value of financial firms is characterized by two broad types of assets—franchise businesses and financial portfolios—we realized that we needed to explicitly measure the evolution of these distinct asset-types differently. (By now, this philosophical view of financial firms, central to the ACPM framework, should be familiar to readers.) Financial firms are able to expand and contract the franchise side of their businesses quickly by pursuing new franchises and then divesting from them as markets change. As a result, they can materially alter their asset volatility profile over a short period of time. With unusual market periods such as the technology IPO boom, many financial firms enjoyed a marked increase in IPO activity and thus saw their franchise-business value volatility spike. When the boom ended, these businesses contracted, thereby changing the volatility profile again. However, the estimation process in use at that time retained the volatility spike in the estimate. Thus, the asset volatility tended to be overestimated, and this overestimate created an upward bias in the PD estimate. Since this impact tended to affect groups of firms similarly (e.g., large banks), the final ranking was not significantly changed. Thus the PD retained its discriminatory power—it just did not produce a PD that was consistent with observed credit spreads for those firms.

In the end, based on this insight and motivated by our observation of the divergence of prices for this sector, we modified the asset volatility estimation method to reflect a longer-term, stabilized volatility estimate for some financial firms (we did not find this effect across the whole sample—mostly in the largest banks and investment banks), thereby minimizing volatility spikes that appeared with regularity in the time series. For more details on the research underlying the modified model for estimating PDs for financial firms, please refer to Sellers and Arora (2004).

Some may argue that other aspects of the model framework should be modified or that these types of difficulties indicate the general weakness of the structural approach. We disagree. Structural models provide a coherent framework within which economic principles can drive model choices and model estimation. The approach does this at the cost of some accuracy in some instances. We discuss in Chapter 6 the benefits of the reduced-form model in better reflecting actual prices. The example in this section highlights how market data not only can be used as an input to the structural approach, but can also provide another dimension of validation that offers clues to causes of model underperformance. Based on these clues, a structural model can be modified to mirror economic insight with respect to firm behavior. Many other modeling approaches do not share this feature. As a result, and as we state often in this text, we recommend developing multiple models within any strong ACPM or risk management function.

STOCHASTIC INTEREST RATES: LONGSTAFF-SCHWARTZ

The previous section mixed together ideas on modifying the BSM and BC frameworks and on empirical estimation. We will spend most of the rest of this chapter focused on several modifications to the BSM framework that were introduced in the 1990s. While the modifications we cover in the final sections of this chapter can be difficult to implement in practice (the difficulties can arise from computational constraints, lack of data, or parameter instability), it is useful to understand the directions in which this framework has been and may continue to be taken. These modifications and extensions also provide insight into the underlying economics of the structural model's underpinnings.

The first modification we consider deals with the BSM assumption that interest rates are constant (or at least deterministic).

Under BSM, default-risk-free interest rates are assumed fixed. Even the VK extension assumes interest rates are deterministic. Relatively recent work in this area reflects the relaxation of this assumption. In 1995, Longstaff and Schwartz included stochastic interest rates in a BSM framework using a Vasicek process (Vasicek 1977) for the default-risk-free interest rate:

$$dr = \kappa(\mu_r - r)dt + \sigma_r dz$$

This specification requires an estimate of the correlation between the firm's asset value and the interest rate. This correlation turns out to be empirically unstable but is typically in the range of zero to a moderately large negative number.

In some economies such as Japan, long periods of extremely low interest rates have made this model extension less relevant; however, recent trends toward more normal interest rates in Japan may result in conditions better captured with this expanded model framework. The United States has also seen periods of relatively low and stable interest rates for a number of years. Recent increases in interest rates coupled with more interest rate volatility may also increase the relevance of this kind of model extension. Although in general the impact of this extension on the levels of spreads *themselves* may be small, the impact on the *shape* of the credit-spread term structure may be significant.

A second challenge arising from adding stochastic interest rates involves the narrow range of functional forms that lend themselves to convenient analytical solutions. While some researchers and practitioners argue that computing power eliminates the need for closed-form solutions, our experience is that the ability to diagnose a model is quite important in application and that this is far easier when dealing with analytic rather than numerical solutions.

CORRELATION OF INTEREST RATES AND FIRM ASSET VALUES

In the structural model framework, a firm's asset value is a key driver of the riskiness of its debt and thus ultimately drives the firm's credit spread. Thus the relationship of interest rates and credit spreads can be evaluated indirectly in terms of the correlation of interest rates and firm asset values.

The relationship of interest rates and firm asset values has been a longstanding area of research interest. In theory, an increase in interest rates should reduce firm asset values as future expected cash flows are discounted at a higher rate. However, the actual behavior of asset value defies this simple characterization. In countries such as Japan where interest rates have been quite low for an extended period of time, this relationship appears to break down, resulting in a correlation near zero. Even in the United States where interest rate behavior is much more variable, the evidence is mixed with respect to this interest-rate/asset value relationship. The success of models such as MKMV's EDF model suggests that the interest rate assumption in the model framework may be less important than other aspects of the model, such as asset volatility. That said, the interest-rate regime of recent years has shifted to one in which we see both higher interest rates and higher volatility in those rates.

We now turn to the Longstaff-Schwartz (LS) model itself. If we start with the partial differential equation (PDE) generated in the BSM framework, we can add the specification of a stochastic process for the default-risk-free interest rate to arrive at the PDE governing the value of debt or equity (both derivatives on the underlying value of the firm). Using the Vasicek process (Vasicek 1977) for the default-risk-free interest rate, we arrive at the following equation. (The equation is written here with respect to E, but has a similar form for the debt, D, except that the boundary conditions are different, which results in different valuation solutions.)

$$\frac{1}{2}\frac{\partial^2 E}{\partial A^2}\sigma_A^2 A^2 + \frac{\partial E}{\partial A}rA + \frac{\partial E}{dt} - rE + \frac{\partial^2 E}{\partial A \partial r}\rho\sigma_A\sigma_r A + \frac{1}{2}\frac{\partial^2 E}{\partial r^2}\sigma_r^2$$
$$+ \frac{\partial E}{dr}(\kappa\mu_r + \lambda_r - \kappa r) = 0$$

where λ_r is the market price of interest rate risk.

Similar to the procedure described in the prior section, we back out asset value and asset volatility from equity prices and calculate DD as was done in the BSM framework. In this case, though, we include a richer characterization of default-risk-free interest rates. The difficulty that results in this characterization, relative to BSM, is that we have many more parameters to estimate and thus require much more involved numerical methods. A modeler must determine whether the increased complexity is justified in terms of a more useful model in practice, given a specific application.

Under LS, we can also calculate directly the value, D, of a risky, zero-coupon bond as follows:

$$D(X, r, T) = B(r, T)(1 - LQ(X, r, T))$$

where $B(r, T)$ is the value of a default-risk-free bond with rate r and time to maturity T,[19] $X = \frac{A}{K}$, with K as the threshold value at which the asset value will result in default $Q(X, r, T)$ is the risk-neutral PD.

The value of the default-risk-free bond first published by Oldrich Vasicek in 1977 is as follows:

$$B(r, T) = e^{a_r(T) + b_r(T)r}$$

where the parameters a and b are equal to the functions described in the accompanying box.

---

[19] Within the BSM framework we had assumed a constant interest rate. Now the value of the default-risk-free bond is not constant and is driven by the stochastic model defined by the Vasicek process.

FUNCTIONAL FORM OF A VASICEK TERM STRUCTURE MODEL

Affine models of interest rate term structures have been well developed since the original Vasicek model. The functional form for default-risk-free bonds is generally $B(T) = e^{a(T)+b(T)X(T)}$ with the parameters defined as follows:

$$a(t) = \frac{2\kappa\mu_b}{\sigma_b^2} \ln\left(\frac{2\gamma e^{(\gamma+\kappa)T/2}}{2\gamma + (\gamma+\kappa)(e^{\gamma T}-1)}\right); \quad \gamma = \sqrt{\kappa^2 + 2\sigma_b^2}$$

$$b(t) = \frac{-2(e^{\gamma T}-1)}{2\gamma + (\gamma+\kappa)(e^{\gamma T}-1)}$$

For a more detailed discussion of this solution see the relevant appendixes in Duffie and Singleton (2003) and Lando (2004). (The notation varies sometimes from text to text.) Benninga and Wiener (1998) describe practical implementations of these term structure models.

While the default-risk-free bond component has a closed-form solution in this framework, we are not as lucky in the case of the default-risky side. Even though we cannot describe a closed-form solution for the risk-neutral probability of default, Longstaff and Schwartz develop a semi-closed-form approach based on a recursive solution technique using the following relationships:

$$Q(X, r, T) = \lim_{n \to \infty} Q(X, r, T, n)$$

where

$$Q(X, r, T, n) = \sum_{i=1}^{n} q_i$$

$$q_1 = \Phi(a_1)$$

$$q_i = \Phi(a_i) - \sum_{j=1}^{i-1} q_j \Phi(b_{ij}), \, i = 2, 3, \ldots, n$$

Refer to Longstaff and Schwartz (1995) for the details of the functions. The equations essentially constitute a numerical approximation method for integrating a function that arises in the context of the problem. Longstaff and Schwartz recommend $n = 200$ as an approximation to the infinite sum. Note, however, that this calculation would require 19,900 [that is, $\frac{1}{2} \times 200(200 - 1)$] evaluations of the cumulative standard normal distribution—a very expensive computation. An alternative is to use some form of finite-difference approximation to the differential equation introduced in this framework.

The default probabilities that are derived in this approach are risk-neutral. In the case where we back out PDs from debt prices, we may not be able to use these directly. If our objective is valuation of other securities, then we can in fact use the PDs directly estimated from this approach, as risk-neutral PDs are what we require. However, if our objective is to build a portfolio risk model, we need physical PDs, so some transformation will be necessary based upon an estimate and functional form for the market price of risk.

In practice, modelers either rely on the functional form discussed in this chapter:

$$cpd_T^Q = \Phi \left(\Phi^{-1} \left(cpd_T \right) + R\lambda\sqrt{T} \right)$$

or use simpler linear transformations.[20] However, for applications involving capital allocation, portfolio risk assessment, and so on, the probability measure required is the physical, not the risk-neutral, PD.

Longstaff and Schwartz's extension introduces dynamic interest rates into the BSM framework, which is desirable. The disadvantage of doing so, however, is the high associated computational cost. As computing power continues to increase, this disadvantage becomes less of an issue. Nonetheless, the amount of computing power required to solve equations associated with this model continues to make LS impractical for many large estimation efforts typical of an ACPM team or risk management group managing a large financial institution's portfolio. Furthermore, the task of accurately

---

[20] Even for some risk applications, though, risk-neutral PDs may still be acceptable. For example, one might use the risk-neutral probabilities for risk *assessment* of individual obligors without modification since the *ranking* of obligor quality may not likely change too much with the transformation (with the exception of comparing firms that have similar risk-neutral default probabilities, but very different measures of systematic risk, R). For example, a large firm may have a much higher R-squared than a smaller firm even though they have similar risk-neutral PDs.

estimating the correlation between interest rates and asset value continues to present implementation challenges. We expect that future research will continue to inform researchers' ability to characterize this relationship and improve the collective understanding of integrating stochastic interest rates into this framework.

JUMP-DIFFUSION MODELS: ZHOU

In our discussion of why DD is non-normally distributed, we highlighted the possibility that the stochastic process governing a firm's asset value may not be geometric Brownian motion. One can go even further and actually reformulate a structural model after incorporating additional stochastic processes into the representation of the asset process.

An important class of such models includes the inclusion of a *jump* term in addition to the diffusion term that serves to shift the parameters of the diffusion for some period of time—a so-called *jump-diffusion* process. Recent work in 2001 by Zhou and work by Hilberink and Rogers (HR) in 2002 suggest this kind of modification. In the Zhou (2001) framework, a numerical scheme is required to solve the system. In the HR (2002) framework, debt is assumed to be perpetual and the asset value follows a jump-diffusion Levy process with only downward jumps. These approaches are attractive theoretically, but in practice they can be quite difficult to implement.

The primary difficulty in implementation involves the instability of parameters governing the jump risk. The rare-event nature of credit data makes it difficult to estimate precisely the components of the jump process. Consequently, the estimates can vary widely depending on the sample chosen and, unlike the models discussed thus far, in the case of jump-diffusion models it can be difficult to diagnose the nature of the problem. Outliers may overwhelm the parameter estimates or the model may be misspecified with respect to the way in which asset values behave in practice.

A secondary difficulty relates (again) to computational cost. Like the LS model, jump diffusion models typically take substantially more computational power to estimate. This combination of parameter instability and computational cost often make them impractical for large financial institution credit portfolios. Even so, jump-diffusion models may be useful when looking at very short-dated instruments (e.g., less than three months). More standard structural models are well-known to be unable to generate sensible spreads observed at short tenors. We see a number of benefits arising from more research in the area of integrating jump processes into the characterization of the asset value process for structural models.

ENDOGENOUS DEFAULT BARRIER (TAXES AND BANKRUPTCY COSTS): LELAND-TOFT

The final modification of BSM that we consider in this chapter goes to the heart of corporate finance: the search for an optimal capital structure. In 1994, Leland, later joined by Toft in 1996, introduced taxes and bankruptcy costs into the BSM framework in an effort to introduce more friction into the behavior of firms in the structural modeling framework. In this way, the authors sought to move closer to reflecting the factors driving a firm's choice of its capital structure. The result is an *endogenous* default barrier that in turn results in a richer analytical structure. In this framework, Leland and Toft (LT) allow for dividend payments and coupon payments. Both debt and equity are assumed to be perpetual. As a consequence, the trade-off between the tax advantage of debt and the cost of bankruptcy can lead to normative characterizations of a firm's capital structure.

One challenge in this framework is the accurate estimation of taxes and bankruptcy costs, which can both be difficult to size based only on publicly available financial statement data. Moreover, recent empirical work suggests other factors may also drive optimal capital structure. Nonetheless, this framework provides a useful frame of reference for evaluating capital structure determination.

This model also begins with the assumption that the firm asset value follows geometric Brownian motion, with the modification (similar to BC) that the firm pays out some portion of its cash flows, p:

$$dA = (\mu_A - p)Adt + \sigma_A Adz$$

Debt is now assumed to be perpetual (i.e., no finite maturity) and to continuously pay a constant coupon C. If we assume the company faces a tax rate, τ, the tax benefit to issuing debt is τC per unit of time where the debt is issued (since interest payments are tax-deductible).

Without a cost to issuing debt, this framework would suggest 100 percent debt financing. But there is a disadvantage to issuing debt, and that is the risk of bankruptcy. Similar to the other variations in the structural framework, we assume a default barrier, X. That is the point at which a fall in asset value results in liquidation of the firm, causing the equity holders to lose everything and the debt holders to end up with whatever residual firm asset value is left.

Constant Default Barrier

To describe the LT framework, we will begin with a characterization of the debt value, D, in a simplified version of this framework by first assuming the default barrier, X, is constant. Consider first the building blocks of this model (refer to Leland and Toft 1996 for the derivations; note that there are differences between the notation that we use and that used in the original paper). The value of the debt can then be calculated as follows:

$$D = \frac{C}{r}\left(1 - \left(\frac{A}{X}\right)^{-\gamma}\right) + (1 - L)X\left(\frac{A}{X}\right)^{-\gamma}$$

where

$$\gamma = \alpha + \xi$$

$$\alpha = \frac{r - p - \frac{1}{2}\sigma_A^2}{\sigma_A^2}$$

$$\xi = \frac{\left(\left(r - p - \frac{1}{2}\sigma_A^2\right)^2 + 2\sigma_A^2 r\right)^{\frac{1}{2}}}{\sigma_A^2}$$

The LT equation is similar to the Black-Cox setup. The first part of the debt equation is the value of the coupon cash flows paid until the default time. The second part is the amount the debt holders will receive at the time of default. It is important to remember that this version of the formula derives its simplicity from the assumption that X is constant and exogenously determined.

Now let us see how the function changes when we assume the default barrier is determined endogenously—that is, when the firm manages its capital structure based on the trade-off between tax savings and bankruptcy costs (both determined, in large part, by entities outside the firm).

Endogenous Default Barrier

Assume the firm issues debt at a rate of $f = \frac{F}{T}$, where the new debt has a maturity of T and F is the total face value of all outstanding bonds. These bonds pay a constant coupon rate, $c = \frac{C}{T}$, per year. As long as the firm is not in default, the total outstanding debt will be F. By making the par amount of debt a *choice* in the context of the trade-off between tax savings and bankruptcy costs, we arrive at a much more involved equation:

$$D = \frac{C}{r} + \left(F - \frac{C}{r}\right)\left(\frac{1 - e^{-rT}}{rT} - I(T)\right) + \left((1 - L)X - \frac{C}{r}\right)J(T)$$

where the following functions are defined as follows:

$$I(T) = \frac{1}{rT}\left(G(T) - e^{-rT}H(T)\right)$$

where

$$G(t) = \left(\frac{A}{X}\right)^{-\alpha+\xi}\Phi[q_1(t)] + \left(\frac{A}{X}\right)^{-\alpha-\xi}\Phi[q_2(t)]$$

$$q_1(t) = \frac{\left(-\beta - \xi\sigma_A^2 t\right)}{\sigma_A\sqrt{t}}; \quad q_2(t) = \frac{\left(-\beta + \xi\sigma_A^2 t\right)}{\sigma_A\sqrt{t}}; \quad \beta = \ln\left(\frac{A}{X}\right)$$

$$H(t) = \Phi[h_1(t)] + \left(\frac{A}{X}\right)^{-2\alpha}\Phi[h_2(t)]$$

$$h_1(t) = \frac{\left(-\beta - \alpha\sigma_A^2 t\right)}{\sigma_A\sqrt{t}}; \quad h_2(t) = \frac{\left(-\beta + \alpha\sigma_A^2 t\right)}{\sigma_A\sqrt{t}}$$

$$J(T) = \frac{1}{\xi\sigma_A\sqrt{T}}\left(-\left(\frac{A}{X}\right)^{-\alpha+\xi}\Phi[q_1(T)]\,q_1(T) + \left(\frac{A}{X}\right)^{-\alpha-\xi}\Phi[q_2(T)]\,q_2(T)\right)$$

In this framework, the market value of the firm, A, equals the asset value generated by the firm's cash flow opportunities plus the value of the firm's tax benefits, less the value of bankruptcy over the infinite horizon. Recall that the tax benefits accrue at a rate of τC as long as the firm's asset value stays above its default barrier. The equation seems a bit daunting, but essentially it reflects the balancing of the tax benefits and the costs of bankruptcy in the context of a first-passage default time framework.

The total value of the firm with these benefits and costs is designated as A_{LT}:

$$A_{LT} = A + \frac{\tau C}{r}\left[1 - \left(\frac{A}{X}\right)^{-\gamma}\right] - LX\left(\frac{A}{X}\right)^{-\gamma}$$

From here we can derive the equity formula using the accounting identity in market value terms:

$$E = A_{LT} - D$$

Unlike versions of the model with an exogenously specified default barrier, we still need to solve for the equilibrium bankruptcy trigger value for X.

The mechanism is a function known as the "smooth-pasting condition":[21]

$$\frac{\partial E(X, T)}{\partial A}\Big|_{A=X} = 0$$

From this setup, LT derive the following (involved) equation for the optimal default barrier:

$$X^* = \frac{\frac{C}{r}\left(\frac{A}{rT} - B\right) - \frac{AP}{rT} - \frac{\tau C\gamma}{r}}{1 + L\gamma - (1 - L)B}$$

$$A = 2\alpha e^{-rT}\Phi\left(\alpha\sigma_A\sqrt{T}\right) - 2\xi\Phi\left(\xi\sigma_A\sqrt{T}\right) - \frac{2}{\sigma_A\sqrt{T}}\phi\left(\xi\sigma_A\sqrt{T}\right)$$

$$+ \frac{2e^{-rT}}{\sigma_A\sqrt{T}}\phi\left(\alpha\sigma_A\sqrt{T}\right) + (\xi - \alpha)$$

$$B = -\left(2\xi + \frac{2}{\xi\sigma_A^2 T}\right)\Phi\left(\xi\sigma_A\sqrt{T}\right) - \frac{2}{\sigma_A\sqrt{T}}\phi\left(\xi\sigma_A\sqrt{T}\right) + (\xi - \alpha) + \frac{1}{\xi\sigma_A^2 T}$$

where $\phi(\cdot)$ is the standard normal density function.

Note that when the time to maturity goes to infinity, this formula simplifies to the following:

$$X^* = \frac{(1 - \tau)C\gamma}{(1 + \gamma)r}$$

In this context, X^* depends on the debt's time to maturity. In other models such as Longstaff and Schwartz, the model setup implies that X^* is independent of debt maturity. Assuming the data are available to parameterize all aspects of this model, the LT model provides more insight into choice of debt maturity and its potential impact on debt value.

LT in Application

While the standard BSM framework produces PD estimates that are much too low relative to those implied by the data for credit spreads, the LT

---

[21] *Smooth-pasting* refers to the condition associated with the change of equity value as the asset value slides into the default barrier. At that point, the limit on the derivative of the change of the equity with respect to the change in asset value is zero since the barrier constitutes the point at which the firm's equity value can no longer change—that is, it stays at zero. This condition indicates that this circumstance happens in a smooth way and the asset value is "pasted" into the barrier.

framework produces a different estimate of the cumulative default probability to time T, or cpd_T:

$$
cpd_T = \Phi \left(\frac{-\beta - \left(\mu_A - p - \frac{1}{2}\sigma_A^2 \right) T}{\sigma_A \sqrt{T}} \right) +
$$

$$
e^{\frac{-2\beta\left(\mu_A - p - \frac{1}{2}\sigma_A^2 \right)}{\sigma_A^2}} \Phi \left(\frac{-\beta + \left(\mu_A - p - \frac{1}{2}\sigma_A^2 \right) T}{\sigma_A \sqrt{T}} \right)
$$

While this formulation moves us closer to actual spreads, it still turns out to underestimate PDs—particularly at shorter maturities. We can still make use of the framework in a manner similar to the other models in this chapter—that is, we can use LT's functions to estimate debt directly or use equity prices to back out implied asset value and asset volatility. The drawback with this formulation is the addition of a relatively large number of new parameters and variables coupled with the more complex set of functions. In practice, for example, the tax rate can be quite difficult to specify accurately.

However, if we are comfortable with the complexity of the LT framework, it provides a rich machinery to analyze a variety of fundamental aspects of firm behavior (beyond just default probability and straight debt valuation), ranging from capital structure to the interaction of the drivers of debt valuation. Some of these applications include:

- Determining optimal leverage for a firm (or, alternatively, determining how far away a firm is from its optimal leverage).
- Understanding debt value as a function of leverage and different maturities.
- Analyzing a firm's debt capacity.
- Analyzing term structure of credit spreads as a function of leverage.
- Evaluating multiple classes of debt with different tenors. This extension is accomplished by assuming each class of debt follows its own schedule of issuance. The amount received at bankruptcy $(1 - L)$ will be determined by the seniority of each debt class.
- Developing a more reasonable assessment of the risk of *asset substitution* (in which equity holders seek to increase the risk of the firm, thereby transferring value from existing debt holders), which can be done since in LT the value of the firm is not just a function of the underlying firm asset value, but also the benefit of the tax deduction (which is lost in bankruptcy).

The LT framework brings us a step forward in understanding the real drivers of optimal leverage. While we pay for this understanding with complexity, the endogenization of the default point provides an important tool in analyzing the interaction of the choice variables that firms can change (amount of debt issued, maturity of debt, seniority of debt, degree of leverage, etc.). We may rely on some of the other models discussed in this chapter to estimate PDs for a large number of exposures in a portfolio. However, we can also benefit from more complex models such as LT when we wish to drill into the circumstances of particular firms or groups of firms, and we can therefore afford the time and effort of managing the accompanying model complexity.

CORPORATE TRANSACTION ANALYSIS

An underappreciated application of structural models concerns analyzing the impact of various types of corporate transactions, such as:

- Share repurchases
- Debt restructuring
- Mergers and acquisitions
- Spin-offs

Since we typically begin with the Modigliani-Miller assumption, which separates the asset value from the capital structure, we can analyze how this constant value is shifted among the various claimants to the underlying asset value. This is done in the context of corporate transactions, which change the mix of debt and equity or which combine or break up corporate entities. The structural framework (regardless of which version of the model one chooses) provides a coherent approach to quantifying the changes to a particular corporate structure and it provides the tools for contemplating corporate transactions in a consistent manner.

Another advantage lies in the ability of a structural model to allow users to convert fundamental analyses into components of the framework. For example, the hypothesized synergies of a merger can be recast in terms of higher asset value forecasts, and business uncertainty can be transformed into different asset volatility estimates. Moreover, particular corporate structures that often favor equity holders at the expense of existing debt holders can be seen in stark relief and thus objectively evaluated. The value of this informational edge can have profound implications for the holder of the information. As market participants become more sophisticated in applying such quantitative models, the model variables and parameters have the potential to become clear and concise means of communication (much as we see Black-Scholes volatility as the preferred method of quoting an option price). In any case, analysts involved in structuring or commenting on deals can benefit from instantiating their views in the context of a coherent analytical infrastructure. This approach can also, in some cases, mitigate model risk as more participants in a transaction understand better the nature of the drivers of value in the context of a common analytical framework and thus review the various model inputs and behaviors.

Not all transactions are equally amenable to such analysis. For example, the impact of straightforward changes in capital structure such as a share repurchase is much easier to evaluate than less clearly specified cases, such as an equity issuance. The key factor driving the ease of analysis concerns how cash is used. If a firm sells assets or borrows money specifically for a share repurchase, it is clear how cash is going to be used. Thus, the changes in asset value and Default Point are much easier to determine.

In contrast, a new equity issuance that is ostensibly invested in the business relies on more assumptions regarding whether the cash raised will actually be converted into incremental asset value. The analysis also becomes more dependent on assumptions in the context of mergers, acquisitions, and spin-offs. The reason lies in the assumptions of the post-transaction asset value and post-transaction asset volatility. In the case of asset value, much debate can ensue among analysts, even within the structural framework, about synergy or the lack thereof. In the case of asset volatility, the parameter of interest is correlation (i.e., systematic risk). Is pre-transaction correlation really a good estimate of post-transaction realized correlation? Are there other deals that provide empirical guidance? While we do not have a single answer for these questions (the analysis can be difficult), the structural framework improves the coherence of the analysis and adds much more objectivity to analytical processes that are typically fraught with manipulation and predetermined conclusions.

In our experience, the insight from these types of analyses makes the discussions regarding deal structure much more productive. In the end, the analyst will have specific predictions for value of the claims held by the following stake holders:

- Existing equity holders
- Existing debt holders
- New equity holders
- New debt holders

Market prices are an excellent benchmark for these predictions as an analyst can compare pre- and post-transaction prices.

Consider a brief example that highlights how this framework can be used in corporate transaction analysis. Assume a firm with a $10 billion market value of assets and a $6.8 billion market capitalization evaluates the impact of a share repurchase. Assume that the liabilities other than equity are roughly 50 percent short-term loans from banks and 50 percent longer-term corporate bonds for a total book value of $3.3 billion. The firm's asset volatility is 20 percent.

The firm decides to execute a share repurchase by issuing $1 billion of new corporate bonds. Let us see how this transaction impacts existing debt and existing equity holders. First, we determine the key components of analysis.

Current Situation
- Market value of assets = 10
- Default Point = $1.65 + (1.65 \times 0.5) = 2.475$
- Asset volatility = 0.20

Assuming an expected growth rate of 5 percent, the one-year DD is calculated as follows:

$$DD = \{\ln(10) + [0.05 + (0.5 \times 0.04)] - \ln(2.475)\}/0.20 = 7.1$$

After Proposed Share Repurchase of $1 Billion Funded by Bonds
- Market value of assets = 10.
- Per the Modigliani-Miller (MM) assumption, asset value does not change with change in capital structure.
- Default Point = $1.65 + (2.65 \times 0.5) = 2.975$.
- Since all the funds are long-term debt, only half the debt enters into the default point per the VK approach.
- Asset Volatility = 0.20.
- Again per MM, asset volatility does not change.

Assuming an expected growth rate of 5 percent, the one-year DD is calculated as follows:

$$DD = \{\ln(10) + [0.05 + (0.5 \times 0.04)] - \ln(2.975)\}/0.20 = 6.2$$

This analysis is summarized in Table 3.4.

The approximate increase in PD for this firm may be on the order of 100 percent—for example, it moves from 0.10 to 0.20 percent. Thus, the share repurchase makes existing debt relatively much riskier.

TABLE 3.4 Corporate Transaction Analysis

	Pre-Transaction	Post-Transaction
Market value of assets	10	10
Default point	2.475	2.975
Asset volatility	0.2	0.2
DD	7.1	6.2
Approximate PD	10bps	20bps

Analysis

This transaction is obviously beneficial to the equity holders. They capture value at the expense of existing debt holders. To see why, consider that MM means that the amount of the pie to distribute stays the same before and after the transaction. However, effectively, the transaction makes the firm riskier, which is desirable for the owners of equity since the returns to equity will increase, but at the expense of bringing the firm closer to insolvency.

The structural framework facilitates specific estimates on how much the debt increases and, when combined with a valuation model, an estimate in the change in the value of existing debt and existing equity. These quantities will help make better decisions with respect to the pricing and structuring of these kinds of transactions.

LIQUIDITY

A common concern in credit modeling focuses on disentangling a liquidity premium from a credit risk premium. We have suggested earlier the importance of modeling spreads over swap rates or even a corporate risk-free rate such as an implied 0-cpd rate (i.e., the rate at which a risk-free corporate might borrow; refer to Bohn 2000b for more discussion on a risk-free corporate rate). This choice of a reference curve is a good first step toward sorting out the liquidity component of spread; however, this approach does not help in determining the liquidity premia associated with specific firms in identifying instances where market conditions are less liquid (e.g., fall 1998 and summer 2007 to 2008) and the resulting liquidity concerns overwhelm credit concerns.

A number of approaches to capturing liquidity have been suggested. Most of these tend to endogenize liquidity, making it a direct component of the spread that must be estimated after controlling for other spread components such as default risk and LGD.

One such approach starts with one reasonably liquid asset market, such as the market for large-firm CDSs, and compares the spreads from these contracts to less liquid instruments such as corporate bonds issued by the same firms. Longstaff, Mithal, and Neis (2004) show this approach may have promise, although they highlight that CDS spreads may be a biased

THE TED SPREAD AS A PROXY FOR A LIQUIDITY PREMIUM

The spread between short-dated (e.g., three-month) Eurodollar contracts and short-dated U.S. Treasury securities provides an indication of liquidity concerns throughout the global economy. Often this spread is referred to as the Treasury Eurodollar (TED) spread. This spread tends to spike at times of uncertainty regarding the resilience of the financial system itself. It is important to distinguish concerns about the economy from concerns about the ability to settle trades. The latter issue seems to drive the TED spread even though economic problems sometimes coincide with financial system difficulties (e.g., the oil crisis in the 1970s).

The TED spread reached its highest level during the Herstatt bank collapse in 1974 when this mid-size German bank could not make good on its overnight commitments. Because the global payments system was not prepared for this kind of event, the payments system became dangerously strained. Thus the TED spread exploded to levels never seen before or since. Other periods of high TED spreads coincide with events one would expect: oil crisis in the 1970s; 1987 stock market break; 1994 peso crisis; 1998 Russian debt and LTCM crisis; September 11, 2001; and more recently the credit crisis starting in the summer of 2007 and continuing into 2008. With the advent of better risk management systems and more regulatory oversight of the global payment system, we have not seen levels of the TED spread anywhere near the levels seen in 1974. This suggests that liquidity has been improved relative to those early days. However, this component of the spread can be particularly important in times of market dislocations—especially for the valuation of investment-grade debt.

estimate of the default component of the spread. After controlling for the characteristics unique to each set of instruments, the difference observed across markets for the same obligor can be interpreted as a liquidity-based spread. Occasional marketwide difficulties such as seen in summer 2007 and into 2008 seem to affect both the CDS and corporate bond market. In these circumstances, CDS spreads may no longer serve as a clean estimate of the default component of spread. In any case, such research is new and evolving quickly. As time goes by, we will look for more sophisticated approaches to model this important component of spreads on credit instruments.

Chacko (2005) presents a novel, exogenous approach to modeling liquidity. Instead of focusing on the nature of the traded instruments, Chacko used a special data set of bond holdings and investor classification that allowed him to focus on the type of investor purchasing the credit instrument. In this way, Chacko was able to sort out the impact of "hot money" purchasers such as hedge funds from more stable holders such as insurance companies or pension funds. The former were more likely to trade often while the latter tended to sit on large positions. Chacko's results were recently supported by conversations one of the authors had with credit traders in the fall of 2007, who commented that during the summer of 2007, the spread on debt or even CDSs often seemed to be more influenced by who was purchasing the instruments than any characteristics of the underlying obligor. In these unusual market conditions, credit risk appeared no longer to drive the value of credit instruments.

Chacko's analysis provides some suggestions for how to include liquidity effects when evaluating a credit instrument. Unfortunately, the data are hard to come by (he secured data from custodians). Day-to-day credit trading and portfolio management require more practical solutions. We have found it useful as a first step to develop simple matrices that relate a liquidity spread to characteristics such as company size and amount of the instrument outstanding.

OTHER STRUCTURAL APPROACHES

All of the structural models we have discussed so far in this chapter use market observables (i.e., prices) to imply asset values and volatilities under various assumptions. The resulting quantities are then used to determine, among other things, firm PDs. Some other structural approaches have been developed that focus on other types of variables. We now turn to an exposition of some of these other types of models that can be useful.

Structure without Market Observables: Wilcox (1971)

An early structural model, Wilcox (1971), proposed that a firm would default when its assets become exhausted through sufficiently large cash outflows. Under this framework, when a firm's liquid (book) assets fall to zero the firm is in default. In some ways, this model represents a similar construct to the Merton (1974) model. However, unlike the Merton framework, Wilcox's formulation relies only on accounting data and the relationship between stock and flow accounts. In particular, unlike the Merton formulation which posits the default process as one in which insolvency occurs when the market value of assets falls below the value of liabilities, Wilcox envisions the firm as increasing or decreasing its asset value through positive or negative cash flows and defaulting when negative cash flows exhaust the liquid assets. Thus, a key difference between most structural models of default and the Wilcox approach is that the Wilcox approach takes a cash flow view of default (i.e., a firm defaults when it runs out of money), whereas most other structural models take a valuation view of default (i.e., a firm defaults when the market value of its assets falls below the par value of its liabilities).[22]

In this light, under the Wilcox model, the problem of credit assessment can be formulated in a setting in which firms are ranked based on the probability that they will ultimately default due to having exhausted their assets. This concept is related to the risk of ruin in the familiar Gambler's Ruin probability problem (Epstein 1977). The solution to the Gambler's Ruin problem, the risk of ruin, is the probability of a gambler exhausting his capital given an initial bankroll, L and a fixed bet size, S, while playing a repeated game which has a single trial probability of success of p and failure $q \equiv 1 - p$. One period of the gamble is shown schematically in Figure 3.3.

In such a setting, the risk of ruin, R, is given as:

$$R = \begin{cases} \left(\frac{q}{p}\right)^N & if \frac{q}{p} < 1 \\ 1 & otherwise \end{cases}$$

---

[22] Note that these two views can be related through the observation that changes in asset value result in positive and negative cash flows. The Wilcox model can be viewed as deriving asset value and volatility through cash flow volatility while the Merton approach can be viewed as arriving at cash flow value and volatility through asset valuation. In principle, with clean data, $\Delta A \propto f$ (EBITDA). However, accounting data is often difficult to interpret in this regard. More generally, the relationship between book assets and market assets (implied through a BSM-type framework) is not transparent. For these reasons, we do not discuss the issue of the relationship between the BSM and Wilcox frameworks further here.

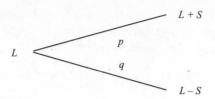

FIGURE 3.3 Gambler's Ruin

where $N = L/S$ is the number of units of initial capital the gambler begins play with, given starting bank roll L and a required bet size of S.

Clearly, if played long enough the game will end in ruin for the gambler with certainty whenever $p < q$; that is, when the probability of success is less than that of failure. Interestingly, even a fair game will end in ruin if played long enough by the gambler against an opponent with infinite capital. An important observation, however, is that given a favorable game $p > q$, a player can make the probability of ruin arbitrarily small by increasing the starting bankroll, L.

Wilcox transforms the Gambler's Ruin problem into a stylized model of default as follows: Suppose that a firm plays a game against the economy. In each period the firm receives a payoff of S with probability p, and a payoff of $-S$ with probability $q \equiv 1 - p$. Thus, L, the level of the firm's (liquid) assets, grows or shrinks by the amount S in each period of the game. The risk of ruin is the probability that the firm will experience a run of losses (negative cash inflows) so severe as to completely consume the initial firm assets as well as any that have been accumulated by the firm during play.

Before developing the full model, we first establish some useful quantities and relationships. If c is the random variable representing the payoff of the game in each period, it follows that the expected value of c, μ, is simply the probability weighted average of S and $-S$:

$$\mu \equiv E(c) = pS - (1 - p)S = (p - q)S$$

Similarly, the variance of c, σ^2, is just

$$\sigma^2 = Var(c)$$
$$= E[S^2] - E[S]^2$$
$$= (pS^2 + q(-S)^2) - (pS + q(-S))^2$$
$$= (p + q)S^2 - (pS + qS)^2$$
$$\sigma^2 = (p + q)S^2 - \mu^2 = S^2 - \mu^2$$

Note that σ^2 has a particularly simple form since the payoff values S and $-S$ are symmetrical and thus their squares are equivalent.[23]

Now, returning to the model, note that since

$$1 - (p - q) = (1 - p) + q = 2q$$

and

$$1 + (p - q) = (1 - q) + p = 2p$$

the gambler's ruin, R, can be rewritten as:

$$R = \begin{cases} \left(\dfrac{1 - (p - q)}{1 + (p - q)} \right)^N & if \, (p - q) > 0 \\ 1 & otherwise \end{cases}$$

and that by the basic relationships we started with,

$$(p - q) = \frac{\mu}{S}$$

and

$$S = \sqrt{\mu^2 + \sigma^2}$$

Finally, combining all of this, we are left with:

$$R = \begin{cases} \left(\dfrac{1 - \dfrac{\mu}{\sqrt{\mu^2 + \sigma^2}}}{1 + \dfrac{\mu}{\sqrt{\mu^2 + \sigma^2}}} \right)^{\frac{L}{\sqrt{\mu^2 + \sigma^2}}} & if \dfrac{\mu}{\sqrt{\mu^2 + \sigma^2}} > 0 \\ 1 & otherwise \end{cases}$$

Wilcox implements this version of R by taking μ as the average cash flow and σ^2 as the estimated variance of cash flow using five years of data.[24]

---

[23] In the case of unequal payouts, where $\sigma^2 = (pS_+^2 + qS_-^2) - (pS_+ - qS_-)^2 = (pS_+^2 + qS_-^2) - \mu^2$, and S_+ and S_- represent the absolute values of the payoffs for a win and loss, respectively.

[24] Wilcox actually suggests deriving the cash flow from the change in balance sheet assets, rather than observing it directly. Note that the formulation here is taken from later versions of the model. The original version included dividend payouts and reinvestments in illiquid assets. See Wilcox (1971), Wilcox (1973), and Wilcox (1976) for comparison.

He measures a firm's liquidation value (L) as a function of the book value of assets, adjusting for the liquidity of the assets:

$$L = \text{cash and marketable securities} + [70\% \text{ of (total current assets} - \text{cash and marketable securities)}] + [50\% \text{ of (total assets} - \text{total current assets)}]$$

In our own work, we have also considered alternative formulations of L, more consistent with the asset position of a leveraged firm and more similar to the default point calculations discussed earlier in this chapter.

In its raw form, the value R represents a credit risk index at no specific horizon, rather than a PD of a specific term. Calibration of the PD can be done in a similar fashion to the DD to PD mappings we discussed earlier. Alternatively, Stein and Jordao (2005) show how the model may be adjusted to reflect a PD at a definite horizon under specific distributional assumptions. In the context of that paper, the objective was to estimate cash flow (EBITDA) volatility more accurately by implying volatility using the model and given a one-year PD. However, the same equations can be used to derive a one-year PD based on an observed volatility. The paper also discusses alternative formulations of L and extending the treatment to optimal liquidity structure, and so on.

In our own experiments, the empirical power of R by itself (in a univariate setting) predicting default is reasonably good. However, in the presence of other financial statement factors, it tends to drop out of statistical models as much of its behavior is captured by various aspects of other factors that, in combination, have higher overall predictive power. Nonetheless, the model is instructive in what it tells us about cash flow and its relationship to solvency. The model can also be used to explore balance sheet issues such as the impact of holding more or less liquid assets.

Hybrid Structural Models

The conventional structural model framework provides an important link between market observables such as equity prices and credit measures such as PDs. While not always comprehensive or accurate enough to be the only type of model used in risk assessment and ACPM, these models are an important part of a well-rounded toolkit.

A key assumption, starting with Merton and flowing through to many of the modifications, is that a firm's underlying asset value is the only driver of a firm's equity price. One can decompose this further into the firm's expected cash flows, the discount rate used to calculate the present value of those cash flows, and the risk premium associated with the uncertainty in those cash flows. To the extent that the equity price becomes de-linked from these underlying drivers, noise can enter the estimates used in a structural model. Equity market conditions such as those witnessed during the huge sell-offs seen in summer 2007, fall 2008, or October 1987 may reflect real changes in cash flow and interest rate expectations or may reflect supply-demand imbalances as other factors independent of asset value (such as margin calls for large investors or basic fear about hidden losses) weigh on market participants. The difficulty is sorting out the drivers impacting asset value from the drivers impacting the equity trading environment. These problems are magnified in the traded markets for debt.

These concerns highlight the possibility that the typical structural models may miss key factors impacting default risk. Said differently, the assumption that equity prices are only affected by changes in the firm's underlying asset value may lead an analyst astray when the equity price becomes overwhelmed by liquidity or market bubble issues or when the information that informs the prices (e.g., the value of inventories, etc.) is observed imperfectly by market participants. The increasingly well documented anomalies in the behavioral finance literature support the notion that more than just underlying firm asset value may ultimately drive a firm's equity price. In developed markets with high levels of transparency, the standard, structural model assumption makes more sense, but even in these markets we occasionally see bubbles and liquidity difficulties mixing in with the more classic economic explanations of equity price movement. In particular, equities with only a small amount of their shares available to trade and equities from emerging markets can be more susceptible to non-asset-value sources of equity price uncertainty.

How might these real-world frictions be accommodated in credit models?

In recent years, some researchers have suggested that we incorporate multiple sources of uncertainty by specifying a *hybrid* model that combines a structural framework with additional factors impacting either the equity or debt markets (or both), or additional financial statement factors that help resolve the uncertainty in the information that informs them. (See Sobehart, Stein, and Mikityanskaya 2000 and Stein 2005a for discussions of some reasonable approaches to building hybrid models.)

It is worth noting that the word *hybrid* has been defined in many ways by various authors. For example, the KMV and MKMV implementation of the VK model constitutes a hybrid model as many modifications are made to the estimation process to incorporate other information (e.g., modeled volatility) that may be generated by sources of uncertainty other than the firm's underlying asset value. Said differently, the VK model incorporates information in a way that improves the model's predictive power and constitutes the overlaying of data other than just the specific firm's equity price in a way that modifies the more standard structural model framework. Another type of hybrid model introduced in the next section begins with the assumption that data are imperfectly observed. This model possesses the intriguing property that it acts like both a structural and reduced-form model.

Regardless of how we define *hybrid*, the challenge continues to lie in sorting out which hybrid model will perform the best. This question can only be settled with empirical evidence. In general, hybrid models trade off performance for transparency. By adding additional elements to a structural model, we increase the number of factors driving the model's prediction and thus often create multiple sources of potential explanations for a model's output. We also tend to lose both the ability to perform transaction analysis in a straightforward manner and in some cases ease of parameter estimation. This may or may not be important to users, depending on their applications.

In our experience, many of these hybrid models are useful to the extent that the modeler is careful to drill into the underlying model behavior. One can sometimes be lulled into accepting model output only to find that the parameterizations were unique to a particular time or particular data set. Once again, as so often is the case in this text, we return to the importance of rigorous validation, which we discuss in Chapter 7. In any event, hybrid models are likely to become more popular in the coming years, particularly as the economic theory supporting their application develops. As such, the final model we present in this chapter is an example of a hybrid model that spans both the structural and the reduced-form modeling frameworks and provides a strong economic rational supporting its use.

Imperfect Information Model: Duffie and Lando

Duffie and Lando (DL) in 2001 begin with the Leland-Toft (LT) structural model framework (incorporating a firm's market value of assets, the coupon on its debt, and its default barrier). Like the more common structural models, Duffie and Lando (2001) assume that a firm defaults when the asset value hits the default barrier. Unlike the common structural models, however, this model introduces the notion of imperfect information.

In our prior discussions, we developed structural model frameworks under the implicit premise that we can observe, without error, the actual quantities used to estimate each model (e.g., long-term debt, and so on). While much of the time this premise makes general sense, the extent to which firms revise disclosed financial statements should also lead us to consider cases in which it is not strictly the case. DL explicitly assumes that we *cannot* observe the asset process directly, so debt holders do not know *exactly* when the asset value has hit the default barrier. This can be because either the information is imperfect or reported with error, or because we may just not know exactly what to observe (e.g., other models may be needed to provide an indication of the firm's asset value). The interesting consequence of this imperfect information assumption is that the default time becomes *unpredictable* as in a reduced-form model (see Chapter 6) even though the rest of the model looks and acts like a structural model.

A key advantage of this particular hybrid model approach lies in the fact that the assumption of incomplete information improves the probability that short-maturity spreads generated by the model are nonzero. Recall that the weakness of some structural models was that as the maturity on a liability approaches zero its spread also approaches zero. Empirically, we observe positive spreads for even the shortest (i.e., one-day) maturity debt instruments. While the DL model will still produce zero spreads at some particular (very short) time horizon, the rate of convergence to zero is slower than the perfect information model reflected in LT. With this slower convergence, we are likely to retain a more realistic characterization of the very short end of the credit-spread term structure with the DL model while still benefiting from the economic interactions underlying the model framework. This unpredictability of the default time creates the reduced-form nature of this model.

In the remainder of this section, we outline the Duffie-Lando model. Readers interested in a more technical description of the model are encouraged to refer to Duffie and Lando (2001); note that we have changed some of the original notation in this exposition to make the formulae more consistent with others throughout this text.

DL's model framework begins with the Leland and Toft (1996) framework, which we introduced earlier. Recall that in the LT framework debt is assumed to be perpetual (i.e., no finite maturity) and continuously pays a constant coupon, C. If we assume the company faces a tax rate, τ, the tax benefit to issuing debt is τC per unit of time where the debt is issued (since interest payments are tax-deductible). The LT framework relies on the trade-off between risk of bankruptcy and value of a tax benefit to determine an equilibrium level of debt (i.e., a default barrier), thereby resulting in the following formula for the firm's PD and the value of its debt (refer back to the previous section for the details of the formula):

$$cpd_t = \Phi\left(\frac{-\beta - \left(\mu_A - p - \frac{1}{2}\sigma_A^2\right)t}{\sigma_A\sqrt{t}}\right) +$$

$$e^{\frac{-2\beta\left(\mu_A - p - \frac{1}{2}\sigma_A^2\right)}{\sigma_A^2}}\Phi\left(\frac{-\beta + \left(\mu_A - p - \frac{1}{2}\sigma_A^2\right)t}{\sigma_A\sqrt{t}}\right)$$

The innovation in the DL model centers on the addition of noise to the observation of firm value:

$$\log \hat{A}_t = Y_t = Z_t + U_t$$

where $U_t \sim \Phi(\bar{u}, a)$ and Z_t and U_t are independent

$$\log A_t = Z_t$$

where A_t follows geometric Brownian motion or

$$dA = \mu_A A dt + \sigma_A A dz$$

For ease of writing down the formula, we follow DL's notation and define

$$m = \mu_A - \frac{1}{2}\sigma_A^2$$

Essentially, we take the core asset value process and add noise to it to produce a measure that reflects data we can actually observe rather than the true value of the quantities. The DL model characterizes this noise as accounting noise (e.g., imperfectly observed inventory levels). The challenge in this framework lies in estimating a, a measure of accounting noise in the market. This value will likely be specific to each obligor. Techniques for specifying this measure of accounting noise must still be more fully developed at this point. That said, this model has potential for addressing the impact of accounting noise and developing a more rigorous sense of the confidence interval around estimates of PDs and spreads.

The PD formula that arises from this framework is given as

$$cpd_{t,s} = 1 - \int_{\underline{A}}^{\infty} (1 - \pi(s - t, x - \underline{A}))g(x|Y_0, Z_0, t)\,dx$$

where $\pi(s - t, x - \underline{A})$ reflects the first passage probability of a Brownian motion with drift m and volatility parameter σ_A from an initial starting point $x > 0$ to a level below 0 from time t to time s, conditional on the firm having survived to t, as follows:

$$\pi(s - t, x - \underline{A}) = 1 - \left[\Phi\left(\frac{x - \underline{A} + m(s - t)}{\sqrt{s - t}} \right) \right.$$
$$\left. - e^{-2m(x - \underline{A})}\Phi\left(\frac{-(x - \underline{A}) + m(s - t)}{\sqrt{s - t}} \right) \right]$$

The density function in the integral for the PD calculation becomes quite a bit more complicated in this framework. For ease of writing down the formula, we define the following variables in a similar manner as DL:

$$\tilde{x} = x - \underline{A}$$

$$\tilde{Y}_t = Y_t - \underline{A} - \bar{u}$$

$$\tilde{Z}_0 = Z_0 - \underline{A}$$

In this notation, DL results in the following expression for the density function:

$$g(x|Y_t, Z_0) = \frac{\sqrt{\dfrac{\beta_0}{\pi}} e^{-J(\tilde{x}, \tilde{Y}_t, \tilde{Z}_0)} \left[1 - e^{\left(\frac{-2\tilde{x}\tilde{Z}_0}{\sigma_A^2 t} \right)} \right]}{e^{\left(\frac{\beta_1^2}{4\beta_0} - \beta_3 \right)} \Phi\left(\dfrac{\beta_1}{\sqrt{2\beta_0}} \right) - e^{\left(\frac{\beta_2^2}{4\beta_0} - \beta_3 \right)} \Phi\left(-\dfrac{\beta_2}{\sqrt{2\beta_0}} \right)}$$

$$J(\tilde{x}, \tilde{Y}_t, \tilde{Z}_0) = \frac{(\tilde{Y}_t - \tilde{x})^2}{2a^2} + \frac{(\tilde{Z}_0 + mt - \tilde{x})^2}{2\sigma_A^2 t}$$

$$\beta_0 = \frac{a^2 + \sigma_A^2 t}{2a^2 \sigma_A^2 t}$$

$$\beta_1 = \frac{\tilde{Y}_t}{a^2} + \frac{\tilde{Z}_0 + mt}{\sigma_A^2 t}$$

$$\beta_2 = -\beta_1 + 2\frac{\tilde{Z}_0}{\sigma_A^2 t}$$

$$\beta_3 = \frac{1}{2} \left(\frac{\tilde{Y}_t^2}{a^2} + \frac{(\tilde{Z}_0 + mt)^2}{\sigma_A^2 t} \right)$$

The interesting link of this model to the reduced-form modeling framework is the fact that the imperfect information assumption makes the default time *inaccessible* (i.e., a surprise). Duffie and Lando (2001) prove that given a particular set of information (i.e., information available at the time of the calculation) and the conditional distribution, f, of Z_t based on that information, an intensity process, h, can be defined as follows:

$$h(\omega) = \frac{1}{2} \sigma_A^2 f_X(t, \underline{A}, \omega)$$

where $0 < t < \tau(\omega)$.

The details of the proof can be found in Duffie and Lando (2001). The important point is that we can arrive at an intensity process (refer to the reduced-form model descriptions in Chapter 6 for more details on intensity-based modeling) from a model that begins with a structural-model framework. In many ways, this model highlights the convergence of the data issues in credit modeling, the usefulness of the structural view of default, and the power of reduced-form modeling. While this model is quite new and we have not seen many implementations used in practice yet, we expect that it will serve as the foundation for more powerful modeling applications in the future.

CONCLUSION

While some researchers continue to debate the degree to which structural models are realistic enough to adequately model the nuances of various quantities of interest, these models will continue to provide important background and insights into the interactions of drivers determining capital structure and debt valuation. It is therefore fortunate that for many applications, these models perform very well. The interpretive power constitutes a key advantage of these models as does their flexibility for supporting corporate transaction analysis. This capability will continue to be a key area in which structural models distinguish themselves by facilitating better insight into how particular corporate actions shift value among claimants to the firm's asset value. We will see later in Chapter 8 when describing portfolio modeling that in addition to being useful for stand-alone analysis they also easily integrate into a comprehensive portfolio risk model that can be used for modeling the risk of large portfolios of credit exposures.

APPENDIX 3A: DERIVATION OF BLACK-SCHOLES-MERTON FRAMEWORK FOR CALCULATING DISTANCE TO DEFAULT (DD)

Definitions

$A \equiv$ Market value of a firm's assets

$\sigma_A \equiv$ Volatility of a firm's asset value

$E \equiv$ Market value of a firm's equity

$D \equiv$ Market value of a firm's debt

$T \equiv$ Time to maturity for D

$X \equiv$ Default point

$r \equiv$ Default-risk-free rate

$\mu_A \equiv$ Asset-value drift (expected growth rate for market value of assets)

$dz_t \equiv$ Wiener process (We will typically drop the t subscript to improve readability of equations.)

We must find two typically unobservable values for a company's distance to default: A and σ_A. If all the firm's debt and equity were traded, we could calculate A by adding up the market value of all the firm's debt and equity. Unfortunately, this simple calculation is not available for most (if not all) firms. Instead, we rely on option pricing theory and the Black-Scholes-Merton (BSM) insight that equity is a call option on the underlying firm's assets:

$$E = f(A, \sigma_A, r, X)$$

At this point, we must choose a particular option pricing framework for defining the relationship between E and A. In this derivation, we assume the framework outlined by BSM (see Black and Scholes 1973 and Merton 1974).

Key Assumptions

No arbitrage: Risk-free profits are not available by trading in both the option (in this case equity) and the underlying (in this case firm asset value).

Single source of uncertainty: The uncertainty driving the risk in the underlying asset value is the single source of uncertainty affecting the firm's equity and debt.

Ability to rebalance continuously: As the underlying asset value changes, an equity position in an arbitrage trade with the asset value can be rebalanced continuously.

Asset value process follows geometric Brownian motion: $dA = \mu_A A dt + \sigma_A A dz$

Equity value is an option on asset value: Payoff at time T is defined as

$$E = \max(A - X, 0)$$

We now need to find dE using Ito's lemma given that equity is a function of the asset value's stochastic process. (Ito's lemma is necessary for determining the differential equation for a variable that is a function of a random or stochastic process.) Basic results of Ito's lemma are

$$dt^2 = 0; dt\,dz = 0; dz^2 = dt$$

(Refer to Neftci 2000 for the details of the derivation for Ito's lemma.)

$$f = E = g(A, t); f_A = \frac{\partial E}{\partial A}; f_t = \frac{\partial E}{\partial t}; f_{AA} = \frac{\partial^2 E}{\partial A^2} dA = \mu_A A\,dt + \sigma_A A\,dz$$

$$dA^2 = \mu_A^2 A^2 dt^2 + 2\mu_A \sigma_A A^2 dt\,dz + \sigma_A^2 A^2 dz^2 = \sigma_A^2 A^2 dt\,df$$

$$= f_A dA + \frac{1}{2} f_{AA} dA^2 + f_t dt$$

Substituting back into the equation for key variables, we arrive at:

$$df = dE = \frac{\partial E}{\partial A}(\mu_A A\,dt + \sigma_A A\,dz) + \frac{1}{2}\frac{\partial^2 E}{\partial A^2}\sigma_A^2 A^2 dt + \frac{\partial E}{\partial t} dt$$

$$dE = \left(\frac{\partial E}{\partial A}\mu_A A + \frac{\partial E}{\partial t} + \frac{1}{2}\frac{\partial^2 E}{\partial A^2}\sigma_A^2 A^2\right) dt + \frac{\partial E}{\partial A}\sigma_A A\,dz$$

Next we will look at the no-arbitrage argument in terms of discrete quantities. The idea is to create a portfolio that consists of the option (in this case equity) and the underlying (in this case the firm asset value) that would generate a risk-free return. Note that in practice, A is not directly tradable, so the applicability of this type of model is sometimes questioned. Suitably extending the BSM model as is done with the Vasicek-Kealhofer approach has been shown to overcome this doubt and has demonstrated the approach's usefulness in estimating empirically defensible default probabilities (see Bohn 2000b, Kealhofer 2003a, and Kealhofer 2003b for details). We will use the symbol Δ to designate the change in portfolio positions in discrete terms. (You can consider Δ to be the discrete analog of ∂.)

$$\Delta A = \mu_A A \Delta t + \sigma_A A \Delta z \,\Delta E = \left(\frac{\partial E}{\partial A}\mu_A A + \frac{\partial E}{\partial t} + \frac{1}{2}\frac{\partial^2 E}{\partial A^2}\sigma_A^2 A^2\right) \Delta t$$

$$+ \frac{\partial E}{\partial A}\sigma_A A \Delta z$$

Note that the Wiener process driving the asset value and equity value are the same. We can use this relationship as the basis for constructing a portfolio that eliminates the randomness from the Wiener process: -1 unit of equity and $\frac{\partial E}{\partial A}$ units of the underlying firm assets. In other words, we construct a portfolio where we are short the equity and long the underlying assets. Since this portfolio eliminates the randomness, it is considered risk-free.

The risk-free portfolio is as follows:

$$\Pi = -E + \frac{\partial E}{\partial A} A$$

Change in value of this portfolio can be represented as follows:

$$\Delta\Pi = -\Delta E + \frac{\partial E}{\partial A} \Delta A$$

By substitution, we arrive at the following:

$$\Delta\Pi = \left(-\frac{\partial E}{dt} - \frac{1}{2}\frac{\partial^2 E}{\partial A^2}\sigma_A^2 A^2 \right)\Delta t$$

The risk-free return for portfolio Π during Δt can be calculated as follows:

$$\Delta\Pi = r\Pi\Delta t$$

By setting the risk-free return for portfolio Π equal to the change in value of this portfolio, we arrive at the following equality:

$$\left(-\frac{\partial E}{dt} - \frac{1}{2}\frac{\partial^2 E}{\partial A^2}\sigma_A^2 A^2 \right)\Delta t = r\left(-E + \frac{\partial E}{\partial A} A \right)\Delta t$$

Rearranging terms, we arrive at the key differential equation for this model:

$$\frac{1}{2}\frac{\partial^2 E}{\partial A^2}\sigma_A^2 A^2 + \frac{\partial E}{\partial A}r A + \frac{\partial E}{dt} - rE = 0$$

Since equity is assumed to become worthless if the asset value of the firm falls below the face value of the debt at the time of maturity, we add the following boundary condition:

$$E = \max(A_T - X, 0)$$

One can solve the partial differential equation directly or use the notion of risk-neutral expectation (written as E^Q). Let us consider the latter solution technique. A risk-neutral payoff can be valued by discounting back the expected payoff at the risk-free rate. For equity, we write down the following equation in this framework:

$$E = e^{-rT} E^Q[\max(A_T - X, 0)]$$

Given our assumption of geometric Brownian motion for the asset value process, $\ln A$ is normally distributed. We can use this fact to solve for a firm's equity value by invoking Ito's lemma ($dt^2 = 0; dtdz = 0; dz^2 = dt$) to determine the mean and standard deviation for $\ln A$.

$$dA = \mu_A A dt + \sigma_A A dz$$

$$f = \ln A; \quad f_A = \frac{1}{A}; \quad f_{AA} = -\frac{1}{A^2}$$

$$dA^2 = \mu_A^2 A^2 dt^2 + 2\mu_A \sigma_A A^2 dtdz + \sigma_A^2 A^2 dz^2 = \sigma_A^2 A^2 dt$$

$$df = f_A dA + \frac{1}{2} f_{AA} dA^2 + f_t dt$$

Substituting back into the equation for

$$df = d \ln A = \frac{1}{A}(\mu_A A dt + \sigma_A A dz) + \frac{1}{2}\left(-\frac{1}{A^2}\sigma_A^2 A^2 dt\right)$$

$$= \left(\mu_A - \frac{1}{2}\sigma_A^2\right) dt + \sigma_A dz$$

As an aside, why do we adjust the drift by the volatility?

This adjustment reflects the geometric mean, which is less than the arithmetic mean. (For example, consider the following return series, given in percentages: 40, 40, 40, −50, 40. The arithmetic mean is 22 while the geometric mean is 14. The adjustment makes the overall asset growth rate more accurate given the actual growth rate of an investment.) Note that this drift reflects the expected continuously compounded rate.

Next we integrate $d \ln A$ from time 0 to time T:

$$\ln A_T - \ln A_0 = \int_0^T \left(\mu_A - \frac{1}{2}\sigma_A^2 \right) dt + \int_0^T \sigma_A dz$$

$$\ln A_T = \ln A_0 + \left(\mu_A - \frac{1}{2}\sigma_A^2 \right) T + \sigma_A(z_T - z_0)$$

$$E(\ln A_T) = \ln A_0 + \left(\mu_A - \frac{1}{2}\sigma_A^2 \right) T$$

$$\text{var}(\ln A_T) = \sigma_A^2 T$$

If we replace the asset value drift, μ_A, with the risk-free rate, r, we can write down the risk-neutral distribution for $\ln A_T$:

$$\ln A_T \sim N\left[\ln A_0 + \left(r - \frac{1}{2}\sigma_A^2 \right) T, \sigma_A\sqrt{T} \right]$$

Let q be the risk-neutral normal density function for $\ln A_T$. We can now solve for the equity value as follows:

$$E = e^{-rT} \int_X^\infty \left(e^{\ln A_T} - X \right) q(\ln A_T) \, d\ln A_T$$

Regardless of the solution technique, the resulting formula can be written as follows:

$$E = A_0 N(d_1) - Xe^{-rT}N(d_2) \quad d_1 = \frac{\ln A_0 + \left(r + \frac{1}{2}\sigma_A^2 \right) T - \ln X}{\sigma_A\sqrt{T}}$$

$$d_2 = \frac{\ln A_0 + \left(r - \frac{1}{2}\sigma_A^2 \right) T - \ln X}{\sigma_A\sqrt{T}} = d_1 - \sigma_A\sqrt{T}$$

The resulting solution provides the foundation for relating asset value, asset volatility, equity value, and (by implication) equity volatility. We will return to this relationship shortly to derive asset value and asset volatility. At this point, we use this framework to directly determine the probability that the asset value is below the debt value (strike price) at time to maturity, T. Mathematically, we want to evaluate $pd = P(A_T \leq X)$.

Since we know the distribution and parameters for $\ln A_T$, we determine the default probability, *pd*, as follows:

$$pd = P(\ln A_T \leq \ln X) = N\left(\frac{\ln X - \left(\ln A_0 + \left(\mu_A - \frac{1}{2}\sigma_A^2\right) T\right)}{\sigma_A\sqrt{T}}\right) = N(-DD)$$

where

$$DD = \frac{\ln A_0 + \left(\mu_A - \frac{1}{2}\sigma_A^2\right) T - \ln X}{\sigma_A\sqrt{T}}$$

APPENDIX 3B: DERIVATION OF CONVERSION OF PHYSICAL PROBABILITY OF DEFAULT (PD) TO A RISK-NEUTRAL PROBABILITY OF DEFAULT (PD^Q)

Definitions

$\mu_A \equiv$ Asset-value drift (expected growth rate for market value of assets)

$\sigma_A \equiv$ Volatility of firm's asset value

$r \equiv$ Default-risk-free rate

$\mu_M \equiv$ Expected market return where the market is assumed to be the market for all corporate assets

$\sigma_M \equiv$ Volatility of market return

$r_A \equiv$ Return to holding all of firm assets

$r_M \equiv$ Return to holding the market portfolio of firm assets

Based on Black-Scholes-Merton (BSM), a physical PD can be calculated as follows (see BSM derivation for details):

$$pd = \Pr(A \leq D^*) = N(-DD)$$

where

$$DD = \frac{\ln A_0 + \left(\mu_A - \frac{1}{2}\sigma_A^2\right) T - \ln X}{\sigma_A\sqrt{T}}$$

A risk-neutral PD reflects a drift of the default-risk-free rate, r, instead of μ_A. We denote a risk-neutral PD with a Q superscript:

$$pd^Q = N\left(-DD^Q\right)$$

where

$$DD^Q = \frac{\ln A_0 + \left(r - \frac{1}{2}\sigma_A^2\right) T - \ln X}{\sigma_A\sqrt{T}}$$

The key point in the derivation is moving from DD to DD^Q. Essentially, we find a way to relate r and μ_A. We can construct this relationship by assuming the capital asset pricing model (CAPM) holds:

$$\mu_A - r = \beta \, (\mu_M - r)$$

where

$$\beta = \frac{\text{cov}(r_A, \, r_M)}{\sigma_M^2}$$

Define a measure of systematic risk, R^2, as follows:

$$R^2 = \left(\frac{\text{cov}(r_A, \, r_M)}{\sigma_A \sigma_M} \right)^2$$

R can be interpreted as the correlation of the firm's asset value with the overall market for firm assets.

Next define a measure of the market price of risk as

$$\lambda = \frac{\mu_M - r}{\sigma_M}$$

Alternatively, one can interpret this measure as the compensation investors demand in terms of excess return per unit of volatility risk to which they are exposed.

Using the CAPM relationship and substitution, we arrive at the following:

$$\frac{\mu_A - r}{\sigma_A} = \frac{\text{cov}(r_A, \, r_M)}{\sigma_A \sigma_M} \frac{\mu_M - r}{\sigma_M} = R\lambda$$

From this relationship of asset drift, default-risk-free rate, systematic risk, and market price of risk, we can substitute

$$r = \mu_A - \sigma_A R\lambda$$

into the formula for DD^Q:

$$DD^Q = \frac{\ln A_0 + \left(\mu_A - \frac{1}{2}\sigma_A^2 \right) T - \ln X}{\sigma_A \sqrt{T}} - \frac{\sigma_A R\lambda T}{\sigma_A \sqrt{T}} = DD - R\lambda\sqrt{T}$$

The risk-neutral DD is smaller than the physical DD, reflecting the adjustment that results in a higher PD, all else equal.

Now we have the necessary components to make the transformation:

$$pd^Q = \Phi(-DD^Q) = \Phi\left(\Phi^{-1}(pd) + R\lambda\sqrt{T}\right)$$

where we have made substitutions per the previous equations. Since we have a negative argument in the parentheses of the normal distribution function, we are adding an amount based on the firm's systematic risk, the market price of risk, and the time to maturity. That produces a larger number, which leads to a higher default probability since we are modifying a negative.

REVIEW QUESTIONS

1. Name at least two criticisms of the structural model framework.
2. Name at least two advantages of the structural model framework.
3. What is it about credit spreads that makes them particularly difficult to model?
4. Why do we prefer to use the LIBOR or swap curves as reference curves instead of U.S. Treasuries when calculating a spread?
5. If equity is considered a call option on the underlying firm assets, how can we characterize debt?
6. Explain why the premium on a CDS contract is considered a spread.
7. The Black-Scholes-Merton (BSM) framework for building a structural model to calculate a firm's default probability results in the distance to default being normally distributed. Provide a plausible explanation for why the distance to default is *not* normally distributed. Discuss your answer in terms of the BSM model framework.
8. What is one simplifying assumption about LGD to create a more parsimonious valuation equation?
9. What causes investors to demand a risk premium to take on credit risk?
10. Describe a potential problem with the simple BSM framework for valuing longer-dated debt securities.

EXERCISES

1. If a firm borrows money to repurchase equity, how does it impact the firm's probability of default?
2. Consider a firm with $148 of market asset value, $48 of short-term liabilities (i.e., maturity is less than one year), $20 of long-term liabilities (i.e., maturity is more than one year), and $100 of market equity value. This firm's asset volatility is 100 percent. The firm does not pay

dividends and its asset value drift is assumed to be 50 percent. The prevailing default-risk-free rate is 5 percent. Note the following table for the natural logarithm (ln) function:

Amount	28	38	48	58	68	78	88	98	108	118	128	138	148	158
ln	3.3	3.6	3.9	4.1	4.2	4.4	4.5	4.6	4.7	4.8	4.9	4.9	5.0	5.1

a. What is the one-year distance to default (to one digit beyond the decimal point) for this firm, assuming a simple Black-Scholes-Merton model (BSM) with the Vasicek-Kealhofer (VK) suggestion for default point specification? (Write out the components of your calculation in addition to the final number.)

b. A banker analyzes this firm and calculates the leverage ratio as follows: Book liabilities divided by the sum of equity value and book liabilities, which is approximately 40 percent. The banker concludes the firm is a moderate- to low-risk borrower based on his experience looking at this leverage ratio. Do you agree with the banker's analytical approach and assessment of the borrower's credit quality? Defend your answer within the context of the BSM model.

c. How much is the market value of the book liabilities?

d. The banker hires a quantitative analyst who educates him on the value of using market-based measures. The analyst calculates the risk of the firm and determines that it has too much debt. The banker turns down the loan. The firm approaches an investment banker, who advises it to repurchase shares and pay down debt over the next year and then return to the bank once the firm has demonstrated its growth pattern and accumulated more asset value. The investment banker further suggests the firm should pay down enough debt so that its default probability is less than 5 percent, which he calculates to be empirically associated with a DD of 1.7. How much debt should the firm repay with a new equity issuance? Be specific about which liabilities will be paid down and explain your answer in terms of the BSM model.

e. In the course of these capital restructuring discussions, the investment banker suggests the firm look at a strategic merger with a competitor. You are brought in to add analytical rigor to the discussion. Describe the conditions of the deal in the context of the BSM structural model that will need to hold for the merger to be beneficial for the existing equity holders. (Hint: Consider each component of the structural model calculation that ultimately drives the value of equity.)

3. In the context of the BSM framework, make one economically meaningful change (i.e., the change will affect the results in a way that has significant economic impact) that you consider more consistent with the real world, and re-derive the expression or system of expressions that describes the calculation for the probability of default.

4. Outline a procedure for estimating the market price of risk in a simple, Merton-based structural model of default. Include a derivation of the mathematical relationships and be specific about what data you would use.

5. In the BSM framework, what drives the shapes of credit spread curves?

CHAPTER 4

Econometric Models

*Can we bridge the gap, rather than sever the link, between
traditional "ratio analysis" and the more rigorous statistical
techniques which have become popular among academicians in the
recent years?*

—Edward Altman, 1968

This cape does not give the wearer the ability to fly.
—Warning label on a Halloween Batman costume

Objectives

After reading this chapter, you should understand the following
concepts:

- The definition of an econometric model of default.
- Some of the academic work on default prediction using econometric
  approaches.
- How to estimate econometric models of default.
- How to calibrate models to probabilities of default and ratings.
- Some strategies for identifying and correcting common data problems.

Thus far in this book, we have described structural models in terms of the
asset value of the obligor and reduced-form models primarily in terms
of default intensities. A third model family provides another approach for
developing a view on the credit risk of an obligor. We have loosely defined
this model family as *econometric* based on the techniques used to estimate

them.[1] In some ways, econometric models share characteristics with both structural models and reduced-form models. Given that econometric models do not necessarily rely on a causal argument for default (though the variables that enter the models are often chosen for their theoretical causal relationship to default), they are closer to reduced-form models in approach. In this chapter, we do not assume the availability of market information that relates to the price or risk of the firms being modeled. For many asset classes such as small and medium enterprise (SME) loans, credit cards, and consumer loans, econometric models provide powerful approaches to evaluating the risk of default.

Analysts typically specify bottom-up econometric models by representing the default process using one of two general approaches: *discrete-choice* specifications (either probability- or classification-based) or *hazard rate* (duration or survival) approaches. Discrete-choice models (e.g., logit, MDA, and so on) tend to be more popular, but hazard-rate approaches have attracted significant interest among practitioners in recent years as well. This is due to their more efficient use of rare default events and their relationship to more general default intensity specifications, such as those used in the reduced-form literature (see Chapter 6). In particular, duration models often provide a more flexible analytic framework for use within pricing and other credit-dependent applications, allowing predictions to be made over multiple horizons using a single model.

In practice we expect the performance of both classes of model to be similar with respect to predictive power as the likelihood functions are closely related (Agresti 1990). There are, however, some differences. For example, with respect to discrete-choice models, Efron (1975) showed that the efficiency of logit is lower than that of multiple discriminant analysis (MDA), even though the two are related through Bayes' rule. However, it is not clear that these theoretical results hold up in practical settings. For example, Lo (1986) concluded that despite the relationship through Bayes' rule, the actual empirical performance of logit and multiple discriminant analysis (MDA) depends on the degree to which certain normality assumptions are met. More specifically, Lo found that in cases where normality holds, MDA should be preferred for its econometric properties, but where they are

---

[1] In principle, all of the models we discuss are *econometric* models since they rely heavily on the use of (sometimes advanced) econometric techniques to estimate their parameters. However, in this section, we focus on models that are largely driven by the treatment of (typically) financial statement data, rather than market information, and that principally integrate this information using various regression or other statistical methods.

not, logit may be preferred for its robustness. Thus, the question of model specification is decided through empirical analysis of the subject data, and Lo's paper provides a specification test for normality in this regard. As a practical matter, in recent years MDA has fallen out of use as a discrete-choice approach, with most practitioners now favoring logit for such applications.

On the other hand, the relative benefits of hazard-rate versus logit-type models is still an area of active discussion among modelers. Shumway (2001) conducted a similar analysis to Lo (1986) but rather than comparing MDA and logit, the author compared logit models and hazard approaches. The paper, which we discuss in more detail later in this chapter, showed that the likelihood function for a multiperiod logit model can be equivalent to a discrete-time hazard specification assuming independence of observations in the discrete-choice setting, but that the hazard-rate specification was both more consistent (in the statistical sense) and less biased.

In practical terms (with some guidance from theory), it is generally not obvious which approach will yield the highest predictive power in any specific case. In our own testing, we have found the results to be quite close on the noisy data sets typically found at banks and other financial institutions, particularly with respect to private firms. Our assessment is that, all else equal, when an application requires a specific prediction horizon (e.g., one year), a properly specified and estimated discrete-choice model will tend to outperform slightly a similarly well-designed hazard-rate model, but that hazard-rate models will tend to exhibit higher predictive power at all other horizons than the specific-horizon discrete-choice model.

It is important to note, however, that the differences we observed were generally not large and, since all else is seldom equal, we find it most practically useful, absent meaningful differences in performance, to choose a modeling approach based on the desired application and the risk management or valuation framework within which the model will be used, rather than on simple performance statistics.

In this chapter, we will try to give a flavor of how these techniques can be used to build PD models from financial statement data. However, our focus is primarily on the nuts and bolts of how models and data must be adjusted to produce reasonable PD models, rather than on the various statistical theories underlying the estimation methods. For a more detailed exposition of the statistical theory and discussion of the variants of the techniques we discuss here, there are numerous detailed treatments (see, for example, Altman et al. 1981, McCullagh and Nelder 1989, Agresti 1990, Hastie and Tibshirani 1990, Greene 1998, Hosmer and Lemeshow 2001, or Kalbfleisch and Prentice 2002).

DISCRETE-CHOICE MODELS

A common approach to modeling default behavior is to use a framework based on discrete-choice (probit and logit) longitudinal models.[2] The dependent variable under such a specification is an indicator describing whether a firm experienced a default event within a certain time window. For example, a default model might produce estimates of one-year or five-year probabilities using such a framework. An advantage to this approach is that events over different horizons can be modeled separately, which allows for flexibility in the relative importance of the different variables for predicting default. (For example, liquidity may be more important for shorter horizons and leverage may be more important for longer horizons.)

Conceptually, the most general discrete-choice setting structures the problem of identifying default behavior as one in which we are trying to choose to which of a number of classes a particular firm belongs (in the case of default, the number is two: default and nondefault). In the case of MDA, this choice is done through classification, while in the case of logit or probit, it is done by assigning probabilities to each class. The most basic of these approaches is that of (non) linear discriminant analysis which takes as its objective the separation of two or more classes along (non) linear boundaries in one or more related factors. In the most basic case, the governing assumption is that the observations in the two subgroups in the population (i.e., surviving firms and defaulting firms) are normally distributed with different means of the factor in each subpopulation.

For example, in Figure 4.1, we show a hypothetical distribution of leverage ratios for a number of firms, some defaulted and some nondefaulted. Here we can see that the firms with lower leverage ratios have a lower probability of defaulting since the defaulting firms, shown here as x's, are clustered further to the right (higher leverage) than the nondefaulting firms, shown as o's. Under the normal assumption, the discriminant analysis approach searches for a value of leverage to separate defaulting from nondefaulting firms. In cases where more than one independent variable is involved, the line becomes a (hyper) surface that partitions the space of all variables to separate defaulting from nondefaulting firms. Unfortunately, the assumption of normality appears unrealistic in many settings. In addition, unlike alternative discrete-choice models that may be based in probabilistic frameworks, discriminant analysis does not provide as direct a probability

---

[2] There typically is one observation per firm per fiscal year and thus multiple observations per firm.

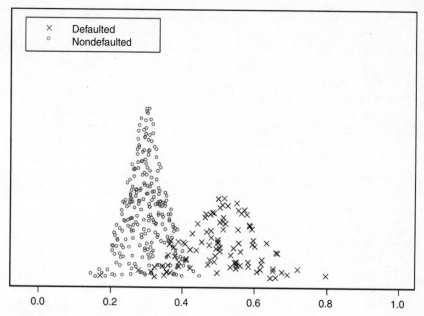

FIGURE 4.1 Hypothetical Example of Distribution of Firms Based on Leverage Ratio

estimate and thus may be less attractive for probabilistic applications and interpretations.[3]

In Figure 4.1, firms represented by x's default over the course of the following year while those represented by o's do not. It is useful to consider how we might assign probabilities of default to a firm, based only on the

---

[3] Note that as mentioned earlier, it can be shown using Bayes' rule that the linear discriminant function for firm i, $f(x_i)$, is itself also the *a posteriori* odds ratio of (in the case of default prediction) defaults versus nondefaults since the discriminant function,

$$f(x_i) = \ln\left(\frac{\pi_i}{(1 - \pi_i)}\right)$$

where π_i is the probability of default for firm i (Efron 1975), can be converted to a probability as

$$\pi_i = \frac{e^{f(x_i)}}{1 + e^{f(x_i)}}$$

Many modern statistical software packages provide class probability estimates for MDA analysis.

information available from Figure 4.1. First observe that in the figure, the only firm with a leverage ratio above 0.8 is a defaulting firm. We might posit that firms with leverage above 0.8 are very likely to default. Similarly, the only firms with leverage below 0.2 are nondefaulters, suggesting a low probability for firms with this leverage level.

Conceptually, we can think of the sample as being ordered by leverage ratio and then divided up into very small buckets so that each bucket contained only firms with identical leverage ratios. The probability of a default for a firm with a given leverage ratio is related to the percentage of firms that default in the bucket for that leverage ratio—that is, firms that have a leverage ratio at or below a specified level. It is simply the empirical frequency of default in each subpopulation (adjusted for the baseline default rate for the sample).

In Figure 4.2, we show this graphically. In this figure, the ascending line shows the cumulative percentage of defaulting firms that are captured by each leverage level. For example, about 80 percent of the defaulting firms had leverage ratios worse than 0.6.

In Figure 4.2 we follow the same convention as in Figure 4.1: firms represented by x's default over the course of the following year while those

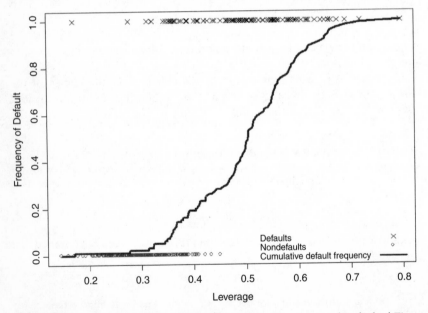

FIGURE 4.2 Hypothetical Example of Cumulative Frequency of Defaulted Firms, Sorted by Leverage Ratio

represented by o's do not. The line indicates the cumulative frequency of defaulted firms at each leverage level. In practice, there are many factors (leverage, liquidity, profitability, size, etc.) that we typically wish to include in a default model, so the simple two-dimensional representations we have been discussing breaks down. Fortunately, as the references at the beginning of the chapter suggest, there is a long history in the statistical literature of modeling discrete-choice probabilities in a multivariate setting and methods for estimating these models are widely available in commercial statistical software packages. In what follows, we focus on the logit-style discrete-choice models as these are most widely used in practice.

Under the logit specification, the dependent variable, y, is an indicator of whether a specific event took place over the horizon of interest. More formally, define an indicator of the status of the ith firm, at time t, y_{it} as:

$$y_{it} = \begin{cases} 0, & \text{if the firm has not defaulted by time } t \\ 1, & \text{if the firm has defaulted by time } t \end{cases}$$

The estimation problem then becomes one of estimating the probability that y_{it} is equal to 1.

Another way to consider this problem is as one in which there is a latent factor, y^*, that cannot be directly observed by the modeler. The latent variable is assumed to be less than zero if the firm is insolvent and greater than zero if it is solvent. (Under a structural framework (Chapter 3), this variable might, for example, be some measure of the distance to default.) In this setting,

$$y_{it} = 1(y_{i\tau}^* < 0), \tau < t$$

where $1(\cdot)$ is an indicator (or *heavy side*) function taking on the value 1 if the term inside the function is true and zero otherwise, and y^* is the latent factor.

The objective then becomes the estimate of the expected value of the outcome, $\hat{y}_i$, given a set of explanatory variables $\mathbf{x}_i$:

$$\hat{y}_i = E\left[y_i \,|\, \mathbf{x}_i\right]$$

(Note that for simplicity we have dropped the time subscript.) Said another way, we estimate the conditional mean of y_i, given the explanatory variables, $\mathbf{x}_i$:

$$\mu_i = E\left[y_i \,|\, \mathbf{x}_i\right]$$

Because y_i is binary, μ_i is bounded by zero and 1 and represents the probability of class membership in class 1.

The class of *generalized linear models* (GLM) (McCullagh and Nedler 1989) has developed for estimating μ_i. Given a matrix of predictors, $\mathbf{X}$, and a vector of outcomes, $\mathbf{y}$, the general form of the GLM specification is

$$G(\mu_i) = \boldsymbol{\beta}'\mathbf{x_i} + \varepsilon_i$$

where $G(\cdot)$ is a (typically nonlinear) *link function* that links the linear model on the right-hand side to μ_i, the expected value of the outcome. Here, if $\mathbf{X}$ is an $N \times k$ matrix describing k independent variables, observed on N firms, then $\mathbf{x_i}$ is a vector of independent variables for firm i, and ε_i is the firm-specific idiosyncratic error term. Since μ_i is an expectation, it is continuous, even though the outcome is binary. Under a suitable link function, therefore, $E[y_i]$ becomes a continuous probability taking on values in [0,1], which is what we are seeking. Note that this is simply a more formal multivariate formulation of the heuristic example we saw in Figure 4.2. Even more generally, these approaches are members of the class of *generalized additive models* (GAM), which can take on a variety of flexible, sometimes nonparametric forms through a suitable definition of the link function (Hastie and Tibshirani 1990) and transformations of both the independent and dependent variables.

In practice, though the specification is a general one. In PD estimation settings, one of two link functions are widely used: the logit (*logistic*) and probit (normal *probability*) links. These make logistic (binomial) and Gaussian assumptions, respectively, about the relationship of the probability of default to linear combinations of the independent variables. The probabilities produced by these two link functions are typically quite similar. The primary motivation historically for the choice of the logit over probit probably related more to the computational tractability of the logit model relative to the probit model in the years before cheap computing power was available.

The probit model is of the form:

$$\Phi^{-1}(\mu_i) = \boldsymbol{\beta}'\mathbf{x_i} + \varepsilon_i$$

where $\Phi(\cdot)$ is the inverse cumulative normal distribution function[4]

$$\Phi(z) = \int_{-\infty}^{-z} \frac{1}{\sqrt{2\pi}} e^{\left(-\frac{t^2}{2}\right)} dt$$

---

[4] Here we assume that z is standard normal with mean zero and variance one. If this is not the case the familiar form becomes $\Phi(z) = \int_{-\infty}^{-z} \frac{1}{\sqrt{2\pi}\sigma} e^{\left(-\frac{(t-\mu)^2}{2\sigma^2}\right)} dt$, where μ and σ are the mean and standard deviation of the distribution of z.

The logit specification replaces the harder to compute expression for Φ with the easier to compute

$$\text{logit}(z) = \log\left(\frac{z}{1-z}\right)$$

With the ready availability of both powerful desktop computers and mature statistical software applications, the choice of logit versus probit is most often one of aesthetics and preference since the historical issues of computation time have largely disappeared and since most models are calibrated after estimation, making the specific choice of the link less relevant.

Importantly, logit-type models are typically horizon-specific. It is not uncommon for a bank to implement, for example, a one-year PD model and a five-year PD model. These implementations allow modelers to include certain factors for short-term default prediction and others for longer-term prediction. Furthermore, the weights on even common factors can also vary from horizon to horizon.

However, this flexibility comes at a cost. Both the estimation and application of such models introduces challenges. From an estimation perspective, extending prediction to overlapping periods (e.g., a five-year period may overlap the previous five-year period by as many as four years) introduces additional correlation into the data set which must be addressed. From an implementation perspective, it is not trivial to create coherent term structures of default probabilities from two (cumulative) points on a curve. This is particularly true in the case when the models are calibrated individually to optimize predictive accuracy over a specific horizon, since, for example, the predicted five-year cumulative probability for a specific borrower could in principle be lower than the one-year predicted probability due to different calibrations and model specifications (Dwyer and Stein 2004). In reality, of course, the true (cumulative) PD for a longer time horizon cannot be lower than that of a shorter horizon.

EARLY DISCRETE-CHOICE MODELS: BEAVER (1966) AND ALTMAN (1968)

It is natural now for professional risk managers to think in terms of quantitative measures of firm performance such as leverage, profitability, liquidity, and so on, and of the statistical relationships that relate these to credit events. However, this approach to credit analysis is a relatively recent advent. While lenders often used rules of thumb to determine when and at what price to provide credit to borrowers, it is only in the past half century or so that this practice was examined rigorously in a formal statistical context.

Probably the first attempt to address this problem formally was in a 1966 *Empirical Research in Accounting* article by W. H. Beaver. In this article, the author set the stage for what would become the standard approach to developing and testing predictive models. Though by today's standards, the experimental design, data handling, and statistical techniques the author applied appear dated, the basic idea of parameterizing and testing a model using financial statements collected from a paired sample of healthy and defaulted firms is still in use today, as are ideas of the definition of a *cutoff* for separating healthy from distressed firms.[5]

Beaver's models were univariate: The author examined individual financial ratios five years prior to default and sought to distinguish defaulting from nondefaulting firms. In his study, he found that a single ratio, cash flow/total debt (CF/TD), provided significant discriminatory power in differentiating future defaulting from nondefaulting firms.

However, shortly after the publication of Beaver's article, Altman published what is still considered to be a seminal article on statistical default prediction in his 1968 *Journal of Finance* paper. This article was the first widely read analysis of how a practical *multivariate* statistical default prediction model might be constructed by applying what were, at that time, state-of-the-art statistical and computational techniques.

Altman's innovation was to expressly cast the default prediction problem as multidimensional and thus accommodate the influence of multiple factors on default. Altman reasoned that firms can fail due to a number of factors (excess leverage, diminished liquidity, declining profitability, etc.) rather than due to a single dominant cause. Instead of selecting a single dimension along which to evaluate a firm, various factors could be weighted to create a more balanced analysis. Doing this requires a means to derive optimal weights (with respect to the sample at hand), and Altman proposed multiple discriminant analysis (MDA) for this purpose.

As we mentioned earlier, in recent years MDA has fallen out of use in favor of more explicitly probabilistic frameworks such as logit or probit formulations. In addition, aspects of the sample selection and validation methodologies used by Altman have been replaced with more sophisticated formulations as research in this domain has advanced. Nonetheless, Altman's study and the various versions of his model, called the *Z-Score*, still

---

[5] As we discuss in Chapter 7, such cutoffs are suboptimal in realistic environments, and more sophisticated methods are available, also based on Type I and Type II error analysis and on the costs of these errors.

stand as prototypical in the default prediction literature, and the models are still used as benchmarks by many researchers.[6]

To this end, we present the broad strokes of Altman's model(s).

The basic Z-score was developed for use on publicly owned manufacturing firms and accommodated five factors: WC/TA, RE/TA, EBIT/TA, MVE/TD, Sales/TA. (See Appendix 4A for full specification of this and other versions of the Z-Score.)

Altman reported that in his sample a lower bound of $Z = 1.81$ captured all defaulting firms (below) and an upper bound of 2.99 captured all nondefaulting firms (above). However, between the two bounds both defaulting and nondefaulting firms could be found. Conceptually, this region is similar to the region shown in Figure 4.1 in which both x's and o's can be found. (Note that the original Z-score model did not include an intercept; users wishing to create a "zero/one" lending framework could recenter the function using either one (or both) of the thresholds.)

In his original study, Altman chose a paired sample design to estimate and test his model: 33 nondefaulting firms and 33 defaulting firms were selected, with the nondefaulters chosen to be "similar" to the corresponding defaulting firms in industry and size. The defaulted and nondefaulted firms were selected over a multiyear period, with each firm being used once. Firm financial statements were observed one year prior to default for the defaulting firms.

Altman has subsequently revised and extended the Z-Score along a number of dimensions, creating new versions for various industry and geographic segments as well as recalibrating the original model. More recently, an updated variant of the Z-score model has been published (Altman and Rijkin 2004). This model, which the authors characterize as "inspired by" Z-score, replaces raw values of some factors with log transformations of these factors; adds an age factor and a size factor, scaled by aggregate equity market size to the model; and reestimates the coefficients using a logit rather than an MDA framework, thus producing a probability estimate. In addition, Altman has proposed a calibration approach in which the Z-scores produced by MDA can be mapped, through ratings, to derive a PD (see "Calibrating to PDs" later in this chapter).

Altman and co-authors also developed versions of the Z-Score for private firms and for emerging markets and nonmanufacturing firms. The specifications of these models, as well as for the quasi Z-score, are given in Table 4 in the Appendix to this chapter.

---

[6] Variants of the Z-score are also available through various financial software vendors and terminal packages.

PAIRED SAMPLES

Default data are often limited since default events are rare. One way some modelers address this is to create a paired sample, as in Altman (1968), in which each defaulted firm is paired with another similar nondefaulted firm. From a practical perspective, a paired design can create problems in some settings because it is not obvious how to sample nondefaulted firms in a meaningful fashion. It is almost always the case that the quality of the nondefaulted firms will be much better than that of defaulters in most populations where default is related to financial factors. This is because most firms are not near default, so most firms will be generally healthy.

While some would argue that this is the point of statistical analysis, consider that in the worst case, the nondefaulted firms might be all of high quality (e.g., Aaa-rated entities) while the defaulters are all one year from failure. Clearly, it is easier to tell the difference between a Aaa and a defaulting firm than between a lower-quality firm and a defaulter. In fact, using the Aaa sample could lead to both unreliable parameter estimates and an overly optimistic evaluation of model performance.

This has practical implications. We find that industry lenders are typically fairly comfortable in their abilities to identify "clearly troubled" and "clearly solvent" borrowers. Rather, lenders seek insight into those firms whose financial profile is not obvious—those that may not be "clearly solvent" but may or may not still be far from default.

Interestingly, Altman has found suggestive evidence of this issue in subsequent validation of the original model. He reports (Altman and Hotchkiss 2006, p. 244; Altman and Rijkin 2004) that prior to recalibration, while Type I error was still acceptable, Type II error (nondefaulting firms classified as defaulting) was quite high, which would be consistent with the aforementioned scenario. However, as the authors of these studies observe, there had also been drift in the underlying financial profiles of firms which could also explain this behavior, so the evidence, while suggestive, is still inconclusive.

In addition to issues of estimation, for probabilistic frameworks such as logit and probit, the use of a matched sample increases the need for recalibration to population priors (see the end of this chapter).*

*Note that Altman did investigate this issue to some degree by selecting a number of unhealthy firms that had had negative profits in the recent past but that did not default. He reported that the majority of these were classified correctly as nonbankrupt.

MULTICOLLINEARITY

Factor selection in econometric modeling can be influenced by a number of objectives and constraints. Economic, intuition, data availability and statistical power are all important criteria that we discuss later in this chapter. However, the factor must also exhibit stable behavior in the model.

Statistical stability (and the soundness of statistical inferences based on a model) can be affected by *multicollinearity*. In its simplest form, multicollinearity arises when two factors are highly correlated and thus are competing to explain the same variance. When this happens, the two factors may have large coefficients with opposite signs. Thus, they largely cancel each other out, except for the small part of the variance that is unique to each. The result can be that small changes in one or the other of the factors can cause large changes in the output. In addition, the parameters associated with the collinear factors may be unstable across different data sets or time periods.

Of course, any linear combination of factors that is correlated with another factor is also collinear but in such cases, the correlation may not be immediately obvious. One way to explore the cause of such behavior, and to identify which potential factors may be driving it, is through the use of various statistical diagnostics for multicollinearity. Such tests include casual inspection of correlation matrices and the use of variance inflation factors (VIF).*

---

*The VIF is defined as $\frac{1}{1-R_i^2}$, where R_i^2 is the R^2 of the regression of the *i*th independent variable on all the other independent variables in the model. In general, a high VIF implies a large standard error for the parameter estimate associated with the variable. Chapter 7 on PD model validation discusses parameter stability and provides some heuristic guidelines for the interpretation and use of factor VIFs. While we do not discuss regression diagnostics in detail in this text, Chapter 7 does provide some strategies for identifying parameter instability in PD models and gives a number of references to more indepth treatments of this type of diagnostic for those readers wishing more detailed treatments of these statistics and their application.

In our own testing, the various versions of the Z-score's performance on large data sets is reasonably good. However, our experiments suggest that the models generally tend to result in lower performance than models specified for individual market segments and geographies and developed using larger data sets. Despite its early beginnings and its simple form, the Z-score has retained popularity among researchers and among some bankers as a simple, quick tool for screening and evaluating borrowers. It is ubiquitous in both the academic literature and the vernacular of industry. This ubiquity makes it also valuable as a benchmark for testing the performance of other models and a useful supplement to (though not a replacement for) more specialized models that an analyst may use to evaluate credit quality of an obligor.

HAZARD RATE (DURATION) MODELS

One clear shortcoming of the discrete-choice approach is that it does not provide a straightforward means of dealing with *censored* observations. Censorship in data can take many forms. Perhaps the most obvious form that arises often in the discrete-choice context, is the case of an incomplete observation period. For example, if default is defined as the occurrence of a credit event within, say, five years of the date of the observation, then observations that occur within five years of the end of the data collection period will not have had a full five years in which to express their tendency to default or not to default. The technical term for this is *right censoring*, and it is a common feature of many default data sets.

In a discrete-choice setting there is no obvious mechanism for dealing with censored data since a nondefault observation has an outcome whose meaning is different for censored versus uncensored observations. In the case of an uncensored record, the meaning is that the record was observed—for the full horizon of interest—for a full five years in our example (i.e., the noncensored observations have had a full five years in which to default, whereas censored observations have not). Excluding censored observations would clearly eliminate this problem, but doing so would also eliminate valuable information (it would also introduce bias) since most firms do not default, and a running theme in our credit modeling is the amount of effort we bring to bear in general to retain as much data as possible.

Within the discrete-choice framework there may be a number of alternative approaches to addressing censorship.[7] In cases where the horizon of

---

[7] Shumway (2001) proposes one alternative approach. Note, however, that this author's approach makes use of discrete-choice estimation techniques; this is done

interest is short, say one year, as it often is in practice, this specific type of censorship is less of an issue and the degree to which this choice matters in practice may be small. However, the development of credit portfolio management has put pressure on analysts to produce more sophisticated analyses of longer-dated exposures. More effort is necessary to address the challenges associated with estimating PDs at time horizons exceeding three years.

The example of the incomplete observation period we provide demonstrates intuitively where discrete-choice models may be misspecified. More generally, it may be natural not to think of a specific horizon by which firms either default or do not, but rather to think of *all* firms as defaulting at *some point* in the future if they do not otherwise exit the market (e.g., wind down, become acquired, etc.). In such a setting, it is reasonable to view data as containing firms that have defaulted and those that have *not yet* defaulted (in the observation period).

In this context, we might be more concerned with how long a firm survives prior to default than with whether the firm defaulted before a certain arbitrary point in time. Viewed this way, discrete-choice models do not take full advantage of the data since *every* observation provides some information about future default (or survival), and knowledge about when defaults (do not) happen within some observation period is key to extracting this additional information.

A second potential drawback of discrete-choice models is the manner in which they are applied in practice. It is typical for modelers to prepare a data set that is partitioned into *firm years*. A firm year is one unit of time in a firm's history. For example if we had only two firms, ABC and XYZ, in our data set, and we observed ABC for 20 years and XYZ for 12 years, we would have a total of 32 firm years—one observation for each firm for each year. It is attractive to partition firm histories in this fashion since many default prediction applications require a one-year horizon and firm years provide a natural means to make this representation. Using firm years also allows the inclusion of the most recent financial information in close proximity to the default outcome.

However, including multiple observations from the same firm implies that there is correlation between some of the observations in the sample since a firm's capital structure and business model do not vary randomly from year to year. On the contrary, the firm's capital structure and business model tend to maintain some degree of their previous structures in most

---

for convenience, and the underlying model is more appropriately characterized as a hazard rate or survival model.

WHEN DOES A FIRM YEAR START?

Setting up data for default modeling involves a number of subtle choices. What is the definition of *default*? Should a defaulted firm that reemerges from bankruptcy be included a second time in the data set and, if so, is it the same firm or another separate firm? And so on.

Perhaps one of the most fundamental questions in a discrete-choice setting is that of how to actually define a *firm year*.* At first blush, this seems straightforward: The year starts in January and ends in December.

However, after a bit of thought, it is less obvious. The key issue is that financial data for, say, fiscal year ending 2007 are actually reported much later. Typically, financial statements for December are reported in March or April of the following year. Thus, information about a firm's leverage in, say, 2005 would not be available until sometime in the first quarter of 2006.

The reason this matters is that when we build a model using firm years, we typically create a matrix with the independent variables in the columns and one observation for each firm for each year in the rows. We then create a vector of default indicators, one for each firm year, which take on values of zero or one depending on whether the firm defaulted, say, one year later. However, unless we control for the late arrival of the financial statement data each year, we will inadvertently peek into the future, using data that we would not actually have had at the time of the prediction.

For example, if we considered a firm's 2005 financial statements, and used this to predict default between January and December 2006, we would be ignoring the fact that the most recent financial data we would actually be able to evaluate in, say, January 2006, would still be the 2005 financial statements. Any model built using FYE 2005 data in January 2006 would appear more predictive than it would actually be in use, when advance notice of financial performance is not available.

To address this, we suggest that modelers use April or May as the start of the one-year period. This implies that the actual financial statement data being modeled is up to 18 months out of date. Unfortunately, this is also the reality.

---

*One can also define *firm quarters*, though this becomes more complicated due to issues of seasonality and annualization. However, the basic topic of defining the beginning of a firm quarter is similar to the one of defining the beginning of a firm year, discussed here.

years. In multiple firm-year settings, the estimates of standard errors and so on tend to be understated, which can make it difficult to make inferences about which factors are predictive (and in some cases even belong in the model). In the next section, we will see an alternative approach to dealing with this issue.

Finally, there is a growing body of finance literature and an ever-increasing set of tools that rely on associated specifications. In particular, the class of *reduced-form* default models discussed in Chapter 6, relating market observables to default processes, relies heavily on the related *default intensity* specification. A number of very useful techniques for estimating correlation and other quantities of interest similarly take advantage of the reduced-form framework.[8]

Duration specifications directly model the duration of survival (rather than the presence or absence of a default event), so that the dependent variable is taken as the *time until default*. If a firm has not yet defaulted, then the time to default is characterized as occurring at some point after the end of the period during which it could have been observed as having defaulted, but it is treated as a *censored* observation in the likelihood function.

Figure 4.3 shows a survival curve for hypothetical firms from their year of inception. The top curve shows firms that have leverage below 0.6, while the bottom curve shows those that have leverage above 0.6. The curves represent the rate at which firms survive at each point in time after inception. The steplike behavior of these curves is induced by defaults. When a firm defaults, the survival rate declines and that produces a step.

In the case of Figure 4.3, we see the survival rate over five years of hypothetical firms with leverage ratios either above 0.6 or below 0.6. As expected, the lower levered firms survive longer, on average, than the higher levered firms. The key distinction here is that rather than looking at firms in terms of those that default and those that do not, this formulation looks at the survival rate of firms or, conversely, the time to default. Note also that there are a large number of firms that do not default during the period of study, but that may default in the future. For example, even among the higher-risk population (leverage > 0.6) a little less than half still survive past year 5. These firms are characterized as *censored*.

In comparing Figures 4.2 and 4.3, we develop a sense for the philosophical differences in the frameworks. Figure 4.2 describes a process in which

---

[8] Later we describe approaches for translating hazard rates into PDs and vice versa; however, it can be cumbersome to do so, particularly for time horizons beyond the original horizon (e.g., one year).

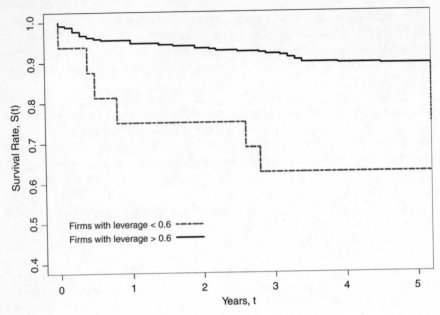

FIGURE 4.3 Hypothetical Example of Survival Curve for Firms

firms either do or do not default, at a specific horizon (in the case of the example, after one year). Firms can be ordered by a factor—in this case, leverage—and we seek to use that factor to assign a probability of default to the firm or to classify firms as future defaulters. Figure 4.3, in contrast, shows the expected survival rate, the time before default, for firms with different leverage profiles. In this case, no horizon is specified, and, in this specific example, we divide the population into two segments based on the factor leverage.[9]

But what happens if some of the firms drop out of the sample due to, say, a merger or acquisition? In this case, adjustments can be made to sample survival functions of the sort shown in Figure 4.3 to account for this censorship. This results in a particular form of survival function estimator called the Kaplan-Meier (sometimes called the *product limit*) estimator which provides a reasonable first pass at a survival function estimator, but which is also known to be potentially biased in finite samples.

---

[9] In both cases, realistic implementations extend the simple univariate case to multi-variate settings.

A number of parametric and nonparametric estimators have been developed to extend the simple hazard-rate modeling framework in various useful ways. While it is beyond the scope of this book to discuss them in detail (see Kalbfleisch and Prentice 2002), for exposition, we review one of the more popular approaches, the *Cox proportional hazards* model.

The hazard function, in the Cox proportional hazards model, is expressed as:

$$h_i(t) = h(t; \mathbf{x_i}) = h_0(t) \exp(\mathbf{x_i'} \boldsymbol{\beta})$$

and the corresponding survival function is

$$S(t; \mathbf{x_i}) = S_0(t)^{\exp(\mathbf{x_i'} \boldsymbol{\beta})}$$

where t is (survival) time

        $\mathbf{x_i}$ is a vector of covariates for the ith observation

        $\boldsymbol{\beta}$ is vector of parameters to be estimated.

In this setting, $h_i(t)$ is the *hazard rate* for firm i at time t: the instantaneous risk of firm i defaulting in period t conditional on having survived up until time t. Finally, the baseline survival function is given as

$$S_0(t) \equiv \exp\left(-\int_0^t h_0(u)du\right)$$

and represents the shape of the average survival rate across all firms, unconditional upon firm-specific attributes.[10]

Under this specification, the shape of the hazard function (and the corresponding survival function) is arbitrary, but the impact ratio of the hazards over time is constant: $h_i(t)/h_j(t) = \exp(\mathbf{x_i'} \boldsymbol{\beta})/\exp(\mathbf{x_j'} \boldsymbol{\beta})$.

Specifically, if

$$S(t_1; x + \Delta) = \lambda S(t_1; x)$$

then

$$S(t; x + \Delta) = \lambda S(t; x)$$

---

[10] See for example Greene (1993), Chapter 20.

ESTIMATING A BASELINE HAZARD FUNCTION: $h_0(t)$

In practice, a fair amount of effort goes into estimating the baseline hazard rate function, $h_0(t)$. Both the level and shape of this function affect how default rates may change over time as firms age. The remaining job of the $h_i(t)$ function is to then adjust upward or downward the relative risk of a specific firm i based on its characteristics, x_i. A common approach to estimating this function uses some form of nonparametric density estimation. For example, we have had good luck using *loess* smoothing (see, for example, Simonoff 1998).

For situations where there is a specific known structure, cubic splines may be more effective since the placement of the splines allows for finer control over the shape of the baseline. For example, when modeling prepayment rates of retail mortgages, the structure of the mortgage dictates to a large degree the general shape of the baseline. A 5/25 loan that offers a low fixed rate for five years and then converts to an often higher floating-rate mortgage would typically demonstrate a spike in prepayments in year five as some mortgage holders refinance their mortgages at the expiration of the fixed-rate period. (There may be a spike in the beginning of this period as well, due to credit curing as first-time borrowers establish credit histories.) In such situations we can think of the model as a semiparametric hazard model with no parametric assumptions about the shape of the baseline hazard rate time distribution.

Making no distributional assumption about the shape of the baseline provides a high degree of flexibility. This differs from simpler, but more constrained, parametric survival models (Weibull, loglogistic, lognormal, etc.). The use of nonparametrics avoids model misspecification and provides much greater control over the baseline hazard shape, which can allow a model to capture the observed peaks and troughs in the empirical distributions more accurately; however, it also increases the chances of overfitting the data, so care is warranted. Importantly, different authors have come to differing conclusions about the degree to which there is a time component in the corporate default behavior and thus whether the baseline is constant.

for all t. Said another way, under this formulation, there is an average hazard rate across all firms that varies with firm age. A particular firm's hazard rate is increased or decreased based on the firm-specific attributes, but the shape of the hazard rate for the firm does not change.

Duration models can be specified to admit either constant covariates or time-varying covariates. Over time several of the independent variables are likely to change—return on assets (ROA) and leverage, for example. Survival modeling with time-varying covariates explicitly incorporates these changes as a function of time so that hazard function becomes a function of both t and the values of the independent variables at time t, $\mathbf{x}_{it}$:

$$h_i(t) = h(t; \mathbf{x}_{it}) = h_0(t) \exp(\mathbf{x}'_{it}\boldsymbol{\beta})$$

In an idealized environment, time-varying covariates would seem to be the most appropriate way to model a firm's hazard function. The problem is that in a forecasting model, the firm's survival function now depends on both t and the evolution of the covariates. In many practical settings, specifying the time-varying covariates is not feasible since (1) there are typically a moderately large set of covariates (e.g., 10 to 15); (2) these covariates are sometimes correlated; and (3) time series of the covariates are typically short.[11]

Many modelers in practice assume constant covariates. However, this restriction is at odds with the conventional wisdom that the best credits tend to become worse credits over time (i.e., they have increasing hazard functions) and that the worst credits tend to become better over time (i.e., they have decreasing hazard functions) if they do not default.[12]

---

[11] For example, it would be unusual in the private credit risk setting to have more than 10 year-end financial statements and quarterly financial statements. In contrast, Duffie and Wang (2004) explicitly model the evolution of covariates when estimating the term structure of bankruptcies for public firms. These authors work with two covariates: U.S. personal income growth and a firm's distance to default. They collect quarterly observations from 1971 to 2001. Therefore, in their setting, the problem of modeling the evolution of covariates is much more tractable given the long history and low-dimensional nature of the covariates.

[12] For example, see the empirical analysis in Bohn (2000b). An additional attribute of the constant covariate hazard rate formulation is that in some cases it permits more efficient (in terms of computing) use of the data as each firm is included in the data set only once (rather than for multiple firm years, as is typical in the case of the discrete-choice setting). This feature can be particularly useful when modeling very large data sets such as are encountered in retail credit applications.

Another simplification (sometimes imposed due to data restrictions) is to require that the same factors be used at all horizons. In some cases, this may be counterintuitive. One example is the case of measures of liquidity, which we would expect to be more useful in predicting default over near-term horizons than over longer ones. When data permit, duration models can be estimated to allow for horizon-dependent parameters. However, in many cases involving corporate credit risk, practical data limitations preclude this approach for private firm default prediction.

EXAMPLE OF A HAZARD-RATE FRAMEWORK FOR PREDICTING DEFAULT: SHUMWAY (2001)

It is instructive to consider one of the better-known applications of hazard-rate models to corporate credit default prediction. In 2001, Tyler Shumway published an article advocating the use of survival models over a certain type of discrete-choice model. In particular, Shumway suggested that logit-type models could be biased and inconsistent in certain settings. Shumway criticized the practice of estimating such models based on paired samples of defaulted and nondefaulted firms one year before default. (Altman's paired sample would be an instance of this approach.) He called such models "static" and his arguments for the alternative approach center around the statistical properties of the estimators.

Shumway shows that under reasonable assumptions, this class of discrete-choice models will produce biased estimates since they ignore the periods prior to default when a defaulting firm did not default but may have had a similar financial profile. In a stylized example, the author shows that parameter estimates of a type of mean in a simple model will be biased upward (due to the exclusion from the denominator of the prior healthy periods of a defaulting firm). The author goes on to show a more elaborate stylized example in which the estimator can also be shown to be statistically inconsistent and, furthermore, that significance tests on variables included in the discrete-choice model may also be incorrect. This in turn implies that inferences based on measures of significance (e.g., factor selection based on chi-squared statistics) will be misleading.

The author implements both a static discrete-choice and several hazard-rate models and demonstrates not only that the hazard-rate models perform better out of sample than their discrete-choice counterparts, but also that many of the factors selected as significant in the discrete-choice framework do not show up as significant in the hazard-rate setting.

It is important to note that Shumway's objections to discrete-choice models are based on a key assumption that is typically not borne out in practice. In characterizing discrete-choice models, he assumes that model builders use one observation per firm, similar to the design of early academic studies. As such, significant information is lost since many firms that do not default in a specific year will contain information about default dynamics years before default. However, in practice, as we have already discussed, most professionals adopt the firm-year approach, which largely avoids this issue.

In fact, Shumway is aware of this. He discusses it and provides examples from the literature of researchers who actually use the firm-year approach within a discrete-choice setting. However, the use of multiple observations from the same firm induces a different concern: correlation in the data. As such, the variance of the discrete-choice models will still be inflated due to this correlation. To address this problem, the author suggests a modification to the chi-square statistics typically produced by logit software that involves adjusting each statistic by dividing it by the average number of firm years per firm in the sample. The rationale for doing this is that in the survival setting, the unit of observation is the firm's observed *lifetime* or nondefault spell, of which there is one for each firm in the data, rather than the firm-year.

This seems reasonable to do, and Shumway reports that this adjustment yields similar results to the test statistics produced by a proportional hazard estimation routine. Note, however, that in situations where the data is fairly complete, this should not change the rank preference for factors in a model. While the absolute significance levels will come down, all test statistics will be adjusted downward monotonically, provided the same data is used to test each model and the same number of observations are used in each case.

Interestingly, Shumway does not actually use a survival estimation routine, but rather adapts a logit framework by including a function of firm age (in the role of a baseline), including one observation for each firm year, and modifying the test statistics as previously discussed. He proposes that this approach is both easier to estimate than some classes of survival functions (particularly those involving time-varying covariates) and more flexible than some classes of parametric survival model. He provides a mathematical proof of the correspondence between his specification and the hazard-rate specification for the simple binary case.

While the author estimates a number of models, they are all of the basic form

$$h_i(t) = \frac{1}{1 + e^{x_i' \beta}}$$

where in some cases $ln(t)$ is included among the x_i. However, Shumway reported not finding age to be a significant factor, suggesting little or no duration dependence in his data. Note that this result is at variance in some sense with other published research (Keenan 1999) showing that newly issued debt tends to have low hazard rates initially which increase over time. Debt seasoning, while not strictly the same as firm age, is related.

The author estimates a number of other models, details of which are given in the Appendix to this chapter.

While Shumway's approach is instructive, his criticism is somewhat misdirected as even at the time of publication, most practitioners and academics no longer used the static framework, preferring instead the firm-year approach. (One reason for this is the need to increase the number of observations to improve estimation—in other words, to avoid the loss of information the author discusses as inherent in using only one observation per firm.) As a result, many of the comparisons he presents, while interesting, may not be as relevant to practitioners. That said, the proposed adjustment to model variance estimates are helpful, as is the characterization of multiperiod logit models as hazard-rate models.

HAZARD RATES VERSUS DISCRETE CHOICE

It is sometimes interesting to ask which specification, discrete-choice or hazard rate, performs better.[13] Given the manner in which discrete-choice models are typically built in industry, particularly with regards to the use of firm years in discrete-choice settings, the distinction between discrete-choice and hazard-rate frameworks may be less mathematical and more pedagogical. For example, in this section we discuss a series of informal tests we conducted by using a database of U.S. private company financials to estimate default prediction models using both approaches and keeping the set of independent variables identical.[14] We compared a Cox model with a probit model and examined predictive power.

We estimated a Cox proportional hazard model and compared the results to those obtained using a probit specification estimated at three

---

[13] This section is based on unpublished work done with D. Dwyer.

[14] Note that this imposes constraints on both models. For the discrete-choice model, it implies that only one set of common factors can be selected at all horizons. For the hazard-rate model, it implies that alternative factors to those selected by the discrete-choice approach cannot be used.

different time horizons (defaults within one, three, and five years). We examined model power (see Chapter 7) as the performance criterion of interest and, since power and rank order are directly related, we also examined the rank correlation of each model with the others.

Not surprisingly, the rank correlations were very high: The correlation of the duration model and the probit models was 0.98 to 0.99 in all cases. The predictive power was similarly close. At a given horizon (e.g., one year), a discrete-choice model optimized for that specific horizon tended to outperform the hazard-rate model ever so slightly. However, in many cases the discrete-choice model optimized for one horizon did not perform as well at an alternative horizon as the hazard-rate model.

We organized the data in this experiment into firm years, so we would not actually expect much of a difference in the model behavior since, as noted in Shumway (2001), with the exception of the baseline (age) factor and inflated significance, these models' specifications are quite similar. However, since in practice most modelers use the firm-year specification, in comparing this to a hazard-rate approach, we were comparing the likely options that a modeler would consider.[15]

PRACTICAL APPLICATIONS: FALKENSTEIN ET AL. (2000) AND DWYER AND STEIN (2004)

A practical commercial implementation of an econometric model was introduced by Moody's in 2000 for modeling private firm default risk in the United States. The model, called RiskCalc (Falkenstein et al. 2000), has since been expanded and revised to accommodate more sophisticated modeling techniques (Dwyer and Stein 2004) and to provide analytics for non-U.S. firms. At the time of this writing, RiskCalc enjoys use at about 300 banks globally and the RiskCalc network of models provides coverage for borrowers in countries comprising approximately 80 percent of the world's GDP.

The RiskCalc models apply a simple but powerful modeling framework that addresses certain problems inherent in private firm middle-market data.

---

[15] It is important to note, however, that we did not select factors independently for each model in this experiment. Had we done so, it might have been the case that some factors selected by the discrete-choice model would not have been selected by the hazard-rate model, and vice versa.

The approach is most similar to that of GAMs, but offers some important differences.

The fundamental steps of the modeling process involve:

- Transformation (nonparametric) of specific variables into density estimates.
- Estimation of default probabilities using the transformed predictors in a logit framework.
- Calibration of the estimated probabilities using a nonparametric mapping. In the case of the newer RiskCalc models described in Dwyer and Stein (2004), a substep of the calibration process involves adjusting estimates for industry and credit cycle effects based on information from equity markets (suitably transformed through a structural model of default as described in Chapter 3).
- Extensive validation of out-of-sample-out-of-time power and calibration, parameter stability, model robustness, and so on. This process is discussed in more detail in Chapter 7.

Perhaps the greatest innovation to corporate credit modeling described in Falkenstein et al. (2000) was the use of transformations to address issues of data noise and nonlinearity between a factor's value and its effect on PD. While this technique had been used in consumer modeling prior to its introduction, and while a rich statistics literature (Hastie and Tibshirani 1990) existed well before the publication of Falkenstein, et al. it does not appear that these techniques had been applied widely for modeling corporate credit.

One reason for this may have been that such approaches, which we describe in a bit more detail in a moment, can be data intensive and most banks historically have not had extensive data sets on loan defaults. The original RiskCalc model was based on a data set that had been pooled from a number of banks and thus provided better data density than had been available in the past. This larger data set permitted the application of more data-driven statistical techniques. This point highlights that having more data in credit expands the number of models and techniques available for estimation. That is one reason that large retail portfolios such as credit cards and consumer loans can often be more easily modeled than smaller portfolios of nontraded corporate borrowers. However, more data will almost always mean more noise. One of the challenges in this type of modeling problem is to draw on or develop robust processes and techniques to deal with the noise found in most credit data samples.

The basic approach to the transformation step in the modeling process involves

* Calculating quantiles of the distribution.
* Estimating the default rate of each quantile.
* Estimating a smooth function of the default rates to derive a transformation function.

For example, say we wished to include a liquidity ratio in the model, and there were N observations in the database. To transform this variable, we would:

* Sort all firms by leverage and create k buckets, each having N/k firms. (The first bucket would have the least liquid N/k firms in the list and the kth bucket would have the most liquid N/k firms.)
* Calculate the number of defaulting firms in each bucket and divide this by N/k to obtain the default rate in each bucket.
* Estimate a (nonlinear) curve that maps quantiles to their default rates and record the value of liquidity associated with each quantile. (If the first N/k firms had liquidity ranging from 0.001 to 0.02, the zero quantile would have the lower bound of 0.001 and the first quantile would have the lower bound of 0.02).

Figure 4.4 provides an example of one such transformation. Note how the transformation function is itself only an estimate of the default rates at each quantile. This is due in part to sampling noise, but also due to the fact that the factor is not a perfect predictor of default and thus some nonmonotonicity is introduced.

The original RiskCalc model described in Falkenstein et al. (2000) used a Hodrick-Prescott filter to estimate the transformation, but later versions replaced this with nonparametric estimators such as loess (Cleveland and Devlin 1988), which turn out to be more flexible and have better statistical properties.

Once the transformation function is estimated, modeling data are then converted to transformed values using the transformation function and interpolation at the quantile level.

If $T(q)$ is the transformation function, and b_i and b_{i+1} are the values of the quantiles q_i and q_{i+1}, respectively, then the interpolation can be made for values of the variable that fall between the two quantiles by estimating

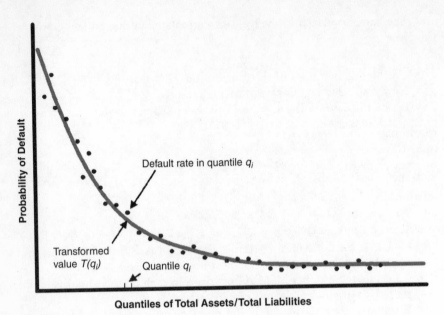

FIGURE 4.4   Example of a Nonparametric Transformation

an interpolated quantile, q^*, as:

$$q^* = q_i + \frac{x - b_i}{b_{i+1} - b_i} [(q_{i+1} - q_i)]$$

or, in the case of k evenly spaced quantiles,

$$q^* = q_i + \frac{x - b_i}{b_{i+1} - b_i} \frac{1}{k}$$

In this example, the transformed value of liquidity for a firm with liquidity of 0.015 would fall between the zero bucket and the first bucket. If there were 100 buckets, the probability of default associated with liquidity of 0.015 would be found by first computing

$$q^* = 0.0 + \frac{0.015 - 0.001}{0.02 - 0.001} \frac{1}{100} = 0.00737$$

and then calculating the probability of default associated with that value using the transformation $T(0.00737)$.

It is reasonable to ask at this point why transformations are useful here. The answer hinges on two main challenges in modeling financial data, particularly for private firms: noise and nonlinearity. Private firm data tend to be incomplete, unaudited, or inaccurate for some firms.[16] From a statistical perspective, this increases the observational error in the data and can lead to estimation problems, particularly in the case of extreme outliers. The transformation process tends to reduce model susceptibility to such issues by creating boundaries between which transformed data fall.

In addition, we observe that most financial variables exhibit nonlinear relationships to default—that is, a variable influences the PD differently in different ranges of the variable. These relationships are generally characterized by monotonic behavior (e.g., higher leverage is always worse than lower leverage). However, this is not true in all cases, particularly with respect to growth- and return-related variables such as sales growth or ROA. This makes intuitive sense. While very low growth is suggestive of a weak business model, very high growth can also be a warning sign as firms that grow too quickly sometimes have trouble managing or sustaining this growth. Transformations of the sort just described capture this nonmonotonicity easily.

Note that in principle, appropriate transcendental or polynomial transformations of each factor could be found that address the issues of nonlinearity. However, searching for these transformations is not simple. The nonparametric form of the transformations we discuss makes them practically attractive as they are flexible and general enough to work in a wide variety of settings.

Also observe that the transformations are nonparametric in two ways. First, the mapping of factors into quantiles naturally stretches and compresses regions of the variable space in proportion to the distribution of the variable in the data set. For example, if the second bucket in the preceding example ranged from 0.02 to 0.025, and the next ranged from 0.025 to 0.027, the mapping would be stretching the data out across the second two buckets, with ranges of 0.005 and 0.002, respectively, and compressing the data in the first bucket with a range of 0.019 $(= 0.02 - 0.001)$. The second way in which the mapping is nonparametric is that the actual function itself that maps quantiles into default rates is derived using nonparametric smoothing techniques such as loess.

---

[16] In our own work, for example, we have seen data on borrowers that were inconsistent from year to year, incomplete, and, in at least one case, heard a colleague recall a financial statement as reported "orally."

In summary, the transformations are useful in that they control for noise in the data and capture nonlinearity in the data without requiring explicit functional or parametric assumptions.

PRACTICAL UNIVARIATE TRANSFORMATIONS

Mechanical algorithms (e.g., loess) for fitting curves to quantile default rates can sometimes exhibit inconvenient behavior in practice. This typically relates to the shape of the curve with respect to the underlying quantile probabilities of default. For example, it is not uncommon for a curve to be bumpy or slightly nonmonotonic in places. It is also not unusual for a curve to fit one portion of the default rates well, but to miss the end sections by over- or underestimating the levels of default probability. Many of these effects are artifacts of the methods used to fit the transformations. Most nonparametric techniques incorporate various smoothing parameters (e.g., degrees of freedom, window width, etc.). Unfortunately, parameter settings that work well for one section of the space may not work well in other regions. The most sophisticated techniques incorporate very flexible parameterizations. However, in many cases, theory for optimal parameter selection is still evolving and parameter choice can still be an empirical issue.

Though perhaps aesthetically distasteful, we have found that in some cases an expedient and often more accurate approach to smoothing bins is simply to select a parameter that fits most of the curve well, to estimate the transformation, and then to manually smooth (through interpolation) the region that is not well captured by the technique. While this is somewhat less scientific than, say, parameter selection through cross validation, it is probably no more arbitrary, as the trade-off between smoothness and accuracy often comes down to judgment.

This may also be the reason that we have found in our own experiments that fully automated algorithms for fitting GAMs produce results that are less robust than those produced using the three-step procedure just described. While optimal fitting parameters or more sophisticated estimation algorithms could be used to achieve better results when using automated techniques, our own sense is that modelers' efforts are best spent thinking about the economic intuition of the models rather than designing progressively more elaborate statistical algorithms.

In the RiskCalc framework, once transformations are completed for all candidate variables, factor selection is done. As it turns out, in addition to making modeling more straightforward, the transformations themselves provide substantial insight and can be useful in guiding variable selection as well. In general, variables that contain substantial information on default will have the property that a small change in their value results in a big change in default probability. Thus, the slope of the transformations of these variables will be large. When evaluating two factors that describe similar behavior (e.g., Total Debt/Total Assets versus Total Liabilities/Total Assets), all else equal, we should prefer the one that has more information about default. We provide recommendations for factor selection later in this chapter.

There is a direct mathematical relationship between power and the transformation of a factor into a default curve, and, as a result, transformations can be used to examine the univariate predictive power of one factor versus another. Later versions of RiskCalc exploited this relationship to facilitate variable selection.[17] For the purposes of understanding the variable selection process in the RiskCalc models, it is useful to observe that transformed variables can be used to determine univariate predictive power directly, by converting these measures to summary statistics such as accuracy ratios or the area under the curve (AUC) of an ROC curve. (See Chapter 7 for more discussion of model validation techniques.)

The estimation step of the RiskCalc modeling process proceeds as described in the discrete-choice section of this chapter. Candidate models are estimated using the candidate transformed variables and are evaluated for their parameter stability and predictive power. Note that it is often the case that the best univariate predictors do not end up in the final model. This is because it is common for factors that show up as important when examined alone drop out of a model in the presence of other factors. One example of this that we have encountered from time to time relates to the use of age as a predictive factor, which sometimes drops out in the presence of size since the two are highly correlated. Since size is typically less prone to observation error than age (which may be stated differently for different firms, particularly in situations where mergers, name changes, etc., have taken place), size is often preferred.

During this phase of model development, the focus is primarily on predictive power, rather than on the calibration of the model. This is for two

---

[17] It can also be shown that there is a direct connection between power and the economic value of a model (Stein 2005). We explore this association more fully in Chapter 7.

SELECTING FACTORS FOR DEFAULT MODELS

In general, the problem of factor selection tends to be solved through a combination of heuristic and empirical processes. While most credit analysts can produce long lists of candidate variables, in environments where data is limited, a structured approach to factor selection is key to avoiding overfitting.

In our own work, we tend to favor clustering factors into broad classes and then evaluating candidate factors within each class in a univariate context before assessing a variable's performance in a multivariate setting. For example, in the case of corporate default prediction (for nonfinancial institutions), we might consider broad clusters of size, leverage, liquidity, and profitability, as well as other measures of financial robustness. Within leverage, we might consider factors such as total liabilities/total assets, total debt/total equity, total adjusted debt/total assets, and so on. Because each of these factors is likely to be correlated with the others in its cluster (both due to common components such as total assets and due to the capital structure and business model of the firm, as in the case of adjusted debt and total debt for firms that do not lease or rent heavily), including many factors from a single category can result in higher collinearity in model.

In evaluating factors, we use a combination of uni- and multivariate techniques. We favor exploratory data analysis in which, for example, the univariate predictive power of a single factor, the shape of the density estimate for this factor, and the variance inflation factor (VIF) of this factor and others are examined. We seek to balance economic intuition with univariate predictive power. Another advantage of this approach is that if a favorite factor in a category turns out to have either statistical or practical problems due to its availability or interaction with other factors, we can substitute an alternative to represent a similar concept from the same category.

reasons. First, as there is a calibration phase in the final step, the absolute levels of the probabilities are less important than their ordinal rank since the calibration creates a mapping from theoretical logit probabilities to empirical probabilities. More importantly, it is far more difficult to achieve high power in a model than it is to calibrate a powerful model once it is estimated.

The final stage, calibration, involves two steps, the first being another transformation of the sort already described, though in this case the variable being transformed is the default probability predicted by the final logit model. This stage involves creating a mapping from the logit probabilities to empirical probabilities in the same manner we discussed for the univariate transformations. The second stage involves adjusting empirical probabilities to reflect differences between the sample default rate and the population default rate that can arise since the sample data is typically not complete and may suffer from systematic censorship of various kinds. We discuss this calibration process in detail in the next section.

It is reasonable to ask why a calibration phase is needed. The discrete-choice methods we have discussed are designed to produce optimal (in a maximum likelihood sense) estimates of probabilities, given the available data. However, our experience is that these estimates rely on distributional assumptions that are typically not met in practice. Though logit and pro-bit models tend to assign probabilities that are generally *ordered* correctly (higher model probabilities correspond to higher empirical probabilities), a nonparametric calibration captures better the empirical default behavior associated with the modeled levels.

In later versions of the RiskCalc models, an additional feature of the calibration was the use of industry-specific adjustments that serve to increase or decrease the probability estimates of the model based on the state of the economic cycle. As a proxy for the economic cycle, the authors use an industry-specific index of aggregate distance to default (see Chapter 3). Deviations from this index indicate high and low points in the credit cycle. This index is incorporated into the estimate of the default probability in the calibration phase and serves to raise or lower the default probability itself rather than the precalibrated model score.

CALIBRATING ECONOMETRIC MODELS

As we have emphasized in a number of sections throughout this book, the first objective of a credit modeler is typically on building models with a high degree of predictive power. With powerful models, we can distinguish the good credits from the bad credits. Remember that a poorly calibrated PD model can still be useful for ranking obligors as long as the model has predictive power.

While a powerful model may be sufficient for simple ad hoc credit analysis, portfolio management requires something more: a well-calibrated model. Calibration leads us to models that can work well in portfolio risk estimation and valuation. In simple terms, a well-calibrated PD model is one in which the estimated PD is an unbiased estimate of the actual PD. In addition to calibrating models to PDs, it is sometimes desirable to map model output to ratings of various sorts either for ease of communication within a bank or to smooth out PD volatility. We discuss calibration to ratings later in this section. We first turn to the question of calibration of PDs, which has application not only for the models discussed in this chapter, but for all PD models.

CALIBRATING TO PDs

Calibration is the practice of shifting a model's predicted probabilities to make them agree with actual outcomes. The goal is to adjust the model's predicted PDs to match actual default rates as closely as possible.

For example, if there were two models, A and B, that each predicted the two rating classes "Good" and "Bad," and the predicted probability of default for A's "Bad" class were 5 percent while the predicted probability of default for B's "Bad" class were 20 percent, we might examine these probabilities to determine how well they matched actual default rates. If we looked at the actual default rates of the portfolios and found that 20 percent of B's "Bad" rated loans defaulted while 1 percent of A's did, B would have the more accurate probabilities since its predicted default rate of 20 percent closely matches the observed default rate of 20 percent, while A's predicted default rate of 5 percent is very different than the observed rate of 1 percent.

While most econometric methods in use today (for example, logit or probit) for default prediction produce natural probability estimates, most practitioners find it necessary to further calibrate these probabilities. Why should this be so?

First, the credit data, particularly default data, tends not to follow regular distributions. As such, the assumptions underlying many econometric approaches are often not met in practice. However, it is still often the case that the rank ordering of the model probabilities is highly correlated with the rank ordering of the empirical probabilities. Thus, if the mapping from the ranking to probabilities can be transformed, while still preserving the ranking, the model output will better reflect the correct probabilities.

The second reason calibration is often necessary is that it is typically the case that the data in the development sample are not fully representative of the population on which the model will be used. It is not uncommon for the base rates (the average default rate) to be different in the development sample due to data gathering and data processing constraints. Examples where this heterogeneity in data gathering is particularly acute include middle-market data from banks, data from institutions in which financial statements and loan performance data are stored in different systems, or in settings where workout groups and servicing groups are in different locations in the organization. (As we just discussed, in extreme cases, modelers use a paired sample that matches one default with one nondefault which, by construction, has a different sample default rate than the target population.) As a result, the default rate in the samples may differ from the overall population, and this in turn will cause the predicted probabilities to be consistently lower or higher than what they should be given a well-calibrated estimate.

To address these two issues, calibration typically involves two steps. The first requires mapping a model score to an empirical probability of default using historical data. For example, the model outputs might be bucketed by score and the default rates for each score calculated using an historical database. The second step entails adjusting for the difference between the default rate in the historical database and the actual default rate (in technical terms, the probability must be adjusted to reflect the true prior distribution).

We begin with the task of mapping model probabilities into empirical probabilities when the assumptions of the econometric model break down. In such situations, simple calibration using nonparametric density estimation techniques can be an effective means of improving the agreement between model predictions and actual default probabilities. This sort of calibration typically proceeds identically to the transformation step discussed in the earlier section on the RiskCalc model. In this case, however, rather than using a financial variable as input to the transformation, the *output* of the probability model (a theoretical probability estimate from a logit model perhaps) is used as input. Thus, for example, a theoretical probability of default of 0.50bps might get mapped to a PD of 105bps. The flexible form of the density estimation approach accommodates nonlinearity in the relationship between the probability estimates produced as output by a model and the empirical default frequencies associated with those outputs. Of course, the cost of this better agreement is more complexity in the model and more difficulty in analyzing driving factors. For this reason, calibration is generally performed after the model is fit rather than in parallel with this process. The details of this type of calibration follow those given in the univariate transformation discussion in the previous section.

Estimating the Prior Probabilities

The second component of calibration involves adjusting the probability produced as raw output by a model to reflect differences in baseline probabilities between the development sample and the target population. This is required in cases where the data set is incomplete in some fashion.

There are many reasons this can arise. For example, the development data set will be incomplete if it is from a vendor that only records bankruptcies but not other forms of default, or it could result from lost historical records for smaller firms that tended not to get archived in a bank. In any event, the difference in incidence rates between the sample and the true population will affect all aspects of the level estimation for the PD model, including the nonparametric calibration described in the previous section.

To gain some intuition for this process, consider a standard example from Bayesian analysis. Though the example does not exactly correspond to the calibration situation, there is enough similarity to provide good insight. Imagine there is a deadly disease "insolventitis" for which your doctor is giving you a test. Fortunately insolventitis is rare and only about 0.01 percent of the population contracts it. Being quantitatively minded, you ask your doctor for some background on the disease and the test. She informs you that the test that she will administer is very reliable: If a patient has the virus, the test will be positive 99.9 percent of the time; and if the patient does not have the disease, the test will be negative 99.9 percent of the time. You make an appointment to see your doctor, take the test and await the results.

A week later the results come back. Your test result is positive. What is the probability you have the disease?

If the base prevalence rate of insolventitis were 0.01 percent in the general population, the odds are pretty good that you do *not* have the disease. To see this, consider Figure 4.5. If your doctor gave the test to 100,000 people, the very accurate test would identify the 10 (0.01% × 100,000) who actually had the disease, since 99.9 percent of 10 is approximately 10. But of the remaining 99,990 who did not, the test would only identify 99,890 (99.9% × 99,890) as not having the disease and so 100 (99,990 − 99,890) would be falsely told they have the disease. In total, 110 people

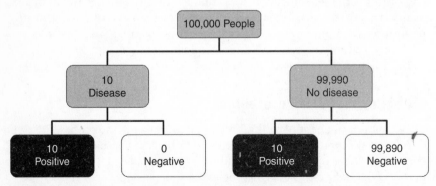

FIGURE 4.5   Schematic of Accuracy of Diagnostic Test

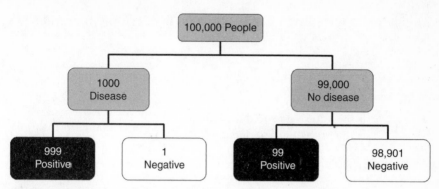

FIGURE 4.6 Schematic of Accuracy of Diagnostic Test with Different Prevalence Rate

would have tested positive, while only 10 would actually have the disease. So the odds of actually having the disease if you tested positive would be only about 9 percent (10/110). Figure 4.5 shows this all graphically.

Now what would your prospects be if the prevalence rate of insolventitis were 1 percent rather than 0.01 percent? In this case the probability that you actually had the disease, having tested positive, would be about 91 percent, or about 10 times higher. (See Figure 4.6.) This is the outcome most people expect when getting a positive result. However it is sometimes surprising to nonmathematicians (and even medical professionals; see Gigerenzer 2003 for a discussion) that the probability of actually having a disease can be so sensitive to the level of the base rate.

Though the situation with PD models is a bit different and the magnitudes of base rate differences and model accuracy can be quite different than in this medical example, the same basic concepts apply. If a model is not calibrated to the correct base default rate, the PDs it generates will be too high or too low.[18] Thus, a recalibration is needed to correct for this.

One simple approach to this calibration is to net out the original base rate used in building the model and then to multiply through by the correct

---

[18] This could in principle be seen as a question of not having enough information to characterize a PD prediction. It might be the case, for example, that a modeler has a sample that is not complete or chooses to use only a subset of the data. In this case, the mean default rate of the sample may not equal the mean default rate of the population due to the missing information. As it turns out, this is quite often the case in practice, particularly for private firm modeling, so this second stage of calibration is typically useful. In cases where a modeler has complete data on both borrowers and defaulters, this second stage is redundant as the true and base rates are equal.

baseline probability (Falkenstein et al. 2000). In this setting, the revised PD becomes:

$$p_i^* = \frac{\pi_T}{\pi_S} p_i$$

where p_i^* is the adjusted probability (final PD)

       p_i is the probability of default from the model

       π_S and π_T are the sample and true probabilities of default, respectively.

For example, if the sample probability of default were 50bps and the default rate in the target population were 150bps, p_i^* would equal $3p_i$.

For the small model probabilities often encountered in practice, this simple approximation works reasonably well. For example, it is not uncommon for the probabilities from an uncalibrated model to be in the single and low double digits, in which case the adjustment works acceptably for many applications.

However, by inspection, if the maximum probability generated by the model is greater than π_S/π_T, p_i^* will be greater than 1.0, which is impossible. More generally, as model probabilities increase, in cases where π_S/π_T is itself greater than 1.0 (the base rate is higher than the sample rate), the adjusted probabilities will become increasingly overstated. We show examples of this phenomenon later in this section. This can be controlled artificially by imposing upper bounds on model probabilities, either through a specific choice of the functional form of the model or through some sort of limiting transformation of the model output.

However, a more complete adjustment would appropriately reflect a fuller Bayesian analysis and is thus preferable in situations where either the ratio of sample to real probabilities is very large or small or when a probability model produces higher probabilities.

Elkan (2001) provides a derivation and proof, in a Bayesian context, of the following adjustment to correct for differences in base rates in different data sets:

$$p_i^* = \pi_T \frac{p_i - p_i \pi_S}{\pi_S - p_i \pi_S + p_i \pi_T - \pi_S \pi_T}$$

where p_i^* is the adjusted probability (final PD)

       p_i is the probability of default from the model

       π_S and π_T are the long-run sample and true probabilities of default, respectively.

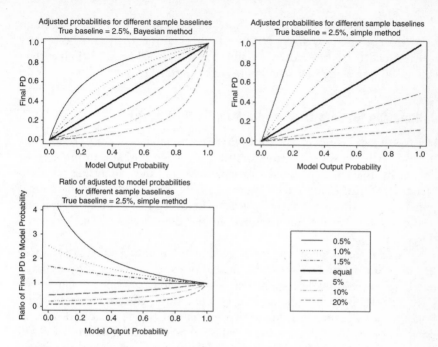

FIGURE 4.7 Comparison of Two Methods for Calibrating Baseline PDs

This adjustment, in addition to being grounded a bit more rigorously in probability theory, has the attractive property that it can never exceed 1.0.

Figure 4.7 gives a better sense of the behavior of the two approaches. The top row of the figure shows the Bayesian approach (left) and the simple approach (right) for different sample baselines versus a true baseline of 2.5 percent. Both the differences in boundedness (below 1.0) and the differences in shape are obvious here, particularly as the sample baseline moves away from the true baseline in either direction. The bottom figure shows the differences in the ratio of adjusted to model probabilities for different values of the sample baseline, again keeping the true baseline fixed at 2.5 percent. The nonlinear shape and nonzero slope of these curves can be contrasted with the linear and constant characteristics of the simple method. Thus, in most settings, the Bayesian approach will be better suited to modeling applications. However, in many practical settings where the base rate probabilities are low, and the sample rate is not too far from the true base rate, the simple approach may be sufficient and offers an easier-to-explain set of calculations.

The question still remains as to how to ascertain the true baseline default rate. Most researchers arrive at this rate through the analysis of secondary sources such as credit bureau data and other published research. Falkenstein et al. (2000) provides a discussion of such approaches.

Calibrating Models to Multiple Sample Databases

In cases where a modeler has two or more databases whose populations overlap, it is possible to gain perspective on the baseline probability of default by analyzing the databases separately and then analyzing the combined databases. Using a technique originally developed for sizing animal populations using *capture-recapture* techniques, the number of missing defaults (i.e., defaults not captured in the databases) can be estimated (Dwyer and Stein 2004).

This approach, originally introduced by Sekar and Deming (1949), was first used to determine birth and mortality rates in India. (The authors' databases were a bit less sophisticated than today's: They compared the birth and death records maintained by the registry to those obtained by a house-to-house canvass in India.) To implement the approach for default databases, we first calculate the number of defaults in each database and then calculate the number of only those defaults that both databases record. Using this information, and some knowledge of basic probability, we can calculate the total number of defaults in the full population.

More specifically, if all of the following are true:

N_1 = the number of defaults in database 1 but not in 2

N_2 = the number of defaults in database 2 but not in 1

C = the number of defaults in both databases

N = the true total number of defaults in the full population

then the paper shows that under the assumption of zero correlation in default collection process, an estimate of the total number of defaults in the full population can be given as $\hat{N} = C + N_1 + N_2 + N_1 N_2 / C$. This follows from the observation that as the population size gets large, the default rate in each database, p_i, can be given as

$$\text{plim}_{N \to \infty} \frac{N_i + C}{N} = p_i$$

and the overlap between the databases, C, can similarly be described as the product of the two database default rates: $C/N = p_1 p_2$. Thus, with some algebraic manipulation, one can solve for $\hat{N}$ with the information given.

In cases where the processes for collecting defaults may be correlated (e.g., both databases were augmented using the same credit bureau data or by tracking the same news services), adjustments must be made to account for this correlation. In this case, if the correlation, ρ, is known, the following expression, which we present without derivation, can be used to estimate the number of hidden defaults:

$$\hat{N} = \frac{-b \pm \sqrt{b^2 - 4ac}}{2a}$$

where

$$a = 1 - \frac{\rho^2 M_1 M_2}{C^2}$$

$$b = -\frac{2 M_1 M_2}{C} + \frac{\rho^2 M_1 M_2}{C^2} (M_1 + M_2)$$

$$c = \frac{M_1^2 M_2^2}{C^2} \left(1 - \rho^2\right) \quad \text{and}$$

$M_i = N_i + C$ is the total number of defaults captured in database i

When the correlation coefficient is positive (negative) the estimate is given by the positive (negative) root.

With two databases it is not possible to estimate ρ; however, with three or more it is (see Dwyer and Stein 2004 for more details as well as derivations of the estimator of $\hat{N}$). In addition, if the databases are biased in some manner—for example, if one or both only contain specific segments of the population (e.g., floorplan lending)—it is not generally possible to estimate missing defaults for the full population although, depending on the amount of overlap in the two database populations, it may still be feasible to do so for the subpopulation that is captured.

In applying this approach to estimate prior probabilities of default, it is important to have a reasonable estimate of the full population size to use for the denominator. For public firms this is typically available information. For private firms, there is less information, but it is often possible to estimate this from various public sources. In principle, the same estimation technique could be used to size the full population (rather than the defaulted population), though some adjustments would be necessary.

Term Structures of Default Probabilities

For some applications, particularly in valuation settings, users of PDs require the full term structure of default probabilities rather than a single (e.g., one year) point estimate. For models developed in the duration framework, this calculation is trivial and can be accomplished by simply varying t, the duration time, under the specification of whichever survival model has been implemented.

For discrete-choice models, however, there is no obvious analog to this operation and additional assumptions are required to produce estimates of the term structure of default probabilities. These assumptions largely involve the shape of the term structures themselves. Historical research suggests that conditional on survival, the probabilities of defaulting in the future converge with the central credit quality probabilities as the horizon becomes longer. For example, conditional on not defaulting, the credit quality of very highly rated firms tends to deteriorate on average while, conditional on not defaulting, low-rated firms tend to improve.[19] This is in line with intuition. In general, it is difficult to maintain high credit quality and firms that have initially high ratings often see these ratings degrade over time. Similarly, for firms that are of very low quality it is difficult to stay solvent and skate along the edge of default. Rather, firms typically either improve their credit quality or default.[20]

Despite this logic, the existence of mean reversion or, more generally, the specific shape of the underlying term structure is an assumption, and modelers must ultimately be comfortable with this assumption before moving forward in choosing a modeling approach for generating full term structures from point estimates of the probability of default. Note for emphasis that since it is likely that the default model parameters and even, in some cases, factors will be different, each firm's term structure of default probabilities will also be different. In fact, firms that have identical, say, one-year PDs may have different, say, five-year PDs and thus different term structures of default probability.

If we *are* willing to make some assumptions, then calibrating a firm-specific term structure to the actual point estimates produced by a PD model is straightforward. We only require a specification of a model for the shape of the term structure, an example of which we discuss shortly, and, for each parameter of that model, we also require a firm-specific probability of default at a unique horizon. (As mentioned in the beginning of this section, a hazard-rate framework is a natural one for representing forward rates and term structures of default probability.)

---

[19] See Lando (1994) for a more formal discussion.

[20] There is some evidence that this behavior is also reflected in yield curves. For example, Bohn (2000) and Agrawal and Bohn (2008) suggest that high-quality credits yield positively sloped term structures and low-quality credits yield negatively sloped term structures.

As an example of how such a calibration might be done, we describe the process using a Weibull survival function. The Weibull is attractive in that it admits mean reversion and produces monotonic hazard rates, which, while perhaps not strictly required, make modeling easier. The survival function using the Weibull is

$$S(t) = \exp\left(-(ht)^p\right)$$

and the companion hazard function is

$$h(t) = hp\,(ht)^{p-1}$$

The goal is now to find a set of parameters that is consistent with the one- and five-year (cumulative) default probabilities produced for a specific firm using the calibrated default models. Recalling the survival function, $S(t) = 1 - CPD_t$, where CPD_t is the (cumulative) probability of defaulting before time t, it is straightforward to rearrange $S(t)$ to get two equations in two unknowns:

$$p = \frac{\ln\left(-\ln(q_1)\right)}{\ln(ht_1)}$$

and

$$h = \frac{\left[-\ln(q_2)\right]^{\frac{1}{p}}}{t_2}$$

where t_i is the horizon ith unique PD
  $q_i = 1 - CPD_i$

For example, to calculate the term structure of default probabilities for a firm with a one-year PD of 75bps and a five-year (cumulative) PD of 3 percent, we might solve for h in terms of p first. Plugging in and solving, we get

$$p = 0.86$$

then substituting this back we get

$$h = 289.8$$

The resulting survival and hazard functions are shown in Table 4.1.

Finally, to provide some appreciation of the degree to which the selection of the survival function and the corresponding assumptions affect the term structure of default rates, in Figure 4.8 we show the results of the term

TABLE 4.1 Example of a Term Structure of PDs Implied from Firm-Specific One-Year and Five-Year PD Estimates

T	S(t)	h(t)
0.5	0.42%	0.72%
1.0	0.75%	0.66%
1.5	1.08%	0.62%
2.0	1.38%	0.60%
2.5	1.66%	0.58%
3.0	1.94%	0.56%
3.5	2.22%	0.55%
4.0	2.48%	0.54%
4.5	2.74%	0.53%
5.0	3.00%	0.52%
5.5	3.25%	0.52%
6.0	3.50%	0.51%
6.5	3.74%	0.51%
7.0	3.99%	0.50%
7.5	4.22%	0.49%

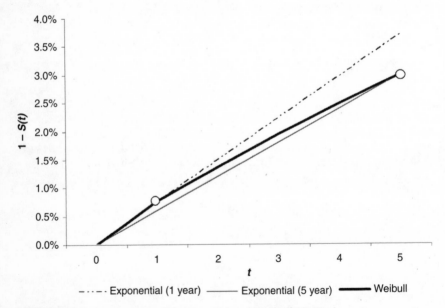

FIGURE 4.8 Comparison of Exponential and Weibull PD Term Structure Estimates

structure analysis using the exponential distribution which admits only a single parameter. To estimate the parameter we used both the one- and five-year probabilities and show the results of doing both.

Note that in the figure, not surprisingly, neither the exponential calibrated with the one-year PD nor the exponential calibrated with the five-year probability match the original probabilities at both horizons. Each matches perfectly the probability on which it was calibrated but under- or overestimates the other.

CALIBRATING TO RATINGS

Calibrating to agency or internal ratings is a different task than calibrating to default probabilities since, unlike default events, ratings themselves are not directly observable in nature, but rather are assigned by rating agencies through their own analysis. Rather than defaulting over some specific horizon that is (generally) an observable outcome for each firm, there is no objective measure of Aaa-ness to allow a researcher to observe the rating of a specific firm. Importantly, ratings serve a number of purposes and a default probability is but one attribute of a rating. Furthermore, rating criteria change over time as agencies and internal credit risk groups conduct research and modify their own methodologies. Despite the challenges, a number of applications in the field of portfolio management require calibration to ratings.

Calibrating to ratings can be done in a number of different ways. A rating calibration typically involves the mapping of a model output (usually a PD) to a rating class label.

Before proceeding, it is important to comment that in mapping a PD to a rating class, we are discarding information since PDs typically offer far higher resolution than do rating scales. However, some organizations find these mappings useful in situations where the staff is more familiar with agency and internal rating scales or where internal policies are based on broad rating categories. Our own view is that when a model produces a PD as output, organizations are best advised to use PD-based policies and practices, particularly in areas of valuation and risk management. This encourages a more natural treatment of the risk implied in the PD and avoids confusion.

Interestingly, we have seen cases in which a bank mapped the output of a PD model to a rating agency rating scale and where users of the scale, requiring probabilities of default, mapped this (mapped) scale back to historical default rates using default studies published by rating agencies! It would have been far more direct (and accurate) in these cases to simply use the original PDs generated by the model.

For many institutions, developing a rating mapping is a requirement for various commercial operations. If rating mappings are required for business purposes, users should be aware of how the mappings are constructed and what information is being compressed into the rating symbols in order to minimize confusion and to avoid the errors that may result from it. In the next few sections, we describe a number of mechanisms for achieving such mappings with the goal of highlighting the differences in philosophy and rating scale behavior in each case.

We can think of the dimensions of the rating calibration approaches as either taking the *rating system* as given (i.e., the gold standard) and mapping PDs into the rating system by matching aspects of the *rating system to the PD* (rating system–centric) or by taking the *PD* as given and calculating the statistical properties of the *ratings with respect to the PD* (PD-centric). As a second dimension, we consider whether the initial definition of the mapping itself begins by characterizing the attributes of ratings or the attributes of the PDs. These are outlined more fully next. More important than the taxonomy, the use to which the rating mapping is being put will determine to a large degree the most effective mapping. Table 4.2 dimensions these attributes and provides some comments on the unique features of each.

Mapping through Historical Default Rates

In practice, it is probably most common for users to map PDs to historical default rates. The mapping is simple to construct and straightforward to implement. To do so, we first obtain some set of historical (raw historical, idealized target, or withdrawal-adjusted historical) default probabilities for each rating class. We then calculate cutoffs $C(,)$ for each rating class based on the rating class default probabilities. Model PDs between the upper and lower cutoffs are mapped to the rating category and those outside are mapped into other categories. The upper cutoff of a rating class is typically the lower cutoff of the next higher rating class.

In constructing the cutoffs, one of three methods is typically used: actual, arithmetic mean (midpoint), or geometric mean. The *actual* cutoffs use the historical rating class probabilities as lower bounds for each rating category. In the case of the *arithmetic mean*, the midpoint (which is equivalent to the mean for two classes) between the current and next lowest rating category is used as a lower bound and, similarly, the midpoint between the current and next higher category is used as an upper bound. Finally, the *geometric mean* is computed in the same fashion as the midpoint method,

TABLE 4.2 Taxonomy of Rating Mapping Approaches

	Rating System–centric	**Model Output (PD)–centric**
From PD to Ratings	*Map PD to default rates of rating classes.* Mapped ratings can be compared across time, etc. Mapped ratings provide quantitative shorthand for PD levels. Rating changes more frequent and sensitive to changes in credit cycle. Requires accurate PD estimates.	*Map PD to rating-model rating class for PD bucket.* Not used often in practice.
From Ratings to PD	*Map model output to quantiles of rating distribution.* Distribution of mapped ratings mirrors rated universe and so avoids clumping. Independent of accuracy of levels of model PD (does not even require PD). Nonparametric mapping may result in disparate model outputs being close together, or vice versa. Rating changes less frequent.	*Map output to rating class with closest average model output.* Mapped ratings are (statistically) most likely given model output. Mapping is independent of accuracy of levels of model PD (does not even require PD). Rating changes less frequent.

but instead of taking the mean of the two adjacent classes the geometric mean is calculated.[21]

Note that these approaches can be ordered from most to least conservative as actual, geometric mean, midpoint.

The procedure for this mapping is given as follows (note that we assume here no exact matches, to conserve space):

1. Calculate historical default rates, DR_j, for each rating category, $j = 1 \ldots J$ where 1 is the best credit quality and J is the worst.
2. For each exposure, i:
   a. Calculate PD_i based on PD model.

---

[21] Recall that the geometric mean of a and b is calculated as $G = \sqrt{a \times b}$.

    b. If $PD_i < DR_1$ assign rating class 1.
    c. If $PD_i > DR_J$ assign rating class J.
    d. Else:
       i. Find two rating classes such that $DR_j < PD_i < DR_{j+1}$.
       ii. Calculate cutoff $c_{j,j+1} = C(DR_j, DR_{j+1})$ using one of the approaches described earlier. (In practice, this can be moved outside of the loop and done only once for each pair of adjacent rating categories.)
      iii. If $PD_i < c_{j,j+1}$ assign rating j; otherwise assign rating $j + 1$.

This method has intuitive appeal as it equates the probabilities predicted by a model to the default rate associated with a specific rating class. However, it is an indirect mapping in that it does not map directly from model to rating as some of the other approaches do, but rather equates the model probability estimate to an *attribute* of the rating scale—the historical (or idealized) probabilities of default. As such, it relies strongly on the accuracy of both probability estimates. In addition, to the extent that probability of default is only one aspect of a rating system (as would be the case if the rating system were designed to represent expected loss rather than probability of default), this approach may miss important characteristics of the rating definitions. Finally, note that because this mapping is an absolute one (the historical default rates are often constant or near-constant for long periods of time), if a particular model produced PD estimates that change frequently with market conditions or other factors, this approach will produce higher transition rates as these model probabilities cross the hard boundaries of the mapping.

Mapping to Quantiles of Rating Distribution

An alternative approach, also driven by the rating system, is to map PDs to ratings using the distribution of ratings as a benchmark and making no assumptions about the validity or distribution of model PDs. Rather than using model PDs to map to rating default rates, this approach is designed to ensure that the distribution of ratings (i.e., the percentage of firms classified in each rating class) matches that of the rated universe.

    This approach works as follows. We first sort the entire population of rated entities by rating. We then calculate the quantiles, Q_j, of the boundaries between ratings. For example, if a rating scale had 2.3 percent of the rated population in the highest rating, rating 1, then the boundary between the highest and next highest rating on our mapping would be 2.3 percent. Once we have the quantiles for all of the rating classes, we calculate the distribution of PDs. We next find the PD associated with the first quantile, the boundary

PD, BPD_1. In the current example, if 2.3 percent of the PDs were lower than 0.20, 0.20 would be the first boundary. We do this for all of the quantiles. The resulting boundary PDs provide cutoffs for model PDs such that a PD between the two boundary PDs that bound a specific rating class are assigned to that rating class. The recipe for this mapping is given as follows (note that we assume here no exact matches, to conserve space):

1. Create J homogeneous buckets of rated firms where the jth bucket contains all of the rated firms with rating $j, j = 1 \ldots J$ (where 1 is the best credit quality and J is the worst).
2. Order buckets from 1 to J.
3. $S = 0$
4. $N =$ total number of rated firms
5. For $j = 1 \ldots J$:
   a. $S = S + n_j$, where n_j is the number of firms in bucket j.
   b. $Q_j = S/N$
6. Order PDs from lowest (best quality) to highest (worst quality).
7. $BPD_j =$ quantile Q_j of the PD distribution (e.g., if $Q_j = 50\%$ then BPD_j would be the median PD).
8. For each exposure, i:
   a. Calculate PD_i based on PD model.
   b. If $PD_i < BPD_1$ assign rating class 1.
   c. Else:
      i. Find two rating classes such that $BPD_j < PD_i < BPD_{j+1}$.
      ii. Calculate cutoff $c_{j,j+1} = C(BPD_j, BPD_{j+1})$ using one of the approaches described previously. (In practice, this can be moved outside of the loop and done only once for each pair of adjacent rating categories.)
      iii. Assign rating j.

This method is attractive in situations where policies or business practices relate to the shape or dispersion of the rating distribution. For example, a bank may wish to underwrite only the top 10 percent of borrowers and the pass-1 category of the rating system may be designed with this in mind. Alternatively, a regulatory guideline might require that a rating system exhibit sufficient granularity to meet some criteria, and this approach would be one way to ensure that there were sufficient rating categories represented in the system in practice.

However, financial institutions implementing portfolio management will find this approach creates distortions in their decision-making process as they attempt to manage against opportunities available in the market. The market does not adapt itself to the idiosyncrasies of a particular distribution of ratings that is not aligned with actual PDs and market prices. The likely result will be lower returns over time for the bank whose PDs and ratings are not calibrated against market observables.

This mapping approach tends to be less sensitive to economywide changes in the credit cycle since it is entirely relative. Should a shock to the economy raise the probability of default for each firm by, say, a factor of two, the ratings would be unchanged (ceteris paribus). In contrast, in the same situation, the historical default rate mapping approach would produce massive downgrades since many PDs would cross the hard boundaries between rating categories.

Mapping to Rating Class with Closest Average PD

Yet another approach takes PDs as given and examines the PD attributes of ratings. This method, also widely used in industry, begins by calculating PDs for all rated entities. Then, within each rating class, some measure of central tendency (mean, median, etc.) is calculated for each rating class. Once this quantity is known, the method proceeds in a similar fashion to the approach of mapping through historical default rates, but instead of using historical default rates, the measures of PD central tendency are used. The recipe for this mapping is given as follows (note that we again assume here no exact matches, to conserve space):

1. Calculate central tendency of distribution of PDs, CT_j, for each rating category, $j = 1 \ldots J$, where 1 is the best credit quality and J is the worst:
   a. Assign a PD to each rated firm.
   b. Calculate CT_j for each rating category j (e.g., for each rating category calculate the median PD for all firms with that rating).
2. For each exposure, i:
   a. Calculate PD_i based on PD model.
   b. If $PD_i < CT_1$ assign rating class 1.
   c. If $PD_i > CT_J$ assign rating class J.
   d. Else:
      i. Find two rating classes such that $CT_j < PD_i < CT_{j+1}$.
      ii. Calculate cutoff $c_{j,j+1} = C(CT_j, CT_{j+1})$ using one of the approaches previously described. (In practice, this can be moved outside of the loop and done only once for each pair of adjacent rating categories.)
      iii. If $PD_i < c_{j,j+1}$ assign rating j; otherwise assign rating $j + 1$.

Calculation of these measures can become quite involved, as the modeler has the flexibility to determine not only the measure of central tendency, but also the historical window over which it is calculated and whether geographic or regional cohorts should be pooled. From a time perspective, calculating the central tendency over longer periods will make the mapping more sensitive to changes in the credit cycle and will thus foment rating transitions, since the boundaries between rating classes become more and more sticky as the window lengthens. Similarly, pooling firms into more homogeneous cohorts will tend to emphasize differences in industry and region and result in more rating dispersion between these cohorts, all else equal.

In terms of appropriate measures of central tendency, most practitioners prefer measures that are less sensitive to both outliers and large differences in the levels of PDs, since PDs often span several orders of magnitude for typical portfolios. In this setting, medians are popular, though other measures such as geometric means and the like are also feasible. When averaging over time and cohort we need to consider an additional dimension in that different time periods, industries, geographies, and so on tend to have different representations in the sample (e.g., there may be more retailers than computer manufacturers in a portfolio or there may be more observations from inflationary periods in history than in recessionary periods in history), so the modeler must take a position on how best to address this challenge. The most agnostic approach is simply to pool the data and calculate the measures over all cohorts. However, this does cause the central tendencies to be driven by the characteristics of the historical population, which may not represent all classes equally.

One popular alternative approach is to calculate the median of each cohort at each point in history and then to calculate the median of these values at whatever level of aggregation is desired. For example, if we were calculating the mapping using five years of monthly data for a cohort, we would calculate the median PD for each rating category for each month over the past five years, giving 60 observations for each rating category. The central tendency for each rating category would then be the median of these 60 observations.

Altman (in personal communication) has advocated for several years a variant of these approaches for use with various versions of the Z-score in which the Z-score is first mapped to a rating category as previously described, and this rating category is then mapped back to an historical default rate based on the historical default frequency for each rating category. Altman recommends using different rating-to-DR mappings, depending on whether a bond or loan is newly issued or more seasoned, as he finds that newly issued bonds have different default characteristics than more seasoned issues. An example of Altman's rating mapping is given in Appendix 4A.

INTERPRETING THE RELATIVE INFLUENCE OF FACTORS IN ECONOMETRIC MODELS

Because of the frequent use of various transformations (nonparametric and nonlinear) in building PD models such as those we have been discussing, it is often difficult to separate the relative influence of a particular factor in a default model. Unlike simpler econometric models, neither the regression coefficients nor the average behavior of the model at the mean are typically sufficient to understand well what drives a particular PD level, given a specific firm's characteristics.

Importance of a Factor with Respect to a Specific Firm's PD

There are a number of approaches to understanding which factors are most influential in arriving at a firm's PD and for measuring the sensitivity of nonlinear functions to changes in inputs more generally. In this section we discuss two that credit analysts have reported finding useful with respect to PDs. In applying one or the other, it is helpful to consider the perspective that will be most useful for a particular analysis.

One way to think about the question of the influence of a specific factor is to ask how the *average company's* PD would change were it to have, say, a leverage ratio equal to that of the current firm, L_i, rather than the typical leverage value, $\overline{L}$. Philosophically, we are asking what makes the current firm *different than expected*. The firm is evaluated on the (high dimensional) surface *near the typical firm*.

An alternative view is to ask how the *current firm's PD* might change were a specific value of leverage L_i *replaced with the sample mean*. In this case, the firm is being evaluated in its neighborhood on the surface and reflects the levels of all of the other factors at the firm's true levels. Here we ask a different question: How would this firm's PD change *if it had a more normal level of a specific factor*? Both of these approaches are useful, and depending on the user's preference, one or both may be used. In practice, we find the second to be a bit more informative as it relates more specifically to the firm, given its placement on the prediction surface.

To calculate the first of these, the change from the mean, define μ as the vector of the development sample means for each factor in the model and define $\mu_{(j),i}$ as the vector of the development sample means of each factor in the model except for the jth factor, which is taken at its own value for observation i. The driving factor evaluated at the mean is given as

$$d_{i,j}^{\mu} = PD(\mu_{(j),i}) - PD(\mu)$$

To calculate the second of these, the firm evaluated at its own values, we can similarly define $\mathbf{x_i}$ as the vector of factor values for firm i and $\mathbf{x}_{\mathbf{i},(\bar{\mathbf{j}})}$ as the vector of the values of each factor in the model for firm i, except that the jth factor value is replaced by the development sample mean. The driving factor evaluated at the firm factors would be given as

$$d_{i,j}^{x} = PD(\mathbf{x_i}) - PD(\mathbf{x}_{\mathbf{i},(\bar{\mathbf{j}})})$$

Note that in some cases, it may be helpful to normalize to values between 0 and 100 percent. If we denote the general driving factor as $d_{i,j}$, the subscript indicating that either factor can be used here, this normalization can be done by simply calculating the sum of the absolute values of the driving factors and dividing each driving factor by this quantity:

$$\langle d_{i,j} \rangle = \frac{d_{i,j}}{\sum_j \left| d_{i,j} \right|}$$

where for convenience we denote this normalized value by $\langle d_{i,j} \rangle$.

PITFALLS IN UNIVARIATE SENSITIVITY ANALYSIS

When calculating firm-specific effects, it is not uncommon for the user of a model to experiment with the impact of changing a specific factor by some amount. However, in practical line applications, the user will often not have access to the model variables directly, but rather provide the basic components of these as inputs. For example, a bank underwriter may provide income statement and balance sheet information to a software interface that feeds the model, and the software will then preprocess these raw values into the various ratios that are required as factors by the model.

As a result, changing certain inputs in isolation can result in counterintuitive behavior.

(Continued)

PITFALLS IN UNIVARIATE
SENSITIVITY ANALYSIS (*Continued*)

For example, imagine a model that contains forms of the factors: size measured as total assets (TA), profitability based on net income (NI) measured as NI/TA, and leverage measured as TL/TA. If a user changes the value of TA, intuitively we would expect the PD to improve since both heuristic reasoning and empirical evidence suggest that smaller firms are riskier than larger firms. However, because this also changes the values for leverage (better) and profitability (worse), the PD may go up or down depending on the specific form of the model. In fact, the result of the analysis becomes sensitive to the coefficients on each of the factors, what types of data transformations may have been used, and even where the rest of the firm's financials place it within each transformation.

This situation is not uncommon. Results of this sort do not necessarily imply that the model is poorly specified. Rather, an alternative explanation is that most firms' financial accounts do not change in isolation, but rather evolve in an interrelated fashion. In our example, we could observe that it would be unlikely for a firm's assets to, say, increase by 50 percent without its revenue also increasing in some sense. Thus the problem is not so much in the model, but in the assumption that we can look at specific accounts independently.

There are adjustments that one could make to address this type of behavior. For example, when assets are increased, the software could automatically increase net income proportionally. However, this is really only feasible for the simplest adjustments. What, for example, should one do if a user wants to make a change to both total assets and net income but in different directions? Even more difficult: what should the software do if a user increases operating income or earnings before interest and taxes (EBIT)?

In general, while warnings and automatic adjustments can be made, it is far more useful for users to have a clear understanding of how the models work so that when they consider performing what-if analysis, they do so in a rational framework. Even better, users should have a framework within which they can make changes to financial statements and other inputs in a coherent fashion that avoids modifying individual components in isolation.

Importance of a Factor for the Model in General

If instead of examining the importance of a factor on a specific firm's PD, we are interested in determining its importance in the model in general, our goal becomes to determine the typical influence that a specific factor has in the model. There are a number of approaches available here as well. We can choose to adopt a convention used in the econometrics literature for examining nonlinear models in which we calculate either (a) the derivative of the PD with respect to the factor at the mean, or (b) the mean, across all observations, of the derivatives of the PD with respect to the factor. For nonlinear functions, because of Jensen's inequality, the results will differ.

In either case, however, this involves calculating a similar quantity to those discussed earlier. To calculate these, we simply calculate $\mu_{(j),i}$ or $x_{i,(\bar{j})}$ but replace the value of the quantity in the jth factor with its current value plus or minus Δ_j. In the case of $\mu_{(j),i}$, this is the result we are seeking. In the case of $x_{i,(\bar{j})}$ we calculate this for each observation and then average the results. We can then use the new evaluations of the PD at the $\pm\Delta_j$ point to calculate the numerical derivative in the usual fashion.

An alternative approach, popularized in the analysis of the RiskCalc models, was to calculate the following quantity for each factor in a model:

$$w_j = \frac{abs(\beta_j)\sigma_j}{\displaystyle\sum_{k=1}^{K} abs(\beta_k)\sigma_k}$$

where w_j is the relative weight of the factor in the PD in a model with K variables

β_j is the coefficient of variable j

σ_j is the standard deviation of the (possibly transformed) variable in the development sample

This provides a reasonable first approximation to the influence of a specific variable on the PD for the typical firm. However, note that this measure is calculated based on the linear interpretation of the coefficient, scaled by the dispersion of the variable. As such, while it does provide a means for accommodating the effect of possible transformations on the PD, it does not take account of either the aggregation function, which is typically nonlinear, or of the calibration steps (also typically nonlinear), and thus ignores some of the important behavior that may affect the model output.

In all analyses involving "typical" or "normal" firm benchmarks, modelers should be mindful that the average firm will typically not have factor values that equal the means of the individual model factors due to the relationships between different factors at the firm level. Thus, financials for the "average" firm is not necessarily a vector of the average for each ratio.

DATA ISSUES

It is said that in the days of the Great Library in Alexandria, the thirst for records and writing was so acute that Ptolemy III of Egypt decreed that any visitors to the city be required to provide all books and other writings they had with them to scribes, who would then copy them for inclusion in the library. Modern financial institutions might similarly consider the value of historical data as they acquire new customers, merge with competitors or even convert database or change loan accounting systems.

By far, the biggest challenge in building econometric models (and for most models more generally, since almost any practical implementation we've ever seen of any of the models we describe in this book requires estimation of model parameters and calibration) is collecting, organizing, and cleaning data. For most modelers, this is also the least exciting aspect of the process. However, our own experience is that there is no more significant determinant of model quality than the amount and quality of the data used to build it.

For example, when we have systematically tested corporate default models on large data sets of public and private firm histories, we have observed that the models that perform best (on average) also happened to be those that were developed using databases that contained the largest numbers of defaults.[22]

For instance, the academic model we often found most powerful was the Shumway (2001) model. This model lagged well behind most commercial models we examined, but among academic models it tended to have an edge. It is perhaps no coincidence that this model was also developed using a data set that contained an order of magnitude more defaults (300) than other studies.[23]

---

[22] We also note that it is likely that researchers who place a higher value on data will not only tend to collect more defaults, but will also likely take more measures to clean the data prior to modeling.

[23] Note that the Shumway (2001) model also used a different modeling framework than other models that had some potentially more attractive econometric properties than traditional approaches. However, as we discussed previously in this chapter, our own experiments suggest that the distinctions in performance attributable to these differences in model structure may not be great. More generally, the finding of increased default data density being associated with increased performance appears to be a stable one, irrespective of the modeling approach taken.

Why is data such an issue? In non-credit-related areas of finance, while authors discuss the importance of data handling, little time is spent discussing acquisition and cleaning.

It turns out that data on credit events, particularly defaults, is *rare*. Most banks for example, spend substantial effort *avoiding* outcomes that lead to default. As a result, most bank databases (of solvent banks) contain relatively few defaults, compared to the number of loans. As it turns out, while the absolute volume of data is important in determining model and test quality, it is the number of default observations that tends to be the constraining factor, particularly in model validation work (see Chapter 7).

One way to think about this is as follows: Say a bank had a database of 10,000 loan histories. Of these 10,000 loan histories, 100 had defaulted. The bank would like to build a model that discriminates between defaulting and nondefaulting firms. Now we add another loan to the data set. If we have added a nondefaulter, we can learn how the new loan is different from the 100 defaulted loans. However, if we add a defaulted loan, we learn how the new loan differs from 10,000 other loans. This is substantially more useful. So the very rare default events turn out to be the most useful for modeling[24] and—because they are rare—the hardest to acquire.[25]

In recognition of this, some financial institutions have begun warehousing their own historical data. This is a fairly new development and firms have only recently begun to systematically track default and recovery information. Until recently, most banks, for example, stored data on performing loans in one business unit (either electronic or paper form) while nonperforming loan information was sent to a separate workout group which stored its data in a different format. Furthermore, until recently, many banks' loan accounting systems only retained the prior three years of data on borrowers. The advent of Basel II and other initiatives has motivated banks to rethink their data strategies; however, many institutions still struggle in collecting historical data on defaults. A related challenge is that banks typically do not retain

---

[24] The results of one simulation study (Peduzzi et al. 1996) suggest that a minimum of ten events (in the PD model context, ten defaults) is required for each variable investigated in a logit analysis. So for example, if one were interested in examining 40 potential factors in a PD model (e.g., different measures of leverage, various macro-economic factors, etc.) one would require at least 400 defaults. However, this study was drawn from the health literature where event rates are much higher than default rates. In this study, for example, the event rate was about 30 percent. It seems reasonable that a larger number of events could be required for data with much lower default rates.

[25] In contrast, researchers and practitioners who work on equity or interest rate models can typically get data at any level of detail and in any volume required. For example, intraday or tick data are readily available for most large equity issues at this point.

data on firms that approached them for a loan but that the bank turned down, which can create selection-biased samples. Fortunately, the recently renewed interest in credit modeling will hopefully improve data collection efforts. As financial institutions begin to come up to speed on systematically organizing credit data, they are taking greater interest in this heretofore less interesting aspect of model building.

However, most firms' data is not just sparse, it is of low quality and located in disparate systems (or paper files).[26] As a result, modelers must contend with an array of database issues, from matching nonstandardized borrower IDs to disambiguating inconsistent use of field codes, to mapping alternative definitions of seemingly obvious variables (e.g., region or industry).

In our work, we have often been called upon to use bank data for modeling or validation purposes. Our experience is that on average, about 70 percent of the data that is initially captured and submitted by banks is unusable due to data quality issues. Many of these issues revolve around seemingly mundane database-related problems such as the inability to match records from different systems; but even if records can be matched, a substantial minority of these matched records have nontrivial data errors.

In light of this, much of the practical work in modeling involves identifying data sources and the issues with them and, where possible, rectifying the errors. Like it or not, modelers must concern themselves with the nitty-gritty detail of data. It is still fairly uncommon to find a database administrator who understands the needs of econometricians well enough to deliver data that is ready to use out of the box.

Data quality depends on both the historical coverage of performance details and financial information of the obligor as well as the use of consistent definitions, the use of consistent data collection practices, and sufficient industry and geographic coverage. In this context, we will discuss two broad types of data problems: (1) the types of data issues that can typically be detected using statistical or business logic rules, and which can often be corrected in this fashion as well; and (2) problems involving biases introduced in the way that data is collected or in the types of borrowers that typically show up in a database. These latter problems may be detectable using automated algorithms, but they probably require some manual research or modeling to fix—if they can be fixed at all without further data collection. In the next two subsections we discuss each in turn.

---

[26] Recall the example in which a record in a bank's database that we were asked to examine was reported to contain a record that listed the source of a financial statement as "oral."

TAXONOMY OF DATA WOES

Entire texts have been written on data problems and data preparation for modeling. However, for our purposes, a practical approach to a discussion of data issues broadly classifies them as shown in Table 4.3. In the table we provide some examples of each type as well.

In this framework, the vertical axis of the table describes the types of basic data problems one might encounter, and the horizontal describes the prospects for fixing them using statistical or logical procedures. As is the case with most frameworks, this stylized view of the world is helpful in discussing the issues, but will almost certainly not accommodate every type of problem a research analyst might encounter.

Automated Diagnosis (and Sometimes Correction)

Before problems can be fixed they must be found. It turns out that many of the problems associated with the left-hand column of Table 4.3 can be caught using reasonably straightforward filtering algorithms. Certainly, basic accounting rules provide a reasonable starting point for such diagnosis. Assets must equal liabilities plus equity, liabilities cannot be negative, and so on. Numerous other accounting-based triggers can be used to flag records as suspicious. Similarly, to the extent that loan- or firm-related codes must

TABLE 4.3 Dimensioning Data Errors

	Automatically Recoverable Errors	Nonautomatically Recoverable Errors
Incomplete Data	Missing loan/firm identifiers (but a number of overlapping fields present) Missing geographic info Missing intermediate accounts	Missing loan performance records Missing default identifier Missing industry classification
Wrong Data	Inconsistent loan identifiers (but a number of overlapping fields) Inconsistent labeling (e.g., loan purpose, industry class, etc.) Business rules violated (e.g, Total assets greater or less than equity plus liabilities)	Incorrect industry codes Multiple inconsistent financial statements for the same reporting period

comply with a specific coding structure and they do not, rules can be used to flag these situations as well.

This is good news since it implies that a significant portion of the work can be done automatically. Even more encouraging is our observation that much of the logic for identifying and correcting data problems can be structured to permit its reuse across different data systems or institutions that may have quite different data structures, but from which we would like to distill common data elements.

AUTOMATING PART OF THE DATA SCRUBBING PROCESS

We have had good success developing databases of data handling rules of the following form:

```
Rule ID::Rule logic::Target universe::Rule
Parameters::Action
```

For example, using pseudo-code:

```
DataProviteARule::Loan_Pmt_Maturity::if
PmtDate>ScheduledPmtDate+GracePeriod and
Status=='CURRENT'::then ACTION:Reject
```

In practice, the "Rule" part would typically be coded in SQL, SAS, or some other data-friendly language and could be considerably more complex, as could the "Action" component.* Note that the parameters and action can be tuned to a particular data source so that this single rule can be reused in different settings as needs require. For example, some banks might not allow a grace period while others located overseas may allow a much longer one.

The key to this type of system is to create a rule engine that can interpret each of the rules and take appropriate action, based on the coding in the rule base. (Those familiar with meta-data management

---

*For example, the "Action" component could itself be a directive to run a statistical test or data augmentation algorithm. For instance, missing values of cash flow might be replaced with calculated values based on EBITDA.

from work in artificial intelligence or business logic management will recognize this basic structure.) As it turns out, while this is not trivial, skilled database programmers can usually implement such systems in a straightforward manner. In fact, today, a number of systems, both commercial and OpenSource, are available for implementing such systems in a more "off-the-shelf" fashion.

However, the harder part is developing the actual rules and actions themselves that accurately reflect the structure of the data and of the business processes that generate the data. Such expertise must be collected both from lending experts and from modelers and can take time to accumulate. Augmenting these filtering rules with statistical outlier detection methods, particularly those that are multivariate in nature, such as the calculation of Cook's Distance or regression leverage points, can be particularly effective for spotting problematic data.

Surprisingly, many institutions look at compiling credit data for modeling as a one-time or perhaps periodic exercise. As a result, they tend not to invest in scalable and reusable data-scrubbing infrastructure. This is a mistake for two reasons.

First, it is seldom the case that institutions will only need to use data a single time. Invariably and inevitably, these firms will need to recalibrate, reestimate, and revalidate the models they build. They will likely also want to use this data for other projects, research, and modeling tasks.

Second, if data scrubbing rules are not organized in a rational fashion, the process of cleaning the data may itself introduce errors into the data or lead to confusing output. In general, when errors are introduced in data handling, all modeling steps subsequent to the point at which the errors were introduced must be redone. Since data scrubbing is one of the first steps in the modeling process, errors here are costly. If a firm is using a hodgepodge of different rules so that the various stages in the data scrubbing process cannot be disentangled, when an error is discovered the data scrubbing will need to be done again from scratch. This is generally expensive, particularly if an audit trail of the data cleaning process is not available.

Importantly, we find that errors in data do not cancel each other out as a general rule. As an example, in one of our own informal experiments (we stress the informal nature of the following study as it was not done for purposes of rigorous research, but rather for expository purposes), we found that data that had not been cleaned could result in substantial errors in model validation and performance analysis.

In this experiment, we segmented default and borrower financial statement data by bank for 10 banks. Each bank had contributed data and we had cleaned the data of each bank for modeling purposes as part of a larger project. However, for this experiment, we backed out the cleaning steps. We then tested various default models on each bank's uncleaned data and then on the pooled clean data sets. We also evaluated the performance of each model on each bank's cleaned and uncleaned data and ranked all models from best to worst using each bank's data. Thus, for each bank, we had a ranking of the models, from most powerful to least powerful, using the unclean data and the clean data. As a benchmark, we used the complete data set: cleaned data from each bank that was then combined with the data from all other banks into a master sample.

The results speak to the effects of data cleaning. On unclean data, only 25 percent of banks produced rankings of eight models that were within two notches of the rankings on clean pooled data versus 75 percent of the banks on the clean samples. In other words, most banks' raw data resulted in tests that ranked most models incorrectly. Once the data were cleaned, however, the rankings improved substantially.

Furthermore, to control for the possibility that some models might perform better on some banks' data (clean or dirty) than on other banks' data (and thus might create the effect just described), we also looked at the agreement of banks' rankings with each other before and after cleaning. We examined the mean interbank rank correlation before and after cleaning. Before the banks' data was cleaned, the average correlation was just under 0.5. In other words, banks' rankings only agreed moderately. One interpretation could be that some banks' portfolios were just better modeled by some models than others. However, once the data was cleaned, the average rank correlation jumped to just under 0.8, suggesting that when the data was cleaned most banks tended to agree on the proper ranking of models, irrespective of their own lending and data practices.

BIASED SAMPLES CANNOT EASILY BE FIXED

While data omissions and errors can be identified and sometimes fixed algorithmically, sampling biases can be elusive to discover and for this reason can be more troubling from an analytic perspective. Here again, much has been written in the statistics literature about sampling and sampling-bias problems.

Perhaps the best-known example of sampling bias occurred during the U.S. presidential election of 1936 when the magazine *Literary Digest* conducted a poll to determine the likely winner of the election. The magazine combined its subscriber list with lists of auto registrations and telephone directories and sent over 10 million mock ballots to these individuals. Over 2.4 *million* of these were returned. From this very large sample of respondents the *Digest* compiled the results of its poll and determined that one of the candidates, Alf Landon, would win the election handily, carrying 32 states and defeating the other candidate, Franklin D. Roosevelt, by a margin of 57 percent to 43 percent. But this was not the way the election turned out. The *Digest* was not only wrong, but it was extraordinarily so. The final results of the election had Roosevelt winning by a landslide of 61 percent to 37 percent, with Landon taking only two states, 8 electoral votes versus Roosevelt's 523.

What went wrong is now a standard case study for statistics students. The *Digest* mistook having lots of data (2.4 million observations!) for having good data. Its sample was biased. By using its own subscribers (affluent Americans) and those who had automobiles or cars (also affluent Americans), the magazine had unintentionally but systematically excluded a large and relevant segment of the population: the middle and lower class. It turns out that in the midst of the Great Depression, these voters had different views than their more affluent compatriots. The problem with the *Digest*'s data was that the method by which the data were generated was biased and therefore the data was as well.

The lesson of the *Literary Digest* is fairly well known among statisticians and a fair number of financial professionals. Surprisingly, though, these same individuals sometimes overlook similar practices in their institutions when they build credit models. To understand how this happens, first consider that most institutions have data on borrowers to whom they have granted credit, but little data on those to whom they have not. Were it the case that institutions' business models remained constant and that the population of borrowers also remained constant, this would probably not be as troubling. However, as institutions seek to enter new markets, cross-sell additional products, and acquire or merge with competitors, both the business model and the client bases become more dynamic. In addition, the introduction of credit models itself changes the process by which credit is granted, implying that some borrowers that might not have gotten credit in the past may now do so (and vice versa).

Consider now what a database of the true population of borrowers might look like in a simplified setting. Here we assume just three attributes: sector, time, and firm asset size.

One way to think about this database of mean default rates is that it produces a hypercube of data buckets, each holding all of the firms that share the same attributes of size, industry, and year of observation. The mean default rate for each industry is then just the weighted average of all of the bins for that industry. This is shown conceptually in Figure 4.9 (adapted from Dhar and Stein 1997), where each bin is represented by a

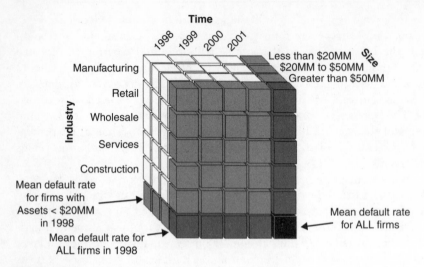

FIGURE 4.9 Schematic of a Three-Dimensional Database

white cube and the means are represented by the grey cubes along the outer edges. So, for example, the farthest cube back on the bottom left represents the mean default rate in 1998 (the value on the "Time" dimension) for all firms whose assets are less than or equal to $20 million (the value on the "Size") and who are in any industry (mean is across all industries).

However, the situation for many institutions is that they do not have a data set that represents the complete universe of potential borrowers. Thus, certain segments of the population are either missing entirely or so severely underrepresented that their impact on the mean is negligible. This situation is represented conceptually in Figure 4.10. Note how the absence of, for example, small firms in Construction and Wholesale affects the calculation of the mean in 1998.

Going back to our simple PD model, the value of the correct PDs would be the weighted average of all of the PDs in each bucket of the full cube.

However, in the case of the sparse data set, we are missing information about the default rates in the missing buckets, and thus the estimate omits the default rates of the missing observations, normalized for the size of this missing subpopulation. It is possible to argue that the data in a specific database is missing at random, and therefore the second term should be approximately the same as the overall mean, and thus the bias should be *de minimus*. However, our own informal analysis suggests that this is not the case.

In one informal study (here we again stress the informal nature of the analysis), for example, we estimated individual models using four banks'

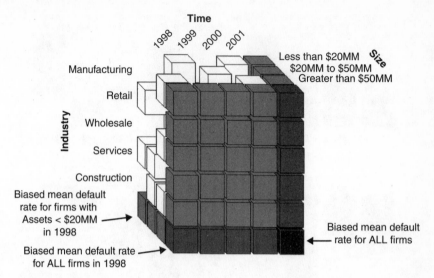

FIGURE 4.10 Schematic of a Sparse Three-Dimensional Database

data sets and compared these results to the performance of the MKMV model (RiskCalc—see discussion in this chapter) which had been developed on a broader data set.[27] We then tested the models on both the banks' data sets and on a broader range of borrowers that was more representative of the full population of the banks' data pooled together. The results are shown in Figure 4.11, which plots the difference in *accuracy ratio* (AR), a measure of model performance (higher accuracy ratios indicate better model power—see Chapter 7). The accuracy ratio was calculated both for RiskCalc (RC) and for the bank-data-only model, and the difference between the two is shown when the calculation was done using the same data. The models built on the banks' data sets generally performed better on the banks' own data than did RiskCalc (top half of Figure 4.11). However, the key observation was that when the models built on bank-data-only data were tested on the broader sample, they performed *worse* than RiskCalc in almost all cases (lower half of Figure 4.11).

The experiment suggests that it is typically *not* the case that data in bank portfolios is missing at random. If this were the case, there would be little difference in performance between models built using the broad sample and those built using only a single bank's data. Rather this study provides

---

[27] The experiment reported here is based on a draft of an unpublished article co-authored with Jalal Akhavein.

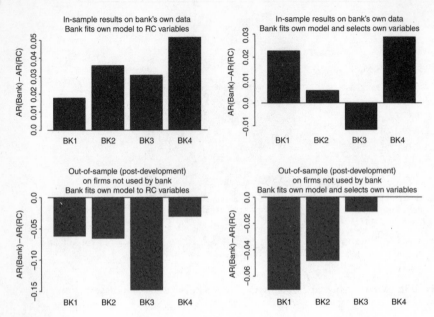

FIGURE 4.11 Performance Comparison Using Pooled versus Unpooled Data (Informal Experiment)

evidence that, as in the case of our simple mean default rate example, *bias* is present in data selection and it can result in substantial differences in performance.

Unfortunately, when data are missing for whole segments of the population there is no easy fix up. Financial institutions whose lending practices are not likely to change much in the near future, and whose client base's characteristics are reasonably stable, might argue internally that the data are sufficient for the immediate business needs. However, for most institutions, both the character of the markets in which they participate and the mechanisms by which they do so are evolving. These institutions ignore sampling bias at their peril.

The basic solution to sampling problems is the acquisition of more complete data. This turns out to be difficult in some markets. Banks can purchase data from vendors in the United States, Japan, and Europe, but the quality of these data sets can vary greatly and they are not without their own issues. Institutions faced with biased data need to consider both the source and effects of these biases before models are deployed and, perhaps, before they are built. If a bank knows that its data is sparse with respect to certain subpopulations, internal guidelines on model usage or data adjustment may help in mitigating the misuse of models.

CONCLUSION

Econometric models boast the longest pedigree of all default modeling frameworks, predating market-based structural models of default by half a decade and reduced-form models by three. These models fill an important gap in credit modeling practice. While typically lacking the theoretical rigor of structural models and the conceptual elegance of reduced-form models, they offer what is sometimes the only practical approach to modeling assets for which market observables are not readily available.

In practice, this is often the type of asset for which no other form of credit assessment, model-based or otherwise, is readily available. For example, unlike large corporations, for which ratings, equity prices, and bond spreads are often observable, small and medium enterprises (SME) loans are typically not traded actively and are issued by smaller, private firms without ratings or publicly traded equity. In such situations, econometric models offer one of the few alternatives to manual credit analysis.

Perhaps in no other modeling framework do modelers need to sift through their data and results more carefully. Because the data is typically of poor quality and incomplete, and because there is typically little ability to triangulate results to determine their reasonableness, all aspects of the modeling process require extreme attention to detail. Factor selection, default definition, sample selection, and so on all loom as challenges in building econometric models. Also, more than in probably any other framework, modelers need to be comfortable making compromises and judgment calls in formulating the problem. This of course highlights the need for rigorous validation practices (see Chapter 7).

However, when these issues are addressed, the resulting models permit portions of a financial institution's portfolio to be evaluated that might not otherwise be feasible, and this allows the quantitative analysis to be integrated into the active portfolio management practices of the institution on a consistent basis, using measures that are common to other asset classes in the portfolio. Ultimately, this then allows risks to be (transfer-) priced and managed more efficiently, not just on the private portion of the firm's exposures, but across the whole portfolio.

APPENDIX 4A: SOME ALTERNATIVE DEFAULT MODEL SPECIFICATIONS

Table 4.4 provides parameter estimates for some published models of default. These can be used, among other things, as benchmarks to aid in the validation of default models. Table 4.5 provides a mapping from the Z-score model to agency ratings.

TABLE 4.4 Parameter Estimates for Some Published Models of Default

Form of model	Z-Score (1968) $Z = \beta'x$	Z-Score (2004) $p = 1 - \dfrac{1}{1+e^{z'\eta}}$ Use log of $\dfrac{RE}{TA}, \dfrac{MVE}{TL}$	Z'-Score Private Firms (1993) $Z = \beta'x$	Z''-Score EM and Non-Manufacturing (1995) $Z = \beta'x,$	Shumway Accounting Only (2001)* $b_i(t) = \dfrac{1}{1+e^{z'\eta}}$	Shumway Market Only (2001) $b_i(t) = b_i = \dfrac{1}{1+e^{z'\eta}}$	Shumway Market and Account (2001) $b_i(t) = b_i = \dfrac{1}{1+e^{z'\eta}}$
Constant		7.72		3.25	−7.811	−12.027	−13.303
$\dfrac{WC}{TA}$	1.2		0.717	6.56			
$\dfrac{RE}{TA}$	1.4	0.52	0.847	3.26			
$\dfrac{EBIT}{TA}$	3.3	3.61	3.107	6.72			
$\dfrac{MVE}{TD}$	0.6						
$\dfrac{MVE}{TL}$		1.34					
$\dfrac{Sales}{TA}$	0.999		0.998				
$\dfrac{BVE}{TD}$		0.420		1.05			

$\frac{TL}{TA}$		4.068	3.593
$\frac{NI}{TA}$		−6.307	−1.982
$\frac{CA}{CL}$			
Ln(age1) Firm age		0.307	
Ln(age2) [min(years since rating, 10)]	0.183		
Alpha$_{t-1}$		−2.072	−1.809
Volatility		9.834	5.791
Relative size 1 ln(mktCap/Tot Mkt)		−0.503	−0.467
Relative size 2 Ln(TL/Tot Mkt)	0.51		

*The author did not propose this model but rather estimated it based on another researcher's model. The author's results suggest this was not a useful specification.

TABLE 4.5 Sample Rating Mapping for Z-Score Based on Compustat Data

S&P Rating	Mean Z-Score 2004–2005	Mean Z-Score 1996–2001
AAA	5.31	5.60
AA	4.99	4.73
A	4.22	3.74
BBB	3.37	2.81
BB	2.27	2.38
B	1.79	1.80
CCC	0.45	0.33

REVIEW QUESTIONS

1. Why might a modeler consider using an econometric model of the sort described in this chapter instead of a structural or reduced-form approach?
2. In choosing the functional form of an econometric PD model, what things should a modeler consider? Why might a hazard-rate approach be preferred to a discrete-choice approach, or vice versa?
3. Why might it be necessary to adjust the output of a PD model by calibrating the base rate? Why would the PD of a model be different if the population PD were different than the sample used to build the model?
4. Why might a modeler elect to perform univariate transformations on factors in a PD model?
5. Why might a bank calibrate PDs to ratings? What are the analytic costs of doing this? What are the various approaches a bank might take to this calibration? Why might a bank choose one ratings calibration approach over another?
6. Why is it often difficult for banks to collect data to build PD models? What are some of the limitations of the data that they do collect? What impact can these limitations have on PD models?

EXERCISES

1. Altman reported that in developing Z-score, values of the Z-score below 1.81 identified all defaulters. If we assume a linear model, then using the definition of the discriminant function we can calculate a probability of default associated with this score. What is this probability?

2. Based on the answer to the preceding question, since Altman's original study used a paired sample (i.e., the sample default rate was 50 percent), if we assume that the true default rate for the population is 1.5 percent, what is the probability associated with the score of 1.81?

3. Assume a firm had a one-year PD of 3 percent and a five-year PD of 7 percent. Under a Weibull term structure of default rates, what would the 2.5-year PD be? What would it be under an exponential term structure of default rates?

4. If Bank A merges with Bank B, with whom it had competed aggressively in a certain market for years, how might the two banks' databases be combined to gain a better understanding of that market? If the total size of the market were 775 firms and the number of defaults each bank experienced were 23 and 38, respectively (of which 10 were in both portfolios), how might the bank estimate the true default rate of the population?

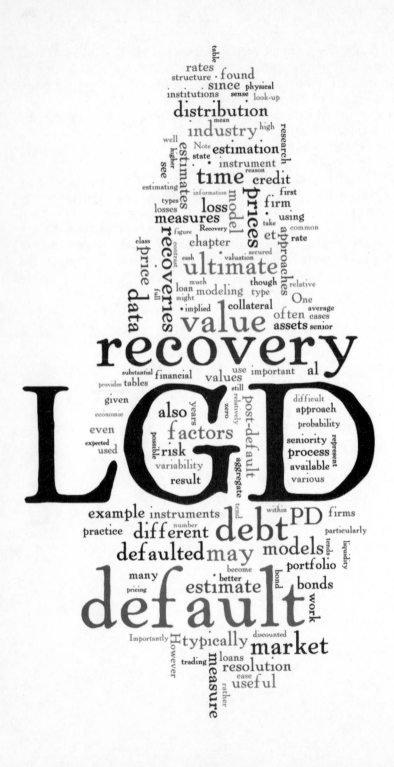

CHAPTER 5

Loss Given Default

Every defeat, every heartbreak, every loss, contains its own seed,
its own lesson on how to improve your performance the next time.
—Malcolm X

Tables are like cobwebs, like the sieve of the Danaides; beautifully
reticulated, orderly to look upon, but which will hold no
conclusion.
—Thomas Carlyle

Objectives

After reading this chapter, you should understand the following
concepts:

- Definitions of loss given default (LGD).
- The difference between post-default price and ultimate recovery.
- Common approaches to estimating LGD.

In this short chapter,[1] we review some of the approaches used in practice to
estimate the severity of the losses experienced in the event of default. This
is a shorter chapter because, unlike other aspects of credit risk discussed
throughout this text, the current state of modeling for loss given default
(LGD, 1 – recovery rate, or *severity*) has lagged that of PD, correlation,
and valuation modeling. While the past several years have shown a marked

---

[1] Portions of the material in this chapter were drawn from Gupton and Stein (2002
and 2005), with permission from Moody's Corporation and/or its affiliates, and are
copyrighted works owned by those entities. All rights reserved.

increase in academic work relating to instrument-level LGD (see Acharya et al. 2003; Davydenko and Franks 2006), much of this work has remained in the academy, with applications in industry focusing on simpler, often more blunt, approaches.

Why is this? We can think of a few reasons. First, until very recently, useful *data* on loss given default was difficult to obtain. This has as much to do with operational practices in organizations as anything else. The lack of systems to track loss after default makes it difficult to assemble meaningful LGD data sets. Second, the *definition* of loss given default can vary widely from institution to institution, market to market, and application to application, which makes standardized approaches harder to achieve. Third, the *calculation* of LGD can be subtle and the value calculated can be fairly sensitive to the assumptions used to calculate it. Fourth, in contrast to the case of default models, there have historically not been attractive theoretical models of LGD around which compelling frameworks could be built. Instead, the large majority of LGD modeling has involved statistical rather than theoretical constructs. Finally, LGD is inherently uncertain. LGD realizations can depend on many hard-to-quantify factors, from the quality of a defaulting firm's assets and franchise to the vagaries of the resolution of legal proceedings and bankruptcy rulings. As a result of this high variability, it is relatively less rewarding to develop sophisticated LGD models than perhaps it is for other aspects of credit risk, since even good models tend to have wide prediction intervals.

Complicating all of this is the observation that most research on LGD tends to be descriptive, rather than predictive. The concepts of a prediction horizon and a prediction interval are relatively new in LGD research, with most work focusing on long-term average behavior or contemporaneous explanation of various co-factors and LGD. In addition, historically much of the work on LGD tends to focus on the analysis of aggregate LGD rates, rather than firm- and instrument-specific LGD.

Our view is that, like probabilities of default (PDs), LGD can and should be predicted over useful horizons on an asset-by-asset basis and that careful attention to LGD is worthwhile. Measures of LGD are essential in lending, investing, trading, or pricing of loans, bonds, preferred stock, lines of credit, and letters of credit. Accurate LGD estimates are important inputs to the calculation for provisioning reserves for credit losses and calculating risk capital.

Consider, for example, the expected loss (EL) equation, which relates EL to PD, LGD, and exposure at default (EAD): $EL = PD \times LGD \times EAD$. Errors in any of the three quantities impact the final estimate multiplicatively. Specifically, misestimating LGD will impact EL, in the same way that misestimating a PD will. A 10 percent relative error in LGD has the same effect on EL as does a 10 percent relative error in PD. It is important to note that the scope for error on LGD estimation is not as large as that on PD estimation. Most LGD estimates fall between 30 and 70 percent, so that an extreme misestimation will be off by a factor of 2 to 3. In contrast, PDs typically range from 1 basis point to 3,500 basis points, which means an extreme misestimation may be off by a factor of a few thousand. This may be more a commentary on the state of precision of our LGD models than on the relative value of PD and LGD estimates.

In principle, estimating LGD with the same precision as we estimate PDs would be quite valuable. However, the current state of our methods, on the one hand, and the inherent subjectivity and idiosyncrasy in the default resolution process on the other, create relatively high variance in LGD outcomes. This translates into estimates for which basis-point precision is not practically significant. As a result, at this point, even though they are multiplicative in nature, from a practical perspective relatively more accurate PD models can be more valuable than relatively more accurate LGD models. Even so, LGD estimates become quite important as the PD accuracies improve and credit traders and portfolio managers look to develop a better characterization of their exposures' risk and value. LGD models are also quite important for evaluating instruments already in or near default.

To give some sense of this, a few years ago we developed the following example (Gupton and Stein 2001).[2] In 2000, senior subordinate corporate bonds had a median recovery (post-default price) of about 32 percent of par. Of course, not every bond that defaulted experienced this recovery; in fact, there was substantial variability. It turns out that the average (median) difference between a bond's actual recovery and this 32 percent figure was about 22 percent, due to changes in the economic cycle, differences in the issuer or industry, and so on. Thus, the typical error from using the average was on the order of 70 percent (22/32 ≈ 69 percent). One way to think about the impact of this is to consider what a 70 percent error in, say, PD would imply.

Using default rates again as of 2000, the same percentage relative error rate (69 percent) in default probabilities (rather than LGD) for a buy-and-hold investor of a Baa-rated senior subordinated bond with, say, a 10-year maturity, would imply a default probability somewhere in the (very wide) Aa-to-almost-Ba range! For most credit-risk professionals this would be an unacceptable level of uncertainty around the probability of default measures. Yet many analysts and portfolio managers tend to routinely accept this level

---

[2] We termed this the "spoonful of raw sewage" example after a favorite metaphor of one of the author's numerical analysis professors. Imagine you have two barrels. One contains a barrel full of fine wine. The other contains a barrel full of raw sewage. If you take a teaspoon of the fine wine and mix it into the raw sewage, you still have a barrel full of raw sewage. Importantly, though, if you take a teaspoon of the raw sewage and mix it into the fine wine, you also have a barrel full of raw sewage.

of estimation error in their calculations of expected recovery, despite the fact that the two sources of imprecision affect the overall estimate of EL symmetrically.

There is nothing wrong with a descriptive representation of recovery data, analyzed in a traditional lookup table format. However, analyses performed on these tables alone may result in much more highly variable estimates of LGD than more precise models. This is a result of the nature of the tables, not the quality of the analysis they contain. Errors in estimating LGD can significantly affect estimates of credit losses and the resulting credit risk exposures. Increasing the accuracy of LGD estimates improves the precision of these estimates, however.

Academic work in this area has tended to focus on three dimensions. The first is a focus on the factors that determine aggregate recovery rates—that is, which factors are most useful in describing average recovery rates for various classes of debt. In particular, there has been some interest in the relationship between average recovery rates and average default rates (Frye 2000; Sironi et al. 2002; Altman et al. 2004). The second stream of research involves extending conceptual frameworks for recovery. Altman et al. (2004 and 2006 update) provides a review of these approaches. These approaches, while interesting from an academic perspective, have not found wide acceptance in practice. Finally, more recent academic work (Acharya 2003; Davydenko and Franks 2006) has focused on instrument-specific recovery prediction. This work, while itself not widely used in industry, provides perhaps the closest analog for what is done in practice. However, these studies tend to focus on the factors that explain LGD rather than on developing stable methods for predicting it.

In this chapter, we focus on the techniques that are most widely used in practice. Unlike work in default prediction, a sense of nascence pervades the work in LGD. Absent a strong theory that can be practically implemented, our preference is to describe the current state of the art and provide pointers to future work in this domain. Importantly, although we will periodically reference research on aggregate recovery rates, our focus in this chapter is on estimating instrument-level recovery since the variability in LGD by instrument- and firm-specific factors is sufficient to warrant individualization of LGD estimates, particularly within a portfolio context.

ROAD TO RECOVERY: THE TIMELINE OF DEFAULT RESOLUTION

In order to understand LGD and the various ways in which one might measure it, it is useful to begin with a description of the default and default resolution process. A simplified view of the bankruptcy process is universal for almost all countries and is broadly composed of two distinct steps:

- *First there is a determination of the aggregate firm-level value of the defaulted entity. This will be the total value available to satisfy all the creditors of the firm.*
- *Second, there is a determination as to how this firm value will be divided up among the creditors.*

Because there is uncertainty about both of these steps, there is typically a good deal of variability in recovery values across firms and industries. Not surprisingly, there are different measures of value that come into play, depending on who is making an assessment and when it is being made. (A true market valuation can take weeks or months from the time of emergence to materialize.)

In Figure 5.1, adapted from Gupton and Stein (2005) we show how this resolution typically proceeds. During this process, there are several points at which investors may have the opportunity to recover some portion of their investments (or, said differently, to realize their losses). This is because there are typically various court and other legal procedures that are invoked upon default, and during this process, some steps may take longer than an investor is willing to wait. Alternatively, some investors may not be able to avail themselves of these opportunities due to the structure of their investment or the dynamics of the market in which the investment is made.

The process begins at default, shown as the two vertical lines on the far left of the figure. (Note that prior to default, there may be one or more "technical events of default," which are considered to be contractual defaults but for which the debtor is able to negotiate nondefault remedies. Different modeling objectives may demand different definitions of default. For example, ACPM may focus more on economic definitions of default while regulatory capital calculations may focus more on legal definitions of default.) Shortly after default, investors in publicly traded instruments get

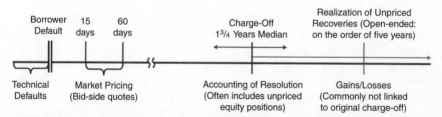

FIGURE 5.1 The Timeline of Default and Resolution

their first opportunity to recover value. Because some instruments are traded in the marketplace, they are valued by other investors on a continuous basis. The market price of a defaulted security is considered to be one measure of recovery since it represents the market estimate of the discounted value of the cash flows expected from the ultimate resolution of the default, which often happens, years later.

At this point, we do not have enough empirical data to determine conclusively whether realized losses contain a systematic component that cannot be diversified away. There appears to be evidence that in aggregate, default and post-default prices are correlated (see Keenan, Carty, and Shtogrin 1998, and Altman 2002); since PDs do exhibit systematic variation, we can infer that there may be systematic factors affecting post-default prices as well. However, how this translates into ultimate recoveries for individual borrowers and assets is a bit less clear since the resolution process can span relatively long time periods, making a recovery event more difficult to relate to one specific economic state of the world. This is in contrast to a default event which occurs (approximately) in a single instant and can thus be more easily associated with various economic factors at a specific point in time. The risk-neutral nature of the post-default price may only be relevant if there turns out to be systematic risk in the ultimately realized loss. If not, then the risk-neutral measure will equal the physical measure.

After this, a second opportunity for measuring recovery takes place, typically one and a half to two years post default. At this juncture, many financial institutions take an accounting charge for the loss, valuing it as fairly as possible given the information available at the time. Recoveries at that point include cash or a variety of settlement instruments including new debt, equity in the new post-emergence entity, and other types of assets.

Finally, some time after default (in most cases), the ultimate realization of the values of assets become known. Due to the vagaries of the recovery process, these are difficult to tie back to the original charge-off, but they do offer residual value—particularly to equity holders.

MEASURES OF LGD (RECOVERY)

In order to understand the various measures of LGD, we find it useful first to consider that conceptually there are two components to any LGD assessment. The first goes in the numerator and describes the actual loss (recovery) in dollar terms. In the previous section, we discussed the various points in the recovery process at which we might measure such a quantity. The estimation of the loss component is complicated by considerations of timing, discounting, choice of measure (physical versus risk-neutral, etc.), and so on.

The other component goes in the denominator and answers the question, "Loss of *what?*" Academics and practitioners have suggested a number of different approaches to characterizing the value that investors might reasonably have expected to receive had there been no default. As it turns out, different measures are appealing for different applications. (We discuss some of the implications of the different recovery assumptions for modeling credit-spread term structures in Chapter 6.)

In the next two subsections we explore each of these components of LGD.

The Numerator: Definitions of Loss

There are two broad ways in which the economic costs of post-default losses are assessed: measures derived from market prices of either defaulted or nondefaulted securities (economic measures) and measures derived from observation of actual cash flows resulting from the resolution of the default proceedings (accounting measures). Figure 5.2, taken from Gupton and Stein (2005), provides a stylized taxonomy of these two measures. In the next several subsections, we describe these measures in more detail.

Accounting Loss Approaches Accounting measures of LGD are generally available only for loans, since banks source these from their accounting records. This information is also scarce because typical bank systems have not historically captured recovery cash flows or tracked the

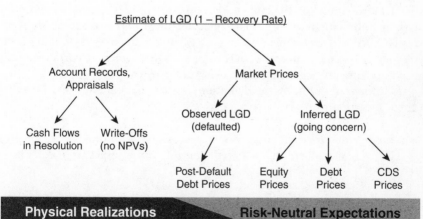

FIGURE 5.2 A Taxonomy of LGD Measures

collateral realizations electronically; so collecting it involves a manual extraction from paper files. Accounting loss is typically calculated using one of two techniques:

- *Charge-off amounts.* This is the lender's write-off value when recovery efforts are exhausted or when it chooses to abandon a particular debt. These values are typically estimates of the ultimate value of the recovery as they are often made years before the full recovery process has been resolved.
- *Cash flows from a default resolution.* Using cash flows permits a more refined analysis of recovery since this representation describes the full profile of when the creditor, typically a lending bank, receives economic value. Naturally, this representation requires the specification of appropriate discount rates, which can be challenging.

We start with the second of these, which attempts to measure the *ultimate recovery* (cash flows from default resolution). This represents the value at resolution. Ultimate recovery is often subjective since equity, rights, and warrants received as payment in resolution commonly have no market price. One study, Hamilton (1999), found that 15 percent of the value of the recoveries for senior secured loans came in the form of equity of the defaulted firm. Since these payments with equity interests (e.g., common stock, preferred, and warrants) commonly do not trade, their value is typically unrealized and unknown for years. When these equity values are eventually realized/known (often well past the write-off date), it would be *atypical* for a bank's accounting systems to track flows back to the original charge-off. Given the lack of a link between the ultimate collection and the original loan, the data are often not available to develop an estimate of what to expect in terms of ultimate losses for a particular defaulted borrower. Recently commercial vendors have begun to make available databases containing both trading price and ultimate recovery data, allowing market participants to begin to compare these values on identical borrowers.[3]

Further complicating the definitions is that there are at least three different measures of ultimate recovery:

1. *Emergence pricing.* These values represent the trading prices of prepetition instruments as observed after the firm emerges from default.

---

[3] Note that the definition of default itself can complicate the assessment of LGD. For example, in some studies about 50 percent of middle-market so-called defaults result in zero LGD.

2. *Settlement pricing.* These values represent the trading value of any instruments that may have been received as part of a settlement, observed at the first opportunity at which they are traded.
3. *Liquidity-event pricing.* These represent prices for assets that are illiquid. These occur at the first so-called *liquidity event*, which is the first time that a price can be determined. Liquidity events are typically triggered by acquisition of the firm, refinancing, subsequent bankruptcy, and so on.

In contrast to ultimate recovery, charge-off amounts represent the amount that an institution charges off for accounting purposes when the loan transitions into a nonperforming state. The problem with using charge-offs is that the charge-off can occur substantially before the final resolution and may not track back to what was actually received in ultimate recovery. Thus, in addition to the difficulties in calculating the ultimate recovery values, the charge-off approach layers on an estimation process. Charge-offs are essentially a best guess by the financial institution on the ultimate recovery, without having market forces to help determine its accuracy. They are, in a sense, the expected value of the ultimate recovery.

Note that *both* accounting approaches suffer similar uncertainties since both fall short of capturing the ultimate realization of all payments typically given in resolution. In addition, it can be exceedingly difficult in practice to capture accurately the timing of cash flows in many cases.

Market Value Approaches   The LGD of an instrument can also be inferred from market prices. Here again, there are broadly two approaches to estimating LGD from market prices: post-default prices for liquidly traded *defaulted* instruments, and implied LGDs for liquidly traded *nondefaulted* instruments.

Post-default prices describe the market price of a liquid security observed at some short interval of time after default. For investors in liquid credit, the market price directly represents recovery, should they elect to sell, as it is the value they would trade out of a defaulted position. Market liquidity is typically good at about one month post-default as many investors that originated or bought the debt are disallowed or disincented, per regulations or their own internal policies, from holding defaulted assets and therefore trade their positions to a group that specializes in defaulted debt. Loan market prices also appear to be robust, based on empirical evidence found by Altman, Gande, and Saunders (2004). These authors find that "... the loan market is informationally more efficient than the bond market around loan default dates and bond default dates."

Given these circumstances, a common measure of recovery is the price of a defaulted instrument and the price is calculated approximately one month after default, since:

1. The time period gives the market sufficient time to assimilate new post-default corporate information.
2. The time period is not so long after default that market quotes become too thin for reliance.
3. This period best aligns with the goal of many investors to trade out of newly defaulted debt.

This definition of recovery value avoids the practical difficulties associated with determining the post-default cash flows of a defaulted debt or the identification and value of instruments provided in replacement of the defaulted debt. The very long resolution times in a typical bankruptcy proceeding (commonly 1.25 to 5 years) compounds these problems. Broker quotes on defaulted debt provide a more timely recovery valuation than requiring the completion of court-ordered resolution payments, potentially several years after the default event. Market quotes are commonly available in the period 15 to 60 days after default.

In contrast to post-default price methods, *implied* LGD methods rely on observing prices (spreads) on liquid bonds and credit default swaps (CDSs) and using these to tease out an estimate of LGD based on some kind of model framework. In both the structural and reduced-form model discussions, we included some measure of LGD (sometimes the value was set at 100 percent). If we have observed prices or spreads and a reasonable measure of an obligor's PD (e.g., from a structural model), we can calculate an implied LGD—in other words, back out an LGD estimate from the model framework. We can often generate more accurate estimates by making use of multiple markets. For example, we can use the equity market to estimate a PD and then use the CDS or bond market to estimate an LGD using the previously calculated equity-based PD as input. If we only have one set of market data, say CDS, we may have to rely on more assumptions to disentangle PD from LGD based on a given set of spreads. This approach is most suited for securities valuation.

A significant complication in implied LGD estimation is that it is often difficult to differentiate residual market premia (e.g., liquidity effects, etc.) from the LGD itself since implied LGD is typically defined as the "remaining" spread, after accounting for the PD. As better methods for estimating liquidity and other effects become more well established (see our discussion on liquidity in Chapter 3), these challenges should begin to abate. Nonetheless, the output of implied LGD estimation usually requires additional scrutiny to ensure that the model estimation process is not inadvertently reflecting (sometimes sizable) liquidity premia.

In practice, it is often very difficult to differentiate statistically between implied LGD and liquidity premia. This can sometimes result in the counterintuitive result of implied LGD estimates that substantially exceed 100 percent. One benefit of using CDSs rather than bond spreads is that the observed spreads for CDSs are generally considered to be less contaminated with liquidity effects since the instruments trade more liquidly than the debt of the underlying names. This is not always the case, however. We do not discuss implied LGD in detail in this chapter, although we elaborate more on this topic Chapter 6 when we talk about reduced-form models.

THE RELATIONSHIP BETWEEN MARKET PRICES AND ULTIMATE RECOVERY

There have been several studies of the market's ability to price defaulted debt efficiently (Eberhart and Sweeney 1992; Wagner 1996; Ward and Griepentrog 1993; Altman, Gande, and Saunders 2004). These studies do not always show statistically significant results, but they consistently support the market's efficient pricing of ultimate recoveries. At different times, we have studied recovery estimates derived from both bid-side market quotes and discounted estimates of resolution value. We find, consistent with other academic research, that these two tend to be reasonable estimates of each other, particularly in the case of loans, as shown in Figure 5.3. This figure is based on two different kinds of recovery data: post-default prices and ultimate recoveries (discounted and nondiscounted). Recovery data is taken from *Moody's Ultimate Recovery Database*. The data shown here are for a sample of revolving bank loans.

From Figure 5.3, several things become apparent. First, looking at the top row, we show histograms of three different measures of LGD. On the left, the distribution of post-default prices is shown for those observations in the database for which they are available. In the middle figure, we show the distribution of recovery values at settlement, discounted by the pre-default note rate; and finally, on the right, we show the settlement values, this time undiscounted. Note the characteristic U-shape of the ultimate recoveries, suggesting that in many cases, recovery can be an all-or-nothing process.

The bottom row of Figure 5.3 provides additional interesting information. The left- and rightmost figures show scatter plots of the post-default price versus the two settlement prices, respectively. Note the strong relationship between the two. Unsurprisingly, we note that there is an obvious impact of discounting on this relationship, which is apparent in the slopes of the

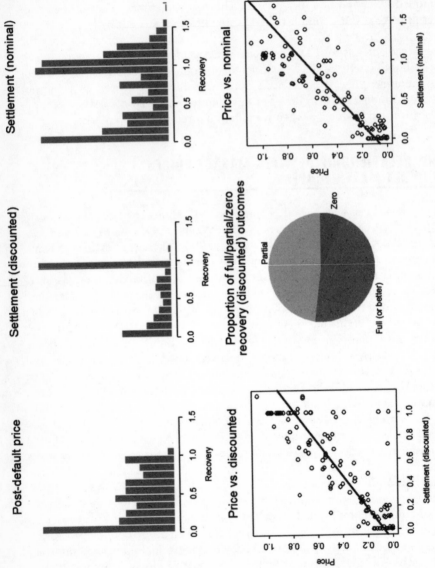

FIGURE 5.3 Comparing Ultimate Recovery and Post-Default Price Recovery

two regression lines we have drawn. The middle figure on the bottom is particularly interesting in light of our observation on the U-shape of the distribution. This pie chart shows the proportion of recoveries that are zero, one, and fractional. Note that a large proportion of recoveries are full (LGD = 0). A smaller but substantial proportion are zero (LGD = 100%). This suggests certain modeling challenges, which we discuss later in this chapter as we do the conceptual linkages between the different realizations of LGD.

Importantly, the question of which recovery estimates are better, 30-day post-default prices or ultimate recoveries, often comes up in practice. The use of the word *better* would seem to imply that one is correct, or more correct, than the other. It is our position that both 30-day post-default prices and ultimate recoveries are important data points. The real question may probably be better posited as "Are 30-day post-default trading prices reasonable proxies for ultimate recoveries?" And which measure is more relevant to a particular user?

We find it useful to cast this argument in terms of the applications of the recovery estimate. If the user of the estimate is using it to determine how much capital to allocate to a portfolio of liquid instruments that must be sold within, say, 30 days of default, the post-default price is *de facto* the appropriate measure as this is the quantity that the portfolio manager will receive upon default. These users can often get valuable indications from trading prices, and these indications, not some discounted measure of ultimate recovery, are the benchmarks that would make the most sense. If, in contrast, the user of the estimate is managing a portfolio of illiquid assets that must be held until maturity or resolution (or is holding a portfolio of liquid assets with the intention of holding for some period of time that might extend through resolution), then an estimate of ultimate recovery may be better suited and trading prices will not be particularly helpful. Interestingly, users who straddle both worlds (e.g., distressed-debt fund managers) may find knowing both measures particularly useful for spotting potential investment opportunities. In these cases, the end user would often want to derive a nominal recovery and compare it to traded prices in order to determine an estimated internal rate of return (IRR) for holding the defaulted debt through an estimated work-out time.

The ultimate recovery of an instrument can be related back to an observable market price by discounting the risky cash flows at an appropriate rate or through calculating the market price of risk and then formulating the price in a risk-neutral setting. Determining a discount rate in the first case, however, is an area of active debate. Some participants use the rate on the instrument just prior to default. Others suggest using various risky rates. In one study (Varma and Cantor 2005) the authors determined that the single B bond spread provided a reasonable proxy for the discount rate that, on average, equated post-default prices with prices at emergence.

It should be noted that other studies of different debt classes (not loans) have found far weaker correspondence between post-default and ultimate recovery observations. While financial theory suggests that there should be a relationship between these two measures, the relationship may be time-varying and it can be more difficult to characterize it in practice (though some market participants have suggested that this is an opportunity for funds that can better characterize this association).

When using post-default prices of recovery, either in a look-up table or through the use of a model, the predicted value is a risk-neutral measure of the expected discounted future recovery. To see why, consider that the ultimate recovery of a defaulted instrument will give a range of possible outcomes. If these possible outcomes are discounted back at, say, the risk-free rate to the expected default date, that will give a range of possible default prices. The risk-neutral, probability-weighted mean of the distribution is the expectation of the market price at default. Figure 5.4 shows this intuition schematically. In the figure, we take market price as an *ex ante*, risk-neutral discounted expectation of ultimate recovery, at time τ, the time of default (for simplicity in notation, we assume for the remainder of this section, without loss of generality, that the risk-free rate is zero):

$$p_\tau = r^Q_{\tau|T}$$

At time t, $t < \tau$, the model estimate of market price at some future time, τ, is an estimate of what the risk neutral expectation will be at time τ:

$$\hat{y}_{t,t<\tau} = E_t[p_\tau] = E_t\left[r^Q_{\tau|T}\right]$$

Because, however, there is also uncertainty around the actual price realization (the variability of the values in the lookup table) and because the

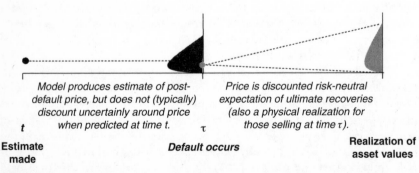

Model produces estimate of post-default price, but does not (typically) discount uncertainly around price when predicted at time t.

Price is discounted risk-neutral expectation of ultimate recoveries (also a physical realization for those selling at time τ).

t τ

Estimate made   *Default occurs*   **Realization of asset values**

FIGURE 5.4   Reconciling Defaulted Debt Value by Time

tables and models do not typically treat this uncertainty analytically, the measure itself can be thought of as a physical expectation. However, for use in valuation, it would be interesting to know directly

$$\hat{y}^Q_{t,t<\tau} = E^Q_t\left[r^Q_\tau\right]$$

or to know equivalently

$$\hat{y}_{t,t<\tau} = E^Q_t[p_\tau]$$

As mentioned before, the question of whether the risk-neutral and physical value of the future ultimate recoveries really differ depends on the extent to which ultimate recovery exhibits systematic risk. Until more empirical data are available, it is a reasonable assumption to treat the post-default price as a risk-neutral value in a valuation context. Of course, some investors will actually receive this value since the post-default price is what they will realize (because they will sell on default).

Recently, substantial interest has arisen in a stressed version of LGD analysis called *downturn LGD*, which describes higher values of LGD during periods of economic stress. This assumption is consistent with earlier research on both aggregate LGD rates (Keenan, Carty, and Shtogrin 1998; Altman et al. 2003) as well as studies of instrument-level LGD (Gupton and Stein 2002, 2005). Recently, regulators have adopted this as a key component of Basel II's treatment of LGD.

Downturn LGD tends to be an obligor-level phenomenon since the fortunes of specific instruments from the same borrower tend to be related more to idiosyncratic instrument structure rather than common macroeconomic factors. Unfortunately, there is substantial heterogeneity in the factors that affect a borrower's fortunes from industry to industry.

Note that the reason some methodologies treat downturn LGD separately is that most approaches to estimating LGD, which we explore more fully later in this chapter, focus on *long-run historical averages* and thus cannot accommodate LGD variation associated with *time-varying factors*. This suggests that a model-based rather than a table-based approach may be particularly useful for LGD.

The Denominator: Loss of . . .

Having outlined the various ways in which researchers characterize the "loss" part of the equation, we now turn to the ". . . of what" component. This section overlaps somewhat with sections of Chapters 3 and 6, where we also discuss the importance of choosing the denominator. In general, there are three broad measures of what an investor "should have gotten":

1. *Recovery of face (par).* The most conceptually straightforward measure of the anticipated payout of a debt investment is the par value of the bond or loan. The recovery of par convention characterizes losses in terms of the original promise made by the issuer.
2. *Recovery of price (market value).* Recognizing that securities are often priced at issuance or in the secondary market at discounts and premia, an alternative convention considers the traded price of the security to be the relevant value for calculating recovery/LGD. This formulation also turns out to make certain calculations, useful in a reduced form setting, more straightforward.
3. *Recovery of Treasury (risk-free value).* Somewhere between these two approaches, a third convention reasons that since defaults typically occur prior to the maturity of an instrument, the time value of money should be incorporated, though perhaps not at a risky rate. This approach considers the relevant measure to be the price of a U.S. Treasury with the same maturity as the defaulted instrument.

As we discuss in various places in this book, the choice of which denominator is used can affect both the interpretation and the tractability of portfolio and valuation models.

With this groundwork in place, we now turn to the estimation of LGD.

Estimating LGD Based on Data, Averages, and Tables

The most widespread practice in industry has been to estimate LGD using some form of historical average. It is interesting to contrast this with the state of PD estimation. In the 1990s market participants expended substantial effort to begin to understand and model probabilities of default. These efforts have paid sizeable dividends in that now, good PD models can be built or bought at reasonable cost. However, the same generally cannot be said of LGD modeling. Ironically, though LGD was considered less challenging to model than PDs, because of the PD modeling efforts, institutions have collected reasonably large samples of default data.[4] In contrast, LGD data

---

[4] This has led in some cases to inefficient underwriting and trading strategies since the primary focus at some institutions is avoiding default rather than maximizing return. As a result, higher (default) risk names may be avoided even in cases where their specific instruments might reasonably be expected to recover nearly 100 percent in default and to do so shortly after default.

is still difficult to come by and, when available, tends to be idiosyncratic in its organization and structure.[5]

Regardless of the data collection challenges, calculating averages across a number of dimensions to produce a look-up table with LGD values continues to be a popular approach for estimating LGD. There are many variants in how averages are constructed: long-term versus moving window, by seniority class versus overall, and dollar weighted versus simple (event) weighted. If data samples are large enough, further granularity can be achieved in the estimates by separating the sample by industry, geography, or size of obligor.

Some institutions use a simple historical average recovery rate as a recovery estimate. Such averages may be dollar weighted, issue weighted, or simply arithmetic averages. In general, some accommodation may be made to control for debt types—with recoveries on secured loans being higher than for unsecured bonds.

For the majority of financial institutions, however, the so-called model used to estimate LGD is a *conditional mean*: a table lookup in which dimensions of the table serve to subset the losses into different buckets. This sometimes reflects expert opinion as to what (physical) LGD *ought* to be, but more commonly LGD lookup tables list historical-average LGDs either from the institution's own experience (usually based on write-offs rather than economic loss) or, not uncommonly, taken from rating agency recovery studies. Some efforts are now under way for groups of financial institutions in various regions to pool data across firms for more robust estimation; however, these projects take many years to complete.

There is a wide variability in recovery values for instruments even when grouped by debt class and seniority. It is common to find table-driven LGD systems that are broken out by debt type, seniority class, collateral type, loan purpose, and business segment. Rapidly, the number of data points available in each category diminishes. Much of the art in constructing these tables lies in balancing number of data points and number of dimensions to arrive at a homogeneous sample. Figure 5.5 gives an example of the range of recoveries for two broad debt types, bonds and bank loans, and further discriminates between secured and unsecured bonds.

---

[5] LGD calculation can become even more complicated for middle-market (SME) firms. One reason for this is that such firms are often (though not always) clients of a single banking institution. When such firms default, their banks often consolidate all of their various loans, lines of credit, and so on, into a single relationship obligation and seek to recover as much as possible of this aggregate exposure. Thus it is often difficult to disentangle the actual recoveries and the factors that affect them at an instrument loan level.

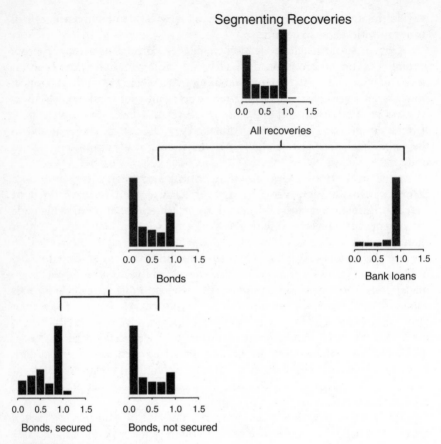

FIGURE 5.5   Segmenting Recoveries

The mobile (hanging) histogram gives a sense of the variability of recoveries in each category. (These data are from *Moody's Ultimate Recovery Database* and represent discounted settlement values.) In this figure, we show a histogram for the full population (top) and then segment by debt type (second row) and then further, for bonds, by whether the debt is collateralized (third row).

We see that the distribution of recoveries for bonds and for loans is quite different. In general, recoveries for loans tend to be more certain and favor full repayment, while those for bonds tend to be more variable. This makes intuitive sense since bank loans tend to be more senior in the capital structure than bonds and also typically enjoy some form of collateralization. Further segmenting the bonds, we distinguish between secured and unsecured bonds and again see a stark difference. Similar to bank loans, the secured bonds exhibit a higher propensity for repayment in full, though to a far lesser degree than loans. In contrast, the distribution of the unsecured bonds is almost a mirror image of the secured, with a high propensity not to repay at all and high variability. Interestingly, none of these subpopulations exhibit a distribution that resembles the full population, suggesting analytic value in refining estimates of recovery and through various statistical techniques (see Figure 5.5).

Importantly, even with this segmentation, the variability tends to be quite high even within subclasses. For example, even though the most common recovery for secured bonds is 100 percent, just under half of the secured bonds in this sample lost 20 percent or more, and more than a third lost more than half their value. Similar bars for other debt types, seniority classes, and collateralizations highlight the wide variability of recoveries even within subsegments of the population. This variability in output makes it more attractive to pursue model-based solutions. While LGD modeling is still in its infancy, the following sections describe early models that are an improvement over the table approach that is still in use.

APPROACHES TO MODELING LGD: THE LOSSCALC (2002, 2005) APPROACHES AND EXTENSIONS

Historical averages, such as those commonly found in lookup tables, broken out by debt type (loan, bond, preferred stock) and seniority class (secured, senior, subordinate, etc.), are important factors in predicting LGD. However, in our own research, we have found that they account for only about 40 percent of the power we are able to attain in predicting levels of recoveries.

Common dimensions for lookup tables include:

- Debt type
- Seniority
- Industry
- Collateral

LGD tables sometimes also blend their recovery history (which is often brief) with subjective adjustments. These approaches typically lack (1) a time-varying factor and (2) a rigorous means of discriminating differences in recovery *within* any given broad cell of the lookup table.

As is the case in most areas of multivariate statistics, tables represent a coarse first approximation to the discrete behavior of LGD that can be extended by using a richer, continuous framework. In this section, we describe work that has been done to extend the traditional lookup table to a more complete statistical representation that accommodates continuous factors and interactions and thereby provides a richer description of the dynamics of LGD.

A Multifactor Approach

Rather than summarizing LGD discretely via a few coarse dimensions, we find multifactor continuous approaches to be far more effective. In addition to providing higher resolution with respect to LGD estimation (statistical models of LGD can account for the relatively high dimensional set of factors affecting it), such models can also appropriately capture the time dimension of LGD.

We typically predict PDs over horizons of one to five years. It is useful to be able to do this for LGD as well. Table formulations do not easily admit a time dimension. This is important in that there are typically two situations in which LGD is required: First, at the time an instrument defaults, a holder of that instrument is interested in knowing the likely recovery value for it. This requires an estimate of the *immediate* LGD. Second, prior to default, for purposes of risk management and valuation, a holder of a credit-risky instrument would like to estimate what the LGD *would be* were the instrument to default over the horizon of interest. This requires a prediction at the horizon. Models that can differentiate between immediate and, say, one year future LGDs are straightforward to estimate econometrically[6] but it is unclear how this would be easily accomplished using table methods.

In our applied work (e.g., Gupton and Stein 2002 and 2005), we have found it most useful to consider factors such that:

1. Each factor is individually predictive.
2. The factors are generally uncorrelated with each other (i.e., they speak to different parts of the puzzle).
3. They are aggregated within a consistent framework.

We first consider the types of factors that can be useful in this regard. As in the case with econometric default modeling (see Chapter 4), we have found it helpful to group factors into categories that each represent a component of risk. In the case of LGD, we find it useful to consider layers of information,

---

[6] This case would involve lagging the independent variables by the time period of the horizon. For example, to create a one-year forward model, we would lag the independent variables by one year. In practice we have found that it is difficult to predict conditional LGD meaningfully beyond one or two years.

starting with the most idiosyncratic (collateral) through the most systematic (state of the economy). One such taxonomy is as follows:

- Collateral and other support.
- Debt type and structure.
- Firm characteristics.
- Industry environment.
- Macroeconomic environment (including geographic variation).

This approach has been pursued in part or in full in other academic literature as well, with respect to both recovery *rates* (for an entire population) and recovery *events* (for individual instruments). Table 5.1 summarizes some of the academic literature on the impact of different factors on recovery.

Collateral and Support

The variability around how financial institutions characterize collateral can be high. That said, most institutions tend to think of collateral value in terms of how liquid it is or, in the case of guarantees, how credible the guarantor is, with higher liquidity/credibility associated with higher value. Thus, for example, cash and marketable securities would be considered more valuable than real estate, and a guarantee from a large parent company more valuable than one from a corporate family member. For larger corporations, pledges of collateral also represent a means through which a lender can exert more control over the borrower (for example, by achieving higher priority).

Of course, collateral is not directly relevant for unsecured debt. However, the recoveries on secured debt types (senior secured loans, senior secured bonds) can vary depending on collateral type. Furthermore, senior unsecured loans also benefit from a type of collateral (subsidiary support) which has value for loan recoveries but is technically not a hard asset. Some of the types of collateral and support include:

- *Cash and marketable securities collateral.* This is cash, compensating balances, linked balances, and liquid instruments held on account.
- *Pledge of "all assets" of the firm.* "All assets" is a general designation and may result in enforceability issues. That is taken into account when assessing its impact.
- *Property, plant, and equipment.* This represents the actual means of production. In the majority of cases it is a physical asset. It can also be extended to include other so-called instruments of production—for example, airport landing rights.
- *Subsidiary support.* This term refers to any (1) guarantees by subsidiaries, (2) pledged stock of subsidiaries, or (3) pledged and substantively sized key assets of subsidiaries.

TABLE 5.1 A Selection of Research on Drivers of LGD

	Support	Differ
Debt type matters	Carty and Lieberman (1996) Van de Castle and Keisman (1999) Gupton (2000) Van de Castle et al. (2000) Gupton and Stein (2002) Acharya et al. (2003) Gupton and Stein (2005)	
Debt structure significant	Carty and Lieberman (1996) Van de Castle and Keisman (1999) Gupton (2000) Van de Castle et al. (2000) Gupton and Stein (2002) Acharya et al. (2003) Gupton and Stein (2005)	
Industry matters	Altman and Kishmore (1996) Hamilton et al. (2001) Gupton and Stein (2002) Acharya et al. (2003) Emery (2004) Gupton and Stein (2005) Varma and Cantor (2005)	Gupton, Gates, and Carty (2000) Citron et al. (2002)
Firm-specific factors affect recoveries	Unal et al. (2001) Gupton and Stein (2002) Acharya et al. (2003) Gupton and Stein (2005) Varma and Cantor (2005)	Citron et al. (2002) (size only)
Macro factors affect recoveries	Hamilton et al. (2000) Fridson et al. (2000) Frye (2000) Altman et al. (2001) Unal et al. (2001) Gupton and Stein (2002) Acharya et al. (2003) Emery et al. (2004) Gupton and Stein (2005) Varma and Cantor (2005)	Hurt and Felsovalyi (1998) Emery et al. (2004)

It is sometimes useful to contemplate a mixture of these and other collateral types, particularly for loans. This reflects the typical practice of bankers who seek to secure as much collateral as possible. Mixing different combinations of collateral can lead to a better estimation of recovery.

Debt Type and Seniority Class

Debt type and seniority class are the bases of most rating agency recovery studies and are also among the most widely used dimensions for creating historical lookup tables in the financial industry. This is for good reason. We have found it useful to include these factors in a multifactor context as well.

Controlling for debt type and seniority classes has several benefits. First, it reflects the likelihood of senior debt holders recovering more than subordinated debt holders and, in North America, it addresses the additional effects of the *Absolute Priority Rule* (APR) of default resolution.[7] Second, even after controlling for seniority, we observe that different classes of debt exhibit different behavior in recovery. Both the central tendency and the dispersion of the distributions of recoveries differ for different debt types even when they have the same seniority. Figure 5.6 demonstrates this.

Another form of seniority analysis involves considering the relative debt cushion below the instrument of interest. In its most basic sense, calculating the relative debt cushion is a simple means to measure the instrument's standing within the firm's capital structure (i.e., are there claimants who stand more senior at the time of default?). For example, preferred stock is the lowest seniority class short of common stock, but it might hold the *highest* seniority rank within a particular firm that has no funding from loans or bonds. In addition, some more senior class of debt may mature, thus revealing another (lower) debt class to be most senior.

Alternative measures of relative debt position are fractional versions of this measure, such as the *amount* of debt that stands more senior, or

---

[7] The APR is a legal construct that provides for the satisfaction of the obligations of a defaulted firm in accordance with the seniority of the lien. Thus, after taxes are paid, the remaining obligations are satisfied, to the extent possible, starting with the most senior debt and working down through the capital structure. In practice, particularly for smaller private firms, the APR is not always followed. For smaller firms, it is more common for the main credit lines to be concentrated with a single financial institution. As a result, the lender tends to think of recovery in terms of the net sum of all obligations that the firm has and effectively consolidates the debt into a single class, the satisfaction of which is accomplished, to the degree possible, by monetizing the assets of the firm, regardless of which particular debt obligation may have been pledged. This practice is more similar to general bankruptcy practices outside of the United States.

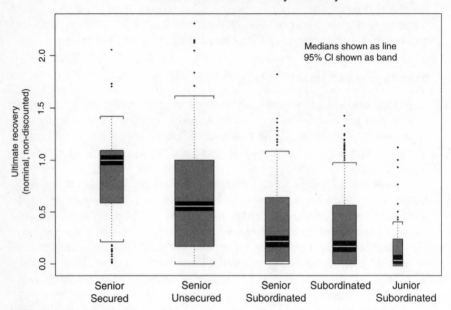

FIGURE 5.6 Bond Recoveries Differ by Seniority

the *proportion* of total liabilities that is more senior. However, though also useful, both the data availability for the components of these continuous measures and the interpretation of them can cause modeling complications. For example, in contrast to the proportion of debt in the capital structure, in bankruptcy proceedings, a junior claimant's ability to extract concessions from more senior claimants is *not* proportional to its claim size. Junior claimants can force the full due process of a court hearing and so have a practical veto power on the *speediness* of an agreed settlement. However, even collecting the data to examine this relationship can be challenging. Claim amounts at the time of default are not the same as original borrowing/issuance amounts since in many cases, borrowers partially pay down their debt before maturity through amortization schedules (for loans) and sinking funds (for bonds). In addition, data on the exposure at default may be unavailable for firms that pursue multiple funding channels.

Firm-Level Information

It is natural not only to think in terms of the structure of the debt and collateral, but also to consider how different firms might fare in financial distress. For example, firms that have strong franchises are likely to continue to generate cash flow after default, even though they were unable to meet all of their obligations in a timely manner.

As an example, often firms default for liquidity rather than solvency reasons. As a result, information about the firm's leverage provides an indication of how much asset value is available to cover the liabilities of the firm. Other factors such as the ratio of short-term debt to total debt may similarly be effective in this regard.

Importantly, when estimating LGD models, the firm level is the most appropriate place to make adjustments for the known estimation biases that may enter into an LGD modeling project since, by definition, only firms that have actually defaulted have an observable (physical) loss (thus the term *loss given default*). This implies that the LGD values we observe are actually *conditional* on default having occurred. However, in practice, LGD models are often applied to firms that have not yet defaulted (for risk management or pricing applications). This introduces estimation bias in models of LGD.

A common econometric result (Heckman 1979) provides a mechanism for correcting this bias by including the probability of entering the default state as a predictor of the ultimate outcome. This approach addresses the potential bias caused by applying a factor that is itself predictive of being in the conditioned state of the world (default). Heckman showed that when this factor is a transformation of the probability (called a *Mills Ratio*) it serves to remove the bias from the estimation.

Industry

Industry turns out to be an important predictor of recovery rates. For this reason, many institutions use recovery averages broken out by industry to refine historical estimates of LGD. However, simply calculating long-run averages by industry produces an estimate that effectively implies that industry characteristics do not change over time. Our own research and that of others, however, suggests that in addition to exhibiting long-run differences in recovery, industries also exhibit time-varying differences in recovery behavior. This is due in part to the correlation of default and recovery that we discuss later in this chapter. Imbalances in the supply and demand for, say, distressed aircraft can serve to depress (or inflate) recovery prices. The static industry-bucket approach alone does not capture the industry-level variability in recovery rates *across time* and across industry. For example, some sectors, such as the telephone industry, enjoy periods of prolonged superior recoveries, but fall well below average recoveries at other times.

The time-varying nature of industry effects in post-default prices suggests that incorporating some sort of dynamic industry factor could be valuable in formulating an estimate. We can look to a number of macro-economic factors as possible candidates—for example, mean industry credit spreads and trailing industry default rates. We have found that examining both the trailing industry recovery experience and some industry-level macro factors is useful as well, each for different reasons. The macroeconomic factors tend to be more dynamic and provide a cross-sectional view of the credit cycle of a specific industry. In contrast, the trailing recovery rates for the industry provide information on the relative values of distressed assets similar to those that might be liquidated in default for the company under study. This historical measure gives some sense of the current supply and demand for these assets. These measures generally exhibit stable predictive behavior across the industries and the country/regions we have examined.

Importantly, the supply/demand nature of recovery appears to be far less pronounced in *ultimate recovery* than in *post-default pricing*. One reason for this may be that the liquidation of the assets that generate the cash flows in the ultimate recoveries need not take place at the same instant. Therefore, to the degree there are a number of liquidations in the same industry, these may be managed in a more orderly fashion than is the case with the inventories of the distressed financial assets that are reflected in post-default prices.

We have observed consistent differences in recoveries in some regulated industries. For example, we found that post-default prices on the defaulted debt of regulated banks tended to be very low in most cases. One reason for this, we believe, is that the banks receive regulatory support while in distress and thus remain technically solvent for longer periods of time than might be the case in other industries. As a result, by the time the firms actually do default, they have run through most of their assets and there is little value left. In contrast, researchers have reported that ultimate recoveries on the debt of defaulted regulated utilities tends to be consistently high.

Macroeconomic/Geographic

Recoveries have been shown to be positively and significantly correlated with default rates, both in an aggregate sense and on a firm-specific basis, particularly in the case of post-default prices. As a result it can be useful to incorporate time-varying information about the state of the credit cycle into LGD modeling and even more useful to do this at both the geographic and industry levels. Indexes of credit indicators such as trailing default rates, Moody's Bankrupt Bond Index, and the change in the index of leading economic indicators (LEI) can all be useful indicators in estimating LGD. We have also found that using a forward-looking measure, such as an aggregate distance-to-default statistic, can substantially increase the predictive power of LGD models. Alternative measures such as aggregate bond spreads or CDS spreads can also be considered. Importantly, the positive correlation between PD and LGD tends to lengthen the tail of a portfolio loss distribution during economic downturns, thus raising economic capital assessments, which can be important in estimating downturn LGD (discussed earlier). It also appears that the correlation between LGD and PD is evident not only in the corporate context but also in the study of other types of credit risk such as residential mortgages.

In some jurisdictions, the local jurisdictional process will turn out to be one of the biggest determinants of recovery (Davydenko and Franks 2006). The reason is that the legal processes governing bankruptcy and default resolution in certain states, provinces, or countries can be more (or less) favorable for borrowers. In these geographies, recoveries are likely to be higher (lower) as a result. This type of geographic effect can be modeled in a number of ways. One of the most straightforward is the inclusion of a jurisdictional flag that designates the relative borrower-friendliness of a jurisdiction. Note that this effect is separate from the cyclical effect we discussed earlier in this section and thus generally benefits from separate treatment when it is present.

An important benefit to including macroeconomic geographic and industry factors is that they provide a natural mechanism for correlating PD and LGD estimates in a portfolio context. To the extent the LGD factors overlap with or are related to those used to model changes in PD, a common correlation model (structural or reduced-form) can be used to generate correlated PD and LGD realizations in a simulation (or analytic) portfolio framework. We discuss factor models in Chapter 8 on portfolio modeling.

A Regression Framework

One aspect of LGD estimation in a portfolio context requires characterization of not just the expected LGD, but also the distribution of possible LGD values. As we explain in Chapter 8, we typically specify a distribution for the LGD in order to more accurately estimate a (simulated) portfolio loss distribution. One common approach to modeling such distributions is to posit a beta distribution as the underlying distribution for the LGD process. A beta distribution is a member of a very flexible family of distributions that can take on a diversity of shapes depending on their parameterization. In particular, the properties of the distribution make it useful for characterizing various ratios and proportions. Importantly, the shape parameters for the distribution can be calculated in practice with knowledge of the lower moments of the empirical sample. Application of a beta distribution has been shown to be robust across many LGD data sets (Gordy and Jones 2002; Onorota and Altman 2003; Pesaran et al. 2003).

Since the beta distribution appears reasonably consistent with empirical LGD data and since this assumption can be easily accommodated in the portfolio frameworks commonly used for ACPM, it can be useful to implement techniques that make use of this distributional characteristic. Gupton and Stein (2002) describe one such regression technique that they found effective when the dependent variable is beta distributed.

The technique involves the following steps:

1. Estimate the shape parameters of a beta distribution, $\hat{\alpha}$, $\hat{\beta}$ from the data set.
2. Calculate the percentile, $p_i^{Beta(\hat{\alpha},\hat{\beta})}$, of each LGD observation, y_i, by calculating the cumulative density function (cdf) of the value of y_i:

$$p_i^{Beta(\hat{\alpha},\hat{\beta})} = Beta(y_i,\hat{\alpha},\hat{\beta})$$

(This is a probability.)
3. Map the new value into a standard normal distribution:

$$z_i = \Phi^{-1}(p_i^{Beta(\hat{\alpha},\hat{\beta})})$$

4. Estimate the parameters, $\hat{\boldsymbol{\delta}}$, of a linear model based on a set of covariates (possibly transformed through a set of functions $q()$), $\mathbf{X}$, such as seniority, industry, and so on, including a Heckman adjustment if desired (mangling slightly notation):

$$\hat{\mathbf{z}} = \hat{\boldsymbol{\delta}}' q(\mathbf{X})$$

5. The final LGD estimate is then recovered by reversing the process: First calculate[8] the probability of $\hat{z}_i$ and then calculate the inverse cdf of the beta distribution that characterizes the original data:

$$\hat{s}_i = Beta^{-1}(\Phi(\hat{z}_i), \hat{\alpha}, \hat{\beta})$$

6. (Optional) A final nonparametric mapping may also be used to further calibrate the modeled LGD to empirical data and correct for any specification error in either the model or the estimation of $\hat{\alpha}$ and $\hat{\beta}$. (See Chapter 4 for a discussion of univariate transformations.)

---

[8] Note that if the mean and variance of the $\hat{z}_i$ are substantially different from standard normal (i.e., mean and variance of 0 and 1, respectively), they can be rescaled to zero mean and unit variance to preserve the mean and variance of the original y_i.

In summary, the form of the model can be described as

$$\hat{s}_i = Beta^{-1}(\Phi(\hat{z}_i), \hat{\alpha}, \hat{\beta})$$

$$\hat{z}_i = \hat{\delta}' q(\mathbf{x_i})$$

where $q(\mathbf{x_i})$ are the transformed factors.

This leaves only the estimation of $\hat{\alpha}$ and $\hat{\beta}$. The beta distribution is specified by two shape parameters, α and β, which can be calculated from the estimated sample mean and standard deviation, $\hat{\mu}$ and $\hat{\sigma}$, respectively. Since, the mean and standard deviation of the beta distribution (in the typical case bounded between 0 and 1) are given as

$$\hat{\mu} = \frac{\alpha}{\alpha + \beta} \quad \text{and} \quad \hat{\sigma} = \sqrt{\frac{\alpha\beta}{(\alpha + \beta + 1)(\alpha + \beta)^2}}$$

it follows that

$$\hat{\alpha} = \hat{\mu}\left[\frac{\hat{\mu}(1 - \hat{\mu})}{\hat{\sigma}^2} - 1\right] \quad \text{and} \quad \hat{\beta} = \hat{\alpha}\left[\frac{1}{\hat{\mu}} - 1\right]$$

Similar variants of these equations can be derived for distributions bounded between zero and an upper value:

$$\alpha = \frac{\mu}{Max}\left[\frac{\mu \cdot (Max - \mu)}{Max \cdot \sigma^2} - 1\right] \quad \text{and} \quad \beta = \alpha\left[\frac{Max}{\mu} - 1\right]$$

Note that in principle, any cdf may be used to estimate the quantiles and invert out again, though the beta distribution has some attractive properties as we have discussed.

Since the publication of Gupton and Stein (2002), more formal techniques for estimating regressions with beta distributed dependent variables have been introduced in the statistics literature. For example, Ferrari and Cribari-Neto (2004) solve the (log) likelihood directly (numerically) for a regression in which the dependent variable is taken to be beta distributed and the log likelihood is given as

$$\ell_i = \log \Gamma(\phi) - \log \Gamma(\mu_i\phi) - \log \Gamma((1 - \mu_i)\phi) + (\mu_i\phi - 1)\log(y_i)$$
$$+ [(1 - \mu_i)\phi - 1]\log(1 - y_i)$$

where

$$\mu_i = \text{logit}(\mathbf{x}'_i\beta) = \frac{e^{\mathbf{x}'_i\beta}}{1 + e^{\mathbf{x}'_i\beta}}$$

and

$$\phi = \alpha + \beta$$

While these techniques enjoy more elegant theoretical foundations, both their implementation and their estimation can be challenging with real-world data. We have implemented and experimented with beta-regression estimators. Our empirical results suggest that the approach produces fairly similar results to that introduced in Gupton and Stein (2002), but that the latter produces more robust estimates when applied to actual loan data, particularly with respect to out-of-sample tests. In addition, the numerical properties of the Gupton and Stein (2002) approach seem better, especially for large data sets where the maximum likelihood approach can fail to converge reliably in our experience.

In more recent work (primarily on retail exposures) we have also examined the viability of implementing additional bias-correcting methods such as that of Heckman (1979) to account for the relatively high number of zero LGD (100 percent recovery) cases. In many cases, LGD may exhibit a beta distribution subject to experiencing a loss greater than zero (see Figure 5.6). We have had relatively good success in specifying LGD models in two stages: the first stage being a discrete choice (probit) model to predict the probability of observing a loss greater than zero, given default; and the second the regression model of the actual LGD including the (transformed) value of the probability estimate from the first.

Note that this approach is different again from that of including the probability of *default* in the LGD model as a predictor. In that case, we are conditioning on the probability of defaulting at all; and in the other, we are conditioning on the probability of having a loss greater than zero, given that a borrower has defaulted and is in the position of having to calculate losses.

In closing this section, we note that we have focused primarily on the LossCalc model of LGD and a few extensions. One reason for this is the relative lack of available commercial research regarding instrument-specific LGD models. While the area of LGD modeling (as opposed to LGD lookup tables) holds substantial promise, we are aware of few efforts to produce commercial LGD estimation models. In recent years, there has been some academic work in this regard and we have come across a number of in-house models used by banks and other institutions, but the lack of availability of commercial products suggests that this area is still a fledgling one, and we expect substantial growth in coming years.

CONCLUSION

LGD is a key quantity in both pricing and risk management applications. It basically tells us how concerned we should be if a firm defaults. If LGD is very low, then default risk is less of a concern. The reason is that even in default, losses will be small. If LGD is very high, then even firms with low default probability may still represent substantial credit risk, particularly for larger exposures. To date, despite its important role in credit-related applications, comparatively little work has been done on LGD, relative to PD estimation, in either the academic or professional realms.

While we continue to learn more about LGD as this research progresses, there are still only a few theoretical models of LGD that are of practical use. Rather, much of our knowledge of recovery appears to come to us through stylized facts. As a result, the state of the art in many financial institutions is not much more advanced than it was a decade ago, with LGD being proxied by standard assumptions (e.g., 60 percent) or through the use of rating agency or internally developed lookup tables.

A recent development in theoretical LGD that shows some promise is research in *firm-level* LGD (Carey and Gordy 2004; Cantor, Emery, and Stumpp 2006). This framework aggregates all of the debt of a firm and contemplates this aggregate amount in the context of the value of a firm at default, the firm's debt structure, and relevant bankruptcy codes. (For example, all three of the major rating agencies now base their debt-level LGD expectations on the analysis of the aggregate value of the firm assets in default and the debt structure of the firm.)

However, implementation may still be lagging, both because of the newness of this approach within many institutions and because of a lack of current and historical data in a convenient form, which reduces the analysis to a firm-by-firm one in many cases. While these approaches are still new, some authors have reported superior forecasting performance using such approaches relative to instrument-level approaches. Additionally, these approaches have provided interesting insights into the relationship between a firm's PD and the ultimate LGD on its defaulted assets. We expect that as the research matures, additional insights will be forthcoming.

As more financial institutions trade credit, LGD estimation has become more important in the valuation context. Understanding implied LGD and developing a better characterization of whether LGD among exposures in a portfolio is correlated will become increasingly important in sorting out trading opportunities. More work needs to be done in expanding existing models to account for the differences in LGD across instruments.

Despite the inchoate nature of LGD models and research, LGD data is slowly becoming more readily available and available in a more systematized format. Banks have begun collecting LGD observations in a more rigorous fashion and commercial databases are for offer in the market. We expect that the modeling of loss given default will become increasingly more important as this data becomes more widely used and analyzed, and we expect that later editions of this book will contain new results and more robust approaches to modeling LGD than are currently state of the art.

REVIEW QUESTIONS

1. What is the difference between post-default price and ultimate recoveries? What are the benefits of each?
2. Assume that in default you receive $950 in recovery. What three quantities might you use to calculate what the recovery rate is, based on a numerator of $950?
3. How does debt structure affect recovery? How can geography affect recovery?
4. A colleague tells you that he will just assume a 40 percent LGD when modeling a portfolio of bonds and loans. What would you advise him?
5. What are the limitations of using table-based approaches to LGD estimation?

EXERCISES

1. Assume you observe a recovery data set with a mean LGD of 40 percent and a standard deviation of 10 percent. What are the parameters of a beta distribution that would describe this data? Under a beta assumption, what is the probability of observing an LGD greater than 55?
2. Assume you have received $950 from selling a defaulted bond with a face value of $1,000 and a maturity in exactly one year. Just before default, the bond was trading at 97.5, meaning each dollar of debt was trading at $0.975, and the one-year Treasury was yielding 5.25 percent. Calculate the recovery under assumptions of recovery of face, recovery of market, and recovery of Treasury.

TABLE 5.2 PD and LGD for Four Structured Loans

Loan	PD	α_{LGD}	β_{LGD}
A	200 bps	6.0	14.0
B	150 bps	14.0	9.2
C	250 bps	0.31	1.2
D	175 bps	1.3	3.0

3. You are shown estimates of PD and LGD for four similarly structured loans to different obligors. The PD and LGD information (assuming beta-distributed LGD) is listed in Table 5.2. Rank these in terms of EL and show the EL for each. Rank them in terms of 0.99 losses. Show 0.99 percentile losses for each. (Assume no information about other portfolio holdings—this evaluation should be done on a stand-alone basis.)

CHAPTER 6

Reduced-Form Models

Complete realism is clearly unattainable, and the question whether a theory is realistic enough can be settled only by seeing whether it yields predictions that are good enough for the purpose in hand or that are better than predictions from alternative theories.
—Milton Friedman

An appropriate appetite for risk is ultimately a matter of judgment, which is informed by quantitative models for measuring and pricing risk and based on a conceptual understanding of the implications of risk.
—Darrell Duffie and Kenneth Singleton (2003, p. 13)

Objectives

After reading this chapter you should understand the following concepts:

- Definition of a reduced-form model of default.
- The basics for building a reduced-form model of default.
- Impact on reduced-form models of using different LGD assumptions.
- Situations in which reduced-form models can be effectively used.
- Empirical challenges of estimating a reduced-form model of default.

Good managers of credit portfolios make use of a variety of models and systems. We spend a good deal of this text discussing structural models and the benefits we see in using them. For example, we discussed in Chapter 3 the power in a structural (i.e., causal) model to capture the economic factors driving an obligor's credit quality and in Chapter 8 we extend this framework to portfolio risk modeling as correlation can be parameterized through factor models as well.

As attractive as they are in theory, however, we have also pointed out that values generated from these types of models often diverge from observed market prices, making them less practically useful for valuation applications in certain markets. In addition, some types of debt instruments (e.g., sovereign debt) do not have simple structural interpretations as the asset processes may not be simple to infer. Thus, despite their theoretical elegance, structural models alone cannot fill all credit modeling needs. In some settings, especially with respect to matching current market spreads, reduced-form models offer an attractive array of modeling options.

This is made clearer when we consider that empirical evidence is mixed on the degree to which structural factors drive credit spreads (Bohn 2000b; Collin-Dufresne, Goldstein, and Martin 2001; Elton et al. 2001; Driessen 2005). While the data, estimation methods, and overall conclusions of various researchers may differ somewhat, most agree that some portion of the credit spread can be modeled by structural factors. The point of disagreement, however, is the *extent* to which economy-wide, systematic factors are important in determining credit spreads. In Chapter 3 on structural models we discussed methods for better integrating economy-wide, systematic factors; however, some applications such as pricing a trading book may require more direct methods. Reduced-form models provide one means for dealing with this type of situation since the model framework can be adapted to accommodate whatever happens to be driving credit spreads.

In Chapter 4 on econometric models, we discussed models that rely on inputs that are easy to understand, but do not always capture the complexities of risk and pricing found in the market. More importantly, these models can be effectively used for evaluating firms that do not have traded securities. They can also be applied to other types of borrowers such as credit card holders. In some ways, the econometric models are an example of a reduced-form approach to modeling credit, and the discussions in Chapter 4 introduced the usefulness of a more widely applicable modeling framework. Structural, econometric, and reduced-form models each have their place in a risk manager's and a portfolio manager's tool kit.

The reduced-form approach presented in this chapter is known for the tractability of its models and for their flexibility. These models generally rely on a stochastic characterization of the *default time* as opposed to a stochastic characterization of a firm's asset value. Consequently, this modeling approach posits that default is essentially unpredictable. This attribute is both a strength and a limitation of these models. It is a strength in the sense that no assumption is necessary to characterize what causes a firm to default. While default could be a result of falling asset value, it could also be a result of a product-liability lawsuit. That makes this type of model more comprehensive in its application. Its weakness arises from firstly the fact that information known to predict default (i.e., falling distance to default) is mostly ignored, at least in terms of directly entering the model; and secondly, the estimates can be quite sensitive to noise in the data used for estimation. As a result of both of these factors, in a number of practical applications, many observations must be pooled with the result that model output may be associated with groups of firms as opposed to specific firms.

In certain contexts, the speed and efficiency of reduced-form models make them more useful than their structural counterparts. In particular, we will show how the mathematical tractability and flexibility of reduced-form frameworks can be useful when market prices contain substantial noncredit information (e.g., liquidity premia). The functional forms of reduced-form models lend themselves to explaining complicated interactions. A big advantage of these approaches is that they offer a tractable and flexible mechanism to interpolate and extrapolate from market observables while still resting firmly on solid financial economics theory.

The tractability of reduced-form models makes them an attractive choice for marking to market illiquid securities using observed prices of more liquid securities, since the models are effective tools for extracting useful information from traded security values that is often obscured by data noise.

REDUCED-FORM MODELS IN CONTEXT

In a sidebar in Chapter 3, we highlighted the evolution of the definition of structural and reduced-form models. We will not review that comparison here, but focus on the current definition of reduced-form models where exogenous variables parameterize intensity processes (often stochastic) that govern the timing of default. Later in this section, we define default intensities and intensity processes with more mathematical rigor. For our purposes at this point, though, the reader can interpret an intensity as simply the probability of default in the next instant of time, *given that default has not yet occurred*. This sounds similar to our definition of a hazard rate in Chapter 4, however, intensities have richer mathematical properties. They represent the propensity of a firm to default conditioned on *all* (sometimes stochastic) information about default. These characteristics allow the models we discuss to represent default risk in a more natural way and to better match the observed pricing behavior than would be the case with simple hazard-rate models. Thus, for infinitesimally small intervals of time, the default probability (given survival to the beginning of that period) over that time interval is the time interval times the intensity. For a fuller and more detailed discussion of the properties of intensities, see Lando (2004, Chapter 5).

Note that as is the case with PDs, a firm with a high intensity is not guaranteed to default; rather, one would expect a group of firms with higher intensities to contain more defaults, on average, than a group of firms with lower intensities (all else equal). To the extent that the intensity itself is estimated from many observations of prices on different firm's debt instruments, or CDS, as is often done in practice due to sparse pricing on many corporate issuers, the intensity itself will not be firm specific.

One approach to characterizing default intensities in the context that we have been discussing is to estimate an intensity directly from pricing and other information. An alternative approach makes use of a transition matrix or a *generator matrix* for a *Markov chain*. These latter representations permit models that admit more than two credit states (beyond default and nondefault) and thus, particularly for higher credit quality issuers, they are sometimes well suited to characterizing default behavior since they can incorporate more information than methods relying on rare default events alone. The Markov setting results in the simplifying assumption that the future evolution of the underlying stochastic process only relies on the current information—it is not dependent on the path taken to arrive at the current state of the world. A generator matrix defines all the transition intensities associated with moving among different possible credit states or rating grades. These ratings may be the external ratings assigned by a rating agency such as Moody's or S&P or they may be internal ratings assigned by a bank's risk group. Recently, some researchers have relaxed (or, more appropriately, generalized) the strict Markov assumption and admitted covariates including prior credit states to good effect.

While the data used to estimate the transitions for this form of reduced-form model may be different, the conceptual framework is the same. We will explore the mathematics later. At this point, the reader can interpret a generator matrix as a compact representation of the propensity of an obligor to transition among several different credit states with the default state included as a *trapping* or *absorbing* state—in other words, once in that state, the obligor can never leave.[1]

In the next several sections we will use these two conceptual tools—default intensities and Markov generator matrices—to describe the framing within which the models were developed. By way of introduction and to provide more intuition around how these models behave, we first put a few of the more important reduced-form models in an historical context.

In 1997, Robert Jarrow, David Lando, and Stuart Turnbull extended work that had been introduced in 1995 by Jarrow and Turnbull to develop

---

[1] The generator approach can also accommodate a nonabsorbing default version of the model; however, most implementations focus on the absorbing barrier version.

a ratings transition approach to modeling credit-risky debt (Jarrow, Lando, and Turnbull 1997). They began their approach by considering the analogy of default risk to foreign exchange. They observed that risky debt could be considered to be an asset denominated in a different currency than risk-free debt. The translation from one currency to another requires a cross-currency exchange rate. In credit terms, this exchange rate effectively constitutes the adjustment necessary to match risky debt prices. This type of adjustment relies on the (credit) *transition intensities* (described through a generator matrix) and the risk premia associated with the uncertainty resulting from the possibility of an obligor deteriorating in credit quality and finally defaulting.

Consider a simple example of the behavior that such transition intensities capture: A firm may be rated investment grade or sub-investment grade. It may also default. The result is a three-state transition matrix with the following states:

1. Investment grade (IG)
2. Sub–investment grade (SIG)
3. Default (D)

The transition intensities characterize the propensity of moving between states (or remaining in the current state). Later in this chapter we provide some numerical examples. The key intuition to gain here is that in addition to defaulting directly, an obligor can transition first from IG to SIG and then to D. Thus, unlike the binary case, there are various shades of credit quality between solvency and default that provide additional information about the default process. A key characteristic of this matrix is the fact that it captures the transitions to other states before default as well as the transition into the default state. Of course, the matrix also captures the propensity of moving directly from IG to D. The matrix captures all the possibilities in this three-state world.

Two important assumptions are made in the 1997 framework to ensure tractable solutions. First, interest rates and credit spreads are assumed to be independent. Second, recovery is calculated with respect to the risk-free (i.e., Treasury) value of the security. While easy to understand and conceptually easy to implement, in practice this framework has suffered from the fact that, from a practical perspective, it ultimately required a fair amount of effort to constrain and modify parameters so that they made practical sense. Sometimes the final estimates became more a function of the constraints than the data. Not much published research is available describing the empirical performance of this type of model; nonetheless, this approach is often used to do preliminary analyses.

Much of the current generation of reduced-form models derives from models introduced both by Lando (1994, 1998) and Duffie and Singleton

(DS) in 1999. The focus of this Duffie-Singleton-Lando (DSL) framework is on an intensity process that is itself stochastic and potentially driven by underlying state variables. DS specified the intensity processes as being a function of underlying state variables and provided practically implementable models. Lando also characterized a similar link to external covariates for either intensity processes or rating transitions. This turned out to facilitate the introduction of correlation between interest rates and credit spreads. The key to this correlation is to link both processes to the same family of state variables. Duffie and Singleton first suggested the recovery specification in which recovery is computed with respect to the predefault price—that is, the market value of the security. (See the section on modeling affine intensity process with fractional recovery later in this chapter, and also Chapter 5.)

For example, say, for simplicity, a model specified default intensity to be a function of the overall debt in the economy and the level of expected GDP growth. By also linking the interest-rate process to these two variables, we induce correlation between default rates and interest rates. In practice, we would likely assume the underlying state variables to be latent (i.e., unobserved) and use market prices in the credit markets to extract information about the parameterization of a model that assumes these latent variables (we discuss how this works in more detail later). The DSL framework can also accommodate liquidity effects by specifying a separate liquidity process, similarly linked to the same set of underlying state variables.

Like structural models, reduced-form models allow for the estimation of both default probabilities and security values. Much of the mathematical infrastructure of the reduced-form framework has been imported from the affine term structure literature, making it easy to find a wide range of formulations that have been solved (analytically or numerically), coded, and tested. The challenge lies in the appropriate application of this infrastructure to credit analysis problems which can often exhibit characteristics quite different from market risk analysis problems.

John Hull and Alan White (HW) proposed another version of an intensity model in 2000 (Hull and White 2000a and 2000b) which has gained popularity in industry due to its tractability and the relative ease with which it can be estimated. Their modification was to focus on the *default probability density* (which is a function of the default intensity). Essentially, the focus is on the same type of parameters except that the formulas are characterized in terms of a function that looks like a density function implying the probability of a credit event. An important contribution of their approach lies in the ease with which the HW model can be used to fit credit default swap (CDS) data effectively. As the demand for mark-to-market algorithms grows, this type of flexible and easy-to-implement model becomes an attractive option for estimating credit curves from CDS data. The curves can then be used to mark all credit-risky securities.

Reduced-form and structural models can also be linked together. As we discussed in Chapter 3, one type of hybrid model is a class of structural models that can be recast as intensity models by introducing a feature that makes default unpredictable (i.e., it breaks the direct causal link). For example, we described the work done by Duffie and Lando (2001) which demonstrates that if a firm's asset value (or the information that can be used to derive this value) is observed with error (so that market participants do not know exactly where the firm's value is with respect to its default barrier), default becomes inaccessible (i.e., unpredictable) even in a model framework that is more akin to a structural characterization of default. While hybrid models such as the Duffie-Lando model have motivated a surge of research activity, most traditional intensity models begin with the assumption (without a theoretical foundation such as the one presented by Duffie and Lando) that a default event is similar to a bolt of lightening—you know it will strike sometime, but when and where are not predictable. This can be both positive and negative.

On the positive side, reduced-form models facilitate effective characterization of pricing tendencies regardless of data quality. An important application of reduced-form modeling lies in the production of generic credit curves that facilitate pricing a wide range of credit-risky securities. This type of application highlights the superior capability of reduced-form models to interpolate—in a meaningful way—real data.

On the negative side, reduced-form models can be hard to fit robustly and can sometimes have a large number of parameters, making them at times difficult to interpret and unstable. Often a mixture of reduced-form modeling and old-fashioned curve smoothing is necessary to produce usable output.

Reduced-form models have become popular in industry because they are relatively easy to implement mechanically and, when CDSs or other credit spreads are available, they produce estimates that are reasonable, even for high-quality credits, an area traditionally difficult for other models. In addition, these models, because of their minimal assumptions, can often be combined flexibly in broader applications.[2]

We now turn to the details of these models.

---

[2] Note a philosophical difference between reduced-form and what we call, for lack of better terms, econometric survival models relates to the use of market observables within a specific framework. In the case of econometric survival models, no relationship between the observed data and the PD (or hazard rate) is specified beyond general directional ones. In the case of reduced-form models, we have a body of economic theory and resulting mathematical constructs, which, while it does not provide guidance on the factors that cause default, does posit specific relationships between risk and spread data, relying on the rational behavior of market participants.

BASIC INTENSITY MODELS

The fundamental building block of most reduced-form models is a default *intensity*. We can characterize an intensity as either approximately the probability of default in the next instant (given survival to the present) or as the mean arrival rate of defaults, assuming the default time is governed by a particular random process such as Poisson. (We will show later how we can transform an intensity into a PD at different time horizons, thus specifically linking an intensity to a PD.) In an intensity-based framework, default is unpredictable and governed by whatever process is assumed to generate the intensity. This underlying process may itself be a multidimensional stochastic process. (This feature provides a convenient means for introducing correlation between, say, default rates and interest rates.) While a default intensity determines the *propensity* for an obligor to default, it does not provide specific information, as does a structural model, about variables or circumstances that create a *causal link* to default.

Intensity models have the advantage of enjoying mathematical tractability that comes from their similarity to a broad class of earlier models in the finance literature that deal with the behavior of interest rates. The highly developed methods for formulation and estimation found in the modeling of affine term structure (of interest rates) literature can often be applied to credit with some modification. The key assumption of reduced-form models is that the intensity process implies a distribution for the *time to default*. Said another way, all firms are assumed to default eventually and the riskier ones default earlier. The default time itself is considered to be a stopping time in the statistical sense (i.e., the time before maturity of the debt security at which default arrives), and this stopping time variable is taken as unpredictable.

The most popular framework assumes that default is governed by a Poisson process parameterized by an intensity, which drives the time of default. In other words, default is considered to be the first arrival time of a Poisson process with some constant mean arrival rate (the intensity). In our discussions here, we adopt the convention of denoting the intensity as h instead of λ so that we avoid confusing it with the market price of risk, which we discuss elsewhere in this book. (Note, however, that many articles and books will use λ to denote intensity.)

A common assumption underlying intensity-based models is that market information is accurate and traders seek to eliminate arbitrage. These models rely on the prices, or more specifically the spreads, of credit securities or credit derivatives for information on the credit riskiness of the underlying entities. These spreads (stripped of risk-free rates) represent the market's collective estimate of the additional credit risk associated with a particular borrower's debt. Unlike structural and econometric models of default, intensity-based models *do not* assume that any firm-specific factors are determinants of default or even that the factors are the same from firm to firm. Rather they assume only that prices distill all relevant factors into estimates of credit risk (which may or may not include common factors and firm-specific information). Subject to an assumption about loss given default (LGD), these credit risk estimates can in turn yield precise estimates of default probabilities.

We will explore two classes of intensity-based models that are similar in some respects to the survival models discussed in the econometrics literature. The first relies on an assumption of a stable default intensity which leads to a deterministic default structure at each time horizon. A stable intensity does not imply that default occurs deterministically. Rather, it implies that the probability of a firm defaulting, which is still random, increases according to a specific set of steps as time gets longer. In contrast, the second approach relaxes this deterministic assumption and allows the actual *intensity* to vary stochastically. These models are called *doubly stochastic* and tend to be better behaved in some practical settings than their deterministic counterparts.[3]

In keeping with the standard approach to these types of models, we assume in the discussions to follow that default arrives according to a Poisson process. It is important to keep in mind throughout this discussion that we do not have any specific information about the *cause* of a particular obligor becoming more or less likely to default—only that the size of its default intensity indicates its propensity to default.

To motivate the discussion, we can show mathematically how, under the assumption of a deterministic intensity process, the cumulative PDs (cpd) are related to a default intensity, h, as follows. The Poisson arrival of n defaults by time t is defined as (Note that some authors use λ rather than h)

$$f(n \mid h,t) = e^{-ht}\frac{(ht)^n}{n!}, n = 0, 1, \ldots; h \geq 0, t \geq 0$$

The probability of *no* defaults (i.e., $n = 0$) by time t (i.e., probability of survival) is thus e^{-ht}. From a PD perspective the probability of no default is $1 - cpd_t$. Thus $1 - cpd_t = e^{-ht}$ or $cpd_t = 1 - e^{-ht}$. Note that if the time to default is exponentially distributed, then the expected (mean) time to default is $\frac{1}{h}$.

---

[3] Doubly stochastic processes are also sometimes called Cox processes (see Lando 1998 for a detailed discussion of Cox processes applied to credit modeling).

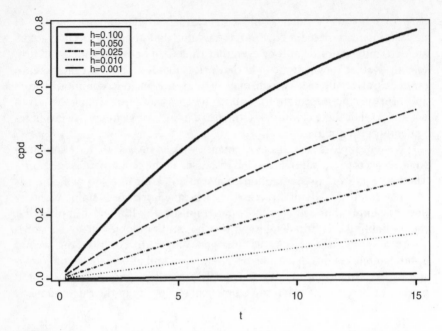

FIGURE 6.1   CPDs for Various Constant Intensities h

Consider the following example of how we convert an intensity into information about the probability of a firm defaulting. Assume we are examining a firm with a constant default intensity of 0.05. Under a model of constant default intensity, this firm will have a one-year ($t = 1$) default probability of 4.9 percent ($= 1 - e^{-ht} = 1 - e^{-0.05} \approx 0.0488$) and an expected time to default of 20 years ($1/h = 1/0.05 = 20$). Figure 6.1 demonstrates graphically the cumulative default probabilities (cpd) that are implied using constant intensities.

We will show later how we can use this framework to calculate security value directly. The output that we estimate will depend on the application of the model. As we discussed in Chapter 3, under a structural framework for valuation we required mathematical functions that move between PDs and security value. In the intensity-based framework, we will reach back one level to develop the functions relating intensities and security value—often written as a spread.

Given this basic definition of the core building block for intensity-based models, we now turn to a discussion of what information we need in order to make use of this type of model.

Default Intensity Model Input

In our discussion of the inputs required for estimating structural models, we focused primarily on data specific to the obligor: asset value, default point, and so on. While such *obligor-specific* data are most important for estimating structural models, ironically we need *large cross-sections* of obligors to efficiently estimate asset volatility and to find an empirical distribution relating DDs to PDs. In contrast, while reduced-form models are mostly focused on attributes found across a large cross-section of obligors, they may not require as large a cross-section of observations as their structural counterparts. Of course, as credit data are noisy, all credit models, regardless of type, will benefit from large cross-sections of observations.

As is the case with PDs, an obligor with a high default intensity will not necessarily default. All one can say is that we expect a group of firms with higher intensities to experience a higher propensity to default than a group with lower intensities. In contrasting reduced-form models with structural models, we find a key difference arising, not so much from this distinction, but from *how* we link the specific characteristics of a firm to the final estimate of the probability of default. In the case of a structural model, we rely more on a specific economic argument that links characteristics of the firm (e.g., asset value, asset volatility, and default point) to the estimate. In the case of a reduced-form model, we rely more on the quantity of data to parameterize general relationships for types of firms and their underlying intensities. As shown in Arora, Bohn, and Zhu (2005) (discussed in more detail later), higher levels of data availability result in reduced-form models outperforming their structural counterparts in explaining credit spreads. The best-in-class versions of both modeling approaches provide important, but different, insights for managing credit portfolios.

Let us now dig more into the details of specifying an intensity-based model. When building an intensity-based model, we look for the following:

- *Intensity process*. As we have emphasized a number of times throughout this book, the probability of default constitutes the most important component of the various components used in credit analysis and credit portfolio management. Intensity-based models begin with the process governing this probability of default. Most of the extensions to the basic intensity-based model focus on specifying more sophisticated processes that produce more flexible functional forms better suited for fitting actual data.
- *Default-free interest rate process*. If we were only interested in PDs, we could stop at the intensity process and would not need to worry about the default-free interest rate. In most applications, however, we

will want to perform valuation, which requires us to specify the process governing default-free interest rates as well. One powerful aspect of the reduced-form modeling approach arises from its flexibility in modeling interest rates. Unlike structural models in which we must identify a corporate risk-free rate to improve the model fit, intensity-based models can accommodate both a reserve-currency (e.g., U.S. dollar or Japanese yen) and a liquidity process to capture the complexities of the component of spread associated with credit risk and the component associated with liquidity risk. As we explained before, one can interpret the risky components of the expected cash flow as something that is exchanged for the risk-free components of the expected cash flow.

- *Characterization of market risk premium.* In a valuation application, we must use risk-neutral PDs and, by extension, risk-neutral intensities. As it turns out, the PDs that reduced-form models recover from spreads are just this: risk-neutral. Thus, if we use a reduced form approach to fit a model to observed spreads or prices for the purposes of valuing another security, we will not need to worry about the market risk premium embedded in the model output. However, for risk management or portfolio analysis applications, we require physical PDs and we therefore need a mechanism for converting the calculated risk-neutral intensities into physical intensities. This calculation requires a characterization of the market risk premium.

- *LGD (possibly a stochastic process).* In a reduced-form setting we can characterize LGD as either a deterministic or stochastic process. One assumption with which analysts often wrestle concerns whether LGD contains systematic risk (see Chapter 5). If we model it as containing a systematic component, then we will further need to be careful to distinguish between actual LGD expectations and risk-neutral LGD expectations. This implies adding another assumption regarding the market price of LGD risk: the market risk premium associated with recovery uncertainty. In practice, we have difficulty specifying these LGD processes so many practitioners tend to make simple, deterministic assumptions.

- *Liquidity process.* The flexibility of this framework allows for rigorous inclusion of a liquidity process. This liquidity process (or premium) is required to reflect the risk generated by the inability to trade often, reflected in the spread between swaps and reserve-currency sovereign curves.

The biggest advantage of the reduced-form approach, its flexibility, can sometimes turn into its biggest drawback. If a modeler chose to include all of the stochastic processes just described (default intensity, risk-free rate, LGD, and liquidity), the resulting model could end up having an unwieldy number of parameters. In our experience, the most comprehensive (expansive) versions of these models often cannot be fit in any meaningful way that ensures robustness and parameter stability—in other words, parameter estimates that are not highly sensitive to the sample on which the model is fit. Consequently, in practice, we must be careful to choose the processes most relevant to the analysis problem at hand. The art lies in balancing a desire to fit the complexities of the real world with the pragmatic constraint of maintaining a manageable number of parameters and a robust fitting algorithm.

We close this section on model inputs with a few words about the data needed to parameterize reduced-form models. Arora, Bohn, and Zhu (2005) illustrate the importance of data in their analysis of two structural models (Black-Scholes-Merton and Vasicek-Kealhofer) and a reduced-form model (Hull-White). The results suggest that the Hull-White reduced-form model performs well (using a variety of power and fitting criteria), provided sufficient data are available. In particular, they provide evidence that firms that issue many bonds (in their paper *many* is defined as more than 10) are better modeled with the reduced-form framework than a structural one for purposes of valuation. The authors conclude that the data for issuers of many bonds tends to be less noisy since several of the quantities are observed multiple times for each observation and this results in more robust estimates. The lack of underlying economic theory driving the functional form of reduced-form models makes them relatively more dependent on the quality and quantity of data used to parameterize them.

In order to fit such models, we usually require at least several hundred observations. Part of the challenge lies in addressing lack of data by grouping data along dimensions such as ratings, industry, and geography to produce buckets of obligors so that we parameterize the reduced-form function for a particular bucket. Another challenge arises from the fact that pricing data on many credit instruments reflects more than just credit. Recall that a bond or loan reflects a package of options ranging from the obvious option to default to the less obvious prepayment option, which may become more valuable as an underlying obligor's credit quality improves. We have highlighted these points in a number of contexts throughout this book. The increasing availability of CDS data has helped to mitigate this problem as CDS spreads reflect only risk-adjusted expected loss, simplifying the modeling problem to separating PDs and LGDs (recall that for bonds expected loss generally equals just PD × LGD, as EAD is one).

Pricing Data Challenges

Building models with spread and price data almost always involves deciphering pricing within sources that sometimes contain mixtures of market prices and matrix or evaluated pricing. *Matrix* and *evaluated* in this context refer to a process that many data vendors take to fill in missing data. Often a firm's bond will not trade on a particular day (some bonds may only trade a few times a month). Since many data vendors sell their data to institutions such as pension funds, asset managers, and insurance companies that must produce a net asset value (NAV) of their fund on a daily basis, matrix prices (usually based on a model or group of models) or evaluated prices (usually based on a modeled price plus an analyst's evaluation) are the data vendors' best guess at what the price would be had the bond traded. This process is useful for reporting NAV; however, it can wreak havoc on data analyses and model fitting. Essentially, unwary modelers may inadvertently end up fitting someone else's model. Moreover, a modeler may mistakenly suppose that a fitted model predicts the vendor's price (model) ahead of time. This often turns out to be a function of the matrix algorithms used by the vendor rather than an actual market phenomenon. Many supposedly profitable trading strategies end up being the result of an inadvertent fitting of a matrix model as reflected in matrix prices reported by a data vendor. It is important to determine collaboratively with the data vendor which data are actual prices, which are matrix or evaluated, and which are quotes, which deserve special mention.

Unlike matrix or evaluated prices, quotes are not the products of the data vendor's data preparation process. Rather they are generated in the context of market interactions and may represent a hypothetical transaction that a vendor asks a dealer to imagine, or a proposed transaction that a dealer hopes to execute but which never actually trades. Often quotes can be a good source of data. However, all quotes are not created equal. Some quotes reflect a dealer's model, which returns us to the problem we face with matrix and evaluated prices. Other quotes may reflect a dealer testing the market rather than actually reflecting the dealer's informed view on where the bond is trading. During the financial crisis of 2007 and 2008, quotes became particularly problematic as the lack of credit trading made it difficult to develop any sense of where prices had settled. Thus, the quality of quotes can vary greatly depending on market circumstances. As always, more data are better than less to combat the potential distortions of data sources. In general, the more instruments issued by a firm, the better chance we have to estimate robust parameter values for a reduced-form model. More importantly, the increasing size and liquidity of the CDS market is now providing a much better source of data free of many of these problems (although the quote versus traded price is still an issue even with CDS data). Even so, events of 2007 and 2008 demonstrate that pricing data out of the CDS market will face periodic difficulties as it grows and matures. Triangulating across multiple markets can help to maximize data quality.

DEALING WITH NOISE IN CREDIT MARKET DATA (AGAIN)

When an analyst is left with a mixture of questionable data (which is often the case), we recommend three important steps in preparing the data for input:

1. Generate histograms, scatter plots, time series plots along dimensions of interest (e.g., credit quality, industry, country, size, etc.). Too often analysts rely on sheets of statistics to understand data issues. We prefer pictures. From these graphical characterizations, we can often quickly identify suspicious data. For example, a time series plot that shows stair-stepped trends in price (i.e., the same price for several days and then a jump to a new level, followed by several days, creating stair steps) will likely reflect matrix pricing as new levels for the price are bled into the reported price, creating auto-correlation in the data.

2. Modify data by calculating medians, producing Winsorized values, or trimming outliers (see Chapter 3). Each of these techniques works to minimize data noise. Before applying any of these techniques, it is imperative to understand as much as possible about the data and the context in which it was collected. That way, it is easier to determine whether the extreme observations are really data errors.

3. Make use of multiple markets to triangulate data for a particular obligor. While the availability of CDS data makes it easier to develop robust parameter estimates, the combination of CDS data, bond data, equity data, and even loan data can provide a means to disentangle various effects: credit risk, interest rate risk, market risk premium, LGD, and liquidity, just to name a few.

Now that we have an understanding of the decisions and techniques associated with the input for estimating a reduced-form model, we turn to a description of some of the more popular models.

Deterministic Default Intensity Models

The simplest class of reduced-form models rests on the assumption that the time evolution of the default intensity is known (i.e., the intensity process is deterministic). The default intensity may be constant over time or it may follow a particular path, but we can mathematically characterize exactly the level of the intensity at any given point in time. Models that make such assumptions tend not to perform as well as some others and are not typically used in practice, but they provide excellent intuition with respect to the interpretation of intensity-based credit models. Their primary weakness lies in their inability to capture the volatility and complexity of actual credit spread behavior exhibited by loans, bonds, and CDSs.

A constant intensity (defined as h) assumption results in a simple model that can be written as follows:

$$1 - cpd_t = e^{-ht}$$

In this setup, the probability of survival, or one minus the cumulative probability of default to time t, relies on just the exponential function. (The reason that this model turns out to be impractical is that it constrains intensity behavior too much; from a practical perspective, it is never the case that a firm's propensity to default will stay constant.)

One possible modification of this approach is to relax the constant intensity assumption and specify a *function* rather than a constant value for the evolution of the intensity over time. This deterministically time-varying version of the model can be written as follows:

$$1 - cpd_t = e^{-\int_0^t h(t)dt}$$

The function is similar to the constant intensity version; however, it facilitates a richer characterization of how an obligor's propensity to default changes over time.

Unfortunately, this extension is only slightly more useful practically, since we can rarely (if ever) know beforehand how the intensity will change over time. So this extended, but still deterministic, version of the model also falls short of explaining actual credit spreads. However, these two simplified deterministic approaches give the general intuition behind the reduced-form approach and demonstrate how default probability and default intensity are related in specific ways through the survival function, the form of which depends on the assumptions underlying the model. We now turn to more realistic versions of intensity-based models.

Mean-Reverting Default Intensity with Jumps Model

As it turns out, the behavior of PDs and credit spreads is more complicated than can be captured by deterministic default intensity models. We can move a step closer to a more realistic model by assuming the intensity process is characterized by more complex behaviors such as jumps and mean reversion. We imagine a given intensity process for an obligor or group of obligors that periodically experiences a shock (i.e., the process that generates the unexpected shock of default is itself shocked) and then trends back to its long-run mean. For example, assume something changes in the competitive environment in an industry such as an inflow of overseas competition or the discovery of health concerns associated with a profitable product class, and this causes the intensity to jump up. This model assumes that this jump occurs and that after the intensity has jumped up, it trends over time back down toward its long-term mean. Now we have a setup that is more realistic. We will refer to this model as *jumps with mean reversion* (JMR).

We begin specifying this model by defining a mean jump size, J, which occurs according to a Poisson process with intensity c (be careful not to confuse this jump intensity with the default intensity). Over time, however, the default intensity trends back to its long-term mean, μ_h, at the rate of κ (taken here as defined on an annualized basis). Mathematically, we can write down the following process for the default intensity in between jump events:

$$dh_t = \kappa(\mu_h - h_t)dt$$

Thus, the further away from the mean intensity the process is, the more quickly it reverts back to the mean, and it does so at a rate of κ.

Given this specification, if $h(0)$ is the time 0 default intensity, the solution for the default probability is as follows (see Duffie and Singleton 2003 for more details on this model and its derivation):

$$1 - cpd_t = e^{a(t)+b(t)h(0)}$$

$$a(t) = -\mu_h\left(t - \frac{1 - e^{-\kappa t}}{\kappa}\right) - \frac{c}{J + \kappa}\left(Jt - \ln\left(1 + \frac{1 - e^{-\kappa t}}{\kappa}J\right)\right)$$

$$b(t) = -\frac{1 - e^{-\kappa t}}{\kappa}$$

The affine structure[4] of this credit model as characterized by a and b is a common result for affine models for the term structure of interest rates.

---

[4] An affine function is characterized by a linear function that does not go through the origin—that is, it has an intercept term. We refer to a class of models developed in the term structure of interest rate modeling literature as *affine* when they have a solution such as the one in this section, where the exponent, $a(t) + b(t)h(0)$, of the exponential function is an affine function. Please refer to Duffie, Filipovic, and Schachermayer (2000) for a more rigorous description of affine processes.

In fact, this model is a special case of a common affine process used in term structure modeling.

Consider the following example to provide more intuition around the way this model becomes specified. First, consider the following values for the input parameters:

$$c = 0.002, \ \kappa = 0.5, \ \mu_b = 0.001, \ J = 10, \ h(0) = 0.002$$

These inputs produce a one-year PD of 33 basis points (0.33 percent). This PD is quite a bit higher than would be the case if the model had instead assumed a constant intensity of 0.002—that is, if the intensity had stayed constant at $h(0)$. The difference, of course, arises from the risk of a shock to the intensity process causing it to jump by a factor of 10. Figure 6.2 shows how the CPD changes as the parameters are varied.

Notice that the cpd is much more sensitive to the mean and the jump intensity than some of the other parameters. This kind of sensitivity analysis

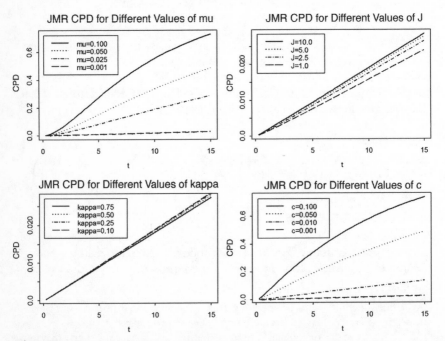

FIGURE 6.2 Cumulative Probabilities of Default (CPD) for a Jumps-With-Mean-Reversion (JMR) Intensity Model with Varying Input Parameters

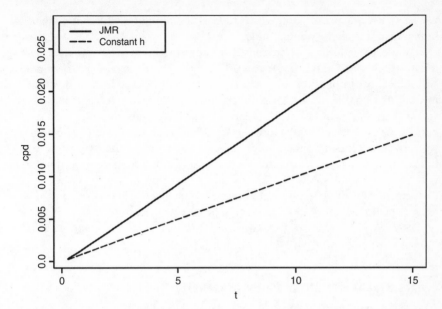

FIGURE 6.3 Comparison of Cumulative Probabilities of Default (CPD) for a Jumps-With-Mean-Reversion (JMR) Intensity Model versus a Constant Default Intensity Model

is quite important in developing intuition around how to evaluate model output. Sometimes models can be simplified by ignoring parameters that do not significantly affect the final output. In our example, JMR appears to offer an improvement over the constant and deterministic versions of the intensity models.

To develop some sense of the impact of the richer structure of the JMR framework versus the simpler constant default intensity approach, consider Figure 6.3.

As we can see in this figure, the constant-intensity model produces relatively smaller PDs as the time horizon of analysis increases. The impact of the JMR model structure becomes more evident at longer tenors since the possibility of substantial moves (i.e., the jumps), in the underlying intensity process increases. Thus, factors that change the credit quality of an obligor and particularly ones that increase the default intensity become more of an issue the longer a portfolio manager holds the securities of that obligor. The constant-intensity model does not provide enough structure to capture these possibilities. In practice, the more sensitive nature of PDs with respect to tenor exhibited by the JMR model turns out to match qualitatively what we see in actual spread data, which reflects the obligor's underlying default intensity and thus the obligor's PD.

While the addition of stochastic jumps to the intensity process itself moves us closer to capturing real-world credit spread variability, the model still falls short in practice. The primary reason lies in the lack of flexibility in the functional form, which reduces the model's ability to capture actual spread variability. In practice, spreads may jump around for extended time periods or even trend away from the long-run mean for a while. The somewhat orderly (and simplified) assumption of a return to the long-run mean following a shock to the default intensity does not adequately capture the volatility in actual spreads. Perhaps the most important innovation from this approach is the suggestion that intensity itself should move around. The next logical step takes us to a stochastic characterization of the intensity process. We now turn to a discussion of *doubly stochastic* reduced-form models.

Simple Stochastic Affine Default Intensity Models

In light of the shortcomings of earlier reduced-form models, researchers moved to richer models of the intensity process. In particular, models that assume that the intensity itself follows a stochastic process turn out to represent more faithfully the dynamics observed in actual credit spreads. Assuming stochastic intensity results in models that look similar to the affine term structure models used for modeling interest rates (see Dai and Singleton 2000 for a detailed discussion of these models). Such models rely on a *doubly stochastic* characterization of default that is also sometimes referred to as a Cox process (see Lando 1998 for a review of Cox processes applied to credit-risky securities).

The doubly stochastic assumption relies on the same setup explained earlier except that now we have yet another alternative specification for the intensity. The stochastic characterization of the intensity process produces a model that can more closely track the variability of actual credit spreads. To understand the setup of these models, it is useful first to consider two of the more common specifications, both arising out of the literature on affine term structure models:

$$Vasicek: dh_t = \kappa \left(\mu_h - h_t \right) dt + \sigma_h dz_t$$

where κ = speed of mean reversion to long-term mean
μ_h = long-term mean for the default intensity
σ_h = volatility of intensity process

This characterization relies on the insight originally introduced by Oldrich Vasicek in 1977 for interest rate modeling. The intensity process is controlled by the mean reversion despite the fact that it randomly experiences shocks, which captures more real-life variability in default risk. The disadvantage to this specification arises from the fact that the intensity process is not bounded, which introduces the possibility of negative intensity realizations. In practice, most data samples result in parameterizations that keep the intensity process in positive territory.

The lucky draws of real samples notwithstanding, the risk of model difficulties leads some researchers to use the following specification, introduced in Duffie and Singleton (1999), which also arises from the term structure literature:

$$Cox,\ Ingersoll,\ and\ Ross\ (CIR): dh_t = \kappa\,(\mu_h - h_t)\,dt + \sigma_h\sqrt{h_t}dz_t$$

The Cox, Ingersoll, and Ross (CIR) specification is quite popular among academics but is less widely used in practice. The behavior of this model is similar to the Vasicek version without the risk of a negative intensity realization (due to the square root of the intensity multiplied by the intensity-process volatility). In either case we can solve analytically (similar to the mean-reverting jump model) for the default probability (or the value) of a credit-risky security. The solution follows the same affine structure found in the term structure modeling literature, and is characterized as follows:

$$1 - cpd_t = e^{a_{CIR}(t)+b_{CIR}(t)h(0)}$$

$$a(t) = \frac{2\kappa\mu_h}{\sigma_h^2} \ln\left(\frac{2\gamma e^{(\gamma+\kappa)T/2}}{2\gamma + (\gamma + \kappa)\left(e^{\gamma T} - 1\right)}\right);\ \gamma = \sqrt{\kappa^2 + 2\sigma_h^2}$$

$$b(t) = \frac{-2(e^{\gamma T} - 1)}{2\gamma + (\gamma + \kappa)\left(e^{\gamma T} - 1\right)}$$

For a more detailed discussion of this solution and a solution for the Vasicek version of the model, refer to Appendix E of Lando (2004). (Note that in Lando's text, $a = \alpha$ and $b = \beta$.) Benninga and Wiener (1998) describe practical implementations of these term structure models. While the affine structure in this version of the intensity-based models move us much closer to capturing real-world spread variability, directly modeling the intensity process reduces our flexibility enough to be sometimes problematic in practice. For one, we have not considered the impact of LGD. More importantly, we do not have the ability in this version of the framework to capture correlation between spreads and interest rates. Before we move on to the more useful versions of these types of models, we digress a bit to discuss valuation again.

A BRIEF INTERLUDE TO DISCUSS VALUATION

Thus far, we have focused on how a default intensity can be converted into a PD. In practice, we typically use prices from bonds, loans, or CDSs to parameterize a reduced-form model. This implies that we need to characterize a valuation equation as well. Once the model is parameterized using market prices, some applications require only a PD calculation (and possibly a change of measure to physical PDs). As we discussed in Chapter 3, PDs by themselves can be used in risk assessment and are inputs to quantitative portfolio models. Other applications will take full advantage of the pricing information in the context of the valuation framework to estimate prices for other assets on which we have no data. These other applications focus on valuing (often illiquid) default-risky securities.

Note again that if our objective is valuation of other securities, we do not need to worry about the transformation between risk-neutral and actual PDs, which vastly simplifies the practical modeling task. In applications such as portfolio risk modeling where we do need physical PDs, we rely on a specification of the market price of risk (explained shortly) that facilitates the extraction of actual PDs from risk-neutral PD estimates. Unfortunately, the risk-neutral transformation within the reduced-form framework can turn out to be challenging. Irrespective of this, the parameterization of the reduced-form model constitutes a useful method to do valuation.

Before we discuss other intensity models, let us review how we arrive at a value for a risky security such as a loan, bond, or credit derivative. The basic pricing relationship for the value, D, of a credit-risky debt instrument is

$$D = f(h, r, l, T)$$

where h is a default intensity
  r is the instantaneous default-free interest rate
  L is the instantaneous loss-given-default
  T is the maturity of debt

If we assume no recovery in the event of default, we can write down the following (the Q superscript denotes risk neutral measures):

$$D(T) = E_0^Q \left[e^{-\int_0^T r(t) + h^Q(t) dt} \right]$$

If we assume some kind of recovery in the event of default, the expression becomes:

$$D(T) = E_0^Q \left[e^{-\int_0^T r(t) + s(t)dt} \right]$$

where $s(t) = h^Q(t) L$ is the (instantaneous) spread to the risk-free rate.

Note that we can imagine a number of variations on this structure:

- LGD becomes time dependent.
- LGD is modeled as a risk-neutral process with the assumption that LGD includes some kind of systematic risk.
- A liquidity process is added to the structure.

As always, the cost of a richer model is more parameters that must be estimated and, typically, less parameter stability. In practice, the preceding specification reflects a fairly good balance of real-world complexity and parameter economy.

Another important component of a valuation framework includes specification of the market risk premium or market price of risk. In the structural BSM framework, the theoretical underpinnings led us to an elegant characterization of how an actual probability can be converted into a risk-neutral probability using a measure of the market price of risk and the extent to which a particular obligor exhibits systematic risk (refer to Chapter 3 for this explanation). In the reduced-form framework, we do not have the same kind of direct connection between the physical and risk-neutral worlds. Instead, we rely on mathematical characterizations that are reasonable and simple to integrate with the larger model framework, but do not have any particular theoretical justification to recommend them.

The first of these is a simple linear transformation, as follows:

$$h^Q(t) = \psi h(t), \psi \geq 1$$

The challenge in using this transformation lies in finding an estimation approach to break out the parameter that reflects the risk premium. This can be done by estimating different sets of parameters from different markets (e.g., bond, equity, and CDS) or using more constraints on a joint estimation of all parameters.

A richer characterization of the transformation ties in a common state variable, X_c, that may or may not be the same state variable driving interest rates and default intensity. This richer formula is as follows:

$$h^Q(t) = \psi_0 h(t) + \psi_1 X_c(t)$$

This specification ties the market price of risk into the larger economy, creating a more defensible model. Again, the challenge is estimating the extra parameters. Note that X_c is considered to be affine under both actual and risk-neutral processes; however, the parameters may differ depending on whether we are estimating physical or risk-neutral quantities.

A good example of this process involves starting with the CDS market to back out the risk-neutral default intensities. One could then use the equity market to estimate an actual default probability and convert this estimate into a physical default intensity. Then the functional form relating risk-neutral to physical default intensities can be used to back out the implied market risk premium parameters. The objective is to triangulate across at least two markets to develop a joint estimate of the parameters of interest.

With this interlude as an introduction, we now turn to a rich and useful version of intensity-based models.

DUFFIE, SINGLETON, LANDO (DSL) INTENSITY MODEL

Thus far, we have discussed fairly simple intensity models where the intensity process is deterministic or follows a simple stochastic process. The real world is generally too complex for this level of simplification. To better capture real-world spread variability, Darrell Duffie, Kenneth Singleton, and David Lando developed modeling approaches that retain a mathematically tractable structure while still capturing the variability of real-world credit spreads. The idea for modeling default intensities and linking this with the affine setting is one that was developed by Duffie and Singleton (published in 1999) and by Lando around the same time, with Lando's work forming part of his thesis (see Lando 1994)—a portion of which was later extended and published as Lando (1998). The models described in the different publications differ in their details (e.g., Lando's model did not contemplate fractional recoveries or the generalizations introduced by Duffie and Singleton; on the other hand, it did extend the framework to include a solution in rating-based settings), though they share common elements in the overall modeling framework. We call this family of models the Duffie-Singleton-Lando (DSL) framework which actually encompasses a number of models all unified by their use of stochastic factors to drive the default intensities underlying credit risk. The DSL framework also provides the means to link important model drivers such as the instantaneous default-risk-free interest rates and an obligor's instantaneous credit (bond or CDS) spread. In addition, the framework's flexibility allows for a wide range of specifications that can include stochastic LGD and specifications of liquidity risk.

No Recovery

The DSL framework itself is similar to the basic affine intensity model described previously except that the model drivers are linked together by a *common (or set of common) stochastic state variable(s)*. In its simplest incarnation, the DSL model assumes no recovery in the event of default and specifies similar processes for both the default intensity and the default-risk-free rate. We discuss richer forms of the DSL model that relax this simplistic recovery assumption in the next subsection; however, it is useful to understand this version of the model first.

DSL use a straightforward mechanism for correlating the default-risk-free rate and the default intensity process. This mechanism is the specification of a common factor, X_c, for both the risk-free rate, r, and the default intensity h^Q,[5] where $D(T)$ is the value of the risky debt maturing at time T. The quantities for this version of the model are specified as follows:

$$D(T) = E_0^Q \left[e^{-\int_0^T \left(r(t) + h^Q(t) \right) dt} \right]$$

$$r(t) = a_r(t) + b_r(t) X_c(t)$$

$$h^Q(t) = a_{h^Q}(t) + b_{h^Q}(t) X_c(t)$$

The state variable is taken to reflect a common factor in the underlying macroeconomy that impacts both interest rates and default intensity. Loosely speaking, we can think of this factor as the common component that drives the underlying business or economic cycle that creates the environment within which interest rates and default intensities are determined.

This model introduces randomness into the behavior of these quantities by specifying a stochastic process for this common state variable, X_c. Note that in this example, we are parameterizing a *process* for the state variable, X_c, as opposed to parameterizing the default intensity and interest rate directly. Similar to the direct parameterization of the default intensity process in the simple stochastic affine intensity models we discussed earlier, we consider two popular functions for parameterizing X_c as follows (we drop the t subscript for ease of notation):

- Vasicek: $dX_c = \kappa \left(\mu_{X_c} - X_c \right) dt + \sigma_{X_c} dz$
- Cox, Ingersoll, and Ross (CIR): $dX_c = \kappa \left(\mu_{X_c} - X_c \right) dt + \sigma_{X_c} \sqrt{X_c} dz$

---

[5] In what follows we continue to use a superscript Q (e.g., h^Q), which indicates the risk-neutral measure of the variable or function (e.g., $E_0^Q(\cdot)$ is the risk-neutral expectation at time 0).

STATE VARIABLES

Throughout this book we often talk about state variables and factors that are the primary drivers of processes that reflect value and/or risk. In the DSL framework, we have introduced another example of a state variable. For many readers, grasping the intuition behind a state variable can be difficult without concrete examples. That is why we often refer to possible interpretations of what the state variable represents—in other words, this state variable may reflect the state of the economic cycle. However, even the example of the economic cycle is still too abstract. We usually refer to specific statistics that tell us something about the state of the world and economic cycle, such as unemployment rate, interest rates, GDP growth, inflation, and so on.

Unfortunately, these common macroeconomic metrics of the state of the economy are measured with too much error (often they are revised after they are reported) and are not available in a timely manner (for the purposes of risk assessment and valuation). The more important problem, however, is that while we have some notion of what it means to be in a particular state of economy, we really do not have a good way of representing all the components of that state with macroeconomic quantities. Consequently, we build models that rely on something (e.g., debt or equity prices) that embed the mix of components that define an economic state. Thus, the state variable itself becomes latent—that is, it is implied in the prices themselves, but we cannot directly observe it. We take advantage of this interpretation in Chapter 8 when we discuss models for correlated default.

When estimating models that include latent factors, the key is to make sure that the parameters scattered throughout the model are estimated in a robust way—in other words, that they do not move around a great deal as we move from sample to sample. We continue to interpret output as if we knew the state of the economy; however, we rely on market prices to provide a lens into what that state might be without defining it in concrete, macroeconomic terms.

Since both the interest-rate process and the default-intensity process are now driven by the same factor, the two processes are correlated through this factor. The a and b parameters are similar to those we described before when introducing the CIR framework. Essentially, we have the same form as would be used for a default-risk-free bond, except that we now have included the risk-neutral default intensity.

Under the DSL model we can determine values of risky and risk-free debt as follows:

- Risky debt (bond or loan): $D(T) = e^{a_D(T) + b_D(T)X_c(T)}$
- Default-risk-free debt: $B(T) = e^{a_B(T) + b_B(T)X_c(T)}$

We need both the risky and risk-free values since we usually analyze spreads, and thus convert the values into spreads, s, as follows:

$$s(T) = -\frac{\ln D(T) - \ln B(T)}{T}$$

By substitution and combining the parameters in the preceding equations, we arrive at a characterization for the spread on a risky credit security as follows:

$$s(T) = -\frac{a_s(T) - b_s(T)X_c}{T}$$

It is important to remember that unlike in the case of the structural model framework, we do not encounter difficulty in identifying the proper spread. In the case of structural models, we improved model fits by very carefully choosing the default-risk-free benchmark, and thus focused on a specific spread that we could confidently interpret as a *credit* spread. In contrast, reduced-form models can be parameterized to handle both credit spreads and liquidity spreads, making it less important to specify the corporate borrower risk-free rate. That is, the reduced-form model exhibits substantial flexibility to capture whatever happens to be driving the spread calculated with respect to any particular benchmark interest rate.

While disentangling the liquidity premium from the credit risk premium in any of these modeling frameworks is fraught with difficulties, the reduced-form framework provides more flexibility to tease out the answer. Remember also that in this form we are typically estimating the risk-neutral default intensity processes. If we need to compute the physical default intensities, we require the extra step (i.e., adjust the physical default intensities for the market price of risk) that was described earlier in the section on valuation.

Fractional Recovery and the Shape of the Term Structure of Credit Spreads

Thus far, we have discussed a model assuming no recovery. In practice, most debt instruments that default have a nonzero recovery (see Chapter 5). Spreads reflect this expectation, and proper characterization of spreads thus requires robust models that specify a nonzero recovery.

We now turn to a more realistic reduced-form specification that assumes fractional recovery—in other words, LGD less than 100 percent. Instead of focusing just on the default intensity, this version of DSL now models the instantaneous, risk-neutral expected rate of *loss of market value*, which is a function of default intensity and instantaneous LGD at time t resulting from default. The instantaneous spread reflects this risk-neutral expected loss and can be specified as follows:

$$s\left(t\right) = h^{Q}\left(t\right) L\left(t\right)$$

where $L(t)$ is the LGD at default time t.

At this juncture, we briefly digress to review again the various ways in which LGD can be calculated. Intuitively, it makes sense to think of LGD as being calculated with respect to the face value of the debt instrument in question. As it turns out, most models do not in fact begin with this face-value assumption. In the various models discussed in this book, we have been working with three specifications for LGD:

1. *Recovery of face value.* While closest to real life, the resulting valuation formula is messy. Most nonquantitative individuals will assume LGD is a percentage of face value. Often, we use one of the two other specifications, and then convert inputs and outputs so that they are ultimately displayed in output reports with respect to face value.

2. *Recovery of market value.* This view of LGD considers recovery as a percentage of a debt instrument's market value an infinitesimally small moment before default. Thus, it reflects the market value just before default. In the DSL model framework, for example, this assumption simplifies the resulting valuation formulae.

3. *Recovery of Treasury value.* This approach distinguishes recovery on longer-dated instruments relative to shorter-dated instruments. This assumption is made in the Jarrow, Lando, and Turnbull model. We also used this assumption in the simple risk-comparable valuation model discussed in the Chapter 3. This represents the percentage of the value of a risk-free security with the same characteristics (maturity, payment structure, etc.) as the one being modeled and thus addresses explicitly the tenor of the security.

We discuss the calculation and specification of LGD for both at moment of default and at ultimate recovery in more detail in Chapter 5.

An interesting consequence of the recovery assumption in these models is their effect on the shape of the term structure of credit spreads. Early research in this area found that while investment grade credits exhibited an upward-sloping spread term structure (i.e., the annualized spreads for longer tenors were higher than for shorter tenors), speculative grade credits exhibited hump-shaped (i.e., very short tenors show smaller annualized spreads than short tenors, but spreads for longer tenors were lower than short to medium tenors) and downward sloping (i.e., annualized spread for longer tenors were lower than for shorter tenors) spread term structures (see Sarig and Warga 1989 and Fons 1994). Helwege and Turner (1999) (HT) demonstrated that these results could be explained, not by the underlying spread dynamics, but by a sample selection bias resulting from the longer tenor bonds in a given credit-rating class actually having better credit quality than shorter tenor bonds. They remedied this bias by looking at bonds of different tenors for the same individual borrowers instead of relying on cohorts within particular agency ratings classes. After controlling in this way for the selection bias in earlier studies, and using new-issue data, they reported that in their analysis credit-spread term structures tended to be upward-sloping regardless of the obligor's credit quality.

In contrast, Lando and Mortensen (2005) reported finding *downward*-sloping curves for speculative-grade obligors using CDS data. Later, Agrawal and Bohn (2008) (AB) used HT's methodology to show that using secondary market data (recall that HT based their work on new-issue data), speculative-grade obligors still tended to have hump-shaped and downward-sloping zero-coupon term structures. Interestingly, they replicate HT's results using par bonds—that is, bonds for which the market price is close to par, which is also typically the case for new issues of the sort that HT studied. Thus, part of the difference in term-structure shapes results from the use of par spreads for the term-structure calculation as opposed to zero-coupon spreads bootstrapped from existing price data. If one assumes recovery of face, it is possible to have an upwardly sloping par curve and still have a hump-shaped or downwardly sloping zero-coupon curve. Based on this research, it would appear that depending on one's choices for constructing a term structure (e.g., zero-coupon versus par; new-issue prices versus secondary-issue prices; recovery assumptions, etc.), one can find empirical support for upwardly sloping, downwardly sloping, or hump-shaped term structures.

It turns out that differing recovery assumptions in the model can drive the shape of the term structure and lead to one of several possible explanations for reconciling these conflicting empirical results. For example, AB show that assuming recovery of *market* or recovery of *Treasury*, the zero-coupon and par term structures can both be upwardly sloping. Interestingly, they then go on to show that if one instead assumes the market prices for bonds are consistent with the recovery of *face* assumption, it is possible for the par term structure of spreads to be upwardly sloping while the zero-coupon term structure is hump-shaped or even downwardly sloping for speculative-grade credits.

An alternative explanation is also available in AB, since in contrast to earlier studies, AB use *the level of credit spreads*, rather than *ratings*, to classify credits as speculative-grade. It may be that in using ratings, HT were not able to analyze a large enough sample of sufficiently low-quality obligors. Using credit spreads, the truly low-quality credits may be distinguished at higher resolution. This second result offers another explanation for reconciling the empirical results.

Most models predict either hump-shaped or downward-sloping term structures for obligors with low credit quality. In particular, the BSM framework suggests that low-quality firms will see their annualized spread fall as they survive past certain time points in the future. That is, obligors of sufficiently low credit quality will already be in a situation where their debt holders are not likely to be repaid unless the underlying asset volatility produces an upswing that puts them in-the-money. In support of the HT findings, Collin-Dufresne and Goldstein (2001) provide a theoretical explanation for all upward-sloping term structures that relies on mean-reverting leverage ratios. We expect that as more empirical work on credit spreads is published, we will develop more clarity in regard to the term-structure shape question.

The reduced-form framework does not necessarily tend toward particular shapes of credit curves as does the structural framework. Nonetheless, insights from the structural framework can provide some guidance when dealing with noisy data in a reduced-form framework. Moreover, the nature of the data (e.g., par spreads versus zero-coupon spreads; ratings-based measures of quality versus spread-based measures) and the interpretation of recovery (e.g., recovery of face, recovery of Treasury, or recovery of market value) lend themselves to particular term structure shapes. The reduced-form framework is flexible enough to handle the different possibilities; however, it remains the task of the analyst to pull together the economic story and develop the intuition for interpreting results.

Returning now to the DSL model framework under the assumption of fractional recovery, we can write down an expression for the value of a credit-risky security similar to the no-recovery version except that we include an estimate of the LGD at time t, $L(t)$, as well:

$$D(T) = E_0^Q \left[e^{-\int_0^T (r(t) + h^Q(t)L(t))dt} \right]$$

We can simplify this expression to obtain an expression identical to the no-recovery version except that instead of the default intensity, we use the instantaneous spread:

$$D(T) = E_0^Q \left[e^{-\int_0^T (r(t)+s(t))dt} \right]$$

The DSL framework allows for specification of multiple state variables driving both the instantaneous default-risk-free short rate and the instantaneous spread. By including more than one state variable, we can develop a richer framework for the correlation between interest rates and spreads. In practice, this correlation is often negative, but it can just as easily move up to zero and become positive.

The actual correlation is a complicated function of the current state of a specific (e.g., geographic) economy in the economic cycle. When interest rates are high and a particular economy is just coming out of recession, the interest-rate-spread correlation may be negative since a drop in interest rates may not immediately result in a drop in the actual rate paid by borrowers throughout the economy, so that the spread widens. However, the opposite result can occur if the dropping interest rates drive improving credit quality as asset values rise. The point is that without actual data, it is difficult to determine the sign of the interest-rate-spread correlation.

As a concrete example, consider the three-state variable (X_1, X_2, X_3) version suggested by DS (1999). In this version, each state variable is assumed to follow, e.g., a CIR process.[6] The model specification is as follows:

$$r = \delta_0 + \delta_1 X_1 + \delta_2 X_2 + \delta_3 X_3$$
$$s = \varphi_0 + \varphi_1 X_1 + \varphi_2 X_2 + \varphi_3 X_3$$

The resulting model structure in matrix form is as follows:

$$d\mathbf{X} = \mathbf{K}(\mathbf{M_X} - \mathbf{X})dt + \mathbf{\Sigma}\sqrt{\mathbf{S}}d\mathbf{Z}^Q$$

where $\mathbf{X}$ is the 3×1 vector of state variables.

$\mathbf{K}$ is the 3×3 matrix that governs the rate at which the conditional means of the state variables revert to $\mathbf{M_X}$. Since $\mathbf{K}$ may be nondiagonal, the different state variables may be used to forecast changes in each other.

---

[6] Note that here, we change slightly our notation and allow vectors of state-variables to be represented in bold capitals.

M_X is the 3×1 vector of long-run risk-neutral means for the state variables.

Σ is the 3×3 matrix of instantaneous correlations.

S is the 3×3 diagonal matrix with instantaneous variances.

Z^Q is a three-dimensional risk-neutral Brownian motion.

Now consider how we can generate negative correlation between interest rates and spreads. One common situation is the one in which the coefficients in the interest-rate process are all positive. In such a setting, one way to characterize negative correlation would be to use a structure in which the first two coefficients in the spread process are negative and the third coefficient is positive. Of course, these estimates would be a function of the data sample used to fit the model. Essentially, negative correlation results when the factors that are driving the spread up are the same ones driving the interest rate down.

One theory is that as interest rates rise, asset values fall, thereby putting upward pressure on spreads (recall from Chapter 3 that asset values falling will result in a smaller DD and thus a higher spread). The data do not always reflect this theoretical prediction. In the next subsection, we describe some topics relating to this empirical estimation and selected published research estimating these coefficients.

Practical Implications

As we have seen thus far, reduced-form models in general and the DSL model in particular are quite flexible. This framework's flexibility and tractability make it suitable for applications that require an accurate reflection of current market conditions regardless of whether these conditions reflect fair value.

For example, a trader pricing a set of illiquid securities using as reference a set of liquidly traded securities may find an intensity model such as DSL quite useful since it would allow him to price those securities for which prices may not be readily observable. Unlike structural models, doubly stochastic intensity models do not superimpose any particular notions of intrinsic economic value, so prices that depart from more fundamental or economically driven values can still be captured in a meaningful way. These differences suggest benefits to considering the output of both kinds of models, structural and reduced-form, to develop a better perspective with respect to questions such as: What is a particular credit instrument's price? What should this instrument's price be?

Traders tend to use the simplest version of these models possible while still meeting minimum criteria for effective management of a trading book. In practice, factor versions of the model, such as the one originally proposed in Duffie and Singleton (1999) can be difficult to estimate. That does not mean that researchers do not find ways to do so in some circumstances. One recent paper by Driessen (2005) details the estimation of one version of this model. Another recent paper, Feldhutter and Lando (2007), presents a six-factor model that accommodates Treasury bonds, corporate bonds, and swap rates, and demonstrates how a larger number of state variables can be included to create a rich model structure and still result in usable parameter estimates. An alternative version of an intensity-based model that demonstrates a particular application of the DSL framework has also been published (see Jarrow 2001a and Van Deventer, Imai, and Mesler 2005 for details).

For example, this latter model defines the default intensity as follows:

$$h(t) = h_0 + h_1 r(t) + h_2 z(t)$$

Here, the default intensity and interest rate are directly related. This model links the state variable back to an observable macroeconomic factor, M, in the following way:

$$dM = M[r dt + \sigma_M dZ]$$

where σ_M is the volatility of the macroeconomic factor.

In this way, a macroeconomic factor such as oil prices, inflation rate, or GDP growth rate can be explicitly used in the framework. If we retain the (sometimes strong) assumption that Z is a standard Brownian motion, we can write down a version of this model with an arbitrary number of macroeconomic factors since the linear combination of these variables will retain similar distributional properties. The balance of this approach follows DSL in terms of specifying *recovery of value* of the security just before the obligor defaults, thus departing from the Jarrow, Lando, and Turnbull (1997) assumptions. This version of the model uses a Vasicek process for the interest rate and includes a generic functional form to handle liquidity.

A lack of data and, more importantly, the problem of noisy data can make parameter estimation difficult and certain specifications of these models unstable. However, while a one-factor version of DSL is easier to manipulate, the interest-rate-spread correlation cannot be estimated as robustly. In Feldhutter and Lando (2007), the convenience yield is shown to be quite important, suggesting that the treatment of liquidity risk in these markets also requires more than one factor. In practice, traders and analysts must make this trade-off when specifying a model. In recent years, the tendency among practitioners has been to use factor models despite the potential difficulties in modeling interest-rate-spread correlation. Recently, as interest rates have started to rise and have also become more volatile, the view that simple one-factor models may not be sufficient has become more prevalent.

It is hard to make strong statements about which modeling decisions are "best," given the relative newness of the models and resulting limited empirical research that has been published in this area to date. We know of one empirical study done by Duffee (1998) on the three-factor version of this DSL model which makes use of an extended Kalman filter that incorporates both the time series and cross-sectional properties of the bond prices (Kalman filters are reviewed in Appendix 6A). The paper showed that φ_1 and φ_2 (the parameters describing the dependence of risky spreads on the first and second state variables) are negative (while the other parameters governing the state variables are positive), supporting the view that the default-risk-free rate and the risky corporate bond spread are negatively correlated. Duffee found the average error in fitting noncallable corporate bond yields with this specification was less than 10 basis points. Unfortunately, his data sample only focused on investment grade borrowers. Later in this chapter, we describe the results of some of our own research in this domain.

However, beyond Duffee's study, much of the other broad-based empirical research in this area is done by practitioners and remains proprietary and unpublished. It would appear that the empirical research in this area continues to be for the most part sample-dependent, supporting a range of conclusions. As more data becomes available and more analysts focus on the empirical questions surrounding these models, we expect to see a clearer consensus develop over time on the degree to which including extra state variables improves performance and where boundaries for trading off increasing model complexity against performance may lie.

One technique that can be used to improve the stability of parameter estimates involves using other characteristics of obligors to either instrument for the parameter estimates, or to form quasi-homogeneous cohorts within the data set. For example, agency ratings or structural model PD values can be used to provide guidance on the credit quality of the underlying obligors issuing particular debt instruments whose pricing is used to parameterize a reduced-form model. In this way, the noise in the data can be mitigated, improving the quality of the parameter estimates.

FITTING AN INTENSITY-BASED MODEL WITH EQUITY-BASED PDs

Improving the fits of any model in the credit arena can be a challenge. As we have pointed out, the reduced-form modeling approach can suffer from parameter instability and parameter excess. Other sources of data that provide a complementary view on an obligor can improve the odds of fitting a model well. PDs estimated from the equity market using a structural model or PDs implied from agency ratings can be used in this context. We discuss two approaches for doing so.

The first approach is to use these measures of credit quality to group data into subsamples. The subsamples can be targeted for specific parameter estimation. As always, the number of observations must be balanced against the homogeneity of the subsample. Refer to the transition probability matrix section later in this chapter for specific recommendations on how to subset the data by either PD or agency rating.

An alternative approach is to estimate the parameters for physical default intensities using the PDs or agency ratings. Recall from the beginning of this chapter that the relationship of a PD to an intensity is:

$$1 - cpd_t = e^{-\int_0^t h(t)dt}$$

Because the PDs tend to suffer from fewer specification problems, we propose to fit one of the standard intensity-based models, in two stages assuming the PD as the input and taking advantage of the relationship between survival probabilities ($1\text{-}cpd_t$) and default intensities. The pricing data from the CDS or bond market can then be used to determine the risk-neutral version of the default intensities. To do this, we use a version of the model relating PDs estimated from an equity-based model or agency ratings to default intensities first through the survival probability relationship to intensities. Then once those parameters governing the intensity process are estimated, we can next use observed credit spreads to set up a functional relationship between spreads, a market risk premium conversion parameter, and the physical default intensities. Finally, we use this system to determine the market price of risk parameters to convert from physical to risk-neutral intensities. By using two (or three or four) different sets of data on the same obligor or groups of obligors, the analyst can assess the parameter estimates across the different subsamples. In addition, the implicit market risk premium parameters can be estimated by looking at both the physical and risk-neutral default intensities for each obligor. Berndt, Douglas, Duffie, Ferguson, and Schranz (2004) use EDF and CDS data to do exactly this sort of estimation.

Sensitivity Analysis

As we have emphasized throughout this book, interpretation of model output and diagnosis of model behavior constitute an essential part of productive credit and valuation analysis. Understanding how the variables and parameters interact provides the foundation for diagnosing a model. It is helpful for researchers and traders to move beyond just consuming tables of numbers. Rather, they can benefit from developing intuition around *what to expect* when estimating a model's parameters.

Sensitivity analysis can provide important guidance in developing this intuition as well as in understanding potential problems or limitations when applying a model to a specific asset. Importantly, while output sensitivity is best analyzed when holding all other parameters constant, this can sometimes lead to results that appear counterintuitive since in a realistic environment often one factor will change in a correlated way to another (so that holding "all else equal" will not reflect realistic behavior). In our judgment, a researcher may still be well served by starting with single parameter changes, with the knowledge that this is sometimes a crude first approximation, but then moving on to correlated parameter changes. At each step, the analyst can carefully evaluate the linkages in the model.

In the case of the DSL model, let us consider how the output changes as we adjust model inputs (see Figure 6.4).

- *Volatility of the intensity process* (σ_b). Increasing the volatility of the intensity process (all else equal) *increases* the dispersion of the default intensity around its mean, thereby increasing the probability of survival (decreasing the PD) since equal dispersion around the default intensity gets translated into a skewed distribution of survival probabilities due to the exponentiation, and the skew is to the low side. This decrease in PD then results in a decrease in spread. This relationship is a bit counterintuitive, as we would normally assume increased volatility to be bad news for a credit. But in this case, the volatility characterizes the *default intensity* and not, say, a firm's asset value. Note that we see the similar impact with respect to the volatility of the state-variable process(es) that drive the default intensity or the instantaneous spread (in the case of nonzero recovery expectations).
- *Mean reversion rate* (κ). *Increasing* the mean reversion rate (all else equal) *decreases* the volatility of the default intensity, thereby decreasing the probability of survival (increasing the probability of default). The intuition is similar to our discussion of directly impacting the volatility of the default intensity. Note, however, that a high starting point for the default intensity may result in a high rate of mean reversion,

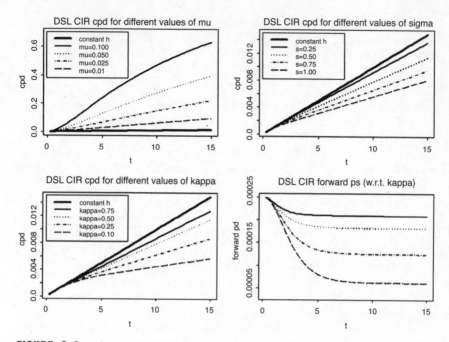

FIGURE 6.4 Changes in DSL Model Output with Adjusted Inputs

resulting in the default intensity process staying close to this initial starting point. Essentially, mean reversion has the effect of reducing the impact of default-intensity volatility on the shape of the forward default probability curve.

- *Long-run mean* (μ_h). The long-run mean directly influences the typical default intensity realized in this type of model. Thus *increasing* the long-run mean *increases* the typical default intensity, thereby increasing the default probability and increasing the spread.

Extensions

Another important advantage of the DSL model's flexibility is the relative ease with which the model can be extended along a number of dimensions. In our discussions so far, we have focused on the most popular specification of the DSL framework. Depending on the market environment and the perspective of the analyst, a number of extensions are possible, each of which can potentially produce a richer modeling infrastructure. As usual, these extensions complicate estimation, primarily due to the increased number of parameters. Nonetheless, extending this model framework can produce useful versions of the model that will help illuminate particular circumstances observed in the market. We will highlight a few of the more popular of these extensions.

Liquidity   *Liquidity* (or lack thereof) can become the primary driver of spreads, as observed most recently in the summer and second half of 2007 and continuing into 2008. For investment-grade obligors, the approach taken to disentangling the premium associated with credit risk from the premium associated with liquidity risk can materially impact the quality of a model's ability to explain spread variability.

One way to address the issue of liquidity is to add a stochastic process for liquidity to the DSL model by specifying a third instantaneous variable, w, using a suitable specification such as Vasicek or CIR. We could also link the liquidity variable to the same set of underlying state variables; however, this strategy may be harder to defend, given the often orthogonal nature of events that drive liquidity crises versus credit crises. That said, the events of 2007 and 2008 have demonstrated that a credit crisis and a liquidity crisis can become highly correlated during certain periods.

To accommodate liquidity, the valuation equation can be modified as follows:

$$D(T) = E_0^Q \left[e^{-\int_0^T (r(t)+s(t)+w(t))dt} \right]$$

While extending the model to reflect liquidity risk seems, on its surface, to be an idea that will only benefit the model, there is currently a lack of strong theoretical guidance as to how to predict shifts in market liquidity, and this introduces challenges that can reduce this extension to mostly a statistical estimation game. The usefulness of the model decreases as parameter instability and lack of coherent stories behind particular estimates make it difficult to interpret the model's parameter estimates. However, the inclusion of liquidity can sometimes have a material impact on model performance. With market data on the recent events of 2007 and 2008 and the liquidity difficulties experienced in the credit markets in 1998, brought on by the Russian default and the demise of Long-Term Capital Management (LTCM), we may start to see research that can draw conclusions about the data from these periods which will, in turn, facilitate better understanding of the interaction of credit and liquidity risks.

LGD (Recovery)   *LGD (recovery)* constitutes another area for extension. We have already discussed the differences in no-recovery models (i.e.,

100 percent LGD) and fractional-recovery models. A rich model extension focuses on casting LGD as another stochastic variable in the model framework. We can choose a particular stochastic process (again, Vasicek and CIR are good candidates), taking into account a view on the behavior of LGD and accounting for its natural bounds (typically from 0 to 100 percent). Modelers may also have to contemplate the possibility of a recovery-risk premium that could drive a wedge between actual expected LGD and risk-neutral expected LGD. Unfortunately, as we have noted elsewhere, we do not have conclusive research on the systematic behavior of actual LGD in wide-ranging samples of corporate borrowers. Here too, as more data are gathered, we hope to develop stronger intuition around how LGD should be integrated into these models. Without such research, LGD assumptions tend to be chosen more for their mathematical convenience.

Richer Stochastic Processes (Factors)   A more substantive change to the DSL framework focuses on the *stochastic processes* driving the intensity process, or the underlying state variables that ultimately drive the intensity process. Thus far, we have opted for straightforward mean-reverting diffusion processes such as Vasicek and CIR. One regular empirical feature of spread data is the presence of *jumps*, as seen in Figure 6.5 where a discontinuity seems to have entered the price process. We have suggested that liquidity risk is one plausible explanatory factor; however, that does not always seem to be the most reasonable explanation.

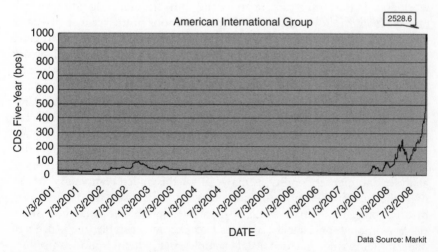

FIGURE 6.5   Example of a CDS Spread Jumping

One mechanism for extending DSL to accommodate such jump behavior (a mechanism that also creates substantially more mathematical and estimation complexity) is to assume that the default intensity, spread, or underlying state variables (depending on the choice of where the diffusion lies) follows an affine jump-diffusion model (see the section in Chapter 3 on jump-diffusion models for additional discussion). This type of modification awaits further research, but constitutes one of the more intriguing extensions.

Obviously, a number of alternative stochastic processes can be defined to create the *doubly* stochastic characteristic of this DSL model framework; however, elegant, closed-form solutions are difficult to find. While some researchers feel that simulation engines and fast computers eliminate the need for such analytic solutions, our own view is that until the baseline level of data noise in financial data is reduced, closed-form models and sensible interpretations of parameter and variable interactions are essential ingredients to reducing model risk in risk and portfolio management. That is, these closed-form models provide more guidance in developing intuition regarding the behavior of actual credit security prices and, importantly, highlight limitations of both the models and the data. While practical implementation may still require quasi-closed-form or outright simulation-based solutions, the availability of analytic solutions for simple cases is still invaluable in testing the reasonableness of models and assumptions.

Forward Rates   A final extension that we touch on only briefly, mirrors the work done in the term structure arena and shifts the modeling into forward-rate space and follows closely similar innovations in the term structure of interest rates introduced in the Heath-Jarrow-Morton (HJM) term structure framework (see Heath, Jarrow, and Morton 1992). The HJM framework typically characterizes the entire forward default-risk-free rate term structure as a state variable, and a similar extension can be made to DSL. In this extension, the forward default rates are estimated conditional on all the information available at each time period. Refer to Duffie and Singleton (2003) for a derivation of the DSL model under these assumptions.

Each of the extensions we have outlined in this section considerably increases the complexity of the basic DSL model. However, certain types of analyses and market conditions may call for this added complexity. Moreover, the quality of experimentation on available data sets will be improved by attempting to estimate some of the newer specifications of these models. Even though parameter estimates may become unstable, the process of understanding when particular data samples and particular models produce parameter instability will assist an analyst in developing useful insight.

as the VK model (see Chapter 3)[12] in the case of obligors with a large number of different outstanding bond issues. In general, the HW model strikes a reasonable balance between model flexibility and parameter-estimation stability. It is useful to consider how this model differs from the other reduced-form models, and we discuss this in the next section. (Our discussion will focus on the "default-at-any-time" version of this model, only. Please refer to Hull and White 2000 for a more detailed explanation of extensions and other model variants.)

Model Setup

An important departure of the HW model (compared to the other reduced-form models discussed in this chapter) is in the way the model solution is expressed. The HW model provides a framework for characterizing the risk-neutral *default probability density*, $q(t)$, instead of the default intensity or intensity, $h(t)$. At its heart, this model is still an intensity-based model. However, the estimation process does not focus on the default intensity directly. The two quantities relate trivially to each other as

$$q(t) = h(t)\, e^{-\int_0^t h(\tau)d\tau}$$

To set up HW, we first characterize the formula for a risky bond, D, and then characterize the formula for a CDS spread.[13] Often, a researcher or trader needs to fit the model on one market (say CDS) and use these parameter estimates to price and/or evaluate the risk of a bond or loan in a different segment of the market. The HW formulation is general enough to handle a variety of assumptions for both interest rates and recovery rates, which can be either deterministic or stochastic. However, HW does make the important assumption that recovery risk is not systematic so that the expectation for recovery in the risk-neutral world is the same as in the physical world.

Assume a bond D matures at time T. The price of a bond that is otherwise similar to D (i.e., same time to maturity, same coupon, etc.)—except that it is default-risk-free—is defined as B. For convenience in writing down

---

[12] Note that for issuers with fewer bond issues outstanding, the HW model did not perform as well as the more theoretically motivated structural model. This highlights the point that when data are plentiful, reduced-form models, which do not rely on heavy theoretical constraints, can perform quite well; but that when data are sparse, the added structure provided by a rich theory can offer a more robust framework.

[13] Note that we have changed some of the notation from that in the original Hull and White (2000) paper for consistency with the notation elsewhere in this text.

the formula, we also define the following terms:

$F(t) \equiv$ Forward price of bond B (i.e., default-risk-free) at time $t < T$

$b(t) \equiv$ Present value of \$1 received at time t with certainty

$C(t) \equiv$ Claim amount at time t to which the expected recovery rate will be applied in the event of default

$R \equiv$ Expected recovery rate or $(1 - \text{LGD})$ in the event of default applied to C

$q_i \equiv$ Constant level of $q(t)$ at time t, $t_{i-1} < t < t_i$

In practice, we typically observe many bonds issued by the same issuer. More generally, we may also find it convenient to create cohorts of issuers and estimate parameters from the group of (approximately) homogeneous borrowers in each cohort. It turns out that HW is particularly helpful in situations in which we do in fact observe more than one bond from a relatively homogeneous cohort, since a larger number of observations provides more information that helps to sort through the noise. This framework lends itself to using the information from a variety of bonds without needlessly watering down the data by averaging across bond issues.

Assume we have a sample of N bonds with the maturity of the ith bond defined as t_i where $t_1 < t_2 \ldots < t_N$. In the version of the HW model we discuss here, any bond can default at any one of the maturity dates. To speak about a specific bond defaulting, we will next add another subscript j to each of the bond related variables (D_j, B_j, F_j, C_j, R_j). This set-up allows for default of any of the j bonds on any of the maturity dates in our sample, even if the jth bond does not mature on that date (as long as the bond is still outstanding on that date). Subsequent formulas can be generalized to allow for default on any date (see Hull and White 2000).

Next we will use the following integral solution relating the forward value of the bond to β_{ij}, which is defined as follows:

$$\beta_{ij} = \int_{t_{i-1}}^{t_i} b(t)[F_j(t) - R_j C_j(t)]dt$$

We can simplify the calculation by making the expected recovery independent of both j and t. We then define the risk-neutral default density as follows:

$$q_j = \frac{B_j - D_j - \sum_{i=1}^{j-1} q_i \beta_{ij}}{\beta_{jj}}$$

HW suggest that "the parameters β_{ij} can be estimated using standard procedures, such as Simpson's rule for evaluating a definite integral." This suggestion and the derivation can also be found in Hull and White (2000).[14]

Bond Valuation and the Recovery of Treasury Assumption

The formula we just derived is quite general. In order to make use of the framework, we need to choose a set of assumptions that facilitate implementation for a particular application. A primary objective in using this framework is to extract parameter estimates from the more liquid portions of the bond or the CDS markets so that various instruments that are less liquidly traded can be valued. This estimation can be simplified dramatically by making several assumptions.

The foremost among these simplifying assumptions is similar to the recovery assumption made in the JLT framework in which we assume that the claim value used to calculate recovery is the default-risk-free (i.e., Treasury) value of the bond. This assumption results in the coupon bond D_j reducing to the sum of the values of the underlying zero-coupon bonds. This property is often called *value additivity*. The advantage of this value additivity is that it makes it possible to calculate zero curves for different categories or cohorts of traded bonds (such as rating categories or PD buckets) and use them to price illiquid bonds. If instead of recovery of Treasury, we assume that the claim value for recovery is the face value of the bond, we can still apply the approach, however, we lose the value additivity property. The cost is more complexity in the calculation.

---

[14] Note that the literature on numerical integration methods is a rich one so a number of methods are typically found in common usage. For example, Simpson's rule, named after the British mathematician, Thomas Simpson, is a numerical technique, similar to the trapezoidal rule, for approximating definite integrals. While the trapezoidal rule uses linear approximations along the function being integrated, Simpson's rule uses quadratic approximations. Simpson's rule is a special case of the more general class of Newton-Cotes formulae for approximating definite integrals. Briefly, we can approximate the integral of a function $f(x)$ between points a and b as $\int_a^b f(x) \approx \frac{h}{3}(f(a) + 4f((a+b)/2) + f(b))$ where $h = (b\text{-}a)/2$. The associated error for this approximation is small: $\varepsilon = \int_a^b \frac{h^5}{90} f^{(4)}(\xi), a < \xi < b$, where $f^{(4)}(x)$ is the fourth derivative of $f(x)$. Higher Newton-Cotes order approximations are also feasible, by adding successively greater numbers of divisions (thus making h smaller). These methods and others can be found in most standard numerical methods texts (see, for example, Press, et al., 2007 or Judd, 1999).

A common problem in the reduced-form framework results from the multiplicative way that default intensity (probability) and expected recovery enter into the equations that describe the spread dynamics under the models. Often, analysts will assume a particular expected recovery rate (40 percent to 50 percent are common estimates) and then estimate the remaining model parameters based on this assumption. The potential trouble arises from circumstances in which the recovery estimates are substantially different from the recoveries implied through market pricing.

How can we determine if this is the case?

The HW framework helps facilitate a more detailed look at underlying model assumptions by making use of upper and lower bounds on the bond yields implied by the model. By comparing the modeled yield ranges to actual market prices, the analyst can develop better intuition regarding reasonable estimates of all parameters in the framework.

To understand how this works and why it is so useful, it is instructive to drill into how we can specify these bond-yield bounds. First, we determine that default probability densities must be greater than zero. This means that based on the formula for the default probability density, the following natural result must be true in this framework:

$$D_j \leq B_j - \sum_{i=1}^{j-1} q_i \beta_{ij}$$

This simply states that the risky bond cannot be more valuable than the risk-free bond which in turn means that the risky bond must yield more than the risk-free bond. If we assume that the maturity date of the bond is t_i, the yield for D_j, r_{D_j} is defined as follows (assuming $D_j = e^{-r_{D_j} t_i}$):

$$r_{D_j} = -\frac{\ln D_j}{t_i}$$

and similarly,

$$r_{B_j} = -\frac{\ln B_j}{t_i}$$

These equations can be used to define a lower bound for the bond yield—that is, r_{D_j} must be no less than r_{B_j} or

$$r_{D_j} \geq -\frac{\ln B_j}{t_i}$$

Next, for any issuer not currently in default, we determine (trivially) that the cumulative risk-neutral probability of default must be less than one. Mathematically:

$$\sum_{i=1}^{j} q_i \, (t_i - t_{i-1}) \leq 1$$

Thus,

$$q_j \, (t_j - t_{j-1}) \leq 1 - \sum_{i=1}^{j-1} q_i \, (t_i - t_{i-1})$$

Again, using the properties of the default probability density, previously shown, we arrive at a second bound:

$$D_j \geq B_j - \sum_{i=1}^{j-1} q_i \beta_{ij} - \frac{\beta_{jj}}{t_j - t_{j-1}} \left[1 - \sum_{i=1}^{j-1} q_i \times (t_i - t_{i-1}) \right]$$

Recasting the bond price in terms of its yield, we arrive at an upper bound for the modeled yield.

The interesting exercise then becomes to compare the actual yields and determine how much a specific assumed input (e.g., expected recovery) would need to change to bracket where the market is trading. This analysis can then be used to assess the reasonableness of the assumption and the sensitivity of the model to this assumption.

CDS Valuation

In practice, we are often interested in estimating parameters from the CDS market and using the results to price or manage bonds or loans. In the next section, we discuss a process for creating *generic curves* from traded CDS prices. The HW model turns out to be an excellent candidate model for generic curve estimation. Before doing this, though, we first derive the appropriate equation for pricing a CDS in the HW framework. To this end, we will make use of the notation and variable definitions defined in the bond pricing equations in the previous section, as well as a few more, which we define as follows:

$s \equiv$ CDS spread
$T \equiv$ CDS maturity
$q(t) \equiv$ Risk-neutral default probability density at time t

$R \equiv$ Expected recovery rate on the underlying obligation (Note the absence of a time subscript on R, indicating the assumption that the recovery is both constant and independent of the time of default.)

$cpd_T^Q \equiv$ Risk-neutral cumulative probability of a credit event (defined per the CDS contract) over the life of the CDS. The relationship to the default density is $cpd_T^Q = \int_0^T q(t)\,dt$.

$b(t) \equiv$ Present value of \$1 received at time t with certainty.

$u(t) \equiv$ Present value of payments of \$1 made each year from time zero to time t. (While this formulation is purposely general to provide flexibility, we can use the basic formula for the present value of an ordinary annuity using a discrete annual default-risk rate of r, which is calculated as $u(t) = \frac{1}{r}[1 - (1/(1+r)^t)]$.)

$e(t) \equiv$ Present value at time t of an accrual payment equal to the amount earned from the previous time period to time t.

$A(t) \equiv$ Accrued interest on the underlying obligation at time t as a percent of face value.

The valuation equation arises out of balancing the present value of the spread payments (i.e., the cost of the implicit credit insurance) and the present value of the risk-neutral expected loss on the contract. By setting these two quantities equal, we can solve for the spread that balances the two expected cash flow streams given the values of the relevant inputs.

The first component is the present value of the expected spread payments. This component can be further broken down into two cases where a default occurs at some time $t < T$ and where no default occurs prior to the CDS's expiration. If default occurs, the present value of payments is the present value of the full payments plus the fractional payment due for the partial period just prior to default:

$$s[u(t) + e(t)]$$

If no default occurs, the present value of payments is:

$$su(T)$$

By attaching the default probability density function to the first part of this component, we arrive at the specification for the present value of expected spread payments to the writer of protection:

$$S(0) = s \int_0^T q(t) [u(t) + e(t)] \, dt + s \left(1 - cpd_T^Q\right) u(T)$$

Essentially, we adjust the payment stream by the default probability density function and the probability of survival to the maturity of the contract.

The second component is the expected payoff in the event of default. This payment amount is calculated as follows:

$$1 - R - A(t) R$$

(Importantly, recall that the recovery rate used in this calculation is assumed to be risk-neutral. This assumption simplifies the modeling. Otherwise, additional modeling is required to move between physical and risk-neutral recovery expectations based on an assumed market price of recovery risk.)

In order to specify the second component of this CDS valuation framework, we make use of the default probability density function to arrive at the following expression for the value to the purchaser of protection:

$$P(0) = \int_0^T b(t) q(t) (1 - R - A(t) R) \, dt$$

To calculate the appropriate spread for this contract, we set *P(0) = S(0)* and solve for *s* to arrive at the following valuation formula for CDS spreads:

$$s = \frac{\int_0^T b(t) q(t) [1 - R - A(t) R] dt}{\int_0^T q(t) [u(t) + e(t)] dt + \left(1 - cpd_T^Q\right) u(T)}$$

In words: we find the spread that forces the risk-neutral expected default payoff to equal the risk-neutral expected payments over the life of the CDS.

Now that we have outlined how to extract the probabilities from both CDS and bond spreads, we have a complete modeling framework for bonds (and, by extension, loans) and CDSs. (Currently, given the liquidity in the CDS and loan markets, we typically have far more access to traded CDS prices than to bond or loan prices, as the liquidity in the CDS market generally continues to improve by the day—despite setbacks in times of difficulty, as was seen in 2007 and 2008.) We can estimate the components of the HW model using CDS prices and then apply them to the valuation and assessment of bonds and loans. The applications range from relative-value analysis supporting credit trading strategies to portfolio risk analysis supporting ACPM. In the next section we show in detail how these methods can be used to construct generic credit curves that can then be used, under certain assumptions, to price illiquid securities.

GENERIC CREDIT CURVES

As we emphasize in Chapter 2 on ACPM in practice, in Chapter 9 (the case study), and in Chapter 8 on portfolio modeling, mark-to-market (MTM) is an important objective for credit analytics. In an ideal world where every security were traded in a liquid market, the need to use models for MTM would become less important. However, at the present time MTM is only mark to *market* in the very best cases, and more often than not, it actually refers to mark to *model*. Reduced-form models fill an important need in this MTM context. For all of their theoretical elegance, structural models often diverge from traded prices, particularly during times of market stress, making them less useful in these cases for MTM.

One way to think about reduced-form models is that they offer a so-phisticated way to interpolate and extrapolate between and beyond observed market prices while enforcing constraints implied by financial economic theory. The result of this extrapolation is often referred to as a *credit curve*—a relationship between tenor and spread that also controls for LGD. Thus, we use the term *generic* credit curve—that is, a credit curve that is generalized to a set of homogeneous obligors defined by characteristics such as geography, size, and industry, but which does not necessarily reflect the collateral or degree of subordination in a specific debt issue. In practice, the specific characteristics of a particular debt issue are commonly applied (i.e., added) to a generic curve to arrive at an estimated spread for a particular exposure.

Before we discuss using a specific model in the context of generic credit curve estimation, for motivation we first consider a very simple approach that does not even require a model. This four-step approach starts with the data gathering and definition of cohorts:

1. Define cohorts.
2. Collect the observable spread data either in the cross-section (for a particular date) or a pooled sample (cross-sectional data across several dates) for each cohort.

3. Bucket the data into tenor categories (e.g., half-yearly intervals—0 to 6 months, 6 months to 1 year, 1 year to 1.5 years, etc.).
4. Determine the median spread for each tenor bucket within each cohort.

This approach will produce a set of discrete points on the curve across tenors. Once we have the discrete points, we can use an interpolation approach such as cubic splines, nonparametric smoothing, or polynomial fitting (e.g., third-order polynomials) to estimate a credit curve across all tenors of interest. Thus, our data is our model. Note that in using these approaches there is nothing special about the fact that we are dealing with financial market data versus any other type of noisy data. Said another way, these simple approaches cannot accommodate the additional information that financial theory provides to improve the interpolation and extrapolation.

As a result, and not surprisingly, a big drawback of this approach arises from the emergence of oddly shaped credit curves (often they become wavy) resulting from noisy data. These shapes often contradict established financial economic theory. In practice, this problem makes these interpolation approaches largely unusable. An even more troubling issue is that of curve *crossing* (e.g., a higher-rated group of obligors has tenors in which the spread exceeds the spreads of a lower-rated group of obligors at the same tenor). Much of the work, even when using a model, lies in fixing the crossovers.

A better approach to estimating generic credit curves relies on using some kind of reduced-form model that benefits from the added structure provided through the large body of theory for asset valuation. One of the models that seems to work well on real CDS data is the HW model. Based on observed spreads, the parameters (in particular, the default probability density) for this model can be estimated and then used to construct the generic credit curves. These curves become the basis for valuing less liquid credit securities. A key step in creating credit curves is to identify cohorts of relatively homogeneous issuers that can be used to identify regularities in market spreads and to then apply these observed regularities to less liquid issuers that are also similar to those in the cohort.

Before any estimation can take place, a good deal of work goes into pooling data that have been scrubbed and otherwise filtered for data quality issues. The pooling is key to the estimation since we use the pooled data to estimate the curves, and in order to increase the stability of the estimates we recommend careful attention to outliers.

In developing cohorts from the cleaned data, we have found it useful to focus on the usual suspects as dimensions for pooling: country or region, industry or sector, size, or credit rating. These dimensions define "homogeneous" pools of data within which the credit curves can be estimated. Note that, subject to the properties of the markets, the characteristics used to construct cohorts can be modified to conform with the desired categories for the credit curves dictated by a particular application. When these curves are used for obligors without traded securities, the characteristics of the target obligors should be chosen so that the sample used to construct the curve is as homogeneous as possible. (In practice, we find that the characteristics are sometimes driven more by data availability than what is theoretically preferred.)

Specifically, a modeler might experiment with cohorts such as the following (note that the cohort dimensions below will almost certainly have to be expanded or collapsed depending on data availability):

- *Regions*: Asia ex-Japan, Europe, Japan, Latin America, Middle East and Africa, North America
- *Ratings*: Either agency ratings or market-based default probabilities from a structural model. At the very least, it is important to segment issuers into investment grade and sub–investment grade. A better option is to move to broad rating groupings such as the following: Aaa and Aa, A, Baa, Ba, B, all else in the lowest rating grades.
- *Sectors*: Banks, nonbank financial institutions, nonservice businesses, service businesses, utilities
- *Size*: Revenue less than 1 billion USD, revenue greater than 1 billion USD.

Tenor is another important consideration in credit curve construction. The final credit curve will be expressed in terms of spreads as a function of tenor for each cohort. Ideally, we want tenors from six months up through 30 years. The data typically cannot accommodate this ideal. What is more typical is the following: 1 year, 2 years, 3 years, 5 years, 7 years, 10 years, 20 years, and 30 years.

But how big should a cohort be? If the subsample is too large, it will likely become too heterogeneous to produce meaningful credit curves. Conversely, if it is too small, the estimates may become unstable or overfit. In our own work, we try to ensure that at least 10 observations remain in each cohort but that the data are not pooled so broadly as to destroy the regularity that we are hoping to model.[15]

---

[15] In practice, there may be limits to how finely the data can be sliced. For example, some banks are faced with privacy laws that make it illegal to subset data so much that an analyst would be able to discern specific information about a particular borrower. While probably not an issue for spreads, this could become an issue for the other attributes used for subsetting spread data.

A modeler should always focus on whether the cohort truly represents a homogeneous view of that type of obligor. Many times, too much data can be concentrated in one or two buckets with the result being that the average or typical obligor in that bucket does not look much like a large portion of the actual sample. For example, choosing industry and country in some cases may produce a cohort that spans substantial differences in size and credit quality. The result is that there may be a bucket, say U.S. manufacturing, that contains both small, risky firms and large, safer firms. The average or representative firm from this subsample will not look like either the small firms or the large firms. The key is to identify the dimensions that are more likely to create homogeneous subsamples.

Once the cohorts have been created, we find it useful to take some time to evaluate various descriptive statistics for each cohort. Though the data have presumably already been scrubbed well, this additional analysis provides guidance as to whether there are outliers that may have been masked in a more heterogeneous sample. Scatter plots and histograms are much better tools for gaining an intuition with respect to the data than are pages of tables of statistics. Data visualization techniques, combined with traditional statistical methods for outlier detection, constitute a useful way to find such outliers. Some outliers will be justified while others will be clear data errors. If there is not an obvious way to fix a known erroneous data record it is typically most useful to simply throw it out. The case of an ambiguous outlier (i.e., an outlier that is clearly different but not clearly an error), the remedy is less clear. Once outliers and data problems have been identified, techniques such as those described earlier in this chapter and elsewhere in the book can be used to reduce the impact of outliers.

The HW framework accommodates multiple CDSs in estimating the default probability density. If the plan is to use all the data, robust estimation techniques can be effective ways to minimize the influence of outliers on the estimates. At some point, however, data sufficiency issues begin to weigh down the analysis, even in the case of robust estimation. In our own work, as we have indicated before, we typically aim to collect more than 10 observations for spread analysis, but at the very least we require three (!) data points at each tenor on the credit-spread term structure. We then use these to calculate a median value before the curves are fit.

Once the data has been appropriately preprocessed and cleaned, we can use a model to fit the data. We discuss one example using the HW model. To review, the observed CDS spread, s, is calculated in the context of the following equation:

$$s = \frac{\int_0^T b(t) q(t) [1 - R - A(t) R] dt}{\int_0^T q(t) [u(t) + e(t)] dt + \left(1 - cpd_T^Q\right) u(T)}$$

However, it is not always obvious how to estimate the quantities in the equation from the noisy data. One technique is to use some statistical framework that incorporates information differentially, depending on data quality. Weighted nonlinear least squares is one simple example since the weighting can be made to depend on some measure of data quality. For example, some data vendors provide information on the depth of the market (i.e., how liquid it is) in a particular name. If fitting to medians, the weight can be a function of the number of data points used to calculate the median. The focus is to use quoted CDS spreads for s together with the relevant information to properly parameterize the equation so that we can estimate parameters such as $q(t)$. Since $q(t)$ is a continuous function and we typically do not have enough data across the full term structure, we focus on fitting intervals. For example, we may decide to estimate the curve with the following eight intervals for t:

0 to 0.5

0.5 to 1

1 to 3

3 to 5

5 to 7

7 to 10

10 to 20

20 to 30

We can perform this fitting exercise for each cohort that we construct. For example, we may decide to look at region, sector, and rating. In this case, if we grouped by rating, broad industry and geography, we might have a single curve fit for North American banks that are in the {AAA or AA} bucket. The HW model accommodates multiple CDSs, making it appropriate for extracting as much information as possible from the market without creating too much incoherence in the final estimates.

Note that under the HW approach, the estimation requires initial or starting values for the q parameters in the equation. These crude estimates can be obtained by using a simple interpolation routine such as cubic splines as we described at the beginning of this section. Alternatively, if the curves are estimated over time, the previous day's estimates can also serve as the initial values once the algorithm goes into production.

Despite its attractiveness, estimating parameters in the HW framework can still be subtle. Improper specification of initial parameter values may cause the estimation algorithm to fail. As with many reduced-form techniques, these algorithms need a fair amount of supervision by analysts in order to avoid incoherent curve estimates. One of the most common manifestations of this need occurs in the context of the problem of crossing that we discussed earlier, which sometimes needs to be addressed in production. Generally, HW-model-based credit curves estimated across the specific cohorts that we have described behave reasonably well. That said, we find it helpful to address this problem by adding parameter bounds for input to the estimation routine. Even so, some manual smoothing at the end may become necessary to achieve monotonically increasing curves across credit quality groups.

CONCLUSION

Term structure modeling has matured over the past decade, and the research into development and estimation of affine models with stochastic characterizations of the short-interest rate are well accepted at most financial institutions around the world. The mathematical infrastructure of these models sets the stage for reduced-form models of the term-structures of credit spreads. The shift from causal models of default to intensity models of default can be difficult for analysts who are used to thinking in structural terms; however, these models are important tools for extracting information from traded securities without worrying too much about fundamental or intrinsic value.

Reduced-form models are heavily used by traders in hedging their trading books and by analysts to price one set of (illiquid) securities with another set of (more liquid) securities. The difficulties that arise in introducing correlation in an intensity-based framework as of the current time make these models less suitable for large portfolio risk modeling though research in this area continues to advance. We discuss these correlation issues in Chapter 8 on portfolio modeling; however, valuation applications can benefit from the flexibility of the reduced-form approach to generating estimates of a security's price.

The computational difficulty in estimating multifactor versions of reduced-form models continues to hamper the introduction of their most sophisticated versions. As computing power improves and econometric techniques evolve, some of these problems are likely to disappear. In the meantime, more computationally straightforward approaches, such as that suggested by Hull and White and one- or two-factor DSL models, will be preferred by some analysts. Importantly, an active stream of the academic work in reduced-form modeling focuses on *explaining* the components of credit spreads, an application we do not discuss in detail in this text, for which they can often provide analytics where other methods fall short. We expect this work to make its way into practice as these results become more well established. Examples include applications to sovereign bond spreads (see, for example, Pan and Singleton 2008). We expect to see continued advances in reduced-form models as credit portfolios continue to expand and encompass a wider array of securities.

APPENDIX 6A: KALMAN FILTER

Reduced-form models are appealing because they aggregate information on an obligor's default risk into a single process. Furthermore, one can estimate not just a default intensity process, but also processes for the recovery rate and liquidity. Given data difficulties and lack of coherent time series, cross-sectional estimation becomes more practical. One strategy is to specify default intensity as a latent variable observed via a pricing function. This approach requires a method that facilitates the estimation of a continuous-time process when data are observed discretely. Note that default is typically recorded on a date close to when a coupon payment is missed. Other empirical evidence that points to observable signals of distress weakens the argument for using an intensity process. Nonetheless, the date at which a firm is beyond hope may be different than the legal or technical default date and may still be sufficiently unpredictable.

Following on this suggestion to treat default intensity as a latent variable, we can use a Kalman filter as the estimation technique, which is well suited to such estimation problems.

Assume a statistical model indexed by a parameter vector ψ. For each value of ψ, we can infer the distribution of the following vector of random variables: $(X_1 \ldots X_T, Y_1 \ldots Y_T)$. The Kalman filter enables us to estimate a likelihood function for a particular ψ. We can then calculate the least-square estimates of the latent variables for each ψ. The challenge here is in finding the maximum value of the likelihood function over possible ψ.

Assume $\mathbf{X}$ is a latent Markov process governed by the following group of transition densities:

$$P(X_t \mid X_{t-1}; \psi)$$

The state variables may be aggregate default intensities themselves (e.g., industry level), or intensities may be a function of the state variables.

We observe a vector $\mathbf{Y}$ of observed yields (derived from debt prices; alternatively we could use CDS spreads) with each yield determined as follows:

$$\mathbf{Y}_t = f(X_t; \boldsymbol{\psi}) + \boldsymbol{\varepsilon}_t$$

Note that the parameter vector, $\boldsymbol{\psi}$, governs the evolution of both the state variables and the prices (yields). Thus, it enters into both the pricing equation and the transition densities.

We can apply the Kalman filter to the following specific system:

$$\mathbf{Y}_t = \mathbf{A}_t(\boldsymbol{\psi}) + \mathbf{B}_t(\boldsymbol{\psi})\mathbf{X}_t + \boldsymbol{\varepsilon}_t$$

$$\mathbf{X}_t = \mathbf{C}_t(\boldsymbol{\psi}) + \mathbf{D}_t(\boldsymbol{\psi})\mathbf{X}_{t-1} + \mathbf{u}_t$$

$$\boldsymbol{\varepsilon}_t \sim \phi(0, \boldsymbol{\Sigma}_Y(\boldsymbol{\psi}))$$

$$\mathbf{u}_t \sim \phi(0, \boldsymbol{\Sigma}_X(\boldsymbol{\psi}))$$

$\boldsymbol{\Sigma}_Y$ and $\boldsymbol{\Sigma}_X$ are variance-covariance matrices of the appropriate dimension. The simplest version of this type of affine model assumes a zero-coupon bond with the yields as an affine function of the state variables as previously specified. That said, any of the reduced-form models can be used to relate the state variables to the observed pricing information, whether it be yields or spreads.

$\mathbf{A}$ and $\mathbf{B}$ are derived from the chosen pricing equation.

$\mathbf{C}$ and $\mathbf{D}$ can be derived from the transition densities over discrete-time intervals in the case of Gaussian diffusions. Even if the process is not Gaussian, as long as it is Markov, affine processes allow for the computation of conditional means and variances of the process over a discrete time period. These means and variances can then be used in a Gaussian approximation of the transition densities. Note the distributions in the system refer to the physical measure. The risk-neutral measure is still relevant for the pricing function.

Now that we have the conceptual framework in place, let us turn to the procedure for estimating the Kalman filter. To estimate the Kalman filter, we need a likelihood function, a starting value in $\mathbf{X}$ assumed to be $\hat{x}_0$, and an associated variance-covariance matrix, $\hat{\boldsymbol{\Sigma}}_0$. While these values are not known, the convention is to choose from the unconditional distribution of $\mathbf{X}$ given the parameters. We start with an estimate of $\hat{x}_{t-1}$ with associated mean-squared error matrix $\hat{\boldsymbol{\Sigma}}_{t-1}$. The key to the estimation is to set up a recursive system as follows (for ease of reading the equations, the parameter vector has been dropped; nonetheless, it is still part of the calculations):

$$\hat{X}_{t|t-1} = C_t + D_t\hat{X}_{t-1}$$

$$\hat{\Sigma}_{t|t-1} = D_t\hat{\Sigma}_{t-1}D_t^{'} + \Sigma_X$$

$$\Gamma_Y = \text{Matrix version of } \varepsilon_t = Y_t - (A_t + B_t\hat{X}_{t|t-1})$$

$$V_\varepsilon = \text{cov}(\Gamma_Y) = B_t\hat{\Sigma}_{t|t-1}B_t^{'} + \Sigma_Y$$

We can then use this system to build the core of the recursion:

$$\hat{X}_t = \hat{X}_{t|t-1} + \hat{\Sigma}_{t|t-1}B_t^{'}V_\varepsilon^{-1}\Gamma_Y$$

$$\hat{\Sigma}_t = \hat{\Sigma}_{t|t-1}^{-1} - \hat{\Sigma}_{t|t-1}^{-1}B_t^{'}V_\varepsilon^{-1}B_t\hat{\Sigma}_{t|t-1}^{-1}$$

With T observations, we can compute the following log-likelihood function for a single ψ:

$$\log L(\psi|Y_1 \ldots Y_T) = \sum_{t=1}^{T}\left(-\frac{1}{2}N_t\log(2\pi) - \frac{1}{2}\log|V_\varepsilon| - \frac{1}{2}\Gamma_Y^{'}V_\varepsilon^{-1}\Gamma_Y\right)$$

$$N_t = \dim(\Gamma_Y)$$

The final step is to maximize the likelihood function over ψ. This maximization process is nontrivial and sometimes quite difficult given the noisy data generally observed in estimating credit valuation models.

Over time we have learned a number of important lessons in using a Kalman filter estimation approach. First, the Kalman filter is well suited for estimating a reduced-form model that assumes a Vasicek process for zero-coupon bonds. In this case, the yields are affine functions of the state variables. Note that the yield of a coupon-paying bond is not an affine function of the state variable. This creates some difficulty for the Kalman filter approach. One can use a first-order Taylor approximation with respect to the estimated state to make use of the Kalman filter approach in this context.

Second, when estimating a CIR model, the structure of the covariance matrix can materially impact the results, sometimes adversely. In practice, the covariance matrix is allowed to be time-varying in the filter. The state can be replaced with the estimated value and substituted back into the expression to generate the covariance matrix.

APPENDIX 6B: SAMPLE TRANSITION MATRICES

TABLE 6.2 Sample Transition Matrices (estimated from Moody's data)

U.S. Firms' One-Year Transitions, 1986–2005

From	To							
	Aaa	Aa	A	Baa	Ba	B	Caa-C	Default
Aaa	93.4%	6.3%	0.4%	0.0%	0.0%	0.0%	0.0%	0.0%
Aa	0.7%	91.1%	7.8%	0.3%	0.1%	0.0%	0.0%	0.0%
A	0.1%	2.2%	91.4%	5.6%	0.5%	0.2%	0.0%	0.0%
Baa	0.1%	0.2%	4.7%	88.8%	4.8%	1.0%	0.2%	0.2%
Ba	0.0%	0.0%	0.7%	6.5%	81.7%	9.5%	0.7%	0.9%
B	0.0%	0.0%	0.2%	0.8%	7.4%	81.7%	5.1%	4.9%
Caa-C	0.0%	0.0%	0.0%	0.1%	3.8%	7.8%	66.9%	21.5%

European Firms' One-Year Transitions, 1986–2005

From	To							
	Aaa	Aa	A	Baa	Ba	B	Caa-C	Default
Aaa	92.6%	7.2%	0.2%	0.0%	0.1%	0.0%	0.0%	0.0%
Aa	1.4%	91.2%	7.3%	0.1%	0.0%	0.0%	0.0%	0.0%
A	0.0%	4.1%	91.1%	4.5%	0.2%	0.1%	0.0%	0.0%
Baa	0.0%	0.3%	6.8%	84.6%	6.5%	1.6%	0.1%	0.1%
Ba	0.0%	0.0%	1.1%	6.3%	80.4%	11.4%	0.2%	0.6%
B	0.0%	0.0%	0.3%	1.1%	9.2%	72.6%	12.0%	4.8%
Caa-C	0.0%	0.0%	0.0%	0.0%	0.6%	21.0%	54.8%	23.7%

Japan Firms' One-Year Transitions 1986–2005

From	To							
	Aaa	Aa	A	Baa	Ba	B	Caa-C	Default
Aaa	90.1%	9.2%	0.7%	0.0%	0.0%	0.0%	0.0%	0.0%
Aa	0.7%	90.6%	8.7%	0.0%	0.0%	0.0%	0.0%	0.0%
A	0.0%	1.3%	94.0%	4.7%	0.1%	0.0%	0.0%	0.0%
Baa	0.0%	0.0%	4.8%	90.2%	4.7%	0.2%	0.1%	0.0%
Ba	0.0%	0.0%	0.0%	7.9%	86.4%	5.4%	0.2%	0.2%
B	0.0%	0.0%	0.0%	0.0%	16.6%	82.9%	0.5%	0.0%
Caa-C	0.0%	0.0%	0.0%	0.0%	0.0%	16.7%	83.3%	0.0%

REVIEW QUESTIONS

1. What are the biggest benefits of using the reduced-form framework for modeling credit risk?
2. What is the biggest difficulty posed in the reduced-form framework for modeling the components of expected loss?
3. In what context is specification of the market risk premium important and in what context is it less important?
4. Identify three ways that recovery can be characterized in an intensity model.
5. Explain why a simple stochastic intensity model does not capture well the behavior of actual credit spreads.
6. Which assumption for recovery creates the most mathematical tractability in a Duffie-Singleton-Lando framework?
7. Explain "doubly stochastic" in the context of a Duffie-Singleton-Lando intensity model.
8. Explain how to generate negative correlation between risk-free rate and the spread.
9. What characteristic of historical, agency rating–based transition matrices leads to likely overestimation of value for a credit instrument using this framework?
10. Describe two difficulties with implementing the JLT framework.
11. What two simplifying assumptions are made in the JLT framework? (Hint: One deals with default-risk-free interest rates and the other deals with recovery.)

EXERCISES

1. Outline a procedure for estimating a parameter for expected recovery in the event of default in a reduced-form model framework. Include the mathematical relationships and be specific about what data you would use.
2. In the context of a simple, affine, reduced-form model of debt, explain the basic underlying mathematical relationships, the key parameters that drive the results, and a simple strategy for estimating these parameters. Be specific about the mathematics of the relationships. (Rather than deriving a model, focus on characterizing the inputs and relationships.)
3. Write down pseudo-code (i.e., it does not necessarily need to be written in a specific computer language syntax) for how you would estimate generic credit curves using a Hull-White model.

4. Construct an example demonstrating how you can have a hump-shaped zero-coupon credit-spread term structure with an upwardly sloping par credit-spread term structure. Be specific about your assumptions.
5. Discuss the specific model differences associated with applying a reduced-form model to corporate bonds versus credit default swaps.

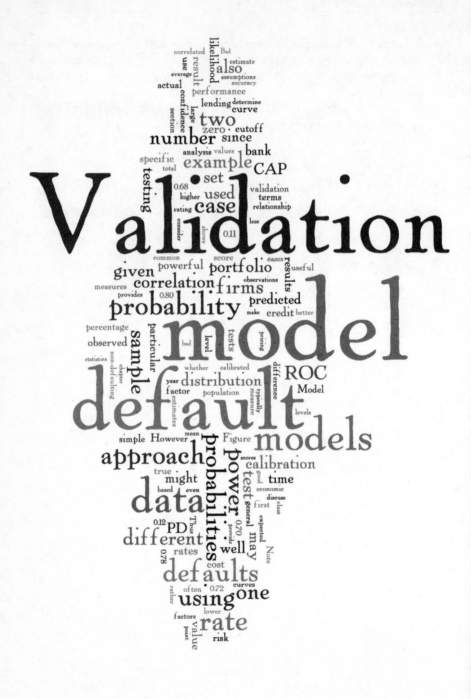

CHAPTER 7

PD Model Validation

The first principle is that you must not fool yourself—and you are the easiest person to fool.

—Richard Feynman

I know that half the money I spend on advertising is wasted. The problem is, I don't know which half.

—John Wanamaker

Objectives

After reading this chapter you should understand:[1]

- The different dimensions along which PD models can be validated.
- How to calculate measures describing how well calibrated and how powerful PD models are.
- How to test PD models for overfitting.
- Whether differences in performance are meaningful, given the data used for testing.
- Techniques for evaluating PD models when there are very few (or no) defaults.
- How PD models can help inform lending decisions and how to determine the economic value of a model.

---

[1] Some portions of the material in this chapter were drawn from Stein (2002, 2003a, and 2003b), with permission from Moody's Corporation and/or its affiliates, and are copyrighted works owned by those entities. All rights reserved. Versions of these articles were also published as Stein (2005b, 2006 and 2007) in *Journal of Banking and Finance*, *Journal of Investment Management*, and *Journal of Risk Model Validation*.

Most of this book deals with implementing and making practical use of models for credit risk. The incentive for doing this, we argue, is that it increases the value of a financial institution by decreasing the potential for catastrophic losses on the institution's credit portfolio. Without adequate objective evaluation criteria and processes, though, the benefits of implementing and using quantitative credit risk models are difficult to realize. This makes reliable validation techniques crucial for both commercial and regulatory purposes. As we have stressed in a number of places, the cornerstone of most credit portfolio systems and procedures is the accurate evaluation of the probability of default for a single obligor. In this chapter, we discuss approaches to validating PD models.

In our own work, we have found it useful to evaluate the quality of a model along a number of dimensions including:

1. *Robustness*: the sensitivity of model outputs to poor-quality data.
2. *Power*: the extent to which we avoid defaults while still designating non-defaulting firms as "good" borrowers.
3. *Calibration*: A model may have strong power but not do well matching actual levels or frequencies of defaults.
4. *Transparency*: The degree to which the interactions of the model's inputs and outputs are easily characterized and interpreted.[2]
5. *Diagnosability*: In conjunction with transparency, the ability to drill into a model's behavior is an important aspect of validation. To the extent that a model's behavior cannot be diagnosed quickly and efficiently, the portfolio manager or risk manager will face more model risk.

An important trade-off faced by a risk modeler pits model complexity against model usability. A more complex model may be more powerful, but so difficult to estimate and diagnose as to make it unusable. In practice, the models used in portfolio and risk management fall somewhere in the middle of the spectrum. An important factor is the set of constraints on the individual using the output. For example, a credit trader may need quick-and-dirty valuation estimates, making model estimation speed and transparency much more important than a high degree of accuracy. (Of course, everyone wants both—but the reality is that trade-offs have to be made.) In contrast, a portfolio manager who runs simulation batches in the

---

[2] Note that as problems become increasingly complex, so too must the models that characterize them. Transparency should be defined with reference to the baseline level of quantitative and financial knowledge associated with a specific problem rather than in absolute terms.

evening or on the weekend may be fine with a more complex model that cannot be run quickly but can still be diagnosed. In general we tend toward parsimonious models in practice, given the increased model risk associated with a complex model. Note that there are a number of broader dimensions along which models can be evaluated as well (see Dhar and Stein 1998; Kumra, Stein, and Assersohn 2001).

In this chapter, we focus on the first three of these dimensions. The last two involve substantial subjective judgment and may depend significantly on the specific business application.

Robustness describes the sensitivity of a model's parameters and output to changes in the underlying data set or to noise in the data as well as the suitability of the parameter estimates of the model. Entire texts have been written on this topic in the statistics and econometrics literature (see, for example, Burnham and Anderson 2002 or Atkinson and Riani 2000). For this reason, we discuss this aspect of model validation only briefly here. The two aspects of robustness we focus on here are: parameter stability, which describes how variable a model's parameters are (i.e., weights, coefficients, lag structure, etc.) relative to changes in either the data set or time; and tests of collinearity, which measure overlap (correlation) among the variables selected for a model. Substantial correlation among factors can cause erratic behavior in model outputs as well as making tests of factor significance difficult to interpret.

Overfitting may also reduce the robustness of the model. Sometimes the availability of too much data leads a modeler to rely too much on the straight statistical output that may hide overfitting. Once such a model is taken to a new sample of data, the overfitted model will not robustly reflect the underlying structure of the new or out-of-sample data. A robust model performs consistently across different data samples.

Though we discuss more traditional econometric validation in the first section of this chapter, the bulk of the chapter considers the two broad dimensions along which default models are typically evaluated: power and calibration.

Power describes how well a model discriminates between defaulting ("bad") and nondefaulting ("good") obligors. For example, if two models produced ratings of Good and Bad, the more powerful model would be the one that had a higher percentage of defaults (and a lower percentage of nondefaults) in its Bad category and had a higher percentage of nondefaults (and a lower percentage of defaults) in its Good category. This type of analysis can be summarized with *contingency tables* and *power curves*, which we describe more fully a bit later.

Calibration describes how well a model's predicted probabilities agree with actual outcomes. That is, it describes how close the model's predicted probabilities match actual default rates. For example, continuing our previous example, if there were two models A and B that each predicted the two rating classes, Good and Bad, and the predicted probability of default for A's Bad class were 5 percent while the predicted probability of default for B's Bad class were 20 percent, we might examine these probabilities to determine how well they matched actual default rates. If we looked at the actual default rates of the portfolios over time and found that 20 percent of B's Bad-rated loans defaulted while 1 percent of A's did, B would have the more accurate probabilities since its predicted default rate of 20 percent closely matches the observed default rate of 20 percent, while A's predicted default rate of 5 percent was very different than the observed rate of 1 percent. This type of analysis can be summarized in terms of *likelihood* measures which we also discuss a bit later in the section.

These techniques are most useful in the context of model development where ample data are available. They also have implications for the validation of third-party models and other internal rating systems used by financial institutions; though data limitations may in some cases make their application less straightforward. Having said this, we feel that where appropriate, these techniques provide several validation components that represent central practices in model development.

We begin our discussion of *power* by looking at simple evaluation tools. These are useful for providing an intuitive foundation but tend to be limited in the information they provide. We go on to show how these measures can be built into more general measures of model power.

In application, model power constitutes the most important test of a model's usefulness for underwriters and for certain risk management applications. For these applications, users ultimately want to steer the institution clear of bad credits. Thus, a model that discriminates well between good and bad obligors is critical. Many powerful models may be difficult to calibrate, though they still may be useful in rank-ordering existing and potential obligors analyzed by a risk manager.

However, as we move to capital allocation and valuation applications, it is not enough for a model just to be powerful. The *probabilities* it generates must also be accurate. For example, PDs are a key input to models for valuing a credit instrument. If the PDs are not well calibrated, the valuation output from the models will not be useful—regardless of its power—as it will diverge too much from observed prices. Going one step further to portfolio risk modeling, a poorly calibrated PD model may result in misleading estimates of the portfolio loss distribution. Thus, calibration becomes an important activity after model power has been established. Remember that a model with low power will not become any more powerful if it is well calibrated.

A BENCHMARKING APPROACH TO VALIDATION

In general, it will not be sufficient to look at default model performance statistics in isolation since performance statistics can vary substantially from data set to data set.

For example, one can imagine testing the power of two models, one on a data set composed entirely of Aaa- and Caa-rated issuers, and another composed entirely of Baa-rated issuers. Clearly we would expect, all else equal, that the model tested on the Aaa/Caa sample would perform better in terms of identifying defaulting and nondefaulting firms than the model tested on the Baa sample since the credit quality of each group is so distinctly different. A better test would be to test both models on the same sample and compare the difference.

For this reason, we advocate using a benchmarking approach in which one or several models are used to *calibrate* the validation results. If a data set is particularly easy (i.e., the obligors in the sample are well differentiated) then most models should do well on it, and if it is particularly hard (i.e., the obligors in the sample are not well differentiated) then most models will perform more modestly. What is interesting in this context is not the absolute level of the performance statistics, but their levels relative to the benchmark. Benchmarks can range from simple financial ratios to more sophisticated models, to a fully developed model (as might be the case in a champion/challenger setting where a bank is deciding whether to keep an existing model or switch to a new one). Appendix 4A in Chapter 4 provides the descriptions and parameter values for some of the models we have found useful to use as standard benchmark models.

However, powerful models can sometimes be effectively calibrated to yield high-quality PD estimates while not affecting their high power. Power should always be evaluated first.[3]

Because accurate PDs are so important, after we describe the tools for validating model power, we look at tools for comparing the calibration of competing models in terms of a model's ability to accurately predict

---

[3] This is not strictly true. Recent work (Dwyer and Stein 2004) has introduced calibration techniques that actually adjust the rankings of firms as well. In this context, the term *calibration* may not fully apply.

default rates. This is done by comparing conditional predictions of default (model-predicted probabilities) to actual default outcomes. We begin with a simple example and compare the predicted average default rates of two models, given a test data set, and then extend this to a more general case of the analysis of individual predicted probabilities, based on firm-specific input data.

It is often desirable to evaluate how good or bad predictions are, either in absolute terms or relative to other models. To facilitate this, we go on to discuss various techniques for estimating confidence bounds on both power statistics and probability estimates. Since business problems are often more easily formulated in terms of profitability than statistical significance, we also discuss how measures of power can be used to determine lending policy and how this policy can be converted into estimates of profitability of one model versus another. We show how this can also be extended to develop simple pricing models based on power curves. Finally, we discuss a validation framework designed to guard against overfitting. This approach helps to ensure that models will perform as expected in different environments.[4]

Importantly, the validation techniques we describe, quantitative though they may be, defy codification in simple checklists. Our experience with some bankers and regulators is that they seek a simple set of generic rules that can be applied across all credit models or asset classes. Unfortunately, this is not a practical goal. In fact, it is our judgment that efforts to create such checklists actually reduce the probability of models being vetted rigorously. This is not to say that regulators will not see benefit in focusing on a handful of broad principles to start financial institutions on the path toward more rigorous assessment of their models and system. These principles will necessarily be high-level rather than detailed and prescriptive. However, such principles can serve to motivate institutions to begin the process of validation. In the end, though, best practice will require each institution to develop a more sophisticated familiarity with and approach to model evaluation that will defy the enumeration of a "one-size-fits-all" approach.

The reason is that validation is an inherently interactive and iterative process. New models, by construction, are developed to address problems that are new to an organization. These range from determining the effectiveness of new approaches to modeling familiar processes, to applying

---

[4] In this book, we often refer to this as "out-of-sample" testing. Because there are many varieties of out-of-sample designs, we note that not all such tests are equally rigorous in our view. In the last portion of this chapter, we discuss in more detail a taxonomy of out-of-sample testing.

established techniques to new markets, and to methods for modeling new asset classes, some of which may not have long histories. Given such situations, it is limiting to predefine methods and practices for validation. Validation approaches that are best practice in some settings are practically impossible in others and not sensible in still others. Each model requires, as part of the model design process, a careful analysis of potential weaknesses and a strategy for determining benchmarks, available data, and testing procedures that are appropriate to test these weaknesses.

THE BASICS: PARAMETER ROBUSTNESS

We begin by discussing some basic practices in statistical model development. As there are extensive texts on model parameter testing and model selection (Greene 1993; Burnham and Anderson 2002), a detailed discussion is beyond the scope of this chapter, though we recommend that interested readers explore these and other standard texts in greater detail. However, to give a flavor of the types of issues that come up in this form of validation, we explore a few simple techniques that we have found useful in selecting model factors and parameters and in testing the robustness of those selections. The focus of this section is on testing the parameters and form of a model, rather than the model's predictive performance.

The key underlying principle of this section is that it is not sufficient that models predict well. They must also permit reasonable economic interpretations for their predictions and they must provide reasonable comfort that their parameters are stable and work well together. These criteria complement the requirements that model power and calibration should be consistently strong over time. Note that this will also tend to favor more transparent models whose parameters themselves are easier to interpret.

We concentrate on two techniques here: One technique is focused on assessing parameter stability and the other is focused on detecting factor multicollinearity. Both techniques can be formalized with decision rules, but they are more generally useful and provide what we might term *guidance* rather than strong acceptance or rejection criteria for model factors and estimates. The first deals with the general stability of parameters and can be used for almost any modeling problem. The second is also useful but lends itself most easily to the analysis of statistical models such as might be estimated using regression techniques, where correlation between factors can radically affect the estimates of the parameters and the explanation of the factors that drive the behavior of the model.

Stability of Parameters

One way to think about the stability of parameter estimates, whether they be the coefficients of a regression or the drift term of a diffusion equation, is that the interpretation of the influence and importance of different factors should not change radically from period to period or from sample to sample.

In the last section of this chapter, we discuss in more detail experimental designs for performance testing that researchers can use to avoid overfitting models. In this section, we anticipate this discussion by focusing only on the parameter estimates, not the model predictions, over different time periods. This analysis can easily be extended to accommodate other types of out-of-sample testing. However, in this section, we are interested only in the stability of the estimates of the model parameters, not, as in most of the rest of the chapter, the model performance.

Traditional statistical and econometric measures of goodness of fit are designed to determine whether a set of parameters is consistent with some hypothesis. The hypothesis being tested is typically the null hypothesis that a parameter or set of parameters is not statistically different than zero. In other words, the tests examine whether including a factor in the model tells us anything additional about the behavior of the variable of interest (and whether it therefore has a zero coefficient.). Wald-type tests[5] of significance are often used in this context, though other, sometimes nonparametric, tests are also popular.

In some cases, researchers may actually use such tests to explore whether a change in process has occurred over time. A Chow test[6] is a common example of such a test. However, more often than not, the tests are used to select factors for inclusion in a model.

---

[5] A Wald test is a general name for a class of statistical tests, named after Abraham Wald, that compare the difference between an observed value with some target value of interest by normalizing by the standard error of the observed value. An example of such a statistic is the commonly used t-statistic produced during regression analysis. In this case, the target value is zero and the test question of interest is whether the coefficient is significantly different than zero. See Green (1993) or Kennedy (1992) for a more detailed discussion.

[6] A Chow test is an econometric test, named for Gregory C. Chow, that is commonly used for examining structural breaks in time series (as well as other relationships). Briefly, the test is an F test that examines the sum of squared errors (SSE) of two regressions, one in which the coefficients are equivalent for all periods and one in which the coefficients are allowed to differ before and after a specific point in time. To the extent the F test shows a significant difference in the regressions, this suggests that there has been a structural break. See Green (1993) or Kennedy (1992) for a more detailed discussion.

An alternative measure of similar interest, though, is the degree to which a model's parameters are generally and practically stable over time or whether they change each time a new bit of information becomes available. A simple way to test for parameter stability is to examine the behavior of the parameters at different historical periods of time. To do this, a modeler can refit the model over various historical time periods and examine the stability of the parameter estimates for the resulting models.[7]

For example, if we fit a model over several different time windows and notice that, say, the magnitude and sign of a key variable's coefficient remained relatively constant and had movements that were well within our expectations for statistical variation, we might be reassured that this parameter estimate and the factor on which it is estimated are robust in our model. Conversely, if we saw that the magnitude of the coefficient moved dramatically or that the sign changed from period to period, we might conclude that the factor was behaving unstably in our model and might consider either working on the model formulation or omitting the factor.

Note that this approach is far less restrictive than more traditional econometric tests that might require that *all* parameters of the model be statistically the same between two test periods. In this case, the interpretation and meaning of the parameters may be similar but, with sufficiently large samples, still be statistically different, if not practically so.

Multicollinearity

If the explanatory variables in a model exhibit multicollinearity, the interrelatedness or correlation of the variables make it difficult to discern the individual effects of each variable or factor. Such correlated factors, when included in a model, also turn out to make estimation difficult as well. One way to explore the cause of such behavior, and to identify which potential factors may be driving the behavior, is through the use of various statistical diagnostics for multicollinearity—or the degree to which factors are linearly correlated.

Multicollinearity is a statistical issue in that it can result in poor estimates of the standard errors of a regression, which in turn creates interpretational problems for tests of significance. Since the individual effects are hard to separate when diagnosing a model, it can be sometimes difficult to determine which variable or factor is really driving the behavior one is testing. This can affect variable selection and the interpretation of factors from an economic intuition perspective. It can also cause the parameters to be unstable over

---

[7] Dhar and Stein (1998) suggest this approach for examining trading models.

time. As it turns out, collinearity can affect not only the interpretation of diagnostics for the variables that are collinear, but also for all factors in the model.

However, a more tangible problem associated with the presence of multicollinearity is that small changes in correlated input factors can result in large changes in model output. This is because when factors are highly correlated they engage in a tug-of-war over which of them gets to explain which components of the behavior of the dependent variable. Since in the end they share the explanatory power for the variance in the dependent variable, the total impact of all factors for the correlated bit must still sum to the same amount. However, how the variables share this explanatory power can be quite sensitive to the idiosyncrasies of the data set used.

As a result, it is not uncommon to observe the two correlated variables that measure the same thing having *opposite* signs in a statistical model. For example, if we included two factors related to profitability, say sales/total assets and net income/total assets, we would expect these two to be highly correlated. Because of this, they would share a large amount of the variability in default outcome. However, because they are not perfectly correlated, there would also be some of this variability that would be uniquely explained by each.

A common outcome in such cases is that one of the two factors would have a large positive estimate for its coefficient and the other would have a large negative one. In a sense, there is only a little extra variance in the combined factors that is not already covered by either one alone. The net result is that the statistical procedures attempt to combine the two factors by *balancing out* their contributions: assigning a too large positive coefficient to one and a too large negative coefficient to the other, with the net result typically being a moderate influence for both. However, when the model is used, if a particular firm exhibits a slightly different relationship between the two factors—a bit more of the part that one or the other factor captured uniquely—the result will be to tip the balance too much in the direction of the negative or positive coefficient and dramatically change the output result, even though the difference in the input factors might be small.[8]

For these and other reasons, it is useful to test not only for bivariate correlation but also for multicollinearity as might occur when some input factors are approximately linear combinations of others. Such tests include

---

[8] See Kennedy (1992) for an intuitive discussion of multicollinearity and in particular how this can be visualized using Balentine graphs.

casual inspection of correlation matrices and the use of variance inflation factors (VIF).

VARIANCE INFLATION FACTORS (VIF)

The VIF is defined as

$$\frac{1}{1 - R_i^2}$$

where R_i^2 is the R^2 of the regression of the ith independent variable on all the other independent variables in the model.

In general, a high VIF implies a large standard error for the parameter estimate associated with the variable. Importantly, a high VIF is a necessary, but not sufficient, condition for evidence of pairwise correlation among individual variables since an independent variable that is highly correlated with a linear combination of the other explanatory variables will have a high VIF. In evaluating VIFs we often use the heuristic of examining closely those variables that produce VIFs greater than 2.0 since this implies that more than 50 percent of the variation in that variable is explained by the other variables in the model.

MEASURES OF MODEL POWER

We now turn to what is perhaps the most common measure of model performance: predictive power. As mentioned earlier, *power* describes how well a model discriminates between defaulting ("bad") and nondefaulting ("good") obligors. If two models produced ratings of Good and Bad, the more powerful model would be the one that had a higher percentage of defaults (and a lower percentage of nondefaults) in its Bad category and had a higher percentage of nondefaults (and a lower percentage of defaults) in its Good category. This type of analysis can be summarized with *contingency tables* and *power curves* and their summary statistics.

Contingency Tables

Perhaps the most basic tool for understanding the performance of a default prediction model is the *percentage right*. A more formal way of understanding this measure is to consider the number of predicted defaults (nondefaults) and compare this to the actual number of defaults (nondefaults) experienced. A common way to represent this is a simple *contingency table* or *confusion matrix*:

	Actual	Actual
Bad	TP	FP
Good	FN	TN

To illustrate, we choose the simplest case of a model that produces only two ratings (Bad/Good). These are shown, along with the actual outcomes (default/no default), in tabular form. The cells in the table indicate the number of true positives (TP), true negatives (TN), false positives (FP), and false negatives (FN), respectively. A TP is a predicted default that actually occurs. A TN is a predicted nondefault that actually occurs (the company does not default). An FP is a predicted default that does not occur and an FN is a predicted nondefault where the company actually defaults. The errors of the model are FN and FP, shown on the off diagonal. FN represents a *Type I* error and FP represents a *Type II* error. A perfect model would have zeros for both the FN and FP cells, and the total number of defaults and nondefaults in the TP and TN cells, respectively, indicating that it perfectly discriminated between the defaulters and nondefaulters.

There have been a number of proposed metrics for summarizing contingency tables using a single quantity for use as indices of model performance. A common metric is to evaluate the true positive rate as a percentage of the TP and FN: $TP/(TP + FN)$, although many others can be used (cf. Swets 1996). It turns out that in many cases the entire table can be derived from such statistics through algebraic manipulation, due to the complementary nature of the cells.

Note that in the case of default models that produce more than two ratings or that produce continuous outputs, such as probabilities, a particular contingency table is only valid for a specific model *cutoff point*. For example, a bank might have a model that produces scores from 1 to 10. The bank might also decide that it will only underwrite loans to firms with model scores better than 5 on the 1-to-10 scale. In this case, the TP cell would represent the number of defaulters worse than 5 and the FP would represent the number of nondefaulters worse than five. Similarly, the FN would comprise all defaulters better than five and the TN would be the nondefaulters better than five. (We discuss how to estimate the optimal cutoff later in this chapter as well as how to extend this approach to determining a type of price so that any loan may be accepted by the bank, subject to appropriate fees.)

Power Curves and Power Statistics

Different cutoffs will imply different relative performances. Cutoff *a* might result in a contingency table that favors model A while cutoff *b* might favor model B, and so on. Thus, using contingency tables, or indices derived from them, can be challenging due to the relatively arbitrary nature of cutoff definitions. It also makes it difficult to assess the relative performance of two models when a user is interested not only in strict cutoffs, but in relative ranking—for example, of a portfolio of credits or a universe of investment opportunities.

Relative or *receiver operating characteristic* (ROC) curves (Green and Swets 1966; Hanley 1989; Pepe 2002; Swets 1988, 1996) generalize contingency table analysis by providing information on the performance of a model at *any* cutoff that might be chosen. They plot the FP rate against the TP rate for all credits in a portfolio.

ROCs are constructed by scoring all credits and ordering the *nondefaulters* from worst to best on the *x* axis and then plotting the *percentage of defaults excluded* at each level on the *y* axis. So the *y* axis is formed by associating every score on the *x* axis with the cumulative percentage of defaults with a score equal to or worse than that score in the test data. In other words, the *y* axis gives the percentage of defaults excluded as a function of the number of nondefaults excluded.

A similar measure, a *cumulative accuracy profile* (CAP) plot (Sobehart, Keenan, and Stein 2000), is constructed by plotting *all* of the test data (defaulting and nondefaulting observations) from "worst" to "best" on the *x* axis. Thus a CAP plot provides information on the percentage of defaulters that are excluded from a sample (TP rate), given we exclude all credits, good and bad, below a certain score.[9]

CAP plots and ROC curves convey the same information in slightly different ways. This is because they are geared to answering slightly different questions.

CAP plots answer the question, "How much of an *entire portfolio* would a model have to exclude to avoid a specific percentage of defaulters?"

---

[9] In statistical terms, the CAP curve represents the cumulative probability distribution of default events for different percentiles of the risk score scale.

CONSTRUCTING AN EMPIRICAL POWER CURVE

A CAP plot is constructed by plotting, for each score k, the proportion of *defaults* with a score worse than k against the proportion of *all* firms with a score worse than k.

An ROC curve is constructed by plotting, for each score k, the proportion of *defaults* with a score worse than k against the proportion of *nondefaulting* firms with a score worse than k.

To plot the power curve for a model:

- Score all the firms with the model.
- For each score, k, calculate the percentage of *all* (in the case of the CAP plot) or *nondefaulting* (in the case of the ROC curve) firms with scores worse than k. This is the x-axis value.
- For each score, k, calculate the percentage of *defaulted* firms with scores worse than k. This is the y-axis value.

Thus, if a particular model gave 5 percent of all (CAP) or non-defaulting (ROC) firms a score worse than k, and 10 percent of all defaults a score worse than k, then its power curve would go through the point (0.05,0.1). This could be interpreted as meaning that if one were to reject all credits with a score in the worst 5 percent (based on the model), then one would exclude 10 percent of all firms who go on to default.

If we consider a particular model for which we bucket the scores into B different bins, then the height of the power curve in a particular bin, b, would be calculated as follows:

$$power\ (b) = \frac{\sum_{i=1}^{b} D(i)}{\sum_{i=1}^{B} D(i)}$$

where $power(b)$ is the height of the power curve in bin b and $D(b)$ is the number of defaults in bin b. Thus the power curve is just the default density over the quantiles of the distribution either of all firms or of nondefaulting firms. For small default rates, as typically encountered in practice, the difference in shape and interpretation for a CAP or an ROC is typically small. Note that ROC curves can also be calculated parametrically, which is computationally more efficient but that requires substantially stronger and often questionable assumptions about the distribution of defaults and nondefaults.

ROC curves use the same information to answer the question, "What percentage of *nondefaulters* would a model have to exclude to avoid a specific percentage of defaulters?"

The first question tends to be of more interest to businesspeople, while the second is somewhat more useful for an analysis of error rates. CAP plots are also a bit easier to use in calibration since they deal directly with the sample probabilities, though this advantage is minor.

In cases where default rates are low (i.e., 1 to 2 percent), the difference between CAP plots and ROC curves can be slight and it can be convenient to favor one or the other in different contexts. The Type I and Type II error rates for the two are related through an identity involving the sample average default probability and sample size (see Appendix 7A) and their summary statistics, which we discuss later in this section, are also related through a simple identity.

Although CAP plots are the representation often used in practice by credit professionals, there is more research available on ROCs, primarily from the statistics and medical research communities. As a result, in a number of places in our discussion, we will refer to ROC curves, since they represent the same information as CAPs. Appendix 7A shows how to convert from points on one type of curve to points on the other. ROC curves generalize the contingency table representation of model performance across all possible cutoff points.

Figure 7.1 shows how all four quantities of a contingency table can be identified on an ROC curve given a specific cutoff point. Each region of the x- and y-axes has an interpretation with respect to error and success rates for defaulting (FP and TP) and nondefaulting (FN and TN) firms.

With knowledge of the sample default rate and sample size, the cells of the table for any cutoff point can be filled in directly by inspecting the ROC. If there are N nondefaulting companies in the data set and D defaulting companies, then the cells are given as:

	Actual	Actual
Bad	TP% $\times$ D	FP% $\times$ N
Good	FN% $\times$ D	TN% $\times$ N

Formulated in this way, it is clear that, *every* cutoff point on the ROC gives a measure of Type I and Type II error as shown in the table. Importantly for validation in cases where the ROC of one model is strictly dominated by the ROC of a second (the second lies above the first at all points) then the second model will have unambiguously lower error for any cutoff.

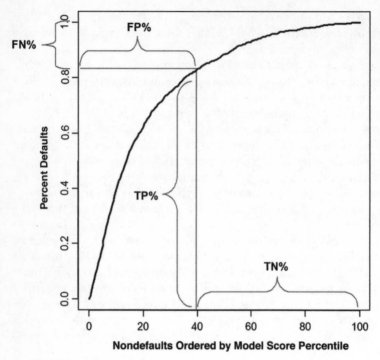

FIGURE 7.1   Schematic of an ROC

The Accuracy Ratio (AR) and the Area Under the Curve (AUC)

A convenient measure for summarizing the graph of the ROC is the *area under the ROC* (AUC or *A*: in subsequent formulas in this section we refer to this quantity as *A*), which is calculated as the proportion of the area below the ROC relative to the total area of the unit square. A value of 0.5 indicates a random model, and a value of 1.0 indicates perfect discrimination. A similar measure, the accuracy ratio (AR), can be defined for CAP plots (Sobehart, Keenan, and Stein 2000) with values ranging from zero (random) to 1.0 (perfect discrimination).

If the ROCs for two models cross, neither dominates the other in all cases. In this situation, the ROC with the highest value of *A* may not be preferred for a specific application defined by a particular cutoff. Two ROCs may have the same value of *A*, but have very different shapes. Depending

CALCULATING AN ACCURACY RATIO

While CAP plots are an intuitive way to visualize model performance, it is often convenient to have a measure that summarizes the predictive accuracy of each risk measure for both Type I and Type II errors in a single statistic. We obtain such a measure by comparing the CAP plot of any set of risk scores with the ideal CAP for the data set under consideration. The closer the CAP is to its ideal, the better the model performs.

The maximum area that can be enclosed above the random CAP is identified by the ideal CAP. Therefore, the ratio of (a) the area between a model's CAP and the random CAP to (b) the area between the ideal CAP and the random CAP summarizes the predictive power over the entire range of possible risk values. We refer to this measure as the accuracy ratio (AR), which is a fraction between 0 and 1. Risk measures with ARs close to 0 display little advantage over a random assignment of risk scores, while those with ARs near 1 display almost perfect predictive power. When comparing the performance of two models on a data set, the more powerful model on that data set will have a higher accuracy ratio.

Mathematically, the AR value is defined as

$$AR = \frac{2 \int_0^1 Y(x)dx - 1}{1 - f}$$

Here $Y(x)$ is the CAP curve for a population X of ordered risk scores, and $f = d/(n + d)$ is the fraction of defaults, where d is the total number of defaulting obligors and n is the total number of nondefaulting obligors.

on the application, even though the areas under the curve are the same for two models, one model may be favored over the other.

For example, Figure 7.2 shows the ROCs for two different models. The ROCs both produce the same value for A. However, they have very different characteristics. In this example, model users interested in identifying defaults among the worst-quality firms (according to the model) might favor model A because it offers better discrimination in this region, while those interested in

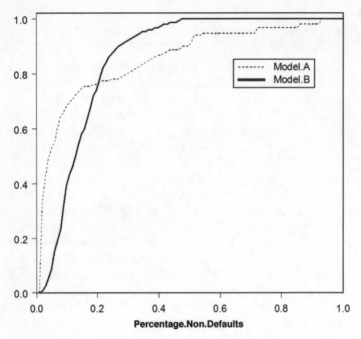

FIGURE 7.2   Two ROCs with the Same Area but Different Shapes

better differentiation among medium- and high-quality firms might choose model B, which has better discrimination among these firms.

The quantity A, the area under the ROC, is equivalent to *the probability that a randomly chosen defaulting loan will be ranked worse than a randomly chosen nondefaulting loan* by a specific model (Green and Swets 1966). This is a useful quantity that is equivalent to a version of the Wilcoxon (Mann-Whitney) statistic (see, for example, Hanley and McNeil 1982).

ROCs provide a good deal of information regarding the ability of a credit model to distinguish between defaulting and nondefaulting firms. The meaning of an ROC graph or a CAP plot is intuitive and the associated statistic A (or AR) has a direct interpretation with respect to a model's discriminatory power. For credit model evaluation, where we are typically most concerned with a model's ability to rank firms correctly, a graphical measure such as an ROC or CAP is usually more useful than simple contingency tables since the graphical measures avoid the need to define strict cutoffs (which can be misleading) and provide much more general measures of model power.

Since both the accuracy ratio (AR) and the area under the ROC curve (A) enjoy popularity, it is useful to be able to translate between the two. Englemann, Hyden, and Tasche (2003) demonstrate the correspondence between the AR and A. Since these rely on the same information, it is not surprising that the correspondence is a simple algebraic one. The paper shows that:

$$AR = 2(A - 0.5)$$

or

$$A = \frac{AR}{2} + 0.5$$

This identity turns out to be a convenient one in that many useful results in statistics relate to the area under the curve (AUC) and can thus be applied to the analysis of CAP plots and the AR as well.

MEASURES OF PD LEVELS AND CALIBRATION

The other main component of model performance is *calibration*. Calibration describes how well a model's predicted probabilities agree with actual outcomes. In the default modeling context, it describes how closely the model's predicted PDs match actual default rates. Reviewing again in the context of our earlier example, if there were two models A and B that each predicted the two rating classes Good and Bad, and the predicted probability of default for A's Bad-rated class were 5 percent while the predicted probability of default for B's Bad-rated class were 20 percent, we would be interested in determining which model produces more accurate PD levels, based on the actual data on hand. To the extent that the default rates predicted by one model seem more reasonable than those predicted by the other, given the actual data, we would have evidence supporting the superior predictive accuracy of that model. Such was the case in our earlier discussion of this example in which the actual default rates of the portfolios were 20 percent for B's Bad rated loans and 1 percent for A's. This type of analysis can be summarized more formally by means of *likelihood* measures as well as by examining the intuitive agreement of predicted probabilities with observed sample frequencies.

The metrics we discussed in the previous section measure how well a model discriminates between defaulting and nondefaulting firms, but they do not provide information on the appropriateness of the *levels* of predicted probabilities. For example, in the context of power, model scores do not necessarily need to be given as probabilities. Scores from 1 to 7 or 10 are common in internal bank models. Models that produce good rankings ordinally will be selected by power tests over those that have poorer power even though the *meaning* of, say, a 6, may not be well defined in terms of probabilities.

Powerful models, without probabilistic interpretations, cannot be used in certain risk management applications such as VaR and hedging since these applications require probabilities of default. Fortunately, as we discuss in Chapters 3 and 4, it is usually possible to calibrate a model to historical default probabilities. In this section we examine measures of calibration accuracy.

We begin with simple measures of calibration, then move on to more formal metrics, and finish up with measures that acknowledge the correlation that may be present in samples and that may change the interpretation of calibration tests.

Evaluation of Predicted Versus Actual Default Rates

We first assume a simple test: A researcher examines whether the observed default rate for borrowers of a certain credit grade is within the expected range for that credit grade. For example, a bank using a model to produce probability of default predictions might wish to know whether the predicted default rate in the "Pass – 2" rating category is correct. The bank might test this by examining all borrowers that were graded "Pass – 2" by the model over a period of time. By calculating the actual number of defaults observed and comparing this with the predicted or target number for "Pass – 2" borrowers, the bank could try to assess the accuracy of the model.

Because probabilities are approximately continuous and default events are rare, this approach is typically applied to buckets of firms all with a common score or whose scores are in some predefined range. In the limit, this range can be the full range of the population and the single statistic would be the average default rate for the population versus the predicted default rate for the population. In fact, a common approach is to evaluate the predicted versus actual default rate for the full population, as a first pass reality check on a model.

This approach is attractive in that it provides a simple, intuitive measure of model goodness: When predicted probabilities are close to actual outcomes, the model seems reasonable, and when they are far apart, we might question the model's calibration. However, the definition of *close* turns out to be complicated. We discuss this in detail later in this chapter.

Before turning to this analysis, though, it is useful to consider what happens when the limit moves in the other direction as the size of the buckets becomes nearly infinitesimal. In this case, there are measures of calibration that evaluate *individual* probability predictions across the population. We discuss these measures in the next section.

A Continuous Approach to Buckets: Likelihood

Likelihood measures evaluate the agreement of the observed data with the hypothetical model predictions. As used here, likelihood measures provide evidence of the plausibility of a particular model's probability estimates.[10] A likelihood estimate can be calculated for each model in a set of candidate models and will be highest for the model in which the predicted probabilities match most closely the actual observed data.

The likelihood paradigm can be used to evaluate which hypothesis or model among several has the highest support from the data. As we have emphasized in other chapters, calibration is particularly important for accurate valuation modeling and meaningful portfolio analysis. This is important for risk management, pricing, and other financial applications. As a result, modelers often spend a fair amount of time *calibrating* models to true probabilities.

Note that tests of calibration are tests of *levels* rather than tests of power and as such can be affected if the data used contains highly correlated default events or if the data represent only a portion of an economic cycle. In particular, the expected default rate will typically be higher than the actual realized default rates in most periods given the correlated nature of these events. The portion of the economic cycle reflected in the data will produce a particular bias with respect to this expected default rate. (After our discussion of likelihood, we will discuss an approach to better understand this effect by using median numbers of defaults, rather than mean default rates, when testing calibration.)

Likelihood measures are most useful in the context of evaluating the calibration of two competing models. For example, two models may be provided by third parties. To gain some intuition for this approach, we

---

[10] A detailed discussion of likelihood approaches is beyond the scope of this chapter. For an introduction, see Reid (2002), which provides a brief discussion; Edwards (1992), which provides more insight and some historical background; or Royall (1997), which provides a more technical introduction along with examples and a discussion of numerical issues. Friedman and Sandow (2003) discuss these measures in the context of credit model validation.

provide a simple example of using likelihood to evaluate two models using a portfolio with 100 loans in it, 4 of which have defaulted.

We begin with the simpler problem of assessing the accuracy of the average predicted default rate with respect to the actual average observed default rate. This is a variant of the analysis we discussed in the previous section, but this time with some more formal framing. In this case our model is just a prediction of the mean default rate.

In our example we wish to determine which of two proposed average probabilities of default, 1 percent or 5 percent, is more consistent with the observed default behavior in the portfolio. Under the assumption that defaults are binomially distributed, the likelihood can be derived directly since

$$b(k; n, p) = \binom{n}{k} p^k [(1 - p)^{n-k}]$$

where p is the probability of an event (default)

     k is the number of events observed

     n is the total number of trials (records in the data set)

     $b(k, n, p)$ is the probability of observing k default events out of n records

Note that the constant (combinatorial) term can be dropped if convenient as it does not depend on the model.

To determine the likelihood of the data having a specific default rate, we simply plug in the probability we wish to test (in our case, 1 percent and 5 percent) and calculate the probability of observing the actual number of defaults (in our example, 4 out of 100). The likelihoods, based on a binomial assumption, are given in Table 7.1.

Using the likelihood paradigm, we would seek the model with the maximum likelihood given the actual data. In other words, we seek the model whose probability of default predictions are most consistent with the empirical data.

TABLE 7.1 The Likelihood of Data Having a Specific Default Rate

Proposed Mean PD	Likelihood of Proposed Mean PD
$\mu = 0.01$	$p(\mu = 0.01) = \binom{100}{4} (0.01^4)(0.99^{96}) = 0.0149$
$\mu = 0.05$	$p(\mu = 0.05) = \binom{100}{4} (0.05^4)(0.95^{96}) = 0.1781$

The default rate of 5 percent has a higher likelihood, given the data used for testing, than the default rate of 1 percent, and thus, the model proposing $\mu = 0.05$ would be favored over the one proposing $\mu = 0.01$, by virtue of this higher likelihood ($0.1781 > 0.0149$).

In this simple case, an analyst would be able to perform this evaluation by simply choosing the default rate closest to the actual observed. However, in most real-world settings, models' estimates of probabilities of default are not constant as in this example, but are conditional on a vector of input variables, x, that describes the company. For heterogeneous PDs, the likelihood approach works identically, but at the record level. Appendix 7B provides a description of the mathematics that extend the simple case to the more general one.

For technical reasons, it is convenient to work with the log of the likelihood so the largest value of the likelihood will be associated with the model that produces the largest value. (Note that this amounts to the value with the *least negative* number.) The model with the highest log likelihood would be the best calibrated.

Note that likelihood measures are designed for making relative comparisons between competing models, not for evaluating whether a specific model is close to being correctly calibrated. For this reason, many analysts find it useful to perform both types of tests of calibration: the default rate test as well as likelihood tests. By doing so, the analyst can get more direct intuition about the agreement and direction of default probabilities in absolute terms, using the default rate approach, while gaining a precise quantitative interpretation of these results for two or more models using likelihood measures. Both analyses can be useful.

Likelihood Alone Is Not Enough

While level calibration is vital to risk model application, the focus on calibration exclusively can lead likelihood methods to incorrectly reject powerful but imperfectly calibrated models in favor of weaker but better calibrated models. This is true even when the poorly calibrated model can be fixed with a simple adjustment.

To see this, consider an example of two models, W and P, that are being applied to an identical portfolio of 11,000 loans with a true default rate of 5 percent. Assume that neither model was developed using the test set, so the test is an out-of-sample test, such as might be performed by a bank evaluating two externally created credit models on its own portfolio. The models themselves are very simple, with only two ratings: Good and Bad. The models have been calibrated so each rating has an associated probability of default.

TABLE 7.2 Log Likelihoods for Two Hypothetical Models

Model	Log Likelihood
W	−2184
P	−2316
(W) − (P)	132

Table 7.2 gives the log likelihoods for these two example models under this data set. Using the likelihood criterion, we would choose model W over model P since a difference of 132 in log likelihood is large.

Now consider how the models that produced these likelihoods performed. Tables 7.3 and 7.4 show the number of defaults predicted by each model and the predicted probabilities under each model for each class, based on the stated calibration of the two models.

Recall that the likelihood approach in this context is being used to determine the effectiveness of model calibration. Now note that the weaker model W, which was preferred under the likelihood selection paradigm, does a far worse job separating defaulting firms from healthy ones. It turns out that Model W's actual performance is *no different than a random model* in that both good and bad ratings have a 5 percent default rate on the test set, and this is the same as the actual central tendency of the test set. Thus, it does not matter which rating the model gives, the actual default rate will be the same: the mean for the population ($50/1000 = 500/10,000 = 5$ percent).

In contrast, model P (the more powerful model) demonstrates very good power, discriminating almost perfectly between defaulters and nondefaulters. Most lenders, if asked to choose, would select model P since, using this out-of-sample test data set, model P gives high confidence that the bank will identify future defaulters.

Why is model W selected over model P under the likelihood paradigm? Because its probabilities more closely match the observed probabilities of the data set. Thus, even though it is a random model that results in the same probability for both Good and Bad classes, this probability is very close to

TABLE 7.3 Performance for Hypothetical Model W

			Actual	Outcome
			Default	Nondefault
Model W	Model PD Prediction			
	5.10%	Bad	50	950
	4.90%	Good	500	9500

TABLE 7.4 Performance for Hypothetical Model P

			Actual	Outcome
Model P	Model PD Prediction		Default	Nondefault
	1.50%	Bad	549	1
	0.01%	Good	1	10,449

what is actually observed, and thus the model probabilities are more likely, given the data, than those of model P.

It appears that model P was miscalibrated and therefore its powerful predictions do not yield the empirical default rates in each class that would be expected given its predicted probabilities of 1.5 percent and 0.01 percent. That is, it is not as well calibrated to its actual performance.

Now suppose that the modeler learns that the true prior probabilities of the sample were different from the probabilities in the real population by a factor of 2, and adjusts the probabilities to reflect this using a simple calibration approach (see Chapter 4). In this case, the log likelihood of model P would change to -1936 and, after this adjustment, model P would be preferred. Note that the model is still badly miscalibrated, but even so, under the likelihood paradigm, it would now be preferred over model W. Thus, a simple (constant) adjustment to the prior probability results in the more powerful model being better calibrated than model W. This example highlights the importance of testing a model's power before evaluating its calibration.

It is reasonable to ask whether there is a similar simple adjustment we can make to model W to make it more powerful. Unfortunately, there is generally no straightforward way to do this without introducing new or different variables into the model or changing the model structure in some other way.

Interestingly, if an analyst were evaluating models using tests of model power rather than calibration, almost any model would have been chosen over model W. To see this, consider that model W makes the same prediction for every credit and thus provides no ranking beyond a random one. Thus, model W would be identical to the random model in a power test. Even a very weak model that still provided slight discrimination would be chosen over model W if the criterion were power.

As a whole, we can say that likelihood measures as we have discussed them here focus on the agreement of predicted probabilities with actual observed probabilities, not on a model's ability to discriminate between goods and bads. In contrast, a CAP plot or an ROC curve measures the ability of a model to discriminate goods from bads, but not to accurately produce probabilities of default. If the goal is to have the most accurate probability estimate, irrespective of the ability to discriminate good credits from bad ones, the maximum likelihood paradigm will always provide an optimal model selection criterion. However, we are not guaranteed that the model selected by the likelihood approach will be the most powerful, or, as the example shows, even moderately powerful.

In contrast, if the goal is to determine which model discriminates best between defaulting and nondefaulting firms, tools such as ROC curves and CAP plots provide a well-established means for doing so. In this case, we get no guarantees on the appropriateness of the probability estimates produced by the model, but we do get an unambiguous measure of the model's power. Fortunately, it is feasible to directly define the calibration mapping from the data for powerful models as discussed earlier. (We discussed approaches to calibration in Chapter 4 where we note that constant calibration is not always ideal.) In general, model power will be of most interest to risk managers; however, credit traders and portfolio managers will demand that a model be both powerful and well calibrated.

An Alternative Approach: Median Default Counts versus Mean Default Rates

In an innovative approach to determining the validity of PD levels, Kurbat and Korbalev (2002) introduce a simulation approach with the objective of estimating the predicted *median number of defaults*, rather than the mean default rate. This approach is motivated by the observation that whenever correlation is present, nondiversifiable skewness appears in the distribution of defaults. While the skewness initially declines as sample or portfolio size increases, it remains nonzero, even in the limit. (We discuss this in more detail throughout this chapter.) As a result, the median of a correlated default distribution will always be smaller than the mean. Said another way, the typical outcome for the number of defaults in any sample will generally be less than the expected outcome.[11]

This suggests that measures of expected central tendency based on the mean will generally overstate default rates in typical realizations of default, while those based on the median should agree more often with observed outcomes. As an alternative to calculating the *mean default rate*, the article suggests simulating the default distribution and using the simulated distribution to estimate the median number of defaults.

Because generation of correlated variables can be expensive computationally for large portfolios, the authors use a factor-based approach similar to the approach we describe in Chapter 8 on portfolio modeling. They take

---

[11] This has led to the rule-of-thumb, "The default rate you expect to observe is usually less than the expected default rate."

advantage of the factor representation but restrict correlation such that all firms have a constant correlation while their PDs may vary. The following algorithm describes the median estimation approach in pseudo-code.

```
for i=1 to numLoans dp_i=Φ⁻¹(PD_i)
for j=1 to numSimus
    ndef_j=0
    for i=1 to numLoans
        z_i=correlated random normal
        if(z_i <dp_i) ndef_j= ndef_j+1
    end for i
end for j
med.ndef=median(ndef)
```

In a sense, this methodology is similar to that introduced by Keenan, Sobehart, and Hamilton (1999) in which the authors use the current distribution of ratings to predict the following year's default rate. However, unlike these authors, Kurbat and Korbalev explicitly address the issue of correlation and the skewness it induces in default rates.

Simulating the distribution requires assumptions about both the levels and homogeneity of correlation. For individual firms these may be obtained from various sources (see Chapter 8). However, the assumption of homogeneity is a strong one. Our own experience is that loss distributions estimated using the mean of the correlations of a portfolio can be quite different from the distribution obtained by using the actual correlations. This is not surprising since correlation typically enters into a loss distribution in a nonlinear fashion—sometimes in an extreme fashion. As a result, Jensen's inequality suggests that we should expect quantities based on averages of the function to be different than a function of the average.

In principle, there is no reason that we need to assume a constant correlation, if sufficient detail is available about the correlation structure of the firms in a portfolio. In such cases, a bit of extra numerical computing can yield similar results with heterogeneous correlations. In the end, the paper concludes that the simulated median number of defaults provides a better benchmark for observed default rates in a given data sample.

A Heuristic Approach: Reasonableness of PDs Based on Bayesian Priors about the State of the Economy

Dwyer (2007) suggests an approach also motivated by observations about correlation but based on a Bayesian analysis. This approach permits an estimate of the *current state* of a common factor (that induces correlation among firm default probabilities) based on observed default rates. This factor can be characterized as a latent macroeconomic factor affecting all firms. The intuition here is that the levels of actual observed default rates can be used to make inferences about the state of the economy, conditional on the predicted levels of a PD model being correct. Said another way, the approach takes *as given* the PD value and a common correlation for all firms and then solves for the required level of the macro factor that makes the observed default rate consistent with these assumptions.

At first, this may seem counterintuitive: If we are trying to test the levels of the model's PD, why do we take these as given? The answer comes in how we interpret the PD. From a Bayesian perspective, we are concerned with the value of the common factor that we would need to assume were true in order for the PD to also be true, given the nature of the underlying correlation and observed data.

For example, if the estimated PD were low but the number of observed defaults were very high, then under this approach the explanation would be that the common factor must be in a very bad state (i.e., a negative state) of the economy that causes the realization to move away from the mean to the tail of the default distribution. If our knowledge of the economy, credit cycle, and so on suggested that the current state was not very bad, we could conclude that the PD levels were inconsistent with the data and with our knowledge of the economy.

The paper assumes a single factor correlation model (based on Vasicek (1991)), in which, as in the previous section, there is one common factor that impacts all firms' credit quality. The observed default rate, given a state of the factor, is given as

$$\Pi(r_m) = \Phi \left(\frac{\Phi^{-1}(PD) + \sqrt{\rho}r_m}{\sqrt{1-\rho}} \right)$$

where $\Pi(r_m)$ is the default rate of the population, given that the common factor describing the economy is in state r_m. (Here, r_m is assumed to be normally distributed with negative values indicating worse than average economic states and positive values indicating better than average states.) Since $\Pi(r_m)$ gives a default rate, we can construct a test based on a normal assumption:

$$\frac{\Pi(r_m) - PD}{\sigma} = z \sim N(0,1)$$

where

$$\sigma = \sqrt{\Pi(r_m)(1 - \Pi(r_m))}$$

To apply the approach, we first solve for the value of r_m that brings the probability of z to some level of confidence (say 5 percent or even a basis point). We can think of r_m as follows: If the actual default rate, $\Pi(r_m)$, were much higher than the model PD, then for the model PD to be correct, there would have to have been a shock as negative as r_m in order to generate an observed default rate on the portfolio of $\Pi(r_m)$. We can then calculate the probability of r_m occurring as

$$\Phi(r_m)$$

where $\Phi(\cdot)$ is the standard cumulative normal distribution.

For example, if r_m were -2, the probability associated with such a large negative shock would be about 2.3 percent. In order to conclude that the model is appropriately calibrated, we would need to believe that the economy was in pretty bad shape. In fact, the state of the economy that generated such a value of r_m would be so bad as to occur approximately 1 out of 43 years (1/0.023) (given the underlying distributional assumptions). If we did not think the economy was in such bad shape, we could conclude that the model might be miscalibrated.

This formulation provides some perspective on the reasonableness of a PD model's predictions beyond what might be achieved using a frequentist approach (i.e., the other types of tests we have discussed). However, the strong reliance on prior assumptions makes the approach challenging to implement in some settings due to the degree of subjectivity involved. This approach might best be thought of as a diagnostic rather than a validation test since, with the exception of severe shocks, there are no clear guidelines for determining when a shock is too big to reject the null hypothesis.

Most required shocks will not be as great as the -2 we showed in our example and, since many of the assumptions underlying the approach are strong and in fact the framework itself presents a stylized view of the portfolio default process, it is difficult to determine how to interpret the shocks that are implied by the approach in typical situations. The introduction of industry effects further complicates this analysis. However, this diagnostic approach can be useful in providing some intuition for the necessary conditions for a particular model to be accurate, and the ability to perform quick reality checks on a model is an attractive feature.

The Relationship between Power and Calibration

Importantly, although they measure different things, power and calibration are related: The power of a model is a limiting factor on how high a resolution may be achieved through calibration, even when the calibration is done appropriately. To see how, consider Figure 7.3, an example of four

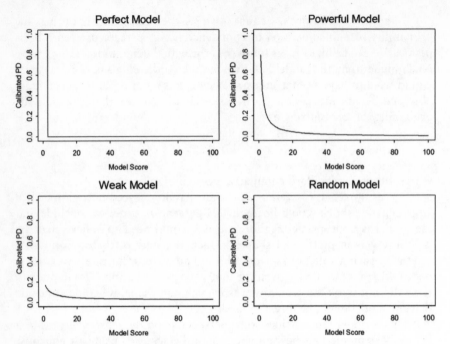

FIGURE 7.3   Calibration Curves for Four Hypothetical Models with Different Power

models, each with different power: a perfect default predictor, a random default predictor, a powerful but not perfect model, and a weak but not random one. Assume that the data used for calibration is a representative sample of the true population.

Figure 7.3 shows calibration curves for four hypothetical models, each with different power. The more powerful a model is, the better resolution it can achieve in probability estimation. Each of these models is perfectly calibrated, given the data, but they are able to achieve very different probability levels because of their differing power. The random model can never generate very high or very low probabilities, while the perfect model can generate probabilities that range from zero to one (although none in between). The more powerful model can give broad ranges, while the weaker model can only give narrower ranges.

The figure shows the calibration curve for these four hypothetical models. In this example, we discuss only the calibration of the very worst score (far left values in each graph) that each model produces since the other scores follow the same pattern.

What does the calibration look like for the perfect model? In the case of the perfect model, the default probability for the worst score will be 1.00 since the model segregates perfectly the defaulting and nondefaulting firms, assigning bad scores to the defaulters. By contrast, what does this calibration look like for the random model? In this case, calibrated default probability is equal to the mean default rate for the population since each score will contain a random sample of defaults and nondefaults. The other two models lie somewhere in between these extremes.

For the powerful model, the calibration can reach levels close to the perfect model, but because it does not perfectly segregate all of the defaults in the lowest score, there are also some nondefaulters assigned the worst score. As a result, even if the model is perfectly calibrated to the data (i.e., the calibrated probabilities for each bucket exactly match the ones in the data set), it cannot achieve probabilities of 1.00. Similarly, the weak model performs better than the random model, but because it is not very powerful, it gives a relatively flat curve that has a much smaller range of values than the powerful model.

These circumstances imply that a more powerful model will be able to generate probabilities that are more accurate than a weaker model, even if the two are calibrated perfectly on the same data set. This is because the more powerful model will generate higher probabilities for the defaulting firms and lower probabilities for nondefaulting firms due to its ability to discriminate better between the two groups and thus concentrate more of the defaulters (nondefaulters) in the bad (good) scores.

There is no simple adjustment to the calibration of these models to improve the accuracy of the probability estimates since they are calibrated as well as possible, given their power. This does not mean that the probabilities of the weaker and more powerful model are equally accurate, only that they cannot be improved beyond their accuracy level through simple calibration unless the power is also improved.

Because of the mathematical relationship between model discriminatory power and probabilities of default for firms with a given score on a power curve, a model may be well calibrated (no bias in its estimates of probability of default) but still not very powerful. We discuss such a case in the next section. To see the relationship between power and probabilities directly, consider how power curves are calculated and how model calibration is done.

Figure 7.4 plots the power curve for a model. In this case we rank-order the firms from risky (left) to less risky (right). This model would quickly have excluded most of the bad companies: a 20 percent exclusion of the worst companies according to the M score would exclude about 70 percent of the future defaulters. We would consider this to be a reasonably good model in terms of power.

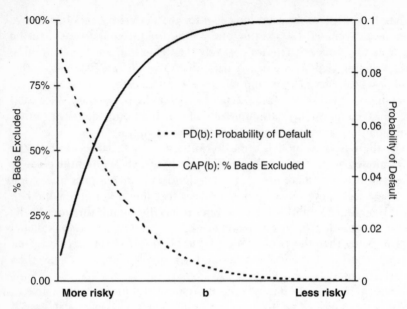

FIGURE 7.4   The Relationship between Power Curves and Calibration Curves for Default Models

Figure 7.4 shows the power curve (CAP plot) as the solid line (left-hand x-axis) for a model *M*. The figure also demonstrates that a CAP plot, together with a baseline default rate, implies a particular calibration curve (this is plotted on the right-hand axis). Thus, the steeper the CAP plot (the more powerful the model), the higher the probability of default will be, assuming the same mean probability. Because calibration and power are related in this way, more powerful models which have steeper CAP plots will also have higher probabilities of default at the low end of the rating scale while having lower probabilities of default at the higher-quality end of the rating scale. An understanding of these characteristics of PD models should be integrated by portfolio and risk managers in order to improve their use and interpretation of these models.

Recently, a discussion has arisen in the credit modeling literature about whether measures of power can be subsumed by measures of probability accuracy. The crux of these discussions is that since, in the case of internal ratings, the *measure* being ranked is also associated with a measure of the actual *probability* of default, power statistics may misrepresent the true predictive power of a model relative to tests of the probabilities themselves. One aspect of the reasoning is that since even the worst-ranked credit in a portfolio only defaults probabilistically, the power curve may distort the true power of the model (White 2002). The second and more often discussed aspect relates to the observation, which we discuss in detail later in this chapter, that for practical purposes, measures of power are sample dependent (Stein 2002, 2007). (This supports our recommendation later in this chapter to consider *differences* in performance between benchmark and candidate models on identical data sets rather than absolute levels of power.)

Lingo and Winkler (2007) discuss this issue in detail and provide analytic results. This paper presents an example of two portfolios under a two-rating class system to demonstrate the effect. In the example, both portfolios experience a default rate for the Good-rated class that is lower than the default rate for the Bad-rated class. In both portfolios, the Good default rate is the same. However, in the first portfolio the default rate for the Bad class is about half as high as the default rate for the Bad class in the second portfolio. In other words, the credit quality of the borrowers in the first portfolio is closer together (harder to discriminate) than for those in the second portfolio. The paper shows that the AR calculated for the first portfolio will be lower than the AR for the second portfolio, demonstrating the sample-dependent nature of these measures.[12] The paper demonstrates that the calibration of the rating categories is related to the power statistics and asserts that calibration alone should determine model quality, providing a permutation test for the confidence bounds of the AUC.

While the analytic results are quite useful with respect to fleshing out our understanding of power and calibration, the focus of the paper is on *rating systems* (i.e., discrete rating categories) rather than *PDs*, and on evaluating such systems across different portfolios. Though this seems to have some utility for regulatory applications, for PD model development and testing both of these conditions appear overly restrictive as typically we avoid both of these constraints by design. Importantly, the authors do not consider that calibrating a powerful model is far easier than increasing the predictive power of a properly calibrated but weak model (as discussed previously),

---

[12] Note that the authors somewhat imprecisely characterize the cause of the change in AR as the "credit quality" of the second portfolio being lower than that of the first. It is easy to show using their example that the overall credit quality of the portfolio (i.e., average default rate) can be preserved, but that a difference in the default rates, not the overall *level* of the default rates, can still cause differences in power: The obligors in the first portfolio are harder to differentiate than those in the second. For example, in the case of an evenly balanced portfolio in which 50 percent of the loans are Good and 50 are Bad, if the default rate on the one class is decreased by, say, 5bps and the default rate on the other is increased by 5bps, the average default rate does not change but the AUC can be increased or decreased by several points.

but rather focus on evaluating models produced by different banks and evaluated on these banks' own portfolios.

Cantor and Mann (2003) introduce a modified version of the accuracy ratio that is defined similarly to the standard AR, but without the adjustment for the baseline default rate $(1 - f)$ in the denominator. The paper argues that a feature of the standard accuracy ratio is that whenever the aggregate default rate changes, the accuracy ratio changes regardless of whether the cumulative accuracy profile has changed. They suggest that the benefit of not including the adjustment for the baseline default rate is that not adjusting for the baseline makes the accuracy ratio invariant to changes in the aggregate default rate, and thus the AR will only change due to shifts in the distribution of default rates. In practical terms, though, there is little empirical difference between the two forms of the accuracy ratio, particularly for low baseline default rates. The paper's objective in developing this measure was to observe the accuracy of rating systems over time where changes in the baseline default rate could complicate the analysis. That said, because in addition to the baseline shifting a typical *population* of obligors is also shifting in time, an alternative approach would be to benchmark the rating system against some reasonable alternative, and to measure the gap in performance on each sample over time rather than measuring the absolute level of the AR. The choice of measure here will depend on the objective of the analysis.

Capital Distortions Implied by Differences in Power

Because of the relationship between model discriminatory power and probabilities of default, a weaker model will typically have a flatter calibration curve than a more powerful one. As a result, the weaker model will systematically tend to assign lower (higher) probabilities of default for its riskiest (safest) segments and correspondingly lower (higher) regulatory capital requirements for that segment. Thus, it may be possible to have two acceptably calibrated (unbiased) models with different power characteristics that will result in different regulatory or economic capital requirements by virtue of their differing probability estimates.[13]

This discussion highlights the importance of calibration for some institutions. If the institution's lending practices result in a portfolio with markedly different risk characteristics than the norm, then depending on the riskiness

---

[13] Note that here we are discussing the expected behavior of the two models since, unless they are perfectly correlated, we would anticipate that a specific firm would be rated differently by each model and thus its location on the respective power curves would not be identical.

of the bank's portfolio and lending practices, the bank may prefer either the weaker or the more powerful model for calculating capital.

To gain intuition for the conflict that banks face, consider Figure 7.5, which shows calibration curves for four hypothetical models, each with different power. To make these graphs consistent with power measures, we have drawn them such that the portfolios are ordered from the worst credits on the left of the x-axis to the best credits on the right.

The graph in the upper left shows the curve for a naïve (random) model. It predicts the baseline default rate for every credit. The model in the upper right is slightly more powerful with two rating classes. The bad class has a PD that is well above the average and the good class has a PD well below the average. Note that without improving the model, there is no obvious way to increase the PDs for riskier firms using the naïve model. Even so, the model is unbiased in its calibration if the average default rate in the population matches its predicted default rate. An important consequence of an unbiased model with less-than-perfect power is that the portfolio-level

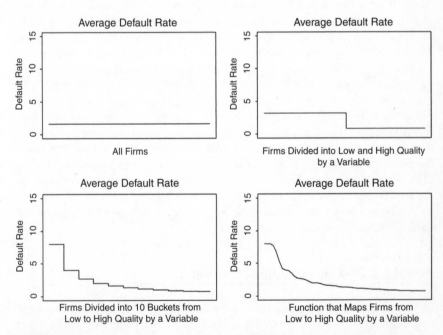

FIGURE 7.5 Calibration Curves for Four Hypothetical Models with Different Granularity and Power

calculations may be reasonably accurate (for representative portfolios) while some of the exposure-level calculations may be misleading.

Similarly, there is no obvious way to have the model in the upper left assign higher probabilities to the very riskiest 1 percent of the population since it cannot distinguish these within its "bad" category. As a result, the model predicts the same PD for the very worst "bad" firms as well as the very best "bad" firms. Again, if the average default rate of all bads in the "bad" category is consistent with the predicted PD, then the model is calibrated as well as it can be, given the model's power. In these two cases, both models are well calibrated, but would produce very different predictions for portfolios made up of mostly good or mostly bad firms.

In the lower half of the figure, we show more refined models that are able to further subdivide the portfolio into meaningfully different segments, each with a more refined probability of default. Here again, note that there is nothing obvious that can be done to assign higher probabilities to the riskier firms in any class without making the model more powerful.

Clearly, most banks seek to minimize losses on their portfolios both for economic and reputation reasons. But consider the (overly simplified) situation of a misguided bank choosing between default models and trying to minimize capital requirements without regard to the true risk. The bank may use either the long-run average (upper left) or a slightly more sophisticated and higher power model (upper right). If the bank knows that it tends to lend to borrowers in the bottom half of the credit spectrum, the (misguided) bank has little incentive to use the more powerful model. In fact, doing so will result in a higher capital charge since, on average, the PD of the naïve model (and thus the capital charges) will be lower than that of the more sophisticated model. Conversely, if the bank knew it would be lending to less risky than average credits, it would be rewarded for using the more powerful model since the naïve model will tend to have higher PDs at the upper end of the credit spectrum. This is one reason that some regulatory treatments require banks to validate models using their own data to demonstrate the appropriateness of the model PD estimates, given the bank's lending practices.

SAMPLE SIZE AND CONFIDENCE BOUNDS

In our discussions with risk managers and regulators, perhaps the most common question we hear is, "How big a difference in power (calibration, PD level, etc.) is important?"

It turns out that there is no single answer to this question. The answer in fact depends on many business issues. It also depends on the nature and quantity of data used to test models. In this section, we focus on answering the question from a data sufficiency (or, conversely, an effect size) perspective.

Practical Considerations

Because most performance measures are sensitive to the data set used to test a model, it is important to consider how they are influenced by the characteristics of the particular data set used to evaluate the model. It is often the case that competing models must be evaluated using only the data that an institution has on hand, and the data may be limited. This limitation can make it difficult to differentiate between good and mediocre models. The challenge faced by many institutions is to understand these limitations and to use this understanding to design tests that lead to informed decisions.

Since in most cases, it is impossible to know how a model will perform on a different sample than the one at hand (if another sample were available, that sample would be used for testing as well), the best an analyst can do is size the magnitude of the variability that arises due to sampling effects. In this section we discuss how we can estimate the impact of this sampling variability. We begin this section by first discussing error bounds on power curves. We then discuss confidence bounds for tests of probability and calibration.

Power Curves and Confidence Bounds

For problems involving rare events (like credit default), it is the _number of occurrences of the rare event_ more than the total number of observations that tends to drive the stability of power curves and other performance measures. For example, if the probability of default in a population is on the order of 2 percent and we test a model using a sample of 1,000 firms, only about 20 defaults will be in the data set. In general, had the model been tested using a different sample that included a different 20 defaults, or had the model used only 15 of the 20 defaults, we would observe quite different results.

Many analysts are surprised to learn of the high degree of variability in test outcomes that can result from the composition of a particular test sample. To demonstrate this more concretely, we present the results of evaluating a simple model using randomly selected samples of 50, 100, 200, and 400 defaults, respectively. The samples are drawn (without replacement) from a large database of defaulting and nondefaulting firms. We did this 100 times for each sample size. These results are shown graphically in Figure 7.6. In the figure, for each sample a separate CAP plot is graphed. Thus, each figure shows 100 CAP plots, each for the same model, but each of

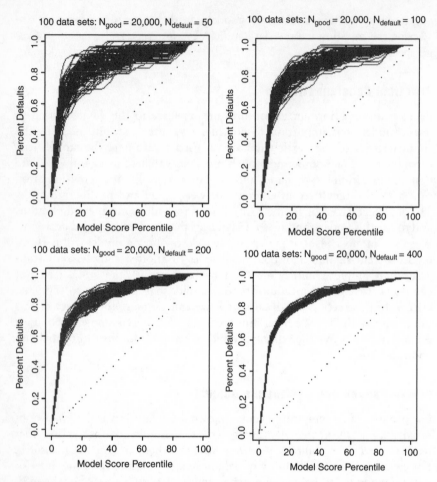

FIGURE 7.6 Variability of Test Results When Different Numbers of Defaults Are Used for Evaluation

which is based on a different sample of 20,000 nondefaulting observations and 50, 100, 200, and 400 defaulting observations.

In examining the figures, note the high degree of variability present. This variability decreases dramatically as the number of defaults is increased and thus is primarily driven by the number of defaults, rather than the total number of observations. Despite the large differences in variability among the graphs, the sample size (total number of firms) for the first and last set of tests (upper left and lower right) differs by less than 2 percent. Note also the wide variability of results, even at relatively high numbers of defaults.

To demonstrate clearly that it is the number of defaults that drives the variability, we present the CAP plots for another group of data sets. These show the results of evaluating the same model using randomly selected samples of 10,000, 15,000, 20,000, and 50,000 nondefaulting financial statements but keeping the number of defaults constant at 100. We do this 100 times for each sample size. These results are shown graphically in Figure 7.7. In this case, it is clear that increasing the number of nondefaulting records, even fivefold, does not materially affect the variability of the results. This outcome stands in contrast to that shown in the previous figure and

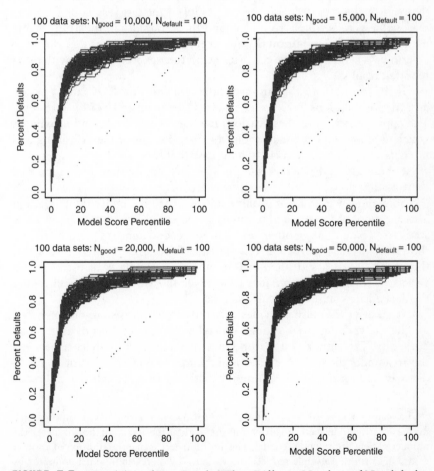

FIGURE 7.7 Variability of Test Results When Different Numbers of Nondefaults Are Used for Evaluation

supports the observation that the key factor in reducing the variability of test results is the number of defaults used to test a model.[14]

If the number of defaults were greater relative to the number of non-defaults, the relationship would be reversed, with nondefaults influencing the variance more dramatically. Similarly, if the number of defaults and nondefaults were about even, they would influence the result to approximately the same degree. In general, it is the minority class (the class with fewer observations) of a sample that will influence the variance most dramatically.

Most institutions face the challenge of testing models without access to a large data set of defaults. Given such a situation, there is relatively little that can be done to decrease the variability of the test results. A far more reasonable goal is simply to understand the variability in the samples and use this knowledge to inform the interpretation of any results they do get to determine whether these are consistent with their expectations or with other reported results.

In the case of sizing the variance of the area under the ROC curve, several analytic formulations have been suggested (see Bamber 1975 for a review). The appropriateness of these various measures tends to depend heavily on which assumptions are made about the distributions of the defaulting and nondefaulting firms, and it is often the case that for a given test, it is unclear what these are and whether sample sizes are appropriate for supporting these assumptions.

Sometimes we wish to examine not just the area under the curve, but also a variety of metrics and a variety of potential hypotheses about these statistics. To do this, we often need a more general approach to quantifying the variability of a particular test statistic. A common approach to sizing the variability of a statistic given an empirical sample is to use one of a variety of resampling techniques to leverage the available data and reduce the dependency on the particular sample.

Bamber (1975) also provides a (semi) closed-form solution for determining the variance of A, though this relies on assumptions of asymptotic normality. The author's estimator derives from the correspondence between the area under the ROC curve, A, and the Mann-Whitney statistic. A confidence bound for the Mann-Whitney statistic can often be calculated directly

---

[14] This is not unexpected. Most of the closed-form solutions that have been suggested for the area under the ROC involve terms that scale as the inverse of the product of the number of defaults and nondefaults. The intuition here is that the addition of another defaulting firm to a sample reduces the variance by increasing the denominator by the (much larger) number of good records, while the addition of a nondefaulting firm only increases the denominator by the (much smaller) number of bad firms.

using standard statistical software which, to some degree, makes this perspective attractive from a calculation standpoint.

Engelmann, Hyden, and Tasche (2003) discuss this approach and also test the validity of the assumption of asymptotic normality, particularly as it relates to smaller samples. They examine the normal assumption both with respect to the evaluation of a single ROC curve and for comparing two ROC curves. To compare the areas of two ROC curves, the authors also suggest that tests of the statistic can be constructed by making an assumption of normality and constructing standard Wald-type significance tests. Following Bamber (1975), they present the details of the calculations required to estimate the variance of A as well as the covariance of the areas of two ROC curves, in this case, based on the work of Delong, Delong, and Clarke-Pearson (1988). Again, this type of two-sample test is also readily available in statistical software packages.

Engelmann, Hyden, and Tasche (2003) test their assumption of normality on a sample of defaulted firms. Their experiments lead them to conclude that the normal approximation is generally not too misleading, particularly for large (default) samples. However, they do present evidence that as the number of defaults decreases, the approximations become less reliable. For very low numbers of defaults (e.g., 20 or even 50), confidence bounds can differ by as much as several percentage points when compared with the normal approximation and the bootstrap estimates. As shown in Stein and Jordão (2003) and discussed later in this chapter, a single percentage point of difference between two models can represent significant economic value. For larger numbers of defaults the results appear more reliable.

It should be noted that a great advantage of the Bamber closed-form confidence bound is the relatively low computational cost associated with calculating confidence intervals based on this measure which enables fast estimation. One reasonable strategy is thus to use the approximations during early work in developing and testing models but to confirm results using bootstrap in the later phases. To the extent that these results differ greatly, an analyst may want to conduct a more extensive analysis of the sample.

In a recent paper, Blume (2008) provides bounds on the projected sample size required to estimate and test the AUC and differences in the AUC. The paper concludes that the empirical estimator is most often used and is probably best. However, in the planning stage, under some homogeneity assumptions, the paper presents a closed-form upper bound for the sample size required to estimate the difference between two possibly correlated AUCs within some level of precision, ε (i.e., the difference between two AUCs is $\pm\varepsilon$).

Specifically, if n_{max} is the maximum number of observations in the minority class (typically the number of defaults for our purposes) required to estimate the difference between two AUCs, A_1 and A_2, using a $100 \times (1 - \alpha)$ percent confidence interval (CI) of length 2ε or less, then[15]

$$n_{max} = \frac{(Z_{\alpha/2})^2}{\varepsilon^2} \left[A_1(1 - A_1) + A_2(1 - A_2) - 2\rho \sqrt{A_1(1 - A_1)A_2(1 - A_2)} \right]$$

where $Z_{\alpha/2}$ is the value of a standard normal associated with the $1 - \alpha/2$ quantile

          ρ is the correlation among AUCs[16]

As it turns out, n_{max} is sensitive to the assumed value of ρ (if we have data, the empirical estimator is used and the bounds are not needed). The value of ρ can be estimated nonparametrically from a subset of the data. For default models, reasonable values of ρ might be taken to be in the range of $[0.2, 0.6]$ in practice.

Similarly, if we are given a data set with n observations in the minority class, we can estimate the maximum possible error for the difference in AUCs (i.e., worst-case scenario) for a $100 \times (1 - \alpha)$ percent CI, as:

$$\varepsilon = \sqrt{\frac{(Z_{\alpha/2})^2}{n} \left[A_1(1 - A_1) + A_2(1 - A_2) - 2\rho \sqrt{A_1(1 - A_1)A_2(1 - A_2)} \right]}$$

Importantly, these are upper bounds and the *practical* number of defaults (or ε given fixed number of defaults) can be dramatically lower than those obtained from these limits. This can be seen in comparing the upper and lower bounds (which must be calculated numerically) under this framework. For example, in the case of a difference of one point of AUC (a 0.01 difference) and a constant correlation, $\rho = 0.35$, then for reasonable values of A_1 and A_2, the upper bound (n_{max}) on the required number of defaults would be calculated to be in the range of 9,000 to 10,000 while the lower

---

[15] Note that we have modified the notation to make it more consistent with the notation in the rest of this chapter.

[16] More generally, an empirical calculation of n_{max} requires estimation of a number of cluster correlations nonparametrically. The form shown here assumes these are all constant across modalities. See Blume (2008) for details. The empirical cluster correlations themselves tend to be sensitive to the underlying data and model ($\rho_{ND} = [P(ND_i < \min(D_i, D_j)) - A^2]/A(1 - A)$ and $\rho_D = [P(D_i > \max(ND_i, ND_j)) - A^2]/A(1 - A))$. Furthermore, for sample sizes on the order of tens of thousands, calculating these empirical estimates fully can be cumbersome or impossible. Resampling approaches appear to give reasonable results for large numbers (e.g., 500,000 or 1 million) of resamples.

bound (n_{min}) would be in the range of 80 to 100! Thus, in practice a fully empirical CI would be preferred and the resulting half-width **will** be smaller than ε under upper bound calculated using the preceding assumptions.

Confidence Bounds for Default Rates

We now turn our focus to confidence bounds for probability estimates. In the next section we discuss the impact of correlation in determining whether a given model's predicted probabilities are accurate. We start this section by reviewing some of the statistical machinery that can be used to help determine the *number of records* required to perform tests on the accuracy of probabilities. As it turns out, the number of records required can be large. For example, when default rates are relatively low, say 50bps, in order to be comfortable at a 99 percent confidence level that a 10 bps (20 percent relative) difference between a default model and actual data were not just due to noise in the data, we would need over 33,000 independent firms!

Furthermore, if correlation is present in the data, there may *never* be enough data to discern at any practically useful level whether the probabilities are right—adding more observations does not necessarily produce a confidence bound that narrows quickly. We also suggest a simple approach using the limiting distribution of Vasicek (1991), which we have previously discussed in this chapter, for evaluating the degree to which we can reduce sampling error, even in the ideal case of infinite data availability. While this relies on a stylized analytic approximation, it provides useful insight.

Error Bounds without Correlation   The mathematical machinery necessary for answering the questions asked in this section is well established in the form of the Law of Large Numbers and the Central Limit Theorem and can be found in most textbooks on probability (Papoulis 2002; Grinstead and Snell 1997). We start by using the limiting properties of the binomial distribution and assume it approaches the normal distribution in the limit as the number of observations gets large. We can then formulate a standard hypothesis test and, with some algebra, solve for the sample size required to be sure that any difference between the true mean and the sample estimate will be small, given some level of confidence.

We start with an assumed predicted default probability, p, perhaps produced by a model, a rating system, or as the target of some underwriting practice. We also have a data set containing n firms, d of which have defaulted. We wish to determine whether the assumed default rate is reasonably close to the true default rate.

We can define the empirical frequency of defaults (the default rate) as

$$f_d = d/n$$

We would like to be certain that

$$P\left(|f_d - p| < \varepsilon\right) \geq 1 - \alpha$$

where α is a significance or confidence level.

For example, we might wish to be sure that the difference between the true default rate and our predicted default rate is less than 20 basis points. We show in Appendix 7E that

$$n \geq \frac{pq}{\varepsilon^2}\left[\Phi^{-1}(1 - \alpha/2)\right]^2$$

where n is the minimum required number of independent firms required to be certain that we will have enough data to determine whether a probability p is accurate to within ε at the α level.

Typically, however, we do not get to choose how many records we have, but rather have a fixed number of records and wish to test a specific prediction using these data. Given that we have n independent firms, we can ask how big a difference between p and f_d we would need to observe in order to conclude at the α level that the assumed probability and the observed default rate differ. Rearranging terms, we get

$$\varepsilon \geq \sqrt{\frac{pq}{n}}\Phi^{-1}(1 - \alpha/2)$$

which gives the desired quantity.[17]

Thus, for a fixed number of firms, the estimate of the default rate that we obtain will be within ε, $100 \times (1 - \alpha)$ percent of the time. This is just the standard confidence bound for a probability estimate.

Note that when p and n are very small, the limiting properties on which this analysis relies may not be present, though other approximations (e.g.,

---

[17] Importantly, an implicit assumption is that the data set accurately captures all relevant defaults. To the extent that this is not true (i.e., there are hidden defaults), the observed empirical probability may not reflect the true frequency of defaults. We discuss how this can be addressed in some cases in Chapter 4 on econometric modeling.

TABLE 7.5 Analytic versus Simulated Levels of ε for Various Sample Sizes When
α = 0.05

n	p	Analytic ε	Simulated ε	% difference
100	0.001	0.0062	0.009	45%
250	0.001	0.0039	0.003	−23%
500	0.001	0.0028	0.003	8%
1000	0.001	0.0020	0.002	2%
50	0.025	0.0433	0.035	−19%
100	0.025	0.0306	0.025	−18%
250	0.025	0.0194	0.019	−2%
500	0.025	0.0137	0.013	−5%

Poisson) or simulation can provide a more reliable mechanism to determine appropriate values of the quantities of interest.

Table 7.5 gives examples of the simulated and analytic results for several selected cases. In the simulations, for each of S simulation iterations, we generate n Bernoulli random variables with a known probability p and then calculate f_d based on the simulated sample. We then calculate the desired quantile (e.g., α = 0.05) of the distribution of $| f_d - p |$ (over all S results) to produce the simulated value of ε. We compare this with the value calculated using an analytic solution. The results in Table 7.5 were generated using $S = 10,000$.

From the table, it is clear that the analytic result provides a reasonable estimate in cases where n or p is fairly large or, more appropriately, not very small. However, the relative difference in predicted values ($[\varepsilon_{simulated} - \varepsilon_{analytic}]/\varepsilon_{simulated}$) can be quite large in cases where the values are too small. For example, even for moderately high default probabilities (e.g., $p = 2.5$ percent), the difference between the analytic approximation to the error bound ε and the simulation result is almost 1 percent in default probability (83 bps) for small samples ($n = 50$).

This result is generally consistent with a common heuristic, which recommends avoiding the approximation unless the quantity npq is a good deal larger than 2. There are also often the cases below which the distribution can become significantly skewed,[18] which complicates the interpretation of the

---

[18] The skewness of the binomial distribution is given, after simplification, as $\frac{1-6pq}{npq}$. For theoretical binomial distributions, the skewness becomes significant just below $p = 1$ percent and $p = 2$ percent for $n = 500$ and $n = 200$, respectively, using a variant of Fisher's test. In both cases, $npq \approx 4$.

results. From our informal experiments, we recommend this approximation only in cases where npq is less than about 4. In the experiments, this resulted in relative errors of less than about 10 percent when estimating ε.

Error Bounds with Correlation   When dealing with correlated assets, such as those found in credit portfolios, it turns out that the correlation makes observed distributions skewed. This means that in most years there is a relatively high probability of losses below the mean (expected value) default rate but there is also a probability of default rate that is very much higher than the expected or average. In general, we think of the lower losses happening in normal or good times and the larger losses happen during times of stress. We anticipate this when we see the distribution. Figure 7.8 shows an example of this set of circumstances. In this example, we simulated a simple credit portfolio containing correlated assets. For simplicity and exposition, we assume the assets can either default or not at the end of a one-year period and that when they default there is no recovery.

In Figure 7.8, each dot represents one possible outcome of the default rate for the portfolio under one economic scenario. Areas with many dots

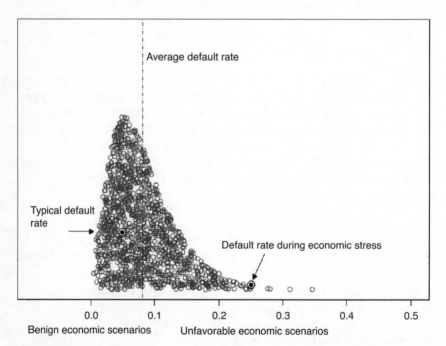

FIGURE 7.8   Hypothetical Correlated Default Distribution

piled up represent the more likely outcomes, and the areas with only a few dots represent the rarer outcomes. This distribution is what we would expect to observe if we examined defaults on an identical portfolio in many different economic states.

Note that the expected default rate, the average, is shown as the dashed line. Because the distribution is skewed, there are actually more outcomes in which the default rate is below the expected loss than there are above it. In fact, the default rate that we expect to see most often is *not* the expected default rate! We also expect from time to time to see losses that are very much larger than the expected loss. As we have discussed, this clustering behavior occurs as a result of the underlying default correlation among obligors.

Of course, we do not know, at the time we estimate this distribution, *which* economic state will occur in the future.

For this reason, estimates of ε and n become understated in the presence of correlation among the data since the binomial distribution only approaches a normal distribution in the limit *when the observations are independent*. Under independence, the results of the previous section allow us to solve analytically for the quantities of interest in many cases. However, there is no simple analytic solution to this problem in general when the observations are not independent. Furthermore, in the nonzero correlation case, we have no guarantee that the bound (ε) goes to zero as the number of observations (n) becomes large.

This result is sometimes surprising to researchers and analysts. However, intuitively, if we have a portfolio containing a single firm and add to it another firm that is 100 percent correlated with the first, we do not get any benefit in terms of reducing the variability of the portfolio losses since the second firm will always default when the first one does and thus, conceptually, represents just a larger position in the same firm. If we add a third and a fourth, the variance similarly does not decline. In fact, we can add an infinite number of 100 percent correlated firms and still not reduce the variance.

To explore the impact of correlation, we performed a second set of simulations. This time, we assumed that there was a hidden factor (e.g., asset value; see Chapter 3 and Chapter 8) that generated the probabilities of default for each firm and that this variable followed a Gaussian distribution. The hidden factor for each firm is correlated across firms in our simulations, and default now occurs when the value of this hidden factor for a specific firm falls below a specific threshold (e.g., a default point) for that firm. In the case of a Gaussian factor, the threshold is chosen so that the probability of default for the firm in the context of the simulation is consistent with the actual probability of default of the firm. Simulation under this model

TABLE 7.6 Required 5 Percent Significance Levels of ε When Firms Are Correlated to Various Degrees

Correlation	n	p = 1%	p = 3%	p = 5%
0.0	500	0.008	0.011	0.018
0.1	500	0.020	0.048	0.070
0.2	500	0.030	0.072	0.106
0.3	500	0.036	0.092	0.136
0.0	1000	0.006	0.008	0.011
0.1	1000	0.020	0.047	0.069
0.2	1000	0.029	0.070	0.106
0.3	1000	0.034	0.091	0.138

involves generating the joint distributions of the firm-level factors for the population and evaluating whether each firm's factor has fallen below the firm's threshold. In the simulations shown here, all default probabilities and correlations are identical, but the same approach can be used for heterogeneous populations.[19]

We then estimated ε assuming different levels of (uniform) correlation among the firms.

We present the results in Tables 7.6 and 7.7.

In Table 7.6, as expected, the estimate of ε with zero correlation is significantly smaller than in the cases in which the correlation is nonzero. We observe that ε increases with the degree of positive correlation. For example, in Table 7.7, we see that the estimate of a 95 percent confidence level for ε using 1,000 firms with a probability of default of 1 percent and no correlation is about 60 basis points. In contrast, ε turns out to be about six times greater, 3.4 percent, when the correlation is 0.3. In Table 7.7 we also see that the reduction in ε is small even as the sample size increases.

Figure 7.9 shows the distribution of ε when we assume uniform correlation at various levels and a uniform probability of default. We chose values of ρ at 0, 0.1, 0.2, and 0.3. Note that as the correlation increases, the distribution becomes increasingly skewed. As a result we observe two effects. Both effects, which we describe in a moment, relate to the change in the shape of the distribution that correlation induces.

---

[19] In the special case of uniform probabilities and correlations, Vasicek (1991) provides an analytic solution. We choose simulation here as it provides a more general solution in the case of more typical portfolios where correlation and probability of default are not uniform.

TABLE 7.7 Required 5 Percent Significance Levels of ε for Various Sample Sizes When Firms Are Correlated (Corr = 0.03, $p = 0.01$)

N	Correlation = 0.3	Correlation = 0.0	Analytic (Correlation = 0.0)
25	0.070	0.030	0.039
50	0.050	0.030	0.028
100	0.040	0.020	0.020
250	0.038	0.010	0.012
500	0.036	0.008	0.009
1,000	0.034	0.006	0.006
5,000	0.034	0.002	0.003

However, it is important to note that as the correlation increases, the distributions of ε resulting from the simulations becomes increasingly skewed. For example, the skewness of the zero correlation case is moderately low at about 0.48 for this set of simulations. In contrast, the skewness of the distributions for the cases of $\rho = 0.1$ and $\rho = 0.3$ are 2.2 and 6.3,

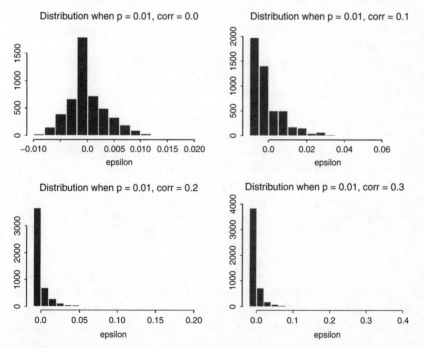

FIGURE 7.9 Distribution of ε at Various Levels of Correlation When $p = 0.01$

respectively. As a result of this skewness, we observe two effects. First, the values of ε increase considerably with the correlation as the right tails of the distributions lengthen and produce more extreme values. Second, as a result of the loss of symmetry, the values of ε become more difficult to interpret since they are mostly generated at the tail on the right side of the mean of the distribution. Here again we note that even in the case of zero correlation, we can see in Table 7.7 that the distributions become quite skewed when n is small, thus making the symmetric interpretation of ε more involved. In this case, it is not until n reaches about 500 that either the theoretical or simulated estimates of ε get smaller than p itself. Since negative values of p are not feasible, this implies that the distribution must be skewed and thus the largest ε are being generated on the right-hand side of the distribution.

Sizing the Effect with Vasicek's Limiting Distribution   It is interesting to ask whether one can *ever* have enough data to be comfortable that a particular sample has specified average default frequency that is close to the predicted probability when the data are highly correlated. Here again, the limiting loss distribution of Vasicek (1991) provides some intuition. For portfolios in which all assets have identical asset correlation and probability of default, the limiting distribution for portfolios with an *infinite* number of loans (or bonds) is given as

$$F(\pi) = \Phi\left(\frac{\sqrt{1-\rho}\,\Phi^{-1}(\pi) - \Phi^{-1}(p)}{\sqrt{\rho}}\right)$$

where π is an arbitrary default frequency and $F(\cdot)$ is the cumulative probability. In words, the expression gives the probability that an infinitely large portfolio of loans with probability of default p and uniform correlation ρ will actually experience a realized default rate of π or less in any particular instance.

We can use the Vasicek limiting distribution to get a quick sense of how much precision we might expect in testing default probabilities. Define $\pi_\alpha(p, \rho)$ as the value of π such that $F(\pi) = 1 - \alpha$ for a given probability p and correlation ρ. For example, $\pi_{05}(p, \rho)$ denotes the value of π such that $F(\pi) = 0.95$ for a given probability p and correlation ρ. Thus, for a given infinitely large portfolio with the probability of default and correlation described, 95 percent of the time the realized frequency f_d will be less than $\pi_{05}(p, \rho)$. In statistical terms, this is the one-sided 95 percent confidence bound.

Now consider the following example: We have a real (i.e., finite) portfolio made up of loans with uniform asset correlation of 0.25 and each loan has a true probability of default of 0.02. We cannot observe the true probability of default. Perhaps we believe that the probability should be 20 bps—possibly due to information from a model or other source. Using the limiting distribution, we solve for $\pi_{05}(0.002, 0.25)$ to get a 95 percent confidence limit on how high the observed default rate might be while still not rejecting our assumption of a 20 bps probability of default. It turns out that $\pi_{05}(0.002, 0.25) \approx 87$ bps, since $F(0.0087) = 0.95$.

Now we can ask, even if we had *extremely large* amounts of data, how often we might falsely accept the 20 bps assumption at a 95 percent confidence level, given that the true (but unobservable) probability of default is 0.02 rather than 0.002 as we hypothesize. By using the limiting distribution again, we find that when the correlation is 0.25 and the probability of default is 0.02, $F(0.0087) = 0.5$. Thus, about half of the time, even with infinite data, we would mistake the default probability for 20 bps when it was actually 200 bps. If we were able to live with only 90 percent confidence, we would still accept the 20 bps hypothesis more than a third of the time.

This suggests that when correlations are higher it becomes more and more difficult to make strong statements about exact default probabilities, particularly when we observe only a single empirical realization of a data set or portfolio, regardless of how many loans it contains. In other words, when correlation is high, ε is typically large.

It bears repeating, however, that while $F(\cdot)$ is a limiting distribution, the limit only applies when asset correlations and default probabilities are both constant and uniform across the data. A similar result holds for finite populations, but again, only in cases where correlations are constant. As discussed earlier, for the more general (and typical) case, no closed-form solution exists.

Further complicating the discussion is the fact that default rates themselves may not be constant in time. If the default rates are themselves shifting, the analysis can become more protracted. Cantor and Falkenstein (2001), for example, explore the case in which the correlation structure is more involved and the estimator of the variance becomes far more elaborate. These authors also show that failing to account for various correlation effects leads to significant underestimation of default rate variance.

Bootstrap Approaches In cases where long histories are available (where *long* is defined as spanning a number of economic cycles), several authors have suggested applying bootstrap techniques (e.g., Efron and Tibshirani

1993) to calculating confidence bounds. Hanson and Schuermann (2006) outline a bootstrap approach that works as follows:[20]

```
for b = 1 to B
    for i = 1 to N
            select with replacement a firm from the data set
    end for i
    calculate the default rate of the bootstrap sample d[i]
end for b
calculate the SD (or quantiles) of s[i]
```

The paper notes that calculating multiyear-horizon default rate confidence bounds can be challenging due to the dependence induced in the sample from year 1 to year 2, from year 2 to year 3, and so on.[21] Cantor, Hamilton, and Tennant (2008) extend this framework to a multiyear horizon as well and calculate (time) marginal default rates (hazard rates).

An important feature of this approach is that it homogenizes the time dependence of the underlying processes. In other words, because the process relies on long histories of many firms, industry- or time-specific shocks will tend to be captured in the statistics. This would not be the case if the calculations were done using only one or a few years of data, as these calculations would likely not incorporate the full variability of default rates as they are manifest over full economic cycles. As such, a bootstrap confidence measure is a measure of uncertainty as it applies to the *long-run* mean default rate. The actual performance of any specific cohort will typically be quite different.

Upper Bound on PDs When the Number of Observed Defaults Is Zero   But what about the case of zero defaults? It often happens that banks or investment grade collateral managers own portfolios of high-quality loans or bonds. By definition, we expect default rates in these portfolios to be very low. For example, the empirical five-year default rate on an Aaa-rated corporate bond is about 8 bps, suggesting that on average over a five-year period, a portfolio containing 100 Aaa bonds would have about a 92 percent chance of experiencing zero defaults. However, if the bonds or loans are unrated,

---

[20] Note that here we present simple summary statistics of the bootstrap samples. However, a number of bias-corrected estimators have been suggested for improving these estimates. (See Efron and Tibshirani 1993 for a discussion.)

[21] The approach could also be extended to incorporate some of the techniques that have been developed to accommodate bootstrapping-dependent data that have been developed in the statistics literature.

managers may have little guidance on the underlying default probability of the assets in their portfolio.

In consideration of these difficulties, several approaches have been proposed for sizing bounds on probabilities of default when no defaults are actually observed. Since probabilities cannot be negative and the observed number of defaults is zero, the lower bound is trivially zero.

To determine the upper bound, in the uncorrelated case, we can start by applying the intuition about the binomial distribution from the previous section. However, since we observe zero defaults, we can use the special case which simplifies the calculation:

$$b(k; 0, p) = \binom{n}{0} p^0 [(1 - p)^n]$$
$$= (1 - p)^n$$

For a desired confidence bound, therefore, we can set this expression equal to that confidence level and, taking logs, solve (approximately) for p.

$$\alpha = (1 - p)^n$$
$$\log(\alpha) = n \log(1 - p)$$
$$\log(\alpha)/n \approx -p$$

For example, for a zero correlation portfolio of n bonds on which we observed no defaults, we could be 95 percent confident that the true default rate of the portfolio would be less than $3/n$ since $\log(0.05) \approx -3$. (At a 95 percent level, this reduces to the "rule of threes"; see van Belle 2008.)

Note that once correlation is introduced, this approach no longer holds. In the correlated case, there are two approaches that one might consider when dealing with PDs. The first relies on the discrete distribution of Vasicek (1991), which can be reduced further in the special case of zero defaults to a single integral over a single expression, analogous to the case of the uncorrelated binomial.

$$P_k = \binom{n}{k} \int \left(\Phi \left(\frac{1}{\sqrt{1 - \rho}} \left(\Phi^{-1}(p) - \sqrt{\rho} u \right) \right) \right)^k$$
$$\times \left(1 - \Phi \left(\frac{1}{\sqrt{1 - \rho}} \left(\Phi^{-1}(p) - \sqrt{\rho} u \right) \right) \right)^{n-k} d\Phi(u)$$
$$P_0 = \int \left(1 - \Phi \left(\frac{1}{\sqrt{1 - \rho}} \left(\Phi^{-1}(p) - \sqrt{\rho} u \right) \right) \right)^n d\Phi(u)$$

This single integral can be solved numerically without too much difficulty so that finding the upper bound at the α level reduces to a numerical search for a value of p that makes $P_0 = \alpha$ (which can be done by brute force or through use of more efficient numerical techniques). For example, with 5,000 bonds in a portfolio and a common correlation of 0.2, a default rate of 0.74 percent is the maximum default rate possible with a 5 percent probability of zero defaults.

Dwyer (2007) introduced an alternative approach which we discussed earlier in this chapter, that also permits a direct numerical solution, but that, as we mentioned, requires some fairly strong prior assumptions (in the Bayesian context) and also requires more involved numerical methods. Dwyer suggests a broader Bayesian adjustment to the preceding assumptions to permit assessments of sample sizes that are far closer to practically useful levels, providing an analyst is willing to make these strong assumptions about the structure of default rates as well as the particular point in the economic cycle that a bank is experiencing. We can, of course, rearrange sample size calculations to arrive at confidence bounds and we explore this in the context of calculating upper bounds on PDs when the observed default rate is zero.

In this approach, one assumes a specific prior distribution of a common systematic factor and then solves for the maximum probability of default attainable, at a desired confidence level, given that D defaults have been observed. This amounts to solving a double integral, where integration is done to achieve the desired $1 - \alpha$ mass. We focus here on the case of zero defaults $(D = 0)$, in which the expression simplifies slightly to

$$K(p|D) = \frac{\int_0^p \int_{-\infty}^{\infty} (1 - \Pi(x, r_m))^N n(r_m) f(x) dy dx}{\int_0^1 \int_{-\infty}^{\infty} (1 - \Pi(x, r_m))^N n(r_m) f(x) dy dx}$$

where $\Pi(x, r_m)$ is the probability of default given a specific shock, r_m, and probability of default, x, and the term $K(p|D)$ represents the probability that the true probability of default is equal to p given that we observe D defaults out of N total observations.

In order to evaluate this expression (which can be done numerically) we need to make assumptions about the distribution of market shocks, $n(y)$, and the distribution of probabilities of default, $f(y)$. Dwyer assumes shocks to be normally distributed and the probabilities of default to be uniformly distributed. For example, in the case of 5,000 observations, zero defaults, and correlation of 0.2, Dwyer reports a maximum PD, at the 95 percent level, of 1.97 percent. This drops to 0.65 percent when the number of observations is 50,000.

Importantly, this Bayesian approach produces quite different results than those obtained using the frequentist approach explained earlier in this section. This is not really surprising since the two approaches use different information sets and answer slightly different questions. The approach using Vasicek directly provides the PD whose 95 percent confidence bound just covers 0. Thus it answers the question, "What is the highest default probability a population could have and still allow one to observe zero defaults 5 percent of the time?"

In contrast, the Bayesian approach answers the question, "Given that I know that I have *already observed* zero defaults, what is the highest probability of default that I could expect with 95 percent certainty?"

In a sense, the second question attempts to take advantage of the information already available to update the assumptions about the distribution of probabilities of default.[22]

It does not appear that the frequentist and Bayesian approaches reconcile. For example, for a portfolio of 5,000 bonds with correlation of 0.2, the 5 percent quantile using the Vasicek distribution is zero when PD = 0.74 percent. As we discussed previously, using the Bayesian approach, the 5 percent quantile is zero when PD = 1.94 percent, more than 2.5 times *larger*. This is somewhat counterintuitive since in the Bayesian case, we actually have more evidence of low-default behavior (we know there were zero defaults) than in the frequentist case (where we speculate on its possibility).

One reason for this may be the selection of a uniform prior for the distribution of probabilities of default, representing a completely uninformed prior.[23] This uninformed prior implies that for zero defaults we would assign equal probabilities to a mean default rate of 87 percent as we would to a mean default rate of 1.5 percent. This is clearly at odds with our experience.

---

[22] This type of framing is familiar in the Bayesian literature. Consider the well-known "Monte Hall Problem" in which a game show host asks a contestant to choose one of three doors. Behind one of the doors is a pot of gold and behind the other two are sacks of beans. Once the contestant chooses, the host reveals that one of the other doors was hiding a sack of beans, and asks whether the contestant wishes to change his selection. Should he? It turns out the answer is yes, though this is not intuitively obvious to many readers. How could the revelation of one of the doors change the probabilities? The intuition becomes clearer if one imagines that there are 100 doors and that after the contestant chooses, the host reveals the contents of 98 of them, leaving just two: the one the contestant originally chose and one more. The host has effectively eliminated 98/99 of the losing doors. The odds of the contestant choosing the correct door the first time were 1 in 100. The odds of the contestant switching to the correct door after the revelation are 1 in 2.

[23] Note carefully the use of the terms "uniform" and "uninformed" which carry different meanings here.

Dwyer presents evidence that for very large portfolios, this assumption is not overly restrictive; however, it is not clear that this holds in general.

One approach would be to consider that the typical distribution of PDs might range from, say, a few basis points to 10 or 15 percent. We could relax the assumption of the uninformed (uniform) prior and adopt, say, a beta distribution (the uniform is actually a special case of the beta) with a somewhat less uninformed prior of a mean near 2 percent and some reasonable standard deviation. (Of course this requires substantial knowledge of the population distribution, which is what we are trying to find!)

For example, for the portfolio we have been discussing with 5,000 bonds and 0.2 correlation, if we assume a beta distribution with shape parameters 0.61 and 30.34 (approximately equivalent to a mean of 2 percent and SD of 2.5 percent with about 95 percent of the default rates in the range [0, 7%]), the PD associated with a 5 percent probability of zero defaults[24] would move from 1.94 percent to 0.70 percent, much closer to the 0.74 percent that we recovered from the Vasicek distribution. However, if we let the SD move to about 4 percent (keeping the mean at 2 percent so that now about 95 percent of the distribution of default rates is in [0, 10%]), the PD associated with a 5 percent probability of zero defaults would move again, this time to about 0.24 percent.

Which value we choose, 1.94 percent, 0.70 percent, or 0.24 percent, depends on our prior assumptions about the distribution of likely default rates.

This highlights the difficulty in some cases of applying Bayesian techniques for validation. The results we observe can be highly dependent on our prior assumptions, and our results can vary substantially as we change these assumptions. This makes it difficult practically to apply this approach to model selection, despite the allure of smaller sample sizes.

However, in some settings this technique can be informative in a descriptive sense (or in the case where the analyst has very strong priors and can defend them well). More broadly, the notion of inverting the relationships to arrive at implications about the state of the economy, as discussed earlier in this chapter, is an interesting reality check for models. We continue to anticipate further developments in this domain, bringing approaches such as this closer to the realm of direct validation testing.

It is not always the case that an analyst wishes to answer the question of the zero-default case PD for an entire portfolio. For example, in the case of portfolios containing (agency or internally) rated instruments, the analyst

---

[24] For convenience, we estimate this through simulation rather than analytically.

may be interested in the default rates for these individual rating classes. As it turns out, this rating information can be used to estimate the PD for those rating classes in which no defaults have been empirically observed. Because there is additional information in the non-default rating classes, this information can be leveraged to produce estimates of the default rate on zero default sub-portfolios.

When considering ratings data, Christensen, Hansen, and Lando (2004) introduce a generator matrix approach to estimating confidence sets for transition probabilities. As a by-product of this process, zero-probability cells of the transition matrix can be bounded. This approach, based on a bootstrap technique, estimates confidence sets for each cell in a transition matrix by first sampling the transition data, then estimating a generator matrix (see Chapter 6), and finally by using the generator matrix to simulate rating trajectories for each observation in the sample. By repeating this process for many iterations, confidence sets can be found for each cell. For the zero default case, however, this approach requires observations on interim (nondefault) rating states in order to recover a generator, so it is *only* applicable to rating systems and not to the case of unrated data. In the case of binary data, with no defaults there is no movement to observe on the underlying firms. Said another way, without observing *some* behavior, we cannot estimate the generator. For multistate ratings data, by contrast, the approach is more directly applicable and offers a robust approach to estimating bounds on the cells of transition matrices, including those with zero observations in the default class.

Pluto and Tasche (2006) suggest an alternative approach to estimating confidence bounds for low- or no-default portfolios. In this approach, they assume there to be k rating classes over which no defaults have been observed. If we assume that there is a monotonic relationship between the rating classes with respect to rating quality, so that the default rates on the rating classes can be ordered monotonically, $\mathrm{PD}(R_1) \leq \mathrm{PD}(R_2) \leq \ldots \leq \mathrm{PD}(R_k)$, the authors provide a simple approach to assessing the *maximum possible* probability of default for each class and they term this estimation *most prudent estimation*. The approach is based on the observation that if there are no defaults to observe, then the most conservative assumption is that the default rates of the classes are equal. In this case, if there are n_i borrowers in rating class i, then one can assume that there are $N_1 = n_1 + \ldots + n_k$ total borrowers, each of which has the same probability of default. One can then set the probability of zero defaults equal to any desired confidence level α as we did in the beginning of this section. The PD that makes this equality true is the upper bound on the probability of default for the first rating category. For the second rating category, we can proceed as before but since we have already defined the upper-bound on the PD for rating class R_1, this time we only consider rating classes $R_2 \ldots R_k$ as having the same PD and take the number of observations as $N_2 = n_2 + \ldots + n_k$, and so on.

In cases where there have been defaults in a specific category, the solution is no longer for zero defaults but for the number of defaults in the target category and all rating classes below. The approach can be extended to accommodate correlation structures as well. The very conservative assumptions (equal PDs for the target class and all classes below the target class) motivate the "most prudent" moniker and in general, even where there are observable defaults, the observed default rate of the portfolio will be well below the modeled default rate using this approach. The authors suggest calibration techniques to reconcile the two default rates.

ASSESSING THE ECONOMIC VALUE OF MORE POWERFUL PD MODELS

While most bankers (except the misguided bankers from our discussion of capital distortions earlier in this chapter) agree that a more powerful model is better when available, obtaining a better model will require incurring more cost. This section provides a rigorous framework for developing a sense of whether that cost is justified. We will describe how the economic benefit can be calculated in concrete terms. In general, the validation of models should be a first step toward determining where a bank should invest in terms of improving its infrastructure to support better decision making. Knowing how much money will be saved or earned in the process makes it easier to justify the initial investment as well as to make cost-benefit trade-offs when evaluating new models.

As it turns out, one way to do this is to define an optimal cutoff (i.e., the cutoff that minimizes costs) for lending policy: a risk score or PD below which a bank will not lend. This can be determined through standard ROC analysis. The approach described in this section also permits the relative value of two models to be quantified and can be extended to accommodate real-world conventions such as relationship lending. Because of the relationship between probabilities and model power we discussed earlier, this analysis can also be related to the familiar lending practice of granting credit when a positive net present value (NPV) is expected and we demonstrate this relationship. Although we begin this section with a discussion of cutoffs, choosing a pass/fail type cutoff is almost always suboptimal. ROC curves can also be used to derive basic "prices," which we show later in this section. These are lower cost and more flexible than simple cutoffs (but still not as complete as the portfolio-referent pricing in Chapter 8).

Deriving Optimal Cutoffs

Cutoff points (loan scores below which loans will not be made and above which they are permitted) are used often by banks since they provide a simple rule by which lending officers can evaluate loans. Cutoff points may also be based on operational business constraints (e.g., there is only enough staff to follow x percent of the total universe), but these are almost always suboptimal from a profit maximization perspective. A more rigorous criterion can be derived with knowledge of the prior probabilities and the cost function, defined in terms of the costs (and benefits) of a false negative (FN) (i.e., process predicts nondefault and the firm defaults) and a false positive (FP) (i.e., process predicts default and the firm does not default) and a true negative (TN) (i.e., process predicts nondefault and the firm does not default) and a true positive (TP) (i.e., process predicts default and the firm defaults).[25]

The key observation is that the economic cost to the organization of a specific type of error (FP or FN) or benefit of a correct prediction (TP or TN) is independent of the model being used. However, the total payoff associated with using a *specific strategy* is dependent on both the cost to the organization of an error *and* the performance of the model. All things being equal, the higher the error rate of a model, the more costly it is to make decisions that rely on that model.

The cost associated with using a particular model to make pass/fail lending decisions is given as the probability-weighted sum of the costs and benefits of the errors associated with the strategy. In our context, we define a strategy as a combination of a specific model and a specific cutoff. Thus the payoff, $P_{m,k}$, of using a combination of specific threshold (cutoff) k with a particular model m is given as the probability-weighted sum of the costs and benefits associated with the rule defined by the cutoff, k:

$$C_s = p(D) \cdot c(FN) \cdot FN_{m,k} - p(D) \cdot b(TP) \cdot TP_{m,k}$$
$$+ p(ND) \cdot c(FP) \cdot FP_{m,k} - p(ND) \cdot b(TN) \cdot TN_{m,k}$$

where $\quad$ $b(\cdot)$ and $c(\cdot)$ are the benefit and cost functions, respectively

$p(\cdot)$ is the unconditional (population) probability of an event

D and ND are default and nondefault events, respectively.

---

[25] Although we take them as given in this discussion, identifying the drivers of these costs is typically nontrivial for banking institutions and is usually institution-specific. In general, the costs of an FP are typically far lower than that of an FN. For example, Altman, Haldeman, and Narayanan (1977) conducted one of the first studies on this topic. The article reported that the ratio of the FN:FP costs was on the order of about 35:1.

Thus the payoff function is the expected benefit of correct decisions less the expected cost of mistakes. Translating into quantities of the ROC in Figure 7.1, we can write down:

$$FP_{m,k} = k$$

$$TN_{m,k} = 1 - k$$

$$FN_{m,k} = 1 - ROC(k)$$

$$TP_{m,k} = ROC(k)$$

$$C_s = [p(D) \cdot c(FN) \cdot (1 - ROC(k))] - [p(D) \cdot b(TP) \cdot ROC(k)]$$
$$+ [p(ND) \cdot c(FP) \cdot k] - [p(ND) \cdot b(TN) \cdot (1 - k)]$$

Setting to zero, differentiating C_s with respect to k, and rearranging terms gives the slope of a line with marginal cost equal to zero.

$$S = \frac{dROC(k)}{dk} = \frac{p(ND)}{p(D)} \frac{[c(FP) + b(TN)]}{[c(FN) + b(TP)]}$$

The point at which the line with slope S, defined above, forms a tangent to the ROC curve for a model will define the optimal cutoff, given a particular set of costs and benefits, as this point will be the one at which marginal payoffs (costs) are zero. Green and Swets (1966, Chapter 1) provide a discussion of this approach and an analytic formulation of the problem as applied to ROC analysis. They show that for any ROC curve and cost function, there exists a point with minimal cost at which both the Type I and Type II errors are minimized within the constraints of the cost function.

A central assumption is that there is a correspondence between the model scores and default probabilities. Fortunately, as we discussed earlier in this chapter, there is a direct relationship between calibration and power. That is, a more powerful model will be easier to calibrate.

A line with a slope S has been termed an *iso-performance* line (Provost and Fawcett 1997). We can use an ROC curve to determine where the optimal cutoff score will be for a given cost function. It is the point where an iso-performance line with slope S forms a tangent to the ROC curve for a particular model. This is the point, k^*, that will minimize this cost function for the particular model.[26]

---

[26] Again, if the ROC curves for two models cross, then neither is unambiguously better than the other with respect to a general cutoff. The preferred model will depend critically on the cost function. When one ROC completely dominates the other (i.e.,

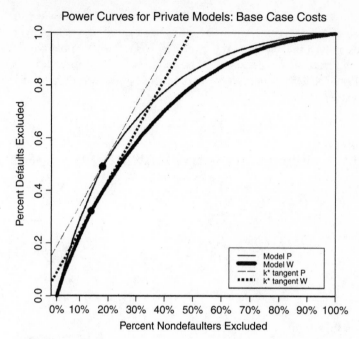

Power Curves for Private Models: Base Case Costs

FIGURE 7.10 Iso-Performance Lines That Define k^* under Base Case Assumptions

Figure 7.10 shows two models and the iso-performance lines that define the optimal cutoff for each under the assumptions outlined for the base case. Dots indicate the points of tangency (and x values) that define k^*.

This methodology is a straightforward application of cost minimization (setting marginal costs equal to zero). However, since this perspective is not always obvious in the context of ROC analysis, it can be useful to frame the discussion in terms of more traditional lending practices.

---

the ROC curve for the dominant model is above the ROC for the other model), in contrast, the dominant model will be preferred for any possible cutoff chosen. For some types of applications, it may be possible to use the two models to achieve higher power than either might independently, through the creation of an *ROC convex hull* that covers both models (Provost and Fawcett 1997). Such approaches may not be suitable for real-world credit problems since these combination approaches require a probabilistic (nondeterministic) choice to be made between the two models for each borrower. However, if this strategy is implemented in the case where the ROCs of two models cross, the expected performance of the combined two models will be superior to either when used separately.

Consider how a lending officer typically views a lending decision in net present value (NPV) terms. Assuming sufficient capital, the officer will make all loans where the NPV of the expected cash flows is positive. If the values of the payoffs are assumed to be given in NPV terms, and the unconditional probability of default is π, then the NPV without a model would be evaluated as

$$NPV = (1 - \pi)V_{ND} + \pi V_D$$

where V_D and V_{ND} are the values of the payoff in the event of default and nondefault, respectively.

Substituting:

$$\pi = p(D)$$

$$(1 - \pi) = p(ND)$$

$$V_{ND} = b(TN) - c(FP)$$

$$V_D = b(TP) - c(FN)$$

we arrive at the following:

$$NPV = p(ND) \cdot b(TN) - p(ND) \cdot c(FP) + p(D) \cdot b(TP) - p(D) \cdot c(FN)$$

How does this change if we introduce a credit scoring model? The model provides additional information about the conditional (borrower-specific) probability of default and allows the user to explicitly define these probabilities. To evaluate the NPV of a loan to a firm that scored in the kth percentile of all firms, using model m, we can use

$$NPV = p(ND) \cdot b(TN) \cdot TN_{m,k} - p(ND) \cdot c(FP) \cdot FP_{m,k}$$
$$+ p(D) \cdot b(TP) \cdot TP_{m,k} - p(D) \cdot c(FN) \cdot FN_{m,k}$$

and we are left with the negative of C_s; note that negative costs are positive cash flows. Thus, assuming a constant cost function and setting a cutoff at the point at which the marginal NPV of zero is equivalent to setting a cutoff at the point on the ROC at which a line with slope S forms a tangent. Assuming a purely economic objective in this simplistic setting, a bank should continue to make loans until the marginal return for doing so is zero.

An example can help illustrate this point. For this example and the others in this section, we use the stylized assumptions in Table 7.8 as the baseline case.

TABLE 7.8 Assumptions for Baseline Underwriting Costs and Profits

	Variable	Baseline Value
1	$P(D)$	2.0%
2	$p(ND)$	98.0%
3	Interest spread (per annum)	1.25%
4	Underwriting fees (up front)	0.50%
5	Workout fees (on default)	2.0%
6	LGD (on default)	35.0%
7	Risk-free rate	4.00%
8	Additional relationship benefit (NPV)	0

The figures in Table 7.8 show the (simplified) assumed costs (and profits) for underwriting to a typical client of a bank. Lines 1 and 2 indicate the assumed baseline probability of default (and its complement) in the bank's model. Lines 3 and 4 represent the fees and revenue the bank will generate by making a loan, and lines 5 and 6 the costs associated with a default. Note also that in this case there is no relationship value to making or not making a particular loan, but that if there were, it would be captured in NPV terms for the life of the loan on line 8. All costs and revenues are quoted as percentages of a dollar loaned.

Consider the case in which a bank has a number of high-profile clients who are identical in all respects to the body of the borrower population except that they provide the bank with significant revenue through the use of additional banking services. What effect should this additional revenue have on the choice of k^*?

Figure 7.11 shows this case under the assumption that the relationship is worth 50 bps per annum. In the figure, we show the iso-performance lines that define the optimal cutoff for both standard clients (dotted line) and relationship clients (dashed line). Dots indicate the point of tangency (and x values); the filled dot represents k^* for the relationship clients and the hollow dot represents k^* for standard clients. Note how k^* is less conservative for clients who also provide relationship revenue. For such clients the cutoff is around the 6th percentile whereas those clients without relationships are optimally cut off at the more conservative 16th percentile.

It is not the case that the relationship clients get preferential treatment as a gesture of goodwill. Rather, since they provide more revenue when they do not default, through their other fees in addition to the loan-related revenues, the opportunity cost of not lending to these borrowers is far greater than for the typical client. Thus, this analysis provides some justification for

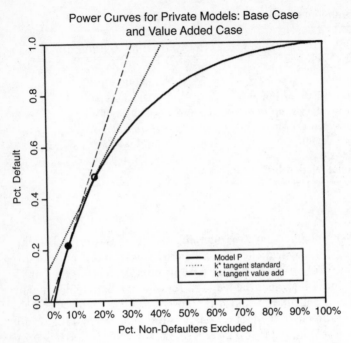

FIGURE 7.11 Iso-Performance Lines That Define k^* When Clients Provide Relationship Revenue

the practice of some bankers who relax lending practices for their better clients, but characterizes the additional cost of doing so as specific minimum additional fees required from adjacent business. As we have discussed in other chapters, the practice of credit transfer pricing is the next step in fully aligning the incentives in the bank so that only clients that add to overall shareholder value are retained. The simple approach described in this section is a first step toward better guidance of what client relationships should be fostered at the bank.

Zero-Cost Lending Cutoffs: Optimal Fees Given Fixed Costs and Capacity and a Single Cutoff

Imagine now that the bank would like to lend at zero expected cost (or better), given a specific cutoff that it has chosen. For example, a bank may determine that it only has staff available to process a specific percentage of the potential applicants. In this case, the bank should optimize its lending policy for the specific cutoff value. If the bank is able to adjust the loan terms to reflect the risk of the specific cutoff policy, it can achieve more efficient lending by designing terms that result in a cost function that ensures that $k = k^*$, the optimal cutoff.

To determine the minimum profit that should be required for a policy based on setting a lending cutoff to a specific value of k, we need to ensure that the marginal revenues at each risk level fully compensate the bank for expected losses. We then solve for $b_{k^*=k}(TN)$, the amount of benefit (spread plus underwriting fees in this case) required at each level of k in order to ensure zero costs (on average) for lending *if that point were used as a cutoff*.

Setting the overall cost, C, to zero and assuming $b(TP)$ is also zero (no benefit for defaulters not granted credit), and rearranging, we obtain the following result for $b_{k^*=k}(TN)$:

$$b_{k^*=k}(TN) = \frac{1}{p(ND)(1 - FP)} \left[p(ND)c(FP)FP_{k,m} + p(D)c(FN)FN_{k,m} \right]$$

This function gives the floor on the NPV of the total expected revenues that must be received to compensate for the associated risks of the lending environment described by the cost function. Importantly, this is the value of $b_{k^*=k}(TN)$ that would be required if k were the cutoff, not if lending were done at all values of k.

Stated more clearly, $b_{k^*=k}(TN)$ is *not the price* that should be charged for a loan with score $s_{(k)}$. Rather, it is the level of revenue that must be received (in NPV terms) for *every borrower granted*, assuming all borrowers with scores above $s_{(k)}$ are granted credit with uniform pricing and none are granted credit with scores below $s_{(k)}$. In other words, $b_{k^*=k}(TN)$ is the value of $b(TN)$ that would be required in a lending policy to make $k = k^*$, the optimal cutoff for that policy.

We note in passing that the approach just described can be extended to a number of other policy applications. For example, in the case where an institution is, in fact, resource constrained and only has enough staff to review x percent ($k = 1 - x$) of the applications, this analysis can also be adapted to determine the cost of setting $k = 1 - x$ versus allowing k to equal k^*.

Since in what follows we are concerned with pricing, we can simplify the preceding expression. In the case of a pricing approach, *no loans* are denied. Rather, any loan can be granted, provided the appropriate revenue (for which we must solve) is received for the loan with $s = s_{(k)}$. If no firms are turned down, lenders are only concerned with true negatives and false negatives. In order to determine the payoff for lending to a specific borrower with a specific score of $s_{(k)}$, we introduce some additional notation, letting tn and fn represent the derivatives of TN and FN with respect to k.

Setting the NPV to 0 and differentiating, we obtain the following:

$$\frac{dNPV}{dk} = p(ND)b(TN)tn(k) - p(D)c(FN)fn(k)$$

Rearranging yields:

$$b_k(TN)p(ND)tn(k) = c(FN)p(D)fn(k)$$

where we now introduce a subscript on $b(\cdot)$ to indicate that, while costs of lending and default remain fixed, the benefits (interest spread, underwriting fees, etc.) must be adjusted to reflect the differing levels of risk associated with each $s_{(k)}$ since here we are charging a different price for each loan. This relationship is consistent with our general intuition: For correctly priced loans, the probability-weighted benefit of the no-default case must be set equal to the cost of a default. (A proof of the relationship to NPV is given in Appendix 7D.)

Rearranging once again, we can solve for $b_k(TN)$, the total revenue that a loan must generate to break even, given its probability of default.

$$b_k(TN) = \frac{c(FN)p(D)fn(k)}{(p(ND))tn(k)}$$

Thus, using only the ROC, information about the baseline default rates, and knowledge of the costs of lending, we can set minimum acceptable prices.[27]

It is useful, at this point, to note that these prices do not reflect the volatility of losses on the transaction in either the market or the portfolio-referent sense (see footnote 27). We have often stressed the importance of considering these factors in determining prices (either market- or transfer-). Despite this, we still find the analysis here quite valuable for a number of reasons: First, it allows institutions that may not yet have implemented full ACPM to begin to see direct benefits of using better PD estimation to influence decision processes. Second, it allows bankers unfamiliar with statistical terminology but familiar with conventional lending practices, to appreciate in clear business terms why PD models can be useful in line lending. Finally, through some additional analysis that we will detail at the end of this section, it provides a basis for senior managers to quantify the financial benefits of making an investment in improving PD estimation practices within the firm.

---

[27] Note that we are using the term *pricing* somewhat loosely here. In particular, the probabilities on which the prices are based are not risk-neutral probabilities but rather actuarial or real-world probabilities. As shown in the main text, a more complete translation from real-world to risk-neutral probabilities can often be made with an estimate of a firm's risk premium (Chapter 3). Transfer prices on the other hand, would reference the bank portfolio (Chapters 2 and 8).

Returning now to the ROC based pricing approach, we note that in moving from cutoff estimation to pricing estimation, our analytic focus shifts. Rather than concerning ourselves with the benefits and costs of *all* borrowers whose scores are below a cutoff, we are now concerned with the benefits and costs of borrowers with a specific score. This shift in perspective results in substantially more flexibility in characterizing the economics of a particular transaction. This perspective shift also motivates the transition in the way we measure *TP* and *FN*. In this case, we have moved from the ROC (cumulative) true positive and false negative to the score-specific equivalent, since we wish to evaluate the cost of lending to clients with scores that are equal to (rather than better than) the particular point on the curve, which also permits tailoring the terms of the transaction to the exact risk of the borrower, rather than taking a single uniform set of terms for all borrowers.

Figure 7.12 shows the required minimum profit for loans with score $s_{(k)}$ using the powerful model. The required profit shifts as expected losses increase (LGD increases). Also note that using this basic pricing mechanism, a bank would be able to grant credit to any borrower by adjusting the terms of the loan. (Lending regulations might prohibit the bank from realizing

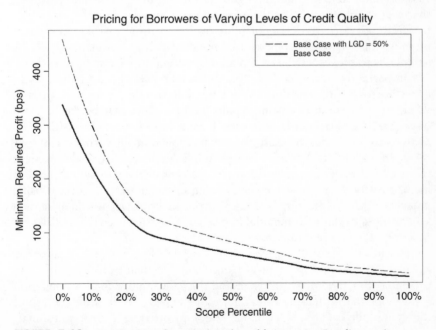

FIGURE 7.12 Required Profit at Each Value of k Assuming Lending to Any Borrower at Zero Cost

revenues in some cases, though, due to restrictions on the permissible levels of interest rates, and so on.)

Here we have shown that pricing curves can be derived from a fixed cost function and an ROC, but it is straightforward to extend the approach to arbitrary cost functions that need be neither linear nor constant. If, rather than defining the pricing curve, we instead take only $p(D)$, $fn(k)$, and $tn(k)$, we can use these directly in a cost function to derive a price.

For example, it is reasonable to contemplate a borrower-specific (non-constant) LGD. In this case, the price for a loan to the ith borrower, with score $s_{(k)}$, might be given as

$$b_k(TN) = \frac{c_i(FN)\,p(D)\,fn(k)}{(p(ND))\,tn(k)}$$

where $c_i(FN)$ is now the *borrower-specific* cost of default. In general, any cost function of $p(D)$, $fn(k)$, and $tn(k)$ could be used.

Users of a weak model will systematically overcharge (undercharge) higher (lower) credit quality borrowers, creating competitive opportunities for those who use the more powerful models. This can be detrimental in the case of relationship lending, since good customers may be asked to pay more than they should using pricing policies based on a weaker model. Conversely, in the riskiest portions of the portfolio, the lender using a weaker model will often not be adequately compensated for the levels of lending risk. (This is analogous to the discussion of capital distortion that we presented earlier.)

Importantly, since models with different power, by definition, rank-order borrowers differently, it is not possible to imply from this analysis what the differential in pricing would be for a *particular* borrower without actually evaluating the borrower. Even if both banks were using ROC analysis to set prices, for example, it is possible that each bank might give the borrower different relative scores. While Bank A using model A might classify a borrower as in the riskiest 20 percent of the population, Bank B might classify the same borrower as being in the riskiest 10 percent using model B. Pricing differentials for the particular borrower would arise then as a result of both the differential in pricing curves between the models *and* (possibly) the different rankings of firms by the models.

What is the value of a more powerful model? In 2003, Stein and Jordão calculated the costs for a typical bank using different models. This paper presented a methodology for extending the ROC approach to a simulation framework that generates a distribution of expected values for the use of different models. The simulation methodology provides a means of estimating the typical benefit (cost), in cash terms, of using a more powerful model over a weaker one.

The approach works by simulating the actual decision process that lenders might undertake in lending. Depending on which aspects of performance we are testing, different versions of the experiment might be used. For exposition, we describe here the design of one such experiment.

In this example, we consider the case in which banks compete for deal flow. Borrowers are assumed to be rational when seeking credit. Since models of different power cannot be perfectly correlated, a borrower that might be rejected by one bank might be accepted by another if the banks were using different models. This is true even in the case where both banks are using optimal (for their model) cutoffs.

To conduct the simulation, Stein and Jordão propose the following steps:

1. Score all loans in the data set using both models.
2. Calculate the optimal cutoff k^* for each model, given the cost function of the bank.
3. For each simulation, repeat the following steps until the portfolios of both models are the desired size:
   a. Randomly select a loan.
   b. Randomly select a model (i.e., a bank).
   c. If the loan's score using that model is above the cutoff for the model, add it to that model's portfolio.
   d. Otherwise, compare its score using the other model to that model's cutoff, and if it is above the cutoff add it to that model's portfolio.
   e. Otherwise, discard the loan.
4. Calculate profits and losses on both portfolios based on actual behavior of the loans.

This approach can be extended as well to pricing by considering how a rational borrower would behave. The risk category assigned to a borrower for pricing by one model might be different than the risk category assigned to it using another model, and this could lead to differential pricing between the two banks. All things being equal, a rational borrower would opt for the bank offering cheaper loan terms.

In a sense, this approach is similar to a bootstrap approach that takes advantage of real data and makes few assumptions about the underlying processes driving default. Blöchlinger and Leippold (2006) provided an alternative simulation approach that does not require data, given a number of simplifying assumptions about the processes driving default, but does require knowledge of the correlation of two models' scores with an unobserved systematic factor, and thus suggests that at least knowledge of the data, if not the data themselves, is required for calibrating the simulation.[28]

Stein and Jordão present an example where they compare two loan scoring models. To give a flavor of the Stein and Jordão (2003) simulation results here, they found that the performance of two models they tested differed in accuracy ratio by about five points. Of course these results are model-specific and, to some degree, bank-specific since the outcomes we describe here do not generalize beyond the two models, economic conditions, and cost structures they examined. In other words, it is not possible to draw specific inferences about the value of a particular power differential (e.g., five points of accuracy ratio) and a particular economic benefit since the value of one model versus another is sensitive to both the economic conditions and the lending opportunity set under which the models would be used, and the shapes of the two power curves. That said, the example and process they outline provide a realistic window into how this analysis could be done at a bank evaluating a number of default models.

Let us consider the conclusions they draw from this example. The simulations showed that if the bank evaluating these two models switched to the more powerful model but a competing bank did not, the revenue differential would be about 11 bps, considerably higher than the 4.1 bps expected when the bank simply switched in isolation. Furthermore, if the banks were competing using a pricing approach, rather than the cutoff approach, the difference in return would be on the order of about 16 bps, which would equate to approximately $6.8 million per year for a prototypical medium-size bank.

More generally, the experiments showed a very conservative estimate of the additional profit generated per point difference of accuracy ratio to be 0.97 bps when using the cutoff approach and 2.25 bps when using the pricing approach. Thus, a conservative estimate of the additional profit for a bank using a model that was five points better than its competition's would be around 5 basis points per dollar granted if the bank were using the cutoff approach, and 11 basis points per dollar granted if the banks were using the pricing approach. For the prototypical medium-size bank described earlier, this would equate to additional profits of about $2.1 million and $4.8 million, respectively, in 2002. Table 7.9 shows some additional estimates of the economic impact of using more or less powerful models in lending. Of

---

[28] In the case where it is further possible to calculate the correlation between two models' scores, the authors present an extension that models how banks might behave if they learn about the scores of other banks and incorporate this in their decision process.

TABLE 7.9   Estimated Additional Profit Earned for Use of Model with Five Points Higher Accuracy Ratio (Simulation Example)

Size of Bank (Total Consolidated Assets)	Estimated New Origination ($MM) in 2002 (CRD)	Estimated Additional Profit ($MM) Cutoff	Estimated Additional Profit ($MM) Pricing
$600b	$20,200	$7.8	$18.2
$50b	$4,275	$1.7	$3.8
$10b	$3,406	$1.3	$3.1

course, these are based on simplified assumptions, and more involved cost functions give other results as would portfolio-referent pricing.

AVOIDING OVERFITTING: A WALK-FORWARD APPROACH TO MODEL TESTING

The previous section marked a digression into a framework for assessing the economic value using validation as a step toward increasing the profitability of the bank. In this final section, we summarize an overall strategy for designing validation tests, regardless of the statistics being calculated. We have found that performance tests are most reliable when models are developed and validated using some type of out-of-sample and out-of-time testing.[29]

Though it has not always been the case, it has now become common practice for models to be developed and tested using some form of *holdout testing*, which can range from simple approaches such as saving some fraction of the data (a *holdout sample*) for testing after the model is fit, to more sophisticated cross-validation approaches. However, with time- (sector-, geography-, etc.) varying processes such as credit, holdout testing can miss important model weaknesses that may not be obvious if a model is fit across time (and other dimensions) since simple holdout tests average information on performance and parameter values through all dimensions.

In this section, we describe a validation framework introduced in Sobehart, Keenan, and Stein (2000) that accounts for variations across

---

[29] *Out-of-sample* refers to observations for firms that are not included in the sample used to build the model. *Out-of-time* refers to observations that are not contemporaneous with the training sample.

time and across the population of obligors. It can provide important information about the performance of a model across a range of economic environments.[30]

This approach is most useful in validating models during development and less easily applied where a third-party model is being evaluated or when data is more limited. The approach is easiest to implement when the model developers are part of the testing process since it typically involves reestimating alternative parameter specifications on different subsets of the data, which can be challenging if the researchers performing the tests must treat the model itself (or the data used to fit the model) as a black box. All in all, however, the technique is extremely useful for ensuring that a model has not been overfit and, where data permit, is a valuable component of model building and validation exercises.

Forms of Out-of-Sample Testing

A schematic of the various forms of out-of-sample testing (Dhar and Stein 1998) is shown in Figure 7.13. The figure breaks up the model testing procedure along two dimensions: time (along the horizontal axis) and the population of obligors (along the vertical axis). The least restrictive out-of-sample validation procedure is represented by the upper left quadrant, and the most stringent by the lower right quadrant. The other two quadrants represent procedures that are more stringent with respect to one dimension than another.

Testing strategies are broken out based on whether they account for variances across time (horizontal axis) or across the data universe (vertical axis). Dark circles represent training data and white circles represent testing data. Gray circles represent data that may or may not be used for testing. (Reproduced from Dhar and Stein 1998.)

The upper left quadrant describes the approach in which the testing data for model validation is chosen completely at random from the full model-fitting data set. This approach to model validation assumes that the properties of the data remain stable over time. Because the data are drawn at random, this approach validates the model across the population of obligors but does not test for variability across time.

The upper right quadrant describes one of the most common testing procedures. In this case, data for model fitting are chosen from any time period prior to a certain date, and testing data are selected from time periods

---

[30] Portions of the presentation in this section follow closely that of Dhar and Stein (1998), Stein (1999, 2002), and Sobehart, Keenan, and Stein (2000).

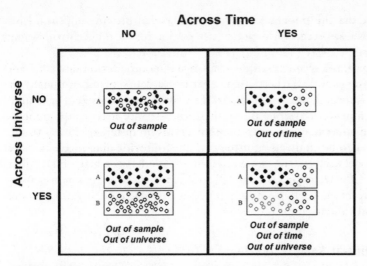

FIGURE 7.13 Schematic of Out-of-Sample Validation Techniques

only after that date. Because model validation is performed with out-of-time samples, the testing assumptions are less restrictive than in the previous case, and time dependence can be detected using different validation subsamples. Here it is assumed that the characteristics of the population do not vary across the population.

The lower left quadrant represents the case in which the data are segmented into two sets containing no firms in common, one set for building the model and the other for validation. In this general situation the testing set is out-of-sample. The assumption of this procedure is that the relevant characteristics of the population do not vary with time but they may vary across the companies in the portfolio.

Finally, the most robust procedure is shown in the lower right quadrant and should be the preferred sampling method for credit risk models. In addition to being segmented in time, the data are also segmented across the population of obligors. Nonoverlapping sets can be selected according to the peculiarities of the population of obligors and their importance (out-of-sample and out-of-universe sampling).

Out-of-sample, out-of-time testing is beneficial since it helps prevent overfitting of the development data set, but also prevents modelers from unintentionally including information about future states of the world that would not have been available when developing the model. For example, default models built before a market crisis may or may not have predicted default well during and after the crisis, but this cannot be tested if the data used to build the model were drawn from periods before and after the crisis. Rather, such testing can only be done if the model were developed using data prior to the crisis and tested on data from subsequent periods.[31]

Because default events are rare, it is often impractical to create a model using one data set and then test it on a separate holdout data set composed of completely independent cross-sectional data. While such out-of-sample and out-of-time tests would unquestionably be the best way to compare models' performance if default data were widely available, it is rarely possible in practice. As a result, most institutions face the following dilemma:

> *If too many defaulters are left out of the in-sample data set, estimation of the model parameters will be seriously impaired and overfitting becomes likely.*
>
> *If too many defaulters are left out of the holdout sample, it becomes exceedingly difficult to evaluate the true model performance due to the severe reductions in statistical power discussed earlier in this chapter.*

We now describe an approach that leverages the sparse data that is typically available for credit model development, while also permitting reasonable out-of-sample testing. The approach is termed *walk-forward* testing.

The Walk-Forward Approach

In light of these problems, an effective approach is to *rationalize* the default experience of the sample at hand by combining out-of-time and out-of-sample tests. A testing approach that focuses on this last quadrant and is designed to test models in a realistic setting, emulating closely the manner in which the models are used in practice, is often referred to in the trading model literature as *walk-forward* testing.

It is important to make clear that there is a difference between walk-forward testing and other more common econometric tests of stationarity

---

[31] It can be argued that there is no truly *honest* out-of-sample test since most modelers use portions of the data to test early models as they converge on a functional form for the model. To the extent that the search for the appropriate form of the model is guided by knowledge of the events or data from future time periods, the out-of-sample test is compromised. Unfortunately, it is almost always the case that modelers have at least knowledge of events and dynamics that would not have been known prior to the out-of-sample period.

or goodness of fit. For example, when testing for goodness of fit of a linear model in economics, it is common to look at an R^2 statistic. For more general models, a likelihood-related measure (e.g., Akaike Information Coefficient [AIC]) might be used.

The key difference between these statistics and tests and statistics derived from walk-forward tests is that statistics such as R^2 and AIC and tests such as Chow tests are all *in-sample* measures. They are designed to test the agreement of the parameters of the model or the errors of the model with the data used to fit the model during some time period(s). In contrast, walk-forward testing provides a framework for generating statistics that allow researchers to test the *predictive power* of a model on data not used to fit it.

The walk-forward procedure works as follows:

1. Select a year, for example, 1997.
2. Fit the model using all the data available on or before the selected year.
3. Once the model's form and parameters are established for the selected time period, generate the model outputs for all the firms available during the following year (in this example 1998).
4. Save the prediction as part of a result set.
5. Now move the window up (e.g., to 1998) so that all the data through that year can be used for fitting, and the data for the next year can be used for testing.
6. Repeat steps 2 through 5, adding the new predictions to the result set for every year.

Collecting all of the out-of-sample and out-of-time model predictions produces a set of model performances. This *result set* can then be used to analyze the performance of the model in more detail. Note that this approach simulates, as closely as possible given the limitations of the data, the process by which the model will actually be used. Each year, the model is refit and used to predict the credit quality of firms one year hence. The process is outlined in the lower left of Figure 7.14.

In this example, we used a one-year window. In practice the window length is often longer and may be determined by a number of factors including data density and the likely update frequency of the model itself, once it is on line.

In walk-forward testing, a model is fit using a sample of historical data on firms and tests the model using both data on those firms one year later and data on new firms one year later (upper portion of figure). Dark circles represent in-sample data and white circles represent testing data. This approach results in walk-forward testing (bottom left) when it is repeated

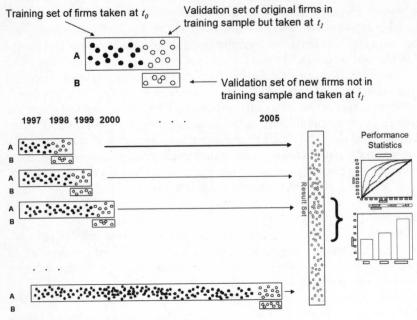

FIGURE 7.14   Schematic of Walk-Forward Testing Approach

in each year of the data by fitting the parameters of a model using data
through a particular year, and testing on data from the following year, and
then moving the process forward one year. The results of the testing for each
validation year are aggregated and then analyzed (lower right) to calculate
particular statistics of interest.

The walk-forward approach has two significant benefits. First, it gives a
realistic view of how a particular model would perform over time. Second,
it gives analysts the ability to leverage to a higher degree the availability of
data for validating models. In fact, the validation methodology not only tests
a particular model, but it tests the entire modeling approach. Since models
are typically reparameterized periodically as new data comes in and as the
economy changes, it is important to understand how the approach of fitting
a model, say, once a year, and using it in real-time for the subsequent year,
will perform. By employing walk-forward testing, analysts can get a clearer
picture of how the entire modeling approach will hold up through various
economic cycles.

Two issues can complicate the application of the walk-forward approach. The first is the misapplication of the technique through the repeated
use of the walk-forward approach while *developing* the model (as opposed

to testing a single final model). In the case where the same out-of-sample data is used repeatedly to garner feedback on the form of a candidate model as it is being developed, the principle of out-of-time is violated.

The second complication can arise when testing models that have continuously evolved over the test period. For example, banks often adjust internal rating models to improve them continuously as they use them. As a result, it is often impossible to recreate the model, as it would have existed at various points in the historical test period, so it can be difficult to compare the model to others on the same test data set. Importantly, a similar issue can arise in the case of models whose inputs (e.g., volatility estimates, etc.) themselves require estimation from historical data. In such situations, it is sometimes feasible to test the model only in a period of time after the last change was made. Such situations are reflected in the upper right quadrant of Figure 7.14. This approach tends to limit the number of defaults available and, as a result, it can be difficult to draw strong conclusions.

Though the walk-forward approach to testing is straightforward to implement, it turns out to provide a rich framework for determining not only how a model performs, but also how the approach to modeling performs. In practice, models are periodically updated to reflect new data. Walk-forward testing simulates this while also testing the models themselves.

CONCLUSION

In this chapter, we have described some useful techniques for characterizing the behavior and performance of default prediction models. Measures of power and calibration provide a convenient means of communicating model attributes, and it is possible to make more precise the variability around model performance or differences in model performance using the techniques we discuss for estimating confidence bounds. Importantly, we can convert this statistical insight into economic terms directly using the relationships between power, profitability and pricing that we present. This economic framing can lead directly to basic decision rules and pricing policy. Finally, we show how all of the pieces can be used within the framework of walk-forward testing—an approach that provides an effective method to control for overfitting.

Validation is necessarily an iterative process and it stubbornly defies a formulaic approach. More than anything, good model validation is about problem formulation: setting up tests that tease out and isolate the behaviors we are interested in understanding. Nothing can substitute for experience with data and domain on the part of the analyst doing the validation. In the end, a model without validation is only a hypothesis.

APPENDIX 7A: TYPE I AND TYPE II ERROR: CONVERTING CAP PLOTS INTO CONTINGENCY TABLES

A common tool for evaluating default prediction models is the use of power curves and CAP plots which graphically show the power of various models on a set of test data. These diagnostics are often summarized through power statistics and accuracy ratios.

However, for some purposes, analysts and researchers are interested in understanding Type I and Type II error rates for specific cutoffs. With knowledge of the sample default rates, these error rates are fully described by the CAP plots. In this Appendix, we describe the calculations for inferring Type I and Type II error rates from these diagnostic plots.

For reference, we repeat that the CAP plot is constructed similarly to the ROC curve. Like an ROC curve, the CAP plot describes the percentage of defaults excluded by a particular model for a given cutoff criterion on the y-axis. Unlike ROC curves, a CAP plot displays the percentage of the entire sample excluded by a cutoff criterion on the x-axis (as opposed to only showing the nondefaulting credits on the x-axis, as in the ROC).

Thus the x and y coordinates display the percentage of the sample excluded and the true positive rate, respectively, as shown in Figure 7.15.

With knowledge of the sample default rate, there is a straightforward transformation that can be used to construct a table of Type I and Type II errors (and false negative and false positive results) from the CAP plot for any cutoff criteria of interest. This in turn permits an analyst to determine what percentage of a portfolio would need to be excluded in order to capture a desired percentage of defaults or, conversely, to determine the percentage of defaults that would be excluded for a given exclusion of a portfolio.

To derive the transformation, first note that the true positive and false negative rates are defined directly on the y-axis of the CAP plot. The true negative and false positive rates are not directly observable from the x-axis, due to the fact that the x-axis of a CAP plot contains both nondefaulted and defaulted firms: the entire sample $[S\%(k)]$.

Since we are interested in percentages in terms of the total number of nondefaults, rather than the percentage of all firms in the sample, we need to back out the defaulted firms. To do this, we need to know how many of them are contained in the region between zero and the cutoff, k. This is just the true positive rate times the total default rate, r percent, since TP percent (k) of the total defaults were excluded and r percent of the total sample

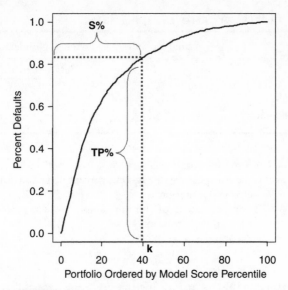

FIGURE 7.15 A Schematic Representation of a CAP Plot

represents the total percentage of the sample that defaulted. This quantity

$$S\%(k) - (TP\%(k)^*r\%)$$

gives the total proportion of the entire sample that were nondefaulters, below the cutoff.

Finally, the preceding expression is still given in units of the total sample, rather than in units of the nondefaulters only. For true and false negatives, since we are interested in the proportion of the nondefaulters that are excluded for a particular cutoff criterion, rather than the proportion of the total sample, we need to normalize this expression to put it in terms of total nondefaults only. To do this, we adjust the percentage so that it is a percentage not of the total sample, but of the total sample minus the defaulters, or $1 - r$ percent. This yields the following expression for false positives:

$$FP\% = \frac{S\%(k) - (TP\%(k)^*r\%)}{1 - r\%}$$

The remaining terms can be calculated directly.

TABLE 7.10 Contingency Table

	Actual Default	Actual Nondefault
Predicted Default	$TP\%(k)$	$\dfrac{S\%(k) - (TP\%(k)^{*}r\%)}{1 - r\%}$
Predicted Nondefault	$1 - TP\%(k)$	$1 - \dfrac{S\%(k) - (TP\%(k)^{*}r\%)}{1 - r\%}$

where k is a specific cutoff criterion

$TP\%(k)$ is the true positive rate (y-axis: percent of defaults captured) associated with criterion k

$S\%(k)$ is the percentage of the full sample (x-axis: percent of sample excluded) with criterion k

$r\%$ is the sample default rate

A contingency table incorporating the preceding transformation is presented in Table 7.10.

APPENDIX 7B: THE LIKELIHOOD FOR THE GENERAL CASE OF A DEFAULT MODEL

In the case of a model predicting a binary event (default/no default), the model's estimate of the probability of a single event y happening given data x is:

$$prob(y|x) = p(x)^{y}[1 - p(x)]^{(1-y)}$$

where $p(x)$ is the probability (of default) predicted by the model, conditional on the input x, and the event y is defined as follows:

$$y = \begin{vmatrix} 1 & \textit{if the firm defaults and} \\ 0 & \textit{if the firm remains solvent} \end{vmatrix}$$

Note that since either y or $(1 - y)$ will always be 0, this reduces to the simple predicted probability of the outcome, according to the model, conditioned on x.

For a given set of data, the *likelihood* of the model, $L(model)$, is calculated by computing the model's predicted probabilities, given the data inputs to the model, and calculating the appropriateness of these predictions for each observation, given the *actual* outcomes. Here we assume the model is evaluated using a specific data set and that the likelihood is thus with respect to this data set.

To do this we generalize the preceding probability by taking advantage of the fact that the overall likelihood of a model for a pooled data set is the product of the individual likelihoods of any disjoint subsets of the data:

$$L(\text{model}) = \prod_{i=1}^{n} prob(y_i | x_i) = \prod_{i=1}^{n} p(x_i)^{y_i} (1 - p(x_i))^{(1-y_i)}$$

In general, it is easier to work with summations than products, particularly for more complicated likelihood functions, so by convention we work with the log of the likelihood, $l(model)$. This is also convenient since for large data sets and small probabilities, the likelihoods can become very small in their raw form. The log likelihood is:[32]

$$l(\text{model}) = \sum_{1}^{n} y_i \ln[p(x_i)] + (1 - y_i) \ln[1 - p(x_i)]$$

APPENDIX 7C: TABLES OF ROC ε AND n_{max}

Importantly, these are upper bounds, derived based on Blume (2008), and the *practical* number of defaults and levels of ε can be dramatically lower than those obtained from these limits. In practice, a fully empirical CI would be preferred and the resulting half-width will be smaller given n than ε under the upper bounds in Tables 7.11 and 7.12.

APPENDIX 7D: PROOF OF THE RELATIONSHIP BETWEEN NPV TERMS AND ROC TERMS

We wish to show that

$$b_k(TN)p(ND)tn(k) = c(FN)p(D)fn(k)$$

can be manipulated to yield the familiar NPV relationship

$$NPV = (1 - \pi)V_{ND} + \pi V_D = 0$$

---

[32] Note that since y_i is always either zero or one, this can also be written as $ln[y_i p(x_i) + (1 - y_i)(1 - p(x_i))]$, which is computationally slightly more convenient.

TABLE 7.11 Maximum Values of ε Given AUCs A_1 and A_2, Constant Cluster Correlation ρ, and Number of Defaults n_D in Data Set; $\alpha = 0.05$

$\rho = 0.25$

A_1	0.68	0.68	0.68	0.68	0.68	0.68	0.70	0.70	0.70	0.70	0.70	0.72	0.72	0.72	0.72	0.74	0.74	0.74	0.76	0.76	0.78
A_2	0.70	0.72	0.74	0.76	0.78	0.80	0.72	0.74	0.76	0.78	0.80	0.74	0.76	0.78	0.80	0.76	0.78	0.80	0.78	0.80	0.80
ε																					
0.005	49,281	48,322	47,280	46,158	44,958	43,686	47,438	46,389	45,259	44,052	42,771	45,411	44,273	43,056	41,765	43,199	41,972	40,670	40,803	39,488	38,223
0.010	12,321	12,081	11,820	11,540	11,240	10,922	11,860	11,598	11,315	11,013	10,693	11,353	11,069	10,764	10,442	10,800	10,493	10,168	10,201	9,872	9,556
0.020	3,081	3,021	2,955	2,885	2,810	2,731	2,965	2,900	2,829	2,754	2,674	2,839	2,768	2,691	2,611	2,700	2,624	2,542	2,551	2,468	2,389
0.030	1,369	1,343	1,314	1,283	1,249	1,214	1,318	1,289	1,258	1,224	1,189	1,262	1,230	1,196	1,161	1,200	1,166	1,130	1,134	1,097	1,062
0.040	771	756	739	722	703	683	742	725	708	689	669	710	692	673	653	675	656	636	638	617	598
0.050	493	484	473	462	450	437	475	464	453	441	428	455	443	431	418	432	420	407	409	395	383
0.060	343	336	329	321	313	304	330	323	315	306	298	316	308	299	291	300	292	283	284	275	266
0.070	252	247	242	236	230	223	243	237	231	225	219	232	226	220	214	221	215	208	209	202	196
0.080	193	189	185	181	176	171	186	182	177	173	168	178	173	169	164	169	164	159	160	155	150
0.090	153	150	146	143	139	135	147	144	140	136	133	141	137	133	129	134	130	126	126	122	118
0.100	124	121	119	116	113	110	119	116	114	111	107	114	111	108	105	108	105	102	103	99	96

$\rho = 0.35$

A_1	0.68	0.68	0.68	0.68	0.68	0.68	0.70	0.70	0.70	0.70	0.70	0.72	0.72	0.72	0.72	0.74	0.74	0.74	0.76	0.76	0.78
A_2	0.70	0.72	0.74	0.76	0.78	0.80	0.72	0.74	0.76	0.78	0.80	0.74	0.76	0.78	0.80	0.76	0.78	0.80	0.78	0.80	0.80
ε																					
0.005	42,712	41,886	40,992	40,035	39,020	37,952	41,115	40,212	39,245	38,218	37,138	39,358	38,379	37,340	36,245	37,442	36,388	35,278	35,366	34,238	33,131
0.010	10,678	10,472	10,248	10,009	9,755	9,488	10,279	10,053	9,812	9,555	9,285	9,840	9,595	9,335	9,062	9,361	9,097	8,820	8,842	8,560	8,283
0.020	2,670	2,618	2,562	2,503	2,439	2,372	2,570	2,514	2,453	2,389	2,322	2,460	2,399	2,334	2,266	2,341	2,275	2,205	2,211	2,140	2,071
0.030	1,187	1,164	1,139	1,113	1,084	1,055	1,143	1,117	1,091	1,062	1,032	1,094	1,067	1,038	1,007	1,041	1,011	980	983	952	921
0.040	668	655	641	626	610	593	643	629	614	598	581	615	600	584	567	586	569	552	553	535	518
0.050	428	419	410	401	391	380	412	403	393	383	372	394	384	374	363	375	364	353	354	343	332
0.060	297	291	285	279	271	264	286	280	273	266	258	274	267	260	252	261	253	245	246	238	231
0.070	218	214	210	205	200	194	210	206	201	195	190	201	196	191	185	192	186	180	181	175	170
0.080	167	164	161	157	153	149	161	158	154	150	146	154	150	146	142	147	143	138	139	134	130
0.090	132	130	127	124	121	118	127	125	122	118	115	122	119	116	112	116	113	109	110	106	103
0.100	107	105	103	101	98	95	103	101	99	96	93	99	96	94	91	94	91	89	89	86	83

TABLE 7.12 Maximum Values of n_D Required to Detect a Difference of ϵ Given AUCs A_1 and A_2 and Constant Cluster Correlation ρ; $\alpha = 0.05$

$\rho = 0.25$																				
A_1	0.68	0.68	0.68	0.68	0.68	0.68	0.70	0.70	0.70	0.70	0.70	0.72	0.72	0.72	0.72	0.74	0.74	0.74	0.76	0.76	0.78
A_2	0.70	0.72	0.74	0.76	0.78	0.80	0.72	0.74	0.76	0.78	0.80	0.74	0.76	0.78	0.80	0.76	0.78	0.80	0.78	0.80	0.80
n_D 25	0.22	0.22	0.22	0.21	0.21	0.22	0.22	0.22	0.21	0.21	0.21	0.22	0.21	0.21	0.20	0.21	0.21	0.20	0.20	0.20	0.20
50	0.16	0.16	0.15	0.15	0.15	0.15	0.16	0.15	0.15	0.15	0.15	0.15	0.15	0.15	0.15	0.15	0.15	0.14	0.14	0.14	0.14
75	0.13	0.13	0.13	0.12	0.12	0.12	0.13	0.13	0.12	0.12	0.12	0.13	0.12	0.12	0.12	0.12	0.12	0.12	0.12	0.12	0.11
100	0.11	0.11	0.11	0.11	0.11	0.11	0.11	0.11	0.11	0.11	0.10	0.11	0.11	0.10	0.10	0.10	0.10	0.10	0.10	0.10	0.10
125	0.10	0.10	0.10	0.10	0.09	0.09	0.10	0.10	0.10	0.09	0.09	0.10	0.09	0.09	0.09	0.09	0.09	0.09	0.09	0.09	0.09
150	0.09	0.09	0.09	0.09	0.08	0.08	0.09	0.09	0.09	0.08	0.08	0.09	0.08	0.08	0.08	0.08	0.08	0.08	0.08	0.08	0.08
175	0.08	0.08	0.08	0.08	0.08	0.08	0.08	0.08	0.08	0.08	0.08	0.08	0.08	0.08	0.08	0.08	0.08	0.07	0.08	0.08	0.07
200	0.08	0.08	0.08	0.08	0.07	0.07	0.08	0.08	0.08	0.07	0.07	0.08	0.07	0.07	0.07	0.07	0.07	0.07	0.07	0.07	0.07
250	0.08	0.08	0.07	0.07	0.07	0.07	0.07	0.07	0.07	0.07	0.06	0.07	0.07	0.07	0.07	0.07	0.07	0.06	0.06	0.06	0.06
300	0.07	0.07	0.06	0.06	0.06	0.06	0.06	0.06	0.06	0.06	0.06	0.06	0.06	0.06	0.06	0.06	0.06	0.06	0.06	0.06	0.06
400	0.06	0.06	0.06	0.06	0.05	0.05	0.06	0.06	0.06	0.05	0.05	0.06	0.06	0.05	0.05	0.06	0.05	0.05	0.05	0.05	0.05
500	0.05	0.05	0.05	0.05	0.05	0.05	0.05	0.05	0.05	0.05	0.05	0.05	0.05	0.05	0.05	0.05	0.05	0.05	0.04	0.04	0.04
750	0.05	0.04	0.04	0.04	0.04	0.04	0.04	0.04	0.04	0.04	0.04	0.04	0.04	0.04	0.04	0.04	0.04	0.04	0.04	0.03	0.04
1000	0.04	0.04	0.03	0.03	0.03	0.03	0.03	0.03	0.03	0.03	0.03	0.03	0.03	0.03	0.03	0.03	0.03	0.03	0.03	0.03	0.03
A_1	0.68	0.68	0.68	0.68	0.68	0.68	0.70	0.70	0.70	0.70	0.70	0.72	0.72	0.72	0.72	0.74	0.74	0.74	0.76	0.76	0.78
$\rho = 0.35$																					
A_2	0.70	0.72	0.74	0.76	0.78	0.80	0.72	0.74	0.76	0.78	0.80	0.74	0.76	0.78	0.80	0.76	0.78	0.80	0.78	0.80	0.80
n 25	0.21	0.21	0.20	0.20	0.20	0.20	0.20	0.20	0.20	0.20	0.19	0.20	0.20	0.19	0.19	0.20	0.19	0.19	0.19	0.19	0.18
50	0.15	0.15	0.14	0.14	0.14	0.14	0.14	0.14	0.14	0.14	0.14	0.14	0.14	0.14	0.14	0.14	0.14	0.13	0.13	0.13	0.13
75	0.12	0.12	0.12	0.12	0.11	0.11	0.12	0.12	0.11	0.11	0.11	0.12	0.11	0.11	0.11	0.11	0.11	0.11	0.11	0.11	0.11

(Continued)

TABLE 7.12 (Continued)

n_D																					
100	0.10	0.10	0.10	0.10	0.10	0.10	0.10	0.10	0.10	0.10	0.10	0.10	0.10	0.10	0.10	0.10	0.10	0.09	0.09	0.09	0.09
125	0.09	0.09	0.09	0.09	0.09	0.09	0.09	0.09	0.09	0.09	0.09	0.09	0.09	0.09	0.09	0.09	0.09	0.08	0.08	0.08	0.08
150	0.08	0.08	0.08	0.08	0.08	0.08	0.08	0.08	0.08	0.08	0.08	0.08	0.08	0.08	0.08	0.08	0.08	0.08	0.08	0.08	0.07
175	0.08	0.08	0.07	0.07	0.07	0.08	0.07	0.08	0.08	0.07	0.07	0.07	0.07	0.07	0.07	0.07	0.07	0.07	0.07	0.07	0.07
200	0.07	0.07	0.07	0.07	0.07	0.07	0.07	0.07	0.07	0.07	0.07	0.07	0.07	0.07	0.07	0.07	0.07	0.06	0.07	0.07	0.06
250	0.07	0.07	0.06	0.06	0.06	0.06	0.06	0.06	0.06	0.06	0.06	0.06	0.06	0.06	0.06	0.06	0.06	0.06	0.06	0.06	0.06
300	0.06	0.06	0.06	0.06	0.06	0.06	0.06	0.06	0.05	0.06	0.06	0.06	0.06	0.05	0.05	0.06	0.05	0.05	0.05	0.05	0.05
400	0.05	0.05	0.05	0.05	0.05	0.05	0.04	0.05	0.04	0.05	0.04	0.05	0.05	0.04	0.04	0.05	0.04	0.04	0.04	0.04	0.04
500	0.05	0.05	0.04	0.04	0.05	0.04	0.04	0.04	0.04	0.04	0.04	0.04	0.04	0.04	0.04	0.04	0.04	0.04	0.04	0.04	0.04
750	0.04	0.04	0.04	0.04	0.04	0.04	0.04	0.04	0.04	0.04	0.04	0.03	0.04	0.03	0.04	0.03	0.04	0.03	0.03	0.03	0.03
1000	0.03	0.03	0.03	0.03	0.03	0.03	0.03	0.03	0.03	0.03	0.03	0.03	0.03	0.03	0.03	0.03	0.03	0.03	0.03	0.03	0.03

Note that these are upper bounds (worst case) on the size of the difference detectable given a fixed number (n_D) of defaults in data or ε differences in AUC (equivalent to $0.5*$ difference in AR). Practical values of these quantities may be smaller.

We start by assuming that the baseline default rate is neither zero nor 1 so that there is at least one default and one nondefault. We also assume that $fn(k)$ is not zero for at least one value of k.

At point k, we are considering the default rate of all firms whose scores fall between percentiles k and $k + \delta$. Let N be the total number of observations, n_k^D be the number of defaulters between percentiles k and $k + \delta$, and n_k^{ND} be the number of nondefaulting firms between percentiles k and $k + \delta$. Then:

$$n_k^{ND} = Np(ND) \cdot tn(k) \cdot \delta$$

and

$$n_k^D = Np(D) \cdot \int_k^{k+\delta} fn(\tau)d\tau$$

since $fn(k)$ is the density of the bads at k and $tn(k)$ is the density of the goods at k.

Therefore, the probability of default, p_k, for firms with a score between k and $k + \delta$ is:

$$p_k = \frac{n_k^D}{(n_k^D + n_k^{ND})}$$

Substituting, we arrive at the following:

$$p_k = \frac{Np(D) \cdot \int_k^{k+\delta} fn(\tau)d\tau}{N\left[p(ND) \cdot tn(k) \cdot \delta + p(D) \cdot \int_k^{k+\delta} fn(\tau)d\tau \right]}$$

$$(1 - p_k) = \frac{Np(ND) \cdot tn(k) \cdot \delta}{N\left[p(ND) \cdot tn(k) \cdot \delta + p(D) \cdot \int_k^{k+\delta} fn(\tau)d\tau \right]}$$

Note first that N cancels out in both cases. Now we take the limit of p as δ goes to zero. Applying a special case of the Leibniz Integral Rule, we note that

$$\lim_{\delta \to 0} \frac{\partial n_k^D}{\partial \delta} = \lim_{\delta \to 0} p(D) \cdot fn(k + \delta)$$
$$= p(D) \cdot fn(k)$$

Now applying L'Hôpital's Rule,

$$\lim_{\delta \to 0} p = \frac{p(D) \cdot fn(k)}{p(ND) \cdot tn(k) + p(D) \cdot fn(k)}$$

and

$$\lim_{\delta \to 0}(1 - p) = \frac{p(ND) \cdot tn(k)}{p(ND) \cdot tn(k) + p(D) \cdot fn(k)}$$

Substituting these expressions into the first equation in this appendix yields

$$b_k(TN)(1 - p_k)A = c(FN)p_k A$$

where $A = (p(ND) \cdot tn(k) + p(D) \cdot fn(k))$, a normalization term that cancels out.

The profit in default, V_D, and nondefault, V_{ND}, are $b(TN)$ and $c(FN)$, respectively, so we obtain:

$$(1 - p_k)V_{ND} = p_k V_D$$

or

$$(1 - p_k)V_{ND} - p_k V_D = 0$$

Note that uncertainty can be incorporated by transforming p_k into a risk-neutral measure.

APPENDIX 7E: DERIVATION OF MINIMUM SAMPLE SIZE REQUIRED TO TEST FOR DEFAULT RATE ACCURACY IN UNCORRELATED CASE

In the case of a binomial distribution where f_d, the frequency of defaults, and the defaults are independent, we can appeal to the Central Limit Theorem (CLT) and obtain a convenient (Gaussian) limit which facilitates calculations. Using the CLT, if $q \equiv (1 - p)$, we get the familiar result:

$$P\left(np_L \leq np \leq np_u\right) \cong \frac{1}{\sqrt{2\pi}} \int_{\frac{n(p_L-p)}{\sqrt{npq}}}^{\frac{n(p_U-p)}{\sqrt{npq}}} e^{-x^2/2} dx$$

$$= \Phi\left(\frac{n(p_U - p)}{\sqrt{npq}}\right) - \Phi\left(\frac{n(p_L - p)}{\sqrt{npq}}\right)$$

where $\Phi(\cdot)$ is the standard cumulative normal distribution.

Since here we are assuming that $p_U - p = p - p_L = \varepsilon$, this simplifies to

$$2\Phi\left(\frac{n\varepsilon}{\sqrt{npq}}\right) - 1 \geq 1 - \alpha$$

or, more conveniently,

$$\Phi\left(\frac{n\varepsilon}{\sqrt{npq}}\right) \geq 1 - \alpha/2$$

yielding:

$$\frac{n\varepsilon}{\sqrt{npq}} \geq \Phi^{-1}(1 - \alpha/2)$$

Rearranging terms gives the result shown:

$$n \geq \frac{pq}{\varepsilon^2}\left[\Phi^{-1}(1 - \alpha/2)\right]^2$$

APPENDIX 7F: TABLES FOR LOWER BOUNDS OF ε AND N ON PROBABILITIES OF DEFAULT

Table 7.13 gives the lower bound on the difference, ε, between the predicted and actual default rates that must be observed to conclude that a significant difference exists at the $\alpha = 5$ percent level between the two, given n firms are available to test. This assumes no correlation in the default rates. Estimates are made assuming the limiting properties of the binomial including zero correlation.

Table 7.14 gives the lower bound on the difference, ε, between the predicted and actual default rates that must be observed to conclude that a significant difference exists at the $\alpha = 1$ percent level between the two,

TABLE 7.13 Analytic Lower Bound on Deviation, ε, That Must be Observed for Level p and Fixed Sample Size n; $\alpha = 0.05$

N	p = 0.0005	0.0010	0.0050	0.0100	0.0250	0.0500	0.0750	0.1000	0.1250	0.1500	0.2000
50	*	*	*	*	*	*	*	0.0832	0.0917	0.0990	0.1109
100	*	*	*	*	*	0.0427	0.0516	0.0588	0.0648	0.0700	0.0784
250	*	*	*	*	0.0194	0.0270	0.0326	0.0372	0.0410	0.0443	0.0496
500	*	*	*	0.0087	0.0137	0.0191	0.0231	0.0263	0.0290	0.0313	0.0351
1,000	*	*	0.0044	0.0062	0.0097	0.0135	0.0163	0.0186	0.0205	0.0221	0.0248
2,500	*	*	0.0028	0.0039	0.0061	0.0085	0.0103	0.0118	0.0130	0.0140	0.0157
5,000	*	0.0009	0.0020	0.0028	0.0043	0.0060	0.0073	0.0083	0.0092	0.0099	0.0111
10,000	0.0004	0.0006	0.0014	0.0020	0.0031	0.0043	0.0052	0.0059	0.0065	0.0070	0.0078
25,000	0.0003	0.0004	0.0009	0.0012	0.0019	0.0027	0.0033	0.0037	0.0041	0.0044	0.0050
50,000	0.0002	0.0003	0.0006	0.0009	0.0014	0.0019	0.0023	0.0026	0.0029	0.0031	0.0035
75,000	0.0002	0.0002	0.0005	0.0007	0.0011	0.0016	0.0019	0.0021	0.0024	0.0026	0.0029
100,000	0.0001	0.0002	0.0004	0.0006	0.0010	0.0014	0.0016	0.0019	0.0020	0.0022	0.0025

*Indicates those cells in which $npq < 4$ and tended to be unreliable.

TABLE 7.14 Analytic Lower Bound on Deviation, ε, That Must be Observed for Level p and Fixed Sample Size n; $\alpha = 0.01$

N	p = 0.0005	0.0010	0.0050	0.0100	0.0250	0.0500	0.0750	0.1000	0.1250	0.1500	0.2000
50	*	*	*	*	*	*	*	*	0.1205	0.1301	0.1457
100	*	*	*	*	*	0.0561	0.0678	0.0773	0.0852	0.0920	0.1030
250	*	*	*	*	0.0254	0.0355	0.0429	0.0489	0.0539	0.0582	0.0652
500	*	*	*	0.0115	0.0180	0.0251	0.0303	0.0346	0.0381	0.0411	0.0461
1,000	*	*	0.0057	0.0081	0.0127	0.0178	0.0215	0.0244	0.0269	0.0291	0.0326
2,500	*	*	0.0036	0.0051	0.0080	0.0112	0.0136	0.0155	0.0170	0.0184	0.0206
5,000	*	0.0012	0.0026	0.0036	0.0057	0.0079	0.0096	0.0109	0.0120	0.0130	0.0146
10,000	0.0006	0.0008	0.0018	0.0026	0.0040	0.0056	0.0068	0.0077	0.0085	0.0092	0.0103
25,000	0.0004	0.0005	0.0012	0.0016	0.0025	0.0036	0.0043	0.0049	0.0054	0.0058	0.0065
50,000	0.0003	0.0004	0.0008	0.0012	0.0018	0.0025	0.0030	0.0035	0.0038	0.0041	0.0046
75,000	0.0002	0.0003	0.0007	0.0009	0.0015	0.0020	0.0025	0.0028	0.0031	0.0034	0.0038
100,000	0.0002	0.0003	0.0006	0.0008	0.0013	0.0018	0.0021	0.0024	0.0027	0.0029	0.0033

*Indicates those cells in which $npq < 4$ and tended to be unreliable.

TABLE 7.15 Analytic Lower Bound on Sample Size, n, for Level p to Consider Deviation of ε Significant; $\alpha = 0.05$

ε	$p = 0.0005$	0.0010	0.0050	0.0100	0.0250	0.0500	0.0750	0.1000	0.1250	0.1500	0.2000
0.0001	191,977	383,762	1,911,126	3,803,044	9,363,556	18,246,929	26,650,121	34,573,129	42,015,956	48,978,600	61,463,341
0.0005	*	15,350	76,445	152,122	374,542	729,877	1,066,005	1,382,925	1,680,638	1,959,144	2,458,534
0.0010	*	*	19,111	38,030	93,636	182,469	266,501	345,731	420,160	489,786	614,633
0.0025	*	*	*	6,085	14,982	29,195	42,640	55,317	67,226	78,366	98,341
0.0050	*	*	*	*	3,745	7,299	10,660	13,829	16,806	19,591	24,585
0.0100	*	*	*	*	*	1,825	2,665	3,457	4,202	4,898	6,146

*Indicates those cells in which $npq < 4$ and tended to be unreliable.

TABLE 7.16 Analytic Lower Bound on Sample Size, n, for Level of p to Consider Deviation of ε Significant; $\alpha = 0.01$

ε	$p = 0.0005$	0.0010	0.0050	0.0100	0.0250	0.0500	0.0750	0.1000	0.1250	0.1500	0.2000
0.0001	331,579	662,826	3,300,861	6,568,548	16,172,560	31,515,759	46,029,595	59,714,069	72,569,182	84,594,932	106,158,346
0.0005	*	26,513	132,034	262,742	646,902	1,260,630	1,841,184	2,388,563	2,902,767	3,383,797	4,246,334
0.0010	*	*	33,009	65,685	161,726	315,158	460,296	597,141	725,692	845,949	1,061,583
0.0025	*	*	*	10,510	25,876	50,425	73,647	95,543	116,111	135,352	169,853
0.0050	*	*	*	*	6,469	12,606	18,412	23,886	29,028	33,838	42,463
0.0100	*	*	*	*	*	3,152	4,603	5,971	7,257	8,459	10,616

*Indicates those cells in which $npq < 4$ and tended to be unreliable.

given n firms are available to test. This assumes no correlation in the default rates. Estimates are made assuming the limiting properties of the binomial including zero correlation.

Table 7.15 gives the lower bound on the number of independent observations, n, that would be needed to be certain that an observed difference, ε, between the predicted and actual default rates was a significant difference existing at the $\alpha = 5$ percent level. This assumes no correlation in the default rates. Estimates are made assuming the limiting properties of the binomial including zero correlation.

Table 7.16 gives the lower bound on the number of independent observations, n, that would be needed in order to be certain that an observed difference, ε, between the predicted and actual default rates was a significant difference existing at the $\alpha = 1$ percent level. This assumes no correlation in the default rates. Estimates are made assuming the limiting properties of the binomial including zero correlation.

REVIEW QUESTIONS

1. What is model power?
2. What is calibration?
3. How are power and calibration related?
4. Define out-of-universe testing and contrast it with out-of-time testing.
5. Compare two types of out-of-sample testing (e.g., cross-validation) and suggest strengths and weakness of each.
6. Describe why lending cut-offs are inefficient.
7. Explain the difference between an ROC and a CAP.

EXERCISES

1. A member of the loan origination group at a bank is dissatisfied with the PDs that potential lenders are being assigned in his branch. He examines the data for the past 18 months and determines that the average default rate for the bank's portfolio was about 75 percent of the average default rate predicted by the bank's models. Based on this analysis, he asserts that the model's PDs are too high. Is he right? Why or why not? How might one explore this quantitatively?

2. You are asked to evaluate a two-class rating system in which the target default rate for class A is said to be 65bps. The observed default rate is 35bps. Under the assumption of a 15 percent correlation, if you had an *infinite* amount of data, could you reject the 65bps assertion at a

95 percent confidence level? Why or why not? Justify your answer by showing your calculations.

3. A company produces a PD model it wishes to sell commercially. The researchers at the company test their model and derive an accuracy ratio of 79 percent. They note that a competitor's report states that the competitor's model, model X, has an accuracy ratio of 74 percent. Since the accuracy ratio on model X is lower than the accuracy ratio of its model, the company asserts that its model is clearly better. Should you believe the assertion? Why or why not?

4. A modeler has developed a very complicated default prediction model that uses cutting-edge statistical methods and very complex finance theory. His method requires 15 years of continuous daily equity price data, a current financial statement, and two quarters of data about the GDP. He claims his model is able to select firms from the general population that are highly unlikely to default. Since the model is so complicated, he demonstrates the utility of the model by testing it on a large sample of firms. Using a walk-forward analysis, he tests the model on firms that meet the data requirements over the full 30 year test period. Surprisingly, over a test period of 30 years, the default rate on the portfolio his model selected is far lower than that of either the bank or any of the rating agency or academic corporate default studies. Should you buy his model? Why or why not?[33]

5. A bank determines that for standard borrowers, it costs about 42 times as much when a loan defaults as when the bank refuses to make a loan to a borrower who ultimately would have paid. The baseline default rate in the population to which the bank lends is 1.75 percent. If the bank wished to create a cutoff for lending, what would the slope of the iso-performance line be? What would it be for preferred clients who provide double the revenue that the standard clients do (i.e., the cost in the preferred case 42:2 or 21:1 rather than 42:1)?

6. You are investigating the predictive power of two models. Using your own data, you calculate that one has an accuracy ratio of 0.52 and the other has an AR of 0.6 (note these are ARs, not AUCs). Your data set has 250 defaults and 30,000 nondefaults, and you estimate the cluster correlations to be about 0.35. In a worst case, what is the smallest difference between the ARs that you will be able to detect? (Hint: Convert to AUC first.) How many more defaults would you need in order to cut that in half?

---

[33] A version of this example was first introduced to one of the authors by Andrew Lo.

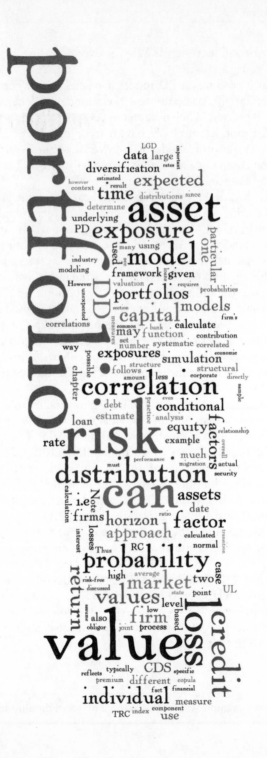

CHAPTER 8

Portfolio Models

A good portfolio is more than a long list of good stocks and bonds. It is a balanced whole, providing the investor with protections and opportunities with respect to a wide range of contingencies.
—Harry Markowitz

By applying the statistical method we cannot foretell the behavior of an individual in a crowd. We can only foretell the chance, the probability that it will behave in some particular manner.
—Albert Einstein

Objectives

After reading this chapter[1] you should understand the following concepts:

- Structure of a factor-based portfolio model.
- How to calculate correlation in a structural framework.
- Analytics used for portfolio risk management and measurement.
- How to use reduced-form models in a portfolio framework.

Portfolios of corporate liabilities often suffer from a lack of diversification due in part to the relatively small number of liquidly traded corporate

---

[1] The framework, techniques, and methodologies relating to the structural approaches outlined in this chapter were first developed by researchers at KMV and MKMV. We have attempted to indicate alternative sources where possible for non-MKMV material. Much of the material in the general portfolio sections is based on Kealhofer and Bohn (2001), with permission from Moody's Corporation and/or its affiliates, and are copyrighted works owned by those entities. All rights reserved.

debt instruments. Unfortunately, selling corporate liabilities can be difficult given the institutional constraints of portfolio holders (and uneven liquidity for many corporate debt instruments). This limitation on selling corporate debt instruments makes active portfolio management difficult.

With the advent of credit default swaps (CDSs) and collateralized debt obligations (CDOs), the potential to achieve much better portfolio diversification is slowly being realized. Structured credit in both cash and synthetic form, when used responsibly for hedging, offers efficient means for adjusting the portfolio. The principles underlying portfolio analysis extend to the modeling of CDS. In fact, as we have discussed in other chapters, corporate debt can be considered a combination of an otherwise default-risk-free security plus a position (i.e., selling protection) in a CDS on the corporate obligor. The crux of credit portfolio analysis focuses on modeling CDS, whether explicitly (as a CDS contract itself) or implicitly (as part of a credit-risky security) in the portfolio.

Typical holders of corporate liabilities are banks, mutual funds, and pension funds. Recently credit hedge funds have also entered the corporate debt markets. These market participants tend to hold debt issued by obligors with relatively low levels of default risk. These same market participants have started including CDSs and CDOs (in particular, synthetic collateralized loan obligations, CLOs) in their portfolios. The recent credit crisis of 2007 and 2008 is radically restructuring these markets and changing the players; however, the instruments will continue to be available as options for managing portfolios of credit risk.

For the typical high-grade borrower, default risk is small, perhaps one-tenth of 1 percent per year. For the typical bank borrower this risk is about one-half of 1 percent. Although these risks do not *seem* large, they are in fact significant. First, they can increase quickly and with little warning. Second, the margins in corporate lending have historically been very tight, and even small miscalculations of default risks can undermine the profitability of lending or owning corporate bonds or loans. But third, and most importantly, many lenders are *themselves* borrowers, with high levels of leverage. Unexpected realizations of default risk have destabilized, decapitalized, and destroyed lenders in numerous instances. Banks, finance companies, insurers, investment banks, lessors: none have escaped unscathed.

The *systematic* component of default risk cannot be hedged away, or structured away. It is a reflection of the substantial risk in companies' futures, tied to the general fortunes of the economy. Credit default swaps and other credit derivatives can be used to shift risk, but in the end, someone must bear this risk. It does not net out in the aggregate.

Although generally a poor long-term investment strategy, it is possible to be rewarded for taking on large concentrations of risk in *equities* because these concentrations at times produce large returns. However, overwhelming evidence of the ineffectiveness of this *stock-picking* strategy has been available since the early 1970s (see Rubinstein 2001 and 2006 for an overview and references regarding the arguments for and against efficient markets, concluding with a strong statement in support of market efficiency) and, as a result, the majority of equity investments are managed in diversified portfolios.

Unlike equities, however, debt has no upside potential to offset the potential for large losses, and thus the case for managing default risk in well-diversified portfolios is even more compelling. The limited upside potential of debt spreads means that there are no practical circumstances under which an investor or counterparty can be rewarded for taking on concentrations of default risk. Like other rare events with high costs, default risk can only be effectively *managed* in a portfolio, not eliminated. Default risk is reduced and managed through diversification. As a result, all else equal, those who can diversify default risk most effectively for certain types of exposures will ultimately own the exposure to the default of those risky assets.

Every lender knows the benefits of diversification.[2] Every lender works to achieve these benefits. However, until recently lenders have been reluctant, or unable, to implement systems for actually measuring the amount of diversification in a debt portfolio. Portfolios have *concentrations*, which become apparent *ex post*. *Ex ante*, however, lenders must look to models and software to help quantify concentrations. Until recently, these types of models have not been generally available. Thus it should not come as a surprise that there have been many unexpected default events in lenders' portfolios in the past.

Quantitative methods for portfolio analysis have been available since Markowitz's pioneering work in 1950. These methods have been applied successfully in a variety of areas of finance, most notably to equity portfolios. Portfolio methods demonstrate the dramatic amount of risk reduction achievable through diversification. They provide tools to measure the amount of risk contributed by an individual asset, or group of assets, to a portfolio. By extension, they also show the amount of diversification provided by a single asset or group of assets. Portfolio methods have been designed to maximize the return to a portfolio while keeping the risk within acceptable bounds. This maximization requires a balancing of return to risk within the portfolio, asset by asset, group of assets by group of assets, while maintaining a global view of the portfolio.

---

[2] For the balance of this chapter, the word *lenders* should be interpreted broadly to include not just commercial banks, but also investors such as insurance companies, mutual funds, hedge funds, and pension funds which purchase corporate bonds, secondary market loans, and other structured corporate credit instruments.

This logic can be illustrated by imagining what would happen were this not the case. If a low-return-to-risk asset were swapped for a high-return-to-risk asset, then the portfolio's expected return would be improved with no addition to risk, which is desirable. What prevents this process from continuing indefinitely is the change in risk that then obtains after the swap is made. As the low-return asset is swapped out of the portfolio, it changes from being a source of concentration to being a source of diversification—that is, its risk contribution to the overall portfolio falls. The reverse applies as the high-return asset is swapped into the portfolio. Thus, if this trade were repeated over and over again, the return-to-risk ratio would steadily increase for the low-return asset (as its diversification benefit decreases its risk) and would decrease for the high-return asset (as its concentration risk increases), until their return-to-risk ratios are equal. At that point, no further swap can raise return without also raising risk. This then characterizes the optimal portfolio or, equivalently, the optimal set of holdings.

This conceptual model applies to the default risk of debt and CDSs as surely as it applies to equities. Equity practitioners, however, have used the past 25 years to develop the techniques for measuring the asset attributes that are necessary for accurately managing and analyzing real portfolios. Until recently, the same development effort has not occurred in the case of debt portfolios because of the greater analytical and empirical difficulties. In particular, it is necessary as a first step to quantify the level of default risk in a single asset. Further, the relationship between each pair of assets in the portfolio (i.e., correlation) also requires quantification, which turns out to necessitate the use of different, less convenient mathematics than is the case for equity portfolios.[3]

As we introduced at the start of this book, the elements of portfolio credit risk can be grouped as follows:

Stand-Alone Risk
- *Probability of default* (PD): the probability that the obligor will fail to service its obligations. Note that we use PD to designate the annualized quantity and cpd to designate the cumulative quantity.
- *Loss given default* (LGD): the extent of the loss incurred in the event the obligor defaults.

---

[3] Because equity returns are symmetrical (i.e., probability of loss is about the same as the probability of gain), the mathematics for equity-portfolio modeling are less difficult and tend to make use of Gaussian (or at least spherical) distributional assumptions. It is true that equity-return distributions have fatter tails than are implied by a Gaussian or normal distribution; however, the high degree of skewness in addition to fat tails observed in credit-return distributions makes modeling credit portfolios much more challenging.

- *Migration risk*: the probability and value impact of changes in PD.
- *Exposure at default* (EAD): the amount of an obligation still actually outstanding at the time of default.

Portfolio Risk
- *Default correlations*: the degree to which the default risks of obligors in the portfolio are related.
- *Value correlations*: the degree to which the values of the securities in the portfolio are related.
- *Exposure weight*: the size or proportion of the portfolio exposed to the default risk of each obligor.

Due to a variety of technical developments in finance, it has become more feasible and practical to estimate these quantities. A good portion of this research was done through direct and indirect collaboration between academics and analytics providers and academics and market participants. As we will discuss, a strong portfolio model requires dynamic PD estimates and a method of correlating the defaults that permits us to analyze and manage portfolios of credit-risky assets. The result of the collaborations on these fronts is that practical and conceptually sound methods exist for measuring actual diversification, and for determining portfolio holdings and position sizes that minimize concentrations and maximize return in credit portfolios.

In this chapter, we largely focus on models that use the *structural* framework. Toward the end of the chapter, we touch on methods and challenges of portfolio modeling in a reduced-form framework. Our experience is that in practice, the structural approaches, with their longer history and more readily available data, result in portfolio models that are easier to estimate and tend to be more stable. Nonetheless, work on reduced-form portfolio models is progressing rapidly and showing great promise, particularly in the context of CDS portfolios. As we have emphasized throughout this book, a portfolio management group will benefit from using multiple models. Even so, at this time, structural approaches to portfolio modeling tend to be more widely implemented and easier to use in practice. We now turn to an explanation of the structural approach that was originally developed at KMV (now MKMV).

By way of warning, this chapter attempts to bring together all of the components we have been discussing throughout the text and to discuss how to do so in a practical fashion. Unfortunately, bringing this much material together is necessarily involved and the realistic issues of implementation are many. As a result, this chapter is a bit more expansive than most of the others and also includes more digressions than other chapters. The reader will also notice that the discussion moves back and forth between more intuitive descriptions of the modeling approach and the specifics of the models and their implementation. At times, this approach to presenting the material will make the chapter a bit repetitive and the transitions a bit more pronounced. This is somewhat intentional. We have attempted both to address the demand for details on how to implement models as well as provide the intuition along the way.

Finally, we note that the gaps in our knowledge of correlation express themselves most clearly in estimates of extreme tail risk. In this chapter, we discuss a number of ways to estimate loss distributions and each provides a mechanism for sizing the tail at any quantile. However, our view is that the processes that drive credit risk during times of extreme stress may be quite different than those that drive credit risk during normal or even "pretty bad" times. Further, it is all but impossible to empirically validate extreme tail estimates. For these reasons, we advocate using the techniques we discuss in this chapter for general risk management, but combining them with stress testing and business judgment when applications require extreme loss scenarios.

A STRUCTURAL MODEL OF DEFAULT RISK

In Chapter 3, we described the conceptual foundations of a structural model of default risk. The key points from that discussion vis-à-vis what ensues in this chapter are as follows:

- An obligor is assumed to default when its market value of assets falls below its default point, which is a function of its debt obligations.
- A distance-to-default (DD) measure can be calculated reflecting the difference between an obligor's market value of assets and its default point, which is then scaled by the obligor's asset volatility.
- A probability of default (PD) and an exposure value can be calculated from an obligor's DD.

Knowing the market value and volatility of the obligor's assets is critical, as we have seen, to the determination of the probability of default. With these quantities, we can also estimate the correlation of two firms' asset values. These correlations play an important role in the measurement of portfolio diversification. One of the great benefits of the structural framework is the linking together of a model for default and a model for portfolio risk.

MEASUREMENT OF PORTFOLIO DIVERSIFICATION

Defaults translate into losses. The loss associated with a single default depends on the amount recovered. For the purposes of this exposition, we will assume that the recovery in the event of default is known, and that this recovery is net of the expenses associated with collecting the debt (including the time value of the recovery process).[4] Using, for example, recovery as a percent of the face value of the loan, we can also specify the loss given default as one minus the expected recovery. (See Chapter 5 for a more detailed discussion of the ways in which LGD may be specified.)

Using this structure, the expected loss for a single exposure is the probability of default times the loss given default. Interestingly, in the case of a single exposure, the *unexpected loss* depends on the same variables as the expected loss. For a simple model of default or nondefault (i.e., no modeling of credit migration), unexpected loss equals the loss given default times the standard deviation of the default probability (the square root of the product of the PD times one minus the PD—see the next section). The unexpected loss represents the volatility of loss.

The impact of credit risk on a portfolio's value has two components: the risk of loss of *principal and interest* due to possible default, and the risk of loss of *value* due to credit deterioration, both of which are characterized at a specific horizon. The typical case in portfolio risk management is to assess a portfolio with respect to a single time horizon. Establishing one horizon for analysis (we usually refer to the time horizon in portfolio analysis with the variable H) forms the basis of a framework for comparing the attractiveness of different types of credit exposures on the same scale. While this book focuses on credit portfolio management, the specification of one time horizon and the use of a factor model (to be explained shortly) make this framework extensible to a variety of asset classes and security types.

Credit instruments from the same obligor with different maturities (as long as the maturity is at or beyond the horizon) have the same default risk at the horizon, but the value risk (i.e., uncertainty around the value of the instrument at horizon) depends upon the remaining time to maturity. The longer the remaining time, the greater the variation in value due to credit quality changes. The introduction of value deterioration as a component of the portfolio's risk requires us to model credit migration for the instruments in the portfolio. We will start with the simpler version (without credit migration) and then develop the more sophisticated version of this model.

PORTFOLIO RISK ASSUMING NO CREDIT MIGRATION

The simplest version of the model relies on the assumption that the maturities of all instruments are the same as the horizon date for analysis (e.g., one year). While this will eliminate maturity as an aspect of credit risk, it will

---

[4] Some CDS contracts define specific payments in the event of default, making this assumption even more appropriate.

not change the qualitative nature of any of the results. Modeling change in value at horizon requires a model of credit migration, which substantially increases the complexity of the calculations. Although maturity effects are important in practice, they are generally of lesser importance than the risk due to default. (Credit migration will still be an important component of a comprehensive portfolio risk modeling tool kit, which is why we will move on to that consideration after discussing the simpler, single-maturity case.)

We now turn to the specifics of how we model some of the key metrics associated with a credit portfolio's risk and pull together the individual concepts we have been developing in earlier chapters. We do this in the context of a unified mathematical framework that facilitates the calculation of some important measures ranging from a portfolio's expected loss to its loss distribution.

Measuring the diversification of a portfolio implies that we specify the range and likelihood of possible losses associated with the portfolio. All else equal, a well-diversified portfolio is one that has a smaller likelihood of generating large losses than does a poorly-diversified portfolio. The average expected loss (EL) for a portfolio is the exposure-weighted average of the expected losses of the assets in the portfolio. It would be convenient if the volatility, or unexpected loss, of the portfolio were simply the weighted average of the unexpected losses of the individual assets, but it is not. This is because portfolio losses depend not only on the mean and variability of losses on individual assets, but also on the relationship (correlation) between possible defaults. Unless all assets are perfectly correlated, the portfolio unexpected loss (UL) will be different from the sum of the individual ULs.

In order to make this first set of calculations (assuming no credit migration—i.e., only default or nondefault at horizon), we define the following variables and relationships for individual obligations in the portfolio. (Note that for ease of exposition, when referring to variables reflecting individual exposures we include an i subscript, whereas the portfolio-level version of the variables will have a P subscript.)

$cpd_{iH} \equiv$ cumulative probability of default to the horizon date for exposure i

$L_i \equiv$ loss given default (percent of face) for exposure i

$EL_i = cpd_{iH} \times L_i \equiv$ expected loss for exposure i

$UL_i = L_i \sqrt{cpd_{iH}(1 - cpd_{iH})} \equiv$ unexpected loss for exposure i at the horizon date

Importantly, we do not characterize EL as a measure of *risk*, but rather as a measure of the *cost* of undertaking the business of extending credit.

In contrast, UL measures the volatility of the losses and is more properly considered a measure of risk. The stand-alone risk of an exposure is reflected in that obligor's UL. While this is useful to know, in a portfolio context, we will be more focused on how much the exposure contributes to the *overall portfolio risk* after accounting for its diversification benefit, which we will calculate later. For now, we emphasize the difference between UL, a measure of stand-alone risk, and EL, one cost of extending credit.

Figure 8.1 provides some intuition regarding the difference in the relationship of both probability of default (PD) and LGD to EL and UL, respectively. Expected loss rises in proportion to the size of the PD and LGD, while UL exhibits nonlinear behavior. At lower PD levels, UL can rise quite quickly as the PD rises. Note that in this figure we are focused just on the relationship of these measures with PD. Later we will be looking at UL for a portfolio as a function of the underlying exposure correlation and risk contribution for the individual exposures, which is also a function of the underlying exposure correlation among other drivers.

A simple example illustrates this point: Consider a mythical island on which it always rains on either one side or the other in a given year, but never on both, with each side equally likely to receive rain. Consider two farms on the island, one on each side, each with debt on which they will default if it does not rain. A portfolio holding both loans in equal amounts, and nothing else, will have an expected default rate of 50 percent. Each borrowing will have an unexpected default rate of 50 percent: $\sqrt{0.5 \times (1 - 0.5)}$. In other words, each of the individual assets is quite risky. But the portfolio as a whole has an unexpected loss rate of zero since in every year the portfolio is guaranteed to lose the investment in one loan but not the other—no more

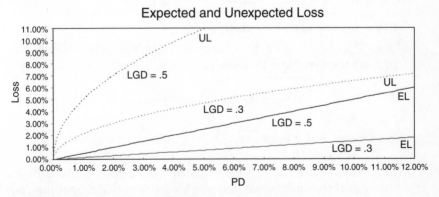

FIGURE 8.1 Expected and Unexpected Loss

and no less. There is a perfect negative correlation and a huge benefit from diversification.

The alternative extreme is that it only rains half of the years on average, but when it rains, it always rains on both sides. This is perfect positive correlation; the farms will default in exactly the same years so that each year we will get either all of our investment back or none of it. Holding one loan is equivalent to holding both loans: There is no risk reduction from diversification. (This is the only case in which the portfolio UL is a weighted sum of the individual ULs.)

An intermediate case is that raining on one farm makes it no more likely or less likely that it will rain on the other. The events of rainfall are independent. In this case, in one-fourth of the years both loans will default, in one-fourth neither will default, and half the time only one will default. There is now substantial diversification versus the perfect positive correlation case, since the likelihood of both defaulting is reduced by half. In this case, the UL for the portfolio is substantially lower than the perfectly correlated case but not as low as the negatively correlated case.

Now let us extend this intuition about diversification to the more general case of a portfolio with multiple risky securities—specifically n securities. The portfolio loss measures can be calculated as follows:

$X_i \equiv$ face value of security i

$P_i \equiv$ price of security i (per \$1 of face value)

$V_P = P_1 X_1 + P_2 X_2 + \ldots + P_n X_n \equiv$ total portfolio value

$w_i = \dfrac{P_i X_i}{V_P} \equiv$ proportion of security i in portfolio (i.e., *weight*)

$\rho_{i,j} \equiv$ loss correlation between security i and security j

Note that $w_1 + w_2 + \ldots + w_n = 1$

$EL_i \equiv$ expected loss for security i

$EL_P = w_1 EL_1 + w_2 EL_2 + \ldots + w_n EL_n \equiv$ portfolio expected loss

$UL_i \equiv$ unexpected loss for security i

$$UL_P = \sqrt{\sum_{i=1}^{n} \sum_{j=1}^{n} w_i w_j UL_i UL_j \rho_{i,j}} \equiv \text{unexpected loss for portfolio}$$

Note that $\rho_{i,j} = 1$ when $i = j$.

The portfolio expected loss is the weighted average of the expected losses of the individual securities, where the weights are the value proportions. By contrast, the portfolio's unexpected loss is a more complex function of the

ULs of the individual securities, the portfolio weights, and the pairwise loss correlations between securities.

In practice, actual defaults on different securities are positively, but not perfectly positively, correlated. Diversification, while not flawless, conveys significant benefits even though negative default correlations are rare to nonexistent (except in unique winner-take-all settings, for example).

Framed this way, the unexpected loss is a straightforward measure of portfolio diversification. Though easily stated, actually measuring diversification can be challenging as it requires good estimates of default correlations and, ultimately—if we are to account for the possibilities of credit migration—the correlations in instrument values.

STRUCTURAL MODELS OF DEFAULT CORRELATION

Default correlation measures the strength of the default relationship between two obligors. If there is no relationship, then the defaults are independent and the correlation is zero. In such a case, the probability of both obligors being in default at the same time is the product of their individual probabilities of default. When two obligors are correlated, this means that the probability of both defaulting at the same time is heightened—that is, it is larger than it would be if they were completely independent. In fact, the correlation is just proportional to this difference. Thus, holding their individual default probabilities fixed, stating that two obligors are highly correlated and stating that they have a relatively high probability of defaulting in the same time period are equivalent statements.

The basic structural default model assumes that the firm will default when the market value of its assets falls below the face value of obligations (the *Default Point*). This means that the joint probability of default for two firms is the probability of both firms' market asset values falling below their respective default points in the same time period. This probability can be determined directly with knowledge of (1) the firms' current market asset values; (2) their Default Points; (3) their asset volatilities; and (4) the correlation between the two firms' market asset values. In other words, the structural framework that we discussed in Chapter 3 enables us to use firms' asset correlation to obtain their default correlation.

Is it the case that exposure correlation cannot be estimated in more direct ways? In fact, the occurrence of the joint default of two obligors is such a rare event that it is exceedingly difficult to observe it directly, making it difficult to estimate exposure correlation directly. In contrast, the correlation, for example, between equity returns (or implied asset returns) can be directly calculated because the histories of the firms' stock returns are easily observable and the data describing them is plentiful. This observable information can be harnessed to develop estimates of the unobservable default correlation.

Default correlations cannot be successfully measured for individual firms from default experience. The historically observed joint frequency of default between two solvent companies is usually zero. For instance, Exxon and Chevron have some chance of jointly defaulting, but nothing in their default history enables us to estimate the probability since neither has ever defaulted. For large, high-quality firms, in particular, a single name defaulting is quite rare; observing two such firms defaulting at the same time is many times rarer.

One fix for this limitation is to consider grouping firms to estimate an average default correlation in the group using historical data. As it turns out, the estimates so obtained can be highly inaccurate. In fact, our own experiments with these approaches suggest that even with large samples, the estimates can have wide confidence bounds. Often, the grouped firms do not exhibit sufficient homogeneity along the dimensions needed for correlation estimation, making the results unstable. In practice, enough idiosyncratic risk exists in the underlying drivers of default that historical observation of correlation is just as likely to reflect idiosyncratic behavior for that time period and a particular data sample as it will reflect systematic behavior.

In fact, no fully satisfactory procedure currently exists for directly estimating default correlations. Not surprisingly, this has been a major stumbling block to portfolio management of default risk. However, the structural approach enables us to measure the default correlation between two firms indirectly, using their asset correlations and their individual probabilities of default. Oldrich Vasicek and Stephen Kealhofer at KMV pioneered this application of structural modeling to the problem of indirectly modeling default correlation by looking directly at the relationship of two firms' asset values to their respective default points. The historical correlation between the two firms' asset values can be empirically measured by first converting their equity values to asset values (as described in Chapter 3) and then using these asset values to calculate correlation. We build this model of correlation by developing an estimate of the probability that both firms' asset values jointly fall below their respective default points based on the distributions of asset values and their correlation. In this way, the default correlation estimation challenge is pushed back to the more tractable estimation of the two firms' asset value movements.

Figure 8.2 illustrates the ranges of possible future asset values for two different firms. The two intersecting lines represent the default points for the two firms. For instance, if Firm 1's asset value (x-axis) ends up being below $180 million (the point represented by the vertical line), then Firm

Default and Nondefault Ranges

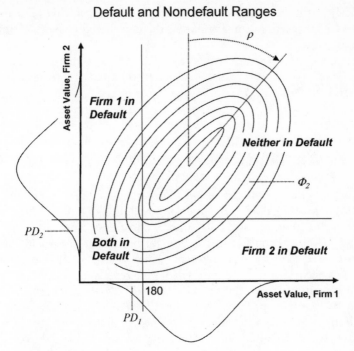

FIGURE 8.2 Default and Nondefault Ranges

1 will default. The intersecting lines divide the range of possibilities into four regions. The upper right region represents those asset values for which neither Firm 1 nor Firm 2 will default. The lower left region represents those asset values for which both will default. The probabilities of all these regions taken together must equal one.

If the asset values of the two firms are independent, then the probabilities of the regions would be determined simply by multiplying the individual probabilities of default and nondefault for the two firms. For instance, suppose that Firm 1's default probability is 0.6 percent and Firm 2's is 0.3 percent. Then the probability of both defaulting, if they are independent, is the product of the default probabilities, or 0.0018 percent. If the two firms' asset values are positively correlated, then the probability of both asset values being high or low at the same time is higher than if they were independent, and the probability of one being high and the other low is lower. For instance, using the previous default probabilities, the probability of both defaulting might now be 0.01 percent, if their asset values are positively correlated.

What is the default correlation that is implied by this joint default? Using basic properties of probabilities, the correlation of two defaults, ρ_D, is given as:[5]

$$\rho_D = \frac{cpd_{X \wedge Y} - cpd_X cpd_Y}{\sigma_X^{cpd} \sigma_Y^{cpd}}$$

where

$$\sigma_X^{cpd} = \sqrt{cpd_X[1 - cpd_X]} \quad \text{and} \quad \sigma_Y^{cpd} = \sqrt{cpd_Y[1 - cpd_Y]}$$

and $cpd_{X \wedge Y}$ is the probability of both Firm 1 (X) and Firm 2 (Y) defaulting in the same period—that is, the joint probability of default.

(Note the addition of the D subscript in the notation for correlation and the cpd superscript in the notation for both correlation and volatility. These are used to distinguish these quantities as they apply to default from the more typical use in the text in which they refer to firm assets.)

This equation shows that the correlation of two default events is defined entirely by the values of the probabilities of the individual events and by the probability of joint default. Thus, given a pair of unconditional probabilities of default and a probability of joint default, we can calculate the correlation of any two default events.

By knowing the individual firms' estimated default probabilities, and knowing an estimate of the correlation of their asset values, the probability of both defaulting at the same time can also be estimated. As described in Chapter 3, the time series of a firm's asset values can be determined from its equity values. By assuming a joint distribution such as bivariate normal, Φ_2 (see box), we can develop an estimate of two firms' joint default probability based on the default probabilities of each firm and the correlation in the assets of the two firms. The correlation between two firms' asset values can be calculated from their respective time series. While this is reasonable as a first pass at a correlation estimator, historical estimation of correlation turns out not to be the best approach for estimating asset correlation. In the next section, we go into more detail about how to arrive at a more robust estimate of firm asset-value correlations. Again, the challenge lies in disentangling the systematic from the idiosyncratic components.

---

[5] See Lucas (1995, 2006) for a more detailed discussion and an empirical application to calculating default correlation based on these relationships as well as for intuitive Venn diagram representations of default correlation.

BIVARIATE NORMAL FUNCTION

Often the bivariate normal is our workhorse distribution for modeling joint behavior. While many data processes appear to be jointly normal, this assumption is sometimes tenuous in finance applications. That said, the mathematical flexibility of the bivariate normal continues to make it useful. The bivariate distribution function is given as:

$$\Phi_2(x_1, x_2, \mu_1, \mu_2, \sigma_1, \sigma_2, \rho) = \frac{1}{2\pi\sigma_1\sigma_2\sqrt{1-\rho^2}} e^{-\frac{b}{2(1-\rho^2)}}$$

where

$$b = \frac{(x_1 - \mu_1)^2}{\sigma_1^2} + \frac{(x_2 - \mu_2)^2}{\sigma_2^2} - \frac{2\rho(x_1 - \mu_1)(x_2 - \mu_2)}{\sigma_1^2\sigma_2^2}$$

In the case of standard normal distributions,* we can simplify this notation to

$$\Phi_2(z_1, z_2, \rho) = \frac{1}{2\pi\sqrt{1-\rho^2}} e^{-\frac{z_1^2 + z_2^2 - 2\rho z_1 z_2}{2(1-\rho^2)}}$$

*A standard normal variable has a mean of zero and a variance of one. Thus, if $x \sim \Phi(\mu, \sigma^2)$, the standardized value of (x, z) is given as $z = \frac{(x-\mu)}{\sigma}$.

The mathematical components for calculating default correlation include the following:

$\Phi^{-1}(\cdot) \equiv$ inverse normal distribution function

$\rho_A \equiv$ correlation of Firm 1's asset value and Firm 2's asset value

$jpd = \Phi_2\left(\Phi^{-1}(cpd_1), \Phi^{-1}(cpd_2), \rho_A\right) \equiv$ joint default probability of Firm 1 and Firm 2—that is, actual probability of both firms defaulting together. This is the joint normal equivalent to $cpd_{X \wedge Y}$ mentioned earlier.

With these in hand, we can calculate ρ_D, as before:

$$\rho_D = \frac{jpd - cpd_1 cpd_2}{\sqrt{cpd_1(1 - cpd_1)\, cpd_2(1 - cpd_2)}}$$

$\equiv$ default correlation for Firm 1 and Firm 2

The numerator of this formula represents the difference of the actual probability of both firms defaulting and the probability of both defaulting if they were independent. Note that if the asset values are independent (i.e., $jpd = cpd_1 cpd_2$), then the default correlation is zero.

In practice, we typically need to extend this basic model to handle not only the correlation in the default behavior of the assets in a portfolio, but also the correlation in the *value* of these assets. This extension moves us into a model framework that assumes credit migration—in other words, a change in value not necessarily associated with the event of default. The default state corresponds to a particularly low realization for the value of a loan or bond issued by the defaulted firm. In addition to a model of credit migration for the securities in the portfolio, this extension requires estimation of the *joint value distribution* between each pair of *credit-risky assets* in the portfolio. In this way, the correlated credit migration over time can be captured to determine a more accurate measure of possible losses in the future since we incorporate both losses due to default and credit losses due to deterioration of credit quality prior to default. Before we discuss how to estimate security value correlation, we first consider how to model credit migration.

CREDIT MIGRATION

If we assume a range of values in the nondefault state at horizon, each implying different valuations, then to model changes in value accurately, we must model the dynamics of the migration to different states. In the context of a portfolio model, we are looking for both an expected path for the security's value (i.e., a mean) and an expected distribution of values conditional on the firm ending up in the nondefault state at the horizon date. In the structural framework, we link the normalized market leverage, the distance to default, and the value of a credit exposure.[6]

Thus, DD becomes a primary component of analysis. By focusing on the conditional distribution of DD at the horizon date (assuming no default), we can develop a model of credit migration. Once we know the terminal state of an exposure at the horizon, we can use the resulting DD to value the exposure, as discussed in Chapter 3. Because the valuation process for defaulted securities is distinct from that of the securities of solvent firms, we find it useful to model the security's value in the default state separately.

In the default state, the exposure value is a function of the assumed recovery process. LGD can be characterized in a number of ways (see

---

[6] This approach, based on the dynamics of DD, was developed at KMV (now MKMV).

Chapter 5). However, in settings where we are performing simulation, it is sometimes convenient to start with approximations. As a first approximation, we can assume that loss given default (LGD, or 1 − recovery) follows a beta distribution (refer to Chapter 5 on LGD for details), $B(\alpha, \beta)$ with an expected value of L. We choose this function given its flexibility to represent a range of possible distributional states. Consider, for example, that by changing the parameters of the beta distribution, we can achieve either a bimodal outcome that reflects a high likelihood of receiving nothing in default or receiving back all the principal or a symmetric rounded distribution that assigns a reasonable level of probability across all possible LGD outcomes; both of which represent shapes that match some samples of loss data. With these parameters and definitions, we arrive at the density function used to generate an LGD realization in the default state:

$$f(L; \alpha, \beta) = \frac{L^{\alpha-1}(1-L)^{\beta-1}}{B(\alpha, \beta)}$$

which we use to value all instruments that have defaulted at the horizon.

It is the nondefault state where the credit migration model is more difficult to specify. In the nondefault states, a credit migration model requires us to map possible realizations of DD to a value of the exposure. The problem can be restated as one of estimating the distribution of possible values for the exposure (and the mean) of this distribution. The overall expected value at horizon should be driven by the term structure of PDs. Either structural or reduced-form models are good candidates to estimate this term structure. The volatility around this mean can be more difficult to estimate. While it would be best to build this distribution with the assumptions of a particular model, our experience is that empirically calibrated DD-transition densities do a better job capturing the actual likelihood of dramatic change in credit quality.

A structural model can be used by calibrating it to transitions in ratings or DDs. In Chapter 6 on reduced-form models, we discussed transition-probability matrices typically calibrated to data on changes in agency ratings over time. One approach to modeling credit migration is to use such matrices. In this case, we can make use of ratings transition matrices to determine the conditional evolution of the value of portfolio exposures. However, the high degree of discreteness in the matrices and the lack of time homogeneity in them can make transition agency ratings-based matrices less attractive for some applications. Without sufficient granularity in the states, it can become difficult to distinguish which exposures are most beneficial to the portfolio. This discreteness also tends to produce jumps in value as the process transitions from one state to another. In addition, the lack of time homogeneity in the matrices can create difficulties when comparing exposures of different maturities.

Some of these shortcomings can be addressed with matrices based on market-implied PDs (e.g., equity-based or CDS-based) by constructing similar transition matrices. In this case, instead of an agency rating, an equity-based PD or CDS spread is used as a measure of credit quality. Even here, though, the lack of granularity (high level of discreteness) still makes transition matrices somewhat unattractive. A better option is to consider estimating *transition densities*, which are essentially transition matrices where the number of states is infinite instead of 8 or 21.

Conceptually, transition densities fit well with the framework we have developed. Unfortunately, we do not have much theoretical guidance on how to characterize these distributions. In our own work with this model, we have sometimes used the normal distribution to characterize the transition density. To do this, we assume that the probabilities associated with landing in different DD buckets (i.e., different credit qualities that will lead to a different value of each credit-risky security) at the horizon date are described by a normal distribution. Since we will need to calibrate to a particular term structure of PDs (that is a function of the term structure of DDs), we need to ensure that the expected path of the security's value follows the input PD term structure, so the normal distribution's mean, in this case, must be shifted to match this parameterization. The variance around that mean will be governed by this distribution. Essentially, we must estimate a family of transition densities that are conditional on where each security's value (i.e., PD level and DD level) starts.

Unfortunately (from an ease-of-implementation perspective), though mathematically tractable, the normal distribution does not appear to put enough probability into dropping into lower grades. The result is an unusually high probability of migrating to a high credit grade, which in turn results in an upward bias in value at the horizon.

A simple example will illustrate this problem. Assume we are modeling the credit migration of a loan to a medium-quality obligor (i.e., PD is around 0.50 percent and the security has a rating of Baa). Assume that this obligor's DD is around 3.5. In a portfolio analysis context, we now need to understand the likelihood that this obligor will migrate to different credit qualities (i.e., different DDs) by the horizon date, say one year out. The simple distributional assumption we have been discussing implies a normal distribution of DDs at the horizon date conditional on starting at a DD of 3.5. We also need to ensure that this conditional distribution is consistent with the term structure of PDs for this obligor, which is likely to be slightly upwardly sloping because the forward PDs tend to rise (see Chapter 3).

In practice, the normal distribution assumption results in too much probability assigned to landing in a higher DD bucket because the conditional DD distributions for investment grade credits are much more skewed with more probability density (relative to the normal) associated with moving to smaller DD levels—that is, higher PDs and lower security values. The result is that for this crossover obligor, we will overestimate the likelihood that it will become very high quality (i.e., PD of 0.01 percent or rating of Aaa).

Part of the difficulty arises from the complex relationship between a firm's market value of assets and the firm's default point. Since a firm's market value of assets tends to be correlated with its default point (refer to the discussion in Chapter 3), the conditional DD distribution is much more skewed than a normal distribution in practice. Under the normal, the probability of moving from a DD of 3.5 to a DD of 0.5 is low. However, the joint movement of asset value and default point together may result in a much higher probability of that kind of substantial change in DD value. Thus, the normal distribution places too much probability weight on improving relative to deteriorating. The difficulty here is similar to the one faced when converting DDs into PDs (again refer to Chapter 3 for detail). Without theoretical guidance, we return to an empirical characterization (as we did for mapping DDs into PDs) of the transition density: We call these *DD transition densities*.

For single-obligor risk, we discussed using empirical default data to specify an empirical DD to PD mapping. In an analogous manner, we can use historical data to estimate empirical DD transition densities. These densities facilitate proper calibration of the conditional forward PD term structure conditioned on the particular DD draw arising from each iteration of the simulation, and they better reflect actual probabilities of migrating to different credit states. This approach minimizes the tendency of structural models to overestimate the probabilities of improving to a near-risk-free state.

Empirically, DD transition density functions are skewed (i.e., starting from a low DD state or high default probability leads to a relatively higher likelihood of improving in credit quality, and starting from a high DD state or low default probability leads to a relatively higher likelihood of deteriorating in credit quality). This makes them better suited to accurately model firm transitions than, say, the simpler normal assumption. The transition densities are typically conditional on the one-year DDs at the as-of date and calculated for the horizon period. In theory (and with enough of the relevant data), a richer set of conditioning characteristics would be better. For example, we might condition on industry or country. Later in this chapter, we return to our discussion of DD transitions and provide a hypothetical example of the transition densities visually in Figure 8.6.

ESTIMATING DD TRANSITION DENSITIES

The conceptual approach to estimating DD transition densities is straightforward:*

1. Use a structural model to construct DD values for a large sample of firms. Typically, we prefer at least 10 years of data for a diverse sample of firms with at least 1,000 firms.
2. Starting at the beginning of the sample, group firms into a reasonable number (e.g., 25 to 50) of DD buckets. We have had good luck using buckets that run from 0 to 16 incremented by 0.5, which produces 32 DD buckets. (Recall that negative DDs are considered to be in default.)
3. Track each group (a *group* is defined here as consisting of firms in a particular DD interval) over a subsequent time period, such as one, three, or five years (note that data limitations will dictate the time horizons that can be credibly estimated), and record the *new* DD for each firm at the end of the time horizon. Repeat this process for the entire sample time series (e.g., record the DD three years later for each firm that started with a DD of 0.5).
4. Collect these results and build a frequency distribution. From here, the density can be fit (often nonparametrically) to the frequency distributions for each DD interval.

This process conditions only on starting DD level. With more data, one can conceivably add other conditioning dimensions. For example, one might want to estimate DD transition densities for different countries, industries, or company size groups.

*This approach was originally pioneered by KMV (now MKMV).

Once we have the empirical DD densities, we have a meaningful characterization of credit migration. These densities can also be used to value credit-risky exposures in the context of a *lattice model*, discussed later in this chapter, and can be incorporated into simulation algorithms to estimate a portfolio loss distribution. We discuss the simulation approach in a later section as well.

A MODEL OF VALUE CORRELATION

An important strength of the structural model of default presented here is its ability to generalize relationships in a way to create a comprehensive credit portfolio model. In addition to the cumulative probability of default (cpd) values for each firm, the joint probability of default (*jpd*) must be calculated to determine a value correlation. In the context of the structural model already explained, the jpd can be calculated by focusing on the relationship between a firm's market asset value and its respective default point. The cpd values capture this information on an individual firm level. The remaining piece of the puzzle is the correlation, ρ_A, between the firms' market asset values.

Pairwise Correlations

A number of applications require knowledge of pairwise correlations. Estimating pairwise asset correlations for publicly traded firms can be done in a number of ways. One method is to calculate a time series of asset values for each firm and then calculate the (Pearson) sample correlation between each pair of asset value series. While this method seems reasonable in theory, in practice it is the least effective way to calculate correlations for credit portfolio modeling. To see why, consider that for portfolio purposes, we are most interested diversifying away the idiosyncratic risk and thus we concentrate on the remaining systematic co-movement. Thus our focus is on efficiently estimating this co-movement over a subsequent time horizon. Because the movement in a typical firm's asset value is mostly driven by factors idiosyncratic to that firm, sample correlations will reflect co-movement that is unique to that sample period. This type of estimate is not very useful for predicting *ex ante* correlation over a subsequent time horizon. Given this (and the data problems that can arise as a result of there not always being a sufficient number of observations to even calculate sample correlations), we turn to factor modeling to calculate correlations. Factor models also turn out to be far more computationally efficient for practical applications.

Factor Models

Correlation (that we can observe) can be considered a consequence of the co-movement in the systematic or nondiversifiable components of the economy that drive changes in asset value. Factor models link these components. For example, the entire economy may follow a business cycle, which affects most companies' prospects. The impact may differ from company to company, but they are affected nonetheless. Determining the sensitivity of changes in asset values to changes in a particular economic factor provides the basis for estimating asset correlation.

Changes in a firm's asset value constitute an asset value return or firm return. We can decompose this return schematically as follows:

$$\begin{bmatrix} \text{Firm} \\ \text{Return} \end{bmatrix} = \begin{bmatrix} \text{Composite} \\ \text{Factor} \\ \text{Return} \end{bmatrix} + \begin{bmatrix} \text{Firm-} \\ \text{Specific} \\ \text{Return} \end{bmatrix}$$

The composite factor return proxies for the systematic risk factors in the economy. There are various approaches to estimating this component. We will focus on one popular approach developed by KMV in which we can further decompose this factor return as follows:

$$\begin{bmatrix} \text{Composite} \\ \text{Factor} \\ \text{Return} \end{bmatrix} = \begin{bmatrix} \text{Country} \\ \text{Factor} \\ \text{Returns} \end{bmatrix} + \begin{bmatrix} \text{Industry} \\ \text{Factor} \\ \text{Returns} \end{bmatrix}$$

$$\begin{bmatrix} \text{Country} \\ \text{Factor} \\ \text{Return} \end{bmatrix} = \begin{bmatrix} \text{Global} \\ \text{Economic} \\ \text{Effect} \end{bmatrix} + \begin{bmatrix} \text{Regional} \\ \text{Factor} \\ \text{Effect} \end{bmatrix} + \begin{bmatrix} \text{Sector} \\ \text{Factor} \\ \text{Effect} \end{bmatrix} + \begin{bmatrix} \text{Country-} \\ \text{Specific} \\ \text{Effect} \end{bmatrix}$$

$$\begin{bmatrix} \text{Industry} \\ \text{Factor} \\ \text{Return} \end{bmatrix} = \begin{bmatrix} \text{Global} \\ \text{Economic} \\ \text{Effect} \end{bmatrix} + \begin{bmatrix} \text{Regional} \\ \text{Factor} \\ \text{Effect} \end{bmatrix} + \begin{bmatrix} \text{Sector} \\ \text{Factor} \\ \text{Effect} \end{bmatrix} + \begin{bmatrix} \text{Industry-} \\ \text{Specific} \\ \text{Effect} \end{bmatrix}$$

Firm-asset correlation can then be calculated from each firm's systematic or composite factor return. This is similar in many respects to the multifactor versions of the capital asset pricing model (CAPM). In this way, we relate the systematic components of changes in asset value, which produces a better estimate of future co-movements in asset values. Note that the manner in which the systematic component is decomposed into its constituent drivers is not as important as the underlying data used to estimate the underlying systematic behavior. The method of decomposition is related to how the systematic co-movement can be most easily explained.

Importantly, regardless of how large the portfolio becomes, the correlation calculation using a factor model scales linearly in the portfolio's size since each firm's asset values are correlated through the common factor model. Correlation between firms occurs due to their common dependence on the same factors rather than through the direct (pairwise) correlation between their individual asset values. For example, calculating pairwise correlations for a portfolio with 5,000 borrowers would require (5,000 × 4,999)/2 ≈ 12.5 million correlations. In contrast, calculating the correlation using a factor model would only require at most 5,000 vectors of factor loadings being calculated on the same portfolio, about 0.04 percent of the pairwise case.[7] In practice, since most firms do not load on all factors, the number of required calculations will be much lower.

Now consider how we might construct the underlying industry and country indexes to use as factors in the decomposition we outlined before. These industry and country indexes can be produced from aggregations of individual firm market asset values for publicly traded firms (e.g., estimated from their traded equity prices together with each firm's liability information). For most robust results, we recommend including at least 15,000 traded firms from around the globe.

The indexes estimated from these data are used to create a *composite factor index* for each firm depending on its country and industry classifications. Mathematically, the following relationship is constructed:

$$w_{kc} \equiv \text{weight of firm } k \text{ in country } c$$

$$w_{ki} \equiv \text{weight of firm } k \text{ in industry } i$$

[Note that $\sum_{c=1}^{C} w_{kc} = \sum_{i=1}^{I} w_{ki} = 1$ where C is the number of countries for which factors are calculated in the sample (typically between 40 and 50) and I is the number of industries in the sample (typically between 40 and 80).]

$r_c \equiv$ asset return index for country c (estimated from publicly traded firms)

$r_i \equiv$ asset return index for industry I (estimated from publicly traded firms)

$\phi_k \equiv$ composite (custom) market factor index for firm k

$$\phi_k = \sum_{c=1}^{C} w_{kc} r_c + \sum_{i=1}^{I} w_{ki} r_i$$

Once the custom index is calculated for a particular firm (we discuss in more detail how to construct custom indexes later in this chapter), the

---

[7] A more accurate comparison would take account of the fact that calculating correlations and calculating factor decompositions and loadings require different computational operations.

sensitivity (i.e., beta) to the market factors reflected in this index can be estimated. It is important to note that any type of index can be constructed as long as it captures the drivers of the systematic movement in each firm's asset values. The approach described here is one that works reasonably well. The relationship used for this estimation is written as follows:

$$r_k \equiv \text{return for firm } k$$

$$\beta_k \equiv \text{beta for firm } k$$

$$\varepsilon_k \equiv \text{firm-specific component of return for firm } k$$

Thus:

$$r_k = \beta_k \phi_k + \varepsilon_k$$

We can similarly estimate the sensitivity or beta ($\beta_{c,F}$ and $\beta_{i,F}$) of countries and industries on common factors, F, that we specify. For example, we might choose two global factors, five regional factors, and seven sectoral factors; since industry and country-specific factors may exist (i.e., those not linked through the 14 common factors), the model might use country- and industry-specific factors. An example of calculating the sensitivity of firm k to a global common factor, G, is given as:

$$\beta_{kG} = \beta_k \left(\sum_{c=1}^{C} w_{kc} \beta_{cG} + \sum_{i=1}^{I} w_{ki} \beta_{iG} \right)$$

This calculation produces the parameters necessary to estimate the firm asset value correlation. We can develop this further as follows:

$$\sigma_{jk} \equiv \text{covariance between firm } j \text{ and firm } k$$

$$\rho_{jk} \equiv \text{correlation between firm } j\text{'s and firm } k\text{'s asset value returns}$$

$$\sigma_k \equiv \text{standard deviation of firm } k\text{'s asset value return}$$

$$\sigma_{jk} = \sum_{G=1}^{2} \beta_{jG} \beta_{kG} \sigma_G^2 + \sum_{R=1}^{\bar{R}} \beta_{jR} \beta_{kR} \sigma_R^2 + \sum_{S=1}^{\bar{S}} \beta_{jS} \beta_{kS} \sigma_S^2$$

$$+ \sum_{i=1}^{\bar{c}} \beta_{jc} \beta_{kc} \sigma_c^2 + \sum_{i=1}^{\bar{i}} \beta_{ji} \beta_{ki} \sigma_i^2$$

$$
\begin{bmatrix} \text{Return} \\ \text{Covariance} \\ j \text{ and } k \end{bmatrix} = \begin{bmatrix} \text{Global} \\ \text{Economic} \\ \text{Factors}(G) \end{bmatrix} + \begin{bmatrix} \text{Regional} \\ \text{Economic} \\ \text{Factors}(R) \end{bmatrix} + \begin{bmatrix} \text{Industrial} \\ \text{Sector} \\ \text{Factors}(S) \end{bmatrix}
$$

$$
+ \begin{bmatrix} \text{Country--} \\ \text{Specific} \\ \text{Factors}(c) \end{bmatrix} + \begin{bmatrix} \text{Industry--} \\ \text{Specific} \\ \text{Factors}(i) \end{bmatrix}
$$

$$
\begin{bmatrix} \text{Return} \\ \text{Correlation} \\ j \text{ and } k \end{bmatrix} = \frac{\begin{bmatrix} \text{Return} \\ \text{Covariance} \\ j \text{ and } k \end{bmatrix}}{\begin{bmatrix} \text{Return} \\ \text{Volatility } j \end{bmatrix}\begin{bmatrix} \text{Return} \\ \text{Volatility } k \end{bmatrix}}
$$

The covariance calculation depends on the sensitivities or betas ($\beta_{Company, Factor}$) for each firm combined with the factor variances (σ^2_{Factor}). To arrive at the correlation we must scale the covariance by the standard deviation of the returns as shown in the final equation of the preceding group.

Simply said, the factor model focuses attention on the components driving co-movements. These components can be separated into the effects previously listed; however, the important aspect of this process is identifying the total systematic component. To the extent that it is correctly estimated, the subsequent decomposition into constituent effects is only necessary for gaining *intuition* about the source of correlation between any two firms. This approach relies on the embedded systematic components reflected in the data on publicly traded firms around the world.

Returning to the jpd calculation, if we combine this asset value correlation with the individual firm cpd values and an assumption about the distribution, we arrive at a default correlation. However, while default correlation is sufficient to model a two-state world (default/nondefault), if we wish to model possible credit migration over our horizon of analysis, we need to calculate not only the jpd but also the joint version of the DD dynamics implied values among all of the assets in the portfolio. Explicitly calculating this relationship requires calculation of a double integral (over all possible firm asset values) for each pair of firms in the portfolio.

For most sizable credit portfolios, this approach is computationally cost prohibitive. Instead, we can again make use of the factor structure previously explained to construct a Monte Carlo simulation, which draws the individual factors over and over again to sample the possible portfolio value realizations. Each of these portfolio value realizations embeds the loan

EXPLAINING THE SYSTEMATIC COMPONENT DRIVING CORRELATION

As we have emphasized, the data from which a factor model is estimated reflects the underlying correlation structure of the firms' asset values. Once we have extracted the systematic component in this framework, we also need to build a decomposition that improves our intuition of what is driving this systematic risk.

One approach is to use Gram-Schmidt orthogonalization (sometimes called Gram-Schmidt construction: see Cantrell 2000 for more detail). The idea is to choose one vector to start (e.g., a particular index of interest) and then subtract the projection of that vector from each of the other vectors. This can be done by simple regression of the asset-value return time series on the first index. Then choose a second vector and repeat the process using the residuals of the previous regression until a desired set of vectors or orthogonalized indexes is achieved. In general, an analyst will want to look across dimensions such as the following: macro-economic, sector, industry, region, and country.

This process will provide insight into what is driving the systematic risk. Note that, except for perfectly orthogonal industries, regions, and the like (which do not occur in practice), the order in which this orthogonalization is done matters. To the extent a particular industry effect is picked up by one vector or index, it will not show up later when another index is extracted. In any case, the resulting sensitivities will provide an idea of which characteristics of the firm are resulting in its systematic behavior from an asset-value perspective. By decomposing the drivers of co-movement into dimensions that are easily understood, a portfolio manager as well as a bank executive can understand better the specific sources of concentration risk in the portfolio. Without this kind of decomposition, the discussion of systematic risk and correlation deteriorates into a morass of difficult-to-interpret statistics.

value correlations since each loan value is calculated based on its DD state at the horizon and this in turn is based on the relationship of each firm's asset value to the systematic factors. These asset values derive from the sensitivity to each of the common risk factors.

A simple example makes this process clearer. Assume we are analyzing a portfolio of three loans to three different companies. We determine that the asset values of company A and company B increase (decrease) whenever interest rates decline (rise). Company C is unaffected by changes in interest rates. In this economy, we have only one factor—interest rate movement. We then simulate this one factor. Whenever this interest rate factor is high, A's and B's asset values are small. These low asset values result in the loans to A and B being valued at a discount; C's loan value is unchanged, since C is not affected by the interest rate factor. If the interest rate factor is low, A's and B's loans will be valued at a premium. The key to the correlation arises from the similar behavior in loan value whenever a particular factor level is drawn.

Clearly, the movements in the value of A's and B's loans are correlated while C's loans are uncorrelated with the rest of the portfolio. The process of simulating different factor realizations generates a sample of portfolio value realizations, one for each path simulated. These value realizations can then be transformed into a loss distribution. The extent to which loan values move together links back to the sensitivities to the different risk factors in the factor model.

PROBABILITY OF LARGE LOSSES

We are all familiar with the properties of the normal distribution from our introductory statistics courses. If portfolio losses had such unimodal, symmetrical distributions, we could accurately specify the probability of large losses simply by knowing the expected and unexpected loss for the portfolio. The problem is that individual debt assets have very *skewed* loss distributions. Most of the time the borrower does not default and the loss is zero. However, when default does occur, the loss is usually substantial. Given the positive correlation between defaults, this unevenness of loss never fully smoothes out, even in large portfolios. There is always a large probability of relatively small losses, and a small probability of rather large losses.

This skewness leads to an unintuitive result: A very high percentage of the time (say 80 percent), the *actual* losses will be less than the average loss (expected loss). The reason is that the average is pulled upwards by the potential for large losses. There is a great danger of being lulled by a string of low losses into believing that the portfolio is more diversified than it actually is.

Fortunately, however, from an analytic perspective, the frequency distribution of portfolio losses can be determined using the information we have already discussed. Knowing this distribution for a given portfolio gives an alternative characterization of diversification: Portfolio A is better diversified than portfolio B if the probability of loss exceeding a given percent is smaller for A than for B, and both portfolios have the same expected loss.

Figure 8.3 contrasts the loan loss distribution we would estimate for a credit portfolio using a normal assumption ("bell-shaped") with a loss distribution having the same EL and UL but assuming correlated defaults. This example is similar to credit portfolios that are typical of many large financial institutions. There are two striking differences in the distributions. The most obvious is that the actual loan loss distribution is asymmetric. There is a small probability of large losses and a large probability of small losses. If losses were determined per the normal distribution, then losses would exceed the expected loss about half the time, and the other half of the time they would be less than the expected loss. For the actual loss distribution, realized losses will be less than the expected loss approximately 75 percent of the time. There is a significant likelihood that even a risky portfolio will generate consecutive years of low realized losses.

The second major difference is that the probability of very large losses approaches zero much more quickly for the normal distribution than for the skewed distribution. In fact, for a portfolio with a skewed loss distribution there is an economically significant chance of realized losses that are six to eight standard deviations in excess of the expected loss. For the normal distribution, there is virtually no chance of a four standard deviation event occurring (less than one half of one basis point). This relatively high

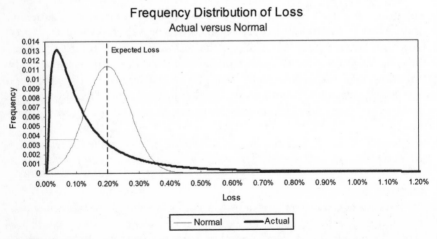

FIGURE 8.3   Frequency Distribution of Loss: Actual versus Normal Losses

probability of large losses highlights the diversification benefit of adding another low-correlation exposure into a portfolio with a skewed loss distribution. As more of these low-correlation exposures are added to the portfolio, the degree of skew and density in the tail will slowly fall, though, again, due to common systematic factors, the skewness we persist even for very large numbers of loans.

Figure 8.4 contrasts two loan loss distributions for different portfolios. The two portfolios have the same level of expected loss, but portfolio A has a higher average asset correlation (lower diversification) and thus a higher unexpected loss. In loss terms there is a significantly higher chance of incurring a large loss in portfolio A than in portfolio B. These probabilities can be seen by looking at the areas under the respective curves. For instance, the probability of a 4 percent loss in portfolio A is 0.1 percent, but the probability of a 4 percent loss in portfolio B is only 0.05 percent.

This view of diversification has an immediate concrete implication for capital adequacy. Given the frequency distribution of loss, we can determine the likelihood of losses that exceed the amount of capital held against the portfolio. This probability can be set to the desired level by varying the amount of capital a financial institution retains. For example, a bank targeting an Aa1 rating would retain the necessary capital to ensure that the probability of the portfolio losing more than the capital amount were consistent with an Aa1 probability of default and expected loss.

To illustrate how this can be done in practice, it is necessary to consider the market value, rather than the book value, of the portfolio. To do that,

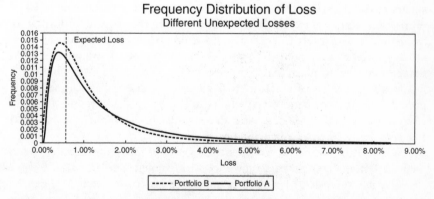

FIGURE 8.4 Frequency Distribution of Loss: Different Unexpected Losses

we need to be able to determine the current market value of a security. Ideally, we would use data from a deep and liquid market in the security we are modeling. In the case of most bonds and loans, though, the markets are typically neither deep nor liquid. While the increasing liquidity in the CDS market provides a new, useful source of data regarding valuation of many corporate debt instruments, for most large portfolios of corporate debt, we must still rely on models to determine a mark-to-market value. We next consider this challenge for the case of determining a value for a loan.

VALUATION

Credit portfolio analysis requires a model for valuation. Tracking changes in a portfolio's market value is key to managing a portfolio and evaluating a portfolio manager's performance. While an actual market price of a particular debt instrument or contract is always preferred at the starting date of analysis, a model is typically used to generate values conditional on simulated states of the world at the time horizon of analysis as we discussed earlier in this chapter.

When direct prices are not available, equity and CDS prices can be used to estimate the key drivers of value for many kinds of credit-risky corporate instruments. In particular, equity provides a *clean* estimate (i.e., separated from loss given default and a market risk premium) of a firm's default probability. CDS prices provide an estimate of risk-neutral expected loss; however, a model is needed to break apart the default probability, the LGD, and the market premium that drives the expected loss. Chapter 5 presents a number of alternatives for estimating LGD (also see the discussion of risk-neutral versus physical LGD). That said, a simple estimate for LGD such as 50 or 60 percent is often a starting point for extracting the requisite information from the CDS market. Chapters 3 and 6 on structural and reduced-form models, respectively, present the details for a variety of valuation models that can be used to mark loans to market.

In all, the value of a credit-risky security requires specification of expected cash flows, a default probability, a loss given default, and a market risk premium. In the case of most cash instruments, the implicit default-risk-free security is taken as a benchmark.

With this background, consider the process of modeling a security with credit risk in the context of a simple loan instrument.

The market price of a loan is simply the price for which it can be bought or sold. Although there is a loan sales market, loans by and large are not actively transacted for extended periods. The result is that current market prices do not exist for most loans and when market prices do exist, they are often clouded with liquidity effects. The objective of valuation is to determine at what price a loan would sell, were it to trade. The value cannot be determined in some absolute sense, but only by comparison to the market prices of other financial instruments that are traded. Valuation consists of extrapolating actual market prices to nontraded assets, based on the relationship between their characteristics. In the case of loans, the process involves consideration of the borrower's traded equity, CDSs available on that borrower, and traded debt (should it exist). Bank instruments also involve a variety of complexities: default risk, utilization, covenants, priority, and so forth. Many of these complexities can be viewed, and valued, as options belonging to the borrower or lender.

To make concrete the basic idea of benchmarking, consider the simple example of an option-free fixed-term, fixed-rate corporate loan. If this loan were not subject to material default risk, then it could be valued readily by comparison with the pricing on similar term Aaa-rated notes since the level of default risk in Aaa-rated notes is very small, making them a good market benchmark. By contrast, Treasury notes, which are assumed to have literally no default risk, are not as good a benchmark for corporate liabilities, due to persistent and unpredictable differences between corporate and government debt issues. The market for U.S. Treasury notes is deep and liquid. Even in times of general market distress, Treasury issues continue to trade smoothly. In contrast, corporate debt can be heavily impacted by market conditions. This liquidity factor causes the difference between Treasury notes and the safest corporate debt to change in a way that is not captured in most of the models used in practice. Thus, in our experience, it is better to use benchmarks that are closer to the corporate debt world.

The so-called pricing on a loan is the set of fees (both up-front and ongoing) and spreads that determines the promised cash flows between borrower and lender which is analogous to the coupon rate on a bond. The value of the loan is obtained by discounting the loan cash flows by an appropriate set of discount rates. The discount rates, in the absence of default risk, would simply differ by increments of term, according to the current term structure of the risk-free curve.

In the presence of default risk, however, the discount rates must contain two additional elements. The first is the expected loss premium. This reflects an adjustment to the discount rate to account for the actuarial expectation of loss. It is based on the (physical) probability of default and the loss given default. The second is the market risk premium. This is compensation for the nondiversifiable loss risk in the loan. If the loan did not contain a risk premium, then on average it would only return the risk-free base rate. The key point is the qualifier: *on average*. In years when *default did not occur*, the loan would return a little more due to the expected loss premium. However, *in the event of default*, it would return much less.

Since an investor could obtain the risk-free base rate not just on average, but all the time, by buying the risk-free asset, the risky asset must provide additional compensatory return. This would not be the case if default risk were completely diversifiable, but (as we have discussed) it is not. The market will provide compensation for unavoidable risk bearing—that is, the portion of the loan's loss risk that cannot be eliminated through diversification. The amount of nondiversifiable risk can be determined from knowledge of the borrower's probability of default and the risk characteristics of the borrower's assets. The market price for risk bearing can be determined from the equity, corporate debt, and CDS markets. This approach, based on option valuation methods, can be used to construct discount rates, specific to the obligor, that correctly account for both the time value of money and the expected and unexpected loss characteristics of the particular borrower. Refer back to Chapter 3 for a discussion of how quantities such as the market price of risk can be estimated.

In the case where a particular CDS can be considered comparable to the implicit CDS in a loan position, the CDS spread can be used to build an appropriate discount rate to arrive at the appropriate, risk-adjusted price of the loan. Unfortunately, practical applications are a bit messier. The LGD assumptions are likely to be different for the loan and the CDS. Moreover, the pricing in the two markets may differ due to a *liquidity premium*. Another possibility (although less defensible) is that the *market risk premium* differs in the loan and CDS markets. In order to resolve these issues and develop more confidence regarding a particular modeled price, we can use a model framework that economically relates each driver of value as we discussed in the context of structural models. Here we will review the approach at a high level from a slightly different perspective, that of return.

There are only two possible outcomes for a loan. Either it is repaid, or the borrower defaults. The loss distribution for a single loan made for one period (assuming that the maturity of the loan and horizon of analysis are the same) is simply:

Event	Probability
Default	cpd
No default	1 − cpd

In the event of default, we expected to lose a percentage of some measure of the face value of the loan equal to L (see Chapter 5 on LGD). If the yield on the loan is y and the risk-free base rate is r_f, then one way the return distribution can be characterized is as follows:

Event	Probability	Return
Default	cpd	$r_f - L$
No default	$1 - \text{cpd}$	y

The expected return is the probability: weighted average of the returns.

$$E(r) = cpd(r_f - L) + (1 - cpd)y$$

The required compensation for the actuarial risk of default is equal to $\frac{L \times cpd}{1 - cpd}$. This is called the expected loss premium. If the loan yield equaled the risk-free base rate plus the expected loss premium, then

$$y = r_f + \frac{L \times cpd}{1 - cpd}$$

and

$$E(r) = cpd(r_f - L) + (1 - cpd)\left(r_f + \frac{L \times cpd}{1 - cpd}\right)$$
$$E(r) = r_f$$

The expected loss premium provides just enough additional return when the borrower does not default to compensate for the expected loss when the borrower does default. The preceding calculation shows that if the only additional compensation were the expected loss premium, then the lender on average would receive only the risk-free base rate. It would be much better for the lender to just lend at the risk-free base rate (e.g., purchase U.S. Treasury bonds), since it would get the same average return and would incur no default risk. There must be additional compensation for the fact that the realized return is risky even for a large, well-diversified portfolio of loans. That additional compensation is called the *risk premium*.

The required pricing on a loan is thus the risk-free base rate plus the expected loss premium plus the risk premium.

$$y = r_f + EL \text{ premium} + \text{risk premium}$$

Subtracting the appropriate EL premium from the credit spread (i.e., spread to r_f) on debt securities or CDSs yields the market risk premium.

If we think of the yield on a loan as being an average of these various discount rates (as yield to maturity is for a bond), then the value of the loan is simply its promised cash flows discounted at its yield. If the yield exceeds the loan rate, then the loan will be priced at a discount that will be just sufficient so that the coupon rate relative to price paid just achieves the market rate of return. An increase in the probability of default will push up the yield required in the market, and push down the price of the loan. Other factors remaining the same, loan value moves inversely to changes in default probability.

By combining data from equity, traded debt, and CDS markets, each driver of value can be estimated to provide a robust tool kit for assigning value to credit-risky exposures found in a credit portfolio. For example, default probabilities can be estimated out of the equity market and LGD can be estimated based on corporate bond loss experience or from a database of historical recovery information. These results can be combined with observed CDS spreads to estimate an implied market risk premium. The art lies in discovering which driver is best estimated in which market. These topics were discussed at length in earlier chapters.

RETURN CALCULATIONS

Thus far, we have introduced the conceptual framework for analyzing credit portfolios from a risk perspective. Of course, risk is only one half of the story in portfolio management. In this section, we identify some specific approaches for calculating and interpreting the other half: the *return* on a portfolio.

Note that the approaches outlined here are not the only ways to calculate meaningful return analytics. That said, the calculations we describe are commonly used by credit portfolio managers today in practice. The conceptual framework is flexible and can serve as a foundation for a variety of calculations, and as an analyst develops more familiarity with the approach, other metrics may suggest themselves for specific settings.

The underlying principle we try to formalize here is that *the return on a credit exposure is the compensation an institution earns for taking credit risk.* The details vary only in how we measure risk and return, how we combine them, and how we benchmark the resulting metrics.

As before, our first step is to determine a time horizon over which to calculate return. Generally, most institutions choose one year as the time horizon since it typically corresponds to the time the institutions estimate they would need to take measures to respond to an extreme loss. For some applications, such as CDO analysis, our time horizon may be as many as 5 or even

10 years, if that is the time over which we are analyzing the performance of the CDO collateral portfolio.

In this framework, we define *return* as the cash payouts plus the expected change in the credit exposure's value (i.e., we add the gain in the security's value or subtract loss in the security's value over the time horizon of analysis). This second part of the return calculation requires us to specify the *migration in value* of the credit exposure in the nondefault states. As discussed earlier, the assumption of credit migration requires us to model the expected value at horizon in the nondefault state.

We now turn to an example of how to calculate return. First, we begin with the value of the asset at the as-of date (i.e., the date we assume to be time 0): V_0. This value will depend on the assumptions used in the analysis; often we assume the book value of the exposure.[8] Next, we determine the expected value at the horizon date, $E[V_H]$. The approach we have emphasized in this chapter decomposes the valuation problem into valuation conditional on the default state, $E[V_H|D]$ and valuation conditional on the nondefault state, $E[V_H|ND]$. We can characterize the calculation of $E[V_H]$ as the probability of default times the value in the default state and the probability of nondefault times the value in the nondefault state, which is determined by expected credit migration. Alternatively, $E[V_H]$ can be calculated as the (probability weighted) sum of any cash flows expected from the as-of date to horizon plus(minus) any expected gain(loss) in the future.

Now we have the components necessary to calculate return: the value at the as-of date, the cash payouts from the as-of date to the horizon date, and the expected value at the horizon date, broken down into the default and nondefault states. One final component that we must calculate in order to isolate the risk premium for a given exposure is the expected loss (EL).

The simpler default-nondefault model assumes maturity equals horizon, resulting in the following intuitive EL calculation: $EL = L \times cpd_H$. When we move to the credit-migration framework, maturity is allowed to exceed the time to horizon, resulting in the following more involved expression:

$$EL = \frac{E[V_H|ND] - E[V_H]}{V_0}$$

---

[8] Alternatively, we can construct a mark-to-market or mark-to-model (MTM) waterfall in which we begin with actual prices if available and then move to generic credit curves or other models when prices are not. The structural and reduced-form models discussed in previous chapters are candidates for choices for this kind of MTM waterfall (see Chapter 9 for an example of such a waterfall).

It is important to emphasize that we normalize the numerator, which reflects the difference in what the creditor receives in the nondefault state less the (probability-adjusted) expected value. (In the simpler case it is already normalized since LGD is given in percentage rather than absolute terms.) The normalization is simply a division by an appropriate measure of exposure size. For typical credit instruments, the as-of date value of the instrument is the appropriate denominator with which to normalize the value. For derivative instruments, the as-of date value is often zero, so we turn to other candidates with which to normalize the value. Two possible such candidates are the maximum exposure over the life of the derivative and the average exposure over the life of the derivative. Conceptually, the calculation is similar; however, comparing return metrics for standard credit instruments such as loans and bonds with return metrics for derivatives can be challenging since they measure potentially different things.

Returning to our discussion of return calculation, we look to calculate a total spread that reflects the premium earned in excess of the risk-free return. If we are comfortable that the term structure of interest rates from the as-of date to the horizon date is reasonably flat, then we can calculate TS as follows:

$$TS = \frac{1}{H} \ln \left(\frac{E[V_H | ND]}{V_0} \right) - r_H$$

(Note that we are using the risk-free rate from the as-of date to the horizon date, which is different than the forward rates referenced in earlier expressions.) This version of the TS calculation can be described as a return-spread calculation in that we look to the value in the nondefault state (including the coupons paid from the as-of date to the horizon date) as the target value and essentially subtract off the risk-free rate to horizon from the expected gain assuming no default.

If, however, we *are* concerned about the shape of the term structure of interest rates from the as-of date to the horizon date, we can use a more complicated formula to extract TS. Basically, we assume a valuation formula in which each future cash flow is discounted by the assumed default-risk-free rate plus the TS. We then solve for the value of TS that satisfies the valuation equation. This TS calculation can be described as the *yield spread* in that we are calculating the spread that satisfies the discounting in much the same way that we calculate a yield to maturity for a bond. The advantage is that we capture the impact of a nonflat term structure from the as-of date to the horizon date. For very short horizons (i.e., less than six months) and when term structure curves are relatively flat, both the return spread and the yield spread will be approximately equal. The return spread calculation is more intuitive, but the yield spread will provide the more accurate characterization of TS.

Note that we have moved beyond a two-state, default-nondefault world and are now developing analytics in the context of a more general framework that assumes credit migration. Effectively, we have decomposed expected return into three analytical components:

1. The difference between the expected return and the return from holding an otherwise default-risk-free security. The difference between the expected return and the risk-free rate is defined as the *total spread* (TS).
2. The *expected loss* (EL) over the time horizon: EL = PD × LGD. (We are assuming away exposure at default, EAD, which is the amount of the total face value exposed at the time of default.) Note again that EL is not considered a measure of portfolio *risk* as the portfolio manager should be provisioning for this expected loss. EL is the primary *cost* of being in the business of taking on credit exposure.
3. The *expected* spread (ES): TS − EL = ES. The expected spread is the premium earned for taking risk associated with an individual credit exposure.

Because a rational investor should demand a premium in excess of the risk-free return and the expected loss, it is natural to seek a way to quantify this, and ES measures just this premium. As we evaluate portfolio performance, we focus on the ES that we earn by taking particular levels of risk. The portfolio ES, ES_P, is the weighted average of all individual exposure ES values, ES_i:

$$ES_P = \sum_i^n w_i ES_i$$

where there are n exposures, each with a portfolio weight of w_i. Similarly, the value of the entire portfolio value at the as-of date (i.e., date of analysis) is the weighted average of the individual exposure values. The ease of aggregating ES makes the return calculations far easier than the risk calculations that we will discuss a bit later. ES becomes a key focus for evaluating portfolios and determining portfolio composition.

RISK CALCULATIONS

Earlier in this chapter, we walked through the conceptual building blocks of modeling portfolio risk. In this section, we return to our discussion of risk to put more mathematical rigor around it. Most performance metrics place the return quantity in the numerator of a ratio and the risk quantity in the denominator of the ratio. Risk measures for credit require more complex calculations given the nature of diversification.

The overall portfolio risk can be understood by evaluating the portfolio loss distribution. In addition, we can use this same structure to assess the *portfolio-referent* measures of individual exposure risk. Recall that portfolio-referent measures evaluate the contribution and value of each individual exposure, *given the other constituents of the portfolio.* It turns out that, because of the great difficulties that we have discussed in constructing and holding the market credit portfolio, most credit portfolios will not look like the market portfolio and thus the incremental value of a specific addition to the portfolio will vary depending on the portfolio structure. We return to this after discussing overall measures of portfolio risk.

One common measure of portfolio risk that we have discussed is *unexpected loss* (UL which is defined as a one standard deviation move in the distribution). Sometimes we refer to UL as the *volatility* of the portfolio distribution. Note that we typically start by estimating a portfolio value distribution and then determine a loss point (e.g., the risk-free value of the portfolio at the horizon date) to calculate the portfolio loss distribution. We usually characterize risk in terms of the loss distribution, but the value distribution can provide all the necessary measures as well. That is, the portfolio loss distribution is a simple transformation of the portfolio value distribution using a particular loss point.

We can calculate a UL for each individual exposure in the portfolio. However, in the case of a diversified portfolio, the risk in the portfolio is less than the average of each asset's stand-alone risk. Some part of each asset's stand-alone risk (i.e., a portion of the idiosyncratic risk) is diversified away in the portfolio. Thinking of it in this way, we can divide the stand-alone risk of an asset into the part that is diversified away and the part that remains. This latter part is the risk contribution of the asset to the portfolio, and the risk of the portfolio is the holdings-weighted sum of these risk contributions.

The residual risk contribution of an asset changes as the composition of the portfolio varies. In particular, as the holding of the asset increases, its risk contribution increases. The percentage of its stand-alone risk that is not being diversified away increases in proportion to the value weight of the asset in the portfolio.

Figure 8.5 shows the loss risk of a single asset. The total height of the bar represents the unexpected loss of the asset. The bottom segment of the bar represents the portion of the unexpected loss that could not be eliminated through diversification even in the broadest possible portfolio. This is called the nondiversifiable, or systemic, risk of the asset. When we speak of the *beta* of an asset, we are referring to the behavior of this portion of an asset's risk.

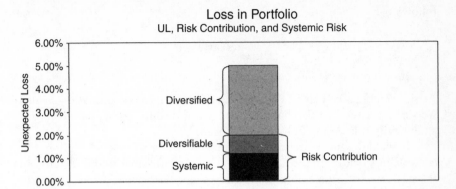

FIGURE 8.5 Loss in Portfolio

In the context of an actual portfolio, diversification is generally less than optimal, and some portion of its risk that could be diversified away has not been. The second segment of the bar represents this portion. The sum of the bottom two segments is the risk contribution of the asset to the portfolio. It represents the risk that has not been diversified away in the portfolio. Some has not been diversified away because it cannot be (the systemic portion); some has not been diversified away because the portfolio is less than optimally diversified.

The portfolio's unexpected loss is simply the holdings-weighted average of the risk contributions (*not* the ULs) of the individual assets. Risk contribution is an appropriate measure of the risk of an asset in a portfolio because it is net of the portion of risk that has been diversified away. As the holdings change, the risk contributions change. For instance, if the proportionate holding of an asset were increased in the portfolio, less of its risk would be diversified away, and the risk contribution would go up.

Systemic risk is measured relative to the whole market for risky assets. Risk contribution in contrast is specific to a particular portfolio: the particular set of assets and the particular proportions in which the assets are held. This means that unlike the case of, say, equity markets, two portfolio managers could agree on the stand-alone risk of a loan but could still disagree on the price that each was willing to pay for the asset since its risk contribution to each manager's portfolio could be different.

Portfolio managers and analysts constantly look at both portfolio-wide risk measures such as portfolio UL and individual exposure risk measures such as exposure UL. To do this, one first places the stand-alone risk on the same scale as that of return by expressing the UL for exposure i as follows:

$$UL = \frac{\sqrt{\text{var}(V_H)}}{V_0}$$

In practice, we often calculate portfolio UL using a simulation, which we discuss later in this chapter. Here we introduce the components for analytically calculating individual exposure UL.

As we did with the return computations, we break the calculation into components conditional on default and then conditional on nondefault. In this case, we focus on conditional variance calculations. In this way, we can analytically calculate the total variance more easily. That is, breaking the calculation into two conditional components—one conditional on default and one conditional on nondefault—we can construct an equation that is easier to estimate and interpret.

First, let us look at variance in the default state, assuming again that the default value is pulled from a beta distribution with parameters α and β and thus mean $L = \alpha/(\alpha + \beta)$. Then the variance in the default state can be parameterized per the beta distribution.

Next, we calculate variance in the nondefault state: In this component, we make use of the mathematical relationship that the conditional variance equals the second moment less the square of the conditional expectation. This reflects what is known as the *law of total variance*.

The second moment requires a specification for the DD-transition densities that we discussed in the credit migration section. (As we indicated before, our recommendation is to estimate these transition densities empirically.) In practice, the extreme DD buckets (e.g., 1 and 12 to 16) suffer from small sample problems so that the empirical density estimate is not nearly as smooth as the others. The key point is to try to make sure the functions do not cross over each other (sometimes, we have to live with some crossover in extreme buckets). The densities give the probability of ending up in a higher DD bucket conditional on starting in a particular bucket (see Figure 8.6).

With these components defined, we need a way to combine the two variances which describe different distributions in the default and non-default states (beta and DD-transition density). This is where the law of total variance is particularly useful. Mathematically we write this result as follows:

$$\sigma_X^2 = E\left[\sigma_{X|Y}^2\right] + \sigma_{E[X|Y]}^2$$

With this mathematical result, we can calculate the variance at horizon for an exposure by characterizing each of the conditional components of the

Example of DD Transition Densities

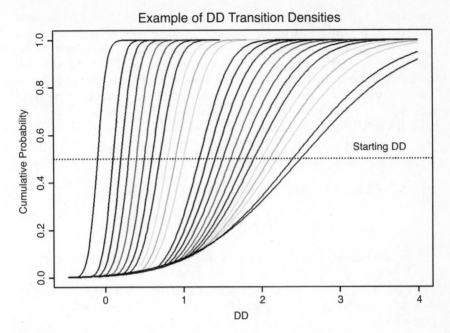

FIGURE 8.6 Example of DD Transition Densities

calculation. The focus is to break apart both the expectation and variance separately for the default state from the nondefault state.

We can calculate the total portfolio's UL from the individual ULs if we have the correlations among all exposures in the portfolio. The UL for two exposures (which is easily generalized to n exposures) is calculated as follows:

$$UL_{ij \in P} = \sqrt{\omega_i^2 UL_i^2 + \omega_j^2 UL_j^2 + 2\omega_i \omega_j \rho_{ij} UL_i UL_j}$$

While it is tempting to conclude that these analytical calculations can form the basis of a portfolio risk model, the size of typical financial institutions' portfolios (usually more than several tens of thousands obligations and as large as several million) make such pairwise (and n-wise) analytics unwieldy. That is why we introduced the factor model for calculating correlations. Rather than calculating the loss distribution analytically, we will use the factor model in the context of a simulation approach. A simulation algorithm does not have the same kind of computational limitations and is much easier to manage. Moreover, a simulation engine facilitates the combination of many categories of asset classes, not just plain vanilla loans and bonds. We will return to the details of the simulation in the next section.

As we evaluate individual exposures, recall that stand-alone UL is not quite as useful for a portfolio manager as portfolio-referent risk measures—that is, measures that reflect the risk of an exposure in the context of a particular portfolio. One important portfolio-referent risk measure that we have been discussing is risk contribution (RC), which measures the post-diversification contribution of an individual exposure to a portfolio's UL. (See Figure 8.5.) Typically, an individual exposure's RC will be less than 50 percent of that exposure's stand-alone UL (the range for large financial institutions' portfolios are typically 5 to 70 percent of individual exposure UL). Now define RC more formally as the following derivative:

$$RC_i = \partial UL_P / \partial \omega_i = \text{cov}(i, P)/UL_P$$

As we highlighted at the start of this chapter, portfolio UL is not a weighted sum of individual exposure UL values—correlation structure impacts this relationship. Risk contribution, by contrast, has the nice property that the weighted sum of individual exposures' RCs does, in fact, equal the portfolio UL:

$$UL_P = \sum_{i=1}^{n} w_i RC_i$$

To gain some intuition for the RC measure, consider the key drivers of RC:

- PD.
- LGD.
- Correlation of exposure i with the rest of the portfolio, P.
- Concentration or exposure weight of exposure i in P.

Obviously, a higher PD or higher LGD will increase RC, all else equal. Correlation directly impacts diversification. Geography and size tend to be dimensions over which correlation is lower, as opposed to industry which is often cited as an important dimension for driving diversification. For example, the RC of a high-yield (i.e., high PD) bond issued by a UK company will likely have a lower RC in a Japanese bank portfolio than will a lower-risk loan to another Japanese company that is in an industry different from what is typically found in that bank's portfolio. The lower correlation results in more diversification and a lower RC. The final driver—weight—should not seem counterintuitive: Increase the weight of the exposure in the portfolio and the RC will rise. Unfortunately, the *rate* at which RC increases as weight increases does not comport with the intuition of experienced analysts.

Why should this be the case? Mathematically, the RC function is concave in portfolio weight. This means that as weight increases, RC increases at a decreasing rate. In practice, the function is only very mildly concave and is often almost linear. As a result, the minima and maxima for this function are not well suited for traditional optimization algorithms. This mathematical property, in turn, can make RC unsuitable for developing portfolio optimization algorithms.

As we have emphasized throughout this book, the skewed, fat-tailed nature of credit return distributions makes them amenable to portfolio selection and optimization, with the implication that a portfolio manager should never have too much of one exposure as this increases concentration (and fattens tails). In our experience, the weight of any one exposure exceeding 2 percent of the whole portfolio can rarely be justified. However, since RC does not increase at an increasing rate as exposure weight increases, an exposure with a moderately high ES will be (inappropriately) heavily weighted in most standard portfolio optimization algorithms, to the point that some exposures will draw a recommended weight well above the 2 percent. While RC can be a useful metric to develop some intuition around which exposures are driving a portfolio's volatility, it turns out that we still need to combine it with other metrics that track an exposure's contribution to extreme-loss risk. Let us turn next to one of these extreme-loss risk metrics called *tail-risk contribution* (TRC).

Tail risk contribution is analogous to RC in the sense that an individual exposure's risk is calculated with reference to a particular portfolio: As the weight of the exposure increases, the measure also increases. However, in the case of the TRC, the impact on the risk is measured in terms of *extreme* loss in a particular region of the portfolio loss distribution, rather than in the UL. The TRC is the post-diversification contribution of an individual exposure to losses above a specific point (typically in the tail region) of the loss distribution. We calculate it using the following derivative:

$$\partial C_P / \partial \omega_i$$

where C_P can be considered the capital for the portfolio assuming a particular targeted portion of the loss distribution. Unlike the case of UL, where the weighted sum of individual RC values equals *portfolio UL*, the weighted sum of individual TRC values equals the portfolio capital for the specified region of the loss distribution.

PORTFOLIO LOSS DISTRIBUTION

The risk measures we just described come from the portfolio loss distribution. It turns out that we run into computational difficulty in aggregating individual exposure ULs. However, rather than calculating these explicitly, we can instead take advantage of any one of a number of alternatives ranging from far simpler analytic models to full-blown simulation. We will focus primarily on the simulation approach later in this section. First, however, we will discuss an innovative approach introduced by Oldrich Vasicek in 1991 (see Vasicek 1987 and 1991) that relies on an analytical derivation.

Analytical

Recall from Chapter 7 that Oldrich Vasicek in 1991 derived a limiting loss distribution for portfolios in cases where all assets have identical asset correlation and probability of default. The limiting distribution holds for portfolios with infinite numbers of loans (or bonds) and is given as

$$P(Loss \leq xL) = \Phi \left(\frac{\sqrt{1-\rho}\,\Phi^{-1}(x) - \Phi^{-1}(cpd_P)}{\sqrt{\rho}} \right)$$

where cpd_P is an aggregate measure of default probability for the portfolio
           x is an arbitrary default frequency
           L is a (constant) LGD assumption
           $P(.)$ is the cumulative probability that an infinitely large portfolio of loans with probability of default cpd_P and uniform correlation ρ will actually experience a realized loss of xL or less in any particular instance. (For applications of this distribution in model validation, see Chapter 7.)

For finite portfolios, a similar, though computationally more involved form is gotten by summing the discrete probability $P(Loss = (k/n)L)$, over $k = 0..K$, where K is the number of defaults:

$$P(Loss = (k/n)L) = \binom{n}{k} \int_{-\infty}^{\infty} \left(\Phi \left(\frac{1}{\sqrt{1-\rho}} \left(\Phi^{-1}(cpd_P) - \sqrt{\rho}u \right) \right)^{k} \right.$$
$$\left. \times \left(1 - \Phi \left(\frac{1}{\sqrt{1-\rho}} \left(\Phi^{-1}(cpd_P) - \sqrt{\rho}u \right) \right) \right)^{n-k} \right) d\Phi(u)$$

where n is the number of (equally sized) exposures in the portfolio
           k is the number of defaults experienced

Vasicek's approach requires a number of sometimes unrealistic assumptions to arrive at this closed-form solution. If the portfolio is homogeneous in the dimensions of correlation, credit quality, maturity, and exposure weight, then analytical approximations may do fine. Unfortunately, many real-world portfolios have enough heterogeneity that the approximations are unrealistic. In our experience, moderate deviations from these homogeneity assumptions along the dimensions of size and PD do not overly affect the results. In contrast, deviations along the dimension of correlation tend to affect the results substantially.

Even if the portfolio *is* homogeneous enough, it can sometimes be difficult to parameterize the analytical characterization of the loss distribution. The advantage of the analytical approach is the speed of calculation once the parameters are estimated. Unfortunately, it is difficult to estimate accurate parameter values without running a simulation. That is, typical portfolios depart enough from the underlying assumptions that it makes it difficult to determine how best to parameterize this distribution for real portfolios.

While the preceding formula assumes a large, homogeneous portfolio of loans, it often generates surprisingly plausible distributions. In fact, many analysts use this distribution to model the risk of CDOs. The specific difficulty with parameterizations lies in the fact that the aggregate systematic risk measure and aggregate PD are not simple statistical calculations such as median, average, or weighted average applied to the underlying exposures in the portfolio, and that the tails of loss distributions can often be thicker than implied by the Vasicek model.

Given the great speed advantage to the analytic solution, it is useful to consider in what settings it might productively be used. One way to use this distribution is to first run a simulation (see next section for details), estimate the parameters of the Vasicek distribution from the simulated distribution, and then assuming a reasonable fit, use this distribution for the portfolio risk calculations, as long as the portfolio exposure weights do not depart materially from the portfolio on which the parameters were estimated. In these cases, fitting the parameters to a simulated loss distribution can be useful for analytical estimates for future portfolios that are similar to the original simulated portfolio. We have found that this simulate-then-estimate approach works quite well in some settings and quite poorly in others. For example, we have found that for some distributions, a single Vasicek distribution cannot fit both the body and the tail of an empirical or simulated distribution. For such situations, full-blown Monte Carlo simulation may be the only practical approach to sizing the risk of a portfolio. However, in settings where the fit is better, it can serve as a reasonable first approximation at the full distribution for quick analysis.

Simulation Approach

The process of Monte Carlo simulation is conceptually simple: we generate many hypothetical paths for the portfolio from the present time to some future horizon and then evaluate the portfolio at the hypothetical future time for each case to generate a distribution of losses, returns, and so forth. Unfortunately, it can be sometimes difficult to engineer practical simulations when we are faced with tens of thousands or millions of exposures in a portfolio. The most basic simulations involve using a correlation matrix of the individual pairwise exposures in the portfolio. The difficulty here (among others) is that the correlation matrix can rapidly explode to a large size when analyzing typical bank portfolios of thousands or millions of exposures. We have also discussed how this underlying correlation structure can be distilled into a multifactor structure that makes it much easier to simulate portfolio loss distributions for large portfolios as well as dramatically reducing the computing time. Even here, though, simulation time can be quite long for large portfolios.

Simulation approaches differ depending on how values are generated. For example, we could simulate loan values directly. Alternatively, we could simulate factors and then transform factor realizations into values. In this section, we look at three different simulation approaches. We discuss the following types of approaches in this context:

1. Direct asset value simulation
2. Multifactor-based asset value simulation
3. Single/Multifactor-based asset value simulation, a technique developed at MKMV for further reducing simulation time.

We review the first two of these three approaches and then discuss the third in detail.

Simple Structural Model

In the mid-1990s, KMV pioneered work in understanding how structural models of default could practically accommodate correlation across exposures in a portfolio. Gupton, Finger, and Bhatia (1997) were aware of this work and produced a public domain model that relied on the structural-model assumption of default probabilities being driven by the levels of obligor asset values, A_i, relative to their individual default points, X_i. The joint distribution of N asset values, $(A_1, \ldots, A_N)$, for the obligors represented in the portfolio is assumed to be multivariate normal with the asset value correlations proxied by equity correlations.[9] Thus, a correlation matrix of asset values is one input necessary in this approach. Note that instead of the raw equity correlations proposed by Gupton et al., we could also transform equity data into asset value data using option-pricing models as discussed in Chapter 3 and directly create an actual asset-value correlation matrix. In either case, we end up with an $N \times N$ correlation matrix.

As is the case in all structural versions of portfolio simulations, we simulate the asset value realizations for each obligor and compare them to a barrier (Default Point). This implies the need for a firm specific barrier for each exposure in the portfolio we are analyzing. We can rely on PDs (calculated in any manner deemed accurate) and invert these through the inverse normal distribution to determine an implied barrier. (Even though strict normality probably does not hold, as long as the real underlying distribution has similar curvature to the normal in the area in which we are focused, the result is often reasonably close despite the fact that the normal distribution does not match empirical data in practice.) We rely on the following functional relationship for default probability:

$$P(A_i < X_i) = cpd_i$$

Making use of the normal distribution, we back out a scaled default barrier as follows:

$$X_i = \Phi^{-1}(cpd_i)$$

We pause here to note that nothing in our setup requires a structural model be used to derive PDs and correlations. Said more strongly, even if our PD model is not a structural model (e.g., ratings) and our correlations are derived outside of the structural framework (e.g., equity correlations), we can still use a structural approach to model the portfolio.

Now, with all the requisite inputs, we run the (single period) simulation for each iteration as follows. First, draw asset values from a multivariate normal distribution with asset value correlations defined by the correlation matrix. Next, determine default indicators, Y_i, for each obligor based on the relationship of each obligor's simulated asset value and its implicit default barrier:

$$Y_i = 1\{A_i < X_i\}$$

---

[9] Note that this assumption can be relaxed when estimates of asset values are available in quantity from a structural model directly.

Note that the joint distribution of default indicators, $(Y_1, \ldots, Y_N)$, does not preserve the linear correlations of the joint asset values distribution; however, since the transformation is monotone, the default correlations are preserved.

Based on the default indicator, determine the value of each exposure as we described in the earlier part of this chapter:

- If it is in default, then draw from an LGD distribution (as we discuss in Chapter 5, a beta distribution is often a reasonable assumption for LGD). Using this LGD draw, determine the conditional recovery value, $1 - \text{LGD}$.
- If it is not in default:
  - If we are running a default-nondefault simulation, record a value of par or the face value of the security.
  - If we are running a credit migration simulation, find the rating state associated with the DD of the firm, conditional on the realization of the asset value. Each DD is associated with a rating grade in a transition probability matrix. This may require mapping the DDs into PDs if we are not using a DD-based transition matrix. (In many cases, the matrix relies on agency ratings so that the DD realization is first converted into a PD and then into a rating based on a PD-to-rating mapping.) A common method to convert the simulated DD (realized asset value relative to the implied default point) into a PD is through the normal distribution since we generated the implied default point with the normal inverse function.
  - From here we can build more sophisticated valuation models based on the matrix-based transition probabilities of moving into different rating states from the horizon date to the date of each cash flow from horizon to maturity of the instrument.

While straightforward in principle, this approach suffers from a number of weaknesses that make it less well suited for sophisticated portfolio managers:

- The requirement of specifying a correlation matrix rapidly creates storage and memory problems as the number of cells multiplies. At some point (probably in the thousands) the management and manipulation of this matrix becomes impractical.
- While we will continue to rely on multivariate normality in other aspects of our preferred approach, the transformation back to a conditional PD in this case results in too many exposures exhibiting unusually low, conditional PDs. This problem can sometimes be remedied by using different distributions, but typically the mathematics quickly become

distanced from defensible economic theory and strange output becomes increasingly hard to analyze and explain.[10]

- The underlying drivers of correlations are quite opaque to the analyst. As a portfolio manager becomes more accustomed to ACPM practices and seeks more sophisticated characterizations of correlated risk, this lack of transparency can become limiting.

We now turn to an extension of this simple model to the richer structure advocated in Gupton, Finger, and Bhatia (1997) which set the stage for future innovation: the multifactor version.

Multifactor Model

One way to reduce the complexity of the simple structural model portfolio approach is to move from pairwise asset correlations to an equivalent (in expectation) factor representation. We stay with the basic approach as outlined in the previous section except that now, instead of using a correlation matrix to parameterize the joint distribution of underlying asset values, we distill the correlation structure into the multifactor structure we discussed at the beginning of the chapter by decomposing the individual firm asset value movements into movements of a set of factors common to all firms. This means that each firm's asset value change is a composite of the changes in a set of common factors, weighted appropriately to represent the firm's exposure to these factors. Two firms with similar weights or *factor loadings* will exhibit correlated asset value movements.

Thus, the asset value of a firm in the simulation context becomes characterized as a function of several factors:

$$A_i = \sum_{j=1}^{k} \beta_{ij}\phi_j + \varphi_i \nu_i, \quad i = 1, \ldots, N$$

where

$$\phi_j, \nu_i \sim \Phi(0, 1)$$

$$\sum_{j=1}^{k} \beta_{ij}^2 + \varphi_i^2 = 1$$

Note that ϕ_j are independent random variables.

Everything else follows the same recipe outlined for the simple structural model simulation except that the asset value is simulated by simulating k

---

[10] Note that as we explain later, we can use this approach with different copulas than the multivariate normal to capture loss distribution tail dependence in a richer way. However, we still lack transparency into what is ultimately driving this dependency.

factors and then using these to determined the conditional value based on the factor loadings defined in the coefficients β_j and the idiosyncratic risk for the obligor determined by the draw for v_i. We can continue to back out an implied default barrier using the normal inverse function applied to an input PD.[11]

The biggest challenge in applying a multifactor model lies in estimating the factor loadings. To do this, we first need a large sample of data on the asset values of typical obligors found in the portfolio. One way to get this sample is to apply a structural model to equity data. Data are typically available for about 25,000 firms around the globe.

Once we have the asset value data we can use these data to estimate a multifactor model using one of two general approaches. *Explicit* factor models rely on fundamental economic factor representations (e.g., GDP, unemployment). *Implicit* factor models assume that asset movements are driven by common (possibly latent) factors that are not directly modeled.

Explicit factor models relate the asset values to observable information such as interest rates, GDP growth, inflation, and so on. The big benefit of this class of models is that we can use them to ask and answer explicit questions about both the drivers of default behavior and the impact of specific states of the world on the portfolio. For example, we can assess the impact of a drop in GDP on the portfolio. Unfortunately, in some cases it can be difficult to use explicit factor models to fully characterize the asset movements without also using additional information about the borrower characteristics, and so on. For some corporate portfolios, these models may explain less than 10 percent of the variance in asset value.[12] This means that

---

[11] Note that one extension not widely explored in published research to date involves simulating not only the asset value but also the default barrier. The difficulty lies in the fact that we do not yet have a clear picture of how the asset value and the default barrier should move together stochastically. We could assume an arbitrary distribution from which to draw the default barrier; however, in practice, this kind of model produces less coherent results than relying on the normal inverse function applied to an input PD. As we highlighted in Chapter 3, the relationship between asset value and default barrier is quite rich: negative correlation at low asset values, positive correlation at moderate asset values, and a near-zero correlation at high asset values.

[12] However, for some asset classes, explicit factor models are the preferred modeling approach. For example, in many cases, it is not possible to observe underlying asset values or proxies for underlying asset values, but much richer characterizations of the loan structure and so on are possible. In such settings, particularly if scenario analysis and economic what-if analysis is a requirement, explicit models suggest themselves.

without additional modeling work, simulation tends to be mostly driven by the idiosyncratic draws for the obligors, and much of the correlated risk becomes washed out in the noise.

Implicit factor models remedy this explanatory-power problem. Instead of forcing external variables into the equation, we assume the factors are latent in the data and we extract the latent relationships reflected in the co-movement of the asset values over time. Often, we try to determine what each latent factor represents (e.g., global macrofactor, sectoral factor, etc.); but the correlation reflected in the underlying factor framework is directly extracted from the asset value data without imposing any other assumptions on what those factors might be. In this way, we increase our ability to explain the variance of asset values and see much more differentiation in the nature of firms. For example, large banks are much more affected by the common factors than is a small software firm. Of course, the increase in power comes at a cost: It is far more difficult to determine the impact of, say, a 3 percent increase in unemployment on the expected loss of a portfolio. That said, given the relative ease with which asset values may be observed for corporate exposures, and the relatively simpler implementation in simulation, we will focus our discussion on the implicit factor model approach.

Single-Factor/Multifactor Model

Despite the speed improvement of factor models over the simple structural simulation, simulating large portfolios is still time-intensive. While a number of techniques exist to improve the speed of simulation, such as importance sampling and variance reduction,[13] we will discuss one more computational approach to simplify model implementation. This approach involves collapsing the multiple factors into a custom index that reflects the firm's industry and country. KMV (now MKMV) pioneered the application of this approach to credit-risk modeling. We sometimes call this framework a *single-factor/multifactor framework*. What we mean by single-factor/multifactor is that we first estimate a multifactor framework, but implement it with a custom index for each exposure based on its industry and country of incorporation. Thus, the implementation, from a mechanical perspective, can be done as if the custom index were a single factor, even though it incorporates information from a multifactor correlation model.

---

[13] We enthusiastically recommend implementing these techniques to improve the simulation speed; Glasserman (2004) is a good reference for these and other simulation techniques.

This approach was developed in order to make it easier to implement a factor model across a large number of heterogeneous obligors and maintain an updated estimate of the underlying factor structure of a large number (if not most) publicly traded firms, globally. Whether we use all factors together or collapse them into a single composite index, the initial step of estimating the factor model is the same: we first define the factors and then decompose the individual firm asset returns using these factors. The difference is the final step where we construct the conditional asset value using a composite index.

We have experienced the most success in practical settings with the single-factor/multifactor model approach due to its ease of implementation and richness of structure. The creation of a composite index based on industry and country of incorporation (or sector and region—depending on how much data is available) allows for much easier integration of obligors where no data exists. Rather than having to guess the factor loadings for a firm without data, we can use industry and country as a proxy. For firms with publicly traded equity, the factor loadings on each individual factor can be directly estimated. In all cases, we need to determine just how much of the overall asset value is driven by systematic factors, but it is much easier to estimate this than it is to estimate each factor loading without time series of data for that specific firm. If we do not have data from traded securities to estimate factor loadings, the single-factor/multi-factor approach facilitates a comparable approach by allowing for a factor relationship based on a firm's industry and country. In this way, even obligors without time series of asset-return data can be efficiently integrated into the same factor framework. An important point to remember in this discussion is that the use of a composite index is just one of several ways to implement a multi-factor model. However implemented, a multi-factor model can provide a rich characterization of a portfolio's underlying correlation structure.

In addition to facilitating simulation, this setup also provides one measure of systematic risk. In this context, this measure is the R^2 from the regression of firm asset value returns on the firm's composite index. It is a measure of systematic risk for the firm since a high R^2 suggests that a large portion of the movement in the asset value of the firm is attributable to movements in systematic factors.

In the following description we provide a general characterization of each step in this process of creating single-factor/multifactor custom factors and subsequently using them for simulation, along with an example of how the approach can be implemented. Note that alternative approaches are reasonable as long as the factor draws are appropriately linked to exposure value realization.

This is an important point. Thus far, we have focused on generating asset value as the bridge between the initial and ending (conditional) value of the exposure. In actuality, our ultimate objective is the value of the exposure conditional on a particular set of factor draws. The simple model used asset value as the link. We can generalize this particular approach to directly generating the DD itself, rather than the asset value, which takes asset value and the default barrier as inputs. As it turns out, though we can generalize the approach, our experience suggests that simulating asset value as a means to DD produces stable models in most settings.

Earlier, we assumed the existence of some kind of valuation framework that transformed the asset value draw into an exposure value at the horizon. Here we provide more detail on how that transformation is made in simulation. Note that any model that produces conditional factor draws can be used with the valuation models we discussed earlier. The key is to build a simulator that is as rich as possible in terms of reflecting the portfolio's underlying correlation structure, given the practical constraints in terms of computing time and power.

It is generally better to link factor draws to firm asset value, calculate DD, and convert DD into security value via some kind of valuation function (for speed purposes, this function can be implemented as a valuation grid where DDs are assigned to different values). The steps for implementing a simulation are as follows:

1. Determine the appropriate (systematic) factor loadings for a particular exposure.
2. Transform factor realizations into a DD based on the chosen modeling approach (in this section, we describe an approach based on asset-value modeling), which relies on simulating an *obligor-specific residual* that gets incorporated with the *deterministic components* of each obligor's asset-value function. The process is as follows:
   a. Generate the *systematic component* of each obligor's asset-value residual based on the number of factors decided in step 1.
   b. Generate the *idiosyncratic component* of each obligor's asset-value residual.
   c. Transform both systematic and idiosyncratic factor realizations into residuals for each obligor and combine with the deterministic components of the asset-value function to generate asset values for each obligor.
   d. Combine each realized asset value with each obligor's implied default point (based on input PD data) to generate DD values for each obligor in the portfolio.

3. Transform (via a valuation formula) DD realizations into an exposure value.
4. Aggregate exposure values.

Now let's look at each of these steps in more detail.

Determining the Appropriate Factors for an Exposure   Before creating the composite index (i.e., representative single factor) from a multifactor model, we must first determine the number of factors that drive the asset value of a specific firm. We have already explained the generic specification for a multifactor framework in which there are k factors. We will now discuss how we actually determine *what* k should be and *which* k factors we should use. We will explain this approach in the context of an implicit factor framework in which the systematic variation in asset value can be estimated from a global sample of traded firms (a diverse sample of, say, 15,000 should be sufficient).

While the number of factors is important for the final implementation of the simulation, this framework assumes the factor-driving processes are implicitly reflected in the data. That is, we have sufficient data such that we may extract information about the underlying systematic risk from the data using as many factors as required without limitation. The number of factors that we choose depends on how much granularity we desire for explaining what is driving the co-movement in underlying asset value. At some point, specifying too many factors produces a spurious level of differentiation, so we have to balance between differentiating how each firm is impacted differently and the fact that at some point, we will lose the ability to statistically tease out the impact of a particular factor.

Once the factors are determined, there is often a desire to label them with intuitive names that give some theoretical comfort. However, the data-driven nature of the implicit factor creation process implies that the characterization of the factors after the fact is an interpretive exercise, not a model-building exercise. Here is an example of useful category labels for implicit factors:

- 1 to 2 common global factors
- 5 to 10 sectoral factors
- 5 to 10 regional factors
- 60 to 70 industry-specific factors
- 40 to 50 country-specific factors

As we touched on earlier, when we start labeling factors in this way and developing a means to explain their impact, unless they are orthogonal (perfectly uncorrelated), the order in which we remove the factors matters. That is, the global factors will contain some components that may be considered industry- and country-specific. For example, an underlying global economic process associated with the business cycle will also impact each industry in some way. Thus, this type of explicit ordering produces the industry- and country-specific factors after we have extracted what is common to all industries and countries. The same is true for sectoral and regional factors: Some portion of the industry and country will be found in these factors. The industry- and country-specific factors reflect what is left over after extracting the common components in each of the previous categorizations.

Essentially, we recommend grouping firms by these particular characteristics (i.e., industry and country) to arrive at a sense of how the factors are behaving. Our experience is that k should be somewhere in the (wide) range of 20 to 120, depending on how much data is available. In fact, a 20- to 30-factor model will typically capture most of the variation at a level of granularity needed to provide useful guidance to diagnose the source of correlation risk in a portfolio.

Transforming Factor Realizations into a DD Having converged on the appropriate number and content of the factor model itself, we next need to build the model infrastructure to transform the factor realizations into the DD-input. In the simulation, we will be drawing the factors from a particular distribution to generate a conditional DD based on the draw. While there are a number of ways to transform factor realizations in DD, we focus on a structural approach, which centers on asset value.

As asset value is the target, we assume it is generated by a deterministic component and a random (stochastic) component. We use geometric Brownian motion as the underlying stochastic process (similar to the specification for many of the structural models, such as BSM, BC, and VK, described in Chapter 3). The deterministic component reflects the expected trajectory of the asset value, which is a function of the firm's asset value drift and its volatility. The random component is driven by a residual, $\tilde{\varepsilon}$, composed of a systematic component, $\tilde{f}$, and an unsystematic or idiosyncratic component, $\tilde{u}$.

Mathematically, we can use the following model to describe asset value movements. (Note that we drop the i subscript to improve readability of the equations; we will do this calculation for all N obligors in the portfolio.)

$$\ln\left(\frac{A_H}{A_0}\right) = \left(\mu_A - \frac{1}{2}\sigma_A^2\right)H + \sigma_A\sqrt{H}\tilde{\varepsilon}$$

where

$$\tilde{\varepsilon} = \tilde{f} + \tilde{u}$$

Generating the Residual In this framework, the residual, $\tilde{\varepsilon}$, is the most important part of the simulation because this quantity essentially defines the realized asset value that is used to calculate the conditional DD, PD, and the value that ends up resulting in each realization of the simulation; this is where the systematic risk enters into the asset process simulation. We need to develop a method to weight the systematic portion (which reflects systematic risk in the economy) differently from the unsystematic or idiosyncratic portion (which reflects risk specific to the firm).

As we explained at the start of this section, in the single-factor/ multifactor framework we use a custom index to estimate a coefficient of determination, R^2, which reflects the extent to which the systematic factors are driving the asset value. This R^2 coefficient is estimated from a regression of the asset return series for a particular firm on its custom index. The custom index is defined by the firm's industry or industries and country of incorporation. The R^2 provides the wedge to differentiate the systematic piece, which reflects the correlated nature of the asset value from the unsystematic piece. When we generate a simulation path, we perform factor draws once for each factor in the framework. Most firms will not load up on all the factors, so some (or many) factor loadings for a given firm will be zero. They roll up to produce the systematic component of the residual as follows:

$$\tilde{f}_i = \left(\frac{R_i^2}{\sum\limits_{j=1}^{k} \beta_j^2 \sigma_j^2} \right)^{\frac{1}{2}} \sum_{j=1}^{k} \beta_j \sigma_j \phi_j$$

where

$$\phi_j \sim \Phi(0, 1)$$

The next step is to perform a separate draw for the firm-specific or unsystematic component (one draw per firm in each path):

$$\tilde{u}_i = \sqrt{1 - R_i^2} v_i$$

where

$$v_i \sim \Phi(0, 1)$$

For each iteration, we are then able to generate an asset value conditional on the simulation draw. In practice, we assume the other pieces of the DD calculation (namely default point and asset volatility) do not change to horizon, so at this point we can directly calculate the DD given the simulated asset value, the PD, and the asset volatility. Finally, we evaluate whether this residual draw from the simulation puts the firm in default or not. As we indicated, more complicated simulation algorithms are conceivable; however, in our own work, the increased complexity did not appear to improve the quality and precision of the risk measures but did decrease transparency.

Transforming DD into Exposure Value   Once we have transformed the residual draws into a DD, we next transform conditional DD into an exposure value at horizon. We do this to capture any change in value for all exposures that have not yet matured, given their ending (as a result of the factor draw) credit quality, which may be different than their original credit qualities. This transformation requires us to calculate a conditional term structure of PDs if the firm is in the nondefault state, and a recovery value if the firm is in the default state. The conditional term structure is required to calculate the present value of the exposure through maturity. Both a valuation function and a credit migration function such as DD transition densities are necessary to make this calculation. Structural valuation models are well suited for this step. In order to accommodate optionality that is typically attached to some types of loans (e.g., spread changes based on change in credit quality, prepayment options, etc.), a *lattice model* can be convenient (see box).

Lattice models can also be used to integrate stochastic interest rates; however, computation time increases substantially as dimensions are added to the lattice. One speed-improving method involves converting the valuation function into a valuation grid where DD is attached to specific values in a table. Usually a 20-cell grid (with linear interpolation between nodes) will be sufficient to obtain suitable granularity in valuation.

Aggregating Exposure Values   For each iteration in the simulation, we draw factor realizations and use these to calculate DDs and, ultimately, conditional values for each exposure in the portfolio. We record the conditional exposure values for all portfolio exposures and report that calculation as one simulated value for the portfolio. We then repeat the process again for as many iterations as is specified. Because we are focused on the tail events for credit analysis, we typically require at least 500,000 simulations, but this number will vary greatly depending on the structure of the portfolio. Some financial institutions will run millions of simulations in a distributed

LATTICE MODELS OF DD

Lattice models are the logical extension of binomial tree models, familiar in options pricing (see Hull 2005). Conceptually, a tree becomes a lattice as the number of paths emanating from and terminating at each node becomes large. To create a valuation model using DDs, we first construct a lattice of DD values. We then use this lattice to estimate the conditional exposure value at each node in the lattice (where the value of a specific portfolio exposure is conditional on the DD).

A one-dimensional lattice starts with an implicit barrier, calculated as we suggested in the subsections on simulation: We start with a PD and then use the normal inverse to extract the value of a DD barrier such that for values of DD above the barrier, the probability is greater than the PD, and for values below it is less than the PD. We then use the lattice to construct possible paths for the asset value in which each step in the lattice is defined by a conditional transition density (conditional on the current value of DD) that determines the possible next value of the DD (of which there are an infinite number). As we progress along the lattice, we create paths for the evolution of the DD. Additional optionality, such as prepayment, can then be built into each node of the lattice.

Two-dimensional lattice models can also be constructed usefully (assuming the processing speed and other calculation-reducing simulation techniques are in place), where the second dimension of the lattice represents the evolution of the interest rate, which is used to calculate the present value at each node. To complete the valuation, a model is used to transform the DD into PDs and then into risk-neutral PDs. These risk-neutral PDs can be used in the context of a valuation model (see Chapter 3 and Chapter 6) to produce an exposure value.

fashion. Additionally, variance reduction techniques and importance sampling methods can greatly reduce computing time (see Glasserman 2004).[14]

Note that the number of iterations is orders of magnitude larger than what is typical in simulations for market risk analysis. The difference arises

---

[14] Some market participants have suggested that recent advances in accelerator cards, typically used for graphics in high-end video games, may be another avenue for increasing simulation speed, assuming the simulation code can be ported to the cards. At the time of this writing a C compiler for these cards has been released.

from the skewed, long-tailed nature of credit distributions. Unfortunately, the precision (i.e., the size of the confidence interval) of the simulation estimates in the distribution's tail (i.e., the last 10 to 100 basis points of the distribution) does not collapse very fast, so that the 99 percent confidence interval at a target probability of 15 basis points (i.e., 99.85 percent probability that the loss will be less than this level) may still be as much as plus or minus 5 percent (the error rates for tail estimates can be particularly sensitive to the distributional assumptions and correlation estimates used.)

Note that the implicit pairwise covariance of returns for any two firms *a* and *b* can be calculated as follows:

$$\sigma(a, b) = \sum_{j=1}^{k} \beta_{aj} \beta_{bj} \sigma_j^2$$

$$\text{correlation} = \rho(a, b) = \sum_{j=1}^{k} \frac{\beta_{aj} \beta_{bj} \sigma_j^2}{\sigma_a \sigma_b}$$

As we have emphasized before, the factor model provides us a parsimonious method for reflecting correlation without explicitly calculating the covariance matrix.

Putting It All Together Again To review the steps in the simulation from the top, one last time, the approach proceeds as follows:

1. Draw factors to generate the systematic component of the firm's asset value residual.
2. Draw the idiosyncratic component of the firm's asset value residual.
3. Calculate the firm's asset value conditional on the simulated factor draws.
4. Determine if the firm is in default conditional on the simulated factor draws. If in default, calculate the security's default value by drawing an LGD. If not in default, calculate the security's nondefault value based on the valuation and credit migration model.
5. Aggregate all securities' values in the portfolios conditional on the factor draws and record this value as one possible value realization for the portfolio.
6. Repeat the process from step 1 with a new set of factor draws. Repeat for the specified number of iterations and use the resulting portfolio values to construct a simulated loss distribution.

The process described here produces a portfolio *value* distribution. For risk purposes, our analysis requires a portfolio *loss* distribution. Thus, we specify a suitable *loss point* from which we can transform the value distribution into a loss distribution. A loss point is the point at which the portfolio will begin to use an institution's available excess capital and experience a loss. Possible loss points could be:

- The *risk-free value* of the portfolio at the horizon. We expect to earn at least the risk-free rate so that any dollar of value below that level at horizon can be interpreted as loss. This loss point implies that both the EL and the ES (effectively the total spread or TS) are available to absorb adverse value changes before we start counting losses. For example, assume a portfolio value of 100 at time 0 and a risk-free rate of 5 percent. We start counting loss for any portfolio value at horizon (equal to one year) that is less than 105. Thus 103, which is a 3 percent *absolute* gain, would still imply a loss of 2 under this measure.
- The value of the portfolio at the horizon at which we earn *the risk-free rate plus the expected spread*. In this case, we start counting losses immediately after exhausting the expected loss cushion (thus giving no credit for ES). While not as theoretically appealing, calculating loss after losing EL reflects a more conservative view that argues ES is not really available to absorb losses in practice, particularly if much of the ES reflects a gain in value over the time horizon—not received cash.

Once we determine the loss point, we can easily convert the portfolio value distribution into a portfolio loss distribution. The loss distribution can then be used to determine how much capital the financial institution must hold such that its target probability of default equals a prespecified level that will be consistent with the institution's target credit quality objective. We discuss approaches to determining this level in more detail in Chapter 2 on ACPM in practice.

CAPITAL

Once we have estimated the portfolio loss distribution, we can use it to generate analytics that support decision making.

One of the most important of these is the amount of *economic capital* required to support a portfolio and how this capital is allocated to individual exposures. For clarity, although we have discussed a number of measures of capital, in this section we assume capital is calculated as the amount of cushion available to absorb extreme losses at some target percentage of (idealized) future states of the world. For example, it might be the amount of capital required to absorb extreme losses 99.85 percent of the time.

To determine this capital number, we first determine a target probability of default for the portfolio as a whole. This target probability should coincide with the credit quality the financial institution believes will maximize its value as a business. The key drivers (related to this target probability) are cost of funding, reputation, the impact on the firm's ability to act as a counterparty, and the impact on the firm's ability to create and develop service businesses. Typical target probabilities might range from 10 bps to 50 bps. With a target probability in hand, we can calculate the present value of the loss amount corresponding to this target probability (as defined by the simulated loss distribution). This amount is the economic capital necessary to ensure that the estimated probability of default for the portfolio is equal to the target probability. We denote this capital number C_P.

Once the overall portfolio capital number has been calculated, economic capital can be allocated to individual exposures. The economic capital allocated to each exposure, C_i, should reflect the amount of capital put at risk to support each exposure i.

There are a number of approaches to doing this, including:

1. The contribution to volatility or RC method:

$$C_i = \frac{RC_i}{UL_P} C_P$$

where $RC_i = \partial UL_P / \partial \omega_i = \text{cov}\,(i, P)/UL_P$ (discussed earlier)

2. The contribution to tail risk or TRC method:

$$C_i = \frac{\partial C_P}{\partial V_{i0}} = TRC_i = E\,[Exposure\ Loss | Loss_{LB} < Loss_P]$$

where $Loss_{LB} \equiv$ Lower bound for overall portfolio loss that is consistent with the target probability of insolvency for the portfolio.

$Loss_P \equiv$ Portfolio loss realization for a given iteration in the simulation.

RC can be calculated analytically or via simulation. For TRC, however, we are not aware at this time of any practically useful analytical approximations to the TRC calculation that do not make unrealistically restrictive simplifying assumptions. Thus, we generally estimate TRC via a simulation. In fact, the method is quite easy to grasp; however, the mathematical derivation (which we leave to interested readers) is not quite so straightforward. The process for using the simulation to estimate TRC is as follows:

1. In each simulation path, check whether the simulated portfolio loss falls beyond the lower bound set for the definition of the tail.
2. If the portfolio loss exceeds the lower bound, then for each exposure, record the individual loss on that position.
3. After the simulation is completed, calculate the average loss experienced by each exposure conditional on the overall portfolio loss falling into the tail region of the distribution (i.e., exceeding the lower bound).
4. This average conditional loss is the TRC.

Consider a simple example to illustrate how TRC varies for different types of borrowers. Assume two exposures are identical with respect to their outstanding amount, PDs, LGDs, and so on, except that one exposure is to a bank with a (high) R^2 of 65 percent, and the other exposure is to a biotech firm with a (lower) R^2 of 10 percent. Assume further that we are interested in the portion of the loss distribution that is associated with the last 100 basis points in target probability terms (i.e., target probability is 99 percent). The higher R^2 for the bank exposure will imply that each time the portfolio experiences a loss that exceeds the loss point associated with 100 basis points of probability, it is more likely that that particular set of factor draws will also affect the bank exposure so that it experiences a large drop in value. In contrast, the changes in value for the biotech firm will be far less a result of the systematic factors affecting the portfolio and far more a result of the idiosyncratic factors affecting only the firm. When TRC is calculated for the bank exposure, it will tend to be higher, on average, than for the biotech exposure, given that the more systematic nature of the exposure resulted in it often contributing (along with the other highly correlated exposures) to extreme loss events for the overall portfolio. Here we see the default clustering phenomenon directly.

Recall that economic capital is different from *regulatory capital* in that economic capital reflects an expectation about the institution's ability to absorb extreme loss, while regulatory capital represents a rule-based approach to determining the capital required to meet regulatory standards. As we consider how to allocate capital to individual exposures, the objective should be how best to encourage value-creation activities at a financial institution (subject to the constraint of also staying within regulatory guidelines). If we use RC, we have a bias toward exposures that do not add to the overall volatility of the portfolio. As we have indicated, a drawback of the RC measure is that it does not rise as fast as the TRC measure as an exposure's weight in the portfolio increases. For this reason, many institutions may benefit from considering TRC as a basis for allocating capital.

In fact, specifying TRC so as to capture the contribution to a particular region of the loss distribution's tail (e.g., everything to the right of 100 bps) results in a measure that is equal to the exposure's expected shortfall or *conditional value-at-risk* (CVaR). This level reflects the expected loss for a particular exposure *conditional on the portfolio experiencing an extreme loss* that only occurs in the tail of the loss distribution. We can use TRC in its raw, CVaR form to determine capital allocation. This means that by calculating TRC for each exposure and aggregating the amounts, we can arrive at an estimate of the overall portfolio capital required based on CVaR as opposed to straight value-at-risk (VaR), which is often criticized for its lack of coherence as a risk measure.[15]

Alternatively, we can calculate a VaR-based capital amount for the overall portfolio instead. This measure is more relevant if we judge that the *size* of the loss in the event of extreme loss is not relevant to the equity holders of the institution when we are analyzing the entire institution's portfolio, since the equity holders' primary concern is whether the extreme loss will exhaust all available capital, once the available capital is breached. The problem with VaR arises when we think about the capital allocation at the exposure or subportfolio level. If we do not account for the possible size of loss, a particular business unit, portfolio manager, or trader could unnecessarily put the entire institution at risk by establishing a position that results in a solvency-threatening level of loss if the trade goes bad.

For example, history has shown that the trades placed by a single trader at an institution can result in the entire bank failing. CVaR-based TRC has the potential to better identify these types of positions so that suitable risk-mitigation measures can be taken. In contrast, at the *total* portfolio level, equity holders and management are typically less concerned as to whether the amount by which the capital threshold is breached is small or large. Thus, VaR may be suitable at this firmwide level. However, local regulators may discourage VaR measures as large losses in down-states of the economy may result in significant systemic problems. They may wish to regulate the CVaR-based economic capital of the institution.

If the regulatory constraints are not binding, a financial institution may elect to calculate the straight VaR-based capital for the entire portfolio, but use CVaR-based TRC to allocate capital to individual exposures. This means that the TRC-based capital will need to be rescaled so that it adds up to the VaR-based number for the entire portfolio.

---

[15] Coherence describes mathematical properties of risk measures that ensure consistency. In particular, VaR measures can violate subadditivity.

Consider a simple example of how this might work:

1. Assume a portfolio that has only two exposures, A and B, with corresponding weights in the portfolio of 80 percent and 20 percent.
2. First calculate the VaR-based capital at a target probability of 15 basis points (i.e., the bank wants to hold enough capital to cover loss 99.85 percent of the time), and assume we determine that it should be 5 percent.
3. Next calculate the CVaR-TRC-based capital for each exposure, except that this time we choose a target probability of 100 basis points. Note that we expand the size of the tail region that we target at the individual exposure level to improve the differentiation among exposures. While it is theoretically more consistent to also specify the TRC region as the last 15 basis points of the distribution so that it conforms with the VaR calculation for the entire portfolio, in practice, unless a very large number of simulations is performed, many of the TRC calculations will be 0 (sometimes as much as 40 percent of the portfolio) since it is rarer to observe individual exposure's contribution to loss for such small (low-probability) regions of the value realizations.

   In any case, assume we run a simulation and calculate the 100 bps, CVaR-TRC-based capital for A and B as 15 percent and 5 percent, respectively. The total (weighted sum) TRC-based capital in this case will be 13 percent [0.15(0.8) + 0.05(0.2)] instead of the 5 percent calculated for the VaR. Basically, we are identifying the capital allocated to each position as reflected in the shape of this portfolio's loss distribution.
4. Based on these calculations, we determine that the TRC-based capital amounts will need to be rescaled by a factor of 5/13 or 39 percent. Thus, we rescale the TRC-based capital number for A and B to 6 percent and 2 percent, respectively, so that they now add up (weighted sum) to the 5 percent for the total portfolio.

The objective here is to separate the determination of the total capital necessary for a portfolio from the allocation to each individual exposure. Note that exposure A still requires three times as much capital (in percentage terms) as B, regardless of whether we use the raw TRC-based numbers or the rescaled amounts. Thus, the relative relationships stay intact while the overall total can reconcile to another number. In fact, the total portfolio capital is often exogenously specified based on regulatory guidance or other top-down models, rather than VaR calculations. In this way, the total portfolio capital can become an *input*, while the allocation across exposures will reflect a robust and theoretically coherent approach to capital allocation. Generally speaking, CVaR-TRC is the preferred approach to allocating capital in most settings. In the next section, we shift back to the conceptual discussion of capital, in whatever form we have defined it.

ECONOMIC CAPITAL AND PORTFOLIO MANAGEMENT

As we suggested in Chapter 2, we find it easier to understand how the pieces for capital and portfolio management fit together by conceptually separating a bank into two parts: one part that contains the actual portfolio of assets, and a second part that contains an amalgam of all other bank franchises and functions. For discussion purposes, call the part containing the portfolio "the fund," and think of the fund as containing only a portfolio management function or ACPM function (i.e., no other bank functions). The fund is leveraged. It borrows from the rest of the bank at the appropriate market rate. We may think of it also as borrowing directly in the bond or money markets. The rest of the bank owns equity supporting the fund (although in principle some or all could be owned outside of the bank).

In essence, the fund is an odd sort of leveraged mutual fund. The fund's assets have a market value, either because the individual assets have actual market prices, or because we can value them using valuations, comparable quotes, or through model-based methods. The fund has fixed obligations, namely, its borrowings. These borrowings also have determinable market values. The value of the fund's equity is exactly equal to the excess of the *market value of the fund's assets* over the market value of its obligations. The economic capital of a bank is closely related to the market value of *the bank's equity*. Rather than being simply the excess of the market value of assets over the market value of liabilities, economic capital is the excess of the market value of assets over the market value of liabilities, *assuming the liabilities had no default risk*. For a bank with low default risk, these values are virtually identical. However, for a distressed bank, economic capital can be zero or negative, whereas market equity is always positive. The economic capital fluctuates with the market value of assets. The fund can raise more equity or more debt and invest it in additional assets, or it can make payouts to debt or equity, reducing its assets.

The objective of fund management is to maximize the value of the fund's equity. In a hypothetical world of frictionless markets and common information (i.e., a world without institutional or communications constraints), this would be achieved by purchasing assets at or below market, and selling assets at or above market. Regardless of circumstance, this is a desirable policy, and its implementation requires rigorous measurement of default risk, and pricing which, by market standards at least, compensates for the default risk. However, institutional constraints do exist, and markets are not frictionless nor is information symmetrically dispersed. In fact, it is the existence of these market imperfections that makes intermediation between borrowers and depositors a valuable service. Conceptually, there would be no need for banks or mutual funds to exist in a world of perfect capital markets.

In practice, equity funding is expensive. This may be because equity returns are taxed at the fund level, or because the lack of transparency of bank balance sheets imposes an additional risk cost or *agency cost*.[16] The result is that banks are sometimes constrained, practically, to use the minimal amount of capital consistent with maintaining their ability to freely access debt markets. For wholesale banks, that access is permitted only to banks with extremely low default probabilities (typically 0.15 percent or less per year). In late 2007 and into 2008, this access to funding became even more problematic at times for financial institutions without a sufficiently low PD.

Finally, it is our view that the fund or the bank's portfolio should be managed with the same discipline as would any investment vehicle. In a world where transactions are costly, one of the portfolio's functions is to minimize those costs for ultimate investors. It does this by providing competitive return for its risk. Failure to do this makes it a secondary rather than primary investment vehicle; in other words, if it is less than fully diversified, another layer of investment vehicles (and another round of transactions costs) is required to provide diversification to the investor.

Both of these considerations add two additional objectives for portfolio management:

1. Obtain maximum diversification.
2. Determine and maintain capital adequacy.

Capital adequacy can be determined by considering the frequency distribution of portfolio losses either by an analytical calculation, as suggested by Vasicek's limiting loss distribution, or by simulation. Maintaining capital adequacy means that the desired leverage must be determined for each new asset as it is added to the portfolio. This leverage must be such that the fund's overall default risk remains unchanged. Assets that, net of diversification, add more than average risk to the portfolio must be financed (proportionately) with more equity and less debt than the existing portfolio (see Figure 8.7).

Capital adequacy implies that an institution is using enough equity funding to ensure that the fund's default risk is acceptably low. A conventional measure is the actual or implied debt rating of the fund; the debt rating can be weakly interpreted as corresponding to a probability of default. For instance, an AA-rated fund typically has a default probability less than 0.05 percent. The fund will default if it suffers losses that are large enough to eliminate the

---

[16] The agency literature is vast. Akerlof (1970) and Ross (1973) provide a good overview of the intuition behind agency costs.

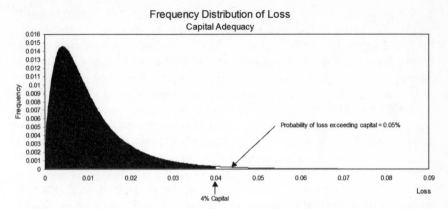

FIGURE 8.7 Frequency Distribution of Loss: Capital Adequacy

equity cushion. The graph in Figure 8.7 shows the loss distribution of the fund's portfolio. For any given level of equity funding, it is possible to determine the probability of losses that would eliminate the equity. For instance, if the portfolio whose distribution is shown in the figure were 4 percent equity funded, then the probability of depleting the equity is 0.05 percent. This is approximately equivalent to the default probability associated with a high debt rating.

Maximum diversification translates into the lowest possible level of portfolio unexpected loss, conditional on a given level of expected return. Note that this is different than minimizing risk without regard to return. (The latter can be accomplished by holding to maturity a portfolio of U.S. Treasury bills!) For each level of return, and for a given set of possible assets, there is a unique set of holdings that gives the minimum unexpected loss. When we depict the expected return and unexpected loss associated with each of these portfolios, the resulting graph is called the *efficient frontier*. The process for determining how much *economic capital* (equity) to use in financing an asset, and the process for maximizing diversification, both require measuring how much risk an individual asset contributes to the portfolio, net of risk reduction due to diversification.

IMPROVING PORTFOLIO PERFORMANCE

In a typical portfolio, there exist assets whose returns are large relative to the amount of risk they contribute. (Note that in practice we must be specific about our measure of portfolio-referent risk—as noted, both RC and TRC have their place in any portfolio performance analysis.) There are also assets whose returns are small relative to the amount of risk they contribute to the portfolio. Both of these types of assets are mispriced relative to the portfolio in which they are being held. Note that when we label these assets *mispriced* we are not making a statement about what their market value should be. It is possible that the market price is efficient in the context of the broad market, but that the asset is mispriced in the context of a particular portfolio. For example, a European bond in a Japanese portfolio may appear to offer a higher return for its contribution to the portfolio risk, given the lower correlation with the Japanese exposures, even if it is bought at market in the bond market. Thus, mispricing in this context relates to a specific portfolio. If, on top of this portfolio-referent mispricing, the market is also pricing the asset inefficiently, there may be an opportunity to earn even more return for a given level of risk (or to take less risk for a given level of return).

In some cases, in fact, this mispricing to portfolio simply reflects that the assets are mispriced in the market, and this type of mispricing is ultimately resolved as the market price adjusts. More often, however, it reflects that the portfolio has too much or too little of the particular assets. If an asset that has too little return for its risk is partially swapped for an asset that is generously compensated for its risk, two things happen. First, the portfolio value is enhanced; without any increase in risk, the portfolio return improves. Second, as the holding of the former asset decreases, its risk contribution goes down (note that similarly, the risk contribution of the latter asset increases). As the risk contributions change, the return-to-risk ratios change for each asset. The former asset is no longer as under-rewarded and the latter is no longer as over-rewarded. Continuing the swap will continue to improve the portfolio until the return-to-risk ratios for each of the assets are brought into alignment with the overall portfolio.

This process, applied to all assets in the portfolio, leads to the maximization of diversification for any given level of return. Thus, a key part of the portfolio management process is to measure the risk contribution of each asset, and its return relative to that risk. An optimized portfolio will not contain the same size allocation of all assets; the holdings will be based upon the risk contribution of each asset relative to its return. In fact, an optimized portfolio is one in which all assets have the same portfolio-referent return-to-risk ratio. Any deviation implies the existence of a swap that could improve the overall portfolio. The availability of CDSs and synthetic CDOs now makes it easier for credit portfolio managers to find trades to improve their portfolios.

Swapping low return-to-risk assets for high return-to-risk assets optimizes a portfolio. Doing this requires that the portfolio manager be able to

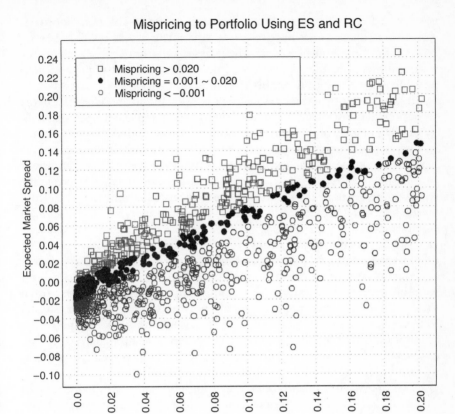

FIGURE 8.8 Mispricing Relative to a Portfolio (Note that KMV (now MKMV) introduced this approach to graphically representing mispricing in its portfolio tools.)

identify which assets are the high and low return-to-risk exposures. Figure 8.8 illustrates for a sample portfolio the return-to-risk characteristics of all the securities in the portfolio; the return to each security is measured by its spread, adjusted for expected loss, while the risk is measured by the risk contribution to the portfolio. Each point in the figure represents one security in the portfolio. The securities represented by the dark circles all have (approximately) average return-to-risk ratios. One can think of this average return-to-risk ratio as defined by a line fit through the middle of the points on the graph. Assets lying above this average ratio level have high values; assets lying below it have low values. As the holding of a low return-to-risk asset is decreased, its risk contribution falls and its return-to-risk ratio improves. The reverse happens for high return-to-risk assets whose holdings are increased. This mechanism serves to move assets into the average range as the portfolio diversification is improved. No further material improvement is possible when all assets lie within the band.

It is key to note that the results of portfolio optimization depend on the set of potential assets that the fund can hold. For example, with the availability of CDS, the set of diversifying exposures has increased substantially for holders of credit portfolios. In the final analysis, it generally does not make sense to maximize diversification over the existing exposures only, without considering the effect of adding new assets into the portfolio. Because of the relatively low default correlations between most borrowers, the gains from broad diversification are substantial and do not decrease quickly as portfolio size increases.

Though the thought of a bank, for example, lowering its risk by *buying* other bank's loans may seem unconventional at first, if we take a step back it is perfectly natural. An equity mutual fund would be poorly diversified if it were limited to only holding those equities that its firm had underwritten itself. This is even more the case for debt portfolios, since there are benefits to diversification in debt larger and more persistent than those in equity. The implication is that funds will benefit from holding the broadest possible set of assets, and to further this objective they must be prepared to buy them when it benefits the fund.

The approaches described here can be used to identify which credit exposures are desirable additions and at which prices. Different holdings of assets in the portfolio result in portfolios with different risk and return characteristics. Recall that we measured risk of the portfolio in terms of UL instead of RC in the example previously discussed. By looking at the stand-alone risk measures or ULs for the individual exposures and the frontier that reflects the portfolio's return-risk possibilities, we see how diversification works. This is illustrated for the portfolio in Figure 8.9.

The dark circles in the figure represent the expected spread versus the unexpected loss for individual assets. A portfolio that consists 100 percent of a single asset will have the same risk and return as that asset. An actual portfolio constructed from multiple assets, depending on their proportions, will produce a specific risk/return combination. The cross in the figure represents one such actual portfolio. Because the assets are positively correlated, all portfolios will have some risk. For a given level of return there must therefore be a portfolio with minimum but still positive risk. The diamond represents the portfolio with the same expected spread as the actual portfolio but the least possible risk. Similarly, there is an upper bound on achievable return at any level of risk. The portfolio represented by the empty circle

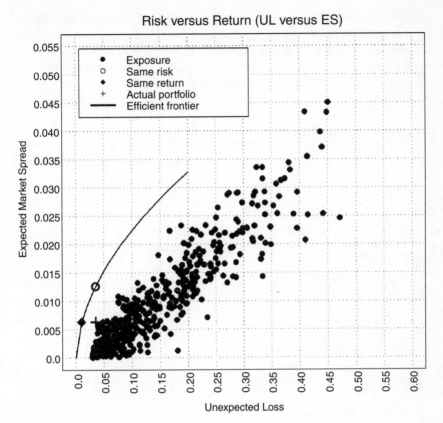

FIGURE 8.9   Risk versus Return

illustrates the maximal return portfolio with the same risk as the actual portfolio. The light line passing through these portfolios is the efficient frontier (estimated, e.g., with market spreads). It represents the expected spread/UL values for those portfolios that have the smallest possible unexpected loss for a given level of expected spread. The unexpected loss of these portfolios lies far to the left of the ULs of the individual assets. This reflects the amount of risk that is eliminated through diversification.

The analytics described in this chapter lend themselves to allowing and encouraging portfolio managers to move their credit portfolios toward the efficient frontier. We have emphasized throughout this chapter that both RC and TRC—especially CVaR-TRC are good measures of risk to use to manage a portfolio. Even if other measures are preferred, the return and risk trade-off concepts continue to be relevant regardless of how return and risk are measured. The key lies in targeting the measures that best set up the portfolio for stable, growing returns and minimize the risk of extreme loss. As we discuss performance metrics, we will focus both on volatility of returns, which is a shorter-term measure of risk, and extreme loss risk, which is a longer-term measure of risk.

PERFORMANCE METRICS

As we have been discussing in the previous section, deciding which exposures to hold, buy, or sell requires the calculation of performance metrics. Moreover, portfolio management is most meaningful when it is done with respect to some benchmark or target for performance. In this section, we provide concrete recommendations for implementing metrics that will fill the requirements we have been discussing in conceptual terms up to this point.

As we have noted in a number of places, several metrics are typically calculated in the context of credit portfolio management:

Sharpe ratio

$\frac{ES_P}{UL_P}$ for portfolio exposure

$\frac{ES_i}{RC_i}$ for individual exposures

Vasicek ratio

$\frac{ES_P}{C_P}$ for portfolio exposure

$\frac{ES_i}{TRC_i}$ for individual exposures

Return on risk-adjusted capital (RORAC)

$\frac{ES_P}{C_P} + (1 + r)^H - 1$ for portfolio exposure

$\frac{ES_i}{C_i} + (1 + r)^H - 1$ for individual exposures

For purposes of calculating these measures, the measures of capital are converted to capitalization *rate* (rather than levels) so that we have the same units as the numerators, which are typically scaled by the mark-to-market value at the as-of date.

The Sharpe ratio measure is one of the most common performance metrics and has found use in a variety of finance calculations. In the credit context, we distinguish a portfolio Sharpe ratio from an individual exposure

Sharpe ratio by using for the denominator UL in the case of the portfolio Sharpe ratio and RC in the case of the individual exposure version of the Sharpe ratio:

$$\frac{ES_P}{UL_P} \text{ for portfolio exposure}$$

$$\frac{ES_i}{RC_i} \text{ for individual exposures}$$

This choice of metric allows the portfolio manager to compare post-diversification contribution to overall portfolio risk. That is, the focus on RC at the individual exposure level allows comparison of each exposure after accounting for how the correlation (or lack thereof) with the rest of the portfolio impacts the overall portfolio diversification. As we have discussed elsewhere, the weighted sum of all the RC quantities in the portfolio is equal to the portfolio UL.

The weakness of the Sharpe ratio as a metric lies in the fact that low-risk, high-concentration (highly correlated) securities will produce a high Sharpe ratio if the ES is a little higher than is typical. For example, a bank portfolio that already has substantial exposure to real estate companies may find a new loan to another large well-capitalized real estate company has a high Sharpe ratio, given that its stand-alone risk is quite low and the ES is moderately high. However, this would be misleading since the correlated nature of the new exposure with respect to the existing portfolio may not be reflected enough in the RC measure. The problem lies in the skewed nature of the return distribution. Equity portfolios, in contrast, have symmetric distributions, making the Sharpe ratio more appropriate. That said, the Sharpe ratio does reveal important information and is a good place to start when evaluating a credit portfolio. The return per unit of volatility provides guidance to how the portfolio will perform over the shorter term.

Because of the skewed nature of portfolio loss distributions, we also look to a second performance metric, such as the Vasicek ratio,

$$\frac{ES_P}{C_P} \text{ for portfolio exposure}$$

$$\frac{ES_i}{TRC_i} \text{ for individual exposures}$$

to evaluate the return per unit of contribution to the risk of *extreme* loss. As we have discussed, TRC, the denominator of the Vasicek ratio, is best calculated based on the CVaR or expected shortfall specification, where we specify the portion of the loss distribution tail in probability space.

For example, we often look at the portion of the tail that runs from 99 percent out to 100 percent—the last 100 basis points of the distribution.

The TRC calculated in this way reflects the average loss experienced by a particular exposure whenever overall portfolio loss is so large that it lies in the region associated with the tail region specified for the calculation. Often, this amount is rescaled so that the weighted sum equals the total capital for the portfolio (refer to the example provided in the section titled "Capital," on using TRC to determine capital allocation). Note, however, that this rescaling does not change the relative ranking of individual exposures based on TRC. The Vasicek ratio indicates the premium earned for taking on extreme-loss risk that typically arises from high concentrations or highly correlated securities. This metric complements well the Sharpe ratio.

A related metric to the Vasicek ratio is return on risk-adjusted capital (RORAC). RORAC uses the capital allocation, C_i, in the denominator, which may be based on either RC or TRC depending on the choice of the portfolio manager.

$$\frac{ES_P}{C_P} + (1 + r)^H - 1 \text{ for portfolio exposure}$$
$$\frac{ES_i}{C_i} + (1 + r)^H - 1 \text{ for individual exposures}$$

The risk-free return is added to the measure since this part of the return is generated without putting (credit) capital at risk. In the early 1990s, risk-adjusted return on capital (RAROC), rather than RORAC, became a popular metric for assessing return per unit of contribution to capital used. RAROC models, however, can be shown to be easily distorted by accounting practices as expenses such as overhead are typically subtracted from the return. Capital in the RAROC calculation will often include more than credit-risk capital (e.g., market-risk capital and operational-risk capital). While reasonable in theory, lingering questions about whether the three types of capital are truly additive, and concerns regarding the best way to calculate operational-risk capital, tend to make this calculation more subjective than the others we have discussed. Often, the operational-risk capital numbers become a plug based on predetermined decisions regarding lending. In the end, the RORAC measure, rather than the RAROC measure, provides a cleaner characterization of return per unit of capital allocated. The Vasicek ratio is an even less muddied measure and the one that we recommend.

In our experience, performance metrics become much more useful if they can be benchmarked. At one level, it is useful to track performance over time in order to compare performance in different time periods. *Ex ante* (i.e., prospective) calculations can be used to drive capital allocation and strategy. Portions of the portfolio with high (low) ratios may be places to invest more (less) capital, and portfolio managers may run various scenarios involving potential investments to assess overall impact on the portfolio. *Ex post* (i.e., retrospective) calculations can be used to evaluate actual performance of a portfolio and to test how well the systems and portfolio managers are doing. However, the performance of external benchmarks, if they can be identified, constitutes the best way to evaluate performance.

The trouble in selecting benchmarks for credit portfolios arises from the fact (once again) that the credit markets do not originate well-diversified portfolios. Thus, broad-based credit market index performance tends to be driven too much by idiosyncratic events such as auto manufacturers suffering huge losses, or an insurance company being debilitated because of exposure to a certain declining sector. Comparing an individual portfolio to this kind of benchmark can result in some arbitrary evaluations that are driven as much by luck as by skill. Some of the newer CDS-based indexes seem to resolve some of this problem and will likely serve as the better benchmarks as long as appropriate comparisons are made. That is, if indexes with portfolios of similar diversification characteristics as an institution's portfolio are used as comparisons to benchmark your portfolio.

While specific levels of performance may be hard to compare from period to period given the changing levels of risk premia, Table 8.1 outlines the Sharpe ratios we have seen in the work we have done during the past 10 years. Note that trading costs can significantly impact portfolio performance in any of these asset classes. These numbers are based on reasonable levels of portfolio turnover.

Different geographies and periods of unusually pronounced spread compression may produce different absolute levels, but the relative performance of these different types of portfolios does not typically change. One weak conclusion that can be drawn is that credit tends to return more per unit of risk than equity portfolios if the credit portfolio is well managed. Note that actively managed equity portfolios do not see much more improvement

TABLE 8.1 Sharpe Ratios

Portfolio Type	Sharpe Ratio to Respective Benchmark
Large bank portfolios	0.1 – 0.3
Improved bank portfolios	0.3 – 0.6
Diversified equity portfolios	0.3 – 0.6
Actively managed debt portfolios	0.5 – 1.5

in realized Sharpe ratios (often they are worse) than fully diversified equity portfolios (even before accounting for the trading costs associated with trading in and out of positions). While every once in a while an equity fund will post astounding performance, that performance is typically short-lived. Credit portfolios, on the other hand, are well suited to active portfolio management. As the credit markets become more efficient and CDS indexes become stronger benchmarks, the financial return to active management of credit portfolios will likely be reduced (if not eliminated).

The difficulty in drawing a *strong* conclusion, though, arises from the fact that we do not have much good data on realized Vasicek ratios. Some suggest that the high Sharpe ratios for actively managed credit funds reflect extra premium for the extreme loss risk. In fact, this may not be an unreasonable assumption. Sometimes, for example, it appears that the results may be driven in some cases from managers maintaining highly concentrated portfolios that would not be recommended. However, many strong, actively managed portfolios still maintain a high level of diversification, so the results in this table are not a consequence of looking *only* at concentrated sectoral or geographic bets. That said, until we have more data, the best we can do is speculate on the drivers of this performance. In the meantime, evaluating the various performance metrics still requires some art mixed in with science if we wish to use these measures to develop a sense of when and how a portfolio has performed well.

REDUCED-FORM MODELS AND PORTFOLIO MODELING

Thus far, we have focused on a structural model approach to portfolio modeling. It is often the case that this type of model makes the most sense for large portfolios held by typical financial institutions since the data needed to parameterize these models is typically more readily available—particularly in high dimensions. Despite this focus, we have highlighted instances, such as in the valuation step of portfolio risk management, where adding a reduced-form model into the mix is attractive.

While more work is required in some cases to apply reduced-form models to large portfolios, in the case of small portfolios such as CDOs or those found in basket swaps, we can model the portfolio behavior directly with reduced-form models—all the way from valuation through to correlation. As with the case of any model, reduced-form models have their limitations. (These limitations were brought to the fore in spring 2005 when changes in the credit quality of some auto manufacturers led to ratings downgrades, which in turn highlighted the rigidness of bankers' rules for indexes on which synthetic CDOs were based, since these indexes contained the auto firms. These rules turned out to be highly prescriptive and were ultimately modified to accommodate more natural market movements.) In the case of reduced-form models, it can sometimes be more difficult to spot cases in which the model is compromised since there is less direct economic intuition for the drivers of default.

Nonetheless, reduced-form models are popular and useful tools and are much more commonly used by analysts supporting traders of CDOs and basket swaps than are structural models because of the ease with which they can be parameterized, and because of their ability to quickly provide estimates of loss distributions even when the full factor structure of the underlying portfolio constituents is not fully known. In the final part of this chapter we touch on topics relevant to using reduced-form models in this context.

CORRELATION IN INTENSITY MODELS

In the reduced-form framework, default is assumed to be unpredictable, driven by an intensity process (the hazard rate of the firm, conditional on not defaulting up until that point) that is typically assumed to be stochastic in nature. The assumption of unpredictable default creates some challenges with respect to modeling the correlation of exposures' values. Since we do not model individual exposure values directly in the reduced-form framework, we need a different model of correlation.

One such approach focuses on creating contagion by creating correlation among the stochastic processes governing the dynamics of each exposure's intensity process (see Duffie and Singleton 2003 and Lando 2004). Much of the work in modeling in this approach is in deciding exactly how to introduce the correlation appropriately, since correlated *intensities* do not directly cause correlated *default times* in the same sense that correlations in asset value cause default correlation in a structural model. The basic principle, which we will describe momentarily, is to correlate the propensities to default (drivers of the intensity functions) across firms. This approach is most natural in reduced-form models specifications involving state variables (Chapter 6). Conceptually the approach involves estimating a matrix of correlations that defines the relationships among each pair of Brownian motions governing the dynamics of each intensity process.

Actually, estimating these correlations under this approach in a way that can be calibrated with observable data or prices can require some work because the dependence structure is quite weak (as correlated intensities do not directly result in correlated default times). Recall that the intensity defines only the propensity to default in a statistical sense—not a specific time of default that can be directly correlated. We next explore some alternative strategies for introducing dependence in a reduced-form modeling framework.

One such strategy is to create a contagion effect by conditioning one component of the intensity on whether another firm has already defaulted (again see Duffie and Singleton 2004 and Lando 2004). Mathematically, the framework can be described as follows:

$$h_t^1 = a_1 + a_2 1_{(\tau^2 \le t)}$$
$$h_t^2 = b_1 + b_2 1_{(\tau^1 \le t)}$$

where h_t^i is the hazard rate (intensity) of firm i at time t

          τ^i is the time to default of firm i

          $1_{(c)}$ is an indicator that takes the value 1 if condition c is true and zero otherwise

          the coefficients $a, b, \ldots$ vary by firm

Essentially, Firm 1's intensity has a component that kicks in when Firm 2 defaults, and vice versa. A matrix of coefficient estimates is required to generate the interactions. This estimation is also difficult given the nature of the data and the underlying processes.

Now consider yet another possible strategy that moves us closer to more realistic dependence. Recall from Chapter 6 that under the Cox-Ingersoll-Ross (CIR) assumptions, we arrive at the following expression for the cumulative probability of default (*cpd*) to time t:

$$cpd_t = 1 - e^{a_{CIR}(t) + b_{CIR}(t)h(0)}$$

If we generalize this expression, we can express the relationship of the *cpd* for a specific firm, i, at a fixed horizon to its default time, τ_i, as follows:

$$F_{\tau_i}(t) = P(\tau_i \le t) = cpd_{it}$$

In the case of the CIR assumptions, F_{τ_i} is defined as above. We have added an i subscript (in addition to the t) to denote the possibility of there being many heterogeneous obligors represented in the portfolio.

We need one more building block for this approach in order to complete the introduction of dependence in this reduced-form modeling framework. This building block relates to a property of the *cumulative intensity* of default defined as $\int_0^\tau h(t)\,dt$. This quantity is exponentially distributed with a mean of one (see Bremaud (1981) for the theorem for this property of the cumulative default intensity). Thus, the default time, τ, for obligor i can be characterized as:

$$\tau_i = \inf \left\{ t \geq 0 : \int_0^t h_i(u)\,du = \xi_i \right\}$$

where ξ_i is exponentially distributed

The trick in this approach is to introduce correlation among the ξ_i for all exposures in the portfolio.

In this way, we can back out correlated default times as follows:

1. Draw correlated ξ_i for all i from a jointly exponential distribution.
2. Calculate an associated vector of uniformly distributed variables, u_i, as follows: $u_i = 1 - e^{-\xi_i}$. Note that the uniformly distributed variables inherit dependence from the correlated ξ_i.
3. Determine default time using a suitable function that incorporates the default intensity as follows: $\tau_i = F_i^{-1}(u_i)$. In this way, we do not have to directly simulate the intensity processes and we still generate dependence among the default times for the portfolio exposures.

See Glasserman (2004) for more details on different techniques for incorporating these approaches into simulations.

While we do not find these approaches used very often in practice to build correlation into a portfolio model, these model frameworks are useful for experimenting with intensity interaction effects. For example, they can be used to gain more insight into the behavior of small CDOs, CDS indexes, and kth-to-default swaps. Importantly, adding this dependency into models for evaluating traded baskets or portfolios can improve the ability to fit actual pricing. An important theme implicit in the prior discussion is the interaction of marginal (i.e., univariate) and joint (i.e., multivariate) distributions. The approaches just described are popular given the ease with which the joint and marginal distributions interact.

As for techniques used in practice, the most common approach to convolute (i.e., correlate) multiple univariate distributions relies on *copula functions*, which we discuss in the next section. We have already introduced the notion of copulas in the context of generating joint distributions. We now explore an interesting characteristic of copulas: Any copula function can be grafted onto any set of marginal distributions.

COPULAS

Copula functions are mathematical tools used to create families of multivariate distributions with given marginal distributions (see, for example, Joe 1997 or Nelson 1999). In other words, a copula function knits together the underlying univariate distributions that drive the values of the portfolio's exposures. Copula functions are a mechanism for reflecting dependence structure. In many applications, the functional form does not relate to any particular economic model or any particular economic intuition, but rather is chosen to produce reasonable correlations and prices or for computational convenience (or both).

Since a copula's role in generating a multivariate (i.e., reflecting correlation) distribution does not arise in the context of a particular set of model assumptions, an analyst is free to superimpose any copula function on any set of univariate distributions desired. This freedom is a double-edged sword.

On the one hand, the lack of restrictions provides flexibility for experimentation and fitting. We will discuss a limited list of copula functions in a moment, but the possibilities are numerous. This means that copulas provide an extremely flexible tool for capturing the relationships between assets in a portfolio, even if the true relationship is unknown or poorly specified.

On the other hand, this freedom implies that the estimation exercise can sometimes become nothing more than calibration, which requires a set of values (typically prices) to which to calibrate. While price data exist for some CDO tranches, the liquidity difficulties in markets for these tranches can overshadow the underlying dynamics at times, creating parameter instability in practical estimation settings. For a typical bank portfolio, we will not have any price data for calibration in many asset classes. Moreover, copula functions sometimes rest on assumptions of homogeneity in the underlying collateral portfolio, which is almost never the case. Nonetheless, in many settings these concerns can be addressed, making copulas another useful tool in an analyst's tool kit.

The most popular copula function is the Gaussian copula or multivariate normal distribution. (Note that with homogeneous correlation and PDs, the single-factor Gaussian copula reduces to the Vasicek 1987 model.) Some criticize the Gaussian copula because of the lack of tail dependence. That is, since credit portfolios are characterized by extreme losses, it is critical to understand co-dependence that drives losses in the tail or extreme loss region of the portfolio loss distribution. Some analysts believe the Gaussian copula does not reflect enough of this clustering and co-dependence in the tail region so there is a perceived lack of sufficient tail risk in the loss distribution estimates. Other copula functions can be used to create more tail risk in the final loss distribution estimate. For example, the Student-t copula could be used in conjunction with normal marginal distributions to produce more co-dependence in the tail, thereby increasing the tail risk (i.e., fatter-tailed loss distributions). Even here, though, some evidence suggests that this formulation does not reflect the underlying behavior of portfolios very well.

Mathematically, a copula function,[17] C, specifies the joint distribution function as follows:

$$F(x_1, \ldots, x_N) = C(F_1(x_1), \ldots, F_N(x_N))$$

F_i, $i = 1, \ldots, N$ are the marginal distributions

These marginal distributions can be assumed to have any form that complies with the laws of probability and is related to the assumptions driving the value of the exposures in the portfolio. While there is considerable flexibility in the specification of the marginal distributions, the shape of loss distribution is fairly sensitive to the choice of the C function and how the parameters governing its dynamics are estimated.

In order to develop some intuition of how these functions work in practice, we list several examples of common copula functions:

- Independent: $C(x_1, x_2) = x_1 x_2$
- Perfect correlation: $C(x_1, x_2) = \min(x_1, x_2)$
- Gaussian: $C(x_1, x_2) = P(\Phi(X_1) \leq x_1, \Phi(X_2) \leq x_2)$
  where X_1 and X_2 are jointly normally distributed with correlation $\rho_{1,2}$
- Gumbel: $C(x_1, x_2) = e^{\left[-[(-\ln x_1)^\alpha + (-\ln x_2)^\alpha]^{\frac{1}{\alpha}}\right]}$
- Others: Clayton, Student-t, Double t, Frank (see Cherubini, Luciano, and Vecchiato 2004 for details)

In the spirit of the simulation discussion earlier, we can use copulas to simulate correlated default times. Even if we do not have refined estimates of the parameters of the copula functions, these simple copula-based simulations can be a quick (and sometimes dirty) way to develop some intuition

---

[17] Note that we abuse slightly our notation here by using the symbol C in this case to represent a copula function relating marginal distributions, rather than reflecting the capital number as was the case earlier in this chapter.

regarding portfolio behavior when the individual exposure data are not available. In the CDO context, copula functions become quite useful for developing a method of communicating tranche value (similar to the way that Black-Scholes volatility is used to communicate value in the option market). In the same way that the Black-Scholes option-pricing model is not assumed to reflect the actual market behavior of options, copula measures of tranche value may be highly stylized. In some ways, copula functions become both a means of communication and a straightforward approach to test theories and conjectures.

In order to develop a simple simulation based on a copula function, we start by generating a vector of uniform, random variables $(u_1, \ldots, u_N)$. Next we convert these uniformly distributed variables using the copula function to arrive at the default times, as follows:

$$\tau_1 = F_1^{-1}(u_1), \ldots, \tau_N = F_N^{-1}(u_N)$$

Based on the outcome, we can determine which exposures defaulted when, and record values in the default and nondefault states, similar to our early simulation procedure. We then draw another set of uniform, random variables. The copula function provides the bridge to determine the extent to which defaults cluster.

In implementation, this approach is a bit easier to write down than it is to calibrate. In many cases, the most straightforward approach is to simulate, say, the multivariate normal distribution directly. Correlation in this case is governed by the covariance matrix that characterizes the multivariate distribution.

Of course, the copula drives the outcome based on the way in which it is parameterized and like all models, copula models are only as good as their calibrated parameters. (Please refer to Trivedi and Zimmer 2005 for more detail on the more practical aspects of using copulas.)

FRAILTY

Before we leave our discussion of introducing correlation into reduced-form models, we discuss a new technique that appears to hold great promise. This technique, called *frailty* analysis, is motivated by the frailty survival model literature for health sciences. Conceptually, the approach assumes latent nonobservable factors that can also drive the default process. For example, there may be factors that cannot be observed, but that are common to all firms in a particular industry.

Another way to think about frailty is that there may be common practices, suppliers, and so on among firms in an industry or region (or even in a specific bank's portfolio), the importance of which only becomes clear *ex post*. These latent factors contribute to the covariance of the assets in the portfolio.

Duffie, Eckner, Horel, and Saita (2006) have adapted frailty analysis to produce dependence in a portfolio of credit instruments. This approach assumes both observable covariates that drive obligor default intensities and unobservable, common sources of frailty—that is, default-risk factors that change randomly over time. We will briefly explain the approach described by Duffie et al. (2006). Please refer to that paper for more details.

Again, we assume N obligors have default intensities, h_{it}, $i = 1 \ldots N$ and $t = 1 \ldots T$, in a doubly stochastic, reduced-form model framework. We specify these default intensities as a function of firm-specific covariates, macroeconomic covariates, and unobservable frailty variables.

$$h_{it} = \tilde{h}_{it} e^{\eta y_t}$$

where $\tilde{h}_{it} = e^{\beta w_{it}}$

This component of the intensity is a function of the following observable covariates:

$$\mathbf{w}_{it} = (1, \mathbf{u}_{it}, \mathbf{v}_t)$$

where $\mathbf{u}_{it} \equiv$ Firm-specific vector of covariates
$\mathbf{v}_t \equiv$ Vector of macroeconomic covariates that are observable

Possible candidates for the $\mathbf{u}_{it}$ covariates include distance to default (DD) as calculated with a structural model applied to equity data (see Chapter 3), logarithm of firm's market value of assets, trailing one-year equity return, and amount of short-term debt relative to long-term debt. Duffie et al. find DD to be the most statistically significant. We look forward to more research in this area to develop a better idea of appropriate firm-specific covariates.

Possible candidates for the $\mathbf{v}_t$ covariates include the three-month Treasury bill rate, trailing one-year S&P 500 index return, GDP growth rate, industrial production growth rate, average industry DD, and U.S. dollar swap spread over U.S. Treasuries. Duffie, et al. find the three-month Treasury bill rate and the trailing one-year S&P 500 index return to be the most statistically significant. Again, more research is needed to better understand the interaction of macroeconomic variables and default intensities. This functional relationship can be quite useful in the context of stress testing where specific macroeconomic scenarios can be evaluated in terms of portfolio impact.

$\mathbf{y}_t \equiv$ Vector of unobservable frailty covariates

$\theta = (\beta, \eta) \equiv$ Parameter vector that is common to all firms

Once we have this setup, we are left with a maximum likelihood problem. Duffie, Saita, and Wang (2007) demonstrate that the joint maximum likelihood estimation (MLE) of the parameter vector γ, which determines the covariate time-series dynamics, and the parameter vector θ, which determines the obligors' exit intensities, can be separated into two MLE operations for γ and θ, respectively. Duffie et al. (2006) derive the following equation based on this foundation:

$$L(\gamma, \theta | \mathbf{w}, \mathbf{d}) = L(\gamma | \mathbf{w}) \int L(\theta | \mathbf{w}, y, \mathbf{d}) p_y(y) \, dy$$

where $\mathbf{w} = (\mathbf{w}_{it} : 1 \leq i \leq \mathbf{n})$

for all t in the sample. That is, we simplify notation so that we have the vector of observations over the sample for all obligors in the sample.

We similarly denote a vector of default indicators:

$$\mathbf{d} = (\mathbf{d}_{it} : 1 \leq i \leq \mathbf{n})$$

for all t in the sample over all obligors.

Finally, $p_Y(y) \equiv$ probability density for the path of the unobserved frailty process **y**. Note that we have assumed the frailty process **y** has a fixed probability distribution and is independent of **w**.

With this notation defined, we can go on to solve the MLE system as follows:

$$L(\gamma, \theta | \mathbf{w}, \mathbf{d}) = L(\gamma | \mathbf{w}) E_\mathbf{y} \left[\prod_{i=1}^{n} \left(e^{-\sum_{t=t_i}^{T_i} h_{it} \Delta t} \prod_{t=t_i}^{T_i} [\mathbf{d}_{it} h_{it} + (1 - \mathbf{d}_{it})] \right) | \mathbf{w}, \mathbf{d} \right]$$

where $E_\mathbf{y} \equiv$ Expectation for **y** given probability density $p_\mathbf{y}(y)$

GIBBS SAMPLER

While more standard maximum likelihood methods are available for estimating models with observables, the presence of frailty factors requires a modified set of estimation tools. The challenge for this frailty model is in the maximization of the likelihood in the presence of the component of the likelihood function that relies on the distribution of the frailty factors. Duffie et al. (2006) propose a combination of expectation maximization with the Gibbs sampler. This technique is designed for estimating parameters in models where the data are incomplete or missing. Following is a brief outline of the approach.

We focus on maximum likelihood estimation (MLE) of the default intensity parameter vector, θ. Begin by finding an initial estimate for the parameters. For example, Duffie et al. (2006) suggest applying standard MLE techniques (e.g., Newton-Raphson) to the model without frailty. Specifically, this means finding

$$\theta^{(0)} = (\hat{\beta}, \eta = 0.05)$$

where $\hat{\beta}$ is estimated from the following equation, which reflects the parameter estimates without the frailty factors:

$$L(\gamma, \theta | \mathbf{w}, \mathbf{d}) = L(\gamma | \mathbf{w}, \mathbf{y}) \prod_{i=1}^{n} \left(e^{-\sum_{t=t_i}^{T_i} h_{it} \Delta t} \prod_{t=t_i}^{T_i} [\mathbf{d}_{it} h_{it} \Delta t + (1 - \mathbf{d}_{it})] \right)$$

Based on the current parameter estimate, $\theta^{(k)}$, the observed covariate data, $\mathbf{w}$, and the observed default data, $\mathbf{d}$, generate sample paths for the frailty covariates, $y_t^{(j)}$, where $0 \leq t \leq T$, and for all $j = 1, \ldots, n$. Duffie et al. (2006) suggest using the Gibbs sampler (see Geman and Geman 1984), assuming that $\mathbf{y}$ follows a Brownian process.

The specification for arriving at this conditional distribution:

$$P(y | \mathbf{w}, \mathbf{d}, \theta^{(k)})$$

(Continued)

GIBBS SAMPLER (*Continued*)

can be found in Appendix A in Duffie et al. (2006). We can then proceed as follows:

1. Adopt the following approximation for the posterior distribution of y_t:

$$P(\mathbf{y}_t = y_j | \mathbf{y}_{t-1}, \mathbf{y}_{t+1}, \mathbf{w}, \mathbf{d}) \approx \frac{q_j}{q_1 + \cdots + q_J}$$

where

$$q_j = e^{(c_0 + c_1((y_j - y_{t-1})^2 + (y_{t+1} - y_j)^2) + c_2 e^{\mathbf{w}y_j} + c_3 y_j)}$$

for a finite set of outcomes of $\mathbf{y}$ defined as $\{y_1, \ldots, y_J\}$ (Duffie et al. recommend $J = 321$) and constants c_0, c_1, c_2, c_3 dependent on the default data, D, and covariate data, $\mathbf{w}$, at any point in time. However, these constants do not depend on the latent frailty factor. Rather, they are estimated directly from the default data.

2. Set $\mathbf{y}_t = 0$ for $t = 0, \ldots, T$.
3. For $t \in \{1, \ldots, T\}$, draw a new value of $\mathbf{y}_t$, y, from its approximated, conditional distribution given $\mathbf{y}_{t-1}$ and $\mathbf{y}_{t+1}$ (recall that y will be one of $[y_1, \ldots, y_J]$).
4. Store each sample path and return to step 3 to draw another value until the specified number of paths has been simulated.

Next, we maximize the approximated, expected complete-data log likelihood,

$$\hat{Q}(\boldsymbol{\theta}, \boldsymbol{\theta}^{(k)})$$

(or intermediate quantity) using the sample paths generated by the Gibbs sampler. In this case, we can use Newton-Raphson to find the parameter vector, $\boldsymbol{\theta}$, that maximizes the following function:

$$\hat{Q}(\boldsymbol{\theta}, \boldsymbol{\theta}^{(k)}) = \frac{1}{m} \sum_{j=1}^{m} \log L(\boldsymbol{\theta} | \mathbf{w}, \mathbf{y}^{(j)}, \mathbf{d})$$

where m is the number of sample paths generated with the Gibbs sampler.

We are now in a position to estimate the parameters with MLE. One brute-force approach would involve Monte Carlo integration over the possible paths for the frailty process **y**. Since data are often available monthly (sometimes even weekly), this Monte Carlo approach would quickly become too numerically intensive to use in practice. Another approach, recommended in the paper, is to assume **y** is a standard Brownian motion and estimate parameters using expectation maximization (EM) (Little and Rubin 1987) and the Gibbs sampler (Geman and Geman 1984). (See box.)

While this frailty approach to incorporating dependence is new, it has tremendous potential. The integration of both observable covariates at the firm-specific and macroeconomic levels with unobservable, latent frailty factors provides tremendous flexibility for capturing correlation risk in a reduced-form framework and, importantly, reflects a source of variance that is not captured elsewhere in portfolio models. The drawback lies in the complexity of the estimation approach and the computational cost associated with implementing MLE on latent variables. As computing power increases and computing cost decreases, we expect to see more applications of this technique in the future.

INTEGRATING MARKET AND CREDIT RISK

In recent years, financial institutions have made progress toward developing a comprehensive view of the overall risk reflected in a given portfolio. The management of interest-rate risk became much easier in the 1980s with the advent of interest-rate swaps and other interest rate derivatives. Most financial institutions track their interest rate risk quite well. Global institutions also face foreign exchange (FX) risk in their portfolios. While FX risk can be managed with derivatives such as cross-currency swaps, the jury is still out on whether it is ultimately beneficial to manage FX in a global credit portfolio that is already diversified across currencies. In addition to interest rate and FX risk, some financial institutions also face equity price risk as they build equity portfolios alongside their credit portfolios.

These market risks (interest rates, FX, and equity) require a separate set of models and capital allocation. Until recently, market risks and credit risks were modeled separately and the results of each analysis were combined, if at all, in a simple fashion. Today, most financial institutions are interested in integrating all of the risks they face—both market and credit—and, in so doing, answering the following question: *Should allocated capital be additive across market and credit risks or is there some diversification benefit along these dimensions deep down in the portfolio that mitigates the overall capital necessary to support the more comprehensive portfolio?*

An unparalleled benefit of the factor-model framework described in the first part of this chapter lies in the framework's flexibility to incorporate more complex, higher dimensional factor models. In this section, we return to our discussion of the structural factor model and suggest ways in which some market risks can be incorporated.

If we can link the factor draws to valuation models for other risks, integration of all risk results as a natural outcome. For credit risk, equity value seems like a natural candidate for deriving factors since in a structural framework we model underlying asset value. (The trouble, of course, is that equity value may be driven by more than just underlying asset value.) A reasonable first approximation, as we have argued throughout this book, is to use equity values to infer asset values and then determine how these vary together by geography, sector, and so on. An advantage in doing so is the ease with which credit instruments and equity instruments can be modeled in the same portfolio framework. The factors driving credit risk, having been derived from equity values, can then be used to model equity instruments as well.

Foreign exchange, however, is a different matter. In practice, linking the same set of factors used for driving debt and equity value to FX behavior is something that is not yet fully within reach analytically. As a result, we may not yet be able to satisfactorily link FX risk with the other risks in our portfolio. Fortunately, while FX risk is evasive, for interest rate risk, the more important challenge, we may be a little closer to a usable solution.

In Chapters 3 and 6, we touched on the interaction of default-risk-free interest rates and credit spreads. In any valuation exercise, we discount future cash flows at some kind of discount rate. The extent to which this discount rate and the underlying processes driving the cash flows are correlated can substantially impact credit analysis. In the portfolio context, this interaction can cascade across portfolio exposures and materially change the outcome of our risk analysis. Most financial institutions already have sophisticated asset-liability management (ALM) systems to manage their exposure to interest rate risk. This makes sense since, as we discussed in the early chapters of this text, most financial institutions—banks in particular—are not well suited to take substantial interest rate risk. Thus, ALM is critical to minimizing interest rate risk.

STOCHASTIC INTEREST RATES
IN CREDIT MODELS

In order for the integration of interest rate and credit risk to work, the valuation models the bank uses must contemplate and accommodate stochastic interest rates. This model feature can, however, substantially slow down the simulation. We recommend using a two-dimensional lattice model in which one dimension reflects the DD evolution and the other dimension reflects the interest rate process.

For example, we might assume that interest rates evolve according to a Vasicek interest rate model as follows:

$$dr_t = \kappa(\mu_r - r_t)\,dt + \sigma_r\,dz_t$$

where　$\kappa =$ Speed of mean reversion to long-term mean
　　　　$\mu_r =$ Long-term mean for the interest rate
　　　　$\sigma_r =$ Volatility of the interest rate process

For the DD, we might assume an evolution that behaves according to the DD transition densities that we discussed in the credit migration section. Alternatively, we could model just the evolution of the asset value.

With these two dimensions, DD and interest rates, overlaid on the lattice, we can generate a value based on parameterization of these systems. The fact that we have state-contingent values at each node of the lattice allows for the introduction of optionality such as prepayment for loans, call and put options for bonds, and conditional usage for commitment lines. As long as the option can be related back to a conditional value realization in the lattice, we can incorporate the option into the valuation.

The models used for ALM can often be overlaid on the credit portfolio framework we have laid out by developing a linkage to the factor set driving the asset values. Ideally, an institution's interest rate models and its credit models should be estimated on the same (comprehensive) factor set. This must be part not only of the portfolio model, but of the valuation models for individual exposures.

The relationship of interest rates to credit spreads turns out to be a fickle one. In some years, the relationship is negative, with high rates implying lower spreads. In other years, it moves to the positive region where rates and credit spreads move together. In more recent years (as of the time of this writing), the interest rate and credit spread processes seem to have decoupled and become independent! Even so, recent trends in all developed economies are toward higher interest rates with accompanying higher volatilities of both interest rates and credit spreads, which suggests that the linkage between interest rates and credit spreads may reassert itself. Analysts contemplating integrated modeling of market and credit risk will need to be more vigilant in recalibrating the parameters of the underlying models and will likely need to do so more often. Straight credit modeling with a robust structural framework does not require quite so much recalibration as DD, and its relationship to value can be more stable over time.

COUNTERPARTY RISK IN CREDIT DEFAULT SWAPS (CDS) AND CREDIT PORTFOLIOS

Throughout this chapter we have discussed CDSs in similar terms as bonds and loans. While CDS spreads and bond spreads do, in many ways, behave in a similar fashion, it is important to also emphasize several key differences associated with CDS modeling in a portfolio context. First, whether buying or selling protection (i.e., CDSs), each counterparty is exposed not only to the credit risk of the underlying asset, but also to the credit risk of the other counterparty to the swap itself.[18]

In the case of buying protection, the buyer is interested in both the default probability of the underlying obligor and the default probability of the counterparty. For portfolio risk modeling purposes, an important analytic is

---

[18] Recall that the counterparty to the CDS is the institution that takes the other side of the swap. A seller of protection would have a counterparty who promises to pay premia, and a buyer of protection would have a counterparty who promises to make payment in the event of a default (or other prespecified credit event) on the underlying name. In many cases, counterparties to CDS contracts are high-quality financial institutions with low default probabilities. However, large concentrations to the same set of high-quality counterparties may adversely affect the diversification of certain portfolios. The liquidity difficulties experienced by the credit markets in summer 2007 exacerbated this risk as some counterparties started facing capitalization concerns as their portfolios eroded in value.

the joint default probability of the underlying obligor and the counterparty. This joint default probability will be a function of the individual default probabilities and the correlation between the underlying obligor and the counterparty. Note that buying protection is similar in form to shorting a loan or bond. While the value of the position may behave similarly to a short-loan or short-bond position, the presence of this joint default probability issue makes the CDS analysis a little more involved.

Some may argue that the joint default probability of a high-quality counterparty and a moderate- to high-quality underlying obligor is close enough to zero that it can be safely ignored. This argument ignores potential correlation effects that increase the size of the overall portfolio downside risk. Many portfolios held by financial institutions contain exposures, both directly to the counterparties in the form of debt investments or credit lines, and indirectly via positions in CDSs contracted with the same counterparties.

Properly accounting for this correlation is important, as it may materially impact the credit risk analysis of a portfolio. Said differently, the sheer size of exposures to a group of correlated, high-quality counterparties may result in higher probabilities of extreme portfolio losses. For example, a commercial bank may have several credit lines to other financial institutions and then separately, in its derivatives book, the bank may also have these same financial institutions as counterparties. In difficult market conditions, these risks may result in extreme losses as the counterparty defaults not just on the outstanding credit lines but also on derivatives on which it was obligated to pay.

The "low probability" argument for ignoring counterparty risk also fails when economic conditions affecting a particular group of counterparties materially increase their risk. Recent experience in Japan demonstrates how once-strong financial institutions may suddenly increase in riskiness, resulting in much higher joint default probabilities among the deteriorated counterparties and low-quality obligors. Frequent monitoring of the total risk exposure across a credit portfolio reduces the chance of facing a sudden increase in the joint default probabilities of counterparties and obligors. With suitable analytics, a warning system can be implemented to provide some signals of when to change counterparties for CDSs.

In the case of selling protection, the seller, like the buyer, is interested in the default probability of the underlying obligor. The seller is also concerned with the default probability of the protection buyer because the periodic payment of CDS premiums is dependent on the health of the counterparty. Practically speaking, the cash value of the premium stream is small relative to other types of exposures. If the protection buyer stops paying, the seller no longer has the obligation to deliver on the contract in the event of default. That said, the value of the contract will have changed, given the elimination of the future cash flows when the protection buyer stops paying. Holders of large portfolios of CDSs would be well served to consider modeling the behavior of protection buyers when they sell protection.

The other key difference with CDS contracts is in the implementation of valuation models. These valuations depend critically on the nature of the contract terms with respect to what is delivered in the event of default. For some contracts, a fixed amount is promised. For other contracts, an actual security—sometimes the cheapest to deliver—is promised. These characteristics should be reflected in the valuation models used for CDSs.

Since a CDS contract is only a swap of premiums for an agreement to cover loss (in accordance with the terms of the swap) in the event of default, one has to make an assumption regarding the implicit risk-free rate. Depending on whether the implicit risk-free rate is the U.S. Treasury curve, the dollar swap curve, or some other corporate default-risk borrowing curve (i.e., 0-EDF curve), the interpretation of the premium will change. This interpretation will influence estimates of the market risk premium as well as liquidity premiums.[19]

CONCLUSION

Credit portfolio management has two central features:

1. The measurement of diversification at the portfolio level.
2. The measurement of the degree to which individual assets or groups of assets affect diversification.

These measurements require estimates of (1) probabilities of default for each asset, (2) expected recovery in the event of default for each asset, and (3) default correlations between each pair of borrowers or obligors.

---

[19] Our own research and that of our colleagues suggests that CDS premia can be interpreted as implicit spreads over a *corporate default-risk borrowing curve*, which is typically 10 to 20 basis points below the dollar swap curve. We can construct such a curve by relying on the swap market for the shape of the curve and then on high-quality corporate borrowers to determine an indication of the level of the short, middle, and long tenors.

In this chapter we have tried primarily to describe a consistent conceptual framework and actual methods for determining these quantities.

In particular, these methods enable the credit portfolio manager to assess:

- The overall frequency distribution of loss associated with its portfolio.
- The risk and return contribution of individual assets or groups of assets.
- The risk/return characteristics of the existing portfolio and how to improve it.
- Overall economic capital adequacy.
- The economic capital required for new and existing assets.
- How to maximize diversification and minimize the use of economic capital.

In short, these new methods provide the means by which a portfolio manager can implement a rigorous program for managing his credit portfolio for maximum return while maintaining risk at a desirable level. With the availability of CDSs and synthetic CDOs, portfolio managers now have more ways to act on the results of the type of credit portfolio analysis outlined in this chapter.

However, it is important to realize that both the portfolio methods we describe here and the techniques for estimating the correlations that drive them are very new. Furthermore, the rare but correlated nature of default events makes validating these systems and parameters challenging. These observations taken together suggest that we still have a ways to go in developing portfolio methods, even though we have made tremendous progress in the last decade. In particular, there is still active debate about the appropriate thickness of the extreme tails of loss distributions and what combinations of factors, functions, and parameters is best for modeling them.

This does not mean the models cannot be used; we think they should be used actively. Rather, in using these powerful tools, users need also consider the limitations of the models as they formulate business strategies around the model outputs.

REVIEW QUESTIONS

1. List and describe five elements of individual and portfolio credit risk.
2. Explain why the unexpected losses of a credit portfolio are not equal to the weighted average of the unexpected losses of each individual credit in the portfolio.

3. How does the expected loss of a portfolio change as the correlation in the portfolio is increased? How does the expected loss above a certain capital level (e.g., 99.9 percent) change as the correlation in the portfolio increases? How would the median loss change?

4. Why is estimating pairwise correlations through a sampling of asset time series not a recommended methodology for a large portfolio? What approach might be preferable?

5. How might an institution compute the expected return on a loan or credit facility using PD and loss given default?

6. Describe the key difference between evaluating a short position in a credit-risky bond and a long position in a CDS on the same risky bond.

7. Why are historical pairwise asset correlations poor estimates of future out-of-sample correlation realizations?

8. What is the difference between default correlation and (asset) value correlation?

9. Describe the difference between implicit and explicit factor modeling.

10. Explain the steps for simulating a portfolio loss distribution in the context of a structural framework.

EXERCISES

1. What is the default correlation if firm A's PD is 0.20 percent, firm B's PD is 0.50 percent, and the joint probability of default is 0 percent? If the joint probability of default increases to 0.002 percent, what is the default correlation?

2. If the probabilities of default of Credit 1 and Credit 2 are p_1 and p_2, and the default correlation is ρ, then if ρ is unknown but not negative, what is the largest possible probability of both Credit 1 and Credit 2 defaulting? What is the smallest possible probability?

3. A Japanese bank credit portfolio manager approaches you about improving his portfolio's diversification. He wants to add a corporate bond issued by a large, German obligor; however, he has heard from other Japanese traders that some Japanese institutions have had trouble with understanding the nuances of German corporate law when enforcing the terms of a bond indenture.

   a. Specify a trade using instruments that are not German corporate bonds that will generate the same type of payoff profile as a German corporate bond.

b. Highlight two potential sources of differences in the payoff of the replicating strategy and the corporate bond.

c. Without solving for the actual (at-market) value, write down a generic (i.e., indicate functions with major inputs) reduced-form model from which the replicating strategy could be estimated. Provide clear qualitative definitions of the functions and a short explanation of the intuition behind the mathematical relationship

4. What is likely to happen to the Sharpe ratio for exposures that have been valued at book at the as-of date and then switched to MTM?

CHAPTER 9

Building a Better Bank

A Case Study

An idea that is developed and put into action is more important than an idea that exists only as an idea.

—Buddha

I often say that when you can measure what you are speaking about and express it in numbers, you know something about it; but when you cannot measure it, when you cannot express it in numbers, your knowledge is of a meager and unsatisfactory kind: it may be the beginning of knowledge, but you have scarcely, in your thoughts, advanced the stage of science whatever the matter may be.

—Lord Kelvin (William Thompson)

Objectives

After reading this chapter, you should understand the following:

- Background of a hypothetical bank looking to implement ACPM and economic capital management.
- Motivation behind looking for new systems and new organization.
- Underlying premises of building a more valuable bank.
- Examples of portfolio analysis.
- Characteristics of systems and organizations needed to implement effective ACPM.

While the concepts and models discussed in this book have applicability to many of the participants in the credit markets, it is commercial banks that provide one of the more interesting contexts in which to study credit risk management. In the course of our professional work, we have had the opportunity to work extensively with dozens of commercial banks in this context. Each bank has its own set of strengths and weaknesses. No organization ever implements its credit risk models and systems in the way we would have predicted at the outset of each project. The reason for this is that inevitably, as such projects progress, numerous challenges and work-arounds present themselves. A subset of the issues that arise in such implementations is specific to a particular bank and is unlikely to be encountered at other institutions. Nevertheless, many issues resonate with similar experiences encountered at a variety of banks.

Instead of focusing on a particular bank, we have decided to construct a representative case study that reflects bits and pieces of the many implementations we have seen or done over the years. In this way, we have more flexibility to focus on the issues of primary importance. This case study reflects a hypothetical commercial bank, which we will call Krisalys Bank. This bank, like many real institutions, is in the midst of transitions along the following business dimensions:

- It is moving from qualitative credit assessment to a credit assessment process based on quantitative credit models.
- It is centralizing its credit portfolio to be managed by an active credit portfolio management (ACPM) group.
- It is developing an economic capital methodology to drive strategy and determine incentives.
- It is wrestling with the organizational implications of introducing ACPM and economic capital management.

We start by describing the current situation at this bank.

DESCRIPTION

Krisalys Bank has a global footprint with headquarters in London. Its portfolio spans a variety of asset classes with (unsurprisingly) heavy concentration in large European corporate borrowers. While the bank has a long legacy of profitability stretching back 50 years, its performance has been lackluster in the past decade. The mid-1970s almost brought the bank down as many of its borrowers experienced financial stress at the same time. By selling off some of its subsidiaries and doing some restructuring, it saved itself from bankruptcy. The 1980s and 1990s saw more stable growth in its business, creating momentum to expand its portfolio outside of its core markets in Europe. Its expansion into the U.S. market started in late 1999. In addition to opening up new opportunities for growth, this expansion also resulted in some portfolio losses during the 2001 recession. The tightening of credit spreads in the United States and Europe has made it difficult for Krisalys to meet its equity return targets, and many shareholders have questioned the bank's expansion strategy. At a recent board meeting, the bank's management proposed a further expansion into Asia. Until now, the bank's Asian exposure was predominantly in the form of real estate lending participation with local banks that lend out of small offices located in Hong Kong and Tokyo.

In pockets of the bank, ambitious young managers have created growing businesses in the fields of credit derivatives trading. The bank's experience in building systems has also led to the creation of a respected cash management service offering. The bank's new CEO, brought in less than a year ago, encourages staff to come forward with ideas for new products and services. Managers of the more successful businesses such as real estate lending in Asia have been pressing for permission to expand their lending operations. However, tension has arisen between the Asian lending group and the risk management function. The latter has expressed concern that the real estate portfolio has become too large and has proposed that the bank tighten its standards for approving new real estate loans. The head of the real estate lending team is frustrated because his subportfolio is one of the most profitable in the bank, as measured by operating business profit.

Throughout the bank, loans and commitments are often granted at special prices for large or strategic clients in the expectation that these customers will purchase other services from the bank; however, no formal effort has been made to track whether the other fee-income streams materialize. Each business head operates against an operating business profit (OBP) target.

Recently, the bank has spearheaded some high-profile loans to support large takeovers. The relationship managers responsible for these deals have argued their bonuses should be substantially increased given the boost in interest income that these deals will bring. In the past five years, default rates have been low so the relationship managers have been complaining that the risk group's evaluation of new credits is conservative and has prevented them from participating in some other deals that they think would have been profitable. The risk group insists that large loans should be evaluated not just in terms of their stand-alone risk, but also their concentration risk for the overall portfolio.

The CEO has been approached by several investment bankers about possible acquisitions of smaller banks in regions that are complementary to the bank's core business. He is searching for a rigorous approach to evaluate these opportunities. These same investment bankers are enthusiastically recommending some changes to the bank's capital structure that currently comprises a mix of demand deposits, traded bonds, hybrid debt, preferred equity, and common equity. The chief risk officer (CRO) is concerned that the recent, large transactions that have been adding assets to the balance sheet have also created undue concentration risk in the portfolio. The Corporate and Institutional (C&I) banking head is frustrated that the CRO's group is hampering the growth of some of his key businesses and he is worried that some of his star relationship managers will leave. Meanwhile, the chief financial officer (CFO) has been pushing for a more rigorous assessment of overall return on equity given that the share price has not been performing well in the past two years.

While the CEO appreciates the flood of ideas and recommendations that his encouragement has precipitated, he is finding it increasingly difficult to decide how best and where to employ the bank's capital. To make matters worse, the risk management department has been at odds with some of the business units regarding how to calculate and use Basel II capital. Most business heads appear to ignore the regulatory capital implied by Basel II, but even for calculating economic capital, the bank has only rudimentary models. When the risk management team and the board discuss capitalization, they typically focus on book capital, but the CEO is much more concerned about the bank's market capitalization.

Given this complex mélange of factions and objectives, the CEO engages three senior consultants to discuss how to make sense of these circumstances. Before we describe the consultant's recommendations, we start with a bit more background information on Krisalys Bank so that we can discuss the conclusions in context (see Table 9.1).

CURRENT ORGANIZATION

Krisalys Bank does not currently have a credit portfolio management function. The risk group has started running bankwide portfolio analyses for the senior management team; but this is largely a reporting function, and each business retains responsibility for actually *managing* the exposures generated in the course of its operations. The CEO has asked the CFO and the CRO to develop a plan to improve the capital allocation and performance management process.

The CRO's risk group maintains the models and systems to perform both regulatory and economic capital calculations. The CFO's finance group uses these numbers, together with its management accounting systems, to track each business unit's performance. Occasionally, the two groups disagree on which capital numbers to use for capital allocation discussions. The risk group seems less interested in cooperating with the businesses to

TABLE 9.1 Simplified Financial Statements for Krisalys Bank

Income Statement for Most Recent Fiscal Year

Net interest income	2,500
Net fee income	1,500
Net trading income	500
Total income	4,500
Total general and administrative expenses	(2,500)
Total credit costs	(500)
Net income	1,500

Balance Sheet for Most Recent Fiscal Year

Assets

Cash and other current assets	10,000
Trading assets	5,000
Loans	200,000
Securities	50,000
Other assets	35,000
Premises and equipment	10,000
Reserve for credit losses	(5,000)
Total assets	305,000

Liabilities

Deposits	165,000
Short-term instruments	60,000
Corporate bonds	35,000
Other liabilities	30,000
Equity	15,000
Total liabilities	305,000
Current market capitalization of the bank	25,000

Regulatory Capital Ratios

Tier I capital ratio	7.8%
Total capital adequacy ratio	12.5%

Overview of Allocation of Loans and Bonds	MTM Exposure
Loans to publicly traded nonfinancial corporations	30%
Loans to private small and medium enterprises (SMEs)	25%
Loans to publicly traded financial corporations	15%
Consumer loans	15%
Sovereign corporate bonds	10%
Corporate bonds	5%

Amounts are in millions of Euros.

develop better models. Each business head seems more focused on leveraging whatever system is in place to make his own business appear successful. The finance group meanwhile attempts to sort through this tangle to assist the CEO and senior management in driving the bank's overall strategy. A larger difficulty arises from the fact that the bank does not use one comprehensive framework to calculate economic capital. Instead, the risk group has developed a collection of unrelated models to address each asset class in a way that seems most appropriate for that asset class. This approach may work in the isolated analysis of a particular asset class; however, it leaves much to be desired when comparing products, customers, and business units across the bank.

Organizationally, the bank's operations and IT infrastructure are managed in a separate division that is not well integrated from a management perspective with the rest of the bank. The IT group does not fully understand the bank's capital and performance management approach. This lack of understanding hinders the generation of timely capital reports, given that the necessary data are often not collected or processed. The chief information officer (CIO) does not really understand the goals of the CRO and CFO with respect to the bank's capital allocation system. This organizational confusion adds to the CEO's frustration as his requests for granular analyses of performance by product, customer segment, and business units are difficult to fill.

TRANSFORMING THE CAPITAL ALLOCATION PROCESS

With this organizational background, we now turn to the recommendations for improving how capital is managed and allocated throughout the bank. The consultants meet with the CEO, CFO, CRO, and CIO and propose the following seven initiatives:

1. Develop robust evaluation criteria for determining the quality of various IT and quantitative options that the bank will consider. Internal and external quantitative tools should be vetted where possible both quantitatively and in terms of infrastructure suitability. New models should be built to be consistent with the overall architecture and philosophy of the bank's risk systems and quantitative frameworks. IT systems should be considered both in terms of typical IT requirements, such as robustness and extensibility, but also with respect to the ability to integrate with other risk systems and provide the type of archival data storage and flexible reporting that the institution will require.

2. Implement a bankwide portfolio analysis system that will serve as the basis of an economic capital calculation. Part of this project will require substantial work on the bank's back-office systems since it will be necessary to collect and store transaction-level data, and these data are currently spread across the bank in dozens of business line–specific systems. Eventually, the data for these analyses will reside in an enterprise-wide data management system (described in the next section).

3. Establish an active credit portfolio management group (ACPM) as part of the corporate and institutional banking division.

4. Implement a credit transfer pricing mechanism to reflect the actual cost of risk exposures generated by relationship managers throughout the bank. Each new credit exposure will be "transferred," for management accounting purposes, into the ACPM portfolio. The relationship manager will bear the cost of the credit risk exposure on his profit and loss statement (which will eventually be used for performance management so that a relationship manager's compensation is tied to individual net profit). This means that the relationship managers will need to negotiate fees or a spread that exceeds the transfer price (i.e., spread) demanded by the ACPM group and/or sell other products and services to earn sufficient revenue from the relationship to generate a profit.

5. Develop a management ledger system (MLS), which is part of an enterprise-wide data management system implemented and maintained by the CIO, but primarily residing within the finance group. This MLS will capture transaction-level data across the bank and marry it with other data sources, such as market-based default probability systems, and sources for terms and conditions for each exposure, to create a single version of reality that can drive a business intelligence system that handles capital allocation and performance management.

6. Encourage the CFO and CRO to work together to develop the requisite calculations that the firm will use to manage its risk and profitability, and to ensure that these are reflected in the overall business intelligence system. The capital allocation system should be comprehensive and, wherever practical, based on data observable in the market. The performance metrics should be tied back ultimately to the bank's share price performance. Specifically, the OBP target should be replaced with something like shareholder value added (SVA) that reflects the extent to which relationships and products generate income that exceeds the capital charge that arises from engaging in those particular transactions.

7. Eventually, separate ACPM into its own stand-alone group which will perform the centralized credit portfolio management function for the bank. This organizational change *should not happen* until all credit risk exposure throughout the bank is modeled on the same system *and* the

business heads have developed a degree of familiarity with the mechanics of the various risk and profitability calculations and the incentives underlying the calculation approach.

In the balance of this chapter, we elaborate on the consultant's recommendations for achieving the CEO's goal of implementing ACPM and improving capital management within the bank.

PORTFOLIO ANALYSIS

While the organizational and policy changes may take some time to implement, the analysis of the portfolio can start right away. The bank can start the process by evaluating the current portfolio based on whatever data it can easily collect. These types of initial analyses can be helpful in two ways: First, the results provide a view of the portfolio and may unearth problems and opportunities that need immediate attention. Second, this type of analysis leads to a characterization of the gaps in data. It effectively gives the bank a road map of the challenges it will face in implementing the ACPM plan. Often, bank executives will prefer to delay portfolio analyses until the data issues are resolved. In our experience, this wastes valuable time since even crude first-pass analysis provides some immediate benefits. In this engagement, Krisalys Bank is better off starting right away to jump-start the process of understanding how to improve management of its exposures.

The following are some key points that can serve as the basis for determining what types of reports Krisalys Bank should generate to make the most of its portfolio analysis:

- Given a target default probability of 0.15 percent (felt by management to be sufficient to sustain a strong investment grade rating), how much overall economic capital is needed? How does this amount compare to the current market capitalization? These calculations require an estimate of the loss distribution of the bank's overall portfolio.
- Where are the sources of concentration risk in the portfolio? Which sectors? Which geographies? Which products?
- Among the loans and bonds in the portfolio, what percentage of the borrowers account for 80 percent of the capital usage?
- What are the top 25 obligors that contribute most to the overall bank portfolio risk?
- Which subportfolios have the highest Sharpe ratio and highest Vasicek ratio?
- What are the top 25 and bottom 25 obligors as ranked by Sharpe ratios and Vasicek ratios?

These are just a few of the questions this initial portfolio analysis may begin to answer. From here, senior management will almost certainly want to dig deeper, slicing the data by dimensions of interest such as subregion, sector, customer segment, maturity, credit rating, and so on. These analytic aspirations, when juxtaposed with the initial state of the bank's systems, can be a powerful motivator to push the ACPM initiative forward. When skillfully interpreted, even these initial analyses will serve to guide bank management toward targeting problem areas, building on areas of opportunity, and identifying risk concerns. A secondary benefit lies in setting the stage for the creation of an ACPM team.

For Krisalys Bank, its ROE (calculated with market value of equity) is 6 percent and its ROA (calculated with book assets) is 0.5 percent. Both of these numbers suggest Krisalys Bank is not doing well relative to its competitors since the better banks are generating ROE over 12 percent and ROA over 1 percent. The good news is that its price-to-earnings ratio is almost 17, which suggests things are looking up; however, the market may be reacting to the appointment of the new CEO and this multiple may not persist. Krisalys Bank's market-to-book ratio (25/15) is 1.7, which is on the lower side, compared to its peers. The key to the bank's future success is for it to build sustainable cash-flow growth.

The key transformation will come when the management shifts its focus from return on equity (ROE) and return on assets (ROA), which are still useful metrics, to the details of how the bank's portfolio is performing, the risk of extreme losses that will upset future cash flow streams, and creation of businesses that generate recurring fee income. In this way, ROE and ROA will naturally improve as the bank's share-price performance improves. The power in the recommendations here lies in the tools provided to drive bank strategy and align incentives.

The consultants use an option-pricing model to estimate the market value of Krisalys Bank's assets from its market value of equity. They find that the market value of the bank's assets is €310 billion. When the consultants mark the bank's portfolio to market, they find that the portfolio is worth about 95 percent of the €305 billion book value (approximately €290 billion). This implies that the extra €20 billion of market asset value (€310B − €290B = €20B) reflects the value of the bank's franchise businesses (including its brand, distribution capability, etc.).

The consultants use the model to determine that the bank's overall asset volatility (franchise plus portfolio) is 10 percent. This estimate is derived using a time series of equity prices for the bank. The consultants decompose this by first examining the volatility of the actual financial and hard assets held by the bank. Using a different methodology, the consultants estimate that the portfolio's volatility is about 7 percent. Next, they determine through comparing the franchise businesses to similar businesses traded in the market that the volatility of the franchise businesses' market value is probably around 30 percent.

With these calculations complete, the consultants turn to the bank's capitalization. The current market capitalization is €25 billion against total market value of assets of €310 billion. This equals a little more than 8 percent total economic capital. One goal of the portfolio analysis now becomes to provide some insight into what portion of this 8 percent economic capital is supporting the credit risk exposure of the bank versus the other risks in the bank.

The initial portfolio analysis suggests that despite the expansion efforts, there is still too much concentration in large corporate obligors, particularly in Europe. The consultants determine that the overall economic capital required to support the bank's credit risk in its portfolio so that the bank maintains a strong investment-grade rating is close to 6 percent of the credit-risky portfolio. This recommendation comes from calculating a portfolio loss distribution for the bank's overall credit portfolio and using this distribution and stress testing to determine how much capital is needed such that the probability of an extreme loss event exceeding that capital level is approximately equal to 0.15 percent.

The calculation breaks down as follows:

1. Of the total €290 billion market value of bank assets, approximately 70 percent or €203 billion reflects credit-risky assets. That means that the 6 percent credit risk capital amount is almost half of the 8 percent total economic capital available ($6\% \times \frac{203}{310} = 3.9\%$).
2. Approximately 25 percent of the portfolio assets, or €72.5 billion, is invested in assets exposed to market risk. The consultants determine that this portfolio requires roughly 2 percent capital. That means that the 2 percent market risk capital amount is a small fraction of the 8 percent total ($2\% \times \frac{72.5}{310} = 0.5\%$).
3. The amount left over is €34.5 billion (310 − 203 − 72.5 = 34.5). This reflects the franchise value plus the market value of the assets used in the course of the bank's operations (i.e., nonportfolio assets). For simplicity, the consultants bundle these fixed-asset values in with the franchise value for evaluating the overall value of the bank's noninterest income generating businesses. Since the credit and market portfolios require a little more than half of the overall 8 percent economic capital available, the franchise businesses are implicitly supported with only 3.5 percent capital.

Recall that the consultants estimated the volatility of these franchise business values to be 30 percent. They first calculate the percentage of the total assets reflected in the franchise business, which is about 11 percent of the total capitalization (34.5/310 = 11%). Under the assumption that the value of these businesses follows a lognormal distribution (i.e., returns are normally distributed), they can now directly relate economic capital to multiples of volatility or standard deviation.[1] Considering the 3.5 percent nonportfolio capital separately from the overall 8 percent economic capital only provides coverage for a little more than a one standard deviation move (30% × 11% = 3.3%) in franchise business volatility. Said differently, the implicit availability of 3.5 percent from the overall 8 percent will only absorb losses for one-standard deviation events. This means that about 16 percent of the time (slightly less frequently than one year out of six) the bank can expect to have a franchise value shortfall, given its current capitalization, portfolio holdings, and business model.

In general, the bank would probably want to cover two to three standard deviations of franchise value volatility. The consultants warn that this framework highlights the need for more capital to cover these businesses. To get there, the bank needs to either increase its market capitalization or reduce the capital needed to cover its credit portfolio. The consultants recommend the latter strategy, as several diversifying transactions and/or hedges added to the portfolio can drop the capital requirement significantly. In fact, they show that by diversifying out of Europe into other geographies by either directly engaging in transactions to buy and sell loans and other assets, or by using synthetic CLO structures or even by purchasing small banks while hedging European exposures in the CDS market, the bank can reduce the necessary economic capital supporting its credit portfolio from 6 percent to 3 percent.

The other major recommendation is for the bank to focus on increasing its noninterest (fee) income as a percentage of overall income. This should be done in a way that is systematic, measurable, and strategic. This means not placing the bank's franchises and future revenue streams at risk of catastrophic disruptions that could happen if high numbers of defaults occur at the same time. The twin strategy of improving portfolio diversification while building more fee-income businesses will set the bank on a path to double both its ROE and ROA (important measures for investors). In fact, allocating capital to higher SVA transactions and businesses (i.e., those transactions and businesses that have high operating profit relative to the capital allocated) will naturally lead to a higher multiple and higher ROE.

---

[1] This contrasts with items 1 and 2 where the capital amounts required the estimation of an actual distribution with a simulation engine (although market risk distributions are also typically assumed to be lognormally distributed).

ACTIVE CREDIT PORTFOLIO MANAGEMENT (ACPM)

The most efficient way to achieve the diversification recommended in the previous section is to build the ACPM group. Once a bank's senior management becomes convinced of the value of ACPM, the question of organizational placement can be a tricky one. Per the consultant's seventh recommendation, eventually ACPM should be housed in its own separate division. Initially, however, placing ACPM within the corporate and institutional banking division provides two advantages:

1. The C&I group is the place in the current organization that is most likely to have staff with the knowledge to begin building the ACPM function. While it is true that a number of new hires will likely be necessary, in the short term a bank must work with the staff that it has.
2. By placing ACPM in the business group during the first phases of this transition, the head of the business group will be more cooperative with the ACPM team, creating an improved operation and developing an understanding of, and trust in, the analytics and framework, particularly if the business head has some control over the pace of change. This can be particularly important since corporate lending is typically not profitable by itself when subject to market-based analysis of capital usage, so shifting a bank from a revenue- or profit-based incentive model to a return-on-capital model with credit transfer pricing without appropriate buy-in can be quite difficult.

In addition to a portfolio manager, the ACPM team will need a deputy general manager and several analysts (probably 5 to 10) as well as substantial systems support from IT. With the systems and technology available today, a large portfolio (e.g., more than USD 100 billion with tens of thousands or maybe even millions of exposures) can in some cases be managed with a team of less than 20 people. Krisalys Bank can probably manage its portfolio with a team of this size. The difficulties that the CEO should try to preempt will likely not be analytic; rather they will have more to do with the business heads and relationship managers not wanting to relinquish control of the management of the loan exposure risk. In the end, clear policy guidelines are essential to maintain proper organizational incentives.

The ultimate goal recommended by the consultants is that ACPM become a separate group. In addition, this group's activities should be consolidated with other proprietary trading or portfolio investing that happens at the bank. In this way, systems, quantitative research teams, and portfolio management execution can be combined to save costs and improve efficiency through increased economies of scope. The obstacles to this organizational structure typically lie more in the politics of the situation and how this is managed by the CEO, than with the analytic or technical issues. The compromise of initially keeping ACPM inside one of the businesses will still place the bank on the right path; however, eventually, ACPM should be given its independence.

DATA, SYSTEMS, AND METRICS

Appendix 9A provides a diagram that outlines at a conceptual level the operational infrastructure for a data and performance management system. The consultants point out that the success of this implementation will depend heavily on the management having timely access to clean data. In the new Krisalys Bank, the finance group will have a much broader role than it has traditionally. In addition to financial planning and strategy, it will also be the locus of information and analysis within the firm, allowing it to close the loop between the operations of the banks line businesses, the financial performance of the bank, and the compensation of bank employees which is tied to their contributions to improving the bank's performance. The recommendation is to house the following five components of the overall system within the finance group:

1. *Center of analysis.* The COA constitutes the "factory" that generates, collects, processes, and prepares the data necessary to support business intelligence systems, such as transfer pricing, performance management dashboards, and management, financial, and regulatory reporting. Within the COA is a management ledger that consolidates all the necessary data to run the business intelligence systems throughout the bank.
2. *Data quality control (DQC).* The DQC team will focus on regular assessment of data along the following dimensions:
   - *Business plausibility.* Are the quantities possible given their definition? For example, negative PDs are not possible, so a DQC analyst would flag negative PDs as a data error to be investigated.
   - *Statistical and theoretical plausibility.* Are the quantities implausible given their definition? For example, one would not expect all the PD term structures to be flat (i.e., credit quality not expected to change over time), so a DQC analyst would flag groups of exposures within a portfolio that exhibited this kind of unusual data pattern.
   - *Relational plausibility.* Are quantities implausible given their relationship to each other? For example, one would not expect very high

spreads for low PD exposures, so a DQC analyst would flag these types of exposures.

- In some settings, the DQC team may be structured to include a financial quality assurance (FQA) function that ensures that models are implemented according to the design and that calculations actually produce the results intended before the models are rolled out. Other institutions may house this in a different area.

Note that the DQC team is an example of a function that can be set up off-shore to reduce costs.

3. *Portfolio analysis and capital allocation system.* The initial portfolio analysis project will lay the groundwork for implementation of a bankwide system to do regular calculation of the portfolio performance metrics and capital for use in the performance management system. The consultants recommend a factor-based, structural model for the overall framework. They present a few different vendor options and recommend against building an entirely new system; however, they predict that some customization will be necessary. They also recommend a variety of valuation models to use in conjunction with the structural framework for determining change in value from the analysis as-of date to the horizon date. For exposures to structured securities, they recommend subscription to a deal library containing data on the waterfall structure of various securities and the underlying collateral in the deals. Here, too, they provide guidance on vendor options.

4. *Performance management system (sometimes called an EPMS or expense and profitability management system).* This portion of the system combines engines that calculate portfolio capital (and funds transfer pricing) with other data to arrive at metrics that facilitate comparison of different investments and different business units.

The bank adopts a system based on shareholder value added (SVA), where the net income is calculated less the allocated capital times the cost of capital. (A second project will need to be undertaken to determine proper cost allocation to arrive at the net income number.) The new portfolio system will form the basis of the capital allocation. (A third project may be necessary to calculate the cost of capital.)

5. *Mark-to-model or mark-to-market (MTM) system.* Initially, the consultants agree that a conventional book-value based approach may be necessary to introduce the concepts of ACPM and the portfolio analysis system to the bank. However, they also recommend that as the new framework gains acceptance and understanding throughout the bank, senior management introduce an MTM system. As the systems are put in place, a shadow MTM system (i.e., calculation only) should be implemented. Since market data are not always available, it may be necessary

to use alternative inputs for valuation. To standardize this, the consultants suggest that the bank create a waterfall of business logic specifying a hierarchy of prices such that the best available market prices/model should be used when available (and specifying which they are in each case); that the next best prices/models be used if the best are not feasible due to model or data limitations; and so on. In the end, however, not all securities in the portfolio will be valued in the same way. Such an MTM waterfall (simplified) might look like the following:

- *Observed price.* In the case of liquidly traded bonds or loans that are regularly traded on the secondary market, an observed market price will be the best source of information. In many markets, it is possible to subscribe to services that provide *evaluated prices* for instruments that did not trade on a specific day. Evaluated prices are estimates of prices made by experts in the markets for different securities. These are typically based on observed prices for similar instruments and communication with dealers in these markets.
- *Estimated price from CDS.* The CDS market now provides regular marks of the credit quality on a wide range of obligors.
- *Estimated price from credit curve.* In the case that a specific CDS or tenor is not available, estimated credit curves can be used to determine an appropriate mark. Both the CDS and the equity market can be used to construct credit curves that are typically defined by geography, industry, and rating. These curves relate different tenors to an estimate of the prevailing credit spread for a particular type of borrower.
- *Discounted cash flow based value.* If an instrument is quite complex or very thinly traded (or both), an approximation to the price may be feasible by discounting the cash flows of the transaction by an appropriate risky discount rate. In order for this to be effective, an organization needs to be comfortable with the assumptions used both to generate the cash flows and to create the discount rate. Since valuations will be quite sensitive to these assumptions, these should be vetted and adjusted by the relevant business managers.

The quality of these systems depends on the processes in place to capture the necessary data. The consultants expect that Krisalys Bank will need to make substantial investments in both technology and staff to improve the data capture systems.

In addition, the bank creates a rigorous process for vetting new models and systems that involves collaboration of the quantitative researchers, the IT group, and the ACPM unit. The group begins to systematically evaluate the models currently in use and to compare these to other vendor options.

ACPM AND TRANSFORMING THE BANK

The active credit portfolio management group sets the stage for transforming the way the bank allocates capital. The ACPM group's efforts lead to a better understanding of how credit is priced in the market and how capital is being used at the bank. These data assist the finance group in the capital allocation process. The finance group, under the leadership of the CFO, centralizes the efforts to streamline data collection processes and change the way business units are capitalized, evaluated, and compensated. ACPM injects market discipline into how the cost of capital is calculated and how capital itself is allocated to supporting the credit portfolio. Whereas asset-liability management (ALM) introduces market discipline concerning the *cost of funds* used to support each business, ACPM introduces market discipline concerning the *credit capital* used to support each business.

As we discussed in Chapter 2, by centrally managing the credit risk portfolio, the bank can separate income earned from taking credit risk (i.e., spread income) from income earned from building franchise businesses (i.e., noninterest income). Banks are typically not good vehicles through which to take interest-rate risk, so the primary role of the ALM function should be to eliminate earnings volatility arising from changes in underlying interest rates. Banks are good vehicles to manage portfolios of credit risk and leverage their client relationships to sell financial services and products. Ultimately, credit risk should be managed systematically in one enterprise-wide portfolio rather than as a loose collection of stand-alone exposures.

Ideally, all credit risk exposures should be transfer-priced into the ACPM portfolio. Here the bank faces a choice. On the one hand, the transfer price might be calculated in terms of the spread needed to generate a return per unit of risk level that is at least as large as the average portfolio return per unit of risk. Recall that this approach is called *portfolio-referent* since the transfer prices will differ from portfolio to portfolio for the same exposure, and thus this measure refers to a specific portfolio. On the other hand, the bank may opt to base transfer pricing directly on market prices.

First consider the case of portfolio-referent measures. This approach requires specific estimates of the risk of the specific portfolio the bank is holding. In earlier chapters, we have discussed several methods to calculate portfolio risk. The bank may want to start with contribution to volatility (i.e., risk contribution) and then migrate to contribution to tail risk (i.e., tail risk contribution) or it may want to use both measures of risk. To the extent a business unit originates credit at a spread that results in a return per unit of risk less than the average performance in the bank portfolio, the business will be charged the difference (in the form of a transfer price) to recognize the economic cost of taking on that exposure.

The advantage of this portfolio-referent approach is that the transfer price will reflect not just compensation for that exposure's stand-alone risk, but also compensation for that exposure's contribution to the overall portfolio risk. In this way, an exposure that diversifies the portfolio (i.e., low correlation with other portfolio exposures) will need a smaller transfer price (all else equal) than a similar exposure that does not diversify the portfolio (i.e., high correlation with other portfolio exposures).

While the portfolio-referent approach is theoretically appealing given the way it incentivizes diversifying trades and originations, it also has two distinct drawbacks:

1. It relies on a modeling framework to estimate correlation and risk contribution that can be difficult to explain to most business and relationship managers. Without understanding the models, business leaders will, at best, be highly skeptical of the approach and, at worst, be active opponents.
2. It may provide incentives for diversification that result in an increase in transactions in markets and asset classes where the bank has little expertise. Without strong controls in terms of how new transactions are undertaken, the transfer pricing system may result in a portfolio of instruments with exposure to other types of risks (e.g., liquidity, settlement, legal, model, etc.) since exposures in different geographies and different instruments (from what is currently in the portfolio) are likely to exhibit lower correlations. Thus, the bank may reduce credit risk by lowering correlation while inadvertently increasing business risk by participating in markets that are unfamiliar.

The alternative approach to transfer pricing bases transfer prices on market prices. Basing transfer pricing directly on market prices provides a more objective, easier-to-understand approach. A popular and reliable method involves estimating credit curves from CDSs to use as the basis for transfer-pricing each new exposure. This price can be interpreted directly as the cost of hedging a new exposure. Since the prices are observable, reluctant business and relationship managers will have one less place to focus their criticism. Thus, the market-price approach does not suffer from the first of the disadvantages just discussed. Disadvantage 2 also becomes less of a concern since a market price will often reflect all the known risks of an exposure. Geographies and asset classes for which no market prices exist will be less appealing in this framework as no reliable transfer price can be estimated.

Interestingly enough, though, this second advantage may actually be a disadvantage in disguise: The bank-specific benefit of low-correlated exposures will not be reflected in the incentives for relationship managers, so they will not necessarily work toward diversifying the overall bank portfolio. For example, the CDS market may price protection on a highly rated UK exposure cheaper than that of a medium-grade Japanese firm, even though from a portfolio basis, the Japanese trade may be better from an overall risk perspective for Krisalys.

That said, special program subsidies can be introduced, informed by the portfolio analysis, to counteract this bias so that a new class of exposures can be encouraged: Management can agree to reduce transfer prices for a specific period of time as these new types of exposures are originated.

In the end, the consultants emphasize that a system will only help if it is actually used. Krisalys Bank chooses the market-price approach to transfer pricing given the ease with which it can be explained to the business units. The consultants also emphasize that management can better guide business development by prudent use of subsidies when they determine a particular sector or business should be expanded.

Over time the business units will migrate to the view that transfer prices are an expense to originating credit. If they earn fees in excess of this price or if they earn fees for the service of origination, they will increase their operating profit. They will not be affected by defaults as ACPM will be shouldering all the credit risk in exchange for the transfer-pricing fees. In this sense, ACPM itself becomes another business unit in that it is in the business of maximizing return per unit of credit risk taken in the portfolio.

This framework presupposes a management information system (MIS) infrastructure that facilitates allocating revenue and expenses at the transaction, customer, product, and business unit levels. Each business unit will be rewarded based on its SVA, which reflects net operating profit less the cost of capital allocated. The ACPM unit will be allocated credit capital and the other business units will be allocated operating capital to support their overall business of selling particular products and services. In this way, the bank will make concrete the extent to which a loss-leader loan results in a profitable customer relationship.

Once this infrastructure is in place, the finance group should be able to look across the bank and identify both *ex ante* and *ex post* return on capital allocated to each business unit. Armed with this information, profitable businesses can be allocated more capital and lagging businesses can be restructured or shut down. One key component of this system is allocation of capital to support the business apart from the market and credit risk it may generate. ALM and ACPM provide a means for measuring and managing market and credit risk, respectively. (For completeness, the view of ALM can be broadened to include the management of liquidity risk.)

An important component of moving to this framework for capital allocation involves shifting the institution to a mark-to-market or mark-to-model (both are rendered *MTM*) orientation. With functioning ALM and

ACPM groups, MTM can be targeted at the portfolio risks managed in those groups. In this way, the bank can substantially reduce the number of surprises that lurk in the portfolio and deteriorating positions can be dealt with quickly. Each business unit is then left to maximize its return on operational capital by focusing on leveraging customer relationships to generate fee income.[2]

The primary point in this discussion, and the underlying theme of this text, is that non-ACPM business units should not generally be taking credit risk and thus should not draw credit risk capital. Note that a separate project may need to be undertaken to understand the need for capital to cushion against liquidity risk. In recent years, liquidity risk has become much more important and should be measured and managed, accordingly.

The addition of an ACPM unit to the bank coupled with changes to the incentive structures faced by each business unit should lead to a more valuable bank. Krisalys Bank now must embark on the long process of implementing the systems, organization, and training to realize this vision.

APPENDIX: FIGURES

The overall data flow and system architecture recommended to Krisalys Bank can be seen in Figure 9.1. Sample reports from the portfolio analysis project are found in Figures 9.2 through 9.8. In addition to providing an overview of overall portfolio performance, these reports provide insight

---

[2] While discussions of operational risk have become more convoluted recently (due to the conflicting perspectives arising in the context of debates about new regulation such as Basel II), for the purposes of our capital allocation discussion here, we define operational *capital* as the capital necessary to support each business unit's effort to generate growing noninterest income streams. (For completeness, we note that some operational *risk capital* will need to be allocated to account for operations risk, and that ACPM unit will also use some of this capital since it is a business unit in its own right.)   More succinctly, operational capital is the support used to run and grow a business. Some operational capital should also be allocated to the overall operational support throughout the bank related to management at the corporate level and collection and processing of data used to make decisions, while some capital should be allocated to account for operational risk as well. Developing a sophisticated methodology for allocating this operational risk capital requires an in-depth analysis of each line of business and is well beyond the scope of this text. However, these analyses benefit from an assessment of each business unit's strategy and their associated competitive environments. By combining these strategic assessments with an analysis of the state of the bank's current credit portfolio and the potential impact on the portfolio of new business initiatives, business strategy is tied back to capital allocation.

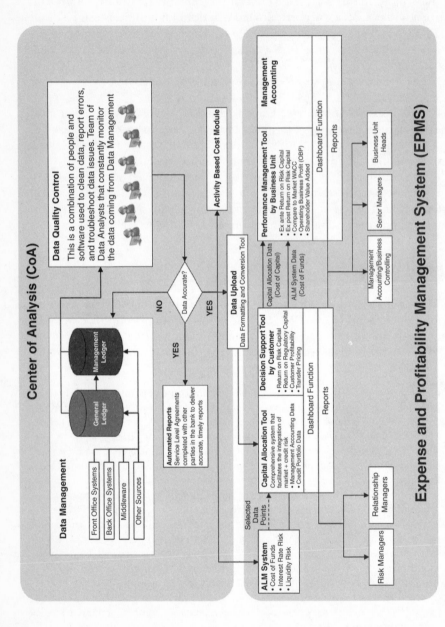

FIGURE 9.1 Example of a Business Intelligence Unit's Operations

	Portfolio Overview
Number of exposures	1,042
Exposure (EUR)	300,000,000,000
MTM exposure (EUR)	299,855,968,991
Market value drawn (EUR)	262,227,447,060
Total spread revenue, annualized (EUR)	11,480,804,490
Unexpected loss (simulated) (EUR)	7,719,076,595
Capital (15.00 bp in excess of expected loss) (EUR)	29,614,970,809
Total spread, annualized	3.83%
Expected loss, annualized	2.36%
Expected spread, annualized	1.47%
Unexpected loss (simulated)	2.57%
Capital (15.00 bp in excess of expected loss)	10.19%
Sharpe ratio	57.13%
RORAC, annualized	20.24%
Vasicek ratio	14.89%

Correlation data from 1992–2007; Capital calculation method; Monte Carlo; run with MKMV
Portfolio Manager™ Software.

FIGURE 9.2   Overall Portfolio Metrics (number of exposures includes aggregated sub-portfolios so that total number of individual exposures will be much higher).

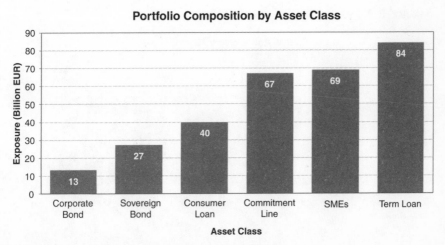

FIGURE 9.3   Portfolio Composition by Asset Class

FIGURE 9.4 Sharpe Ratio by Asset Class

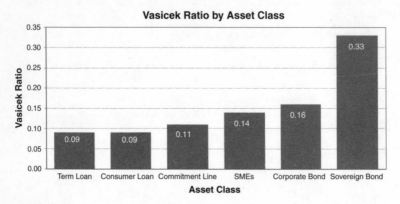

FIGURE 9.5 Vasicek Ratio by Asset Class

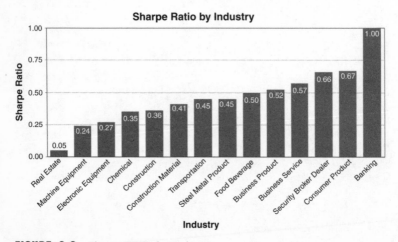

FIGURE 9.6 Sharpe Ratio by Industry

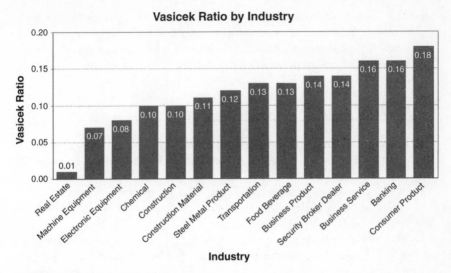

FIGURE 9.7 Vasicek Ratio by Industry

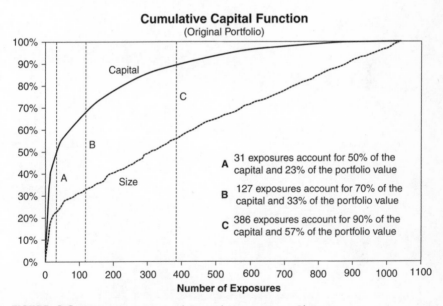

FIGURE 9.8 Characterization of Capital Usage across Clusters of Portfolio Exposures

into the sources of concentration risk as well as the drivers of portfolio performance. Based on these reports the consultants working together with the portfolio manager can devise strategies to best improve diversification and improve the return per unit of risk for the bank's portfolio.

EXERCISES

1. Based on the information in the case, calculate the market value of the bank's outstanding liabilities other than its traded equity. Express the answer both as a total value and as a percentage of par.
2. Name two strategies the bank can take to increase the value of its outstanding liabilities other than its traded equity. Why might the bank choose not to follow those strategies?
3. The consultants determine that Krisalys Bank's cost of equity capital is 8 percent. What is the overall shareholder value added (SVA) for Krisalys? Compare and contrast its SVA with its return on equity (ROE) and return on assets (ROA).

References

Abramowitz, Milton, ed. 1972. *Handbook of mathematical functions with formulas, graphs, and mathematical tables.* New York: Dover Publications.

Acharya, Viral V., Sreedhar T. Bharath, and Anand Srinivasan. 2003. *Understanding the recovery rates on defaulted securities.* Social Science Research Network.

Agrawal, Deepak, and Jeffrey R. Bohn. 2008. Humpbacks in credit spreads. *Journal of Investment Management* 6(3):73–98.

Agresti, Alan. 1990. *Categorical data analysis.* New York: John Wiley & Sons.

Akerlof, George A. 1970. The market for lemons: Quality uncertainty and the market mechanism. *Quarterly Journal of Economics*, 84(3):488–500.

Altman, Edward I. 1968. Financial ratios, discriminant analysis and the prediction of corporate bankruptcy. *Journal of Finance*, 589–609.

Altman, Edward I. 1993. *Corporate financial distress and bankruptcy.* New York: John Wiley & Sons.

Altman, Edward I., and E. Hotchkiss. 2006. *Corporate financial distress and bankruptcy: Predict and avoid bankruptcy, analyze and invest in distressed debt.* Hoboken, NJ: John Wiley & Sons.

Altman, Edward I., and Gabriele Sabato. 2006. Modeling credit risk for SMEs: Evidence from the U.S. market. New York: New York University.

Altman, Edward I., and Herbert Rijken. 2004. How rating agencies achieve rating stability. New York: Stern School of Business.

Altman, Edward I., and Vellore M. Kishmore. 1996. Almost everything you wanted to know about recoveries on defaulted bonds. *Financial Analysis Journal*, 56–62.

Altman, Edward I., A. Gande, and A. Saunders. 2004. Informational efficiency of loans versus bonds: Evidence from secondary market prices. Working paper. New York: New York University.

Altman, Edward I., Andrea Resti, and Andrea Sironi. 2003. Default recovery rates in credit risk modeling: A review of the literature and empirical evidence. Working paper. New York: New York University.

Altman, Edward I., R. A. Eisenbeis, and J. Sinkey. 1981. *Applications of classification techniques in business, banking, and finance.* Greenwich, CT: JAI Press.

Anderson, Ronald, and Suresh Sundaresan. 2000. A comparative study of structural models of corporate bond yields: An exploratory investigation. *Journal of Banking and Finance.*

Arora, Navneet, Jeffrey R. Bohn, and Fanlin Zhu. 2005. Reduced form vs. structural models of credit risk: A case study of three models. Working paper. New York: MKMV.

Atkinson, A., and M. Riani. 2000. *Robust diagnostic regression analysis*. New York: Springer-Verlag.

Bamber, Donald. 1975. The area above the ordinal dominance graph and the area below the receiver operating characteristic graph. *Journal of Mathematical Psychology* 12:381–417.

Beaver, William H. 1966. Financial ratios as predictors of failure. *Journal of Accounting Research*.

Benninga, Simon, and Zvi Wiener. 1998. Term structure of interest rates. *Mathematica in Education and Research*.

Berndt, Antje, Rohan Douglas, Darrrell Duffie, Mark Ferguson, and David Schranz. 2004. Measuring default risk premia from default swap rates and EDFs. Working paper. Palo Alto, CA: Stanford University.

Birdsall, T. G., and D. E. Lamphiear. 1960. Approximations to the noncentral chi-square distributions with applications to signal detection models. Technical Report No. 101. Ann Arbor, MI: Electronic Defense Group, Dept. of Electrical Engineering, University of Michigan Research Institute.

Birdsall, T. G. 1966. The theory of signal detectability: ROC curves and their character. Dissertation Abstracts Int.

Birdsall, Theodore Gerald. 1973. The theory of signal delectability: ROC curves and their character. Ann Arbor, MI: Cooley Electronics Laboratory, Dept. of Electrical and Computer Engineering, University of Michigan.

Black, Fischer, and John C. Cox. 1976. Valuing corporate securities: Some effects of bond indenture provisions. *Journal of Finance* 31:351–367.

Black, Fischer, and Myron Scholes. 1973. The pricing of options and corporate liabilities. *Journal of Political Economy*.

Blochlinger, A., and M. Leippold. 2006. Economic benefit of powerful credit scoring. *Journal of Banking and Finance* 30:851–873.

Blume, Jeffrey D. 2008. Bounding sample size projections for the area under a ROC curve. *Journal of Statistical Planning and Inference*. Forthcoming.

Bohn, Jeffrey R. 2000a. A survey of contingent-claims approaches to risky debt valuation. *Journal of Risk Finance* 1(3):53–78.

Bohn, Jeffrey R. 2000b. An empirical assessment of a simple contingent-claims model for valuation of risky debt. *Journal of Risk Finance* 1(4):55–77.

Bos, R. J., K. Kelhoffer, and D. Keisman. 2002. *Ultimate recoveries in an era of record defaults*. New York: Standard & Poor's.

Bremaud, P. 1981. *Point processes and queues*. New York: Springer-Verlag.

Brennan, Michael J., and Eduardo S. Schwartz. 1978. Corporate income taxes, valuation, and the problem of optimal capital structure. *Journal of Business*.

Burnham, K. P., and D. R. Anderson. 1998. *Model selection and inference*. New York: Springer.

Burnham, Kenneth P., and David R. Anderson. 2002. *Model selection and multimodel inference: A practical information-theoretic approach*. New York: Springer.

Cantor, Richard, Kenneth Emery, and Pamela Stumpp. 2006. Probability of default ratings and loss given default assessments for non-financial speculative-grade corporate obligors in the United States and Canada. New York: Moody's Investors Service.

Cantor, Richard, and Eric Falkenstein. 2001. Testing for default consistency in annual default rates. *Journal of Fixed Income.*

Cantor, R., D. T. Hamilton, and J. Tennant. 2008. Confidence intervals for corporate default rates. *RISK.*

Cantor, Richard, and Chris Mann. 2003. Measuring the performance of Moody's corporate bond ratings. New York: Moody's Investors Service.

Cantrell, C. D. 2000. *Modern mathematical methods for physicists and engineers.* Cambridge: Cambridge University Press.

Carey, Mark, and Michael Gordy. 2004. Measuring systematic risk in recoveries on defaulted debt I: Firm level ultimate LGDs. Washington, DC: Federal Reserve Board.

Carey, Mark, and Rene M. Stultz. 2005. The risks of financial institutions. Working paper.

Carty, Lea V. 1997. Moody's rating migration and credit quality correlation, 1920–1996, Special comment. New York: Moody's Investors Service.

Carty, Lea V. 1997. Three essays on capital market imperfections. New York: Columbia University, Economics Department.

Carty, Lea V., and Jerome S. Fons. 1993. Measuring changes in corporate credit quality, Special report. New York: Moody's Investors Service.

Carty, Lea V., and Jerome S. Fons. 1994. Corporate default rates: 1970–1993, Special comment. New York: Moody's Investors Service.

Carty, Lea V., and Dana Lieberman. 1996. Defaulted bank loan recoveries. New York: Moody's Investors Service.

Chacko, George. 2005. Liquidity risk in the corporate bond markets. Working paper. Cambridge, MA: Harvard Business School.

Cherubini, Umberto, Elisa Luciano, and Walter Vecchiato. 2004. Copula methods in finance. London: John Wiley & Sons.

Christensen, J., E. Hansen, and D. Lando. 2004. Confidence sets for continuous-time rating transition probabilities. *Journal of Banking and Finance* 28:2575–2602.

Citron, David B., Mike Wright, Rod Ball, and Fred Rippington. 2002. Secured creditor recovery rates from management buy-outs in distress. EFMA 2002 London Meetings. Cass Business School Research Paper.

Cleveland, William S., and Susan J. Devlin. 1988. Locally weighted regression: An approach to regression analysis by local fitting. *Journal of the American Statistical Association* 83:596–610.

Collin-Dufresne, Pierre, and Robert Goldstein. 2001. Do credit spreads reflect stationary leverage ratios? *Journal of Finance.*

Collin-Dufresne, Pierre, Robert S. Goldstein, and J. S. Martin. 2001. The determinants of credit spread changes. *Journal of Finance.*

Copeland, Tom, Tim Koller, and Jack Murrin. 2000. *Valuation: measuring and managing the value of companies.* New York: Wiley.

Crosbie, Peter, and Jeffrey R. Bohn. 2002. Modeling default risk. KMV working paper. New York: MKMV.

Crouhy, Michel, Dan Galai, and Robert Mark. 2000. A comparative analysis of current credit risk models. *Journal of Banking and Finance*.

Dai, Qing, and Kenneth J. Singleton. 2000. Specification analysis of affine term structure models. *Journal of Finance*.

Davydenko, S. A., and J. R. Franks. 2008. Do bankruptcy codes matter? A study of defaults in France, Germany, and the U.K. *Journal of Finance* 63, no. 2.

Davydenko, Sergei A., and Julian R. Franks. 2006. Do bankruptcy codes matter? A study of defaults in France, Germany and the UK. SSRN.

Dawes, Robyn M. 1979. The robust beauty of improper linear models in decision making. *American Psychologist* 34:571–582.

Dawes, Robyn M., David Faust, and Paul E. Meehl. 1989. Clinical versus actuarial judgment. *Science* 243(4899):1668–1674.

DeLong, Elizabeth R., David M. Delong, and Daniel L. Clarke-Pearson. 1988. Comparing the areas under two or more correlated receiver operating characteristic curves: A nonparametric approach. *Biometrics* 837–845.

DeRoover, Raymond A. 1948 *The Medici bank: Its organization, management, and decline*. London: Oxford University Press.

Dewenter, Kathryn L., and Alan C. Hess. 1998. An international comparison of banks' equity returns. Working paper. Seattle: University of Washington.

Dhar, Vasant, and Roger Stein. 1998. Finding robust and usable models with data mining: Examples from finance. *PCAI*.

Dhar, Vasant, and Roger Stein. 1998. *Seven methods for transforming corporate data into business intelligence*. New York: Prentice Hall.

Driessen, J. 2005. Is default event risk priced in corporate bonds? *Review of Financial Studies* 18(1):165–195.

Duffee, Gregory R. 1998. The relation between Treasury yields and corporate bond yield spreads. *Journal of Finance*.

Duffie, Darrell, Andreas Eckner, Guillaume Horel, and Leandro Saita. 2006. Frailty correlated default. Working paper. Palo Alto, CA: Stanford University.

Duffie, Darrell, D. Filipovic, and W. Schachermayer. 2000. Affine processes and applications in finance. Working paper. Palo Alto, CA: Stanford University.

Duffie, Darrell, and David Lando. 2001. Term structures of credit spreads with incomplete accounting information. *Econometrica*.

Duffie, Darrell, Leandro Saita, and Ke Wang. 2007. Multi-period default prediction with stochastic covariates. *Journal of Financial Economics*.

Duffie, Darrell, and Kenneth J. Singleton. 1999. Modeling term structures of defaultable bonds. *Review of Financial Studies*.

Duffie, Darrell, and Kenneth J. Singleton. 2003. Credit risk: Pricing, measurement, and management. Princeton Series in Finance. Princeton, NJ: Princeton University Press.

Duffie, Darrell, and Ke Wang. 2004. Multi-period corporate failure prediction with stochastic covariates. National Bureau of Economic Research Working Paper Series No. 10743.

Dwyer, Douglas D. 2007. The distribution of defaults and Bayesian model validation. *Journal of Risk Model Validation* 1.

Dwyer, Douglas W., and Roger M. Stein. 2004. Moody's KMV RiskCalc v. 3.1 technical document. New York: Moody's KMV.

Dwyer, Douglas W., and Roger M. Stein. 2006. Inferring the default rate in a population by comparing two incomplete default databases. *Journal of Banking and Finance* 30:797–810.

Eberhart, Allan C., and Richard J. Sweeney. 1992. Does the bond market predict bankruptcy settlements? *Journal of Finance* XLVII:943–980.

Edwards, A. W. F. 1992. *Likelihood*. London: Johns Hopkins University Press.

Efron, Bradley. 1975. The efficiency of logistic regression compared to normal discriminant analysis. *Journal of the Americal Statistical Association* 70.

Efron, Bradley, and Robert J. Tibshirani. 1993. An introduction to the bootstrap. *Monographs on statistics and applied probability 57*. London: Chapman and Hall/CRC Press.

Elkan, C. 2001. The foundations of cost-sensitive learning. Seventeenth International Joint Conference on Artificial Intelligence (IJCAI'01).

Elton, E. J., M. Gruber, D. Mann, and C. Agrawal. 2001. Explaining the rate spread on corporate bonds. *Journal of Finance*.

Engle, Robert. 2001. GARCH 101: The use of ARCH/GARCH models in applied econometrics. *Journal of Economic Perspectives*.

Englemann, B., E. Hayden, and D. Tasche. 2003. Testing rating accuracy. *RISK*.

Eom, Young H., Jean Helwege, and Jing-Zhi Huang. 2004. Structural models of corporate bond pricing: An empirical analysis. *Review of Financial Studies*.

Ericsson, Jan, and Joel Reneby. 2004. An empirical study of structural credit risk models using stock and bond prices. *Journal of Fixed Income* (March), 38–49.

Falkenstein, Eric, Andrew Boral, and Lea V. Carty. 2000. RiskCalc for private companies: Moody's default model. New York: Moody's Risk Management.

Feldhutter, Peter, and David Lando. 2007. Decomposing swap spreads. Working paper.

Ferrari, S. L. P., and F. Cribari-Neto. 2004. Beta regression for modeling rates and proportions. *Journal of Applied Statistics* 31:799–815.

Figlewski, S., H. Frydman, and W. Liang. 2006. Modeling the effect of macroeconomic factors on corporate default and credit rating transitions. Working paper. New York: New York University.

Fledelius, Peter, David Lando, and Jens Perch Nielson. 2004. Non-parametric analysis of rating transition and default data. *Journal of Investment Management*.

Fons, Jerry. 1994. Using default rates to model the term structure of credit risk. *Financial Analysts Journal*.

Fridson, Martin S., M. Christopher Garman, and Kathryn Okashima. 2000. Recovery rates: The search for meaning. New York: Merrill Lynch Global Securities Research and Economics Group.

Friedman, C., and S. Sandow. 2003. Model performance measures for expected utility maximizing investors. *International Journal of Applied and Theoretical Finance* 5:335–401.

Friedman, Milton. 1953. The methodology of positive economics. *Essays on positive economics*. Chicago: University of Chicago Press.

Frye, Jon. 2000. *Depressing recoveries*. Chicago: Federal Reserve Bank of Chicago.

Geman, S., and Donald Geman. 1984. Stochastic relaxation, Gibbs distributions, and the bayesian restoration of images. *IEEE Transactions on Pattern Analysis and Machine Intelligence* 6:721–741.

Gigerenzer, Gerd. 2003. *Calculated risks: How to know when numbers deceive you*. New York: Simon & Schuster.

Glantz, Morton. 2002. *Managing bank risk*. London: Academic Press.

Glasserman, Paul. 2004. *Monte Carlo methods in financial engineering*. New York: Springer-Verlag.

Gordy, M., and D. Jones. 2002. Capital allocation for securitization with uncertainty in loss prioritization. Federal Reserve Board.

Gorton, Gary, and Andrew Winton. 2002. Financial intermediation. Working paper 8928. New York: National Bureau Economic Research.

Green, David M., and John A. Swets. 1966. Signal detection theory and psychophysics. Los Altos, CA: Peninsula Publishing.

Greene, William H. 1993. Econometric analysis. New York: Macmillan.

Grinstead, Charles M., and J. Laurie Snell. 1997. Introduction to probability. Providence, RI: American Mathematical Society.

Guill, Gene D., and Charles Smithson, eds. 2005. *Sound practices in credit portfolio management*. New York: IACPM.

Gup, Benton E., and James W. Kolari. 2005. *Commercial banking: The management of risk*. New York: John Wiley & Sons.

Gupton, Greg M., Chris C. Finger, and Mickey Bhatia. 1997. CreditMetrics technical document. Working paper. New York: RiskMetrics Group.

Gupton, G. M., D. Gates, and L. V. Carty. 2000. Bank loan loss given default. New York: Moody's Investors Service.

Gupton, Greg M., and Roger Stein. 2001. A matter of perspective. *Credit*.

Gupton, Greg M., and Roger M. Stein. 2002. LossCalc(TM): Moody's model for predicting loss given default (LGD). New York: Moody's Investors Service.

Gupton, Greg M., and Roger M. Stein. 2005. LossCalc V2.0: Dynamic prediction of LGD. New York: Moody's KMV.

Hamilton, David, and Richard Cantor. 2004. Rating transitions and defaults conditional on watchlist, outlook and rating history. *Global Credit Research*. New York: Moody's Investors Service.

Hamilton, David T., and Alexandra Berthault. 2000. The investment performance of bankrupt corporate debt obligations: Moody's Bankrupt Bond Index 2000. New York: Moody's Investors Service.

Hamilton, David T., Greg M. Gupton, and Alexandra Berhault. 2001. Default and recovery rates of corporate bond issuers: 2000. New York: Moody's Risk Management.

Hanley, A., and B. McNeil. 1982. The meaning and use of the area under a receiver operating characteristics (ROC) curve. *Diagnostic Radiology* 143: 29–36.

Hanley, John A. 1989. Receiver operating characteristic (ROC) methodology: The state of the art. *Critical Reviews in Diagnostic Imaging* 29.

Hanson, S. G., and T. Schuermann. 2006. Confidence intervals for probabilities of default. *Journal of Banking and Finance* 30(8).

Hastie, Trevor, and Robert Tibshirani. 1990. Generalized additive models. London, New York: Chapman and Hall.

Heath, David, Robert Jarrow, and A. Morton. 1992. Bond pricing and the term structure of interest rates: A new methodology for contingent claims valuation. *Econometrica*.

Heckman, James J. 1979. Sample selection bias as a specification error. *Econometrica* 47:153–161.

Helwege, Jean, and Christopher M. Turner. 1999. The slope of the credit yield curve for speculative-grade issuers.

Hilberink, B., and L. Rogers. 2002. Optimal capital structure and endogenous default. *Finance and Stochastics* 6(2):237–263.

Hosmer, D. W., and S. Lemeshow. 2001. *Applied logistic regression*. New York: John Wiley & Sons.

Huang, Jing-zhi, and Ming Huang. 2003. How much of the corporate-Treasury yield spread is due to credit risk? Working paper.

Hull, John. 2005. *Options, futures, and other derivatives*. New York: Prentice Hall.

Hull, John, and Alan White. 2000. "Risk-neutral and real-world measures of default Risk" in *Visions of Risk*, ed. Carol Alexander. Upper Saddle River, NJ: FT Prentice Hall.

Hull, John, and Alan White. 2000. Valuing credit default swaps I: No counterparty default risk. *Journal of Derivatives* 8:29–40.

Hurt, L., and A. Felsovalyi. 1998. Measuring loss on Latin American defaulted bank loans, a 27-year study of 27 countries. *Journal of Lending and Credit Risk Management* 80:41–46.

Ingersoll, Jonathan E. 1977. A contingent-claims valuation of convertible securities. *Journal of Financial Economics*.

Jarrow, Robert. 2001a. Default parameter estimation using market prices. *Financial Analysts Journal*, September/October.

Jarrow, Robert. 2001b. Technical guide: Default probabilities implicit in debt and equity prices. Honolulu: Kamakura Corporation Technical Guide.

Jarrow, Robert, David Lando, and Stuart Turnbull. 1997. A Markov model for the term structure of credit risk spreads. *Review of Financial Studies*.

Jarrow, Robert, and Stuart Turnbull. 1995. Pricing derivatives on financial securities subject to credit risk. *Journal of Finance*.

Joe, H. 1997. *Multivariate models and dependence concepts*. London, New York: Chapman & Hall.

Jones, E. Philip, Scott P. Mason, and Eric Rosenfeld. 1984. Contingent claims analysis of corporate capital structures: An empirical investigation. *Journal of Finance*.

Judd, Kenneth L. 1999. *Numerical Methods in Econometrics*. Cambridge, MA: The MIT Press.

Kalbfleisch, J. D., and Ross L. Prentice. 2002. *The statistical analysis of failure time data*. Hoboken, NJ: Wiley.

Kalotay, A., D. Yang, and F. Fabozzi. 2004. An option-theoretic prepayment model for mortgages and mortgage-backed securities. *International Journal of Theoretical and Applied Finance*.

Kane, Edward J., and Haluk Unal. 1990. Modeling structural and temporal variation in the market's valuation of banking firms. *Journal of Finance*.

Kealhofer, Stephen. 2003. Quantifying credit risk I: Default prediction. *Financial Analysts Journal*, January/February.

Kealhofer, Stephen. 2003. Quantifying credit risk II: Debt valuation. *Financial Analysts Journal*.

Kealhofer, Stephen, and Jeffrey R. Bohn. 2001. Portfolio management of default risk. KMV working paper. San Francisco.

Kealhofer, Stephen, Sherry Kwok, and Wenlong Weng. 1998. Uses and abuses of bond default rates. KMV working paper.

Keenan, S., J. Sobehart, and D. T. Hamilton. 1999. Predicting default rates: A forecasting model for Moody's issuer-based default rates. New York: Moody's Investors Service.

Keenan, Sean C., Lea V. Carty, and Igor Shtogrin. 1998. Historical default rates of corporate bond issuers, 1920–1997. *Global Credit Research*. New York: Moody's Investors Service.

Keisman, D., and K. Van de Castle. 1999. Insights into losses from defaults. *Journal of Lending & Credit Risk Management*.

Kennedy, Peter. 1992. *A guide to econometrics*. Cambridge, MA: MIT Press.

Kocagil, Ahmet E., and Jalal A. Akhsavein. 2001. Moody's RiskCalc™ for private companies: Japan. New York: Moody's Investors Service.

Kohn, Meir. 2001. Payments and the development of finance in pre-industrial Europe. Working paper 01-15. Hanover: Dartmouth College.

Koomey, Jonathan G. 2001. *Turning numbers into knowledge: Mastering the art of problem solving*. Oakland: Analytics Press.

Kumra, Roger, Roger Stein, and Ian Assersohn. 2006. Assessing a knowledge-based approach to commercial loan underwriting. *Expert Systems with Applications*.

Kurbat, M., and I. Korablev. 2002. Methodology for testing the level of the EDF™ credit measure. San Francisco: Moody's KMV.

Lando, D. 1994. Three essays on contingent claims pricing. Ithaca, NY: Cornell University.

Lando, David. 1998. On Cox processes and credit risky securities. *Review of Derivatives Research* 2:99–120.

Lando, David. 2004. *Credit risk modeling: Theory and applications*. Princeton Series in Finance. Princeton: Princeton University Press.

Lando, David, and Allan Mortensen. 2005. Revisiting the slope of the credit curve. *Journal of Investment Management*.

Lando, David, and Torben Magaard Skodeberg. 2002. Analyzing rating transitions and rating drift with continuous observations. *Journal of Banking and Finance*.

Leland, Hayne E., and Klaus B. Toft. 1996. Optimal capital structure, endogenous bankruptcy, and the term structure of credit spreads. *Journal of Finance.*

Levy, Amnon. 2008. An overview of modeling credit portfolios: Modeling methodology. Working paper. San Francisco: MKMV.

Lingo, Manuel, and Gerhard Winkler. 2007. Discriminatory power—An obsolete validation criterion? SSRN.

Little, R. J. A., and D. B. Rubin. 1987. *Statistical analysis with missing data.* New York: John Wiley & Sons.

Lo, Andrew. 1986. Logit versus discriminant analysis: A specification test with applications to corporate bankruptcies. *Journal of Econometrics* 31:151–178.

Longstaff, Francis A., Sanjay Mithal, and Eric Neis. 2004. Corporate yield spreads: Default risk or liquidity? New evidence from the credit-default swap market. Working paper. Los Angeles: UCLA.

Longstaff, Francis A., and Eduardo S. Schwartz. 1995. A simple approach to valuing risky fixed and floating rate debt. *Journal of Finance.*

Lucas, Douglas. 1995. Default correlation and credit analysis. *Journal of Fixed Income.* March.

Lucas, Douglas J., Laurie S. Goodman, and Frank J. Fabozzi. 2006. *Collateralized Debt Obligations.* Hoboken, NJ: John Wiley & Sons.

McCullagh, P., and John A. Nelder. 1989. *Generalized linear models.* London, New York: Chapman and Hall.

Megginson, William L., Annette B. Poulsen, and Joseph F. Sinkey Jr. 1995. Syndicated loan announcements and the market value of the banking firm. *Journal of Money, Credit, and Banking.*

Mehta, Dileep, and Hung-Gay Fung. 2004. *International bank management.* London: Blackwell.

Merton, Robert C. 1974. On the pricing of corporate debt: The risk structure of interest rates. *Journal of Finance.*

Modigliani, Franco, and Merton H. Miller. 1958. The cost of capital, corporation finance and the theory of investment. *American Economic Review* 48:261–297.

Nandi, Saikat. 1998. Valuation models for default-risky securities: An overview. *Economic Review*, Federal Reserve Bank of Atlanta.

Neftci, Salih. 2000. *An introduction to the mathematics of financial derivatives.* San Diego: Academic Press.

Nelson, R. B. 1999. *An introduction to copulas.* New York: Springer-Verlag.

Ong, Michael K. 1999. *Internal credit risk models: capital allocation and performance measurement.* London: Risk Books.

Ong, Michael K., ed. 2004. *The Basel handbook: A guide for financial practitioners.* London: KPMG and Risk Books.

Onorota, M., and E. I. Altman. 2003. An integrated pricing model for defaultable loans and bonds. London: City University, and New York: New York University.

Pan, Jun, and Kenneth J. Singleton. 2008. Default and recovery implicit in the term structure of sovereign CDS spreads. *Journal of Finance* 43(5):2345–2384.

Papoulis, A. 2002. Probability, random variables and stochastic processes. Boston: McGraw-Hill.

Peduzzi P., J. Concato, E. Kemper, T. R. Holford, and A. R. Feinstein. 1996. A simulation study of the number of events per variable in logistic regression analysis. *Journal of Clinical Epidemiology* 49(12).

Pepe, Margaret Sullivan. 2002. Receiver operating characteristic methodology. In *Statistics in the 21st Century*, ed. Adrian Raftery, E., Martin A. Tanner, and Martin T. Wells. London: Chapman & Hall/CRC.

Pesaran, M. H., T. Schuermann, B.-J. Treutler, and S. M. Weiner. 2004. Macroeconomic dynamics and credit risk: A global perspective. Working paper. Cambridge: University of Cambridge.

Petroski, H. 1992. *To engineer is human: The role of failure in successful design.* New York: Vintage Books.

Pluto, K., and D. Tasche. 2006. Estimating probabilities of default for low default portfolios. In *The Basel II Risk Parameters*, ed. B. Engelmann and R. Rauhmeier. New York: Springer.

Press, William H., Saul A. Teukolsky, William T. Vetterling, and Brian P. Flannery. 2007. *Numerical recipes: The art of scientific computing, third edition.* Cambridge: Cambridge University Press.

Provost, F., and T. Fawcett. 1997. Analysis and visualization of classifier performance: Comparison under imprecise class and cost distributions. Proceedings of Third International Conference on Knowledge Discovery and Data Mining, Newport Beach, CA.

Reid, N. 2002. Likelihood. In *Statistics in the 21st Century*, ed. Adrian E. Raftery, Martin A. Tanner, and Martin T. Wells. London: Chapman & Hall/CRC.

Ross, Stephen A. 1973. The economic theory of agency: The principal's problem. *American Economic Review.*

Royall, Richard. 1997. *Statistical evidence: A likelihood paradigm.* London: Chapman & Hall/CRC.

Rubinstein, Mark. 2001. Rational markets: Yes or no? The affirmative case. *Financial Analysts Journal.*

Rubinstein, Mark. 2006. A history of the theory of investments. Hoboken, NJ: John Wiley & Sons.

Sarig, Oded, and Arthur Warga. 1989. Some empirical estimates of the risk structure of interest rates. *Journal of Finance* 44:1351–1360.

Saunders, Anthony. 1999. *Credit risk measurement: New approaches to value at risk and other paradigms.* New York: John Wiley & Sons.

Schonbucher, Philipp J. 2003. Credit derivatives pricing models: Models, pricing and implementation. West Sussex, UK: John Wiley & Sons.

Sekar, C. C., and W. E. Deming. 1949. On a method of estimating birth and death rates and the extent of registration. *American Statistical Association Journal* 44:101–115.

Sellers, Martha, and Navneet Arora. 2004. Financial EDF measures: A new model of dual business lines. Working paper. New York, MKMV.

Shumway, T. 2001. Forecasting bankruptcy more accurately: A simple hazard model. *Journal of Business*, 101–124.

Simonoff, J. S. 1996. *Smoothing methods in statistics*. New York: Springer-Verlag.

Sironi, Andrea, Edward I. Altman, Brooks Brady, and Andrea Resti. 2002. The link between default and recovery rates: Implications for credit risk models and procyclicality. SSRN.

Sobehart, Jorge, Sean Keenan, and Roger Stein. 2000. Validation methodologies for default risk models. *Credit*.

Sobehart, Jorge R., Sean C. Keenan, and Roger M. Stein. 2000. Benchmarking quantitative default risk models: A validation methodology. New York: Moody's Risk Management.

Sobehart, Jorge R., Roger Stein, and V. Li L. Mikityanskaya. 2000. Moody's public firm risk model: A hybrid approach to modeling default risk. Moody's Investors Special Comment. New York: Moody's Investors Service, New York.

Starbuck, W. H, and F. J. Milliken. 1988. Challenger: Fine-tuning the odds until something breaks. *Journal of Management Studies* 25:319–340.

Stein, Roger M. 1999. Pattern discovery and simulation methods for evaluating risk control strategies for futures trading systems. New York: New York University.

Stein, Roger M. 2002. Benchmarking default prediction models: Pitfalls and remedies in model validation. Technical Report #030124. New York: MKMV.

Stein, Roger M. 2003a. Power, profitability and prices: Why powerful models increase profits and how to set a lending cutoff if you must. Technical Report. New York: MKMV.

Stein, Roger M. 2003b. Are the probabilities right? A first approximation to the lower bound on the number of observations required to test for default rate accuracy. Technical Report. New York: MKMV.

Stein, Roger M. 2005a. Evidence on the incompleteness of Merton-type structural models for default prediction. Working paper. New York: MKMV.

Stein, Roger M. 2005b. The relationship between default prediction and lending profits: Integrating ROC analysis and loan pricing. *Journal of Banking and Finance* 29:1213–1236.

Stein, Roger M. 2006. Are the probabilities right? Dependent defaults and the number of observations required to test for default rate accuracy. *Journal of Investment Management* 4:61–71.

Stein, Roger M. 2007. Benchmarking default prediction models: pitfalls and remedies in model validation. *Journal of Risk Model Validation* 1.

Stein, Roger M., and Felipe Jordao. 2003. What is a more powerful model worth? New York: Moody's KMV.

Stein, Roger M., and F. Jordão. 2005. Better predictions of income volatility using a structural default model. Working paper. New York: Moody's Investors Service.

Stigum, Marcia. 1990. *The money market*. New York: McGraw Hill.

Swets, J. A. 1988. Measuring the accuracy of diagnostic systems. *Science* 240:1285–1293.

Swets, John A. 1996. *Signal detection theory and ROC analysis in psychology and diagnostics*. Mahwah, NJ: Laurence Erlbaum Associates.

Swets, John A., Robyn M. Dawes, and John Monahan. 2000. Better decisions through science. *Scientific American*.

Tamaki, Norio. 1995. *Japanese banking: A history 1859–1959*. Cambridge: Cambridge University Press.

Therneau, T. M., and P. M. Grambsch. 2000. Modeling survival data: Extending the Cox model. New York: Springer.

Trivedi, Pravin K., and David M. Zimmer. 2005. Copula modeling: An introduction for practitioners. *Foundations and Trends in Econometrics*.

Unal, Haluk, Dilip Madan, and Levent Guntay. 2001. A simple approach to estimate recovery rates with APR violation from debt spreads. College Park, MD: University of Maryland.

Van Belle, G. 2008. *Statistical rules of thumb*. Hoboken, NJ: John Wiley & Sons.

Van de Castle, K., D. Keisman, and R. Yang. 2000. Suddenly structure mattered: Insights into recoveries from defaulted debt. *Standard & Poor's Credit Week* May 2000.

Van Den Castle, K., and D. Keisman. 1999. Recovering your money: Insights into losses from defaults. *Standard & Poors Credit Week* June 16, 1999.

Van Deventer, Donald R., Kenji Imai, and Mark Mesler. 2005. *Advanced financial risk management*. New York: Wiley Finance.

Varma, Praveen, and Richard Cantor. 2005. Bond prices at default and at emergence from bankruptcy for U.S. corporate issuers. *Global Credit Research*. New York: Moody's Investors Service.

Vasicek, Oldrich A. 1977. An equilibrium characterization of the term structure. *Journal of Financial Economics*.

Vasicek, Oldrich A. 1984. Credit valuation. Working paper. New York: KMV.

Vasicek, Oldrich A. 1987. Probability of loss on loan portfolio. New York: KMV.

Vasicek, Oldrich A. 1991. Limiting loan loss probability distribution. New York: KMV.

Vassalou, Maria, and Yuhang Xing. 2002. Default risk in equity returns. Working paper. New York: Columbia University.

Wagner, Herbert S. III. 1996. The pricing of bonds in bankruptcy and financial restructuring. *Journal of Fixed Income* 40–47.

Ward, David J., and Gary L. Griepentrog. 1993. Risk and return in defaulted bonds. *Financial Analysts Journal* 61–65.

White, Alan. 2002. Measuring default probability. New York: Moody's Academic Research and Advisory Committee.

Wilcox, Jarrod W. 1971. A Simple Theory of Financial Ratios as Predictors of Failure, *Journal of Accounting Research* 9:389–85.

Wilcox, Jarrod W. 1973. A prediction of business failure using accounting data, empirical research in accounting: Selected studies 1973. *Supplement to Journal of Accounting Research* 9:163–179.

Wilcox, Jarrod W. 1976. The Gambler's ruin approach to business risk. *Sloan Management Review* Fall: 33–46.

Wilmott, Paul. 2001. *Paul Wilmott introduces quantitative finance*. West Sussex: John Wiley & Sons.

Wilson, Thomas C. 1997. Measuring and managing credit portfolio risk: Part I: Modelling systemic default risk. *Journal of Lending and Credit Risk Management* 79:61–72.

Yago, Glenn, and Donald McCarthy. 2004. The U.S. leveraged loan market: A primer. Santa Monica: Milken Institute.

Zhou, Chunsheng. 2001. The term structure of credit risk with jump risk. *Journal of Banking and Finance*.

About the Authors

Jeffrey R. Bohn, Ph.D., leads the Financial Strategies group at Shinsei Bank in Tokyo. Previously, he led Moody's KMV's (MKMV's) Global Research group and MKMV's Credit Strategies group. After Moody's acquired KMV, he and Roger M. Stein co-headed MKMV's research and product development. Dr. Bohn also serves on the board of directors for the International Association of Credit Portfolio Managers (IACPM).

Roger M. Stein, Ph.D., is Group Managing Director of the newly formed Quantitative Research and Analytics group at Moody's Investors Service in New York. After Moody's acquired KMV, he and Jeffrey R. Bohn co-headed MKMV's research and product development. Before this, he was head of research for Moody's Risk Management Services. Dr. Stein also serves on the editorial boards of a number of credit and finance related journals.

Index